Frommer's®

P9-DZP-236

New York State

5th Edition

by Marc Lallanilla,
Neil Edward Schlecht &
Brian Silverman

WILEY

John Wiley & Sons, Inc.

Published by:

JOHN WILEY & SONS, INC.

111 River St.

Hoboken, NJ 07030-5774

Copyright © 2012 John Wiley & Sons, Inc., Hoboken, New Jersey. All rights reserved. No part of this publication may be reproduced, stored in a retrieval system or transmitted in any form or by any means, electronic, mechanical, photocopying, recording, scanning or otherwise, except as permitted under Sections 107 or 108 of the 1976 United States Copyright Act, without either the prior written permission of the Publisher, or authorization through payment of the appropriate per-copy fee to the Copyright Clearance Center, 222 Rosewood Drive, Danvers, MA 01923, 978/750-8400, fax 978/646-8600. Requests to the Publisher for permission should be addressed to the Permissions Department, John Wiley & Sons, Inc., 111 River Street, Hoboken, NJ 07030, 201/748-6011, fax 201/748-6008, or online at http://www.wiley.com/go/permissions.

Wiley and the Wiley logo are trademarks or registered trademarks of John Wiley & Sons, Inc. Frommer's is a trademark or registered trademark of Arthur Frommer. Used under license. All other trademarks are the property of their respective owners. John Wiley & Sons, Inc. is not associated with any product or vendor mentioned in this book.

ISBN 978-1-118-09601-7 (paper); ISBN 978-1-118-20428-3 (ebk); ISBN 978-1-118-20427-6 (ebk); ISBN 978-1-118-20429-0 (ebk)

Editor: Jessica Langan-Peck with Linda Barth
Production Editor: Katie Robinson
Cartographer: Guy Ruggiero
Photo Editor: Richard Fox
Production by Wiley Indianapolis Composition Services
Front Cover Photo: Beached canoe in the Adirondacks ©4 Eyes Photography / Getty Images
Back Cover Photo: Horse racing in Saratoga Springs ©SportsAction / Alamy Images

For information on our other products and services or to obtain technical support, please contact our Customer Care Department within the U.S. at 877/762-2974, outside the U.S. at 317/572-3993 or fax 317/572-4002.

Wiley also publishes its books in a variety of electronic formats. Some content that appears in print may not be available in electronic formats.

Manufactured in the United States of America

5 4 3 2 1

CONTENTS

LIST OF MAPS

ABOUT THE AUTHORS

Neil Edward Schlecht is a writer and photographer who frequently travels along the Hudson River between an old farmhouse in northwestern Connecticut and New York City. He is the author of more than a dozen travel guides—including *Spain For Dummies;* Frommer's Day by Day guides to Buenos Aires, Mallorca and Menorca, and Barcelona; and Frommer's guides to Texas, Cuba, and Peru—as well as art catalogue essays and articles on art and culture.

Marc Lallanilla has written extensively on science, health, the environment, design, architecture, and travel. A resident of New York's Hudson Valley, he is also a co-author of *Frommer's 500 Adrenaline Adventures*. His work has been published in the *Los Angeles Times,* ABCNews.com, About.com, and other online and print publications.

Brian Silverman is a freelance writer whose work has been published in *Saveur, The New Yorker, Caribbean Travel & Life, Islands,* and *Four Seasons.* Among the many topics he writes about are food, travel, sports, and music. He is the author of numerous books including *Going, Going, Gone: The History, Lore, and Mystique of the Home Run,* and the *Twentieth Century Treasury of Sports.* For Frommer's, he has written Complete, Portable, and Budget guides to New York City, as well as *New York City For Dummies.* He lives in New York City with his wife and two sons.

HOW TO CONTACT US

In researching this book, we discovered many wonderful places—hotels, restaurants, shops, and more. We're sure you'll find others. Please tell us about them, so we can share the information with your fellow travelers in upcoming editions. If you were disappointed with a recommendation, we'd love to know that, too. Please write to:

Frommer's New York State, 5th Edition
John Wiley & Sons, Inc. • 111 River St. • Hoboken, NJ 07030-5774
frommersfeedback@wiley.com

ADVISORY & DISCLAIMER

Travel information can change quickly and unexpectedly, and we strongly advise you to confirm important details locally before traveling, including information on visas, health and safety, traffic and transport, accommodations, shopping, and eating out. We also encourage you to stay alert while traveling and to remain aware of your surroundings. Avoid civil disturbances, and keep a close eye on cameras, purses, wallets, and other valuables.

While we have endeavored to ensure that the information contained within this guide is accurate and up-to-date at the time of publication, we make no representations or warranties with respect to the accuracy or completeness of the contents of this work and specifically disclaim all warranties, including without limitation warranties of fitness for a particular purpose. We accept no responsibility or liability for any inaccuracy or errors or omissions, or for any inconvenience, loss, damage, costs, or expenses of any nature whatsoever incurred or suffered by anyone as a result of any advice or information contained in this guide.

The inclusion of a company, organization, or website in this guide as a service provider and/or potential source of further information does not mean that we endorse them or the information they provide. Be aware that information provided through some websites may be unreliable and can change without notice. Neither the publisher nor author shall be liable for any damages arising herefrom.

FROMMER'S STAR RATINGS, ICONS & ABBREVIATIONS

Every hotel, restaurant, and attraction listing in this guide has been ranked for quality, value, service, amenities, and special features using a **star-rating system.** In country, state, and regional guides, we also rate towns and regions to help you narrow down your choices and budget your time accordingly. Hotels and restaurants are rated on a scale of zero (recommended) to three stars (exceptional). Attractions, shopping, nightlife, towns, and regions are rated according to the following scale: zero stars (recommended), one star (highly recommended), two stars (very highly recommended), and three stars (must-see).

In addition to the star-rating system, we also use **eight feature icons** that point you to the great deals, in-the-know advice, and unique experiences that separate travelers from tourists. Throughout the book, look for:

special finds—those places only insiders know about

fun facts—details that make travelers more informed and their trips more fun

kids—best bets for kids and advice for the whole family

special moments—those experiences that memories are made of

overrated—places or experiences not worth your time or money

insider tips—great ways to save time and money

great values—where to get the best deals

warning—traveler's advisories are usually in effect

The following abbreviations are used for credit cards:

AE	American Express	DISC	Discover	V	Visa
DC	Diners Club	MC	MasterCard		

TRAVEL RESOURCES AT FROMMERS.COM

Frommer's travel resources don't end with this guide. Frommer's website, **www.frommers. com,** has travel information on more than 4,000 destinations. We update features regularly, giving you access to the most current trip-planning information and the best airfare, lodging, and car-rental bargains. You can also listen to podcasts, connect with other Frommers. com members through our active-reader forums, share your travel photos, read blogs from guidebook editors and fellow travelers, and much more.

THE BEST OF NEW YORK STATE

V isitors to New York State who venture both down-state and upstate have an array of options unequaled elsewhere in the country. Besides the urban allure, culture, and shopping of Manhattan, much of New York State is still, in many ways, waiting to be discovered on a grand scale. The state is endowed with outstanding beauty and diversity of scenery from one end to the other. Although New Yorkers have long vacationed in the Catskill and Adirondack mountains, and at Long Island beaches, most have seen too little of the state between its tourist bookends, New York City and Niagara Falls. The historic Hudson Valley, a majestic river lined with elegant estates, is finally positioning itself as a destination, not just a day trip from the city. The great wilderness of the Adirondack and Catskill mountains is magnificent for outdoors and sporting vacations, but those spots are also home to the easygoing charms of small towns. The pristine, glacial-lake beauty and outstanding wineries of the Finger Lakes make it one of the state's most spectacular, yet lesser-known destinations. And Long Island is home to splendid sandy Atlantic Ocean beaches, but also the gulf of New York economic extremes, ranging from blue-collar immi-grant enclaves to palatial summer homes in the Hamptons.

Planning a trip to a state as large and diverse as New York involves a lot of decision making, so in this chapter we've tried to give some direction. Below we've chosen what we feel is the very best the state has to offer—the places and experiences you won't want to miss. Although sites and activities listed here are written up in more detail elsewhere in this book, this chapter should give you an overview of New York State's highlights and get you started planning your trip.

—*Neil Edward Schlecht*

THE best HOTELS

- **The Ritz-Carlton New York, Central Park** (50 Central Park South; © **212/308-9100**): The combination of a great location across from Central Park: large, well-outfitted rooms, and excellent Ritz-Carlton service is as good as it gets. See p. 75.
- **Casablanca Hotel** (147 W. 43rd St.: © **888/922-7225**): In the The-ater District, the Casablanca not only offers clean, well-outfitted rooms

New York State

Legend:
- 86 Interstate
- 90 Toll Highway
- 62 US Highway
- State Road
- ✪ State/Province Capital
- ✪ National Capital

USA — New York

ONTARIO

Toronto

Lake Ontario

Kingston

Oswego
Fulton
Baldwinsville
Syracuse
Auburn
La Fayette
Geneva
Genoa
Cortland
Ithaca
Richford
Johnson City

Manitou Beach
Ontario-on-the-Lake
Medina
Albion
Greece
Rochester
Brighton
Alton
Newark

Lewiston
Lockport
Niagara Falls
Buffalo
Cheektowaga
Batavia
Canandaigua
Finger Lakes
Ovid

West Seneca
Geneseo
LETCHWORTH SP
Wayland

Angola
Hamburg
East Aurora
Lake Erie
Dunkirk
Caneadea
Genesee R.
Hammondsport
Bath

Fredonia
Ellicottville
Hornell
Corning
Elmira

Chautauqua L.
Chautauqua
Randolph
ALLEGANY SP
Olean

Jamestown

Allegheny Res.
Warren

Oil City
Clarion

Punxsutawney

Allegheny R.

PENNSYLVANIA

W. Br. Susquehanna R.

Williamsport

Susquehanna R.

Altoona

Juniata R.

Susquehanna R.

Harrisburg
Hershey
Reading

0   25 mi
0   25 km

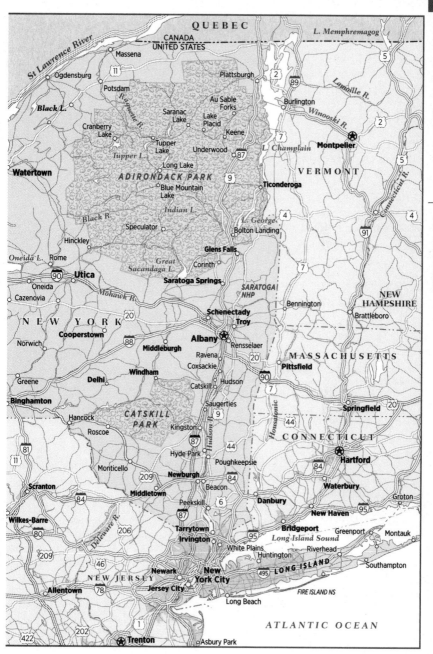

at value rates, but also includes such extras as complimentary breakfast, bottled water, free high-speed Internet access, and a lovely roof deck perfect for a cocktail on a balmy evening. See p. 87.

o **Buttermilk Falls Inn + Spa** (Milton-on-Hudson; ✆ **877/746-6772**): Secluded among 70 acres along the Hudson River, this soothing boutique hotel is an excellent choice to get away from it all or to use as a base for exploring the Hudson Valley or the eastern edges of the Catskills. Part historic inn (the main house is a 1764 Colonial), part posh day spa, and part rustic retreat—with wooded trails, waterfalls and ponds, gardens, and separate cottage houses—there's something for almost everyone. Rooms are elegant without being fussy. The great new restaurant, Henry's Farm-to-Table, makes it a place you may never want (or have) to leave. See p. 210.

o **Mohonk Mountain House** (Lake Mohonk; ✆ **800/772-6646**): A legendary Victorian castle perched on a ridge overlooking the Catskill region's Shawangunk Mountains, the Mohonk Mountain House is more than a hotel; it's a destination unto itself. In the midst of the 6,400-acre Mohonk Forest Preserve, its setting is beyond compare and outdoor activities include something for everyone. The spa is spectacular. See p. 234.

o **The Saratoga Hilton at City Center** (Saratoga Springs; ✆ **888/866-3591**): Saratoga is loaded with charming Victorian B&Bs, but, until recently, it didn't have anything approaching a modern luxury hotel. This large, chic business hotel, right on the main drag, fills that niche nicely. See p. 271.

o **The Otesaga** (Cooperstown; ✆ **800/348-6222**): The grande dame of central New York sprawls majestically along the shores of Lake Otsego. While renovations have brought the bathrooms and air-conditioning into the 21st century, the hotel is firmly rooted in the past, maintaining its historic feel with high ceilings and formal furniture. Still, with a plethora of patios and balconies, this seasonal hotel is focused on the equally gorgeous outdoors that surround it. See p. 295.

o **Aurora Inn** (Aurora; ✆ **866/364-8808**): This small boutique hotel is the centerpiece of a sweet little town on the east bank of Cayuga Lake. Although small, the inn has the superb service and style of a luxury hotel, as well as stunning water views. Its small sister hotel, the **E.B. Morgan House,** offers similar elegance. See p. 320.

o **Sherwood Inn** (Skaneateles; ✆ **800/3-SHERWOOD** [374-3796]): Occupying a prime position in the most delightful town in the Finger Lakes, this longtime small hotel—a stagecoach stop from the early 19th century—looks out onto Skaneateles Lake and exudes a relaxed, genteel feel. The old staircase, wide-plank floorboards, and colorfully designed rooms may seem old-world and old-money, but travelers can stay for moderate prices. See p. 363.

o **Hotel Skyler** (Syracuse; ✆ **800/365-4663**): Unexpected in snowy Syracuse, this environmentally progressive and exceedingly cool midsize hotel sports a chic design that respects the architectural integrity and 1920s character while making it a model for the city and future hotel development. See p. 367.

o **Lake Placid Lodge** (Lake Placid; ✆ **877/523-2700**): Sitting on the shores of secluded Lake Placid, this exclusive getaway features meticulous and personalized service, along with rooms filled with one-of-a-kind pieces of furniture, many built by local artists. With lots of quiet nooks and a gorgeous stone patio, you can grab your own corner of the 'dacks and feel like you have the place to yourself. See p. 386.

o **Athenaeum Hotel** (Chautauqua; ✆ **716/357-4444**): For sheer Victorian grandeur, it's hard to beat this historic landmark, perched on a hill overlooking Chautauqua Lake and located on the grounds of the Chautauqua Institution. All guests are on the American plan, which includes three meals a day—not a problem when the hotel is home to one of the most innovative restaurants in the region. See p. 425.

THE best INNS & B&BS

o **Mount Merino Manor** (Hudson; ☎ **518/828-5583**): A grand, late-19th-century manor house just outside of Hudson, this lovely B&B is almost too luxurious and refined for the category; it's essentially a top-of-the-line boutique hotel. The secluded location offers serenity and beautiful views, while its proximity to Hudson's restaurants and antiques shops makes it an ideal getaway. See p. 220.

o **The Inn at Lake Joseph** (Forestburgh; ☎ **845/791-9506**): A first-class country estate in the southeastern quadrant of the Catskill region, this secluded Victorian inn is elegant and peaceful. It has manor house rooms in a 19th-century summer getaway, as well as splurge-friendly carriage and cottage houses that are more like princely private apartments. See p. 257.

o **The Stone House Bed & Breakfast** (Hurley; ☎ **845/339-4041**): Not far from the famed stone houses of Huguenot Street, this remarkable house is 3 centuries old, and it's been masterfully converted into one of the most unique and beautiful small inns upstate. Its aesthetic aims are made obvious by rooms named for paintings by the Dutch master Vermeer; luxuriously designed and outfitted, they live up to the lofty monikers. See p. 236.

o **Hillcrest Manor** (Corning; ☎ **607/936-4548**): A refined B&B in a gateway town to the Finger Lakes, this gorgeous 1890 Greek Revival mansion is just minutes from the world-renowned Corning Museum of Glass in a peaceful residential neighborhood. The opulent inn, owned by two art collectors, has tasteful parlors and very spacious bedrooms. See p. 331.

o **Hobbit Hollow Farm B&B** (Skaneateles; ☎ **315/685-2791**): Overlooking graceful Skaneateles Lake, this sumptuous and intimate small inn gives you a chance to pretend you're a privileged country gentleman or -woman relaxing on your horse farm. For those on a budget, the smaller rooms are a decent value and you can still imagine yourself the prince of Skaneateles. See p. 363.

o **Seatuck Cove House** (Eastport; ☎ **631/325-3300**): On the edge of the Hamptons, this enormous, beautiful home sits right out on the water with gorgeous views. Because the inn has only five rooms, you'll feel like you own the place. The rooms are painted white and decorated with an appropriately beachy aesthetic. Take a walk along the waterfront or a dip in the pool, then grab one of the best B&B breakfasts on Long Island. See p. 173.

o **The Mansion Inn of Saratoga** (Rock City Falls/Saratoga Springs; ☎ **888/996-9977**): This sophisticated 1866 Victorian inn sits on 4 acres just outside Saratoga Springs and is replete with luxurious details, both in common rooms and in the spacious accommodations. The owners are serious about high-end pampering, making it an ideal weekend getaway. See p. 273.

o **Black Sheep Inn** (Hammondsport; (☎ **607/569-3767**): A new arrival to the Finger Lakes is this inn occupying a rare 1859 octagon house, immaculately restored and converted by the young owners, one a chef devoted to organic cooking and the other an interior designer. The house is lavishly outfitted, but not at all fussy. The location—in a pretty, small town near beautiful Keuka Lake—is a bonus. See p. 335.

o **The Chalet of Canandaigua** (Canandaigua; ☎ **585/394-9080**): This tiny luxury inn has enormous rooms of immense style, a surprise within the walls of a log cabin. Equipped to the nines, it's a perfect blend of rusticity and stylish warmth, with no detail overlooked. Whatever the season, this chalet makes a dignified retreat. See p. 341.

THE best RESTAURANTS

- **Oceana** (Manhattan; ✆ **212/759-5941**): In the heart of Midtown, this seafood mecca combines the freshest fare along with first-rate service. Simple is better, but you really can't go wrong with anything from the sea here. See p. 102.
- **The Mark Restaurant** (Manhattan; ✆ **212/606-3030**): One of Chef Jean Georges Vongerichten's newer ventures, The Mark is less fussy than the very good Jean-Georges, but just as good. In a beautiful, sky-lit room off the lobby of the newly renovated Mark Hotel, The Mark Restaurant is flawless on every level. See p. 108.
- **Peter Luger** (Great Neck; ✆ **516/487-8800**): Hands down, this is one of the best steakhouses in the country. People flock here for one thing and one thing only: porterhouse. In fact, if you try to order anything else (or even ask for a menu), you'll likely get a quizzical stare from your waiter. The dry-aged meat comes brushed with a tasty glaze and is tender enough to make vegetarians reconsider. See p. 149.
- **Culinary Institute of America (CIA)** (Hyde Park; ✆ **845/471-6608**): The most elite training ground in the country for chefs has not one, but four on-campus restaurants run by students—but they're a far cry from what college students typically eat. Choose the sophisticated Escoffier Restaurant (French), Ristorante Caterina de Medici (Italian), American Bounty Restaurant (regional American), or St. Andrew's Café (casual). You'll be impressed, and unsurprised, that so many of America's finest restaurants have CIA chefs at the helm. Plan ahead, though, because reservations are about as tough to come by as admission to the school. See p. 205.
- **Blue Hill at Stone Barns** (Pocantico Hills; ✆ **914/366-9600**): At this farm-to-table complement to the renowned restaurant Blue Hill in New York City, Chef Dan Barber works magic from the freshest ingredients possible from this and other Westchester County farms. The "menu" consists of a prix-fixe Farmer's Feast, assembled from the finest local produce, fish, poultry, and game available that day. The elegant farm setting makes this a destination restaurant worth planning a trip to the Hudson Valley around. See p. 197.
- **Valley** (Garrison; ✆ **845/424-2339**): Ensconced within the gently rolling grounds of a golf course high above the Hudson Valley, this understated but quietly creative restaurant has quickly become one of the finest in the valley. Its seasonal American menu features the best from local Hudson Valley farms, and its wine cellar is peerless in the region. See p. 198.
- **Terrapin Restaurant** (Rhinebeck; ✆ **845/876-3330**): Chef/owner Josh Kroner ambitiously adds creative Mexican and Asian accents to American cuisine in this popular restaurant that inhabits a 19th-century church in the quaint village of Rhinebeck. There's fine dining in the evenings on one side, and a casual bistro on the other, and the well-thought-out wine list is as good as they come in the Hudson Valley. See p. 212.
- **Cucina** (Woodstock; ✆ **845/679-9800**): This rustic, chic Italian trattoria blends warm traditionalism with modern creativity, signaled by the minimalist interior and long community table inside a Victorian farmhouse. Chef Gianni Scappin makes

great use of the local bounty from the Hudson River Valley and Catskills at this new restaurant that pleases nearly everyone, from demanding foodies to comfort-food travelers and families. See p. 238.

- **Alex & Ika** (Cooperstown; ✆ **607/547-4070**): Formerly located in tiny Cherry Valley, this house of culinary masterpieces is now right in the heart of Cooperstown. Fortunately, the food has lost none of its punch—it's still packed with so many flavor combinations that you'll be talking about the meal long after you leave. With a menu that changes weekly, it's hard to believe they can hit a home run with every dish, but somehow they do. See p. 297.

- **Suzanne Fine Regional Cuisine** (Hector; ✆ **607/582-7545**): Suzanne's looks like a harbinger of the future in the Finger Lakes—fine dining to accompany the region's swiftly improving wines. Meticulously crafted American food, using the finest local ingredients, is the calling card at this sophisticated but relaxed country-elegant spot, in an old farmhouse with swoon-worthy views of Seneca Lake. Locals consider it *the* place for a special dinner. See p. 327.

- **The Bistro at Red Newt Cellars** (Hector; ✆ **607/546-4100**): At the forefront of the movement to focus on the bounty of local farms, this terrific and creative bistro restaurant is also keen on matching food with local wines. And why not—the restaurant is intrinsically connected to one of the Finger Lakes' better wineries (which is run by the chef's husband). See p. 326.

- **Dano's Heuriger** (Lodi; ✆ **607/582-7555**): A radical departure from what one might expect to find along the shore of one of the Finger Lakes, this Austrian restaurant, a modern version of a Viennese wine garden, is nonetheless perfectly at home. The menu encourages diners to sample small plates and unique tastes, which pair perfectly with the local wines (or Austrian varietals, such as Grüner Veltliner). See p. 327.

- **North Fork Table & Inn** (Southold; ✆ **631/765-0177**): This outstanding restaurant is a standard-bearer in Long Island's East End for the meticulous preparation of creative, locally sourced meals. The bright space has a romantic country inn feel, with wood plank floors and ceiling beams, but the food—from a kitchen led by Gerard Hayden, formerly of NYC's Aureole—is simply, yet artfully presented. See p. 158.

- **The View** (Mirror Lake Inn, Lake Placid; ✆ **518/302-3000**): This top-notch inn has always served up some of the best dishes in the Adirondacks, and with its change from black-tie to casually clad servers, it fits in better with the area's laid-back atmosphere. Meals are consistently excellent, and they come with a gorgeous view out over Mirror Lake. See p. 389.

- **Tempo** (Buffalo; ✆ **716/885-1594**): With a creative Italian menu and a modern, romantic setting, this restaurant has been at the top of the city's dining scene since it opened. The inventive food is dramatically presented; dig in and you'll see why Western New Yorkers keep coming back for more. See p. 413.

THE best PLACES FOR ANTIQUES HOUNDS

- **Greenport:** This bustling hub out on Long Island's North Fork has one of the best selections of antiques reflecting the old seafaring world on the North Fork. See chapter 6.

o **Southold:** While it may play second fiddle to neighboring Greenport, just-as-cute-but-quieter Southold is a great place to browse antiques with less company. There are a number of treasure-filled shops, including an antique doll hospital. See chapter 6.

o **Locust Valley:** Most antiques hunters head to Port Jefferson, farther east on Long Island's north shore. And that's exactly why you should hit this tiny town that's not even on many maps—the goods are less picked over, and the antiques are of excellent quality. See chapter 6.

o **Hudson:** This formerly run-down town along the Upper Hudson has exploded with high-end and eclectic antiques shops, making it *the* antiquing destination of the Hudson River Valley (indeed of any place in the state north of Manhattan). Almost all the dealers are confined to the long stretch of Warren Street, making it ideal for window-shopping. See chapter 7.

o **Bloomfield Antique Country Mile:** Just west of Canandaigua, this mile-long cluster of antiques dealers along routes 5 and 20 in Bloomfield is one of the best concentrations for antiquing in the Finger Lakes, with several multidealer shops lined up back-to-back. See chapter 11.

THE best HIKES

o **Mashomack Preserve, Shelter Island:** With more than 2,000 pristine acres in the southeastern part of the island, this preserve, run by the Nature Conservancy, is about as remote as you can get on Long Island. There are 11 miles of easy hiking trails that run through the oak woodlands, marshes, ponds, and creeks. Keep an eye out for osprey, ibis, foxes, harbor seals, and terrapins. See chapter 6.

o **Hudson River Valley:** Though the Hudson Valley is more hilly than mountainous, tucked in the southern highlands are several excellent spots for day hikes. Hudson Highlands State Park near Cold Spring has a number of great day trails, as do Bear Mountain and Harriman state parks, some following a section of the Appalachian Trail. Many are surprisingly challenging. See chapter 7.

o **Catskill Region:** Some of the most scenic hiking in New York State is through the dense forests and along the stony ridges lacing the Catskills, where there are nearly three dozen peaks above 3,500 feet. The 6,000-acre Mohonk Preserve, part of the Shawangunk Mountains, has 60 miles of trails. Nearby Minnewaska State Park Preserve offers another 12,000 acres perfect for hiking and mountain biking, with 30 miles of footpaths and carriageways. See chapter 8.

o **Southern Adirondacks:** How adventuresome are you feeling? If the answer is "very," head to Lake George for a crazy steep climb up Black Mountain, an 8.5-mile round-trip with a 1,100-foot vertical rise and some amazing views of the lake and mountains. If you want a great view without so much work, Bald Mountain, east of Old Forge, is also steep but much shorter (2 miles round-trip). For a hike back in the woods, check out Cascade Lake, just north of Eagle Bay. It's an easy 5-mile walk to the lake that takes you past a gorgeous waterfall. See chapter 12.

o **Northern Adirondacks:** New York State's highest peak is Mount Marcy, at 5,344 feet. It's not the easiest climb, but for anyone with aspirations to nab the state's highest spot, it's a must. Just watch out for crowds: Most people hike to the peak from the north, but take the Range Trail and you'll find fewer hikers and better views along the way. For an easier hike, check out High Falls Gorge, which offers a great, relaxing stroll along the Ausable River and its waterfalls. See chapter 12.

- **Letchworth State Park:** This western New York park is home to a stunning 400-foot-deep gorge, with all sorts of hiking trails taking you past views of the deep chasm that's cut by the Genesee River. Trails go either deep into the forest or along the rim of the canyon; the Gorge Trail hits the most scenic spots. It's a 7-mile trail one-way, and moderately difficult, but, of course, you can turn around at any time. Take the kids along the Pond Trail, an easy .75-mile walk that leads you to a small pond stocked with fish. See chapter 13.

THE best FAMILY VACATION SPOTS

- **Shelter Island:** Hardly the raging party scene that exists in the nearby Hamptons, Shelter Island makes for a quiet family retreat on the eastern end of Long Island. Hike, boat, or just relax. And because it's an island, there are very few ways to escape, meaning that—for better or worse—on this family vacation, you'll always be together. See chapter 6.
- **Mount Tremper & Phoenicia:** This spot in the southeastern Catskills—two small towns bunched together off the main road—serves up a surprising roster of activities for families. In Mount Tremper, at Catskill Corners, the Kaatskill Kaleidoscope Theatre is the world's largest kaleidoscope, occupying an old barn silo. In Phoenicia, just a couple of miles up the road, families can rent inner tubes and float down Esopus Creek, which slices the valley between towering mountains. See chapter 8.
- **Delaware & Ulster Railride:** In Arkville, the Delaware & Ulster Railride transports visitors through the Catskill Mountains in a historic train that departs from the old depot. Kids will especially love the special "Great Train Robbery" train, where costumed actors playfully hijack and rob the train. See chapter 8.
- **Saratoga Springs:** This genteel resort town welcomes families with its plenitude of parks, the Saratoga Children's Museum, and Saratoga Spa State Park, a huge and lovely urban park with miles of hiking trails, swimming pools, and a skating rink. But surely the most entertaining feature for kids is the Saratoga Race Course and the opportunity to attend a thoroughbred horse race. Kids can take a walking tour of the stables, learn how horses and jockeys prepare for races, and even dress up like jockeys. See chapter 9.
- **Rochester:** As the northeastern gateway to the Finger Lakes, this amiable upstate city overflows with great family activities. With Lake Ontario beaches, a 96-foot urban waterfall in the High Falls Historic District, and proximity to watersports at any of the Finger Lakes, it has plenty of good outdoor pastimes. But it also has three indoor spots with huge appeal to families, including the Strong Museum, one of the top children's museums in the country; the George Eastman House, a museum of photography in the home belonging to the founder of Kodak; and Genesee Country Village & Museum, a re-creation of a 19th-century village staffed by interpreters in period costume. See chapter 11.
- **Skaneateles:** This charming village at the north shore of the Finger Lake of the same name has tons of shops, restaurants, and inns that parents will love, but also plenty of activities for the entire family. In summer, children are sure to love the nostalgic long pier that extends over the water, as well as swimming and boating in one of the state's most beautiful lakes. But best of all are the winter holidays, when

Skaneateles comes alive with a Dickens Christmas celebration, with costumed Dickens characters taking over the streets, singing Christmas carols. See chapter 11.

o **Lake George:** This southern Adirondacks town is hardly a calm getaway in the summer, but it boasts distractions galore for families, including amusement parks, haunted houses, family restaurants, and all the lake swimming you can handle. See chapter 12.

o **Niagara Falls:** It isn't just for honeymooners anymore—it's also jammed with families. The famous cascading water appeals to people of all ages, and you can see it from high above, behind, or way down below on the ever-popular *Maid of the Mist*. But over on the Canadian side in the Clifton Hill area is where your kids will really want to go: There you'll find haunted houses, theme rides, and fun museums. See chapter 13.

THE best PLACES FOR WATERSPORTS

o **North Fork:** The protected waters of Long Island Sound (to the north of the fork) and Peconic Bay (to the south) make for the perfect place to head out with a boat. Whether it's a canoe, kayak, jet ski, paddleboard, or powerboat, you'll cruise around on relatively calm waters while keeping an eye out for herons, osprey, hawks, fish, seals, and turtles. See chapter 6.

o **Hudson River:** One of the best ways to see the Hudson River, America's first highway and one of the great rivers in the nation, is from the middle of it: on a boat. You can board a sightseeing cruise at Rondout Landing in Kingston on the *Rip Van Winkle*, or in Newburgh on *The Pride of the Hudson;* or take a sunset cruise aboard *Doxie*, a 31-foot sloop, or a traditional-style yacht. See chapter 7.

o **Delaware River:** Fly-fishing is legendary along the Delaware River and nearby Beaverkill and Willowemoc trout streams. The junction pool at Hancock, where the east and west branches join to form the main stem of the Delaware River, has long been celebrated for its preponderance of massive brown and rainbow trout. Pepacton Reservoir, also in the western Catskills, is perfect for open-water brown trout fishing. See chapter 8.

o **Finger Lakes & Erie Canal:** The gorgeous Finger Lakes are incredibly scenic spots for boating, water-skiing, and sailing. Seneca Lake has a picture-perfect port where you can hire a yacht or sailboat, including a vintage 1930 schooner yacht. At Keuka Lake, considered by many locals to be the prettiest of the Finger Lakes, there are boat cruises aboard the *Keuka Maid*. At several Finger Lakes, you can also rent kayaks and canoes if you're looking for an even more intimate experience on the water. Skaneateles Lake has one of the longest cruise-boat traditions in the region, and the lake is perfect for relaxed sightseeing and dinner cruises. See chapter 11.

o **Alexandria Bay, Thousand Islands:** The miles-wide St. Lawrence River, dotted with somewhere between 1,000 and 1,800 islands, comes tailor-made for watersports. Tool around in a powerboat, canoe, or kayak, and check out the castles and mansions that some of America's wealthiest families have built. Just watch out for tankers and other big ships—this is one of America's busiest shipping lanes! See chapter 12.

o **Lake George:** Peppered with islands small and large, 32-mile-long Lake George offers endless exploration, whether you're in a canoe, kayak, powerboat, or paddle-wheel tour boat. Get out and experience the thrill of water-skiing, or just kick back and paddle quietly along the shores. Rent boats in the town of Lake George or in Bolton Landing. See chapter 12.

o **Mirror Lake, Lake Placid:** Surrounded by the gorgeous peaks of the Adirondacks, this lake comes to life in the summer with all kinds of boats plying the waters. The only drawback is that while it's superconvenient (Lake Placid sits right above it), it can get a little too crowded. See chapter 12.

THE best ONE-OF-A-KIND EXPERIENCES

o **Walking the Brooklyn Bridge:** One of the great New York activities of all time. The skyline view heading toward Manhattan from Brooklyn is unparalleled. The walk takes 20 to 40 minutes, depending on your pace, and every minute on this 19th-century architectural marvel is exhilarating. See chapter 5.

o **Sleeping in a Historic Lighthouse:** Several hotels tout their proximity to the Hudson River, but in the Upper Hudson Valley, you can sleep at the 1869 Saugerties Lighthouse (© 845/247-0656), which functions as a B&B and is perched at water's edge. The only way to get to it is by walking a mile-long trail through woods and wetlands. See chapter 8.

o **Reliving America's Glory Days:** Vintage "base ball," a nostalgic sport played by old-school traditionalists partial to the 19th-century rules and uniforms of America's classic sport, is played in several parts of New York. In Roxbury, in the northwest Catskill region, locals take it especially seriously. The best time to see a game is on Labor Day, when the Roxbury Nine hosts a home game and the town celebrates "Turn of the Century Day." Locals turn out in period costume, and the opposing team arrives by vintage train. See chapter 8.

o **Attending a Baseball Hall of Fame Induction Ceremony:** Every July, a new generation of players is transformed from mortal to legendary as inductees take their place alongside Babe Ruth, Lou Gehrig, and the other greats in Cooperstown's Baseball Hall of Fame. See chapter 10.

o **Gorging on Grape Pie in Naples, Finger Lakes Region:** There's a reason grape pie hasn't earned a spot alongside apple, cherry, and peach in the pie pantheon: Peeling grapes is just too laborious. But every year, on the last weekend in September, the attractive little village of Naples near Keuka Lake becomes the grape-pie capital of the world; nearly everyone seems to be selling, buying, and eating them. Grape fanatics and pie pilgrims come from all over to attend the Naples Grape Festival and stuff themselves silly with grape pie. See chapter 11.

o **Soaring the Friendly Skies:** The Finger Lakes are gorgeous from any angle, but a bird's-eye perspective—in a vintage warplane or a silent glider plane—is one of the most unique experiences to be had in New York State. At the National Warplane Museum, near Elmira, you can take to the sky in a PT-17 or even a B-17 bomber. And at the nearby National Soaring Museum, visitors can climb aboard sailplanes for peaceful, quiet rides that soar above the valleys around Corning. See chapter 11.

o **Ice-Skating on the Olympic Rink, Lake Placid:** Slip on your silver skates and take to the same rink where Eric Heiden won his gold medals in the 1980 Olympics. It's a public rink, so there's no pressure to race, just glide at your leisure while taking in the majesty of the surrounding Adirondacks. See chapter 12.

o **Eating Beef on Weck in Buffalo:** We like wings well enough, but you can get decent wings anywhere—including at Buffalo's Anchor Bar, where they were invented. But Beef on Weck—sliced roast beef on *kummelweck,* a German kaiser roll sprinkled with pretzel salt and caraway seeds—is a whole other story. For a true, only-in-Buffalo culinary event, head to Schwabl's (technically in the hamlet of West Seneca), to taste this zesty, delicious sockdolager of a sandwich. See chapter 13.

o **Watching Fireworks over Niagara Falls:** On the Canadian side of the falls every Friday and Sunday from May to September, there's a concert from 8 to 10pm, followed by an amazing show in which the sky lights up with fireworks and colored lights shine on the cascading water. Not going during the summer? No worries: You can see the falls lit up every night of the year. Walk along the railing of the Canadian side for the best view. See chapter 13.

THE best HISTORIC PLACES

o **Grand Central Terminal:** Despite all the steel-and-glass skyscrapers in New York, there are still many historic marvels standing, and the best is this Beaux Arts gem. This railroad station, built in 1913, was restored in the 1990s to recapture its brilliance. Even if you don't have to catch a train, make sure you visit. See chapter 5.

o **Sagamore Hill, Oyster Bay:** Theodore Roosevelt's summer White House still stands out on his beloved stretch of earth overlooking Long Island Sound. The decor of this 23-room Victorian estate reflects the president's travels with the Rough Riders; it's jammed with animal skins and heads, and exotic treasures from East Africa to the Amazon. See chapter 6.

o **Hudson Valley's Great Estates:** American history was made up and down the Hudson River, and not just at Revolutionary War battle sites. The grand estates of important literary figures, railroad magnates, and finance barons—including Washington Irving's Sleepy Hollow, the Lyndhurst Estate, the Rockefeller Family's Kykuit Estate, and the Vanderbilt Mansion—are lasting portraits of a young country's great expansion and riches at the height of the industrial age. See chapter 7.

o **Huguenot Street Stone Houses, New Paltz:** Founded in 1678, New Paltz is built around one of the oldest streets of surviving stone houses in North America. Along Huguenot Street are a half-dozen original Colonial-era stone houses built by French religious refugees, the Protestant Huguenots. The earliest was built in 1692, and all have been restored with period furnishings and heirlooms and operate as house museums (but guided tours of the houses are conducted in summer months only). See chapter 8.

o **Seneca Falls:** The small town of Seneca Falls is where the women's and civil rights movements got their start in the mid–19th century. The first Women's Rights Convention was held here in 1848, and today the Women's Rights National Historical Park has a museum erected next to the chapel where such brave activists as Elizabeth Cady Stanton, Lucretia Mott, and Frederick Douglass formalized the women's rights and abolitionist movements that would ultimately redefine the concept of individual liberty. See chapter 11.

o **Great Camp Sagamore:** Back when wealthy industrialists were exploring the concept of leisure travel, they discovered the Adirondacks. Of course, "roughing it" to the Vanderbilts wasn't exactly sleeping in a lean-to. This camp, 4 miles south of Raquette Lake, is a 27-building "Great Camp" filled with rustic luxury—there's even a bowling alley. Today, you can check out what this camp in the woods was all about. See chapter 12.

- **Downtown Buffalo:** It's hard to believe that 100 years ago, this area was home to more millionaires per capita than anywhere else in the U.S. Fortunately, those wealthy industrialists left behind a wonderful architectural legacy, and buildings designed by the likes of E. B. Green and H. H. Richardson still grace the city's skyline. From City Hall to the amazing Ellicott Square building, it's worth walking around downtown and checking out the sites. See chapter 13.

THE best PLACES TO COMMUNE WITH NATURE

- **Fire Island, Long Island:** This slender island protecting the mainland is replete with trees, wilderness, and one entire side of gorgeous golden-sand beach. Best of all, cars aren't allowed, meaning bikes and little red wagons are the only things that can run you over. And because the island is 32 miles long but just a half-mile wide, you're never more than a short walk from the ocean's waves and beach. For a truly remote wilderness experience, head to the eastern end, where it'll likely just be you and the deer in the gorgeous environment. See chapter 6.

- **Howe Caverns:** Not all of Mother Nature's handiwork is aboveground—deep beneath the earth's surface you'll discover a wonderland of mysterious rock formations in every color, size, and shape at New York's most popular natural attraction after Niagara Falls. A variety of tours will thrill everyone, from families with young kids to hard-core adrenaline junkies. See chapter 10.

- **Kaaterskill Falls:** The Catskill Mountains are all about the great outdoors, providing lots of invitations to hike, bike, ski, boat, and fish. But one of those unique spots where everyone is sure to feel just a little closer to nature is Kaaterskill Falls, the highest waterfall in New York State. It's not nearly as powerful and massive as Niagara Falls, though it is indeed higher. An easy but beautiful walk, wending along a flowing creek, takes you to the bottom of the falls. See chapter 8.

- **Shawangunk Mountains:** Rock-climbing enthusiasts from across the country descend on the white 1,200-foot-high cliffs of the 'Gunks, as they're known locally, for spectacularly sheer climbing opportunities. Combine that with some hiking in the 6,000-acre Mohonk Preserve, and then venture to Skytop for panoramic views of the Catskills and as many as six states on a clear day. See chapter 8.

- **Montezuma National Wildlife Refuge, Finger Lakes Region:** Smack in the middle of the Atlantic Migratory Flyway, at the north end of Cayuga Lake, this 7,000-acre wetlands nature park, established in 1938, is superb for birding and a spectacular nature experience for families. The marshes draw thousands of Canada geese, blue herons, egrets, wood ducks, and other water birds on their sojourns from nesting areas in Canada, reaching temporary populations as great as two million birds during the fall and spring migrations. You can drive, cycle, or walk along a road that takes you up close and personal with birds and other creatures. See chapter 11.

- **Watkins Glen State Park:** There are too many great nature spots in the Finger Lakes to even discuss or hope to visit on a single trip, starting with the sinewy lakes themselves, but this 776-acre park is surely at the top of any list. Its centerpiece is an amazing slate gorge carved out of the earth at the end of the last ice age, gradually shaped by the waters of Glen Creek. Along the beautiful walking trails are 19 waterfalls. See chapter 11.

o **St. Regis Canoe Wilderness:** It's not easy these days to find a single body of water expressly reserved for nonmotorized boats, and it's even harder to find several bodies of water for the canoer/kayaker. But this remote area, tucked deep in the heart of the Adirondacks, is just that. Take your boat out on these waters and it'll likely just be you and the birds as you cruise quietly through this amazing backcountry. See chapter 12.

THE best LEAF-PEEPING

o **Hudson River Valley:** Fall is one of the best times to visit the Hudson Valley. Temperatures are perfect and the great estates, many of them set among large old trees and gardens with gorgeous views of the Hudson, are splendid for aesthetic visits. The light is always great on the Hudson, but it's really special during the fall. See chapter 7.

o **Catskill Mountain Region:** Pick a county and go on a hike. Or kayak down the Delaware River. This extremely rural region is ideal for fall leaf-peeping. It's full of dairy farms and farmers' markets, emboldened by mountains and laced with lakes. The dense Catskill Forest Preserve is a kaleidoscope of color in autumn. See chapter 8.

o **Finger Lakes Region:** Autumn in the Finger Lakes region is impossibly scenic, with the golden hues of vineyards gracing the banks of deep-blue lakes, all set off against autumnal colors. It's a perfect time to visit the excellent wineries, take a boat cruise, or bike around the lakes. One of the prettiest routes, whether by car or by bike, is Route 54A around Keuka Lake. See chapter 11.

o **Warrensburg to Indian Lake:** This drive north nets you some amazing scenery and even more amazing fall colors. From I-87, take Route 73 through Keene Valley and Keene and you'll head straight into the Adirondack High Peaks area, one of the most scenic in the state, even without fall colors. You'll see mountains ablaze with oranges and reds; once you hit Lake Placid, go north on Route 86 and you'll be driving along the west branch of the Ausable River, also bright with color. See chapter 12.

o **Letchworth State Park:** Long and slender, the park's central feature is a 400-foot-deep cavern; the water from the Genesee River feeds tons of deciduous trees that absolutely light up with color during the fall. Go on a hike deep in the woods, or see it all from above in a balloon. See chapter 13.

THE best FOUR-SEASON TOWNS

o **Saratoga Springs:** Although summer is the star season in Saratoga, this small city is also an excellent year-round destination. In warm months, the one-time "Queen of the Spas" sees thoroughbred racing at the famed Race Course, where the season lasts from the end of July to Labor Day; open-air concerts in the park; the New York City Ballet and Philadelphia Orchestra in residence; and boating and fishing on Saratoga Lake. However, Saratoga is eminently enjoyable in spring, fall, and even winter, when visitors can enjoy cross-country skiing and ice-skating. See chapter 9.

o **Ithaca:** This college town is a great place to visit no matter what season, with its varied menu of sports and culture available year-round. The great hikes along Cayuga Lake and to nearby gorges are perfect ways to enjoy spring, summer, and fall. Cornell University's attractions, including the Herbert F. Johnson Museum of Art and Cornell Plantations' botanical garden, wildflower garden, and arboretum, can easily be enjoyed at any time of year. The nearby wineries of the Cayuga Wine Trail make great visits in any season (though they're perhaps best in fall during harvest). In winter, there are nearby downhill skiing and lots of cross-country skiing. See chapter 11.

o **Lake Placid:** In the summer, go boating on Mirror Lake, hike the many trails just outside town, or canoe along your own quiet stretch of lake. In winter, things really swing: The home of two Olympic Games, Lake Placid offers the opportunity to ski Whiteface Mountain, ice-skate, try the bobsled run, or go dog-sledding on Mirror Lake. See chapter 12.

o **Buffalo:** Okay, it might be a little crazy to visit Buffalo in the depths of snowy winter, but things never shut down here. At any time of year, you can walk (or drive) downtown to check out the city's gorgeous architecture, stroll through its amazing Albright-Knox Art Gallery, take in a professional football or hockey game (in the right season, of course), and finish off the day with some of the city's famous wings in one of its many atmospheric old bars. See chapter 13.

THE most ADORABLE TOWNS

o **Greenport:** This is the cutest town on Long Island's North Fork. Filled with Colonial buildings, inns, homes, and shops, the town sits right on the protected waters of Peconic Bay. There's a strong sense of the town's history as a fishing village, with the smell of salt in the air, but there are also nice galleries and restaurants that line Main Street. See chapter 6.

o **Cold Spring:** Perhaps the most visitor-friendly small town on the Hudson, warm and inviting Cold Spring has something for everyone. The historic waterfront, equipped with a Victorian band shell and park benches, has unequaled views of the Hudson River; Main Street is packed with antiques shops, cafes, and restaurants; and the nearby mountains are perfect for surprisingly rigorous hikes. Cold Spring is within easy reach of lots of historic estates along the river, and the town's excellent handful of restaurants and inns could easily entice you to a much longer stay than you had planned. See chapter 7.

o **Aurora:** A tiny, picture-perfect village hugging the east shore of Cayuga Lake, Aurora, now in the throes of full-scale revitalization, could be a movie set. It pretty much consists of a main street, a village market, a pizza restaurant, an ice-cream parlor, a historic inn, a whimsical ceramics factory, and a women's college. The town owes its startling makeover to the efforts of the Aurora Foundation, set up by a single benefactor who made it big with American Girl dolls and set about overseeing the restoration of the village's historic buildings, including the beautiful 1833 Aurora Inn (like the town, on the National Register of Historic Places). Visiting the campus of ceramics maker MacKenzie-Childs is about as close to a Willy Wonka wonderland as you'll get. See chapter 11.

- **Cooperstown:** This chain store–free town is best known for being home to the Baseball Hall of Fame. But sitting on the shores of Lake Otsego, it's also one of the state's cutest small towns. Tiny buildings and shops line the short Main Street, and you can walk its length in just a few minutes. You'll find quaint inns, good restaurants, and plenty of baseball-card shops; then walk down to the water and have a picnic lunch overlooking the quiet, undeveloped lake. See chapter 10.

- **Skaneateles:** They don't come any cuter (or harder to pronounce—it's "skinny atlas") than this graceful town, which is more reminiscent of New England than upstate New York. The historic downtown, an attractive mix of 19th-century Greek Revival and Victorian homes and appetizing boutiques and antiques shops lining East Genesee Street, sits right on the north shore of Skaneateles Lake. The beautiful and crystal-clear lake is one of the prettiest and cleanest in the state, and charming inns and restaurants back right up to it. In summer, bands play on the lakefront at a picturesque gazebo; in winter, costumed actors create a Dickensian holiday. See chapter 11.

- **Saranac Lake:** Less hectic than its neighbor, Lake Placid, this town boasts a charm all its own. With tiny clapboard shops mixed in with cute brick structures, the town has a couple of good restaurants, along with a pretty inn and clean streets. See chapter 12.

THE best ODDBALL ATTRACTIONS

- **Reviving the Borscht Belt:** The Catskill region has come a long way from the Borscht Belt vacationland where New York City families once retreated to day camps in the mountains. But there are still some of those old-school, all-in-one resorts—many of them ethnic enclaves of group entertainment and back-to-back activities like bowling, shuffleboard, and pale imitations of yesteryear game shows. One stands out: Scott's Oquaga Lake House, where generations of one family have been entertaining visitors, incredibly, since 1869. The resort is best known for the singing Scott family's nightly cabaret revues in which everyone from the costumed grandkids to the grandparents plays a rousing part. See p. 250.

- **700 Mormons Interpreting the Bible in Full Technicolor:** The Mormon Church, also known as the Church of Jesus Christ of Latter-day Saints, got its miraculous start in the Finger Lakes region before heading west. Every year in July, hundreds of thousands of the faithful and curious make pilgrimages to witness the Hill Cumorah Pageant, a giant spectacle that constitutes the largest outdoor theatrical production in the U.S. The show sports a costumed cast of 700, a nine-level stage, and music by the Mormon Tabernacle Choir. It has to be seen to be believed, but even nonbelievers enjoy the over-the-top show. See p. 339.

- **The Winery Impersonating Hooters:** Wine tasting is all about protocol and pompous, highbrow terms like *bouquet, nose,* and *body,* right? Not at Hazlitt 1852 Vineyards, in the Finger Lakes, where a visit to the vineyard is occasionally more akin to something you'd stumble upon at a college frat house. To start, the winery's bestseller is the mass-market "Red Cat," a low-rent party wine that has earned a reputation as an everyman's aphrodisiac. The winery revels in party atmosphere, rock-'n'-roll music, and irreverence toward traditional wine-tasting etiquette. See p. 322.

- **Kazoo Museum, Eden:** Who would go through the trouble of collecting wooden kazoos, gold kazoos, and liquor-bottle-shaped kazoos (celebrating the end of Prohibition)? People driven indoors by the brutal western New York winters, that's who. This museum has the oddest collection of this peculiar little instrument and, until recently, was making even more. See chapter 13.
- **Town of Mediums, Lily Dale:** This haven for those in touch with otherworldly spirits has been celebrating its odd collection of residents for nearly 130 years. You can stop by for a private reading any time of year, or come in the summer for daily events, along with meditation and healing services. See chapter 13.

NEW YORK STATE IN DEPTH

by Neil Edward Schlecht

For many people across the globe, New York—or perhaps more specifically, New York City—is the United States. Much of what is identifiably American, from commerce to art and popular culture, has a New York imprint.

As home to the Statue of Liberty and Ellis Island, New York paved the way for the U.S. model of immigration and integration. Baseball was invented upstate in Cooperstown, and the New York Yankees are among the most fabled sports teams ever to take the field. New York's distinctive language has thoroughly infiltrated American and international culture, from the working-class New Yawk accents of Brooklyn and Queens and the urban street slang appropriated from the worlds of jazz and hip-hop to Latino-inflected English (by virtue of large Puerto Rican and Dominican populations) and Yiddish words that have filtered down from New York City's Jewish community.

Even though New York may represent the U.S. in the eyes of many, New York is two wildly disparate things: the city—New York, New York—and the rest of the state. New York is perhaps the most international city in history, and though Manhattan is an island just 14 miles long, it and the other four boroughs cast a giant shadow across the state. New York is nearly 30 times as large as (and 7 hr. by car from) the next biggest city, Buffalo.

New York State has lived up to the sobriquet George Washington himself reportedly gave it: the Empire State. Although crucial early events took place in Massachusetts, Pennsylvania, and Virginia, the nation was effectively built in New York. Henry Hudson navigated the first great American river (later named for him), strategically important during the American Revolutionary War. The engineering of the Erie Canal enabled the opening of the West. And Ellis Island received generations of immigrants who formed a national labor force and gave the young country strength through diversity. While New York is no longer the most populous state in the country, having surrendered that title to California, it has hardly relinquished its place of honor among states.

Impressions

New York is to the nation what the white church spire is to the village—the visible symbol of aspiration and faith, the white plume saying the way is up!

—E. B. White

A beacon for visitors and immigrants for 2 centuries, New York City remains one of the most ethnically diverse and dynamic cities on the planet. A global capital of big business, banking, and the arts, it has set new standards for urban culture and living (and in many cases, prices). New York City has given the world Madison Avenue advertising, Broadway theater, SoHo contemporary art, and Wall Street finance. Yet the disparity between the hyperurban environment of the city and the vast majority of New York State, overwhelmingly rural and agricultural, could not be greater.

Apart from Manhattan's megawatt tourist attractions, much of New York State is still waiting to be discovered. Although New Yorkers have long vacationed in the Catskill and Adirondack mountains, for too long too few other visitors have seen what lies between its two tourist bookends, New York City and Niagara Falls. The historic Hudson Valley is finally positioning itself as a destination, not just a day trip from the city. The great wilderness of the Adirondacks and Catskills and the pristine glacial-lake beauty of the Finger Lakes are magnificent for outdoors and sporting vacations, and home to easygoing small towns. And Long Island is home to splendid sandy Atlantic Ocean beaches, excellent wineries, and the gulf of economic extremes, ranging from blue-collar immigrant enclaves to elite summer homes in the Hamptons.

NEW YORK TODAY

For New Yorkers, the upstate/downstate divide is the foundation for an occasionally uneasy relationship. Many residents of New York City, which they dare to call, with typical humility, "the City," lump anything north of Manhattan into "upstate" and think of it as an unappealing mix of wilderness and blue-collar towns. While some Manhattanites owe their sanity to weekend and summer houses upstate or on the East End of Long Island, other city dwellers recoil at the thought of peace and quiet—and critters. Addicted to asphalt and yellow cabs, those urbanites find bewilderment in the country, not escape.

Most recently, New York became the sixth state in the country to make same-sex marriages legal, on June 24, 2011. Greenwich Village, for many the epicenter of the gay rights movement since the days of the Stonewall riot in 1969, erupted this time in joy, with exuberant gay-marriage supporters filling the streets after midnight as soon as the State Senate's decision was announced. The first gay couples married in New York a month later, on July 24, 2011.

New York City is inextricably tied to the rest of the state, and not just because of what does (or does not) go on in the capital, Albany. New York depends on the watershed of the Catskill Region for its freshwater supply, a fact that has preserved much of the natural beauty upstate but also precluded development. Even if upstaters resent that critical relationship, they also know how linked their economic fortunes are to weekenders, visitors, and economic resources flowing north from the City. Of course, that doesn't stop upstaters from mocking city residents who believe they can pop over to the Finger Lakes (5 hr. by car) for lunch as if they were crossing the 59th Street Bridge to check out a new ethnic restaurant in Queens.

Not unexpectedly, New York also plays an outsize role in national politics. After leaving the White House, former First Lady Hillary Rodham Clinton became the junior senator of the Clintons' adopted state (they reside in Westchester County's tony Chappaqua), a position she used as a platform to run for president against her fellow senator, Barack Obama. When former Governor Eliot Spitzer, a crusader for cleaning up Wall Street, was busted for frequenting an uptown call girl, it was national news and fodder for comedians. The theme of New York politician behaving badly was revisited in 2011 when Congressman Anthony Wiener from Queens was discovered to have been sending lewd photos of himself to female followers on Twitter.

And of course, Wall Street continues to make national news, from its role in the recent economic crisis, with the collapse of such major banks as Lehman Brothers, the absorption of Merrill Lynch by Bank of America, and the federal bailout of the mammoth insurer AIG, to record bonuses for some trading firms, such as Goldman Sachs. With continuing job losses, a declining real estate market, and revelations that Bernie Madoff, a former chairman of NASDAQ, swindled investors out of $50 billion in a Ponzi scheme, New Yorkers—outside of members of that rarified breed who are in a position to award themselves massive year-old bonuses—perhaps aren't feeling as on top of the world as they once were. The same could be said for many of their upstate counterparts, in areas that have been hit hard in the past by economic down-swings and are again.

That said, resilience and certain toughness are almost a prerequisite for being a New Yorker—whether a resident of the biggest and most dynamic city in the country or the vast state that lives in its massive shadow.

LOOKING BACK: NEW YORK STATE HISTORY

New York State's original inhabitants were Native Americans, with the two largest groups the Algonquins and the Iroquois. The Six Iroquois Nations—the Mohawks, Oneidas, Onondagas, Cayugas, Senecas, and Tuscaroras—formed the Iroquois Con-federacy in 1570 at a meeting of the Great Council in Onondaga, in upstate New York, and established joint rule of the area west of the Hudson River and east of Lake Erie.

France commissioned an expedition by the Italian explorer Giovanni da Verrazano in 1524, and he is credited as the first European to sail into the New York Harbor. Henry Hudson, under contract to the Dutch East India Company, was searching for the fabled Northwest Passage to the Orient in 1609 when he sailed the great river that would later be named for him. The enterprising Dutch claimed the new lands and called the area *New Netherland*, though the Frenchman Samuel de Champlain, exploring the region around the same time, claimed the same land for France.

Colonial History & Revolutionary War

In 1624, Dutch settlers established a colony in Fort Orange (now Albany), the first permanent European settlement. The governor of the Dutch colony purchased Man-hattan Island from the Algonquins, for the bargain sum of the equivalent of about $25 in skins and furs, and called it New Amsterdam. The colony, under constant threat from Native Americans, existed solely for trade but did not exactly flourish. Four decades later, in 1664, the Dutch surrendered the colony to the English with no resistance. The new English colony was named New York, for the Duke of York (later King James II).

France and England would battle for control of North America for the better part of a century. The French and Indian War, declared by England in 1756, allied the Iroquois with the British and ended in the Treaty of Paris in 1763, effectively ending the French threat to British sovereignty in the colonies.

New York was the crown of England's American empire. With the Hudson the principal highway for transport of goods and men, New York was of pivotal strategic importance during the Revolutionary War, which began in 1776. The New York colony was divided, with many Patriots rebelling against British policies and rule, and others, Loyalists, supporting the crown. New York was the principal battleground in the Revolutionary War; about one-third of all battles, including some of the fiercest and most important, such as the tide-turning Battle of Saratoga in 1777, took place on New York territory.

Independence & the Empire State

On July 9, 1776, New York approved the Declaration of Independence and established an independent government; the New York Senate met for the first time in Kingston in 1777. New York ratified the Constitution and became the 11th state of the Union on July 26, 1778.

British troops evacuated New York City, their longtime stronghold, November 25, 1783, and England recognized the independence of the United States. General George Washington famously bade farewell to his officers 10 days later at Fraunces Tavern in Manhattan.

After ratification of the Federal Constitution, New York City became the first capital of the new nation, a title it would hold for 5 years. President George Washington was inaugurated in New York on April 30, 1789. The state's economic and industrial progress prompted George Washington to nickname it the Empire State— "the seat of our Empire." The New York Stock Exchange, founded in 1792, transformed New York into a center of global finance.

Industrial Growth

The Erie Canal, an engineering marvel completed in 1825, opened the west of the state, linking New York City to Buffalo, and transformed the port of New York into the world's busiest commercial port. New York State quickly became the gateway to the west and the economic engine of a rapidly industrializing nation.

New York played a pivotal role in growing political consciousness. The Underground Railroad that carried slaves to freedom in Canada had many supporters and important stops in New York, and Frederick Douglass published the abolitionist paper *The North Star,* in Rochester, in 1847. In 1848, the first Women's Rights Convention—the origin of the women's suffrage and civil rights movements in the U.S.—was held in Seneca Falls.

Presidential Birthplaces

Four of forty-four American presidents were born in New York State, including (no. 8) Martin Van Buren, 1837–41 (b. Dec. 5, 1782, Kinderhook); (no. 13) Millard Fillmore, 1850–53 (b. Jan. 7, 1800, Locke Township [now Summerhill]); (no. 26) Theodore Roosevelt, 1901–09 (b. Oct. 27, 1858, New York, New York); and (no. 32) Franklin Delano Roosevelt, 1933–45 (b. Jan. 30, 1882, Hyde Park).

LOCAL LINGO PRIMER

One of the most distinctive elements of New York City–speak—apart from the gruff, in-your-face style epitomized by Robert De Niro in the movie "Taxi Driver" ("You talkin' to me?") and the Long Island and Brooklyn cliché "fuggedabout it'"—is the preponderance of Yiddish words dropped into conversation by Jews and non-Jews alike. Here's a quick glossary:

chutzpah guts, daring, audacity

kvetch complain, gripe

mazel tov congratulations

mensch good person, stand-up guy

meshugeneh crazy person

oy vey exclamation of grief or horror

putz idiot

schlep drag or haul; to make a tedious journey

schmo jerk

schmuck fool

schmear spread (for instance, cream cheese on a bagel)

schmutz grime, dirt, the stuff that gets in New York City windows

shvitz sweat

By the mid-1800s, New York was the capitol of capitalism, with great fortunes amassed in trade, shipping, and railroads. The United States' industrial growth attracted millions of poor immigrants from Europe during the 19th century, transforming New York City into a "melting pot" of cultures, races, and religions. The Statue of Liberty, a gift from France, was placed in the New York harbor on Ellis Island and dedicated in 1886, its famous inscription, "Give me your tired, your poor, your huddled masses yearning to breathe free," a testament to the country's new global position. New York was by then the most populous state in the nation. By 1925, more than 12 million immigrants had passed through Ellis Island.

In October of 1929, the New York Stock Exchange crashed, leading to the Great Depression. New York Governor Franklin Roosevelt was elected President and initiated the "New Deal" jobs program.

New York City became the epicenter of the art world in the 1950s and 1960s. However, the state gradually lost population to the growing exodus south and west. New waves of immigrants, though, have continued to flock to New York City, predominantly from Latin America and Asia, and filter out across the state and country.

New York's global stature was tragically reaffirmed on September 11, 2001, when two large commercial airplanes, hijacked and piloted by terrorists, destroyed the Twin Towers of the World Trade Center in Lower Manhattan, killing nearly 2,700 people. The symbolism of striking New York was certainly not lost on the terrorists, nor was it lost on the rest of the world. (Reconstruction of the site continues at a frustratingly slow pace, after much deliberation and arguing over the Freedom Tower and memorial site, which led to the discarding of many features from the original 2002 design competition.) On a much more positive note for the city and nation involving the

Impressions

When it's 100 degrees in New York, it's 72 in Los Angeles. When it's 30 degrees in New York, in Los Angeles it's still 72. However, there are six million interesting people in New York, and 72 in Los Angeles.
—Playwright Neil Simon

crash of an aircraft, in January 2009 Capt. "Sully" Sullenberger gently landed a US Airways plane on the Hudson River, a masterful landing that saved the lives of all aboard—exactly 400 years after Henry Hudson first sailed the river, providing a neat symbolic bookend.

NEW YORK IN POPULAR CULTURE

Books & Literature

New York City has famously nurtured hundreds of famous writers (and been home to countless more who've struggled to survive and publish their art), many of whom portrayed the city in their works. **Edith Wharton** (NYC) chronicled the concerns and foibles of turn-of-the-20th-century Manhattan and Hudson Valley elites in such books as *The House of Mirth, The Age of Innocence,* and *Old New York.* **Washington Irving** (NYC/Tarrytown) coined the nickname "Gotham" for New York City and set *Legend of Sleepy Hollow* on the banks of the Hudson River; he also wrote the *Knickerbocker's History of New York,* a fictionalized history of the city when it was Dutch. **Henry James** (NYC) examined the psyches of New York residents in *Washington Square* and many essays, and **F. Scott Fitzgerald**'s *The Great Gatsby* was set on Long Island's North Shore (the Gold Coast). **Ralph Ellison**'s *Invisible Man* unforgettably wandered the streets of New York, while Holden Caulfield in **J. D. Salinger**'s *The Catcher in the Rye* had memorable encounters in the city after being expelled from prep school. **Mario Puzo** wrote *The Godfather,* the quintessential portrait of the New York Mafia families; and **Jay McInerney,** in *Bright Lights, Big City,* and **Tom Wolfe,** in *The Bonfire of the Vanities,* captured the ethos of 1980s New York, from the drugged-out club scene to "masters of the universe" and their trophy wives. For a look at upstate New York, don't miss the novels of **William Kennedy** (Albany), who penned an entire series of novels about life upstate in the capital, including *Ironweed;* and Pulitzer Prize winner **Richard Russo,** including *Nobody's Fool, Straight Man, Empire Falls,* and *Bridge of Sighs.*

Film

Woody Allen, Martin Scorsese, and Spike Lee are the three modern auteurs most closely identified with New York, not only because they hail from the city, but also because they've made New York a vital character in virtually all their films. **Woody Allen** (NYC) has repeatedly portrayed his native city with acerbic wit and charm—essentially making Manhattan a leading character—in movies like *Manhattan,*

New York Theater

For much of the English-speaking world, New York City's **Broadway** *is* theater (London's West End is its only rival). Besides being host to the biggest and most legendary dramatic plays and musicals, New York is also home to most of its finest actors, directors, and producers, as well as the setting for (and, really, a character in) many a memorable production, including *West Side Story, A Chorus Line, Angels in America, Rent, In the Heights, The Normal Heart,* and many, many more.

Annie Hall, Hannah and Her Sisters, Crimes and Misdemeanors, and *Manhattan Murder Mystery.* The visceral films of **Martin Scorsese** (New York's Little Italy), such as *Mean Streets, Taxi Driver, Raging Bull, The Age of Innocence, Goodfellas,* and *Gangs of New York,* exposed the rituals, fight for survival, and underbelly of urban life in New York. And **Spike Lee,** the inveterate New York Knicks fan, has delved into the city's complicated race relations and aspirations in lower-middle-class neighborhoods in Brooklyn's Bed-Stuy neighborhood, most memorably in *Do the Right Thing, Malcolm X,* and *She's Gotta Have It,* as well as *Crooklyn* and *Summer of Sam.*

A list of films set in and about New York City, often celebrating the city, is very long indeed; in addition to those of Scorsese, Allen, and Lee, a sampling of the most notable includes these: *King Kong* (1933); *On the Waterfront* (1954); *Rear Window* (1954); *The Apartment* (1960); *Breakfast at Tiffany's* (1961); *The Odd Couple* (1968); *Barefoot in the Park* (1967); *Funny Girl* (1968); *Midnight Cowboy* (1969); *The French Connection* (1971); *The Godfather* (1972); *Serpico* (1973); *The Way We Were* (1973); *Dog Day Afternoon* (1975); *Saturday Night Fever* (1977); *Once Upon a Time in America* (1984); *Desperately Seeking Susan* (1985); *Moonstruck* (1987); *Wall Street* (1987); *Working Girl* (1988); *When Harry Met Sally* (1989); *Eyes Wide Shut* (1999); *Requiem for a Dream* (2000); *The Squid and the Whale* (2005); and *Julie & Julia* (2009). In fairness to those who believe New York has been over-romanticized in the movies, there are several dozen, including *Independence Day* (1996) and *Planet of the Apes* (1968), in which the city has been cinematically destroyed! Fewer films are featured in the New York that extends beyond the city, though *Ironweed* (1987) is, like the book it's based on, set during the Great Depression in Albany; *You Can Count on Me* (2000) depicts small-town family troubles in the Catskills; *Eternal Sunshine of the Spotless Mind* (2004) takes place in large part in Montauk (East End of Long Island), even when it's inside the heads of its principals; and *Frozen River* (2008) examines the desperate transportation of illegal immigrants across the Canadian border into upstate New York. *Synecdoche New York* (2008) is Charlie Kaufman's story of a blocked theater director from upstate New York who creates a life-size replica of New York City inside a warehouse for a new play; in *Taking Woodstock* (2009), Ang Lee depicts the true story of how one young man tries to stage a small musical festival in the Catskills and sees it become the generation-defining Woodstock Festival; and Angelina Jolie filmed action scenes for the spy movie *Salt* (2010) in downtown Albany.

Music

Music is as much a part of the New York land (and sound) scape as art and theater. Great composers and musicians from New York include **George Gershwin** (Brooklyn), famous for "Rhapsody in Blue" and songs that celebrate New York City, including "Harlem River Chanty," "Union Square," and "New York Serenade." The New York jazz scene revolutionized pop culture in the '50s and '60s, with **John Coltrane, Miles Davis,** and **Thelonious Monk** playing and experimenting at the Village Vanguard and other downtown haunts. **Bob Dylan** hit the ground running in Greenwich Village in 1961, launching a soundtrack to a countercultural movement, and **Beatlemania** landed on U.S. shores at Shea Stadium. Other members of the pop-music pantheon include **Lou Reed** (Freeport, Long Island), a founding member of the **Velvet Underground,** a scene-defining New York City band; and the Forest Hills, Queens, band **Ramones,** who jump-started punk rock with their "Blitzkrieg Bop." **Billy Joel,** who wrote "New York State of Mind," is now almost as well known for his automobile accidents in the Hamptons as his songbook. New York's hip-hop

Impressions

[Manhattan is] skyscraper national park.
—Kurt Vonnegut

artists, from **Run-DMC** to **Jay-Z,** defined the East Coast street sound. The indie rock scene of the 21st century has taken firm hold in Brooklyn (and specifically Williamsburg), providing a fertile home to buzzed-about bands like **Yeah Yeah Yeahs, The National,** and **Sufjan Stevens.** And if you've ever attended a sporting event in New York, you've undoubtedly heard your share of Frank Sinatra's "New York, New York" (and its signature lines, "If I can make it there/I'll make it anywhere/It's up to you/New York, New York"), surely the most famous song ever about the city (even though he hailed from across the Hudson in Hoboken, NJ). Jay-Z's "Empire State of Mind," featuring local girl **Alicia Keys,** is something of the modern-day version.

TV

While it may seem as though two of every three sitcoms on television is set in New York City, several shows over the past 4 decades, which include the most popular and acclaimed series ever on TV, elevated New York into a character that nearly outshone the stars. **"I Love Lucy"** was set in New York, until Lucy and Ricky Ricardo moved to Connecticut, and **"The Honeymooners"** was a portrait of marital strife and working-class life in Brooklyn. **"The Dick Van Dyke Show"** was set in the suburbs of Westchester County. **"All in the Family,"** about Archie Bunker and his lower-middle-class family in Queens, and **"Taxi"** defined the 1970s. The **Cosbys** lived in Brooklyn, and the cast of **"Friends"** lived in ridiculously large apartments downtown. **"NYPD Blue"** set the standard for gritty cop shows. The self-centered nut-jobs on **"Seinfeld"** lived and breathed the city's narcissism and obsessions on the Upper West Side; the fashion-, cocktail-, and man-obsessed girlfriends on **"Sex and the City"** paraded Manhattan streets in designer shoes (and the show's legacy and commercial voyeurism continues to draw themed tours to the bars and shopping haunts featured in the series); and the filming of **"Law and Order"** and its multiple spinoffs in real life long wreaked havoc with car owners who continually had to move their automobiles from choice parking spots to accommodate filming. The newest TV darlings to use New York City as a vital backdrop are **"30 Rock"** and **"Mad Men,"** the latter about 1960s advertising execs and their daily habits of martinis, cigarettes, and girlfriends in the city and wives in Westchester.

EATING & DRINKING

New York has left its mark on the national menu. The **hot dog** was born on Coney Island, Brooklyn, in 1871. **Bagels,** the thick salted **pretzels** sold on street corners, and stacked **pastrami deli sandwiches** are New York classics; locals argue about which are the best and visitors scramble to try them. Up in Buffalo, you'll find the same feelings toward their eponymous chicken wings and beef on weck. The Hudson Valley's **Culinary Institute of America** trains the finest chefs and food-industry professionals in the country and has several excellent student-operated restaurants on its campus that are open to the public. And of course New York City comprises one culinary ethnic enclave after another. The city's roster of Italian, Chinese, Indian, Middle Eastern, Vietnamese, Korean, Polish, German, and Ukrainian eateries established international cuisine in this country. With estimates of some 30,000 or more restaurants in the city, it would take more than a lifetime of eating out every night to get to them all. And top chefs from around the world, from Alain Ducasse and Thomas Keller to Nobu and Daniel Boulud, still fight for the prestige of having a signature restaurant in New York on their resume. Upstate and on Long Island, in country towns and midsize cities, restaurants take care to use fresh produce and meats from local farms and farmers' markets; the locavore and farm-to-table movement has taken root across New York State.

New York is home to the nation's oldest winemakers and is today the third-largest wine producer in the U.S.—even though relatively few people are aware of the range or quality of New York wines. Mostly, that is a problem of national distribution, but New York wines are definitely on the way up. The number of wineries continues to expand, and there are now more than 200. The state has three major grape-growing and wine-producing regions (which together produce nearly three dozen varieties of grapes): Eastern Long Island (principally the North Fork), the Finger Lakes, and the Hudson Valley. While some people quickly assume that New York is too far north and too cold to provide the right climatic conditions, New York wine regions are "cool climate" regions roughly parallel in latitude to the famed Burgundy and Bordeaux regions in France.

Most New York wineries are small operations, but most welcome visitors, and more than three million people visit each year for tours and tastings. Entire vacations can be constructed around winery visits; a new trend, especially in the Finger Lakes and on the North Fork, is to hire a limousine to take you around to as many wineries as you dare. To make it even easier, many independent wineries have joined one of the dozen wine trails across New York State.

Long Island is New York's newest and fastest-growing wine region, just 3 decades old. The moderate climate produces some notable, low-alcohol reds, including "meritage" blends and merlots, and excellent whites, including what some wine writers have called among the best chardonnays currently produced in the U.S. All but three Long Island wineries are located on the North Fork (the others are on the South Fork, near the Hamptons). Wineries in the **Finger Lakes** produce outstanding rieslings, gewürztraminers, cabernet francs, ice wines, and other hard-to-find European varietals well-suited to the lakes' microclimates. Though it trails the other two regions in both quantity and quality, the **Hudson Valley** was the first wine-producing region in the U.S. (the French Huguenots planted the first vines near New Paltz in 1677, at least a century before vines were planted in what is today California). Today the Hudson Valley is home to two dozen wineries and two wine trails, the Dutchess and the Shawangunk. Finally, far upstate, Lake Erie has about a dozen wineries in the area that produce rieslings, seyvals, and ice wines.

WHEN TO GO

Because New York State is a four-season destination, the best time to visit depends on what you want to do.

Summer is peak season, accounting for about 40% of New York State tourism. New York City is swamped with tourists most of the year, but the number really swells in summer months with vacationing students, families, and foreign visitors—when the city can be truly stifling. Beyond New York City, summer weather is ideal for travel. If you have watersports on your mind, in the Adirondacks or along Long Island, this is of course the time to go. Parklands and campgrounds are filled with vacationers, especially on weekends. Cities throng with sightseers, making for long lines, sold-out events, and high prices.

Autumn is also a huge draw in much of the state, and leaf-peeping is a major touristic activity in the Hudson River Valley, the Catskill Mountain Region, the Adirondacks, and the Finger Lakes. New York's beautiful fall foliage is a huge draw, especially in mid-October—the best time to catch trees sporting brilliant reds and golds. Expect country inns, B&Bs, and state and national parks to be particularly busy over Columbus Day weekend.

Although statistically winter is the slowest time for tourism in New York, it is high season for the state's ski destinations, and parks are still active with winter-sports lovers. Those drawn to winter sports have plenty of choices, from skiing to snowshoeing, and the holiday season in many towns and cities, such as Skaneateles and New York City, is magical. Manhattan is extra jammed during the holidays thanks to Christmas festivities at Rockefeller Center, holiday shopping, and New Year's Eve in Times Square.

If you enjoy the quietly melting snow and fresh spring breezes, spring may be your golden opportunity to indulge in outdoor activities before the summer rush. New York City is especially pleasant before the summer heat begins.

WEATHER

From June to August, the weather is pleasant and mostly sunny, though it tends to be humid. Temperatures usually remain below 85°F (29°C), except in the vicinity of New York City and Long Island, which is about 10° warmer than the rest of the state year-round.

Average Monthly Temperatures

ALBANY	JAN	FEB	MAR	APR	MAY	JUNE	JULY	AUG	SEPT	OCT	NOV	DEC
°F	22	25	35	47	58	66	71	69	61	49	39	28
°C	-6	-4	2	8	14	19	22	21	16	9	4	-2

BUFFALO	JAN	FEB	MAR	APR	MAY	JUNE	JULY	AUG	SEPT	OCT	NOV	DEC
°F	25	26	34	45	57	66	71	69	62	51	40	30
°C	-4	-3	1	7	14	19	22	21	17	11	4	-1

NEW YORK CITY	JAN	FEB	MAR	APR	MAY	JUNE	JULY	AUG	SEPT	OCT	NOV	DEC
°F	33	35	42	52	62	72	77	76	69	58	48	38
°C	12	6	11	17	22	25	24	21	14	9	3	

SYRACUSE	JAN	FEB	MAR	APR	MAY	JUNE	JULY	AUG	SEPT	OCT	NOV	DEC
°F	23	25	34	45	57	66	71	69	61	50	40	29
°C	-5	-4	1	7	14	19	22	21	16	10	4	-2

Fall, from September to November, is another extremely popular time to visit. Upstate, the air turns to crisp jacket weather in September, but farther south, summertime lingers until early October. Contrary to popular belief, winter temperatures aren't miserable—they normally range from about 15°F (–9°C) to as high as 40°F (4°C) in New York City. The snow, on the other hand, can be brutal. Infamous lake-effect snowstorms can dump several feet at once on Buffalo and surrounding towns, prompting Thruway and airport closings. Most of upstate New York is blanketed in snow from December to March.

The spring thaw begins in March, but it's not unusual for snow to fall in April, or even May. There are spring showers, but the average amount of precipitation is no heavier than in summer or fall. Rainfall remains fairly constant from May to November at approximately 3 to 4 inches per month.

HOLIDAYS

Banks, government offices, post offices, and many stores, restaurants, and museums are closed on the following legal national holidays: January 1 (New Year's Day), the third Monday in January (Martin Luther King Day), the third Monday in February (Presidents' Day), the last Monday in May (Memorial Day), July 4 (Independence Day), the first Monday in September (Labor Day), the second Monday in October (Columbus Day), November 11 (Veterans Day/Armistice Day), the fourth Thursday in November (Thanksgiving Day), and December 25 (Christmas). The Tuesday after the first Monday in November is Election Day, a federal government holiday in presidential-election years (held every 4 years, and next in 2012).

Calendar of Events

For an exhaustive list of events beyond those listed here, check http://events.frommers.com, where you'll find a searchable, up-to-the-minute roster of what's happening in cities across New York State as well as all over the world.

JANUARY

Nature Valley Freestyle World Cup, Lake Placid. The world's best aerial skiers take off and fly, tucking and spinning their way to a championship. You'll see mogul action, too, as the athletes' skis zigzag among the mounds of snow. Call ✆ **518/523-2202,** or visit www.whiteface.com/events/freestyle.php. Mid- to late January.

FEBRUARY

Chinese New Year, New York City. Every year, Chinatown rings in its own new year (based on a lunar calendar) with 2 weeks of celebrations, including parades with dragon and lion dancers, plus vivid costumes of all kinds. Call ✆ **212/484-1222;** contact the Asian American Business Development Center at ✆ **212/966-0100,** or visit www.aabdc.com. Late January to mid-February.

Olmsted Winterfest, Buffalo. Delaware Park becomes a magnet for fun seekers, with sledding, skating, snowmobiling, softball, ice sculpting, a chili cook-off, and races taking place all over the park. There's a Friday Fish Fry, naturally, as well as fireworks. Call ✆ **716/838-1249,** or visit www.bfloparks.org. Four days in mid-February.

Empire State Winter Games, Lake Placid. The games for New York State's premier amateur athletes. Call ✆ **518/523-2445,** or visit www.empirestatewintergames.com. Early to mid-February.

MARCH

St. Patrick's Day Parade, New York City. More than 150,000 marchers join in the world's largest civilian parade, as Fifth Avenue from 44th to 86th streets rings with the sounds of bands and bagpipes. The parade usually starts at 11am, but go extra early if you want a good spot. Irish bars throughout the city throb with revelers (who are known for their completely out-of-hand, intoxicated, and usually inappropriate behavior). Call ✆ **212/484-1222,** or visit http://nyc-st-patrick-day-parade.org. March 17.

APRIL

Easter Parade, New York City. No marching bands, no baton twirlers, no protesters. It's more about flamboyant exhibitionism, with hats and costumes that get more outrageous every year—and anybody can join right in for free. It's along Fifth Avenue from 48th to 57th streets on Easter Sunday, from about 10am to 3 or 4pm. Call ✆ **212/484-1222.**

MAY

Lilac Festival, Rochester. More than 1,000 lilac trees in Highland Park, with dozens of varieties of fragrant lilacs in full bloom, are the excuse for a big civic party. There are music and food, but the highlight is easily the lilacs. Visit www.lilacfestival.com. Mid-May.

Bike New York: TD Bank Five Boro Bike Tour, New York City. The largest mass-participation cycling event in the United States attracts about 30,000 cyclists from all over the world. Call ☎ **212/870-2080,** or visit www.bikenewyork.org to register. First Sunday in May.

Tulip Festival, Albany. For more than 50 years, Albany has celebrated its Dutch heritage with this colorful festival, where, in addition to thousands of beautiful tulips in Washington Park, there is plenty of food, entertainment, and crafts—not to mention the annual crowning of the tulip queen! Call ☎ **518/434-2032,** or visit www.albany events.org. First or second week of May.

Falls Fireworks & Concert Series, Niagara Falls, Ontario. Every Friday and Sunday, you can enjoy free concerts by the falls at 8pm, followed by a fireworks show at 10pm, which bathes the falls in color. Call ☎ **877/642-7275,** or visit www.niagara parks.com. Mid-May to mid-September.

Fleet Week, New York City. About 10,000 U.S. Navy and Coast Guard personnel are "at liberty" in New York for the annual Fleet Week, an event immortalized in *Sex and the City.* Usually from 1 to 4pm daily, you can watch the ships and aircraft carriers as they dock at the piers on the west side of Manhattan, tour them with on-duty personnel, and watch some dramatic exhibitions by the U.S. Marines. Visit www.fleetweeknew york.com. Late May.

JUNE

Belmont Stakes, Elmont (Long Island). The third jewel in the Triple Crown is held at the Belmont Park Race Track. If a Triple Crown winner is to be named, it will happen here. For information, visit www.belmont-stakes. info. Early June.

Shakespeare in the Park, New York City. The Delacorte Theater in Central Park is the setting for first-rate free performances (often with marquee actors, such as Meryl Streep, Al Pacino, or Anne Hathaway) under the stars—including at least one Shakespeare production. Call ☎ **212/539-8500,** or point your browser to www.public theater.org. Early June to early September.

Caramoor International Music Festival, Katonah (Hudson River Valley). This idiosyncratic house-museum and performing arts center hosts one of the state's best music festivals, with a full slate of summer outdoor chamber and symphonic music concerts. Call ☎ **914/232-1252,** or visit www.caramoor.com. Late June to early August.

Hudson Valley Shakespeare Festival, Garrison (Hudson River Valley). On the gorgeous grounds of Boscobel Restoration, one of the prettiest spots along the Hudson, the summer theater performance of Shakespeare seems suitably grand, and perfect for a summer's-eve picnic. Call ☎ 845/265-7858 (845/265-9575 for tickets), or visit http://hvshakespeare.org. Mid-June to early September.

Shakespeare in Delaware Park, Buffalo. Free Shakespeare under the stars has been a Buffalo tradition for almost 30 years. Call ☎ **716/856-4533,** or visit www.shakespeare indelawarepark.org. Mid-June to mid-August.

Chautauqua season opens, Chautauqua Institution. This arts camp in western New York is one of the most prestigious in the nation. Its extensive grounds, right on the shores of Chautauqua Lake, play host to all manner of arts classes, lectures, and performances. Call ☎ **800/836-ARTS** (2787), or go to www.ciweb.org. Late June to end of August.

Museum Mile Festival, New York City. For New York City's "Biggest Block Party," Fifth Avenue, from 82nd to 105th streets, is closed to cars from 6 to 9pm as 20,000-plus strollers enjoy live music, street entertainers, and free admission to nine Museum Mile institutions, including the Metropolitan Museum of Art and the Guggenheim. Call ☎ **212/606-2296,** or visit www.museum milefestival.org. Second Tuesday in June.

Lesbian and Gay Pride Week and March, New York City. A week of cheerful happenings, from simple parties to major political fundraisers, precedes a zany parade commemorating the Stonewall Riots of June 27, 1969, which for many marked the beginning of the gay liberation movement. Call ✆ 212/80-PRIDE (807-7433), or visit www.nycpride.org. Late June.

Lake Placid Horse Show, Lake Placid. Watch horses take to the air in this prestigious horse show set against the gorgeous Adirondacks. Call ✆ 518/523-9625, or visit www.lakeplacidhorseshow.com. Late June to early July.

JULY

Glimmerglass Opera, Cooperstown. Central New York's famous opera gears up for another impressive season. Call ✆ 607/547-2255, or go to www.glimmerglass.org. Mid-July to end of August.

Hill Cumorah Pageant, Palmyra (Finger Lakes region). Near the site where the Mormon religion was founded, the Church of Jesus Christ of Latter-day Saints puts on an amazing theatrical spectacle, in the tradition of Middle Ages pageants, with 700 actors. Call ✆ 315/597-5851, or visit www.hillcumorah.org/pageant. First 2 weeks of July.

Macy's Fourth of July Fireworks Spectacular, New York City. Start the day amid the patriotic crowds at the Great July Fourth Festival in Lower Manhattan, and then catch Macy's great fireworks extravaganza (one of the country's most fantastic) over the East River or the Hudson River (after several years over the former, in 2009 the show lit up the sky over the Hudson, in honor of Henry Hudson's voyage 400 years earlier). Call ✆ 212/484-1222 or Macy's Visitor Center at 212/494-4495, or visit www.ny.com/holiday/july4. July 4.

Hurley Stone House Tour, Hurley (Catskill region). Unlike New Paltz, where the ancient stone structures are open in season to visitors, Hurley's collection of two dozen stone houses, most privately owned, open only once a year for visits. Call ✆ 845/331-4121, or visit www.stonehouseday.org. Early to mid-July.

Finger Lakes Wine Festival, Watkins Glen International Racetrack. The Finger Lakes is one of the country's great (but still up-and-coming) wine regions, and everybody gets together—locals, visitors, and some five dozen or so wineries—for tastings, crafts,

food, and good spirits. It's anything but stuffy, though, as the annual toga party (or "Launch of the Lakes") attests. Call ✆ 607/535-2486, or visit www.flwinefest.com. Mid-July.

Windham Chamber Music Festival, Windham (Catskill region). Opera stars from the Metropolitan in New York City descend upon the Catskill Mountains for some high culture at a higher altitude. Call ✆ 518/734-3868, or visit www.windhammusic.com. July to August.

Maverick Concert Series, Woodstock. America's oldest summer chamber music series, continual since 1916, is this agreeable version of "Music in the Woods." Call ✆ 845/679-8217, or visit www.maverickconcerts.org. July to early September.

Belleayre Music Festival, Highmount (Catskill region). The ski mountain of Belleayre races in summer with a wide-ranging mix of highbrow and popular music and entertainment, from classical and opera to folk and puppetry. Call ✆ 845/254-5600, or visit www.belleayremusic.org. July to early September.

Annual Wine Country Classic Boat Show & Regatta, Hammondsport (Finger Lakes region). At the southern end of Keuka Lake, this antique- and classic-boat show features more than 100 boats, with judging, water parades, and demonstrations. On Sunday is the race regatta. Call ✆ 585/526-6934, or visit www.hammondsport.org/events.htm. Mid-July.

Saratoga Summer Culture, Saratoga Springs. In July, the New York City Ballet makes its off-season home at the National Museum of Dance & Hall of Fame, and during the month of August, the Philadelphia Orchestra is in residence at the Saratoga Performing Arts Center (SPAC). Who would think that high culture could compete stride-for-stride with the horses over at the track for the big event of the summer? Call ✆ 518/584-2225 or 584-9330, or visit www.saratoga.com. July and August.

Baseball Hall of Fame Induction Weekend, Cooperstown. Come see which legendary swingers will make it in this year. Call

888/HALL-OF-FAME (425-5633), or visit www.baseballhalloffame.org. Late July.

Thoroughbred Horse Racing, Saratoga Springs (Capital region). At the famed Race Course, the oldest in the country, the race season lasts 6 weeks and turns the town upside down. Call ☎ **518/584-6200,** or visit www.nyra.com/index_saratoga.html. End of July to early September.

Bounty of the Hudson, Hudson Valley. A 2-day food and wine festival showcasing the best of the Hudson Valley, including cooking workshops and live music held at one of the local wineries. Tickets and more information are available at ☎ **845/256-8456** or **888/241-0769,** or www.shawangunkwinetrail.com. Last weekend in July.

AUGUST

Antique Boat Show & Auction, Clayton (Thousand Islands). It's the country's oldest antique boat show in the world—you can even bid on a boat at the auction. Cruise the commercial marketplace and flea market, sit in on an educational forum, listen to music, and sample food. Lots of kids programs, too. Contact the Antique Boat Museum at ☎ **315/686-4104,** or visit www.abm.org. Early August.

Harlem Week, New York City. The world's largest black and Hispanic cultural festival actually spans almost the whole month to include the Black Film Festival, the Harlem Jazz and Music Festival, and the Taste of Harlem Food Festival. Call ☎ **212/484-1222.** Throughout August.

NASCAR Sprint Cup Series at the Glen, Watkins Glen. Among legions of race fans, this huge event is unparalleled in the Northeast, and it draws NASCAR fans from across the state and region, filling up just about every bed in the Finger Lakes. Call ☎ **607/535-2486** (for tickets, **866/461-RACE** [7223]), or visit www.theglen.com. End of first week/beginning of second in August.

National Buffalo Wing Festival, Buffalo. This festival features many restaurants and sauces from Buffalo and around the country. Best wing and sauce competitions, wing-eating contests, and more. Call ☎ **716/565-4141,** or visit www.buffalowing.com. Late August/early September/Labor Day weekend.

New York State Fair, Syracuse (Finger Lakes region). New York State's massive 12-day agricultural and entertainment fair, with all kinds of big-name music acts and tasty fair treats you'll ultimately be glad come 'round only once a year. Call ☎ **800/475-FAIR** (3247), or visit www.nysfair.org. Late August to early September.

US Open Tennis Championships, New York City. The final Grand Slam event of the tennis season is held at the Arthur Ashe Stadium at the USTA Billie Jean King National Tennis Center, the largest public tennis center in the world, at Flushing Meadows Park in Queens. Tickets go on sale in May or early June, and the event sells out immediately. Call ☎ **888/OPEN-TIX** (673-6849) or 718/760-6200 well in advance; visit www.usopen.org or www.usta.com for additional information. Two weeks around Labor Day.

SEPTEMBER

Turn-of-the-Century Day, Roxbury (Catskill region). Reliving the glory days of baseball and hoop skirts, the town of Roxbury sheds about 100 years and celebrates with a vintage "base ball" game, horse-drawn wagon rides, and period foods and costumes on the former estate of Helen Gould Shepard in this Labor Day tradition. Call ☎ **607/326-7641,** or visit www.roxburyny.com/wordpress Labor Day weekend.

West Indian–American Day Parade, New York City. This annual Brooklyn event is New York's largest and best street celebration. Come for the extravagant costumes, pulsating rhythms (soca, calypso, reggae), bright colors, folklore, food (jerk chicken, Caribbean soul food), and two million hip-shaking revelers. Call ☎ **212/484-1222** or 718/625-1515. Labor Day.

Adirondack Balloon Festival, Glens Falls, Queensbury, and Lake George. Watch a rainbow of colors soar into the sky as 60-plus hot-air balloons lift off at New

York's largest hot-air balloon festival. Tons of activities surround this annual event. Visit www.adirondackballoonfest.org. Mid- to late September.

Naples Grape Festival, Naples (Finger Lakes region). To celebrate the harvest of the grape in this grape-growing and wine-producing region, grape pie lives for a weekend in the tiny town of Naples. Con-noisseurs rejoice, scarfing down as much pie as possible, and there are a "World's Greatest Grape Pie" contest and live enter-tainment. Visit www.naplesgrapefest.org. Third week in September.

OCTOBER

Legend Weekend at Sleepy Hollow and Philipsburg Manor, Tarrytown (Hudson River Valley). At Washington Irving's Sun-nyside home, as well as up the road at Philipsburg Manor, the specter of the Head-less Horseman returns for one last ride for Halloween. So as not to scare all concerned, there are also walks in the woods, storytell-ing, and puppet shows. Call 914/631-8200, or visit www.hudsonvalley.org. Last week in October.

Halloween at Howe Caverns (near Utica). Come check out the underground scare-a-thon with pumpkin-decorating contests, scary stories, and a special kids' buffet. Call 518/296-8900, or visit www.howe caverns.com. October 31.

Greenwich Village Halloween Parade, New York City. This is Halloween at its most outrageous. You may have heard Lou Reed singing about it on his classic album *New York*—and he wasn't exaggerating. Drag queens and assorted other flamboyant types parade through the Village in wildly creative costumes. Visit www.halloween-nyc.com or http://halloween.villagevoice.com/parade.php for the exact route so you can watch—or participate, if you have the threads and the imagination. October 31.

NOVEMBER

ING New York City Marathon, New York City. Some 30,000 hopefuls from around the world participate in the largest U.S. marathon, and more than a million fans cheer them on as they follow a route that touches on all five New York boroughs and finishes at Central Park. Call 212/423-2249 or 212/860-4455, or visit www.ing nycmarathon.org or www.nyrr.org, where you can find an application to run. First Sunday in November.

Lights in the Park, Buffalo. Delaware Park is transformed into a colorful wonderland throughout the holidays, with animated lighting displays and a collection of holiday scenes. Call 716/856-4533. Begins mid-November.

Winter Festival of Lights, Niagara Falls, Ontario. A visual lighting extravaganza fea-turing Disney's motion light displays in Queen Victoria Park. Call 800/563-2557 or 905/374-1616, or visit www.wfol.com. November to early January.

Macy's Thanksgiving Day Parade, New York City. The procession of huge hot-air balloons from Central Park West and 77th Street and down Broadway to Herald Square at 34th Street continues to be a national tradition. The night before, you can usually see the big balloons being blown up on Central Park West at 79th Street; call in advance to see if it will be open to the public again this year. Call 212/484-1222 or the Macy's Visitor Cen-ter at 212/494-2922, or visit http://social.macys.com/parade2010/#/home. Thanks-giving Day.

Christmas Traditions, New York City. Look for these holiday favorites: Radio City Music Hall's Christmas Spectacular (212/247-4777; www.radiocity.com); the New York City Ballet's staging of *The Nutcracker* (212/870-5570; www.nycballet.com); *A Christmas Carol* at the Theater at Madison Square Garden (212/465-6741; www.thegarden.com); and the National Chorale's singalong per-formances of Handel's *Messiah* at Avery Fisher Hall (212/875-5030; www.lincoln center.org). Call for schedules. Late Novem-ber to December.

Dickens Christmas, Skaneateles (Finger Lakes region). Sweet nostalgia takes over this quaint Finger Lakes town as costumed characters—Father Christmas, Mother

Goose, and Scrooge—roam the streets. Locals go door-to-door caroling, and there are carriage rides and free roasted chestnuts. Call © **315/685-0552,** or visit www.skaneateles.com. Last weekend in November to just before Christmas.

DECEMBER

Great Estates Candlelight Christmas Tours, Hudson River Valley. Some of the grandest mansions lining the Hudson River—Boscobel, Sunnyside, Van Cortlandt Manor, Lyndhurst, Olana, and others—get all decked out for the holidays, with special candlelight house tours, caroling, bonfires, and hot cider. It's one of the best times to experience the pageantry and customs of another era. Visit www.hudsonvalley.org. Throughout December.

Holiday Trimmings, New York City. Stroll down festive Fifth Avenue and you'll see doormen dressed as wooden soldiers at FAO Schwarz, a 27-foot sparkling snowflake floating over the intersection outside Tiffany & Co., the Cartier building ribboned and bowed in red, wreaths warming the necks of the New York Public Library's lions, and fanciful figurines in the windows of Saks Fifth Avenue and Lord & Taylor. Madison Avenue between 55th and 60th streets is also a good bet; Sony Plaza usually displays something fabulous, as does Barneys New York. Throughout December.

New Year's Eve, New York City. The biggest party of them all happens in Times Square, where thousands of raucous revelers in unison count down the year's final seconds until the new lighted ball drops at midnight at 1 Times Square. Hate to be a party pooper, but this one, in the cold surrounded by thousands of very drunk revelers, is a masochist's delight. Call © **212/768-1560** or 212/484-1222. December 31.

RESPONSIBLE TOURISM

Traveling "green," seeking sustainable tourism options, is a concern in almost every part of the world today. New York State, with its large expanses of nature upstate and the massive resources consumed in New York City, is no different. Although one could argue that any vacation that includes an airplane flight or a rental car can't be truly "green," you can go on holiday and still contribute positively to the environment. All travelers can take certain steps toward responsible travel. Choose forward-looking companies that embrace responsible development practices, helping preserve destinations for the future by working alongside local people. An increasing number of sustainable tourism initiatives can help you plan a family trip and leave as small a "footprint" as possible on the places you visit.

The American Conservation Movement began in New York. Much of New York State's eco-tourism activities are naturally focused on trips to 176 state and 24 national parks, including Adirondack Park, the Appalachian National Scenic Trail, the North Country National Scenic Trail, and Upper Delaware Scenic and Recreational River, among others.

Road Scholar (Elderhostel © **800/454-5768;** www.roadscholar.org) organizes a number of guided tours for naturalists and outdoors types. Those include explorations of Adirondacks flora; boating, kayaking, and canoeing at Adirondacks camps; nature hiking at Sagamore's Great Grand Camp (the Vanderbilt estate); paddling along historic water routes of the Adirondacks; hiking in the Adirondacks; fly-fishing in the Catskills; and hiking in the Catskills and Finger Lakes.

You can also find eco-friendly travel tips, statistics, and touring companies and associations—listed by destination under "Travel Choice"—at The International Ecotourism Society (TIES) website, **www.ecotourism.org**. Also check out **Conservation International** (www.conservation.org)—which, with *National Geographic*

Traveler, annually presents **World Legacy Awards** to those travel tour operators, businesses, organizations, and places that have made a significant contribution to sustainable tourism. **Ecotravel.com** is part online magazine and part eco-directory that lets you search for touring companies in several categories (water-based, land-based, spiritually oriented, and so on). Here are a few options for a sustainable trip in New York State:

The Omega Institute for Holistic Studies ★★★, 150 Lake Dr., Rhinebeck ℂ 877/944-2002; www.eomega.org), offers yoga and meditation retreats and workshops and is committed to green living and sustainable initiatives. The Institute's pioneering **Omega Center for Sustainable Living (OCSL),** inaugurated in July 2009, is an education center and natural wastewater treatment facility, and a model of sustainable architecture: Omega has deluxe green cabins with organic bedding and linens, local sustainable building materials, low-flow shower heads and dual-button toilets, compact fluorescent lighting, and air-conditioning and heat offset by wind-powered energy.

The **Apple Pond Farm and Renewable Energy Education Center ★★** (ℂ 845/482-4674; www.applepondfarm.com), 80 Hahn Rd., Callicoon (southwestern Catskill region), is a horse-powered organic farm that produces its own renewable energy. It offers demonstrations of milking; goat-cheese-making classes; farming for kids; and seminars and workshops on wind, photovoltaic, solar thermal, geothermal, and microhydro systems renewable energy. For family-friendly farm vacations (especially for city kids), guests stay at the three-bedroom guesthouse (which sleeps up to five; $400 for 2-night stay, $950 for week) and help out with daily chores and experience life on a working farm.

Kinderhook Farm ★★★ (ℂ 505/603-1815; www.kinderhookfarmstay.com), Route 21, Ghent NY (15 min. north of Hudson), offers farm stays in a beautifully renovated and decorated 18th-century farmhouse, on a 1,200-acre working farm. Children and adults can gather eggs in the morning, visit with lambs, and feed baby chicks, horses, and Ginny the donkey. Guests have their own kitchen garden to pick items for cooking their own dinner (farm-fresh eggs and produce are included), and they can visit the FarmStore for organic meat. Rates (for up to four adults and two children) are $285 per night, 2-night minimum; or $1,800 for a week.

Other New York farm stays are listed on **ILOVENY,** the official New York State tourism site: www.iloveny.com/Where-To-Stay/Listings.aspx?cat=fdr.

There are many more possibilities for "agrotourism," on **WWOOF,** the "World Wide Opportunities on Organic Farms" exchange program that facilitates opportunities to work on a farm and learn about organic farming practices and sustainable living. The organization counts several dozen farms in New York State among its participating members, including in Garrison, on Shelter Island, Chatham, Hurley, New Paltz, Saugerties, Callicoon, Trumansburg, and East Syracuse, among other communities. In exchange for volunteer help, WWOOF hosts offer food, accommodations, and learning opportunities. For information, visit www.wwoof.org and www.wwoofusa.org.

TOURS

Academic & Learning Trips

Although it's difficult not to learn a little something while visiting New York City, **Smithsonian Journeys** (ℂ 877/338-8687 or 800/528-8147; www.smithsonian

journeys.org) will make sure you do, with tours that include visits to "green" architectural landmarks, art collections, and artist studios; there are also art-themed cruises along the Hudson River and trips focusing on the performing arts and Broadway theater educational trips. History and architecture buffs should check out the trips offered by **National Trust for Historic Preservation Tours** (✆ 800/944-6847; www.preservationnation.org), which include Hudson River Valley fall foliage cruises (with visits to Revolutionary War Sites, historic estates along the Hudson, and immersion into the Hudson Valley School of Painting), and a trip focusing on "Architectural Preservation in New York City." **Road Scholar (Elderhostel)** ★★★ (✆ 800/454-5768; www.roadscholar.org) offers a wide variety of New York educational trips, ranging from historic Hudson Valley arts and mansions to Jewish history and humor, theater arts, and explorations of rural 19th-century frontier living. Their roster includes nearly 100 trips large and small to New York City and across the state. Students interested in group trips sans parental units can explore New York City while learning about its history, architecture, and culture with **Educational Tours, Inc.** (✆ 800/962-0060; www.educationaltours.com/Destinations/New-York-City).

Adventure & Wellness Trips

For adventure travel to New York State, check out **GORPtravel** (✆ 877/440-GORP [4677] or 303/516-1153; http://gorptravel.away.com), which offers several New York trips, including road biking along the Erie Canal, cycling the Hudson River greenway, biking the Finger Lakes, a Bronx walking tour (now there's real adventure!) and a Brooklyn Bridge bike tour. See also the variety of outdoors and educational trips offered by **Road Scholar,** the program arm of Elderhostel (see above).

ILOVENY, the official New York State tourism site, is a good source of information for those planning outdoor recreation in the state. It lists dozens of outdoor and adventure guided trips, from Adirondack trout fishing to canoeing and kayaking and hiking trips; visit www.iloveny.com and search for "outdoors guides."

Yoga, spiritual, and wellness retreats have found a niche in upstate New York, particularly in the Hudson River Valley and rural Catskill Mountain Region. The highly regarded **Omega Institute for Holistic Studies,** 150 Lake Dr., Rhinebeck (✆ 877/944-2002; www.eomega.org), has a massive campus on 185 acres. Among their weekend and weeklong wellness programs are "Rest and Rejuvenation Retreats," featuring meditation, yoga, tai chi, and other classes (p. 209). **New Age Health Spa,** 658 Rte. 55, Neversink (✆ 800/682-4348; www.newagehealthspa.com), on 280 acres in Sullivan County, is a relaxed, all-inclusive destination spa at the edge of the Catskills State Forest Preserve. It features a 10,000-square-foot yoga and meditation center and a full menu of yoga, meditation, spa treatments, and week and miniweek schedules. **Karma Triyana Dharmachakra Tibetan Buddhist Monastery,** 335 Meads Mountain Rd., Woodstock (✆ 845/679-5906; www.kagyu.org), offers Buddhist teaching, practice, and meditation retreats, including accommodations at the guesthouse, and vegetarian meals. Other upstate monasteries and ashrams offering stress-relieving meditation, Zen studies, fasting, and yoga retreats/vacations (as well as largely spartan, dorm-style accommodations) include these: **Vivekananda Retreat, Ridgely,** Leggett Road, Stone Ridge (✆ 845/687-4574; www.ridgely.org); **Zen Mountain Monastery,** Plank Road, Mount Tremper (✆ 845/688-2228; www.mro.org); **Sivananda Ashram Yoga Ranch,** Budd Road, Woodbourne (✆ 845/436-6492; www.sivananda.org/ranch); **Dai Bosatsu Zendo,** 223 Beecher Lake Rd., Livingston Manor (✆ 845/439-4566; www.daibosatsu.org); **Blue Cliff**

Monastery, 3 Mindfulness Rd., Pine Bush (© **845/733-4959;** www.bluecliff monastery.org); **Ananda Ashram,** 13 Sapphire Rd., Monroe (© **845/782-5575;** www.anandaashram.org); and **Zen Center of Syracuse Hoen-Ji,** 266 W. Seneca Tpk., Syracuse (© **315/492-9773;** www.zencenterofsyracuse.org).

Food & Wine Trips

Food and wine lovers will have their hands (and mouths) full on a trip to New York. You can enhance the experience with an organized tour that either takes in a city neighborhood's eats or plunges into the food and wine of New York State. **City Food Tours** (© 212/535-TOUR [8687]; www.cityfoodtours.com) offers guided walking tasting tours, ethnic eats trips, and more, while **Foods of New York** (© **212/209-3370** or 917/408-9539; www.foodsofny.com) organizes walking-and-eating tours of Chinatown, Greenwich Village and SoHo, Chelsea Market and the Meatpacking District, and visits to iconic food shops—as well as 3-night packages that take in all of the above. **Road Scholar (Elderhostel;** see above) features longer trips around the state; options include "Wine, Wineries, and the Culinary Institute of America," "Finger Lakes Wine and Geology," "Hudson River Valley/Catskills Food and Wine," and "Tastes of the City: New York's Food Culture." If you're interested in the North Fork of Long Island's burgeoning food and wine scene, which has grabbed a lot of wine writers' attention, and you want to learn more about becoming a oenophile, check out **Wine Camp** (© 631/495-9744; www.winecamp.org), which puts on 4-day immersion camps, teaching campers to taste wine like an expert and pair foods with wines (it's hardly drudgery; for homework you'll visit wineries and lunch at vineyards). Foodies should also check out New York State's Tourism Website (www.iloveny.com/TravelIdeas/VineandDine.aspx) for "Vine & Dine" ideas for food- and wine-oriented trips and events throughout the state, including food festivals and wine trails.

Guided Tours

Most escorted tours focus on short visits in New York City. **GOGO Worldwide Vacations** (www.gogoworldwidevacations.com) organizes short-term (generally 3-night) junkets to New York City and Niagara Falls, all offered through travel agents. **All New York Tours** (© 866/654-1396 or 702/233-1627; www.allnewyorktours.com) has a slew of short, themed tours (including helicopter tours and movie, TV, and music tours) in New York City, while **Get America Tours** (© **800/594-0025;** www.getamericatours.com) offers escorted minitours to New York City and Niagara Falls, including the latter's Festival of Lights in December. **Crosby Tours** (© **718/349-9600;** www.crosbytours.com) does a 3-day "Best of New York State" tour (which is at the very least an idiosyncratic take on that superlative and may be best for New Yorkers wanting to see more of their state), traveling to Howe Caverns, the Thousand Islands, and, finally, the Great New York State Fair. **Gray Line Tours** (© **800/803-5073;** www.grayline.com), one of the largest tour operators in the world, organizes a number of escorted bus trips, package tours, and day trips in New York City and Niagara Falls.

Volunteer & Working Trips

The concept of "voluntourism" has taken off on international trips, and increasingly there are options to do good at home while on vacation. **Earthwatch Institute** (© **800/776-0188;** www.earthwatch.org), which has plenty of options abroad, offers volunteer programs for urban ecosystem research and protecting the environment in and around New York City and the Hudson River. **Together Green,** in association with the National Audubon Society and based in New York City, has a number of environmental and conservation volunteer opportunities and events organized by state; check out the current roster of New York State volunteer gigs at www.togethergreen.org. A truly unique and valuable idea in volunteer trips is **Sprout** (© 212/222-9575; www.gosprout.org), which brings in volunteers to help adults with developmental disabilities to have their own vacations. Since 1979, volunteers have led small groups on 1- to 8-day trips in New York City, the area around New Paltz (Catskill Mountain Region), and Niagara Falls.

Walking Tours

ILOVENY, the official New York State tourism site, lists a number of walking tours (go to www.iloveny.com and search for "walking tours"), from tours of the historic Kingston Stockade district (www.ci.kingston.ny.us) and the Hassidic Crown Heights community (www.jewishtours.com) to culinary walking tours of New York City (www.foodevents.com; see also "Food & Wine Trips," above). **Gotham Walking Tours** (© 646/645-5782; www.walkingnyctours.com) offers a huge variety of themed and neighborhood walks, all led by Lina Viviano, in New York City, from architectural tours and "gay and lesbian Greenwich Village" to "Gangs of New York."

SUGGESTED NEW YORK STATE ITINERARIES

3

To experience the best of a large and diverse state like New York in a relatively short amount of time, you need a workable and efficient travel schedule. That's the point of this chapter. Of course, these are merely suggestions, and infinite variations and combinations are possible. We suggest you concentrate primarily on one region—the Adirondacks or the Finger Lakes, for example—rather than try to cover too much ground in one trip (or perhaps combine two geographically close regions, like the Hudson Valley and Catskills, or New York City and the East End of Long Island). These itineraries are designed for travel in a car—the most convenient way to get around the state—and some of the highlights below are particular to summer (or, to a lesser degree, spring or fall); winter in New York State may be ideal for skiers, but parts of the state virtually close up in the dead of winter.

THE REGIONS IN BRIEF

NEW YORK CITY   Residents in the surrounding areas of New York, New Jersey, and Connecticut refer to it simply as "the City," as if there were no other. The city comprises about 300 square miles divided into five boroughs—the Bronx, Brooklyn, Manhattan, Queens, and Staten Island. Best known for world-class museums, Broadway theater, Madison Avenue shopping, five-star cuisine, and glamorous nightlife, it's also a great place for more low-key adventures, like grabbing a hot dog at Yankee Stadium or spending a sunny afternoon in Central Park. For more about New York City, see chapter 5.

LONG ISLAND & THE HAMPTONS   At 188 miles, "long" is an accurate description of the island situated to the east of Manhattan, dividing the waters of the Long Island Sound from the Atlantic Ocean. As you may have guessed, the sea is the dominant theme here—charming ports, sandy beaches, and fresh seafood abound. Surprisingly, it's also an agricultural area that supports numerous farms and vineyards. The north shore, or "Gold Coast," is strewn with mansions that once belonged to Astors and Vanderbilts, now transformed into museums open to the public. See chapter 6.

THE HUDSON RIVER VALLEY   The stunning landscape along the 100-mile stretch of the Hudson River from Albany to New York City has been immortalized on canvas by the painters of the Hudson River School and on paper in classics such as *The Legend of Sleepy Hollow* and *Rip Van Winkle*. The Appalachian Trail cuts through the valley, offering hikers an up-close view of the river and wilderness. Antiquing is a favorite pastime here, as is touring the grand historic estates built by America's great industrialists. See chapter 7.

THE CATSKILL MOUNTAIN REGION   The Catskill Park and Forest Preserve lies in the heart of the Catskill Mountains, about 100 miles to the northwest of New York City. Nature lovers can explore 300 miles of trails up and down mountain peaks and amid unspoiled forests, lakes, and rivers. The Borscht Belt image of yesteryear is subsiding as more sophisticated ventures take root. See chapter 8.

THE CAPITAL REGION: SARATOGA SPRINGS & ALBANY   Albany's impressive architecture reflects its status as the state's capital since 1797. Saratoga Springs, about 20 miles north of Albany, is named for the natural mineral waters that have drawn visitors to the town's spas and baths since the 1800s. It's also home to the Saratoga Race Course, the oldest thoroughbred racetrack in the U.S. See chapter 9.

CENTRAL NEW YORK   Just west of the Finger Lakes, this largely rural area is legendary among sports fans for the National Baseball Hall of Fame and Museum in Cooperstown. See chapter 10.

THE FINGER LAKES REGION   Bounded by Lake Ontario to the north and the Pennsylvania border to the south, the aptly named Finger Lakes region has 11 long, slender lakes plus rivers, streams, waterfalls, and smaller bodies of water. The lakes offer lots of water-related fun, from swimming to kayaking to fishing. Finger Lakes wine is another big attraction here; more than 70 wineries are located around Canandaigua, Keuka, Seneca, and Cayuga lakes. See chapter 11.

THE NORTH COUNTRY   Massive Adirondack Park, full of lakes, hiking trails, and rustic "camps," accounts for the majority of land in New York State north of I-90. At 6.1 million acres, the park is almost the size of the neighboring state of Vermont. See chapter 12.

WESTERN NEW YORK   On its journey from Lake Ontario to Lake Erie, the Niagara River pours between 50,000 and 100,000 cubic feet of water per second over spectacular Niagara Falls. Buffalo—the second-largest city in New York State and a good bet for restaurants and nightlife—is just a 30-minute drive from the falls. See chapter 13.

THE BEST OF NEW YORK CITY IN 2 DAYS

Seeing the best of New York City in 2 days requires endurance, patience, perseverance, very good walking shoes, a daily fun pass MetroCard (p. 68), and a good map of the city subway system. You'll also need to get an early start and have a plan of attack. If you've seen many or all of these sites before, try some of the other listings in chapter 5. Or pick a few neighborhoods you don't know as well, and explore. See *Time Out New York* and *The New York Times* for festivals and events. **Start:** *42nd Street at Twelfth Avenue.*

Day 1: Major Buildings & Landmarks

On Day 1, take the **Circle Line Sightseeing Cruise** ★ (p. 128) for an overview of Manhattan and a view of the Statue of Liberty. Then take the M42 42nd Street cross-town bus to Fifth Avenue and head to the **New York Public Library** ★★ (p. 122). Don't miss the incredible reading room. While you're here, take a look at the library's backyard, **Bryant Park.** (If tents are up, you're visiting during one of the two Fashion Weeks held yearly in the park.) Head east on 42nd Street to Lexington Avenue for a view of our favorite skyscraper, the **Chrysler Building** ★★ (p. 121). Take a stroll through **Grand Central Terminal** ★★ (p. 112), then walk down Fifth Avenue into the **Empire State Building** ★★★ (p. 111), and head to the top for a pristine panoramic view. Take the B or D train uptown to Seventh Avenue, and walk east across 53rd Street to the completely renovated **Museum of Modern Art** ★★ (p. 113). Yes, the $20 suggested admission is outrageous, but this is New York and you are slowly getting used to outrageous. Then spend the rest of the afternoon strolling around **Rockefeller Center** ★★ (p. 114) and **Fifth Avenue** (p. 134). (In winter, you can squeeze in a spin on the ice at either Bryant Park's or Rock Center's rinks.) If your timing is right, you may be able to catch the 70-minute **NBC Studio Tour** (p. 114). Finally, cap off the evening with dinner, then a **Broadway show in Times Square** (p. 135 for ticket details) and see the area in all its noisy, illuminated glory.

Day 2: Downtown & Major Museums

On your second day, head downtown in the morning and explore the city where it began. Take the no. 1 subway to South Ferry or no. 4 or 5 to Bowling Green, and check out **Wall Street** attractions (p. 117), including the impressive **U.S. Customs House,** which houses the **National Museum of the American Indian,** and the **New York Stock Exchange.** Take the A or C train at Broadway/Nassau Street to High Street, the first stop in Brooklyn, and take a half-hour stroll back to Manhattan over the **Brooklyn Bridge** ★★ (p. 110), an absolute must, with a spectacular view of the skyline. You'll exit the bridge near the no. 6 train at Brooklyn Bridge/City Hall, which you can take uptown to 77th Street and Lexington Avenue. There, you can explore a few Upper East Side attractions, like the exciting (and manageable in size) **Whitney Museum of American Art** ★★ (p. 117) and sprawling, spectacular **Metropolitan Museum of Art** ★★★ (p. 112). Take an hour-long museum highlights tour, or stick with exploring a few rooms. The Met's backyard is **Central Park** ★★★ (p. 123), which you enter at either 79th Street or 85th Street. If you have time, check out the fantastic **American Museum of Natural History** ★★★ (p. 110) at the western side of the park. As with the Met, pick a few highlights. At night, check out a comedy club, or try a bar-hop and bond with the locals.

THE HUDSON VALLEY & SARATOGA SPRINGS IN 3 DAYS

The Hudson River is more than 300 miles long and the Valley on either side is loaded with historical homes, museums, Victorian hamlets, and outdoor sporting opportunities, so you have a lot to choose from during a 3-day trip. If you are primarily visiting, or live in or around, New York City, you could easily make a day trip or a weekend in any of these spots. See chapter 7 for more ideas, and watch for wineries along your route. **Start:** *New York City.*

Day 1: Lower Hudson Valley

Drive north from Manhattan up the east side of the Hudson River, quickly entering Westchester County (take either I-87 or the Sawmill Pkwy. to Rte. 9N) and traveling through Tarrytown. (If traveling with kids, you may want to squeeze in **Philipsburg Manor** ★★, p. 186, a surprising living-history museum in Sleepy Hollow.) Perhaps the biggest attraction in the Lower Hudson Valley is **Kykuit** ★★★ (p. 187), the famed Rockefeller estate, where you'll need at least 2 to 3 hours to enjoy one of the tours of the house, gardens, and modern artwork. For lunch, head upriver (25 miles, Rte. 9N) to the quaint riverside town of **Cold Spring** (p. 189), which has several nice restaurants on or near Main Street. After lunch, check out some of the antiques shops or stroll down to the river for a great view of the Hudson. In the afternoon, visit **Boscobel Restoration** ★★ (p. 187), a mansion not only handsomely restored, but picked up and moved to its spectacular current site, on the banks of the Hudson in nearby Garrison. Fans of contemporary art may prefer to head upriver to **Dia:Beacon** ★★★ (p. 200), a huge repository of minimalist art housed in an old factory. For a special dinner outing, check out **Valley** ★★★ (p. 198) or **Tavern at Highlands Country Club** ★★ (p. 199). Spend the night at one of the inns in either Cold Spring or Garrison.

Day 2: The Mid-Hudson Valley

Continue your Great Estates tour of the Hudson Valley in Hyde Park, home to the **FDR Presidential Library and Museum (Springwood)** ★★★ (p. 202), as well as **Eleanor Roosevelt's Val-Kill Cottage** and FDR's private getaway **Top Cottage** ★ (p. 203). You'll need most of the morning to explore all three. Have lunch at one of the restaurants at the esteemed **Culinary Institute of America** ★★ (p. 205). (Foodies should check the tour schedule in advance for a behind-the-scenes look at one of the foremost culinary-arts programs in the country.) After lunch, head to the storied **Vanderbilt Mansion** ★★★ (p. 202), one of the finest estates of the Gilded Age. *Note:* Fans of modern art may wish to take a different tack for Day 2 and head west across the Hudson (take I-84W toward Newburgh and the bridge) for one of the most unique art museums in the country, **Storm King Art Center** ★★★ (p. 188), 500 acres of rolling hills and monumental sculpture by the top names of 20th-century art. (To get to Storm King, head south from Newburgh on Rte. 9W to Mountainville, near Cornwall.) A great spot for dinner is the picturesque village of **Rhinebeck.**

Day 3: Upper Hudson River

Head north on Route 9W or 9G, up to **Hudson** ★★ (p. 218), and shop on Warren Street, the best spot in the state for antiquing. You can easily spend a morning and an afternoon here. Also check out the Persian castle architecture and panoramic landscapes of the **Olana State Historic Site** ★★★ (p. 216). If you have time, venture out to the **Mount Lebanon Shaker Society** ★★★ (p. 218). Then you can eat and sleep in either Tivoli or Hudson (and take the 2½-hr. trip back to NYC in the morning via the Taconic State Pkwy.). Hudson and a couple of inns in the surrounding area are perfect for spending the night.

But if you don't have another night to spend in the region, you could leave the Upper Hudson in late afternoon and make your way south along the west side of the river (along either I-87, the faster route, or 9W), perhaps stopping for dinner in the attractive town of **Nyack** ★ (p. 191) before making your way back to New York City.

THE ADIRONDACKS & THE NORTH COUNTRY IN 1 WEEK

For outdoors lovers, the North Country is the heart of New York State. Blessed with deep pine forests, softly rounded mountain peaks, and isolated islands set on quiet lakes, the Adirondacks and the Thousand Islands region can make for endless days of adventure. If you're staying in hotels, settle in Old Forge before starting off, then switch lodgings throughout the tour as you see fit. For camping information, see listings in chapter 12. *Start: Old Forge.*

Days 1 & 2: Blue Mountain Lake & Raquette Lake Area

From Old Forge, drive east on Route 28 and go north on Route 30 to start off the week with a great overview of the park at the **Adirondack Museum** ★★ (p. 374). Along with the history, flora, and fauna you'd expect, you'll also find great interactive exhibits, making this museum perfect for kids as well as adults. It's easy to spend a full morning here. Be sure to pack a picnic lunch and enjoy it out on the shores of gorgeous **Blue Mountain Lake.** Then strap on your hiking boots, make sure you have drinking water, and tackle **Bald Mountain,** just east of Old Forge—it's a short but steep climb, and the summit will reward you with a great view. With your remaining energy, drive back to Old Forge and wander the town, enjoying the kitschy rides and games.

On the second day, hit the water. This area is famous for its chain of lakes; the only way to really get a sense of them is to go out with a canoe or kayak. **Mountainman Outdoor Supply Company** (p. 372), in both Old Forge and Inlet, can set you up with the equipment; then spend the morning paddling as the mist rises from the lake. Drive over Route 28 to Raquette Lake and see how the Vanderbilts went "camping" (in 27 rooms, with a bowling alley!), at **Great Camp Sagamore** ★★ (p. 373). You can tour what was their retreat for more than 50 years, just south of Raquette Lake.

Day 3: Lake George

Part of this park's appeal is that it makes for great driving. Take your time heading east on Route 28 over to the Lake George area. Then go out onto the lake with **Lake George Steamboat Company** (p. 371) on one of its narrated cruises aboard a steamship paddle-wheeler. Drive up to Bolton Landing and enjoy a drink or dinner at **The Sagamore** ★★★ (p. 375), one of the few historic hotels left in the park.

Day 4: Lake Placid

Meander up I-87, then cut over Route 73 and take Route 86 into the town of Lake Placid, which is famous for hosting both the 1932 and the 1980 Winter

Olympics and remains a center for Olympic training. Get a taste of history in the **Winter Olympic Museum ★** (p. 382) at the Olympic Center, and check out the rinks where Sonja Henie and Eric Heiden captured hearts and gold medals. Then get ready for some Olympic adventures yourself, out at the Verizon Sports Complex, 20 minutes west of town. You can jump in a bobsled (don't worry, professionals drive it), either on wheels or on ice. Grab a bite in town, then go off to **High Falls Gorge** (p. 384), 8 miles east of town, which allows for a great stroll along the **Ausable River.** The trail runs past 700 feet of waterfalls and across bridges as you admire the water spilling over ancient granite cliffs. Come back into town as the sun starts to set and casts its rosy glow over Mirror Lake. Enjoy dinner and stay overnight in Lake Placid.

Days 5, 6 & 7: The Thousand Islands

Spend the morning saying goodbye to the Adirondacks aboard the **Adirondack Scenic Railroad ★** (p. 385) on a 1-hour journey through the forest between Lake Placid and Saranac Lake. Then say a longer goodbye as you drive west on Route 86, out of the park on Route 3 to Watertown, then on Route 12 up to the Thousand Islands region. Count on a few hours for the drive. You have a few options for the rest of Day 5: Delay your departure from the 'dacks by stopping in a few towns, such as Childwold and Cranberry Lake; or test out the **St. Regis Canoe Wilderness Area** (p. 380); or just head straight to the Thousand Islands, to **Clayton,** the center of the area's activity, and explore the town. Dine and stay in Clayton.

On your second day here, check out some of the area castles, built by wealthy industrialists in the early 20th century. Pack a picnic lunch for your castle outing, then hop on the two-castle tour run by **Uncle Sam Boat Tours ★★** (p. 395). You'll get a good overview (or rather, water view) of the many islands that lie in the middle of the **St. Lawrence River.** You'll stop off at Dark Island and take a guided tour of **Singer Castle ★★** (p. 395), built by the director of the Singer Sewing Company and opened to the public in 2003. Then it's over to **Boldt Castle ★★** (p. 393), on Heart Island, built by Waldorf=Astoria owner George C. Boldt. Enjoy your picnic lunch on the 5 acres of grounds, then explore the turrets, admire the 365 windows, and wander among the formal gardens. You have an unlimited stop here, so whenever you're ready, just catch the shuttle back to the mainland. In the late afternoon, head over to the **1000 Islands SkyDeck ★** (p. 395), 400 feet off the ground and with a 25-mile view over the St. Lawrence River. It's over the Canadian border, so bring your passport.

Start off Day 3 with a fine tradition here—**fishing,** followed by a **shore dinner** (p. 401). Many of the fishing charter companies run these trips, and they've been happening up here since the early 1900s. You'll spend the morning fishing, and then stop on a deserted island. Your guide fries up the just-caught fish, then serves it up with potatoes, corn, and dessert. Walk off your decadent lunch by heading over to the **Antique Boat Museum ★★★** (p. 393), which boasts the largest collection of inland freshwater boats in the U.S. You'll see more than 200 boats, from a 19th-century dugout canoe to 1920s racing boats. The sunset is gorgeous, so grab a table on the water to enjoy it.

weekend EXCURSIONS FROM NEW YORK CITY

When New Yorkers tire of the "city," it only takes a couple of days in the "country," as they call it, and they're refreshed and ready to come back. Here are some popular getaways, also handy for travelers in the city on extended business.

Long Island History & Wine Tour   On Day 1, head out of New York onto the Long Island Expressway (LIE) to exit 41 north (NY 106 north). Take 106 north to Oyster Bay and follow signs to **Sagamore Hill** ★★★ (p. 144), Theodore Roosevelt's 23-room Victorian estate—full of animal trophies and other things masculine—which he used as the summer White House from 1902 to 1908. It's an easy drive to **Planting Fields Arboretum/Coe Hall** ★★ (p. 144), a grand expanse of historic buildings and greenhouses. Have lunch in tiny **Locust Valley,** peruse its collection of antiques shops, and then head out to the **Vanderbilt Museum and Planetarium** ★★ (p. 145) in Centerport. Have dinner and overnight in the **Centerport** area. On Day 2, try hopping between some of the 50 wineries on the North Fork. Fortunately, lots of wineries are east on Route 25,

which is a much nicer drive than the LIE. Out past Jamesport, you can stop at **Bedell Cellars** and sample its merlot; then it's just a half-mile to **The Lenz Winery,** which makes excellent chardonnays and merlots. See p. 152 for more wineries. End up in the town of Greenport for dinner.

Beach Party in the Hamptons   Note that the quickest way to get here by train is the express off-peak train from Hunter's Point in Queens (near the 7 subway stop). If you're driving, take the LIE. Remember, it's best to choose your beach before you go. In Southampton, **Cooper's Beach** is the main public stretch of sand, beautiful but crowded and with pricey parking. **Old Town Beach** is less crowded but parking can be a problem. **Main Beach** in East Hampton is gorgeous and in view of some giant mansions. **Montauk** is away from the crowds, at the end of the island. Then dine among the celebrities in **East Hampton** and go clubbing in town. On Day 2, check out the **chic shops of East Hampton,** drive by the enormous estates in Southampton's **Gin**

THE FINGER LAKES & WESTERN NEW YORK IN 1 WEEK

This itinerary covers a large swath of central and western New York. It begins with the natural beauty of the Finger Lakes, a series of deep, slender bodies of water formed by glaciers many thousands of years ago at the end of the ice age. The local wine industry, the state's biggest, is deservedly winning accolades for its cool-climate wines, and a tour of the wineries hugging the banks of the lakes is one of the most scenic (and delicious) trips in the state. You'll see more scenic beauty at the spectacular gorges of Watkins Glen and Letchworth, as well as the world-famous Niagara Falls. *Start:* Ithaca *(Cayuga Lake).*

Day 1: Ithaca

Hugging the southern shore of Cayuga Lake, Ithaca ★ is an attractive, relaxed college town with a superb setting, and it's a good place to start your tour of the region. In the morning, visit the campus of Ivy League **Cornell University** ★★

Lane and **Coopers Neck,** and then have a happy-hour home brew at the **Southampton Publick House** ★★ (p. 176). Have dinner in Southampton, then check out some live music at the **Stephen Talkhouse** (p. 177) in Amagansett. See coverage in chapter 6 for complete Hamptons details.

Catskill Mountain Region **Ulster County,** just 90 minutes by car from New York City, is not the most pastoral part of the Catskills, but it offers the greatest diversity of attractions in a relatively compact area. Cross the George Washington Bridge, then take the Palisades Parkway to I-87 north about 80 miles to **New Paltz** ★★ (p. 229) and explore the town. After lunch, outdoorsy types can hike or bike in the **Mohonk Preserve** ★★★ or **Minnewaska State Park Preserve,** or even rock-climb the awesome **Shawangunk Mountains** ("the 'Gunks"). Or take a scenic drive from New Paltz to Gardiner and up **Route 44/55,** just beyond the Minnewaska Preserve. Watch for a handful of nearby wineries. Stay at the legendary **Mohonk Mountain House** ★★★ (p. 234), a

Victorian fantasy on a cliff with activities galore, or return east toward High Falls or nearby Rosendale for dinner. Spend the night in Stone Ridge, Gardiner, along the Hudson in Milton, or even in Mount Tremper, about 35 to 40 miles northwest. On Day 2, head up I-87 to Route 28 west, toward Mount Tremper (or Rte. 213 to 28A, which is more scenic but longer). Off Route 28 is the beautiful **Ashokan Reservoir** ★★ (p. 232). Then, Mount Tremper's **Emerson Place** ★ or the town of **Phoenicia** ★ (a mile west) is perfect for shopping (or inner tube rafting down the river). After lunch, head east along Route 212 (just outside of Mt. Tremper) toward **Woodstock** ★ and check out the town, or explore the legendary **Byrdcliffe Arts Colony** ★ (p. 231). Then head east along the road (Rte. 212) to **Saugerties** ★, about 10 miles away, where you'll find a host of homegrown antiques stores. Or head across the river to **Hudson** (I-87N to Rte. 23E, about 20 miles), site of the best antiques shopping in upstate New York. Enjoy dinner, then head back to the city. (The drive will take 2–2½ hr.)

(p. 311), which sits on a hilltop above town. Its **Johnson Museum of Art** ★★ has a particularly strong collection of Asian art and spectacular fifth-floor views of Cayuga Lake. From the museum, you can take a short walk along a path leading to a suspension bridge over deep **Fall Creek Gorge** ★ (p. 311). Also part of the university is **Cornell Plantations,** a wonderful spot for garden lovers. You could then head up to Sheldrake Point Winery, along Route 96, for a relaxing lunch at **Simply Red Lakeside Bistro** ★★ (p. 318).

In the afternoon, families will enjoy a visit to **Sciencenter** (p. 313), a hands-on science museum with a walk-in camera, an outdoor playground, and "piano stairs." The **Sagan Planet Walk** (p. 313) is an outdoor scale model of the sun and nine planets, built as a memorial to Cornell astronomer Carl Sagan. Have dinner in town at **Maxie's** ★★ (p. 318). Alternatively, if you want to see some of southern Cayuga Lake, take the 7-mile drive up Route 89 to **Taughannock Falls State Park** ★★ (p. 311), with an easy hike to a free-falling waterfall that outdoes even Niagara Falls, followed by dinner at **Taughannock Farms Inn** ★ (p. 316).

Day 2: Wineries of Cayuga & Seneca Lakes

If you didn't visit **Taughannock Falls State Park** on Day 1 (see above), you can catch it on your way to exploring the wineries that dot Cayuga Lake.

Getting a taste of the Finger Lakes means exactly that: tasting some of the excellent wines that come from this respected viticultural region. Starting out on the west side of Cayuga Lake, you can visit a few of the wineries that belong to the **Cayuga Wine Trail ★** and several on the east side of Seneca Lake, part of the **Seneca Lake Wine Trail ★★★** (p. 322). Sheldrake Point, Hosmer, and Goose Watch, all about halfway up Route 89 on the west side of the lake, are some of our favorites on Cayuga. Head south along Route 414 past Lodi to visit some of the wineries on the Seneca trail, such as Lamoreaux Landing, Wagner, Standing Stone, and Red Newt. Depending on which wineries you visit and the hour, Sheldrake Point, Wagner, and Red Newt all have restaurants and are good spots for lunch (a handful of the best restaurants in the region are near Hector and Lodi, as well). Spend the night at an inn near Watkins Glen, along either the east or the west side of Seneca Lake.

Day 3: Watkins Glen/Keuka Lake

Begin by trekking through **Watkins Glen State Park ★★★** (p. 322), a 776-acre park with a walking trail that wends through a spectacular gorge formed at the end of the last ice age. Then drive west toward **Keuka Lake ★★★** (p. 334). You can stop at more wineries along the way, or merely enjoy the drive around perhaps the prettiest of the Finger Lakes. Head north along Route 54, on the east side of the lake, toward Penn Yan. **Route 54A ★★** (p. 335), which travels between the two prongs of the lake and south along the west side of the lake, is a gorgeous drive, one of the best in the region. Stop at Esperanza Mansion for lunch and magnificent lake views. After lunch, hit perhaps the most famed winery in the region, Dr. Frank's, and a couple of the other wineries of the **Keuka Lake Wine Trail ★★** (p. 336), and then head down to the cute town of **Hammondsport ★** (p. 335) for shopping and dinner at the Village Tavern Restaurant. Spend the night here, either in one of the rooms owned by Village Tavern or at Black Sheep Inn. You could also base yourself just west, in another adorable Finger Lakes town, **Naples** (along Rte. 53), where the place for dinner is Brown Hound Bistro.

Day 4: Letchworth Park

Starting in Corning, drive on the New York State Thruway (I-90) west to Route 400 south and take the East Aurora exit. Turn left onto Route 20A east. Follow 20A to Warsaw. Make a right onto Route 19 south to Route 19A, to Denton Corners Road. Turn left on Denton Corners Road and into the park. **Letchworth State Park** (p. 422) is a gorgeous gash in the earth and has been formed over the millenniums by the Genesee River. You'll find 66 miles of trails here, but it's best to stick to the southern end, where cliffs climb as high as 600 feet. Pack a snack and hike on the **Gorge Trail,** a 7-mile one-way trek that's moderately difficult, so don't do the whole thing unless you're feeling adventuresome. Then reward yourself with a great all-American dinner at the **Glen Iris Inn ★★★** (p. 423) in Castile. You can even spend the night here.

Days 5 & 6: Buffalo

Head back to I-90 and drive west to **Buffalo.** This city may just surprise you with its collection of famous architecture. It's worth taking a walking tour of downtown to check out some of these buildings. Start at **Market Arcade** (p. 406) on Main Street and walk south—you'll see neoclassical, Beaux Arts, and Art Deco buildings galore. Stop off for lunch at the **Ellicott Square Building** (p. 406) and try some "Beef on Weck" (p. 415) done right by Charlie the Butcher. Then head over to the **Darwin D. Martin House ★★★** (p. 409), where a painstaking restoration is beautifully showcasing the mastery of the home's architect, Frank Lloyd Wright. If your passion tends more toward painting and sculpture, visit the **Albright-Knox Art Gallery ★★★** (p. 408), a winner of a gallery that houses some 5,000 works. Finish up the daytime hours with a stroll through **Delaware Park,** designed by Frederick Law Olmsted, creator of Central Park. Today it's a 350-acre gem. For dinner, drop by the home of the city's original namesake chicken wing, **Anchor Bar** (p. 413). Honestly, the wings are nothing special, but when in Buffalo . . .

Then, the area surrounding Buffalo has more than enough cool and quirky museums and sites to keep you occupied for another day. Start off at **Graycliff ★★★** (p. 417), a stunning Frank Lloyd Wright creation. Then drive over to the tiny, charming town of **East Aurora,** where Elbert Hubbard started his furniture-building movement and founded the **Roycroft Arts and Crafts Community** (p. 418) more than 100 years ago. Browse some of the craft shops, then have lunch at the **Roycroft Inn ★★★** (p. 420). Make a stop at **Vidler's 5 & 10,** which has been selling candy and knickknacks since 1930. Then drive farther west on I-90 to Route 60 and over to America's largest community of mediums, the **Lily Dale Assembly ★★** (p. 417). In summertime, there are public readings, but you can come anytime for a private reading. Don't count on any chairs rattling, but some of these folks are frighteningly good at telling you about anyone who has "passed over." Have dinner and stay overnight back in Buffalo.

Day 7: Niagara Falls

Get back on to I-90 and drive west to check out the beautiful gushing water of **Niagara Falls ★★★** (p. 426). Some daredevils attempt the falls in a barrel, while others just come to admire the view. We recommend the latter. We also recommend bringing your passport because you'll want to see the falls from both the American side and the Canadian side. Pick up the discount card Passport to the Falls at **Niagara Falls State Park** (p. 426), then walk out onto the newly renovated Observation Tower that stretches into the river. At the bottom of the tower is the famous *Maid of the Mist* **boat ride ★★★** (p. 429), a very cool (but very wet) way to see the falls from below. Then visit the **Cave of the Winds ★★** (p. 429) to walk around the base of the falls. Walk over the border (it's faster than driving, especially in summer), have lunch, and check out the stunning Niagara Falls view from the Canadian side. Then peruse the area of **Clifton Hill,** Niagara's answer to Disney. Head back to the American side to have dinner at one of the excellent new restaurants in the **Seneca Niagara Casino & Hotel ★★★** (p. 433), and finish off the day by trying your luck on the casino floor.

THE ACTIVE VACATION PLANNER

by Neil Edward Schlecht

4

Perhaps because New York City is—despite the giant green oasis of Central Park—the ultimate in asphalt adventure, New York State doesn't quite get its due as an outdoors destination. But New York is much more rural, mountainous, and crisscrossed with water than many people realize, and it's a splendid, incredibly diverse state with terrain and opportunities to satisfy the most discriminating outdoors enthusiasts. New York is, after all, where the American Conservation Movement began, and the state has benefited from the active presence of committed environmentalists like native son Theodore Roosevelt, the 26th president of the U.S.

New York has 176 state and 24 national parks. **Niagara Falls State Park** was designated the first state park in the U.S., and state parks and forest preserves in the **Adirondack and Catskill mountains** were declared "forever wild" by the New York State Constitution. **Adirondack Park** (www.visitadirondacks.com), totaling more than 6 million acres of public and private lands—roughly one-fifth of the state—ranks as the largest park in the country.

From Long Island and Great Lakes beaches to Adirondack lakes and Catskill rivers, visitors have myriad opportunities for water fun, including swimming, boating, fishing, canoeing, and kayaking. The Catskill region is famous among anglers as one of the fly-fishing capitals of the world.

The rugged mountains and dense forests that dominate upstate New York beckon avid hikers, mountain bikers, and winter-sports fans. In the Catskills, 35 peaks reach 3,500 feet, while in the Adirondacks, more than 40 mountains rise above 4,000 feet. Lake Placid has hosted the winter Olympics, and ski mountains in the Catskills draw enthusiasts from across the Northeast, as do the hundreds of miles of terrain for cross-country skiing.

In warm months, New York State plays host to professional golf and tennis championships, including the US Open, and an impressive roster of public and private courses makes the state one of the nation's best for golf.

The website of the **I Love New York** Travel and Tourism board—www.iloveny.com—contains exhaustive listings of parks, hiking trails, outfitters, facilities for outdoors adventure, and ideas for outdoor activities in all four seasons.

VISITING NEW YORK'S NATIONAL PARKS

New York State's 24 national parks include splendid natural spots like the Appalachian National Scenic Trail and Fire Island National Seashore, in addition to famous historic monuments. One extremely popular natural area is the **Upper Delaware Scenic and Recreational River,** part of the National Wild and Scenic Rivers System; it runs 73 miles along the New York–Pennsylvania border, making it the Northeast's longest free-flowing river. Perfect for boating and kayaking, the Upper Delaware is known for its Class I and II rapids, public fishing, and wintering bald eagles. An interesting fact: Nearly all the land along the Upper Delaware River is privately owned; only 30 acres belong to the U.S. government. The **Erie Canalway National Heritage Corridor** (www.eriecanalway.org), the newest national park in New York State, comprises four navigable waterways (Erie, Champlain, Oswego, and Cayuga-Seneca) and sections of the first Erie Canal, totaling more than 500 miles in upstate New York. More than 230 trail miles along the corridor have been equipped for biking and hiking. The **Fire Island National Seashore** (www.nps.gov/fiis), located in Patchogue (1 hr. east of NYC), is the site of beautiful ocean shores, an ancient maritime forest, and historic lighthouses and estates. Outdoor activities include backpacking and birding.

Crossing New York State are two of the nation's most important scenic trails. The famous **Appalachian National Scenic Trail** (**A.T.;** www.appalachiantrail.org), which opened as a continuous trail in 1937 and was designated the first National Scenic Trail in 1968, is a 2,167-mile footpath that crosses the Appalachian Mountains from Maine to Georgia. The trail is very popular with day, weekend, and other short-term hikers, section hikers, and through-hikers (who hike the entire length of the trail in one season). The **North Country National Scenic Trail** (**NCT;** www.northcountrytrail.org) crosses seven northern states: New York, Pennsylvania, Ohio, Michigan, Wisconsin, Minnesota, and North Dakota.

Detailed national park information covering travel and transportation, facilities, fees and permits, hours, wildlife, and more is available through the National Park Service website at **www.nps.gov**.

National & State Park Passes

The best way to visit national parks not just in New York State but across the country is with the **National Parks Interagency Annual Pass** ($80, valid for 1 year), which provides admission to any national park that charges an entrance fee. The pass covers the pass holder and three accompanying adults. It can be purchased at national park sites; online at http://store.usgs.gov/pass or www.recreation.gov; by calling ✆ **888/ ASK-USGS** (275-8747), ext. 1; or by sending a check or money order payable to the National Park Service for $80 (plus $3.95 for shipping and handling) to National Park Foundation, P.O. Box 34108, Washington, DC 20043-4108. The new Senior Pass ($10, for seniors only; lifetime membership) replaced the old Golden Age Passport in January 2007 (plastic Golden Age passports are still valid for lifetime; paper passports may be exchanged for the new Senior Pass, free of charge). Other old passes, including the National Parks Pass, Golden Eagle Hologram, and Golden Access and Golden Eagle Passports, will continue to be honored until they expire. For additional information, call ✆ **888/ASK-USGS** (275-8747).

The **Empire Passport** provides unlimited day use and vehicle access to most New York State parks ($65, valid Apr 1–Mar 31 of the following year), and it is available by calling ✆ **518/474-0458** or at www.nysparks.com/passport.

OUTDOOR ACTIVITIES FROM A TO Z

Bicycling

New York State has thousands of excellent roads and mountain trails for cycling. The **Hudson Valley** has moderate hills, Hudson River views, farm landscapes, and the allure of historic estates such as those in Hyde Park. Excellent off-trail riding is popular in the Catskill Mountain region in the **Mohonk Preserve** (✆ **914/255-0919;** www.mohonkpreserve.org) and **Minnewaska State Park Preserve** (✆ **845/256-0579;** http://nysparks.state.ny.us). A great route for hard-core road cyclists in the Catskills is the hilly, 114-mile **Reservoir Loop,** near New Paltz (http://bicycling.trimbleoutdoors.com/ViewTrip/355113). For mountain-biking trails, road-cycling routes, and trip reports in the **Shawangunk Mountains,** at the edge of the Catskills, see www.gunks.com; fat-tire fans should also contact GUMBA (Gunks Mountain Biking Association; ✆ **914/255-3572;** www.gumba.org). The **Finger Lakes** region is ideal for cyclists who want to circle the lakes, perhaps stopping off at wineries en route. Cyclists are very fond of scenic lake loops around several of the larger Finger Lakes, such as the 100-mile loop around **Cayuga Lake,** the 40-mile loop around **Skaneateles Lake,** and the 20-mile loop around **Keuka Lake.** In the Catskills, **Plattekill Mountain** is one of the top five mountain-biking destinations in North America, and other mountains, such as **Windham** and **Hunter,** also cater to mountain bikers in summer. There's easy cycling along the **Catskill Scenic Trail** (✆ **607/652-2821**), a 19-mile "Rails to Trails" pathway. Farther upstate, **The Seaway Trail,** a scenic road route, runs 450 miles from Massena to Niagara Falls and goes along the south shore of Lake Ontario and the St. Lawrence River. Near the shores of Lake Champlain, **Lake Champlain Bikeways** is a series of demarcated bicycling loops.

A terrific cycling option for cyclists of all abilities is along the historic **New York State Canal System,** comprising more than 230 miles of trails across upstate New York. Multiuse trails include the 25-mile **Hudson-Mohawk Bikeway** in the Capital-Saratoga region, the 36-mile **Old Erie Canal State Park** in central New York, the 90-mile **Erie Canal Heritage Trail** in the northern Finger Lakes region, and the 8-mile **Glens Falls Feeder Canal Trail** in the foothills of the Adirondacks near Lake Champlain. For additional information, contact the **New York State Canal Corporation,** 200 Southern Blvd., P.O. Box 189, Albany, NY 12201-0189 (✆ **800/4-CANAL-4** [422-6254]; www.canals.ny.gov). For information on bike tours along the Erie Canal, call ✆ **518/434-1583.** Even New York City has gotten into the game; it's home to a great many dedicated cyclists, who ride the 6.25-mile loop within **Central Park,** a classic urban cycling destination, and the multiuse **Manhattan Waterfront Greenway** (www.nyc.gov/html/dot/html/bicyclists/bikemaps.shtml), which runs 28 miles and nearly encircles the entire island, skirting the edges of the Hudson and East rivers. Another favorite ride of locals is from the city across the George Washington Bridge and up to **Nyack** along the west side of the Hudson River, a perfect 50-mile round-trip. Each May, some 25,000 intrepid cyclists take to the New York streets for the **Great Five Boro Bike Tour,** which covers 42 miles and touches all five of the city's boroughs; get more information at www.bike newyork.org. In an attempt to become more eco-friendly, the city under the Bloomberg Administration is even planning to roll out an ambitious bike-share plan, in which users will be able to use 10,000 city bikes at some 600 stations across the city, officially starting in 2012. The plan has been beset by questions and concerns, with some doubting that New York could ever do what Paris, London, and Barcelona have done with considerable success.

The Guided Outdoors

For guided and organized adventure trips across the state, including bicycling, mountain biking, hiking, canoeing, sea kayaking, whitewater kayaking and rafting, and cross-country skiing, check out the **A1 Trails** website (www.a1trails.com), and specifically its section dealing with guided adventure (www.a1trails.com/guides/gdesny.html).

A great resource, with information on organizations, trails, and guided trips, is the website of **A1 Trails** (www.a1trails.com/biking/bike_ny. html). Most areas have bicycle shops that rent bikes. Among the loads of guidebooks dealing specifically with biking in New York State, the following are recommended: 25 *Mountain Bike Tours in the Adirondacks* (Countryman Press); 30 *Bicycle Tours in the Finger Lakes Region* (Countryman Press); *Bicycling the Canals of New York: 500 Miles of Bike Riding along the Erie, Champlain, Cayuga-Seneca & Oswego Canals* (Vitesse Press); *The Catskills: A Bicycling Guide* (Purple Mountain Press); *Cranks from Cooperstown: 50 Bike Rides in Upstate New York* (Tourmaster Publications); *Paths Along the Hudson: A Guide to Walking and Biking* (Rutgers University Press); and *Ride Guide: Hudson Valley, New Paltz to Staten Island* (Anacus Press).

Boating

New York is blessed with thousands of miles of rivers and streams, as well as 500 miles of the New York State Canal System, hundreds of lakes, and the Long Island Sound. From Saratoga Lake to the Delaware River and the 11 scenic Finger Lakes, there are plenty of great opportunities for boating enthusiasts.

On the **New York State Canal System** (www.nyscanals.gov), you can cruise the waterway's 57 locks. The canal system stretches more than 500 miles and is normally navigable from May to mid-November. There are four canals, all easily accessible by boat. From the south, the Hudson River opens onto the Erie Canal; farther north is the Champlain Canal. The Erie Canal travels east to west, with access to the Great Lakes from the Oswego Canal or the western end of the Erie Canal, with access to Lake Erie. The Cayuga-Seneca Canal connects with the Erie Canal in central New York, allowing access to the Finger Lakes region.

You can rent an authentic, old-fashioned canal boat for a few days or a week. For more information on tour boat and cruise operators, canal passes, boats for hire, and the many sites and attractions (including state parks, canal villages, museums, and urban cultural parks) along the canal system, contact the **New York State Canal Corporation,** 200 Southern Blvd., P.O. Box 189, Albany, NY 12201-0189 (*©* **800/4-CANAL-4** [422-6254]; www.nyscanals.gov). The organization puts out the *Cruising Guide to the New York State Canal System,* which you can purchase by calling ℂ **800/422-1825.** Individual counties also put out canal-specific tourism brochures. See chapters 11 and 13 for additional regional canal information.

Several cruises and riverboat tours are offered along the majestic **Hudson River,** passing some of the great estates, historic river towns, and even West Point Military Academy. Another option is to rent a houseboat in the Thousand Islands and sail the St. Lawrence River, which makes its way around an estimated 1,000 to 1,800 small islands. For more information, contact the **Thousand Islands International Council** (ℂ **800/8-ISLAND** [847-5263]; www.visit1000islands.com/visitorinfo).

Fans of regattas may want to check out the annual **New York YC Regatta** (www. nyyc.org), which has been going on for more than 150 years. **Lake Champlain,** on the New York/Vermont border, plays host to a number of regattas throughout the season.

The free *New York State Boater's Guide* is available from **New York State Parks Marine and Recreational Vehicles,** Empire State Plaza, Albany, NY 12238 (ℂ **518/474-04545**). You may also want to visit www.nysparks.state.ny.us/recreation/boating, where you'll find a link to the **New York State Boater's Guide,** a reference guide detailing the rules and regulations for boating in New York State.

Camping

New York State has more than 500 public and privately owned campgrounds across the state. Above all, the wilderness, forests, lakes, and rivers of the Adirondack and Catskill mountains offer the best backwoods camping in the state. The Hudson Valley and Finger Lakes regions, while not as remote, also offer fine camping with easy access to towns and regional attractions. The **Adirondack Camping Association** (www.adirondackcampgrounds.com) is a good resource for campsite information in that region. **Ausable Point Campground** (ℂ **518/561-7080**) sits on a stunning patch of land overlooking Lake Champlain, with 123 sites. But to really get away from everyone, reserve a spot on one of the **Saranac Lake Islands,** Saranac Lake (ℂ **518/891-3170**), and prepare to canoe there. Detailed listings of campgrounds large and small are available at ℂ **800/CALL-NYS** (225-5697) or www.iloveny.com/Where-To-Stay/Listings.aspx?cat=camp, www.nysparks.com, and www.gocamping america.com.

The Department of Environmental Conservation (DEC) operates 52 campgrounds in the Adirondack and Catskill state parks and publishes the free booklet *Camping in New York State Forest Preserves.* For camping reservations and additional information, call ℂ **518/457-2500,** and for reservations, contact **Reserve America** (ℂ **800/456-CAMP** [2267]; www.reserveamerica.com). Guidebooks include what some consider to be the bible of New York camping, *The Campgrounds of New York: A Guide to the State Parks and Public Campgrounds* (North Country Books), and *Adventures in Camping: An Introduction to Adirondack Backpacking* (North Country Books).

Canoeing, Kayaking & Rafting

New York State has thousands of miles of waterways for canoeing, kayaking, and rafting. In the Adirondacks alone, there are 1,200 miles of rivers designated wild, scenic, and recreational—little-changed since first used by Native Americans. One of the most popular routes is the **Adirondack Canoe Route,** which begins at Old Forge and flows 140 miles through the Fulton Chain of Lakes to Raquette Lake and north to the Saranac Lakes through Long Lake and then on to Tupper Lake, or east to Blue

Mountain Lake. Nick's Lake is excellent for beginning paddlers; the north branch of Moose River is more challenging. Another great spot for canoeing is the **St. Regis Canoe Area** near Saranac Lake, with 57 interconnecting lakes and ponds. For information about canoeing in the Adirondacks, contact the **Department of Environmental Conservation, Preserve Protection and Management,** 50 Wolf Rd., Albany, NY 12233-4255 (✆ **518/457-7433;** www.dec.ny.gov), the **Association for the Protection of the Adirondacks** (www.protectadks.org), or the **Adirondack Regional Tourism Council** (✆ **518/846-8016;** www.visitadirondacks.com). The **Delaware River** in the Catskills is one of the longest (73 miles) and cleanest free-flowing rivers in the Northeast, and it's excellent for tubing, rafting, kayaking, and canoeing. The historic **Hudson River,** especially in the Mid-Hudson Valley around Cold Spring, is excellent for kayaking. For information, contact the **Upper Delaware Scenic and Recreational River** (✆ **570/685-4871;** www.nps.gov/upde), which has a 24-hour River Hotline recording from April to October: ✆ **845/ 252-7100.**

Guided **white-water rafting trips** of varying difficulty, lasting a single day or even less, are available on several New York State rivers. White water is the most challenging in the springtime, although some companies offer rides throughout the summer and fall. In western New York, excellent rafting is done on Cattaraugus Creek through Zoar Valley or the Genesee River in Letchworth State Park. In the Adirondacks, the Black River near Watertown is best for advanced rafters, while Indian Lake is considered "the Whitewater Capital of New York State." Moose River is another favorite of experts, while the Sacandaga River is a long and serene trip through the Adirondacks with an exciting finish.

A detailed list of canoeing, kayaking, and rafting operators is available on www.iloveny.com. You can also visit the **DEC Bureau of Public Lands** website at www.dec.state.ny.us, or call ✆ **518/402-9428.**

Fishing

The trout streams and rivers of the **southwestern Catskills,** such as Beaverkill and the Delaware River, are among the best in North America—or the world, for that matter—for fly-fishing. For additional information, contact the **Delaware County Chamber of Commerce** (✆ **800/642-4443;** www.delawarecounty.org) or **Sullivan County Visitors Association** (✆ **800/882-CATS** [2287]; www.scva.net).

The **Hudson River** is very good for striped bass and trout fishing from mid-March to the end of May. For more information, visit www.hudsonriver.com/stripers.htm.

At the eastern end of Long Island, **Montauk** is a sport-fishing capital known for its shark fishing (peaks in late June). Sport-fishing boat rentals and charters are available. For a list of fishing charters and outfitters, see www.montauk-ny.worldweb.com. Charter fishing on **Lake Ontario,** a celebrated freshwater fishery, brings in large chinook and Atlantic salmon, as well as brown, rainbow, and lake trout; walleye; and smallmouth bass. Contact the **Lake Ontario Sportfishing Promotion Council** (✆ **800/338-7890**).

The **Thousand Islands** isn't a world-class fishing area for nothing. Grab a charter in tiny Clayton—the river serves up walleye, pike, perch, muskellunge (get your muscles ready—these grow up to 35 lb.), and bass. In **Eastern Lake Ontario,** you'll hook onto salmon, lake trout, steelhead, and walleye. For information on fishing charters and guides, see www.visit1000islands.com.

State fishing licenses are required for anyone ages 16 and over for fishing in New York freshwater. Many tackle shops and fishing outfitters issue them, as do town clerk offices. Call © **518/357-2049** or visit www.dec.ny.gov/outdoor/fishing.html for more information on fishing in New York State and specific information on permits. Guidebooks on fishing in New York State include *Flyfisher's Guide to New York* (Wilderness Adventures Press); *Gone Fishin': The 100 Best Spots in New York* (Rutgers University Press); and *Good Fishing in the Catskills: A Complete Angler's Guide* (Countryman Press).

Golf

New York State boasts a preponderance of courses routinely rated by golfing magazines and organizations to be among the country's best. There are more than 600 public and private golf courses, many in gorgeous natural settings. Some of the nation's most prestigious golf tournaments, including the US Open and the PGA Championship, are routinely held in New York (most recently, the 2009 US Open was held at Bethpage Black in Farmingdale). Championship status has been awarded to James Baird and Rockland Lake North in the Hudson Valley, Saratoga Spa and Battle Island in Fulton, Chenango Valley in Binghamton, Green Lakes in Fayetteville, Beaver Island in Grand Island, and Montauk Downs and Bethpage on Long Island.

But throughout the state, in the Catskill region, Long Island, Finger Lakes, Hudson Valley, Adirondacks, western New York, and the area around Saratoga Springs, there are dozens of superb courses for golfers of all abilities. Many of the large resort hotels in regions like the Catskills and Adirondacks have their own golf courses, many of them quite good.

For information about golfing in state parks, contact **New York State Parks** (© **518/474-0456;** www.nysparks.state.ny.us/golf-courses). For complete listings of courses across the state, visit www.iloveny.com/What-To-Do/Reasons-To-Love-NY/Golf.aspx and www.golfguideweb.com/newyork/newyork.html. Golf fans and those looking to play extensively on a trip to New York would do well to consult the **New York State Golf Association** (www.nysga.org), which maintains a ratings list of courses.

Hiking

Few places on the East Coast have the variety of mountains, forest preserves, and hiking trails of New York State, making it a superb destination for anyone from hardcore trail hounds to casual day hikers. The wild, remote **Adirondacks** (www.visit adirondacks.com), an area that covers nearly one-fifth of the state, are the state's top location for hiking, with a great hiking trail system to high peaks, waterfalls, and secluded lakes. Serious hikers will want to head to the High Peaks region. **Mount Marcy,** at 5,300 feet, is New York State's highest mountain, but with a heavy tree cover, there are peaks with better views to be found. One of them is **Bald Mountain,** east of Old Forge, a 2-mile (steep) climb with gorgeous vistas. The trail to **Avalanche Lake** is extraordinary, and **Phelps Mountain** is a moderate climb rewarded by 360-degree views of the high peaks. The DEC's Preserve Protection and Management (© **518/457-7433;** www.dec.ny.gov/outdoor/7865.html) publishes free trail maps and literature. Information on the Adirondacks can also be obtained from the **Adirondack Mountain Club,** or ADK, in Lake George (© **518/668-4447;** www.adk.org), New York's oldest hiking club.

The **Catskill Mountain region** abounds with fantastic hiking possibilities. Particularly good are trails in the Minnewaska Preserve and Mohonk Preserve. Hugely popular with climbers, the **Shawangunks** (commonly known as the 'Gunks), at the southeastern edge of the Catskills, also have great hiking trails. For trail information throughout the region, see www.catskillguide.com/hiking.htm. The **Hudson River Valley** is more hilly than mountainous, but there are great hikes in Bear Mountain, Hudson Highlands, and Fahnestock state parks.

The numerous gorges and glens in and around the lakes make the **Finger Lakes** terrific for hiking. The 16,000-acre **Finger Lakes National Forest** (btw. Cayuga and Seneca lakes) contains nine trails of up to 12 miles in length. See www.fs.fed.us/r9/forests/greenmountain/htm/fingerlakes/f_home.htm for more information. In terms of sheer length, nothing (save the Appalachian Trail and North Country Trail, both of which cross through New York State) is on a par with the **Finger Lakes Trail** (© **716/288-7191;** www.fingerlakestrail.org), a hard-core 559-mile system of wilderness foot trails across the state. It's part of the North Country National Scenic Trail, which, upon completion, will extend 4,200 miles from eastern New York State all the way to North Dakota. The main Finger Lakes Trail connects the Catskill Mountains with the Allegheny Mountains.

The **New York State Canalway System** (www.nyscanals.gov) comprises 230 miles of multiuse trails across upstate, including the 90-mile Erie Canal Heritage Trail; the 36-mile Old Erie Canal Park Trail in central New York; the 25-mile Mohawk Hudson Bikeway in eastern New York; and the 8-mile Glens Falls Feeder Canal Trail in the foothills of the Adirondacks (near Lake Champlain). For a free map of the **Canalway Trail System,** call © **800/ 4-CANAL-4** (422-6254).

A good website for information on hiking in **western New York,** from Letchworth State Park to Niagara Falls, is www.wnyhikes.com.

For trail information and maps, contact the conservation group (composed of hiking clubs, environmental organizations, and individuals) **New York–New Jersey Trail Conference,** 232 Madison Ave., #802, New York, NY 10016 (© **212/685-9699;** www.nynjtc.org). The **New York State Office of Parks, Recreation and Historic Preservation** publishes the comprehensive *Empire State Trails;* for a free copy, contact NYS Parks, Empire State Plaza, Agency Bldg. 1, Albany, NY 12238 (© **518/474-0456**). Trail information is also available online at www.nysparks.state.ny.us/news/public. **New York Parks and Conservation Association** (© **518/434-1583**) has an online trail-finder maps feature, with details on more than 90 trails and over 850 miles of walking, biking, in-line skating, and cross-country skiing. Another excellent resource, with information on organizations, trails, and more, is the **A1 Trails** website, **www.a1trails.com**.

The **Adirondack Mountain Club (ADK),** based in Lake George but with chapters in all major regions in the state, has more than 20,000 members and publishes guidebooks and the *Adirondack* magazine. It also manages trail maintenance and operates two lodges in the Adirondacks. For more information on specific trails, call © **800/395-8080** or visit www.adk.org. **The New York Ramblers** in New York

When You Don't Go It Alone

The New York State Outdoor Guides Association (NYSOGA) offers licensed guide services for guided wilderness trips—whether your interests are hunting, fishing, rock and ice climbing, or cross-country skiing and snowshoeing. Contact NYSOGA, 211 Saranac Ave., #150, Lake Placid, NY 12946 (© **866/ 4-NYSOGA [469-7642]; www.nysoga. com).**

Elmira, in the southern Finger Lakes region, is where the first 13 national soaring contests in the U.S. were held, which is why the city is sometimes called "the Soaring Capital of America." You can hop aboard a glider or soaring plane at the **Harris Hill Soaring Center** (© 607/734-0641 or 734-2752; www.harrishillsoaring.org), which offers soaring rides over the rolling countryside of Chemung County; and check out the **National Soaring Museum** (© 607/734-3128;

www.soaringmuseum.org) in Elmira. If you're more interested in motorized flight, you can take to the air in a PT-17 warplane at the **National Warplane Museum** (© 607/739-8200; www.wingsofeagles.com), in Horseheads, near Elmira. For amazing balloon rides (Apr–Oct) over one of the state's most beautiful parks, contact **Balloons Over Letchworth** (© 585/493-3340; www.balloonsoverletchworth.com) for a trip high above Letchworth State Park.

City offers hiking and snowshoeing trips. Visit www.nyramblers.org. The **Views from the Top** bulletin board has postings on the latest trail conditions across New York State; consult www.viewsfromthetop.com/trail/ny/index.html.

Following are just a few recommended guidebooks devoted to hiking in New York State; local bookstores will have more options: *50 Hikes in Central New York: Hikes & Backpacking Trips from the Western Adirondacks to the Finger Lakes* (W.W. Norton & Co.); *50 Hikes in the Adirondacks: Short Walks, Day Trips & Backpacks Throughout the Park* (Countryman Press); *50 Hikes in Western New York: Walks & Day Hikes from the Cattaraugus Hills to the Genesee Valley* (Countryman Press); *Hiking New York State* (Falcon Press); and *Paths Less Traveled: The Adirondack Experience for Walkers, Hikers & Climbers of All Ages* (Pinto Press).

Hunting

Hunting, especially big-game hunting, is big with New Yorkers upstate and more than a few visitors. The New York State Department of Environmental Conservation estimates that 700,000 New Yorkers and more than 50,000 nonresidents hunt in the state for a large variety of wildlife, including big game, small game, game birds, and fur bearers. Small- and big-game licenses are required in New York State.

For information on hunting in New York State—primarily the Adirondacks and Catskills, the two principal hunting destinations—check out the information on seasons, regulations, licenses, and more at © **518/402-8924** or www.dec.ny.gov/outdoor/hunting.html.

Rock Climbing

The sheer white cliffs of the **Shawangunk Mountains,** colloquially called the 'Gunks, near Minnewaska Preserve in the Catskill/Hudson Valley region, allow for some of the best rock climbing on the East Coast—but this is probably not the place for beginners. Experienced rock climbers will delight in more than 1,000 technical climbing routes. For articles, route suggestions, and information on climbing, see www.gunks.com or www.mohonkpreserve.org. There is also good rock climbing in and around Lake Placid and Lake George in the **Adirondacks;** contact the **Adirondack Mountain Club** in Lake George (© **518/668-4447;** www.adk.org) for locations and outfitters.

Skiing & Winter Sports

Though New York may not be in the league of Vermont or New Hampshire for classic East Coast skiing, it has a considerable number of downhill skiing areas and quite respectable mountains appealing to expert skiers, novices, and families. You'll find the east's only Olympic mountain (and its greatest vertical drop) at **Whiteface Mountain,** Wilmington (© **877/SKI-FACE** [754-3223]; www.whiteface.com), just outside of Lake Placid. The top downhill areas overall are in the Catskills region. **Hunter Mountain** in Hunter (© **888/HUNTER-MTN** [486-8376]; www.hunter mtn.com) and **Windham Mountain** in Windham (© **518/734-4300;** www.wind hammountain.com) have plenty of good trails for practiced skiers, but now also cater to beginners and families. **Belleayre Mountain** in Highmount (© **800/942-6904;** www.belleayre.com) has the highest skiable peak and longest trail in the Catskills, while **Plattekill Mountain** (© **800/NEED-2-SKI** [633-3275] or 607/326-3500; www.plattekill.com) is a small '50s-style resort. There are also good skiing mountains in the Adirondacks and near the Hudson Valley and Finger Lakes regions. Lift tickets are in line with those of most ski resorts in the Northeast (that is to say, not inexpensive), though many offer very good ski packages, especially for beginners.

Cross-country trails are scattered throughout the state, from the grounds of historic homesteads to state parks. Rural areas like the Adirondacks, Catskills, and Finger Lakes, couldn't be better for Nordic skiing, but virtually anywhere you go in upstate New York, you'll find trails. Sections of the massive 559-mile **Finger Lakes Trail** (© **585/658-9320;** www.fingerlakestrail.org) are equipped for cross-country skiing.

NEW YORK CITY

by Brian Silverman

Welcome to the Big Apple . . . wait a minute. So why is New York City called "The Big Apple"? Some say it's a horse-racing reference: The prize for the winning horse was an apple, and in the 1920s, with so many racetracks in New York, it was referred to as the "Big Apple"—the city that jockeys and trainers aspired to conquer. It's also called Gotham, the Empire City, the City that Never Sleeps, the Melting Pot, the Capital of the World, and a city "so nice, they named it twice." After all, when a place is world-class in finance, culture, and media, it's difficult to sum up your grandeur in one moniker.

How do eight million people function, live, work, and even thrive on top of each other? It's mind-boggling. For those of us who do live here, it's best not to ponder the enormity of it all. We're in too much of a hurry.

But forget the monuments, the glass towers, the arenas and theaters; it is the people who make the city—for better, for worse! It's the place to prove yourself; to "make a brand new start of it"; and where "if [you] can make it there, [you can] make it anywhere." And it's the people, and their unique contributions, who keep the city thriving. Whether they are from Ireland, Italy, West Africa, France, Israel, Pakistan, Mexico, Haiti, or Manhattan (Kansas), it's that mix of people and cultures that has always been the city's most solid foundation and source of energy.

The variety and diversity seem to form a collective unifying and feisty spirit that is essential to the city's character.

ARRIVING

By Plane

Three major airports serve New York City: **John F. Kennedy International Airport** (✆ **718/244-4444**) in Queens, about 15 miles (1 hr. driving time) from midtown Manhattan; **LaGuardia Airport** (✆ **718/533-3400**), also in Queens, about 8 miles (30 min.) from Midtown; and **Newark Liberty International Airport** (✆ **973/961-6000**) in nearby New Jersey, about 16 miles (45 min.) from Midtown. Information about all three airports is available online at **www.panynj.gov/airports**. I prefer LaGuardia, because it's the closest airport to Manhattan. However, JFK has the best reputation for timeliness, such as it is, among New York–area airports; Newark has the worst. None will offer the best airport experience of your life. *Note:* As we all know, the experience of flying has gotten more and more complicated. Now we have body scans and pat-downs. This, of course, is not limited to our fair city, but it's best to plan as best you can to deal with it all.

Almost every major domestic carrier serves at least one of the New York–area airports; most serve two or all three.

TRANSPORTATION TO & FROM THE NEW YORK–AREA AIRPORTS

For transportation information for all three airports (JFK, LaGuardia, and Newark), call **Air-Ride** (*©* **800/247-7433**), which offers 24-hour recorded details on bus and shuttle companies and car services registered with the New York and New Jersey Port Authority. Similar information is available at **www.panynj.gov/airports**; click on the airport at which you'll be arriving.

The Port Authority runs staffed Ground Transportation Information counters on the baggage-claim level at each airport where you can get information and book various kinds of transport. Most transportation companies also have courtesy phones near the baggage-claim area.

Generally, travel time between the airports and Midtown by taxi or car is 45 to 60 minutes for JFK, 20 to 35 minutes for LaGuardia, and 35 to 50 minutes for Newark. Always allow extra time, especially during rush hour, peak during holiday travel times, and if you're taking a bus.

By Train

Amtrak (*©* **800/USA-RAIL** [872-7245]; www.amtrak.com) runs frequent service to New York City's **Penn Station,** on Seventh Avenue between 31st and 33rd streets, where you can get a taxi, subway, or bus to your hotel. To get the best rates, book early (as much as 6 months in advance) and travel on weekends.

If you're traveling to New York from a city along Amtrak's Northeast Corridor— such as Boston, Philadelphia, Baltimore, or Washington, D.C.—Amtrak may be your best travel bet now that they've rolled out their high-speed Acela trains. The Acela Express trains cut travel time from D.C. down to 2½ hours, and travel time from Boston to a lightning-quick 3 hours.

By Bus

Busing to and from New York City from major East Coast cities has become the single most cost-effective way to get into town. Originally, these were cheap bus services created by Chinese-Americans as a means of getting between New York City and Boston, Philadelphia, and Washington, D.C. Budget travelers soon discovered the bus lines, and now a number of companies offer service between most of the major cities in the East (and as far west as Buffalo and Toronto) for a fraction of what you'd pay by train or plane. While the Chinatown buses remain the cheapest, I'd recommend that you check out the newer, larger services, which are both more comfortable and offer amenities like Wi-Fi, as well as a safer ride (Chinatown bus lines made the news in early 2011 after two fatal crashes).

From Philadelphia, the average ride might range from $10 to $20; for the other two cities you'll pay $15 to $30, but there are times when specials reduce the fares to just $1. For information about the major lines (Megabus and Boltbus, as well as the Chinatown buses) as well as fare information and bookings, visit the well-designed agency site called **BusJunction** (**www.busjunction.com**).

You will probably wait for the bus to pick you up, or depart from a street corner, rather than a bus station, which some people might count as a bonus if you're not fond of bus stations.

For individual company websites, visit the following:

- **Megabus** (© 877/GO2-MEGA [462-6342]; www.megabus.com)
- **Boltbus** (© 877/BOLTBUS [265-8287]; www.boltbus.com)
- **Vamoose** (© 877/393-2828; www.vamoosebus.com)
- **DC2NY** (© 888/888-DCNY [3269] or 202/332-2691; www.dc2ny.com)

By Car

From the **New Jersey Turnpike** (I-95) and points west, there are three Hudson River crossings to the city's West Side: the **Holland Tunnel** (lower Manhattan), the **Lincoln Tunnel** (Midtown), and the **George Washington Bridge** (upper Manhattan). From **upstate New York,** take the **New York State Thruway** (I-87), which crosses the Hudson River on the Tappan Zee Bridge and becomes the **Major Deegan Expressway** (I-87) through the Bronx. For the East Side, continue to the Triborough Bridge and then down the FDR Drive. For the West Side, take the Cross Bronx Expressway (I-95) to the Henry Hudson Parkway or the Taconic State Parkway to the Saw Mill River Parkway to the Henry Hudson Parkway south.

From **New England,** the **New England Thruway** (I-95) connects with the **Bruckner Expressway** (I-278), which leads to the Triborough Bridge and the FDR Drive on the East Side. For the West Side, take the Bruckner to the Cross Bronx Expressway (I-95) to the Henry Hudson Parkway south.

Note that you'll have to pay tolls along some of these roads and at most crossings. If your state has an **E-ZPass** program (**www.ezpass.com**), as most states in the Northeast do, your pass will allow you to go through the designated E-ZPass lanes.

Once you arrive in Manhattan, park your car in a garage (expect to pay $20–$45 per day) and leave it there. Don't use your car for traveling within the city. Public transportation, taxis, and walking will easily get you where you want to go without the headaches of parking, gridlock, and dodging crazy cabbies.

Visitor Information

INFORMATION OFFICES

For information before you leave home, your best source (besides this book!) is **NYC & Company,** the organization that fronts the New York Convention & Visitors Bureau (NYCVB), 810 Seventh Ave., New York, NY 10019. You can call © **800/ NYC-VISIT** (692-8474) to order the **Official NYC Visitor Kit,** which contains the *Official NYC Guide* detailing hotels, restaurants, theaters, attractions, events, and more; a foldout map; a newsletter on the latest goings-on; and brochures on attractions and services. The guide is free and will arrive in 7 to 10 days. (**Note:** I've received complaints that the packets sometimes take longer to arrive.)

You can also find a wealth of free information on the bureau's website, **www.nycgo. com**. To speak with a live person who can answer specific questions, call © **212/484-1200,** staffed weekdays from 8:30am to 6pm EST, weekends from 9am to 5pm EST.

City Layout

The city comprises five boroughs: **Manhattan,** where most of the visitor action is; the **Bronx,** the only borough connected to the mainland United States; **Queens,** where JFK and LaGuardia airports are located and which borders the Atlantic Ocean and occupies part of Long Island; **Brooklyn,** south of Queens, which is also on Long Island and is famed for its attitude, accent, and Atlantic-front Coney Island; and **Staten Island,** the least populous borough, bordering Upper New York Bay on one side and the Atlantic Ocean on the other.

When most visitors envision New York, they think of Manhattan, the long finger-shaped island pointing southwest off the mainland—surrounded by the Harlem River to the north, the Hudson River to the west, the East River (really an estuary) to the east, and the fabulous expanse of Upper New York Bay to the south. Despite the fact that it's the city's smallest borough (13½ miles long, 2¼ miles wide, 22 sq. miles), Manhattan contains the city's most famous attractions, buildings, and cultural institutions. For that reason, almost all of the accommodations and restaurants suggested in this chapter are in Manhattan.

In most of Manhattan, finding your way around is a snap because of the logical, well-executed grid system by which the streets are numbered. If you can discern uptown and downtown, and East Side and West Side, you can find your way around pretty easily. In real terms, **uptown** means north of where you happen to be and **downtown** means south.

Avenues run north–south (uptown and downtown). Most are numbered. **Fifth Avenue** divides the East Side from the West Side of town and serves as the eastern border of Central Park north of 59th Street. **First Avenue** is all the way east and **Twelfth Avenue** is all the way west. The three most important unnumbered avenues on the East Side are between Third and Fifth avenues: **Madison** (east of Fifth), **Park** (east of Madison), and **Lexington** (east of Park, just west of Third). Important unnumbered avenues on the West Side are **Avenue of the Americas,** which all New Yorkers call Sixth Avenue; **Central Park West,** which is what Eighth Avenue north of 59th Street is called because it borders Central Park on the west; **Columbus Avenue,** which is what Ninth Avenue is called north of 59th Street; and **Amsterdam Avenue,** which is what Tenth Avenue is called north of 59th.

Broadway is the exception to the rule—it's the only major avenue that doesn't run straight uptown–downtown. It cuts a diagonal path across the island, from the northwest tip down to the southeast corner. As it crosses most major avenues, it creates **squares** (Times Sq., Herald Sq., Madison Sq., and Union Sq., for example).

Streets run east–west (crosstown) and are numbered consecutively as they proceed uptown from Houston (pronounced *House*-ton) Street. So to go uptown, simply walk north of, or to a higher-numbered street than, where you are. Downtown is south of (or a lower-numbered street than) your current location.

As I've already mentioned, Fifth Avenue is the dividing line between the **East Side** and **West Side** of town (except below Washington Sq., where Broadway serves that function). On the East Side of Fifth Avenue, streets are numbered with the distinction "East"; on the West Side of that avenue, they are numbered "West." East 51st Street, for example, begins at Fifth Avenue and runs east to the East River, while West 51st Street begins at Fifth Avenue and runs west to the Hudson River.

Unfortunately, the rules don't apply to neighborhoods in Lower Manhattan, south of 14th Street—like Wall Street, Chinatown, SoHo, TriBeCa, the Village—because they sprang up before engineers devised this brilliant grid scheme. A good map is essential when exploring these areas.

Manhattan Neighborhoods in Brief

Lower Manhattan: South Street Seaport & the Financial District Lower Manhattan constitutes everything south of Chambers Street. **Battery Park,** the point of departure for the Statue of Liberty, Ellis Island, and Staten Island, is on the southern tip of the island. The **South Street Seaport,** now touristy, but still a reminder of times when shipping was the lifeblood of the city, lies a bit north on the east coast; it's just south of the Brooklyn Bridge, which stands proudly as the ultimate engineering achievement of New York's 19th-century Industrial Age.

The rest of the area is considered the **Financial District,** but may be more famous now as **Ground Zero.** Until September 11, 2001, the Financial District was anchored by the **World Trade Center,** with the World Financial Center complex and residential Battery Park City to the west, and **Wall Street** running crosstown a little south and to the east.

Just about all of the major subway lines congregate here before they either end up in or head to Brooklyn.

TriBeCa Bordered by the Hudson River to the west, the area north of Chambers Street, west of Broadway, and south of Canal Street is the *Tri*angle *Be*low *Ca*nal Street, or TriBeCa. Since the 1980s, as SoHo became saturated with chic, the spillover has been quietly transforming TriBeCa into one of the city's hippest residential neighborhoods, where celebrities and families quietly coexist in cast-iron warehouses converted into spacious, expensive loft apartments. Artists' lofts and galleries as well as hip antiques and design shops pepper the area, as do some of the city's best restaurants.

Chinatown New York City's most famous ethnic enclave is bursting past its traditional boundaries and has seriously encroached on Little Italy. The former marshlands northeast of City Hall and below Canal Street, from Broadway to the Bowery, are where Chinese immigrants arriving from San Francisco were forced to live in the 1870s. This booming neighborhood is now a conglomeration of Asian populations. It offers tasty cheap eats in cuisine ranging from Szechuan to Hunan to Cantonese to Vietnamese to Thai. Exotic shops sell strange foods, herbs, and souvenirs; bargains on clothing and leather are plentiful.

One of the Canal Street (J, M, N, Q, R, Z, 6) subway stations will get you to the heart of the action. The streets are crowded during the day and empty out after around 9pm; they remain quite safe, but the neighborhood is more enjoyable during the bustle.

Little Italy Little Italy, traditionally the area between Broadway and Bowery, south of Houston Street and north of Canal Street, is a shrinking community today, due to the encroachment of thriving Chinatown. It's now limited mainly to **Mulberry Street,** where you'll find most restaurants, and just a few offshoots. With rents going up in the increasingly trendy Lower East Side, a few chic spots are moving in, further intruding upon the old-world neighborhood. The best way to reach Little Italy is to walk east from the Spring Street station, on the no. 6 line, to Mulberry Street; turn south for Little Italy (you can't miss the year-round red, green, and white street decorations).

The Lower East Side The Lower East Side boasts the best of both old and new New York: Witness the stretch of Houston between Forsyth and Allen streets, where Yoneh Shimmel's Knish Shop sits shoulder to shoulder with the city's newest art house cinema—and both are thriving.

The neighborhood makes a fascinating itinerary stop for nostalgists and nightlife hounds alike. Still, the blocks well south of Houston can be grungy in spots, so walk them with confidence and care after dark.

There are some remnants of what was once the largest Jewish population in America along **Orchard Street,** where you'll find great bargain hunting in its many old-world fabric and clothing stores still thriving between the club-clothes boutiques and trendy lounges. Keep in mind that the

Manhattan Neighborhoods

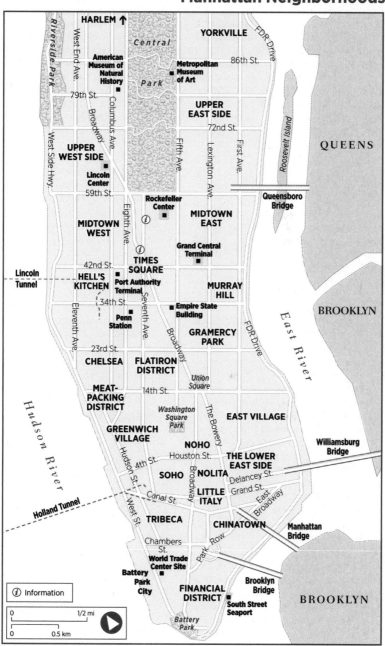

HARLEM ↑

Riverside Park

West End Ave.

Central

YORKVILLE

FDR Drive

American
Museum of
Natural
History

86th St.

Metropolitan
Museum
of Art

Park

79th St.

Columbus Ave.

Broadway

UPPER
EAST SIDE

72nd St.

West Side Hwy.

UPPER
WEST SIDE

Lincoln
Center

59th St.

Fifth Ave.

Lexington Ave.

First Ave.

Roosevelt Island

QUEENS

Rockefeller
Center

ⓘ

MIDTOWN
EAST

Queensboro
Bridge

Eighth Ave.

MIDTOWN
WEST

ⓘ

Grand Central
Terminal

East River

BROOKLYN

Lincoln
Tunnel

42nd St.

TIMES
SQUARE

HELL'S
KITCHEN

Port Authority
Terminal

MURRAY
HILL

34th St.

Seventh Ave.

Empire State
Building

Eleventh Ave.

Penn
Station

Broadway

GRAMERCY
PARK

FDR Drive

23rd St.

CHELSEA

FLATIRON
DISTRICT

Union
Square

MEAT-
PACKING
DISTRICT

14th St.

Hudson River

*Washington
Square
Park*

EAST VILLAGE

GREENWICH
VILLAGE

The Bowery

Williamsburg
Bridge

NOHO

Houston St.

4th St.

Hudson St.

SOHO

Broadway

NOLITA

THE LOWER
EAST SIDE

Delancey St.

Canal St.

West St.

LITTLE
ITALY

Grand St.

East
Broadway

Holland Tunnel

TRIBECA

CHINATOWN

Park Row

Manhattan
Bridge

Chambers
St.

World Trade
Center Site

Battery
Park
City

FINANCIAL
DISTRICT

Brooklyn
Bridge

BROOKLYN

South Street
Seaport

*Battery
Park*

ⓘ Information

0   1/2 mi

0   0.5 km

▶

5

NEW YORK CITY | Manhattan Neighborhoods in Brief

old-world shops close early on Friday afternoon and all day on Saturday (the Jewish Sabbath).

Take the F or M trains to Second Avenue and walk east on Houston; when you see Katz's Deli, you'll know you've arrived. You can also reach the neighborhood from the Delancey Street station on the F line, and the Essex Street station on the J, M, and Z lines.

SoHo & Nolita No relation to the London neighborhood of the same name, **SoHo** got its moniker as an abbreviation of "*So*uth of *Ho*uston Street." This superfashionable neighborhood extends down to Canal Street, between Sixth Avenue to the west and Lafayette Street (1 block east of Broadway) to the east. It's easily accessible by subway: Take the N or R to the Prince Street station; the C, E, or 6 to Spring Street; or the B, D, F, or M trains to the Broadway–Lafayette Street stop.

An industrial zone during the 19th century, SoHo retains the impressive cast-iron architecture of the era. Once a haven for artists seeking cheap rents, SoHo is now a prime example of urban gentrification and is more a ritzy shopping district than an art center.

In recent years SoHo has been crawling its way east, taking over Mott and Mulberry streets—and white-hot Elizabeth Street in particular—north of Kenmare Street, an area now known as **Nolita** for its *No*rth of *Li*ttle *Ita*ly location. Nolita is well known for its hot shopping prospects, which include a number of pricey antiques and home-design stores. Taking the no. 6 to Spring Street will get you closest by subway, but it's just a short walk east from SoHo proper.

The East Village & NoHo The **East Village,** which extends between 14th Street and Houston Street, from Broadway east to First Avenue and beyond to Alphabet City—avenues A, B, C, and D—is where the city's real bohemia has gone. It's a fascinating mix of affordable ethnic and trendy restaurants, upstart clothing designers and kitschy boutiques, punk rock clubs, and folk cafes. A half-dozen Off-Broadway theaters also call this place home. The gentrification that has swept the city has made a huge impact on the East Village, but there's still a seedy element that some of you won't find appealing—and some of you will.

The East Village isn't very accessible by subway, unless you're traveling along 14th Street (the L line will drop you off at Third and First aves.). Your best bet is to take the N, Q, R, 4, 5, or 6 to 14th Street/Union Square; the N or R to 8th Street; or the 6 to Astor Place and walk east.

The southwestern section of the East Village, around Broadway and Lafayette between Bleecker and 4th streets, is called **NoHo** (for *No*rth of *Ho*uston), and has a completely different character. The area has developed much more like its neighbor to the south, SoHo. The Bleecker Street stop on the no. 6 line will land you in the heart of it, and the Broadway–Lafayette stop on the B, D, F, and M lines will drop you at its southern edge.

Greenwich Village Tree-lined streets crisscross and wind, following ancient streams and cow paths. Each block reveals yet another row of Greek Revival town houses, a well-preserved Federal-style house, or a peaceful courtyard or square. This is "the Village," from Broadway west to the Hudson River, bordered by Houston Street to the south and 14th Street to the north. It defies Manhattan's orderly grid system with streets that predate it—so be sure to take a map along as you explore.

The Seventh Avenue line (nos. 1, 2, and 3) is the area's main subway artery, while the West 4th Street stop (where the A, C, and E lines meet the B, D, F, and M lines) serves as its central hub.

The Village is probably the most chameleon-like of Manhattan's neighborhoods. Some of the highest-priced real estate in the city runs along lower Fifth Avenue, which dead-ends at **Washington Square Park.** Serpentine **Bleecker Street** stretches through most of the neighborhood and is emblematic of the area's historical bent. The tolerant, anything-goes attitude in the Village has fostered a large gay community, which is still largely in evidence around **Christopher Street** and Sheridan Square.

The streets west of Seventh Avenue, an area known as the **West Village,** boast a more relaxed vibe and some of the city's most charming and historic brownstones. Three colleges—New York University, Parsons School of Design, and the New School for Social Research—keep the area thinking young.

Streets are often crowded with weekend warriors and teenagers, especially on Bleecker, West 4th, 8th, and surrounding streets.

MIDTOWN

Chelsea & the Meat-Packing District Chelsea has come on strong in recent years as a hip address, especially for the gay community. A low-rise composite of town houses, tenements, lofts, and factories, the neighborhood comprises roughly the area west of Sixth Avenue from 14th to 30th streets. (Sixth Ave. itself, below 23rd St., is actually considered part of the Flatiron District; see below.) Its main arteries are Seventh and Eighth avenues, and it's primarily served by the C or E and no. 1 subway lines.

New restaurants, cutting-edge shopping, and superhot nightspots pop up daily in the still-beefy **Meat-Packing District,** while the area from West 22nd to West 29th streets between Tenth and Eleventh avenues is home to the cutting edge of today's New York art scene. With galleries and bars tucked away in converted warehouses and former meat lockers, browsing can be frustrating. Your best bet is to have a specific destination (and an exact address) in mind, be it a restaurant, gallery, boutique, or nightclub, before you come.

The Flatiron District, Union Square & Gramercy Park These adjoining and sometimes overlapping neighborhoods are some of the city's most appealing. Their streets have been rediscovered by New Yorkers and visitors alike, largely thanks to the boom-to-bust dot.com revolution of the late 1990s; the Flatiron District served as its geographical heart and earned the nickname "Silicon Alley" in the process. These neighborhoods boast great shopping and dining opportunities and a central-to-everything location that's hard to beat.

The **Flatiron District** lies south of 23rd Street to 14th Street, between Broadway and Sixth Avenue, and centers on the historic Flatiron Building on 23rd (so named for its triangular shape) and Park Avenue South, which has become a sophisticated new Restaurant Row. Below 23rd Street along Sixth Avenue (once known as the Ladies' Mile shopping district), mass-market discounters such as Filene's Basement, Bed Bath & Beyond, and others have moved in. The shopping gets classier on Fifth Avenue, where you'll find a mix of national names and hip boutiques.

Union Square is the hub of the entire area; the L, N, Q, R, 4, 5, and 6 trains stop here, making it easy to reach from most other city neighborhoods. Union Square is best known as the setting for New York's premier green market every Monday, Wednesday, Friday, and Saturday.

From about 16th to 23rd streets, east from Park Avenue South to about Second Avenue, is the leafy, largely residential district known as **Gramercy Park.**

Times Square & Midtown West Midtown West, the vast area from 34th to 59th streets west of Fifth Avenue to the Hudson River, encompasses several famous names: Madison Square Garden, the Garment District, Rockefeller Center, the Theater District, and Times Square. This is New York's tourism central, where you'll find the bright lights and bustle that draw people from all over the world.

The nos. 1, 2, 3 subway line serves the massive neon station at the heart of Times Square, at 42nd Street between Broadway and Seventh Avenue, while the B, D, F, M line runs up Sixth Avenue to Rockefeller Center. The N, Q, R, line cuts diagonally across the neighborhood, following the path of Broadway before heading up Seventh Avenue at 42nd Street. The A, C, E line serves the west side, running along Eighth Avenue.

Longtime New Yorkers like to kvetch about the glory days of the old peep-show-and-porn-shop **Times Square.** The area is now cleaned up and there really is not much here for the native New Yorker. The revival, however, has been nothing short of an outstanding success for tourism. Grand old theaters have come back to life as Broadway playhouses. Expect dense crowds, though; it's often tough just to make your way along the sidewalks.

To the west of the Theater District, in the 40s and 50s between Eighth and Tenth avenues, is **Hell's Kitchen,** an area that is much nicer than its ghoulish name, and one of my favorites in the city. The neighborhood resisted gentrification until the mid-'90s, but has grown into a charming, less touristy adjunct to the neighboring Theater District. Ninth Avenue, in particular, has blossomed into one of the city's finest dining avenues; just stroll along and you'll have a world of great cuisine, ranging from American diner food to rustic Mediterranean to traditional Thai.

Unlike Times Square, gorgeous **Rockefeller Center** has needed no renovation. Situated between 46th and 50th streets from Sixth Avenue east to Fifth, this Art Deco complex contains some of the city's great architectural gems, which house hundreds of offices and a number of NBC studios.

Between Seventh and Eighth avenues and 31st and 33rd streets, **Penn Station** sits beneath unsightly behemoth **Madison Square Garden,** where the Rangers, the Liberty, and the Knicks play. Taking up all of 34th Street between Sixth and Seventh avenues is **Macy's,** the country's largest department store; exit Macy's at the southeast corner and you'll find more famous-label shopping around **Herald Square.**

Midtown West is also home to some of the city's most revered museums and cultural institutions, including **Carnegie Hall,** the **Museum of Modern Art,** and **Radio City Music Hall,** to name just a few.

Midtown East & Murray Hill Midtown East, the area including Fifth Avenue and everything east from 34th to 59th streets, is the more upscale side of the Midtown map. This side of town is short of subway trains, served primarily by the Lexington Avenue nos. 4, 5, 6 line.

Midtown East is where you'll find the city's finest collection of grand hotels. The stretch of **Fifth Avenue** from Saks at 49th Street extending to 59th Street is home to the city's most high-profile haute couture shopping.

Magnificent architectural highlights include the recently repolished **Chrysler Building,** with its stylized gargoyles glaring down on passersby; the Beaux Arts tour de force that is **Grand Central Terminal; St. Patrick's Cathedral;** and the glorious **Empire State Building.**

Farther east, swank Sutton and Beekman places are enclaves of beautiful town houses, luxury living, and tiny pocket parks that look out over the East River. Along this river is the **United Nations,** which isn't officially in New York City, or even the United States, but on a parcel of international land belonging to member nations.

Claiming the territory east from Madison Avenue, **Murray Hill** begins somewhere north of 23rd Street (the line btw. it and Gramercy Park is fuzzy) and is most clearly recognizable north of 30th Street to 42nd Street. This brownstone-lined quarter is largely a quiet residential neighborhood, most notable for its handful of good budget and midprice hotels.

UPTOWN

Upper West Side North of 59th Street and encompassing everything west of Central Park, the Upper West Side has **Lincoln Center,** arguably the world's premier performing arts venue, and the **Time Warner Center** with its upscale shops, such as **Hugo Boss, A/X Armani,** and **Sephora.** It's also the home for **Jazz at Lincoln Center.**

Unlike the more stratified Upper East Side, the Upper West Side is home to an egalitarian mix of middle-class yuppiedom, laid-back wealth (lots of celebs and moneyed media types call the grand apartments along Central Park West home), and ethnic families who were here before the gentrification.

Two major subway lines service the area: the nos. 1, 2, 3 line runs up Broadway, while the B and C trains run up glamorous Central Park West, stopping right at the historic

Dakota apartment building (where John Lennon was shot and Yoko Ono still lives) at 72nd Street, and at the Museum of Natural History at 81st Street.

Upper East Side North of 59th Street and east of Central Park is some of the city's most expensive residential real estate. This is New York at its most gentrified: Walk along Fifth and Park avenues, especially between 60th and 80th streets, and you're sure to encounter some of the wizened WASPs and Chanel-suited socialites who make up the most rarefied of the city's population. Madison Avenue from 60th Street well into the 80s is the main shopping strip—so bring your platinum card.

The main attraction of this neighborhood is **Museum Mile,** the stretch of Fifth Avenue fronting Central Park, which is home to no fewer than 10 terrific cultural institutions, including the mind-boggling **Metropolitan Museum of Art.**

The Upper East Side is served solely by the crowded Lexington Avenue line (4, 5, 6 trains), so wear your walking shoes (or bring taxi fare) if you're heading up here to explore.

Harlem Harlem has benefited from a dramatic image makeover in the past few years, and with new restaurants, clubs, and stores, it's slowly becoming a neighborhood in demand.

Harlem proper stretches from river to river, beginning at 125th Street on the West Side, 96th Street on the East Side, and 110th Street north of Central Park. This area is benefiting greatly from the revitalization that has swept so much of the city. The commercial area is served primarily by the A, B, C, D and nos. 2, 3, 4, and 5 lines.

Washington Heights & Inwood Located at the northern tip of Manhattan, Washington Heights (the area from 155th St. to Dyckman St., with adjacent Inwood running to the tip) is home to a large segment of Manhattan's Latino community, plus an increasing number of yuppies who don't mind trading a half-hour subway commute to Midtown for much lower rents. **Fort Tryon Park** and **the Cloisters** are the two big reasons for visitors to come up this way. The Cloisters houses the Metropolitan Museum of Art's stunning medieval collection, in a building perched atop a hill, with excellent views across the Hudson to the Palisades. Committed off-the-beaten-path sightseers might also want to visit the **Dyckman Farmhouse,** a historic jewel built in 1783 and the only remaining Dutch Colonial structure in Manhattan.

GETTING AROUND

Frankly, Manhattan's transportation systems are a marvel. It's simply miraculous that so many people can gather on this little island and move around it. For the most part, you can get where you're going pretty quickly and easily using some combination of subways, buses, and cabs.

But during rush hours, you'll easily beat car traffic while on foot, as taxis and buses stop and groan at gridlocked corners (don't even *try* going crosstown in a cab or bus in Midtown at midday). You'll also see a whole lot more by walking than by riding beneath the street in the subway or flying by in a cab. So pack your most comfortable shoes and hit the pavement—it's the best, cheapest, and most appealing way to experience the city.

By Subway

Run by the **Metropolitan Transit Authority,** also known as the MTA (**www.mta. info/nyct/subway**), the much-maligned subway system is actually the fastest way to travel around New York, especially during rush hours. Some 4.5 million people a day seem to agree, as it's their primary mode of transportation. The subway is quick, inexpensive, relatively safe, and efficient, as well as being a genuine New York experience.

The subway runs 24 hours a day, 7 days a week. The rush-hour crushes are roughly from 8 to 9:30am and from 5 to 6:30pm on weekdays; the rest of the time the trains are much more manageable. *Note:* In December 2009, in order to make up for a $400-million shortfall, the MTA passed a budget that mandates major cutbacks in service on both the subway and bus lines. Subways and buses are running with reduced frequency during weekends, late nights, and weekday afternoons. Some lines have been eliminated altogether (the W and V subway lines). These cuts, many of which took effect in late spring of 2010, have infuriated many New Yorkers, and various groups have been fighting them. Some cuts were restored after public outcry, but a number of bus and subway routes have changed—be sure you have an up-to-date map.

PAYING YOUR WAY

A SingleRide subway fare is $2.50 (half-price for seniors and those with disabilities), and children under 44 inches tall ride free (up to three per adult). *Note:* The prices listed in this section reflect the latest price increase by the MTA, which went into effect in December 2011. The fares are scheduled to go up again in 2013.

Tokens are no longer available. People pay with the **MetroCard,** a magnetically encoded card that debits the fare when swiped through the turnstile (or the farebox on any city bus). Once you're in the system, you can transfer freely to any subway line that you can reach without exiting your station. MetroCards also allow you **free transfers** between the bus and subway within a 2-hour period.

MetroCards can be purchased from staffed token booths, where you can pay only with cash; at the ATM-style vending machines now located in every subway station, which accept cash, credit cards, and debit cards; from a MetroCard merchant, such as most Rite Aid drugstores; at Hudson News, at Penn Station and Grand Central Terminal; or at the MTA information desk at the **Times Square Information Center,** 1560 Broadway, between 46th and 47th streets.

MetroCards come in a few different configurations:

Pay-Per-Ride MetroCards can be used for up to four people by swiping up to four times (bring the entire family). You can put any amount from $4.50 (two rides) to $80 on your card. Every time you put $8 or more on your Pay-Per-Ride MetroCard, it's automatically credited 15%—in other words, spend $20 and you get a free ride, plus a 50¢ balance. You can buy Pay-Per-Ride MetroCards at any subway station; most stations have automated MetroCard vending machines, which allow you to buy MetroCards using your major credit card or debit card. MetroCards are also available from many shops and newsstands around town in $10 and $20 values. You can refill your card at any time until the expiration date on the card, usually about a year from the date of purchase, at any subway station.

Unlimited-Ride MetroCards, which can't be used for more than one person at a time or more frequently than 18-minute intervals, are available in two values: the **7-Day MetroCard,** which allows you 7 days' worth of unlimited subway and bus rides for $29; and the **30-Day MetroCard,** for $104. Unlimited-Ride MetroCards can be purchased at any subway station or from a MetroCard merchant. They go into effect the first time you use them—so if you buy a card on Monday and don't begin to use it until Wednesday, Wednesday is when the clock starts ticking on your Metro-Card. Seven- and 30-day MetroCards run out at midnight on the last day. These MetroCards cannot be refilled.

Tips for using your MetroCard: The MetroCard swiping mechanisms at turnstiles are the source of much grousing among subway riders. If you swipe too fast or too slow, the turnstile will ask you to swipe again. If this happens, ***do not move to a different turnstile,*** or you may end up paying twice. If you've tried repeatedly and really can't make your MetroCard work, tell the token booth clerk; chances are good, though, that you'll get the movement down after a couple of uses.

If you're not sure how much money you have left on your MetroCard, or what day it expires, use the station's MetroCard Reader, usually located near the station entrance or the token booth (on buses, the farebox will also provide you with this information).

To locate the nearest MetroCard merchant, or for any other MetroCard questions, call ✆ **718/330-1234.** Or go online to **www.mta.info/metrocard**, which can give you a full rundown of MetroCard merchants in the tri-state area.

USING THE SYSTEM

The subway system basically mimics the lay of the land aboveground, with most lines in Manhattan running north and south, like the avenues, and a few lines east and west, like the streets.

Lines have assigned colors on subway maps and trains—red for the nos. 1, 2, 3 line; green for the 4, 5, and 6 trains; and so on—but nobody ever refers to them by color. Always refer to them by number or letter when asking questions. Within Manhattan, the distinction between different numbered trains that share the same line is usually that some are express and others are local. **Express trains** often skip about three stops for each one that they make; express stops are indicated on subway maps with a white (rather than solid) circle. Local stops are usually from 5 to 10 blocks apart.

Directions are almost always indicated using "Uptown" (northbound) and "Downtown" (southbound), so be sure to know in which direction you want to head. The outsides of some subway entrances are marked UPTOWN ONLY or DOWNTOWN ONLY; read carefully, as it's easy to head in the wrong direction. Once you're on the platform, check the signs overhead to make sure that the train you're waiting for will be traveling in the right direction. If you do make a mistake, it's a good idea to wait for an express station, like 14th Street or 42nd Street, so you can get off and change for the other direction without paying again.

In 2011, the MTA initiated helpful digital signs inside and some outside of subway stations indicating how long before the next desired train will arrive. These signs are lessening the neck strain on New Yorkers used to judging when a train will arrive by continually staring down the dark subway tunnel waiting hopefully to see the lights of an oncoming train.

By Bus

Cheaper than taxis and more pleasant than subways (they provide a mobile sightseeing window on the city), MTA buses are a good transportation option. However, they can get stuck in traffic, sometimes making it quicker to walk. They stop every couple of blocks, rather than the 5 to 10 blocks that local subways traverse between stops. So for long distances, the subway is your best bet; but for short distances or traveling crosstown, try the bus. Bus stops are located every 2 or 3 blocks on the right-side corner of the street (facing the direction of traffic flow). Watch for the blue-and-white sign with the bus emblem.

PAYING YOUR WAY

Like the subway fare, a SingleRide **bus fare** is $2.50, half-price for seniors and riders with disabilities, and free for children under 44 inches (up to three per adult). The fare is payable with a **MetroCard** or **exact change.** Bus drivers don't make change, and fareboxes don't accept dollar bills or pennies. You can't purchase MetroCards on the bus, so you'll have to have them before you board; for details on where to get them, see "Paying Your Way," under "By Subway," above.

If you pay with a MetroCard, you can transfer to another bus or to the subway for free within 2 hours. If you pay cash, you must request a **free transfer** card that allows you to change to an intersecting bus route only within 2 hours of issue. Transfer cards cannot be used to enter the subway.

By Taxi

If you don't want to deal with public transportation, finding an address that might be a few blocks from the subway station, or sharing your ride with 4.5 million other people, then take a taxi. The biggest advantages are, of course, that cabs can be hailed on any street (provided you find an empty one—often simple, yet at other times nearly impossible) and will take you right to your destination. I find they're best used at night when there's little traffic and when the subway may seem a little daunting. In Midtown at midday, you can usually walk to where you're going more quickly.

Official New York City taxis, licensed by the Taxi and Limousine Commission (TLC), are yellow, with the rates printed on the door and a light with a medallion number on the roof. You can hail a taxi on any street. *Never* accept a ride from any other car except an official city yellow cab (livery cars are not allowed to pick up fares on the street, despite what the driver tells you when he pulls over to see if he can pick up a fare).

Taxi-Hailing Tips

When you're waiting on the street for an available taxi, look at the **medallion light** on top of the oncoming cabs. If the light is out, the taxi is in use. When only the center part (the number) is lit, the taxi is available—this is when you raise your hand to flag the cab. If all the lights are on, the driver is off duty. A taxi can't take more than four people, so expect to split up if your group is larger.

The base fare on entering the cab is $2.50. The cost is 40¢ for every ⅕ mile or 40¢ per 60 seconds in stopped or slow-moving traffic (or for waiting time). There's no extra charge for each passenger or for luggage. However, you must pay bridge or tunnel tolls (sometimes the driver will front the toll and add it to your bill at the end; most times, however, you pay the driver before the toll). You'll pay a $1 surcharge between 4 and 8pm and a 50¢ surcharge after 8pm and before 6am. A 15% to 20% tip is customary.

Most taxis are now equipped with a device that allows you to pay by credit card, though some drivers will claim the machine is broken (there is a transaction fee for credit cards that cuts into their income) and ask you to pay in cash. You can choose to either add the tip to the credit card or tip the driver in cash.

Many, if not most, taxi drivers may not have the best grasp of English. If their driving is scaring you, ask them to slow down, stop slamming on the brakes *quite* so hard, and taking off like a rocket when the light turns green. Wear your seat belt—taxis are required to provide them.

The TLC has posted a **Taxi Rider's Bill of Rights** sticker in every cab. Drivers are required by law to take you anywhere in the five boroughs, to Nassau or Westchester counties, or to Newark Airport. They are supposed to know how to get you to any address in Manhattan and all major points in the outer boroughs. They are also required to provide air-conditioning and turn off the radio on demand, and they cannot smoke while you're in the cab. They are required to be polite.

For all driver complaints, including the one above, and to report lost property, call ℂ **311** or 212/NEW-YORK (639-9675; outside the metro area). For details on getting to and from the local airports by taxi, see "By Plane," under "Arriving," earlier in this chapter. For further taxi information—including a complete rundown of your rights as a taxi rider—point your Web browser to **www.ci.nyc.ny.us/taxi**.

[FastFACTS] NEW YORK CITY

Area Codes There are four area codes in the city: two in Manhattan, the original **212** and **646;** and two in the outer boroughs, the original **718** and the newer **347.** Also common is the **917** area code, which is assigned to cellphones. All calls between these area codes are local calls, but you'll have to dial 1 + the area code + the seven digits for all calls, even ones made within your area code.

Business Hours In general, **retail stores** are open Monday through Saturday from 10am to 6 or 7pm, Thursday from 10am to 8:30 or 9pm, and Sunday from noon to 5pm. **Banks** tend to be open Monday through Friday from 9am to 5pm, with many open Saturday mornings, and some now even open on Sundays.

Doctors If you get sick, consider asking your hotel concierge to recommend a local doctor—even his or her own. This will probably yield a better recommendation than any toll-free telephone number would.

There are also several walk-in medical centers, like **Beth Israel Medical Group,** 55 E. 34th St., between Park and Madison avenues (ℂ **212/252-6000**), for nonemergency illnesses. The clinic is open Monday through Sunday from 8am to 8pm.

The **NYU Downtown Hospital** offers physician referrals at ℂ **212/312-5000.** You can also try the emergency room at a local hospital. Many hospitals also have walk-in clinics for emergency cases that are not life threatening; you may not get immediate attention, but you won't pay the high price of an emergency-room visit.

Pack **prescription medications** in their original containers in your carry-on luggage. Also bring along copies of your prescriptions in case you lose your pills or run out. Don't forget an extra pair of contact lenses or prescription glasses.

If you have dental problems on the road, a service known as **1-800-DENTIST** (ℂ **800/336-8422**) will

provide the name of a local dentist.

Drinking Laws The legal age for purchase and consumption of alcoholic beverages is 21; proof of age can be requested at bars, nightclubs, and restaurants, especially if you're graced with youthful looks. However, this is New York City, which is a most tolerant place. Liquor and wine are sold only in licensed stores, which are open 6 days a week, with some choosing to close on Sunday, others on an early or midweek day. (You can usually find an open liquor store on Sun.) Liquor stores are closed on holidays and election days while the polls are open. Beer can be purchased in grocery stores and delis 24 hours a day, except Sunday before noon. Last call in bars is at 4am, though many close earlier. Do not carry open containers of alcohol in your car or any public area that isn't zoned for alcohol consumption. The police can fine you on the spot.

Electricity Like Canada, the United States uses 110 to 120 volts AC (60 cycles), compared to 220 to 240 volts AC (50 cycles) in most of Europe, Australia, and New Zealand. Downward converters that change 220 to 240 volts to 110 to 120 volts are difficult to find in the United States, so bring one with you.

Emergencies For all emergencies—a fire, police, or health emergency—call **911.**

Family Travel To locate accommodations, restaurants, and attractions that are particularly kid-friendly, look for the "Kids" icon throughout this guide. For more extensive recommendations, you might want to purchase a copy of *Frommer's New York City with Kids,* by Alexis Lipsitz Flippin (Wiley), an entire guidebook dedicated to family visits to the Big Apple.

Good bets for the most timely information include the "Weekend" section of Friday's *New York Times,* which has a section dedicated to the week's best kid-friendly activities; the weekly *New York* magazine, which has a full calendar of children's events in its listings section; and *Time Out New York,* which also has a weekly kids section with a bit of an alternative bent. *Big Apple Parent* is usually available, for free, at children's stores and other locations in Manhattan. For a list of more family-friendly travel resources, turn to the experts at Frommers.com.

Health New York City has some of the best hospitals and doctors in the world. Hopefully, you won't need to avail yourself, but it's good to know, in case.

Hospitals The following hospitals have 24-hour emergency rooms. Don't forget your insurance card.

Downtown: New York Downtown Hospital, 170 William St., between Beekman and Spruce streets (© 212/312-5106 or 312-5000), and **Beth Israel Medical Center,** First Avenue and 16th Street (© 212/420-2000).

Midtown: Bellevue Hospital Center, 462 First Ave., at 27th Street (© 212/562-4141); **New York University Langone Medical Center,** 550 First Ave., at 33rd Street (© 212/263-7300); and **St. Luke's/Roosevelt Hospital,** 425 W. 59th St., between Ninth and Tenth avenues (© 212/523-4000).

Upper West Side: St. Luke's Hospital Center, 1111 Amsterdam Ave., at 114th Street (© 212/523-4000), and **Columbia Presbyterian Medical Center,** 622 W. 168th St., between Broadway and Fort Washington Avenue (© 212/305-2500).

Upper East Side: New York Presbyterian Hospital, 525 E. 68th St., at York Avenue (© 212/746-5454); **Lenox Hill Hospital,** 100 E. 77th St., between Park and Lexington avenues (© 212/434-3030); and **Mount Sinai Medical Center,** 1190 Fifth Avenue at 100th Street (© 212/241-6500).

Internet & Wi-Fi New York is rife with Wi-Fi (wireless fidelity) "hotspots" that offer free Wi-Fi access or charge a small fee for usage. A good directory of free hotspots in the city can be found at **www.openwifinyc.com**.

Your hotel may also provide Wi-Fi or broadband access in your room, sometimes for a hefty daily fee. It's always surprised us that the higher-end hotels are the ones that charge for Internet access, while the budget places are more likely to use free Internet as a selling point.

You can access the Internet for free at **Starbucks** (**www.starbucks.com/coffeehouse/wireless-internet**). So have a cup of coffee and check your e-mail at your leisure. **FedEx Office** (**www.fedex.com/us/office/services/computer/index.html**) has free Wi-Fi at most locations, as well as computers you use for 30¢ per minute. There are dozens of locations around town.

LGBT Travelers Gay and lesbian culture is as much a part of New York's basic identity as yellow cabs, high-rises, and Broadway theater. Indeed, in a city with one of the world's largest, loudest, and most powerful LGBT populations, homosexuality is squarely in the mainstream. So city hotels tend to be neutral on the issue, and gay couples shouldn't have a problem.

All over Manhattan, but especially in such neighborhoods as the West Village (particularly Christopher St., famous the world over as the main drag of New York gay-male life) and Chelsea (especially Eighth Ave., from 16th to 23rd sts., and W. 17th to 19th sts., from Fifth to Eighth aves.), shops, services, and restaurants have a lesbian and gay flavor.

The **Lesbian, Gay, Bisexual & Transgender Community Center,** familiarly known as "the Center," is at 208 W. 13th St., between Seventh and Eighth avenues (📞 **212/620-7310;** www.gaycenter.org). The center is the meeting place for more than 300 lesbian, gay, and bisexual organizations. You can check the online events calendar, which lists hundreds of happenings—lectures, dances, concerts, readings, films—or call for the latest. The staff is also helpful in lending advice on gay-friendly businesses in the area, including hotels and guesthouses.

Other good sources for lesbian and gay events are the free biweekly newspaper *Gay City News* (**www.gaycitynews.com**) and the free magazines **Next** (**www.nextmagazine.com**) and **GONYC** (**www.gomag.com**), which is lesbian-oriented. You'll also find lots of information on their websites.

The weekly *Time Out New York* (**www.timeoutny.com**) boasts a terrific gay and lesbian section. *The Center* (see above) publishes a monthly guide listing many events (also listed on its website).

Newspapers & Magazines

There are three major daily newspapers: the *New York Times,* the *Daily News,* and the *New York Post.* There are also two free daily papers, *AM-New York* and *Metro,* usually distributed in the morning near subway stations and in self-serve boxes around town.

If you want to find your hometown paper, visit **Universal News & Magazines,** at 234 W. 42nd St., between Seventh and Eighth avenues (📞 **212/221-1809**), and 977 Eighth Ave., between 57th and 58th streets (📞 **212/459-0932**). Other good bets include the **Hudson News** dealers, located in Grand Central Terminal, at 42nd Street and Lexington Avenue, and Penn Station, at 34th Street and Seventh Avenue.

There are several weekly and biweekly newspapers and magazines (such as the glossies *New York Magazine* and *TimeOut New York*), as well as the *Village Voice* and *Gay City News,* which are excellent sources of information about events, restaurants, and attractions in the city. We list them and their websites throughout the book.

Police

Dial 📞 **911** in an emergency; otherwise, call 📞 **646/610-5000** (NYPD Switchboard) for the number of the nearest precinct. For nonemergency matters, call 📞 **311.**

Safety

The FBI consistently rates New York City as one of the safest large cities in the United States, but it is still a large city and crime most definitely exists. Here are a few tips for staying safe in New York:

- Trust your instincts, because they're usually right.
- You'll rarely be hassled, but it's always best to walk with a sense of purpose and self-confidence. Don't stop in the middle of the sidewalk to pull out and peruse your map.
- Anywhere in the city, if you find yourself on a deserted street that feels unsafe, it probably is; leave as quickly as possible.
- If you do find yourself accosted by someone with or without a weapon, remember to keep your anger in check and that the most reasonable response (maddening though it may be) is to not resist.

Senior Travel

New York subway and bus fares are half-price ($1.10) for people 65 and older. Many museums and sights (and some theaters and performance halls) offer discounted admittance and tickets to seniors, so don't be shy about asking. Always bring an ID card, especially if you've kept your youthful glow.

Many hotels offer senior discounts; **Choice Hotels** (which include Comfort Inns, some of my favorite affordable Midtown hotels), for example, gives 10% off the published rates to AARP members. Call ✆ **877/424-6423** or visit **www.choicehotels.com**.

Smoking Smoking is prohibited on all public transportation; in the lobbies of hotels and office buildings; in taxis, bars, and restaurants; and in most shops. Most recently, it was banned in all parks and on beaches, too.

Student Travel There are student discounts at almost every museum in New York, for example, and so student travelers should bring their school IDs with them. In this case, "student" means high school or college—or any school, really.

Taxes **Sales tax** is 8.875% on meals, most goods, and some services. **Hotel tax** is 5.875% plus a daily fee up to $2, depending on the cost of your room, per night. **Parking garage tax** is 18.375%. The United States has no value-added tax (VAT) or other indirect tax at the national level. Every state, county, and city may levy its own local tax on all purchases, including hotel and restaurant checks and airline tickets. These taxes will not appear on price tags.

Tipping In hotels, tip **bellhops** at least $1 per bag ($2–$3 if you have a lot of luggage), and tip the **chamber staff** $1 to $2 per day (more if you've left a big mess for him or her to clean up). Tip the **doorman** or **concierge** only if he or she has provided you with some specific service (for example, calling a cab for you or obtaining difficult-to-get theater tickets). Tip the **valet-parking attendant** $1 every time you get your car.

In restaurants, bars, and nightclubs, tip **service staff** and **bartenders** 15% to 20% of the check, tip **checkroom attendants** $1 per garment, and tip **valet-parking attendants** $1 per vehicle.

As for other service personnel, tip **cab drivers** 15% of the fare; tip **skycaps** at airports at least $1 per bag ($2–$3 if you have a lot of luggage); and tip **hairdressers** and **barbers** 15% to 20%.

For help with tip calculations, currency conversions, and more, download our convenient Travel Tools app for your mobile device. Go to **www.frommers.com/go/mobile**, and click on the Travel Tools icon.

Toilets You won't find many public toilets or restrooms on the streets in New York City, but they can be found in hotel lobbies, bars, restaurants, museums, department stores, and railway and bus stations. Large hotels and fast-food restaurants are often the best bet for clean facilities.

Public restrooms are available at the visitor centers in Midtown (1560 Broadway, btw. 46th and 47th sts.; and 810 Seventh Ave., btw. 52nd and 53rd sts.). You can find relief at the New York Public Library's main building on Fifth Avenue just south of 42nd Street. Grand Central Terminal, at 42nd Street between Park and Lexington avenues, also has clean restrooms. There are staffed bathrooms open from early in the morning until fairly late at night in the Times Square subway station (closer to Seventh Ave.). On the Lower East Side, stop into the Lower East Side BID Visitor Center, 54 Orchard St., between Hester and Grand streets (weekdays 9:30am–5:30pm, weekends 9:30am–4pm).

Travelers with Disabilities New York is more accessible to travelers with disabilities than ever before. The city's bus system is wheelchair-friendly, and most of the major sightseeing attractions are easily accessible. Even so, **always call first** to be sure that the places you want to go to are fully accessible.

Most hotels are ADA compliant, with suitable rooms for wheelchair-bound travelers as well as those with other disabilities. But before you book, **ask lots of questions based on your needs.** Many city hotels are in older buildings that have been modified to meet requirements; still, elevators and bathrooms can be on the small side, and other impediments may exist. If you have mobility issues, you'll probably do best to book one of the city's newer hotels, which tend to be more spacious and accommodating. At **www.access-able.com**, you'll find links to New York's best accessible accommodations (click on "World Destinations"). Some Broadway theaters and other performance venues provide total wheelchair accessibility; others provide partial accessibility. Many also offer lower-priced tickets for theatergoers with disabilities and their companions, though you'll need to check individual policies and reserve in advance.

Hospital Audiences, Inc. (📞 **212/575-7676;** www.hainyc.org), arranges attendance and provides details about accessibility at cultural institutions as well as cultural events adapted for people with disabilities. Services include "Describe!" which allows visually impaired theatergoers to enjoy theater events, and the invaluable **HAI Hot Line** (📞 **212/575-7676**), which offers accessibility information for hotels, restaurants, attractions, cultural venues, and much more.

Another terrific source for travelers with disabilities who are coming to New York City is **Big Apple Greeter** (📞 **212/669-8159;** www.bigapplegreeter.org). All of its employees are extremely well versed in accessibility issues. They can provide a resource list of city agencies that serve those with disabilities, and they sometimes have special discounts available to theater and music performances. Big Apple Greeter even offers one-to-one tours that pair volunteers with visitors with disabilities; they can even introduce you to the public transportation system if you like. Reserve at least 1 week ahead.

WHERE TO STAY

New York City may be the most expensive place to live in the United States. It only follows that hotel rates here will also be more expensive than in almost any other city in the country. If you want to spend less than 100 bucks a night, you're probably going to have to put up with some inconveniences, such as possibly sharing a hall bathroom with your fellow travelers. If you want a room with standard amenities, plan on spending at least $150 a night or so. If you do better than that, you've landed a deal.

The Financial District
VERY EXPENSIVE

Ritz-Carlton New York, Battery Park ★★★   Perfect on almost every level, the only drawback to this Ritz-Carlton is that it's so far downtown. But the location, on the extreme southern tip of Manhattan, is also one of its strengths. Where else can you get, in most rooms anyway, magnificent views of New York Harbor from your bedroom—complete with telescope for close-ups of Lady Liberty? This modern, Art Deco–influenced high-rise differs from the English-countryside look of most Ritz-Carltons, including its sister hotel on Central Park (p. 85), but that's where the differences end. You'll find the full slate of comforts and services typical of Ritz-Carlton, from Frette-dressed feather beds to the chain's signature Bath Butler, who will draw a scented bath in your own deep soaking tub. If you don't mind the location and the commute to Midtown and beyond, you won't find a more luxurious choice.

2 West St., New York, NY 10004. www.ritzcarlton.com/batterypark. 📞 **800/241-3333** or 212/344-0800. Fax 212/344-3801. 298 units. $315–$545 double; from $625 suite. Check website for weekend packages. AE, DC, DISC, MC, V. Valet parking $60. Subway: 4 or 5 to Bowling Green. Pets under 20 lb. accepted. **Amenities:** Restaurant; bar; lobby lounge for light meals and cocktails; Ritz-Carlton Club Level w/5 food presentations daily; concierge; state-of-the-art health club w/panoramic views; room service; technology butler and bath butler services. *In room:* A/C, TV w/pay movies and video games, DVD w/surround sound in suites and Club rooms, CD player, fridge, hair dryer, minibar, Wi-Fi.

Downtown Hotels, Restaurants & Attractions

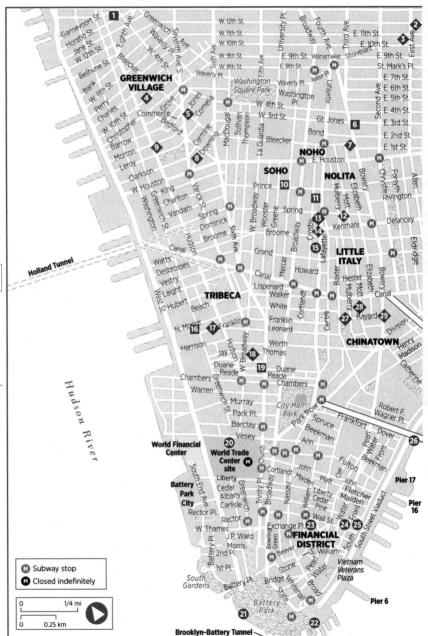

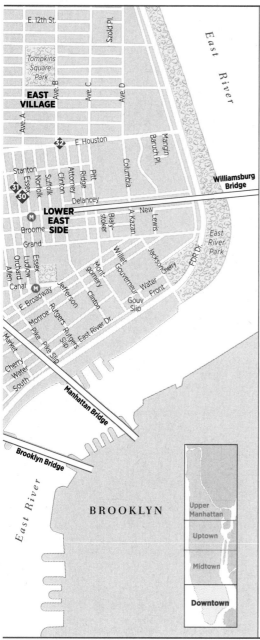

HOTELS ■
Andaz Wall Street **24**
The Bowery Hotel **6**
Crosby Street Hotel **11**
Duane Street Hotel **19**
Greenwich Hotel **16**
Gansevoort Meatpacking Hotel **1**
Hotel on Rivington **30**
The Mercer **10**
Ritz Carlton New York
Battery Park **21**

RESTAURANTS ◆
Big Wong King **28**
Bread **12**
Clinton St. Bakery **32**
Double Crown **7**
En Japanese Brasserie **9**
Ed's Lobster Bar **14**
Hearth **2**
'inoteca **31**
John's Pizzeria **5**
L'artusi **4**
Locanda Verde **15**
Mas **8**
Momofuku Noodle Bar **3**
New York Noodeltown **29**
The Odeon **18**
Osteria Morini **13**
Pho Viet Huong **27**
Thalassa **17**

ATTRACTIONS ●
Brooklyn Bridge **26**
Children's Museum of the Arts **15**
Ellis Island Ferries **21**
South Street Seaport & Museum **25**
Staten Island Ferry **22**
Statue of Liberty Ferry **21**
Wall Street and the New York
Stock Exchange **23**
World Trade Center Site
(Ground Zero) **20**

Midtown Hotels, Restaurants & Attractions

HOTELS ■
Andaz Fifth Avenue **39**
Casablanca Hotel **13**
Gansevoort Park **31**
Gershwin Hotel **29**
Grace Roomate Hotel **46**
Gramercy Park Hotel **26**
Hotel Elysee **52**
Ink 48 **8**
Inn on 23rd Street **17**
Jumeirah Essex House **1**
Le Parker Meridien **54**
The Library **40**
New York Palace **49**
The Michelangelo **5**
The Pierre **57**
Ritz Carlton New York
    Central Park **56**
The Royalton **45**
The Setai **36**
Sofitel New York **45**
Thirty Thirty **32**
Travel Inn **14**

RESTAURANTS ◆
Aldea **22**
Aquavit **53**
BLT Fish **21**
Brgr **16**
Buddakan **19**
Carnegie Deli **2**
Chola **55**
Devi **23**
Frankie & Johnnie's **35**
John's Pizzeria **11**
Keen's Steakhouse **34**
La Pizza Fresca Ristorante **24**
Millesime **30**
Molyvos **1**
Morimoto **20**
New York Burger Co. **15, 28**
Nizza **10**
Oceana **47**
RUB **18**
Sapporo **6**
Shake Shack **31**
Stage Deli **3**
Virgil's Real BBQ **12**
Wondee Siam **4**

ATTRACTIONS ●

Chrysler Building **43**
Circle Line Sightseeing
  Cruises **15**
Empire State Building **33**
Flatiron Building **27**
Grand Central Terminal **42**
Gray Line New York Tours **7**
International Center of
  Photography **41**
Morgan Library **37**
Museum of Modern Art **51**
New York Public Library **38**
Rockefeller Center **48**
St. Patrick's Cathedral **50**
Top of the Rock **48**
United Nations **44**
U.S.S. *Intrepid* **9**

5

Uptown Hotels, Restaurants & Attractions

HOTELS ■
Hotel Beacon **9**
Hotel Newton **1**
Hotel Plaza Athenee New York **14**
The Lucerne **6**
The Mark **19**
The Surrey **17**
Trump International Hotel & Tower **11**

RESTAURANTS ◆
A Voce Columbus Circle **13**
Barney Greengrass, the Sturgeon King **2**
Cascabel Taqueria **19**
Fatty Crab **8**
Flor de Mayo **1**
Good Enough to Eat **4**
Kefi **3**
Noche Mexicana **1**
The Mark Restaurant **18**
Porter House New York **12**
Telepan **10**

ATTRACTIONS ●
American Museum of Natural History **7**
Cathedral of St. John the Divine **1**
Central Park Zoo **13**
Children's Museum of Manhattan **5**
Cooper-Hewitt Museum of Manhattan **22**
The Frick Collection **15**
Metropolitan Museum of Art **20**
Rose Center for Earth and Space **7**
Solomon R. Guggenheim Museum **21**
Whitney Museum of American Art **16**

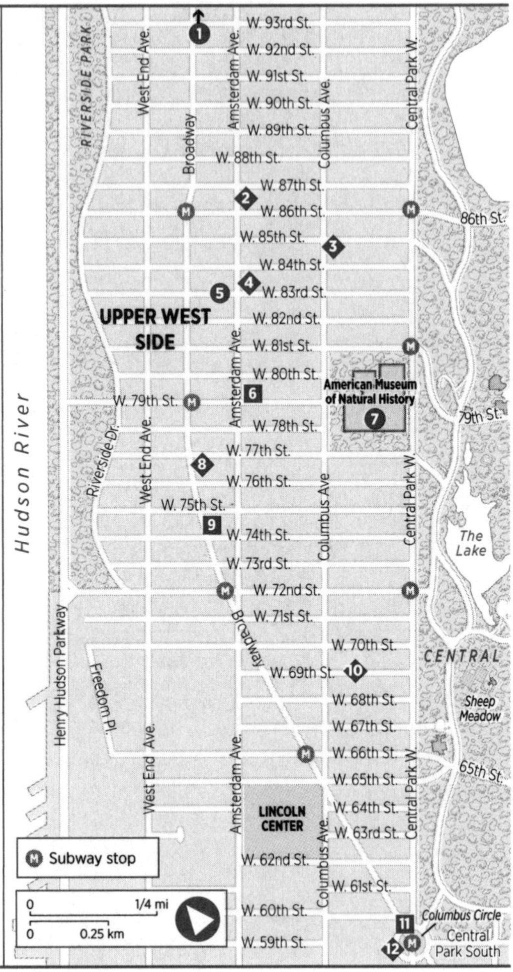

EXPENSIVE/MODERATE

Andaz Wall Street ★★   The first of Hyatt Hotel & Resorts' new Andaz collection to open in New York debuted with a Wall Street address in early 2010. Offering a more personal, less corporate alternative to the Hyatt brand, Andaz delivers with stellar results: personalized check-in; a communal living room–like lobby where wine and coffee are complimentary daily; a state-of-the-art spa and fitness facility; and spacious rooms, many with bathrooms where huge soaking tubs peek into the bedroom. Like its neighborhood, the Andaz is high-tech-y; rooms are economical in their use of space, with a rotating wall that includes a full-size mirror, closet, and minibar. Floor-to-ceiling soundproof windows offer plenty of light, including some with panoramic

5

Where to Stay

NEW YORK CITY

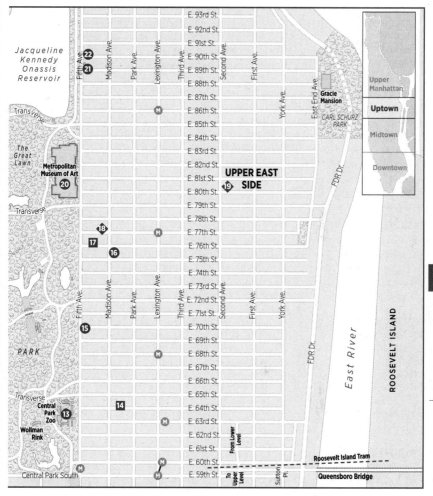

downtown views. The Andaz is a welcome new addition to an area that doesn't offer much boutique lodging.

75 Wall St. (at Water St.), New York, NY 10005. www.andazwallstreet.com. ✆ **212/590-1234.** Fax 212/590-1238. 253 units. From $275 double. AE, DISC, MC, V. Parking from $35. Subway: 2 or 3 to Wall St. **Amenities:** Restaurant; bar; concierge; fitness center and spa; room service. *In room:* A/C, TV, hair dryer, complimentary snacks and nonalcoholic-beverage minibar, Geneva sound system, unlimited local calls, Wi-Fi (free).

TriBeCa
VERY EXPENSIVE

The Greenwich Hotel ★★★ Robert De Niro has already helped establish TriBeCa as a New York destination with his restaurants and film festival. Now he's expanded his TriBeCa empire as a co-owner of this impressive new hotel. Built from the ground up, the Greenwich Hotel, like the Bowery Hotel (p. 83), is a combination of modern-meets-rustic in design. The building was crafted with handmade bricks, reclaimed wood, and furniture from antiques stores and flea markets throughout the world. No guest rooms are alike, whether it is a Tibetan silk rug in one or the Moroccan tile in the bathroom in another. The rooms are airy and quiet; some have Hudson River views. The hotel has a Japanese-inspired spa including a pool surrounded by a 250-year-old Japanese farmhouse assembled without using a single nail. You might find the TriBeCa location a bit too far away from the heart of the city, but maybe in this case, that's just the point.

377 Greenwich St. (btw. N. Moore and Franklin sts.), New York, NY 10013. www.thegreenwichhotel.com. ⓒ **212/941-8900.** Fax 212/941-8600. 88 units. $450–$725 double. AE, DC, DISC, MC, V. Valet parking $55. Subway: 1 to Franklin St. **Amenities:** Restaurant; bar; lobby lounge and outdoor courtyard; concierge; fitness center; pool; room service; spa. *In room:* A/C, TV, hair dryer, complimentary minibar (alcoholic beverages excluded), MP3 docking stations, Wi-Fi (free).

Lower East Side
EXPENSIVE
The Hotel on Rivington ★★ The contrast of a gleaming 21-story, glass-tower luxury hotel in the midst of 19th- and early-20th-century Lower East Side low-rise tenement buildings is striking, but an accurate representation of what the neighborhood has become. From the floor-to-ceiling windows of your room, surrounded by amenities such as flat-panel televisions, Japanese soaking tubs in the bathrooms, and Tempur-Pedic mattresses, not only do you have incredible and unobstructed city views, but you also can look down and spot ancient Lower East Side landmarks such as the Economy Candy store (est. 1937) or the shops of Orchard Street. Along with the aforementioned views, three-quarters of the rooms have private terraces, the option of in-room spa services, and heated, tiled floors in the large bathrooms, where you can enjoy your view of the city as you bathe—which means someone with binoculars might have a view of you as well.

107 Rivington St. (btw. Ludlow and Essex sts.), New York, NY 10002. www.hotelonrivington.com. ⓒ **212/475-2600.** Fax 212/475-5959. 110 units. From $395 double. AE, DC, MC, V. Parking $50. Subway: F to Delancey St. **Amenities:** Restaurant; concierge; fitness center; room service. *In room:* A/C, TV, CD players and iPod speaker system available, fridge, hair dryer.

MODERATE
Duane Street Hotel ★ 🛏 Small, but cozy, the rooms here are designed with IKEA-ish style furnishings, but, as in the loft apartments in the TriBeCa neighborhood where it is located, the walls are hardwood, the ceilings are high, and the windows are large, providing more of a sense of space. Bathrooms are spacious and well outfitted with showers equipped with rain shower heads. Every room has a good-sized desk and a 32-inch plasma HDTV. Best of all is the personable, extremely helpful staff that seems to enjoy doing the little extras to improve your stay. The Duane Street Hotel is a welcome choice in a vibrant neighborhood with limited midprice hotel options.

130 Duane St. (at Church St.), New York, NY 10013. www.duanestreethotel.com. ⓒ **212/964-4600.** Fax 212/964-4800. 45 units. $259–$799 double. AE, DC, DISC, MC, V. Subway: A or C to Chambers St. **Amenities:** Restaurant; concierge, spa services *In room:* A/C, TV, CD player, hair dryer, spa services, Wi-Fi (free).

SoHo
VERY EXPENSIVE

Crosby Street Hotel ★★ The Crosby Street Hotel features individually designed rooms complete with hand-picked art and furniture combined with the newest in high-tech amenities. The rooms all feature floor-to-ceiling warehouse-style windows—some with amazing downtown Manhattan views, especially from the upper floors. Designed with bright colors, including some in pink and violet, and unusual furniture, the spacious rooms are quirky yet cozy. The lavish bathrooms feature heated towel racks and bidets. A courtyard and garden, screening room, and "drawing room" add to the hotel's wonderfulness. And knowing that the hotel is environmentally responsible and aims for a GOLD LEED certification makes indulging in all that extravagance almost guilt free.

79 Crosby St. (btw. Prince and Spring sts.), New York, NY 10012. www.crosbystreethotel.com. ✆ **212/226-6400.** Fax 212/226-0055. 86 units. From $495 double; from $815 suite. AE, DC, DISC, MC, V. Parking $55–$65. Subway: N or R to Prince St. **Amenities:** Restaurant; bar; concierge; fitness center; room service; screening room. *In room:* A/C, TV, minibar, MP3 docking stations, Wi-Fi (free).

The Mercer ★★★ The Mercer is a place where even those who represent the antithesis of hip (and I'm speaking personally) can feel very much at home. Inside the hotel, there is a pronounced calm—from the postmodern library lounge and the relaxed Mizrahi-clad staff to the huge soundproof loftlike guest rooms; the hotel is a perfect complement to the scene outside your big window. The tile-and-marble bathrooms have a steel cart for storage, and an oversize shower stall or oversize two-person tub (state your preference when booking). Just off the lobby is the Kitchen restaurant, one of Jean-Georges Vongerichten's earlier endeavors that is still going strong.

147 Mercer St. (at Prince St.), New York, NY 10012. www.mercerhotel.com. ✆ **888/918-6060** or 212/966-6060. Fax 212/965-3838. 75 units. $495–$695 double; $710–$895 studio; from $1,600 suite. AE, DC, DISC, MC, V. Parking $55 nearby. Subway: N or R to Prince St. **Amenities:** Restaurant; lounge; food and drink service in lobby; book, magazine, video, DVD, and CD libraries; concierge; free access to nearby Equinox fitness center; room service. *In room:* A/C, ceiling fan, TV/DVD, CD player, minibar, MP3 docking stations, Wi-Fi (free).

East Village, Greenwich Village & the Meat-Packing District
EXPENSIVE

The Bowery Hotel ★★ Despite the history associated with its name and location, the Bowery Hotel is about as far from a flophouse as you could imagine. Standing alone in the heart of NoHo, the Bowery Hotel has that burnished, dark-wood look inside, most evident in the expansive lobby with a fireplace, comfy velvet draperies and furniture, vintage paneling, Moroccan tiles, and an adjoining outdoor area complete with plush lounge chairs. The rooms—and no two are the same—are very large and airy by New York standards with high ceilings and ceiling fans, many with huge terraces, and all with spectacular views. What the Gansevoort Hotel did for the Meatpacking District, the Bowery Hotel is doing for the Bowery—making a once-desolate area a hip destination.

335 Bowery (at 3rd St.), New York, NY 10003. www.theboweryhotel.com. ✆ **212/505-9100.** Fax 212/505-9700. 135 units. From $375 double; from $675 suite. AE, DISC, MC, V. Valet parking $45; self-parking $31. Subway: 4, 6 to Bleecker St. **Amenities:** Restaurant; bar; concierge; room service. *In room:* A/C, HDTV/DVD, hair dryer, iPod stereo and MP3 docking system, minibar, Wi-Fi (free).

Gansevoort Meatpacking Hotel ★★ Despite its potentially excessive trendiness, the 14-floor, zinc-colored Gansevoort offers excellent, personable service. Rooms are a good size with comfortable furnishings in soft tones and high-tech amenities such as plasma televisions. Suites have a living room and separate bedroom, and some have small balconies and bay windows. Corner suites offer adjoining guest rooms for families or larger parties. The generous-size bathrooms are done up in ceramic, stainless steel, and marble and are impeccably appointed. In all the guest rooms and throughout the hotel, original art by New York artists is on display. The **G Spa,** a 5,000-square-foot spa and fitness center, and the indoor-outdoor **O Bar** are destinations unto themselves.

18 Ninth Ave. (at 13th St.), New York, NY 10014. www.hotelgansevoort.com. ✆ **877/426-7386** or 212/206-6700. Fax 212/255-5858. 187 units. From $425 double; from $675 suite. AE, DISC, MC, V. Parking $40. Subway: A, C, or E to 14th St. Pet-friendly floors. **Amenities:** Restaurant; 2 bars; 2 lounges; concierge; fitness center; indoor-outdoor rooftop pool; room service; spa; rooftop garden. *In room:* A/C, TV, hair dryer, minibar, Wi-Fi (free).

Chelsea
MODERATE

Inn on 23rd Street ★★★ 🎒 Behind an unassuming entrance in the middle of bustling 23rd Street is one of New York's true lodging treasures: a real urban bed-and-breakfast with as personal a touch as you'll find anywhere. Each guest room has a king- or queen-size bed outfitted with a supremely comfy pillow-top mattress and top-quality linens, satellite TV, a large private bathroom with thick Turkish towels, and a roomy closet. Rooms have themes, like the Rosewood Room, with '60s built-ins; the elegantly Asian Bamboo Room; and Ken's Cabin, a large, lodgelike room with cushy, well-worn leather furnishings and wonderful Americana relics. The Inn has a lovely library where the complimentary breakfast is served, and it also has an honor bar where you can make yourself a drink for less money than you would pay in any other hotel in the city. The only drawback: The Inn is so comfortable you might be tempted to lounge indoors and miss the city sights.

131 W. 23rd St. (btw. Sixth and Seventh aves.), New York, NY 10011. www.innon23rd.com. ✆ **877/387-2323** or 212/463-0330. Fax 212/463-0302. 14 units. $199–$259 double; $359 suite. Extra person $25. Children 11 and under stay free in parent's room. Rates include continental breakfast. AE, DC, DISC, MC, V. Parking $20 nearby. Subway: F or 1 to 23rd St. **Amenities:** Fax and copy service; cozy library w/stereo and VCR. *In room:* A/C, TV, hair dryer, Wi-Fi (free).

Union Square, the Flatiron District & Gramercy Park
VERY EXPENSIVE

The Gansevoort Park Hotel ★★ Tamer than its Meatpacking District older sister, **Gansevoort Meatpacking Hotel** (p. 84), the Gansevoort Park, which opened in 2010, still retains much of big sister's cool glamour feel. There's the indoor-outdoor rooftop bar and plunge pool, an Exhale spa and gym, and transportation to various city locations on a first-come, first-served basis in a chauffeur-driven Panorama Porsche. Rooms average a spacious 475 square feet with suites topping out at an enormous 1,500 square feet, including some with landscaped terraces and many with open midtown views. All the rooms have big desks and glass-tiled bathrooms with deep soaking tubs.

420 Park Ave. S (at 29th St.), New York, NY 10016. www.gansevoortpark.com. ✆ **888/702-9348.** 249 units. From $495 double; from $725 suites. AE, DISC, MC, V. Parking $50. Subway: 6 to 28th St. Pet-friendly. **Amenities:** Restaurant; 2 bars; concierge; gym; plunge pool; room service; Exhale Spa. *In room:* A/C, TV, hair dryer, MP3 docking stations, Wi-Fi (free).

Gramercy Park Hotel ★★★ More than half of the rooms are suites at this 1925-built legend, some with views overlooking Gramercy Park. All rooms are appointed with mahogany English drinking cabinets where the minibar and DVD player are hidden, some variation of the overstuffed lounge chair, and a portrait of Schnabel's friend, the late Andy Warhol. Beds are velvet upholstered, tables feature leather tops, and photos by world-famous photojournalists adorn the walls. Bathrooms are large and feature wood-paneled walls. If you choose to leave your room, the hotel's magnificent **Rose Bar** is where you should venture first, followed by the Danny Meyer–run restaurant, **Maialino.**

2 Lexington Ave. (at 21st St.), New York, NY 10010. www.gramercyparkhotel.com. ☏ **212/920-3300.** Fax 212/673-5890. 185 units. From $595 double; from $700 suite. AE, DC, DISC, MC, V. Parking $55. Subway: 6 to 23rd St. **Amenities:** Restaurant; 2 bars; concierge; fitness center and spa; room service. *In room:* A/C, TV/DVD, CD player, hair dryer, minibar, MP3 docking station, Wi-Fi (free).

INEXPENSIVE

Gershwin Hotel ★ ☺ This Warholesque hotel caters to up-and-coming artistic types—and well-established names with an eye for good value—with its bold modern-art collection and wild style. The standard rooms are clean and bright, with Picasso-style wall murals and Philippe Starck–ish takes on motel furnishings. Superior rooms are best, as they're newly renovated, and well worth the extra $10; all have a queen bed, two twins, or two doubles, plus a newish private bathroom with cute, colorful tile. If you're bringing the brood, two-room suites (or family rooms) are a good option. For the *very* low-budget traveler, the Gershwin also offers hostel-style accommodations (called "Bunkers") from $39 a night in 10-bed or 6-bed rooms. The hotel is more service-oriented than you usually see at this price level, and the staff is professional.

7 E. 27th St. (btw. Fifth and Madison aves.), New York, NY 10016. www.gershwinhotel.com. ☏ **212/545-8000.** Fax 212/684-5546. 150 units. $109–$355 double; $329–$405 Family Room. Extra person $20. Check website for discounts or other value-added packages. AE, MC, V. Parking $25 3 blocks away. Subway: N, R, or 6 to 28th St. **Amenities:** Bar; coffee bar; babysitting. *In room:* A/C, TV, hair dryer, Wi-Fi (free).

Times Square & Midtown West
VERY EXPENSIVE

Ritz-Carlton New York, Central Park ★★★ ☺ There's a lot to like about this hotel—from its location overlooking Central Park to the impeccable, personable service—but what I like best is that this luxury hotel manages to maintain a homey elegance and does not intimidate you with an overabundance of style. Rooms are spacious and decorated in English-country style. Suites are larger than most New York apartments. Rooms facing Central Park come with telescopes, and the marble bathrooms are oversize and feature a choice of bathrobes. For families who can afford the steep prices, the hotel is extremely kid-friendly. Suites have sofa beds, and cribs and rollaway beds can be brought in. Children are given in-room cookies and milk. The adults can be pampered with services at the Switzerland-based **La Prairie Spa** or dine at the hotel's restaurant, **BLT Market.**

50 Central Park South (at Sixth Ave.), New York, NY 10019. www.ritzcarlton.com/centralpark. ☏ **212/308-9100.** Fax 212/207-8831. 259 units. $595–$1,195 double; from $995 suite. Package and weekend rates available. AE, DC, DISC, MC, V. Parking $55. Subway: N or R to Fifth Ave.; F to 57th St. Pets under 60 lb. accepted. **Amenities:** Restaurant; bar; babysitting; lobby lounge for tea and cocktails; Ritz-Carlton Club Lounge; concierge; fitness center; room service; La Prairie spa and facial center; butler and bath butler services. *In room:* A/C, TV/DVD, hair dryer, high-speed Internet, minibar.

EXPENSIVE

Le Parker Meridien ★★ ☺   Consider the many attributes of this hotel: Its location on 57th Street is not too far from Times Square and a short walk from Central Park and Fifth Avenue shopping; there's a 17,000-square-foot fitness center, **Gravity,** featuring basketball and racquetball courts, a spa, and a rooftop pool; three excellent restaurants, including **Norma's,** for breakfast, and the aptly named **Burger Joint** (rated by many as the best burger in the city); and a gorgeous lobby that also serves as a public space off of which **Knave,** the hotel's excellent espresso bar, is located. The spacious rooms, though a bit on the IKEA side, have a fun feel, with hidden drawers and twirling television platforms, making an economical use of space. Many have fantastic Central Park views.

119 W. 56th St. (btw. Sixth and Seventh aves.), New York, NY 10019. www.parkermeridien.com. ✆ **800/543-4300** for reservations, or 212/245-5000. Fax 212/307-1776. 727 units. $300–$600 double; from $750 suite. Extra person $50. Excellent packages and weekend rates often available (as low as $225 at press time). AE, DC, DISC, MC, V. Parking $53. Subway: F, N, Q, or R to 57th St. Pets accepted. **Amenities:** 3 restaurants; espresso/cocktail bar; concierge (2 w/Clefs d'Or distinction); fitness center and spa w/Wii studio; rooftop pool; room service; sun deck. *In room:* A/C, TV w/DVD/CD player, hair dryer, high-speed Internet, minibar.

The Michelangelo ★★ ▮▮   Owned by the Italian-based Starhotel, this is the group's only U.S. property, and it offers a welcome dose of Italian hospitality in the heart of New York. From the moment you enter the spacious lobby, adorned with Italian marble, you feel you've left behind the rapid-fire sight-and-sound assault of nearby Times Square. Off the lobby is a lounge where coffee and cappuccino are served all day, and a complimentary Italian breakfast of pastries and fruit is offered each morning. The recently renovated rooms come in various sizes, all of which are more than adequate by New York standards. Among other things, they feature marble foyers, Italian fabrics, king beds, and two television sets (one in the bathroom). The bathrooms are well maintained and feature deep whirlpool bathtubs.

152 W. 51st St. (btw. Sixth and Seventh aves.), New York, NY 10019. www.michelangelohotel.com. ✆ **800/237-0990** or 212/765-0505. Fax 212/581-7618. 179 units. From $395 double; from $625 suite. Visit website for (sometimes substantial) discounts. Rates include Italian breakfast. AE, DC, DISC, MC, V. Valet parking $40 per day; self-parking (1 block away) $32 per day. Subway: N or R to 49th St. **Amenities:** Restaurant; lounge; concierge; fitness center; room service. *In room:* A/C, TV, fax, hair dryer, high-speed Internet, minibar.

Royalton Hotel ★★   The Royalton toned down its fashion-trendy look and style a few years back and now has an understated elegance and sophistication to it. Once you locate the very unassuming entrance (for a hotel), you enter what is a marvel of a lobby, dark and narrow with check-in counters that appear more like coat-check closets, a sprawling lounge area accentuated by a blazing two-sided glass-enclosed fireplace, a very lively bar just off the front entrance, and a restaurant in the rear. Rooms still retain the hotel's original cool Phillipe Starck minimalist feel with categories ranging from the standard (no tub but decent sized) to deluxe standards with fireplaces and soaking tubs, to alcove suites with long couches and big Jacuzzi tubs, to penthouse suites. Despite the bustle of hotel-heavy 44th Street and the action in the lobby, rooms are, thankfully, quiet.

44 W. 44th St (btw. Fifth and Sixth aves.), New York, NY 10036. www.royaltonhotel.com. ✆ **800/697-1781** or 212/869-4400. Fax 212/869-8965. 169 units. $249–$599 double. AE, DC, DISC, MC, V. Subway: B, D, F, or M to 42nd St.–Bryant Park. **Amenities:** Restaurant; 2 bars; concierge; fitness room; room service. *In room:* A/C, TV, MP3 docking stations, Wi-Fi (free).

Sofitel New York ★★★ 🎁 There are many fine hotels on 44th Street between Fifth and Sixth avenues, but the best, in my estimation, is the soaring Sofitel. Upon entering the hotel and the warm, inviting lobby with check-in tucked off to the side, you wouldn't think you were entering a hotel that is this young, which is one of the reasons the hotel is so special. The designers have successfully melded modern, new-world amenities with European old-world elegance. The rooms are spacious and ultracomfortable, adorned with art from New York and Paris. The lighting is soft and romantic; the walls and windows are soundproofed. Suites are extraspecial, equipped with king beds, two televisions, and pocket doors separating the bedroom from a sitting room. Bathrooms in all rooms are magnificent, with separate showers and soaking tubs.

45 W. 44th St. (btw. Fifth and Sixth aves.), New York, NY 10036. www.sofitel.com. © **212/354-8844.** Fax 212/354-2480. 398 units. $235–$599 double; from $700 suite. 1 child stays free in parent's room. AE, DC, MC, V. Parking $45. Subway: B, D, F, or M to 42nd St. Pets accepted. **Amenities:** Restaurant; bar; concierge; exercise room; room service. *In room:* A/C, TV w/pay movies, CD player, hair dryer, minibar, Wi-Fi (free).

MODERATE

Casablanca Hotel ★★ 🗡 Just off Broadway in the middle of Times Square, the Casablanca Hotel is an oasis in the middle of all that mayhem, where, in **Rick's Café,** the Casablanca's homey lounge, you can sit by a fire, read a paper, check your e-mail, watch television on the big-screen TV, or sip a cappuccino from the serve-yourself machine. Or, if it's balmy, you can lounge on the rooftop deck or second-floor courtyard. The rooms might not be the biggest around, but they are well outfitted with ceiling fans, free bottles of water, and beautifully tiled bathrooms. The Casablanca is an HK Hotels property (the Library, Elysée, and Giraffe), and, as at those hotels, service is top-notch. Because of its location, moderate prices, and size (only 48 rooms), the Casablanca is in high demand, so book early.

147 W. 43rd St. (just east of Broadway), New York, NY 10036. www.casablancahotel.com. © **888/922-7225** or 212/869-1212. Fax 212/391-7585. 48 units. $249–$299 double; from $399 suite. Check website for specials. Rates include continental breakfast, all-day cappuccino, and weekday wine and cheese. AE, DC, MC, V. Parking $25 next door. Subway: N, R, 1, 2, or 3 to 42nd St./Times Sq. **Amenities:** Cyberlounge; concierge; free access to New York Sports Club; room service; video library. *In room:* A/C, ceiling fan, TV/VCR, CD player, hair dryer, minibar.

Ink48 ★ If you don't mind the long walk (and sometimes windy, and cold in the winter, conditions) from the subway, this hotel is an intriguing, more serene alternative than those a few blocks east. Being next to car dealers and behind a Verizon truck depot may not seem very serene, but if your room faces west, with floor-to-ceiling views of the Hudson River and the USS *Intrepid,* or the east, with spectacular city views, you might just discover that serenity. The rooms, featuring standard Kimpton, minimalist furniture, are generously proportioned by New York City standards and now offer basic, high-tech amenities like iHome sound systems and flatscreen televisions with Web TV. Though it prides itself as a "boutique" hotel, the term and the design seem outdated. Still, what Ink48 lacks in in-room and design aesthetics, it more than makes up for in service and in those amazing views.

653 11th Ave. (btw. 47th and 48th sts.), New York, NY 10036. www.ink48.com. © **212/757-0088.** Fax 212/757-2088. 222 units. Rates from $279 double. AE, DC, DISC, MC, V. Parking $55–$75. Subway: C or E to 50th St. Pet-friendly. **Amenities:** Restaurant; bar; concierge; fitness center; room service; spa; wine reception daily. *In room:* A/C, TV, wireless and high-speed Internet, iHome sound systems.

Room Mate Grace Hotel ★ 🎣   From its Midtown location to its many extras, such as a swimming pool in the lobby, steam room and sauna, complimentary continental breakfast, and good-size rooms, including a number with bunk beds, Grace Hotel is one of the better moderate options in the Times Square area. The rooms are sparse in tone, but the queen- and king-size platform beds are plush and dressed with Egyptian cotton sheets. The biggest drawback is the bathrooms: There are no doors on the bathrooms—sliding doors conceal the shower (none of the rooms has a tub) and the toilet.

125 W. 45th St. (btw. Sixth Ave. and Broadway), New York, NY 10036. www.room-matehotels.com. ✆ **212/354-2323.** Fax 212/302-8585. 139 units. $179–$350 double. AE, DC, MC, V. Parking nearby $25. Subway: B, D, F, or M to 47th–50th sts./Rockefeller Center. **Amenities:** Bar; complimentary Spanish-inspired breakfast; gym; pool; sauna; steam room. *In room:* A/C, flatscreen TV, CD/DVD players, hair dryer, iHome docking port, free high-speed Internet, minifridge, blackout drapes, 2-line speakerphones w/free local calls.

INEXPENSIVE

Travel Inn ☺ 🎣   Extras such as a huge outdoor pool and sun deck, a sunny and up-to-date fitness room, and *free* parking (with in and out privileges!) make the Travel Inn a terrific deal. The Travel Inn may not be loaded with personality, but it does offer the clean, bright regularity of a good chain hotel. Rooms are oversized and comfortably furnished, with extrafirm beds and work desks; even the smallest double is sizable and has a roomy bathroom, and double/doubles make great affordable shares for families. A total renovation over the past couple years has made everything feel like new, even the tiled bathrooms. Though it's a bit off the track, Off-Broadway theaters and affordable restaurants are at hand, and it's a 10-minute walk to the Theater District.

515 W. 42nd St. (just west of Tenth Ave.), New York, NY 10036. www.thetravelinnhotel.com. ✆ **888/HOTEL58** (468-3558), 800/869-4630, or 212/695-7171. Fax 212/967-5025. 160 units. $105–$250 double. Extra person $10. Children 15 and under stay free in parent's room. AAA discounts available; check website for specials. AE, DC, DISC, MC, V. Free self-parking. Subway: A, C, or E to 42nd St./Port Authority. **Amenities:** Coffee shop; fitness center; terrific outdoor pool w/deck chairs and lifeguard in season; room service. *In room:* A/C, TV, hair dryer.

Midtown East & Murray Hill
VERY EXPENSIVE

The Pierre ★★★   A property of India-based Taj Hotels, the Pierre, along with the St. Regis and the Plaza, is one of New York's grandest of grand dame hotels. The elegant white-glove service, elevator operators, sprawling hallways, and high-ceilinged, sumptuous rooms remain, but now are meshed with a more contemporary feel. Rooms are apartment-like, many with Central Park views, and now feature amenities like Bose wave studio music systems and 40-inch plasma televisions. The marble-clad bathrooms were redesigned, adding glass-walled showers and, in some rooms, tubs decadently equipped with flat-panel televisions. As part of the renovation, high tea is now served, along with cocktails at **2E,** the new lobby lounge off the hotel's 61st Street entrance. A stay at the Pierre, if you can afford it, is a one-of-a-kind New York experience.

Fifth Ave. (at 61st St.), New York, NY 10021. www.tajhotels.com/pierre. ✆ **800/838-8000.** Fax 212/940-8109. 189 units. From $495 double. AE, DC, DISC, MC, V. Parking $60. Subway: N, R to 59th St./Fifth Ave. **Amenities:** Restaurant; 2 bars; concierge; fitness center and spa; room service. *In room:* A/C, TV, Bose Wave studios systems, fax, Wi-Fi (free).

The Setai ★★★ A combination hotel/condo, the Setai offers some of the largest rooms I've seen along with five-star service, a Michael White–helmed restaurant called **Ai Fiori,** a spa featuring four "lunar" treatments, and a Julien Farel salon offering styling for both women and men. Just a few blocks from the Empire State Building, Bryant Park, and Herald Square just adds to the appeal of the Setai. Most guest rooms are larger than 700 square feet and have deep soaking tubs, televisions inset into the bathroom mirrors, and expansive windows. If you want to splurge, book an apartment suite, which includes a state-of-the-art kitchen that might even tempt you to cook something during your stay. The only problem at the Setai is that all this wonderfulness will make it very hard to venture out.

400 Fifth Ave. (btw. 36th and 37th sts.). www.setaififthavenue.com. ✆ **212/695-4005.** 214 units. From $595 double. AE, DC, DISC, MC, V. Valet parking $80. Subway: B, D, F, M, N, R, Q to 34th St. **Amenities:** Restaurant; bar; fitness center; personal assistants; 24-hour room service; spa; complimentary pressing service upon arrival. *In room:* A/C, TV, kitchens in apt. suites, minibar, MP3 docking stations, Wi-Fi (free), espresso machines, washer/dryer in apt. suites.

EXPENSIVE

Andaz Fifth Avenue ★★ 🏨 In mid-2010 the second Andaz hotel (see Andaz Wall Street, p. 80) opened in New York at what couldn't be a more central location on Fifth Avenue—across from the New York Public Library. But it's not just the location that makes the property desirable. Rooms are all spacious with high ceilings, high tech controls, complimentary snack and beverage bar (excluding alcohol), enormous bathrooms with a foot soaking basin (a first in any New York hotel I've visited), and original art by Uruguayan artist Carlos Capelan. Other perks include New York–centric art in the hallways by students at local New York public schools, a subterranean bar, a restaurant featuring local and organic produce, and virtual concierge services.

485 Fifth Ave. (at 41st St.), New York, NY 10017. www.andaz.com. ✆ **212/601-1234.** Fax 212/601-8888. 194 units. From $465 double. AE, MC, V. Parking $60. Subway: B, D, F, M to 42nd St. **Amenities:** Restaurant; bar; concierge; fitness center; room service. *In room:* A/C, TV, hair dryer, MP3 docking stations, Wi-Fi (free).

Hotel Elysée ★★ This romantic gem in the heart of Midtown might be easy to miss: It's dwarfed by glass towers on either side of it. But that it is so inconspicuous is part of the Elysée's immense appeal. Built in 1926, the hotel has a storied past as the preferred address for artists and writers, including Tennessee Williams, Jimmy Breslin, Maria Callas, and Vladimir Horowitz (who donated a Steinway, which still resides in the Piano Suite). Rooms have many quirky features; some have fireplaces, others have kitchens or solariums, and all are decorated in country-French furnishings. Good-size bathrooms are done up in Italian marble and well outfitted. Off the gorgeous black-and-white marble-floored lobby is the legendary **Monkey Bar.** On the second floor is the Club Room, where a free continental breakfast is offered daily, along with complimentary wine and cheese weekday evenings.

60 E. 54th St. (btw. Park and Madison aves.), New York, NY 10022. www.elyseehotel.com. ✆ **800/535-9733** or 212/753-1066. Fax 212/980-9278. 103 units. From $249 double; from $409 suite. Check website for seasonal specials. Rates include continental breakfast and evening wine-and-cheese reception. AE, DC, DISC, MC, V. Parking $30. Subway: E or M to Fifth Ave. **Amenities:** Restaurant; bar; concierge; free access to nearby gym; room service. *In room:* A/C, TV/VCR, DVD on request, hair dryer, minibar, MP3 docking stations/radio/alarm clock, Wi-Fi (free).

The Library Hotel ★★ 🏨 Located 1 block from the New York Public Library, the Library Hotel has a pleasing, informal feel. Each of the Library Hotel's 10 guest-room floors is dedicated to 1 of the 10 major categories of the Dewey Decimal System.

When I visited the hotel, I was appropriately booked into a "Geography and Travel" room. Guest rooms, which come in three categories—petite (really small), deluxe, and junior suites—feature mahogany built-ins, generous desks, and immaculate marble bathrooms; all are extremely comfortable. The Library's public spaces—a reading room where weekday wine and cheese and a complimentary daily breakfast are served, a writer's den with a fireplace and flatscreen TV, and a rooftop terrace—all help make it a welcome refuge in the heart of the city.

299 Madison Ave. (at 41st St.), New York, NY 10017. www.libraryhotel.com. ☎ **877/793-7323** or 212/983-4500. Fax 212/499-9099. 60 units. $239–$289 double; $329 Love Room or junior suite; $619 2-room family suite. Check the website for packages and weekend rates (as low as $329 at press time). Rates include continental breakfast buffet, all-day snacks, and wine and cheese nightly. AE, DC, V. Parking $30 nearby. Subway: 4, 5, 6, 7, or S to 42nd St./Grand Central. **Amenities:** Restaurant; roof garden lounge; free access to nearby health club; room service; video library of American Film Institute's Top 100 films. *In room:* A/C, TV/VCR, CD player, hair dryer, minibar, MP3 docking station/radio/alarm, Wi-Fi (free).

The New York Palace ★★   In perhaps the most prime of prime locations, in the absolute heart of Midtown, the New York Palace has undergone many transformations in the past decade. Now a member of the prestigious, London-based Dorchester Collection of Hotels, the Palace has been spruced up in appearance and service to match that company's esteemed reputation. Rooms have always been grand, some with amazing views of Rockefeller Center and St. Patrick's, but now they have added a sleeker, more contemporary look along with high-tech amenities such as iPod docking stations and high-definition flatscreen televisions. Still, for a hotel this opulent, better window soundproofing should have been part of the renovations; I could hear, clearly, trucks and construction from my room on the 49th floor.

455 Madison Ave. (at 50th St.), New York, NY 10022. www.newyorkpalace.com. ☎ **800/804-7035** or 212/888-7000. Fax 212/303-6000. 899 units. $349–$1,199 double; from $772 suite. AE, DC, DISC, MC, V. Parking $51. Subway: 6 to 51st St. E or M to 53rd St.–Fifth Ave. **Amenities:** 2 restaurants; bar; concierge; fitness center and spa; room service. *In room:* A/C, TV, hair dryer, MP3 docking station, Wi-Fi (free).

INEXPENSIVE

Hotel Thirty Thirty ★ 🍴   Thirty Thirty is just right for bargain-hunting travelers looking for a splash of style with an affordable price tag. The design-conscious tone is set in the loftlike industrial-modern lobby. Rooms are mostly on the smallish side but do the trick for those who intend to spend their days out on the town rather than holed up here. Configurations are split between twin/twins (great for friends), queens, and queen/queens (great for triples, budget-minded quads, or shares who want more spreading-out room). A few larger units have kitchenettes, great if you're staying for a while, as you'll appreciate the extra room and the fridge. There's no room service, but delivery is available from nearby restaurants.

30 E. 30th St. (btw. Madison and Park aves.), New York, NY 10016. www.thirtythirty-nyc.com. ☎ **800/804-4480** or 212/689-1900. Fax 212/689-0023. 243 units. $139–$349 double; $259–$599 suite. Call for last-minute deals, or check website for special promotions (as low as $101 at press time). AE, DC, DISC, MC, V. Parking $30 1 block away. Subway: 6 to 28th St. Pets accepted with advance approval. **Amenities:** Restaurant; concierge. *In room:* A/C, TV, hair dryer.

Upper East Side

EXPENSIVE

Hotel Plaza Athénée New York ★★★   This hideaway in New York's most elegant neighborhood (the stretch of Madison Ave. in the 60s) is elegant, luxurious, and oozing with sophistication. With antique furniture, hand-painted murals, and the

Italian-marble floor that adorns the lobby, the Plaza Athénée has a European feel. In that tradition, service here is as good as it gets, with personalized check-in and attentive staff at every turn. The rooms come in a variety of shapes and sizes, and are all high ceilinged and spacious; entrance foyers give them a residential feel. Many of the suites have terraces large enough to dine on. The Portuguese-marble bathrooms are outfitted with thick robes made for the hotel. The lush, leather-floored lounge is called **Bar Seine** and is a welcome spot for a predinner cocktail.

37 E. 64th St. (btw. Madison and Park aves.), New York, NY 10021. www.plaza-athenee.com. ☏ **800/447-8800** or 212/734-9100. Fax 212/772-0958. 142 units. $790–$825 double; from $1,620 suite. Check for packages and seasonal specials (as low as $495 at press time). AE, DC, DISC, MC, V. Parking $53. Subway: F to Lexington Ave.–63rd St. **Amenities:** Restaurant; bar; Clefs d'Or concierge; fitness center; room service; spa. In room: A/C, TV, fax, hair dryer, high-speed Internet, minibar.

The Mark ★★★ After a spectacular $150-million top-to-bottom renovation, the Mark Hotel has once again established itself as the height in luxury in the already luxurious stretch of Madison Avenue real estate. Gone is the frumpy, grand dame, replaced by a contemporary, art-centric look along with the prerequisite high tech amenities, a Frederic Fekkai salon, and a restaurant helmed by Master Chef Jean Georges Vongerichten (p. 108). This kind of luxury does not come cheap. But for your money you get space; no rooms are less than 400 square feet and suites start at 700 square feet. Rooms are outfitted with Bang & Olufsen LCD televisions, subzero refrigerators and freezer drawers, marble bathrooms with deep soaking tubs, and maid service twice daily.

Madison Ave. (at 77th St.), New York, NY 10075. www.themarkhotel.com. ☏ **212/744-4300** or 866/744-4300. Fax 212/606-3100. 150 units. $875–$1,025 superior rooms; from $1,590 suites. Check website for specials. AE, DISC, MC, V. Parking $55. Subway: 6 to 77th St. Pet-friendly. **Amenities:** Restaurant; bar; concierge; fitness center; room service. In room: A/C, TV, MP3, Wi-Fi (free), cordless phones, touch-screen room control panel.

EXPENSIVE

The Surrey ★ Set among town houses between Madison and Fifth avenues, the Surrey has always reeked of classic Upper East Side elegance. But after a $60-million "re-creation," when you step inside the Art Deco gray-marble lobby and notice graffiti splattered on a large dresser near the elevators, you understand the "re-creation" was to offer elegance with an edge. Rooms vary in size from cozy to spacious suites that offer private terraces. All are very well equipped though most standard rooms do not have tubs and, unfortunately, the re-creation did not soundproof the walls; I could clearly hear incessant Caribbean patois coming from a next-door maid's room. Still, the hotel offers a beautiful rooftop garden; a new, intimate bar; and room service by the very good **Café Boulud.**

20 E. 76th St. (btw. Fifth and Madison aves.), New York, NY 10021. www.thesurrey.com. ☏ **212/288-3700.** 190 units. AE, DC, DISC, MC, V. $450–$575 salon; from $899 suite. Subway: 6 to 77th St. Pet-friendly. **Amenities:** Restaurant; 2 bars; concierge; fitness center and spa; room service; rooftop garden. In room: A/C, TV, high-speed and wireless Internet, minibar, MP3 docking station.

Upper West Side
VERY EXPENSIVE

Inn New York City ★★★ 🛏 Tucked away in an Upper West Side brownstone is a quaint, almost rustic retreat located, ironically, in the shadow of Donald Trump's mammoth and unrustic Trump Place. Featuring four delicious, self-contained units—each has a full kitchen—Inn New York City offers a very different experience than one you will find at your standard New York City hotel. Here, after a day of touring, you can relax in the huge Jacuzzi in the Spa Suite, or sip coffee on the terrace overlooking the tranquil backyard from the Inn's Opera Suite. If you have a family, the very spacious Library Suite comes equipped with a sofa bed and a pocket door that separates the sleeping areas. Along with all the rustic—the quilts, stained glass, and antique furnishings—you also get modern amenities like plasma televisions. A stay at the romantic Inn New York City is as special as it gets.

266 W. 71st St. (btw. Amsterdam and West End aves.), New York, NY 10023. www.innnewyorkcity.com. ✆ **212/580-1900.** Fax 212/580-4437. 4 units. $475–$645 double. Check website for specials. AC, MC, V Parking $38. Subway: 1, 2, 3 to 72nd St. *In room:* A/C, TV, CD/DVD players, kitchen, Wi-Fi (free), complimentary snacks, wine and cheese on arrival.

Trump International Hotel & Tower ★★★   From the outside, it's a tall, dark monolith, hovering over Columbus Circle and lower Central Park. But go inside and spend a night or two, and experience services such as your own "Trump Attaché," a personal concierge who will provide comprehensive services; take advantage of such first-class facilities as the 6,000-square-foot health club with lap pool and a full-service spa; or order room service from the hotel's signature restaurant, the four-star **Jean-Georges.** Guest rooms are surprisingly understated, with high ceilings and floor-to-ceiling windows, some with incredible views of Central Park and all with telescopes for taking in the view, and marble bathrooms with Jacuzzi tubs. But if that's not enough, you also get two complimentary bottles of Trump water, complete with a picture of the Donald on each one. For a hotel this well run, you can forgive the man for his excesses.

1 Central Park West (at 60th St.), New York, NY 10023. www.trumpintl.com. ✆ **212/299-1000.** Fax 212/299-1150. 176 units. From $765 double; from $1,200 1- or 2-bedroom suite. Children stay free in parent's room. Check website for special rates and package deals; also try booking through www.travelweb.com for discounted rates. AE, DC, DISC, MC, V. Parking $48. Subway: A, B, C, D, or 1 to 59th St./ Columbus Circle. Pets allowed. **Amenities:** Restaurant; babysitting; butler (personal attaché); concierge; health club w/spa and pool; DVD library. *In room:* A/C, TV/VCR w/pay movies and video games, DVD/CD player, fax/copier/printer, hair dryer, high-speed Internet, minibar, MP3 docking stations.

MODERATE

Hotel Beacon ★★ ☺ 🏷   For families, you won't find a better location—or value. Close to Central Park and Riverside Park, the Museum of Natural History and Lincoln Center, and major subway lines, the Beacon's location is ideal. Rooms were recently updated and are generously sized, featuring a kitchenette, a roomy closet, and a marble bathroom. Nearly all standard rooms have two double beds, and they're plenty big enough to sleep a family on a budget. The large one- and two-bedroom suites are some of the best bargains in the city; each has two closets and a pullout sofa in the well-furnished living room. The two-bedroom suites have a second bathroom, enough to house a small army—including my own. There's no room service, but a wealth of good budget dining options that deliver, along with such excellent markets as Fairway, Trader Joe's, and Citarella, make the Beacon even more of a home away from home.

2130 Broadway (at 75th St.), New York, NY 10023. www.beaconhotel.com. ✆ **800/572-4969** or 212/787-1100. Fax 212/724-0839. 265 units. From $205 double; from $250 1-bedroom suite. Extra person $15. Children 12 and under stay free in parent's room. Check website for specials. AE, DC, DISC, MC, V. Parking $55 1 block away. Subway: 1, 2, or 3 to 72nd St. **Amenities:** Coffee shop adjacent; concierge; access to nearby health club; Internet center. *In room:* A/C, TV w/pay movies, hair dryer, fully stocked kitchenette.

The Lucerne ★★ As a longtime resident of the Upper West Side, I can easily say the Lucerne, in a magnificent 1903 landmark building, best captures the feel of this special neighborhood. Service is impeccable, especially for a moderately priced hotel, and everything is fresh and immaculate. The rooms are comfortable and big enough for kings, queens, or two doubles, with attractive bathrooms complete with travertine counters. Some of the rooms have views of the Hudson River. The suites are extra special and include kitchenettes, stocked minifridges, microwaves, and sitting rooms with sofas and extra TVs. The highly rated **Nice Matin** offers room service for breakfast, lunch, and dinner. But if you don't want to dine there, you can sample some of the neighborhood food at nearby Zabar's or H&H Bagels.

201 W. 79th St. (at Amsterdam Ave.), New York, NY 10024. www.thelucernehotel.com. © **800/492-8122** or 212/875-1000. Fax 212/362-7251. 250 units. $200–$440 superior queen; $310–$470 superior double; $330–$490 superior king or deluxe double; $360–$520 deluxe king; $390–$600 1-bedroom suite. Extra person $20. Children 15 and under stay free in parent's room. AAA discounts offered; check website for deals as low as $189 at press time. AE, DC, DISC, MC, V. Parking $29 nearby, valet parking $42. Subway: 1 to 79th St. **Amenities:** Restaurant; fitness center; room service. *In room:* A/C, TV w/ Nintendo, hair dryer, Wi-Fi (free).

INEXPENSIVE

Hotel Newton ★ 🍴 On the northern edge of the Upper West Side, the Newton is one of the best choices in the city in the inexpensive category. As you enter the pretty lobby, you're greeted by a uniformed staff that's attentive and professional. The rooms are generally large, with good, firm beds, a work desk, and a sizable bathroom, plus roomy closets in most (a few of the cheapest have wall racks only). Some are big enough to accommodate families, with two doubles or two queen beds. The suites feature two queen beds in the bedroom, a sofa in the sitting room, plus niceties such as a microwave, a minifridge, and an iron, making them well worth the few extra dollars. The bigger rooms and suites have been upgraded with cherrywood furnishings, but even the older laminated furniture is much nicer than I usually see in this price range.

2528 Broadway (btw. 94th and 95th sts.), New York, NY 10025. www.thehotelnewton.com. © **888/HOTEL58** (468-3558) or 212/678-6500. Fax 212/678-6758. 110 units. $75–$175 double or junior suite. Extra person $25. Children 14 and under stay free in parent's room. AAA, corporate, senior, and group rates available; check website for special Internet deals. AE, DC, DISC, MC, V. Parking $27 nearby. Subway: 1, 2, or 3 to 96th St. **Amenities:** Room service. *In room:* A/C, TV, hair dryer, Wi-Fi ($4.95 per day).

Brooklyn

Nu Hotel ★★ 🏨 A few blocks from downtown Brooklyn and subway lines leading quickly into Manhattan, and across the street from Brooklyn's restaurant row, Smith Street, the Nu Hotel couldn't have found a better location. This eco-friendly hotel uses cork flooring in the guest rooms, organic Baltic linen, and recycled teak-wood furnishings. Rooms, though not enormous, have high ceilings and windows that allow an abundance of light; mine had a view of the iconic Williamsburg Savings Bank. The larger rooms, including the "friends suites," have queens and bunk beds for families, while the "urban suites" feature a sitting area and your own personal hammock, making the Nu Hotel the only hotel in New York City that I know of that has hammocks. A well-equipped gym, complimentary breakfast, and business center add to the hotel's enormous appeal.

85 Smith St. (at Atlantic Ave.), Brooklyn, NY 11201. www.nuhotelbrooklyn.com. © **718/852-8585.** 93 units. $199–$249 double. AE, DC, DISC, MC, V. Parking $25. Subway: F to Bergen/Smith St.; A or C to Hoyt/Schermerhorn. **Amenities:** Lounge; complimentary continental breakfast; concierge; fitness club. *In room:* A/C, TV, jack packs to dock audio, video, and computer electronics, Sangean radio, Sonus Satellite music systems (in some rooms).

WHERE TO EAT

Attention, foodies: Welcome to your mecca. No other culinary capital spans the globe as successfully as the Big Apple. *Tip:* Reservations are always a good idea in New York, and a virtual necessity if your party is bigger than two. For some popular spots, you'll need to call a month in advance—or take a chance with a late-night walk-in.

TriBeCa

EXPENSIVE

Locanda Verde ★★★ ITALIAN   It's just simple sheep's milk ricotta sprinkled with herbs and sea salt and served over crostini. Doesn't sound like much, does it? But that simple starter is the one dish everyone raves (deservedly) about after dining at Locanda Verde, the fun and delicious restaurant in the Greenwich Hotel helmed by Daniel Boulud–trained chef Andrew Carmellini. I think what makes Locanda Verde so good is that Carmellini eschews the fancy and sticks with hearty family dishes like "My Grandmother's Ravioli" rigatoni with lamb ragú, or the other "must-try" dish, the porchetta sandwich, thin-sliced roast pork served on hearty bread with vinegar peppers. It's a scene at Locanda Verde—loud, crowded, always busy—but know that going in and hurry up and order that sheep's milk ricotta, and all that background buzz will soon be just a minor irritation.

377 Greenwich St. (at N. Moore St.). ✆ **212/925-3797.** www.locandaverdenyc.com. Reservations highly recommended. Main courses $17–$28. AE, DISC, MC, V. Mon–Fri 11:30am–3pm; Mon–Sun 5:30–11pm; Sat–Sun 10am–3pm. Subway: 1 to Franklin St.

Thalassa ★★ GREEK   Greek food is best when prepared simply with the freshest ingredients, especially fish, and Thalassa does a remarkable job of that. The variety of seafood is staggering: When I visited, the options included fresh langoustines from Scotland, pound-and-a-half shrimp from Mexico, and a number of oyster selections. For starters, the zucchini and eggplant chips were addictive, while the octopus, simply grilled with a red-wine vinaigrette, was as good as I've had west of Astoria (the Greek neighborhood in Queens). The main courses won't disappoint: Seafood *Thalassina*, a stew of shellfish including those aforementioned Gulf shrimp, was a standout, while the grilled branzino, simply prepared with a touch of olive oil and lemon, was exceptional. The knowledgeable sommelier can help you select a Greek wine from the restaurant's cellar, where a number of unusual and good Greek cheeses are also stored. The restaurant is large; tables are spaced well enough apart for intimacy, and service is attentive and pleasant.

179 Franklin St. (btw. Greenwich and Hudson sts.). ✆ **212/941-7661.** www.thalassanyc.com. Reservations recommended. Prix-fixe lunch $24; main courses dinner $28–$42. AE, DC, DISC, MC, V. Mon–Fri noon–3pm; Mon–Thurs 6–11pm; Fri–Sat 6pm–midnight; Sun 5–10pm. Subway: 1 to Franklin St.

MODERATE

The Odeon ★ AMERICAN BRASSERIE   For more than 2 decades, the Odeon has been a symbol of the TriBeCa sensibility; in fact, the restaurant can claim credit for the neighborhood's cachet—it was the first to lure artists, actors, writers, and models to the area below Canal Street before it was given its moniker. Why did they come? They came to drink, schmooze, and enjoy the hearty no-frills brasserie grub such as the country frisée salad with bacon, Roquefort cheese, and pear vinaigrette and the truffled poached egg, steak frites, and pan-roasted cod. Though the restaurant is not quite the celebrity magnet it was in its heyday of the 1980s, the food, the drink, and the inviting, open, Art Deco–ish rooms have withstood the test of time and have surpassed trendy to claim well-deserved New York establishment status.

145 W. Broadway (at Thomas St.). © **212/233-0507.** www.theodeonrestaurant.com. Reservations recommended. Main courses $13–$35 lunch, $19–$35 dinner (most less than $21); fixed-price lunch $27. AE, DC, DISC, MC, V. Mon–Fri noon–11pm; Sat 10am–midnight; Sun 10am–11pm. Subway: 1, 2, or 3 to Chambers St.

Chinatown

INEXPENSIVE

Big Wong King ★ CANTONESE   For more than 30 years, Big Wong has been an institution for workers from the nearby courthouses and Chinese families who come to feast on *congee* (rice porridge) and fried crullers for breakfast. They also come for the superb roasted meats, the pork and duck seen hanging in the window, the comforting noodle soups, and the terrific barbecued ribs. This is simple, down-home Cantonese food—lo mein, chow fun, bok choy in oyster sauce—cooked lovingly, and so cheap. If you don't mind sharing a table and brusque service at best, Big Wong is a must at any time of day.

67 Mott St. (btw. Canal and Bayard sts.). © **212/964-0540.** Appetizers $1.50–$5; *congee* $1.50–$6; soups $3–$5; Cantonese noodles $5.25–$11. No credit cards. Daily 8:30am–9pm. Subway: N, Q, R, 6 to Canal St.

New York Noodletown ★★ CHINESE/SEAFOOD   So what if the restaurant has all the ambience of a school cafeteria? I'm wary of an overadorned dining room in Chinatown; the simpler the better, I say. And New York Noodletown is simple, but the food is the real thing. Seafood-based noodle soups are spectacular, as is the platter of chopped roast pork. Those two items alone would make me very happy. But I'm greedy and wouldn't leave the restaurant without one of its perfectly prepared shrimp dishes, especially the salt-baked shrimp. If you're lucky and your hotel has a good-size refrigerator, take the leftovers home—they'll make a great snack the next day. New York Noodletown keeps very long hours, which makes it one of the best late-night bets in the neighborhood, too.

28½ Bowery (at Bayard St.). © **212/349-0923.** Reservations accepted. Main courses $4–$15. No credit cards. Daily 9am–3:30am. Subway: N, Q, R, 6 to Canal St.

Pho Viet Huong ★ 🍴 VIETNAMESE   Chinatown has its own enclave of Viet-namese restaurants, and the best is Pho Viet Huong. The menu is vast and needs intense perusing, but your waiter will help you pare it down. The Vietnamese know soup, and *pho,* a beef-based soup served with many ingredients, is the most famous, but the hot-and-sour *canh* soup, with either shrimp or fish, is the real deal. The small version is more than enough for two to share, while the large is more than enough for a family. The odd pairing of barbecued beef wrapped in grape leaves is another of the restaurant's specialties and should not be missed, while the *bun,* various meats and vegetables served over rice vermicelli, are simple, hearty, and inexpensive. You'll even find Vietnamese sandwiches here: French bread filled with ham, chicken, eggs, lamb, and even pâté. All of the above are best washed down with an icy cold Saigon beer.

73 Mulberry St. (btw. Bayard and Canal sts.). © **212/233-8988.** Appetizers $3–$8.50; soups $6–$7; main courses $10–$25. AE, MC, V. Daily 10:30am–10:30pm. Subway: N, Q, R, 6 to Canal St.

SoHo & Nolita
EXPENSIVE
Osteria Morini ★★ ITALIAN   From the prolific chef, Michael White (**Marea, Ai Fiori**) comes his take on the cuisine of Emilia-Romagna in northern Italy. That translates to much hearty fare, including lots of pork. Examples include a hockey puck–sized disk of spit-roasted *porchetta,* meat protected by a generous layer of fat on the outside while seasoned with sage and rosemary, and an enormous grilled pork chop resting on a bed of polenta and flavored with balsamic vinegar and sweet cipollini onions. Try the heavenly *cappelletti,* little raviolis filled with truffled mascarpone and prosciutto, or the *tagliatelle* with a ragú, and you'll be very challenged to find room for one of Pastry Chef Heather Bertinetti's dessert creations. Rustic with lots of terra-cotta tiles and rough wood, the restaurant is riotously loud, so don't expect conversation.

218 Lafayette St. (btw. Spring and Broome sts.). © **212/965-8777.** www.osteriamorini.com. Reservations recommended. Main courses $17–$29. Mon–Fri 11:30am–3:30pm; Sat–Sun 11:30am–4pm; Tues–Sat 5pm–1am; Sun–Mon 5pm–midnight. Subway: 6 to Spring St.

MODERATE
Ed's Lobster Bar ★★ AMERICAN/SEAFOOD   You may be a long way in distance (and price) from a roadside shack in Maine when dining at Ed's Lobster Bar, but take a seat at the white marble counter and bite into Ed's signature lobster roll (prepared cold with mayonnaise), and you might think that it's the rocky Atlantic coast outside the window rather than bustling Lafayette Street. After you've tried the over-stuffed lobster roll, if you still have room, try the oysters, raw or delicately fried. Or the fried Ipswich clams, or the steamers, or the chowder. Thankfully unpretentious, Ed's is straight-ahead New England seafood served in a casual, laid-back dining room and whitewashed bar. They even have paper bibs, homemade pickles, and Belfast Bay Lobster Ale on tap. What more could you want in a seafood "shack" in New York City?

222 Lafayette St. (btw. Spring and Kenmare sts.). © **212/343-3236.** www.lobsterbarnyc.com. Main courses $15–$30 (lobster and oysters at market price). Tues–Thurs noon–3pm and 5–11pm; Fri noon–3pm and 5pm–midnight; Sat noon–4pm and 5pm–midnight; Sun noon–9pm. Subway: 6 to Spring St.

INEXPENSIVE
Also consider **Lombardi's Pizza,** 32 Spring St., between Mott and Mulberry streets.

Bread ★ ITALIAN/LIGHT FARE   **Bread** does bread like no other sandwich shop. The bread comes from Balthazar Bakery down the street, but it's what they do with it that makes it so special. They might take a rustic ciabatta loaf, slather it with Sicilian sardines, Thai mayonnaise, tomato, and lettuce, and then turn it over to their panini press. The result is a gooey convergence of flavors that you will attempt to gobble gracefully. It *will* fall apart, but that's okay; someone will be along shortly with more napkins. The 32-seat restaurant is in chic Nolita, and you may even see a model wrapping herself around one of their sandwiches.

20 Spring St. (btw. Mott and Elizabeth sts.). © **212/334-1015.** Reservations not accepted. Breads $7–$9.50; plates $6–$16. AE, DC, DISC, MC, V. Sun–Thurs 10:30am–midnight; Fri–Sat 10:30am–1am. Subway: 6 to Spring St.

The Lower East Side, East Village & NoHo
EXPENSIVE
Double Crown ★ ASIAN/BRITISH   In the now-trendy Bowery, Double Crown's eclectic AvroKo-designed front and back dining areas add to the neighborhood's

appeal. The menu is inventive, and the streaky ham (house cured and delicious) starter with fenugreek-glazed figs to offset the addictive saltiness was excellent. Of the entrees, the steamed snapper in a sesame broth with prawn dumplings was simple perfection, while the British-influenced venison Wellington was probably better than what the former colonists ever experienced. The dining room in the front of the restaurant can get very loud. If you prefer a bit less commotion, try for a table in the back.

316 Bowery (at Bleecker St.). ℂ **212/254-0350.** www.doublecrown-nyc.com. Reservations recommended. Main courses $17–$30. AE, DISC, MC, V. Sun–Wed 6–11pm; Thurs–Sat 6pm–midnight; Sat–Sun 11am–3:30pm. Subway: 6 to Bleecker St.

Hearth ★★ 📖 ITALIAN   If you're in the East Village, you will be doing yourself a great service if you decide to spend some of that time at aptly named Hearth. The restaurant is as welcoming as its name, and the food and drinks, even more so. If you are in the mood for humble Italian food, Hearth's three-course *cucina povera* with its robust *ribollita*, a soup of cabbage, beans, Parmesan, and far-from-humble braised lamb shank, will definitely satisfy that mood. But if you want haughty instead of humble, try the chef's rabbit ballotine or snapper crudo. Along with an excellent wine selection, Hearth features an impressive wine and tequila list. Service is knowledgeable and seating is comfortable, confirming the restaurant's public philosophy that "ALL the needs of the guest have been met and exceeded."

403 E. 12th St. (at 1st Ave.). ℂ **646/602-1300.** www.restauranthearth.com. Reservations recommended. *Cucina povera* $35; seasonal tasting menu $70; main courses $25–$29. AE, MC, V. Sun–Thurs 6–10pm; Fri–Sat 6–11pm. Subway: L at 14th St.

MODERATE

'inoteca ★★ 📖 ITALIAN   The Lower East Side was once the home to many Kosher wine factories, but you'll find only Italian wines at cozy 'inoteca. The list is more than 250 bottles long, but even better are the exquisitely prepared small plates that complement the wines. Though the Italian-language menu is a challenge, servers are helpful. The panini stand out in their freshness and their delicacy, with the *coppa* (a spicy cured ham) with hot peppers and *rucola* (arugula) being the standout. The *tramezzini*, a crustless sandwich, is nothing like the crustless sandwiches served at high tea. Here, you can have yours stuffed with tuna and chickpeas or with *pollo alla diavola*, spicy shredded pieces of dark-meat chicken. The "Fritto" section includes a mozzarella *in corroza*, breaded mozzarella stuffed with a juicy anchovy sauce and lightly fried. 'inoteca is a place to go slow, to savor both wine and food.

98 Rivington St. (at Ludlow St.). ℂ **212/614-0473.** www.inotecanyc.com. Reservations accepted for parties of 6 or more. Panini $8–$17; *piatti* (small plates) $8–$11. AE, MC, V. Daily noon–3am; brunch Sat–Sun 10am–4pm. Subway: F, J, M, or Z to Delancey St. Also at 323 Third Ave. (at 24th St.). ℂ **212/614-0473.** Subway: 6 to 23rd St.

Momofuku Noodle Bar ★ ASIAN   Practically unclassifiable, Momofuku might be put in the Asian noodle category. But you will also find such items as fried veal sweetbreads, spicy honeycomb tripe, grilled beef tongue, country ham and hash browns, and grits and shrimp. Despite the seemingly contradictory menu, the Southern-style Asian noodle combo works. Still, unless you have a craving for offal, come to Momofuku for the noodles, the ramen in particular. And in the Momofuku Ramen, a big bowl brimming with rich broth, noodles, shredded smoky pulled pork, and a poached egg, you actually can get a taste of the South and Asia in one bowl. Service is brisk, but try to get to Momofuku early or for lunch, before the few communal tables fill up and lines begin to form.

171 First Ave. (btw. 10th and 11th sts.). ☏ **212/777-7773.** www.momofuko.com. Reservations not accepted. Main courses $10–$17. AE, DISC, MC, V. Daily noon–4pm; Sun–Thurs 5:30–11pm; Fri-Sat 5:30pm–midnight. Subway: L to Third Ave.

INEXPENSIVE

One of the most famous delis in the world is **Katz's Delicatessen** at 205 E. Houston St., at Ludlow Street (☏ **212/254-2246**).

Clinton St. Baking Company ★ 🎁 AMERICAN   Though they are open all day, breakfast and desserts are the best offerings here. The blueberry pancakes with maple butter and the buttermilk-biscuit egg sandwich are worth braving the morning lines, while the desserts, all homemade and topped with a scoop or two of ice cream from the Brooklyn Ice Cream Factory, are good any time of day.

4 Clinton St. (at Houston St.). ☏ **646/602-6263.** www.clintonstreetbaking.com. Main courses $8–$14. No credit cards. Mon–Fri 8am–11pm (closed 4–6pm); Sat 10am–11pm; Sun 10am–4pm. Subway: F or M to Second Ave.

Greenwich Village & the Meat-Packing District

EXPENSIVE

En Japanese Brasserie ★★★ JAPANESE   At En, they bill themselves as a "modern *izakaya*," a kind of Japanese pub where diners share small plates along with beer, sake, or *shochu* (a vodkalike drink made from various ingredients like barley, sweet potato, and buckwheat). And as a fan of pubs in general, I can truly appreciate this one, where I can sample numerous sakes along with amazing dishes: warm, freshly scooped tofu (at En, they make their own tofu at hour-and-a-half intervals each evening); Japanese mountain vegetables in spicy soy sauce; black cod marinated in miso; and grilled, thinly sliced Kobe-style short ribs grilled on a hot stone. Ordering can be overwhelming, so there are *kaiseki* menus where a selection of dishes are put together by the chef and accompanied with sake and *shochu*.

435 Hudson St. (at Leroy St.). ☏ **212/647-9196.** www.enjb.com. Reservations recommended. Main courses $15–$35; *kaiseki* $65–$85 per person. AE, DC, MC, V. Mon–Thurs noon–2:30pm and 5:30–11:30pm; Fri-Sat noon–2:30pm and 5:30pm–midnight; Sun 5:30–11pm. Subway: 1 to Christopher St.

Mas ★★ FRENCH   This "farmhouse" is in the West Village, and though there are nods to the rustic in the decor, there is also an atmosphere of sophistication. A glass-enclosed wine cellar is visible from the small dining room, the restaurant stays open late, and you'll find hipsters as well as folks in power suits. The dishes are innovative and the ingredients are fresh, many supplied by upstate New York farms. The tender, perfectly prepared braised pork belly is served with polenta and a stew of escargot and lima beans; the duck breast melds magically with apple purée, sautéed Brussels sprouts, and chestnuts. Service is low-key but attentive; and the seating, though somewhat cramped, is not enough to dim the romantic aura.

39 Downing St. (btw. Bedford and Varick sts.). ☏ **212/255-1790.** www.masfarmhouse.com. Reservations recommended. 4-course tasting menu $68; 6-course $95; main courses $32–$36. AE, DC, DISC, MC, V. Mon–Sat 6pm–4am (small-plate tasting menu after 11:30pm). Subway: 1 to Houston St.

MODERATE

L'Artusi ★★ ITALIAN   Offering a staggering range of small plates from *"crudo"* (raw) to *"carne"* (meat), L'Artusi has something for everyone, most of it very good. Seating is a bit cramped at the long, narrow restaurant that features an open kitchen and dining at the bar and at the "crudo" bar, and L'Artusi is noisy and busy. The menu changes frequently, but if you are lucky, the chicory with lemon anchovy dressing will be available, along with the combination pork belly with cockles under the "carne" section. Do not neglect the "small plate" of coconut semifreddo for dessert, which is an absolute revelation. The restaurant features a 2,500-bottle walk-in wine cellar and the servers go out of their way to find the right pairings for your selections.

228 W. 10th St. (btw. Bleecker and Hudson sts.). ℂ **212/555-5757.** www.lartusi.com. Reservations recommended. Main courses $10–$24. AE, DISC, MC, V. Sun–Thurs 5:30–11pm; Fri–Sat 5:30pm–midnight. Subway: 1 to Christopher St.

INEXPENSIVE

The original **John's Pizzeria** (there are now four of them) is at 278 Bleecker St., near Seventh Avenue (ℂ **212/243-1680**); it's the most old-world romantic of the group and my favorite.

Chelsea & the Meat-Packing District

EXPENSIVE

Buddakan ★ ASIAN   My expectations of Buddakan were of a loud dance club scene in a large space where the food would be showy, but flavorless. I was right about the loud scene, but wrong about the food. The "Brasserie" is the main dining room on the lower level, and the steps can seem steep after a few cocktails, such as the signature *Heat*, a combination of tequila, Cointreau, and chilled cucumbers, in the upstairs lounge. To fortify yourself, don't hesitate to order some of Buddakan's superb appetizers, such as the edamame dumplings, the crab and corn fritters, and, most notably, the crispy calamari salad. You could make a meal out of appetizers—the extensive menu at Buddakan works best for large parties and has the now obligatory "communal" table. But if you order one entree, make sure it's the sizzling short rib, tender and removed from the bone and sitting on top of a bed of mushroom chow fun.

75 Ninth Ave. (at 16th St.). ℂ **212/989-6699.** www.buddakannyc.com. Dim sum–appetizers $9–$13; main courses $17–$35. AE, DC, MC, V. Sun–Wed 5:30pm–midnight; Thurs–Sat 5:30pm–1am. Subway: A, C, or E to 14th St.

Morimoto ★★ JAPANESE   The Morimoto experience is like a theme park for foodies. You've seen him on television, but here, in this 12,000-square-foot bi-level space in Chelsea, you can sample Iron Chef Masaharu Morimoto's creations. The problem, however, is how to decide among all the treasures. The tuna pizza, spicy with jalapeño peppers and with anchovy aioli is a good start, while the "duck, duck, duck" entree—a foie gras croissant, roast duck, and a soft duck egg in a red miso sauce—is out of the "Iron Chef" playbook. If it's all too overwhelming, leave it to the chef and order the "Morimoto Omakase" tasting menu. Whatever path you choose, accompany your meal with one of the many sake options and don't skip dessert; the soft chocolate ganache with black-and-white sesame ice cream is memorable.

88 Tenth Ave. (btw. 15th and 16th sts.). ℂ **212/989-8883.** www.morimotonyc.com. Reservations recommended. Main courses $14–$48; Omakase tasting menu $120 per person. AE, DISC, MC, V. Mon–Fri noon–2:30pm; Sat–Sun 5pm–midnight. Subway: A, C, E, or L to 14th St.

MODERATE

RUB ★★ BARBECUE   RUB is short for Righteous Urban Barbecue—a contradiction in terms if ever there was one. The New York arrival of RUB, co-owned by Kansas City pit master Paul Kirk, who has won seven World Barbecue Championships and is a member of the Barbecue Hall of Fame, was eagerly anticipated by those barbecue fanatics who are aware there is a Barbecue Hall of Fame. The smoked turkey and barbecued chicken were the best I've had, moist inside with a distinctive smoked flavor, and the ribs, St. Louis style, were delicate and crispy, yet tender and meaty. The "burnt ends," the fatty part of the brisket, however, were a bit tough. The restaurant is cramped and loud and the prices are urban (meaning high); but the food at RUB will provide all the comfort you need.

208 W. 23rd St. (btw. Seventh and Eighth aves.). ✆ **212/524-4300.** www.rubbbq.net. Sandwiches $9–$12; platters $15–$23; Taste of the Baron $46. AE, MC, V. Tues–Thurs noon–11pm; Fri–Sat noon–midnight. Subway: 1 to 23rd St.

Union Square, the Flatiron District & Gramercy Park

EXPENSIVE

Aldea ★★ 🎁 AMERICAN/PORTUGUESE   At the very pleasant, low-key Aldea, I'm glad to report, chef George Mendes keeps it simple, letting the fresh, first-rate ingredients shine without too much accompaniment. Though he is Portuguese American, only traces of Portuguese cooking can be found in his appetizers and *petiscos* (small bites), where bits of *bacalao* (salt cod) are added to a simple farm egg, or the addition of *pimenton* (Portuguese hot pepper) is included in the preparation of shrimp *alhinho*. The main dishes—original creations like the *arroz de pato,* duck confit, chorizo, duck cracklings and olive, and the monkfish in a stew of fennel, potato, leeks, and mussels over black rice—would be unusual, but very welcome, on any menu east (or west) of the Azores.

31 W. 17th St. (btw. Fifth and Sixth aves.). ✆ **212/675-7223.** www.aldearestaurant.com. Reservations recommended. Main courses $24–$29; chef's tasting menu $85. AE, DC, DISC, MC, V. Mon–Fri 11:30am–2pm; Mon–Thurs 5:30–11pm; Fri–Sat 5:30pm–midnight. Subway: 4, 5, 6, L, N, Q, R to 14th St.–Union Sq.

BLT Fish ★★ SEAFOOD   The seafood branch of the **BLT** (Bistro Laurent Tourondel, BLT Steak, BLT Prime, BLT Market) empire is actually two restaurants with two kitchens. The downstairs is a moderately priced faux-seafood shack with a raw bar, fried fare, and the much-in-demand lobster roll. Upstairs (you can walk the steps or take a glass elevator) is the elegant (higher-priced) dining room. Here you can sit under a skylight or near the open kitchen and watch an army of servers move from the kitchen with huge platters, where whole fish sit, dressed up beautifully, ready for consumption. Check out the crispy red snapper, Cantonese style, that is filleted tableside. Another is the sea-salt-crusted New Zealand pink snapper, which you'll have to crack to get to the tender, juicy flesh underneath.

21 W. 17th St. (btw. Fifth and Sixth aves.). ✆ **212/691-8888.** www.bltfish.com. Reservations recommended. Main courses $25–$35. BLT Fish Mon–Thurs 5:30–11pm; Fri–Sat 5:30–11:30pm. BLT Fish Shack Mon–Fri 11:45am–2:30pm; Mon–Thurs 5:30–11pm; Fri–Sat 5:30–11:30pm; Sun 5–10pm. Subway: 4, 5, 6, L, N, Q, R to 14th St./Union Sq.

Dévi ★★ INDIAN   Few of the many Indian restaurants in the city are like this one. Dévi offers $45 to $85 tasting menus (vegetarian and nonvegetarian), and that's really the way to go. The menu features small courses that will let you sample much of what the restaurant has to offer. Some of the highlights include tender tandoori chicken stuffed with spicy herbs, halibut coated in a cilantro rub accompanied with mint coconut chutney and lemon rice, *zimikand koftas,* delicate yam koftas in a creamy tomato-onion sauce, and the addictive, crispy okra, the Indian equivalent of french fries. With the tasting menus, you get a choice of desserts; I recommend the fabulous *falooda,* an Indian sundae that's a refreshing combination of noodles with honey-soaked basil seeds, mango, and strawberry sorbet in lemon grass–infused coconut milk.

8 E. 18th St. (btw. Fifth Ave. and Broadway). ✆ **212/691-1300.** www.devinyc.com. Reservations recommended. AE, DISC, MC, V. Main courses $15–$30; tasting menus $45–$85. Mon–Sat noon–2:30pm and 5:30–11pm; Sun 5–10pm. Subway: N, Q, R, 4, 5, or 6 to 14th St.–Union Sq.

Millesime ★★ FRENCH/SEAFOOD   On the lush mezzanine lobby of the Carlton Hotel, this intimate and romantic spot serves very good, very fresh seafood. The raw bar is the best place to start, especially the oysters, both east coast and west coast selections. Of the hors d'oeuvres, Millesime's take on the Caesar salad—featuring grilled romaine, smoked black cod with Parmesan cheese, and lime—is a revelation. The fish is prepared simply, either grilled or on a wood plank. My choice was grilled cod and then I had to make another decision: which of the five sauces would best accompany my fish. I went with the sauce vierge, made of olives, tomato, and basil, and it was the perfect complement to the flaky fish. The wine list is extensive and impressive and service is casual, not snooty.

92 Madison Ave. (at 29th St.). ✆ **212/889-7100.** www.millesimerestaurant.com. Reservations recommended. AE, DC, DISC, MC, V. Main courses $15–$24. Daily 11:30am–2pm; Tues–Sat 5:30–11pm; Sun–Mon 5:30–10pm. Subway: 6 to 28th St.

MODERATE

La Pizza Fresca Ristorante ★★ 🍴 PIZZA/ITALIAN   When comparing the top pizzerias in New York, you rarely hear La Pizza Fresca Ristorante mentioned. And that's a mistake. Those who have sampled the genuine Neapolitan pizza (one of only two New York pizzerias certified for authenticity by the Italian organization, *Associazione Vera Pizza Napoletana*) swear by its quality. To achieve certification, they must use a wood-burning oven, San Marzano tomatoes, bufala mozzarella, and hand-pressed dough, and all the ingredients must be cooked with the pizza in the oven. The result is a pizza as good (almost) as you might find in Naples and as good as just about any other in New York. Also impressive is La Pizza Fresca's 800-plus wine list. The restaurant is comfortable and cozy, with low lighting, exposed brick, and the constant glow from the pizza oven.

31 E. 20th St. (btw. Park Ave. and Broadway). ✆ **212/598-0141.** www.lapizzafresca.com. Reservations not accepted. Pizza $9–$19; main courses $12–$28. AE, DC, DISC, MC, V. Mon–Sat noon–3:30pm; Mon–Sat 5:30–11pm; Sun 5–11pm. Subway: 6 to 23rd St.

INEXPENSIVE

For healthy burgers, try either outlet of the **New York Burger Co.,** 303 Park Ave. S., between 23rd and 24th streets (✆ **212/254-2727**), and 678 Sixth Ave., between 21st and 22nd streets (✆ **212/229-1404**). For a burger with boutique-quality meat, try **Brgr,** 287 Seventh Ave., at 26th St. (✆ **212/488-7500**).

Times Square & Midtown West
EXPENSIVE

Frankie & Johnnie's ★★ STEAKHOUSE   When restaurants open other branches, red flags go up. Does that mean the restaurant has become a chain and thus quality has eroded to chain-food status? In the case of Frankie & Johnnie's, the legendary Theater District former–speak-easy–turned–steakhouse, those fears are quickly allayed after one bite of their signature sirloin. It also helps that the dining room on the second floor of the town house is gorgeous, with stained-glass ceiling panels, dark-wood walls, and a working fireplace. Not only are Frankie & Johnnie's steaks underrated in the competitive world of New York steakhouses, but the other options are superb as well. The crab-cake appetizer had an overwhelmingly high crab-to-cake ratio—and that's a good thing in my book—while the side of hash browns was the best I've had. Service is steakhouse old-school, and if you are staying in Midtown, the restaurant provides complimentary stretch-limo service to and from the restaurant.

32 W. 37th St. (btw. Fifth and Sixth aves.). © **212/947-8940.** www.frankieandjohnnies.com. Reservations recommended. Main courses $25–$36. Mon–Fri noon–2:30pm; Mon–Thurs 4–10:30pm; Fri–Sat 4–11pm. Subway: B, C, D, M, N, Q, R, or W to 34th St./Herald Sq. Also at 269 W. 45th St. (at Eighth Ave.). © **212/997-9494.** Subway: 1, 2, 3, 7, A, C, E, N, Q, R, S to 42nd St.

Keens Steakhouse ★★★ STEAKHOUSE   Keens not only serves the basics of a steakhouse—the porterhouse for two, aged prime T-bone steak, and filet mignon with the requisite sides such as creamed spinach and hash browns—but also serves chops: lamb chops, prime rib, short ribs, and, most notably, mutton chops. It is the mutton chop that has made Keens the original that it is. The monstrous cut has two flaps of long, thick, rich, subtly gamy meat on either side of the bone, which looks kind of like mutton-chop sideburns. Keens is no gussied-up remake: It's the real thing, from the thousands of ceramic pipes on the ceiling (regular diners were given their own personal pipes, including celebrities like Babe Ruth, George M. Cohan, and Albert Einstein) to the series of rooms on two floors with wood paneling, leather banquettes, fireplaces (in some), a bar with a three-page menu of single malts, and even the framed playbill Lincoln was reading at the Ford Theater that infamous evening in 1865.

72 W. 36th St. (at Sixth Ave.). © **212/947-3636.** www.keens.com. Reservations recommended. Main courses $26–$45. AE, DC, DISC, MC, V. Mon–Fri 11:45am–10:30pm; Sat 5–10:30pm; Sun 5–9pm. Subway: B, D, F, N, Q, R, or M to 34th St./Herald Sq.

Molyvos ★★ GREEK   This restaurant's success is based on its ability to please those who want traditional Greek food as well as exciting, original Greek-accented creations. For those who like their Greek unadulterated, you won't go wrong with cold *mezedes,* such as the *tzatziki, melitzanosalata,* and *taramosalata,* and hot *mezedes* such as spinach pie or grilled octopus. For Greek food with an edge, there is ouzo-cured salmon on a chickpea fritter or the seafood Cretan bread salad. Just a sampling of the *mezedes* alone should be enough for anyone, but with entrees as good as grilled *garides,* wild head-on prawns barbecued souvlaki-style, and the *chios* pork and *gigante* bean stew, not ordering one would be a mistake. The knowledgeable sommelier will pair your choices with a Greek wine, of which there are many. Or skip the wine and sample one or two of the dozens of ouzos; but don't skip the desserts.

871 Seventh Ave. (btw. 55th and 56th sts.). © **212/582-7500.** www.molyvos.com. Reservations recommended. Main courses $17–$29 at lunch (most less than $20), $20–$36 at dinner (most less than $25); fixed-price lunch $24; pre-theater 3-course dinner $36 (5:30–6:45pm). AE, DC, DISC, MC, V. Mon–Thurs noon–11:30pm; Fri–Sat noon–midnight; Sun noon–11pm. Subway: N or R to 57th St.; B, D, or E to Seventh Ave.

Oceana ★★★ SEAFOOD   In 2009, Oceana moved from its longtime yachtlike home on the east side to a luxury liner of a space in the McGraw-Hill building across the street from Rockefeller Center. I'm happy to report that the new Oceana is as good as or better than its previous incarnation. At Oceana, as its name implies, it all starts with extremely fresh seafood. Start with the restaurant's very good raw bar, composed of a variety of oysters, clams, crab, and mussels. The marinated appetizers—ceviches, crudos, and smoked fish—are delicately flavorful and a few of them would make a fine meal in themselves. But if you have the stamina (and the deep pockets) to continue, the whole branzino, roasted and stuffed with mushrooms, spinach, and olives, will reward you for your grit. Service for such a large restaurant is exceptional and the sommelier and his crew are especially attentive to proper pairings with your selections.

1221 Sixth Ave. (btw. 48th and 49th sts.). © **212/759-5941.** www.livanosrestaurantgroup.com. Reservations recommended. Main courses $28–$34. AE, DC, DISC, MC, V. Mon–Sun 11:30am–3pm; Mon–Sat 5–11pm; Sun 4–10pm. Subway: B, D, F, M to 47th–50th sts./Rockefeller Center.

MODERATE

Virgil's Real BBQ ★★ ☺ BARBECUE/SOUTHERN Located in the heart of the theme-restaurant wasteland known as Times Square is a theme restaurant that actually has good food. The restaurant, sprawling with dining on two levels, is made to look and feel like a Southern roadhouse with good-ol'-boy decorations on the walls and blues on the soundtrack. The spice-rubbed ribs are slow-cooked and meaty, but it's the Owensboro Lamb (smoked slices of lamb) and the Texas beef brisket that are the standouts. Both are melt-in-your-mouth tender; the lamb is sprinkled with a flavorful mustard sauce, while the brisket is perfect with a few dabs of Virgil's homemade spicy barbecue sauce. Virgil's is a great place to bring the kids; they can make as much noise as they want and no one will notice.

152 W. 44th St. (btw. Sixth and Seventh aves.). © **212/921-9494.** www.virgilsbbq.com. Reservations recommended. Sandwiches $10–$13; main courses and barbecue platters $15–$24 (most less than $19). AE, DC, DISC, MC, V. Sun–Mon 11:30am–11pm; Tues–Sat 11:30am–midnight. Subway: 1, 2, 3, 7, N, R to 42nd St./Times Sq.

INEXPENSIVE

If you're looking for the quintessential New York Jewish deli, you have a choice between the **Stage Deli,** 834 Seventh Ave., between 53rd and 54th streets (© 212/245-7850), known for its jaw-distending celebrity sandwiches, and the **Carnegie Deli,** 854 Seventh Ave., at 55th Street (© 800/334-5606), for the best pastrami, corned beef, and cheesecake in town.

There is a very nice outlet of **John's Pizzeria** in Times Square, 260 W. 44th St., between Seventh and Eighth avenues (© 212/391-7560).

Nizza ★★ 🍴 FRENCH/ITALIAN You won't do much better for pre- or post-theater dining than Nizza. It's a restaurant where you can fill up on appetizers and salads, starting with the tangy tapenade of black olives served with freshly baked focaccia chips and *socca,* a chickpea pancake cooked in a brick oven and sprinkled with fresh herbs. Or savor a glass of wine with a plate of *salumi,* a selection of cured meats such as *coppa, mortadella,* prosciutto, and a variety of salamis. Entrees include the delicate *polpette* (meatballs), served on a bed of polenta and garnished with a hot green pepper, and wild boar lasagna that is much less ferocious than it sounds. The restaurant is loud and seating is tight, but you'll love the memorable food and the easy-on-your-wallet prices.

630 Ninth Ave. (at 45th St.). © **212/956-1800.** Main courses $8–$12. AE, MC, V. Tues–Sat 11:30am–2am; Sun–Mon 11:30am–midnight. Subway: A, C, E, or 7 to 42nd St.

Sapporo ★ 🍴 JAPANESE NOODLES Peruse the community bulletin board as you enter Sapporo and you might find a deal on an apartment—that is, if you can read Japanese characters. Thankfully, the menu is in English at this longtime Theater District noodle shop. If the mostly Japanese clientele doesn't convince you of Sapporo's authenticity, the constant din of satisfied diners slurping at huge bowls of steaming ramen (noodle soup with meat and vegetables) surely will. And though the ramen is Sapporo's well-deserved specialty, the *gyoza* (Japanese dumplings) and the *donburi* (pork or chicken over rice with soy-flavored sauce) are also terrific. Best of all, nothing on the menu is over $10 and that's not easy to accomplish in the oft-overpriced Theater District.

152 W. 49th St. (btw. Sixth and Seventh aves.). ☏ **212/869-8972.** Reservations not accepted. Main courses $6–$9. No credit cards. Mon–Sat 11am–11pm; Sun 11am–10pm. Subway: N, R to 49th St.

Wondee Siam ★ 🍴 THAI   Hell's Kitchen offers countless ethnic culinary variations and one of the most prevalent is Thai—there are at least six in a 5-block radius. My favorite among these is the tiny, zero-ambience Wondee Siam. I don't need colorful decorations or a big fish tank to enjoy authentic, uncompromisingly spicy Thai food, and that's what I get at Wondee Siam. Here you don't have to worry that your waiter will assume you want a milder form of Thai. If there is a little red asterisk next to your item, you can be sure it is appropriately spicy. The soups are terrific, especially the sinus-clearing Tom Yum. In fact, there is a whole section of Yum (chiles) dishes on the menu, my favorite being the Larb Gai, minced ground chicken with ground toasted rice. The curries are also first-rate, as are the noodles, including the mild pad Thai. This is strictly BYOB and you'll want to do so to complement the spicy food. If you want a bit more comfort, try Wondee Siam II, 1 block up. But make sure you ask your waiter not to dumb down the spices, but serve up the food authentic Thai style.

792 Ninth Ave. (btw. 52nd and 53rd sts.). ☏ **212/459-9057.** Reservations not accepted. Main courses $8.50–$18 (most under $10). No credit cards. Daily 11am–11pm. Subway: C, E to 50th St. Also, Wondee Siam II, 813 Ninth Ave. (btw. 53rd and 54th sts.). ☏ **917/286-1726.** Same hours.

5 Midtown East & Murray Hill
EXPENSIVE

Aquavit ★★★ SCANDINAVIAN   The restaurant, in the bottom of a glass tower on East 55th Street, is designed in sleek Scandinavian style with modernist furniture. In the front of the restaurant is an informal and less-expensive cafe, while past a long bar is the dining room. The smoked fish—all the fish—is prepared perfectly. I daydream about the herring plate: four types of herring accompanied by a tiny glass of aquavit, distilled liquor not unlike vodka flavored with fruit and spices, and a frosty Carlsberg beer. The hot smoked Arctic char on the main a la carte menu, served with clams and bean purée in a mustard green broth, is also a winner. Most fixed-price menus offer a well-chosen beverage accompaniment option.

65 E. 55th St. (btw. Park and Madison aves.). ☏ **212/307-7311.** www.aquavit.org. Reservations recommended. Cafe main courses $9–$32; 3-course fixed-price meal $24 at lunch, $35 at dinner; main dining room fixed-price meal $45 at lunch, $85 at dinner ($39 for vegetarians); 3-course pre-theater dinner (5:30–6:15pm) $55; tasting menus $58 at lunch, $105 at dinner ($90 for vegetarians); supplement for paired wines $30 at lunch, $80 at dinner. AE, DC, MC, V. Mon–Fri noon–2:30pm; Sun–Thurs 5:30–10:30pm; Fri–Sat 5:15–10:45pm. Subway: E or F to Fifth Ave.

BLT Steak ★★★ STEAKHOUSE   Steakhouses are often stereotyped as bastions of male bonding, testosterone-fueled with red meat and hearty drinks. But BLT (Bistro Laurent Tourondel) Steak breaks that mold; on the night I visited, I noticed more women—slinky and model-like—chomping on thick cuts of beef than men. That doesn't mean men can't also enjoy the beef here; it's served in cast-iron pots and finished in steak butter with a choice of sauces—béarnaise, red wine, horseradish, and blue cheese, to name a few. The signature is the porterhouse for two (a whopping $79), but I recommend the New York strip or the short ribs braised in red wine. Both can be shared, which may be a good idea, especially after devouring the complimentary popovers and sampling an appetizer such as the tuna tartare or a side of onion rings, potato gratin, or creamy spinach.

106 E. 57th St. (btw. Park and Lexington aves.). ℂ **212/752-7470.** www.bltsteak.com. Reservations highly recommended. Main courses $29-$45. AE, DC, MC, V. Mon–Fri 11:45am–2:30pm; Mon–Thurs 5:30–11pm; Fri–Sat 5:30–11:30pm. Subway: 4, 5, 6, N, or R to 59th St.

Pampano ★★ MEXICAN/SEAFOOD   I'm usually wary of overly presented and overpriced Mexican food, much preferring the stuff I can buy from the taco trucks in east Harlem. Pampano, however, does things with Mexican ingredients, especially seafood, that no taco truck has ever done—and the lovely, lush town house location is much more comfortable. The fish is the highlight of the menu. Start with the tasting of either three or four ceviches; they are all spectacular, especially the halibut bathed in lemon juice, cilantro, chilies, and mango. For a rare and special treat, try a lobster taco—you won't find that at your local *taqueria.* Of the entrees, it would be difficult to order anything but the fantastic *camarones pompano,* shrimp in a pepper-tomato sauce resting on an Anaheim chili stuffed with goat cheese. Save room for chocolate flan and maybe a cleansing shot of one of the restaurant's many excellent tequilas.

209 E. 49th St. (at Third Ave.). ℂ **212/751-4545.** www.modernmexican.com. Reservations recommended. Main courses $23-$30. AE, DC, MC, V. Mon–Fri 11:30am–2:30pm; Mon–Wed 5–10pm; Thurs–Sat 5–11pm; Sun 5–9:30pm. Subway: E or M to Lexington Ave./53rd St.; 6 to 51st St.

MODERATE

Chola ★★ 🏫 INDIAN   The food of Chola, which includes a number of hard-to-find dishes from the India's southern regions, is as good as you will find anywhere in Manhattan. The menu is extensive and features many vegetarian and vegan options. Of the starters, the *kurkuri bhindi* (crispy okra and red onions flavored by a lime and *chaat* marsala) is not to be missed, while the cochin lamb chops, rubbed with southern spices and served with onions and garlic, is so good that it might tempt a vegetarian to cross over to the dark side. Long, crispy *dosas* (thin crepes stuffed with spiced potatoes and peas) are also available, and, according to the menu, a favorite of Martha Stewart's. After a few bites, I concurred with Martha. Probably the best way to experience Chola and to sample a wide variety of its dishes is to visit to take advantage of the popular weekend "maharaja" buffet—just don't expect to eat again for a long time.

225 E. 58th St. (btw. Second and Third aves.). ℂ **212/688-4619.** www.fineindiandining.com. Main courses $14-$23; lunch buffet $14. AE, DC, DISC, MC, V. Mon–Fri noon–3pm; Sat–Sun 11am–3pm; daily 5–11pm. Subway: 4, 5, 6, N, or R to 59th St.

Upper West Side
VERY EXPENSIVE

Porter House New York ★★ STEAKHOUSE   The space, located in the Time Warner Center on Columbus Circle, features floor-to-ceiling windows overlooking Central Park. But even if there were no view, this steakhouse would satisfy the essentials of the best red meat emporiums, with a few inventive twists. I gambled by ordering the chili-rubbed rib-eye—would chili obscure the natural flavor of the meat? My gamble paid off; the chili was subtle and actually brought out the cut's essence. If you want your steak straight ahead, the dry-aged prime strip steak, cooked to perfection and bursting with flavor, won't let you down. Sides are unconventional for a steakhouse, such as pieces of thick smoky bacon added to the creamed spinach, and porcini mushrooms on a bed of polenta offered as an alternative to mashed potatoes.

10 Columbus Circle (4th Floor) in the Time Warner Center (at 60th St.). ℂ **212/823-9500.** www.porterhousenewyork.com. Main courses $24-$39. AE, DC, DISC, MC, V. Mon–Sat noon–4pm; Sun noon–3pm; Mon–Thurs 5–10:30pm; Fri–Sat 5–11pm. Subway: A, B, C, D, 1 to 59th St./Columbus Circle.

EXPENSIVE

A Voce Columbus Circle ★★★ ITALIAN   The original A Voce off Madison Park has always been popular, but this one, in the Time Warner Center, with picture windows overlooking Columbus Circle and Central Park, is even better. The room is big, sparkling, and convivial, with to-die-for views. The menu changes periodically, each new menu focusing on a different Italian region; when I visited, the emphasis was on Sicily and the south. The house-cured baccala with pine nuts and raisins was the perfect mix of salt and sweet and a wonderful first course. A pasta course is a must; I still dream about the cavatelli with Brussels sprouts, almonds, and whipped sheep's-milk ricotta. With Sicily in mind, I sampled the *pesce spada*, or swordfish, with fennel, olives, and a chickpea fritter that was cooked to moist perfection. A Voce makes its own gelato, sorbet, and granite (Italian ice), and one or all are irresistible as an accompaniment to any of the restaurant's amazing desserts.

10 Columbus Circle, 3rd Floor. **✆ 212/823-2523.** www.avocerestaurant.com. Reservations recommended. Pastas $19–$25; main courses $22–$38. AE, DC, DISC, MC, V. Mon–Fri 11:30am–3pm; Sun–Wed 5–10pm; Thurs–Sat 5–11:30pm; Sat–Sun 11am–3pm. Subway: A, B, C, D, 1 to 59th St./Columbus Circle.

Telepan ★★ AMERICAN   The venue for Telepan is an Upper West Side town house with a dining room painted in soothing lime green. The cool design complements the menu, which changes seasonally, but always features farm-fresh products. I had the good fortune to dine in the spring and was greeted with fresh ramps, fiddleheads, and young peas in many of the dishes I sampled. Of the appetizers, the standout was the wild green frittata that did indeed come with in-season ramps. Telepan offers Mid Courses, and, of them, the pea pancakes with pea agnolotti looked and, more important, tasted greenmarket fresh. Save room for an entrée, specifically the haddock with a sweet lobster sauce. Whatever you choose to eat, you'll have no problem finding a complimentary wine from the restaurant's long and impressive list. Telepan has become a pre–Lincoln Center favorite, so if you want to avoid the crush, make a reservation for after curtain.

72 W. 69th St. (at Columbus Ave.). **✆ 212/580-4300.** www.telepan-ny.com. Reservations recommended. Main courses $29–$36; 4-course tasting menu $55; 5-course tasting menu $65. AE, DC, MC, V. Lunch Wed–Fri 11:30am–2:30pm; dinner Mon–Thurs 5–11pm, Fri–Sat 5–11:30pm, Sun 5–10:30pm; brunch Sat–Sun 11am–2:30pm. Subway: B or C to 72nd St.

MODERATE

Fatty Crab MALAYSIAN   The loud, busy, somewhat rushed ambience complements the chef's pull-no-punches spicy Malaysian cuisine. If you don't want to venture to Chinatown or Queens for family-run, inexpensive, and authentic Malaysian, Fatty Crab is a pricier but worthy alternative, with a few innovations like the funky Fatty Dog, a pork sausage seasoned with chilies and shrimp paste and served in a potato hot dog bun. The restaurant's signature dish, chili Dungeness crab, is lip-searing good, but a project that requires intricate surgery to remove the delicate crabmeat, not to mention numerous napkins and additional wet wipes. If you don't want to bother, the noodle and rice dishes are exceptional, especially the Lo Si Fun, rice noodles with Chinese sausage and shiitake mushrooms. All the dishes are for sharing and you can make a substantial meal out of the snacks alone.

2170 Broadway (btw. 76th and 77th sts.). **✆ 212/496-CRAB** (2722). www.fattycrab.com. Reservations recommended. Main courses $7–$22. AE, DISC, MC, V. Daily 5pm–midnight; brunch Sat–Sun 11am–4pm. Subway: 1, 2, or 3 to 72nd St. Also at 643 Hudson St. (btw. Gansevoort and Horatio sts.). **✆ 212/352-3590.** Mon–Wed noon–midnight; Thurs–Fri noon–2am; Sat–Sun 11am–midnight. Subway: A, C, E, or L to 14th St.

Kefi ★★★ 🍴 GREEK   Kefi is like your Greek mother's (if you had a Greek mother) kitchen, and, in fact, the restaurant was inspired by chef Michael Psilakis's mother and her traditional recipes. Greek standards such as moussaka, spinach pie, Greek salad, and grilled fish are featured. But oh, what Psilakis does with the standards! The *mezes* (Greek appetizers) are good enough to make up a meal; it's hard to resist the selection of spreads accompanied by pita, the warm feta, tomatoes, capers, and anchovies. But something's gotta give if you want to save room for such entrees as the flat noodles with braised rabbit; the grilled whole branzino with potatoes, olives, tomatoes, and feta; or the slow cooked, comforting lamb shank on a bed of orzo. If it is humanly possible after indulging in all of the above, don't miss out on the desserts, most notably the walnut cake with maple walnut ice cream.

505 Columbus Ave. (at 84th St.). ℂ 212/873-0200. www.kefirestaurant.com. Reservations recommended. Main courses $10–$20. AE, DISC, MC, V. Tues-Fri noon–2:30pm; Sun-Thurs 5–10pm; Fri-Sat 5–11:30pm; Sat-Sun noon–4pm. Subway: B or C to 86th St.

INEXPENSIVE

For breakfast or lunch, also consider **Barney Greengrass, the Sturgeon King,** 541 Amsterdam Ave., between 86th and 87th streets (ℂ **212/724-4707**), one of the best Jewish delis in town.

Flor de Mayo 🍴 CUBAN/CHINESE   Cuban/Chinese cuisine is a New York phenomenon that started in the late 1950s when Cubans of Chinese heritage immigrated to New York after the revolution. Most of the immigrants took up residence on the Upper West Side, and Cuban/Chinese restaurants flourished. Many have disappeared, but the best one, Flor de Mayo, still remains and is so popular that a new branch opened farther south on Amsterdam Avenue. The kitchen excels at both sides of the massive menu, but the best dish is the *la brasa* half-chicken lunch special— beautifully spiced and slow-roasted until it's fork tender and falling off the bone, served with a giant pile of fried rice, bounteous with roast pork, shrimp, and veggies. Offered Monday through Saturday until 4:30pm, the entire meal is just $6.95, and it's enough to fortify you for the day.

2651 Broadway (btw. 100th and 101st sts.). ℂ 212/663-5520 or 212/595-2525. Reservations not accepted. Main courses $4.50–$19 (most under $10); lunch specials $5–$7 (Mon-Sat to 4:30pm). AE, MC, V ($15 minimum). Daily noon–midnight. Subway: 1 to 103rd St. Also at 484 Amsterdam Ave. (btw. 83rd and 84th sts.). ℂ 212/787-3388. Subway: 1 to 86th St.

Good Enough to Eat ★ ☺ 🍴 AMERICAN HOME COOKING   For over 25 years, the crowds have been lining up on weekends outside Good Enough to Eat to experience chef/owner Carrie Levin's incredible breakfasts. As a result, lunch and dinner have been somewhat overlooked. Too bad, because these meals can be just as great as the breakfasts. The restaurant's cow motif and farmhouse knickknacks imply hearty, home-cooked food, and that's what's done best here. Stick with the classics: meatloaf with gravy and mashed potatoes; turkey with cranberry relish, gravy, and cornbread stuffing; macaroni and cheese; and the BBQ sandwich, roast chicken with barbecue sauce, and homemade potato chips. And save room for the homemade desserts; I can never resist the coconut cake. There are only 20 tables, so expect a wait on weekends during the day or for dinner after 6pm.

483 Amsterdam Ave. (btw. 83rd and 84th sts.). ℂ 212/496-0163. www.goodenoughtoeat.com. Breakfast $5.25–$12; lunch $8.50–$15; dinner $8.50–$23 (most under $18). AE, MC, V. Breakfast Mon-Fri 8am–4pm, Sat-Sun 9am–4pm; lunch Mon noon–4pm, Tues-Fri 11:30am–4pm; dinner Mon-Thurs 5:30–10:30pm, Fri-Sat 5:30–11pm, Sun 5:30–10pm. Subway: 1 to 86th St.

Noche Mexicana ★ 🍴 MEXICAN   This tiny restaurant serves some of the best tamales in New York. Wrapped in cornhusks, as a good tamale should be, they come in two varieties: in a red mole sauce with shredded chicken or in a green tomatillo sauce with shredded pork. There are three tamales in each order, which costs only $6 making it a cheap and almost perfect lunch. The burritos are authentic and meals unto themselves. The *tinga* burrito, shredded chicken in a tomato-and-onion chipotle sauce, is my favorite. Each is stuffed with rice, beans, and guacamole. Don't get fancy here; stick with the tamales, burritos, and soft tacos, the best being the taco *al pastor,* a taco stuffed with pork marinated with pineapple and onions.

852 Amsterdam Ave. (btw. 101st and 102nd sts.). © **212/662-6900** or 662-7400. Burritos $6.50–$8.50; tacos $2; tamales $6; Mexican dishes $9.50–$11. AE, DISC, MC, V. Sun–Thurs 10am–11pm; Fri–Sat 10am–midnight. Subway: 1 to 103rd St.

Upper East Side

EXPENSIVE

The Mark Restaurant ★★★ CONTINENTAL   Everything comes together, as it usually does for chef/restaurateur Jean Georges Vongerichten, at his newest New York City venture in the Mark Hotel. Opened in 2010, The Mark Restaurant offers perfection on every level. The long, flowing dining room is airy, with ample comfortable seating including many tables in a recessed glass solarium. Service is low key, not overly formal, but always attentive, while the food, of course, is hard to beat. A simple Caesar salad becomes a memorable taste with just the right combination of lemon, cheese, and aioli in the dressing. A pasta offering of fettuccine with Parmesan, black pepper, and lemon relies on the freshness of the ingredients to get it right. Best of all, the Mark Restaurant, despite its elegant Madison Avenue location, serves a far-from-stuffy selection of pizzas, burgers (albeit with black-truffle dressing and brie), fried calamari, and simply cooked meats and fish.

25 E. 77th St. (at Madison Ave., in the Mark Hotel). © **212/606-3030.** www.themarkrestaurantnyc.com. Reservations highly recommended. Main courses $21–$48. AE, MC, V. Mon–Fri 11:30am–2:30pm; Sat–Sun 11:30am–3pm; Mon–Sun 5:30–11pm. Subway: 6 to 77th St.

INEXPENSIVE

Cascabel Taqueria ★ 🍴 MEXICAN   A real-deal taqueria in the heart of the Upper East Side's Frat row? Now who would've ever believed that? But it's true. Cascabel serves up some of the tastiest tacos south of Spanish Harlem. Sure, you need to fight through the throngs of aforementioned frat brothers and their sorority sisters to get in, but it's worth the raucous scene to sample Cascabel's take on the crab cake with *piquillo* pepper aioli or the zesty guacamole, made very spicy if so desired. The *pescado* taco, a soft corn tortilla stuffed with crispy tuna belly with hearts of palm, is a wondrous mess while the *carnitas,* slow roasted Berkshire pork butt, pickled red onion, and roasted chile *de arbol,* are an absolute must. The beer and cocktail list is extensive, the televisions are plentiful, and the tables are cramped, but you won't go wrong with the grub.

1538 Second Ave. (at 80th St.). © **212/717-8226.** www.nyctacos.com. Reservations recommended. AE, MC, V. Starters $5–$8; tacos $9. Sun–Thurs 11:30am–midnight. Fri–Sat 11:30am–1am. Subway: 6 to 77th St.

Harlem

EXPENSIVE

Red Rooster ★★ AMERICAN/SOUTHERN   The buzz surrounding the opening of one of Harlem's most anticipated restaurants became deafening until, in early

THE SOUL OF HARLEM

There is much soul in Manhattan, but Harlem seems to possess the mother lode when it comes to food, though recently many old favorites have become victims of the recession. Here is one man's primer to what is left of Harlem's soul food:

Amy Ruth's 113 W. 116th St., between Lenox and Seventh avenues (✆ **212/280-8779;** www.amyruthsharlem.com). Claiming to be authentic soul, Amy Ruth's has become a mecca for Harlem celebs, with the kitschy gimmick of naming platters after some of them, such as the Rev. Al Sharpton (chicken and waffles) and the Rev. Calvin O. Butts III (chicken wings and waffles). Most of the celebrities gained their fame in Harlem, as did the chicken and waffles, or fried whiting and waffles, or steak and waffles. You can't go wrong with anything here as long as waffles are included.

Charles' Pan Fried Chicken ★

2839–2841 Frederick Douglass Blvd., between 151st and 152nd streets (✆ **212/281-1800**). One of the saddest days of 2008 was when I learned Charles's Southern Style Kitchen had closed. It was the best soul food restaurant in Harlem, mainly because of chef/owner Charles Gabriel's pan-fried chicken. Imagine my happiness when the news arrived that Gabriel was reopening in late 2009 under

a new name but with the same perfect fried chicken. It's out of the way, but worth the visit.

Miss Mamie's Spoonbread Too

366 W. 110th St., between Columbus and Manhattan avenues (✆ **212/865-6744;** www.spoonbreadinc.com). Entering this strawberry-curtained charmer is like stepping into South Carolina. But you are in Harlem, or at least the southern fringe of Harlem, and you won't be paying South Carolina soul prices, or Harlem soul prices either. Still, despite the cost, Miss Mamie's is the real deal, especially the barbecued ribs, falling off the bone in a sweet peppery sauce, and the smothered chicken, fried and then covered with thick pan gravy.

Sylvia's

328 Lenox Ave., between 126th and 127th streets (✆ **212/996-0660;** www.sylviassoulfood.com). Sylvia is the self-proclaimed queen of not only Harlem soul food but all soul food. In reality, Sylvia is queen of self-promotion. Sylvia's now has become a franchise, with canned food products, beauty and hair products, and fragrances and colognes. With all that attention to merchandising, the food at her original Harlem restaurant has suffered and now has regressed into a tourist trap. If you plan to go, however, make it on Sunday for the gospel brunch, which is an absolute joy.

2011, famed chef Marcus Samuelsson (Aquavit, p. 104) quieted it when the restaurant, after numerous delays, finally opened. Now the sounds you hear are the ooohs and ahhhs over the refined down-home comfort food presented by Chef Samuelsson. Exploring the diversity of Harlem in the menu with nods to Latino, African, West Indian, and, most prominently, the South, Red Rooster is the most exciting and dynamic restaurant to open north of 110th Street. The boisterous, large dining room is highlighted by an open kitchen where, even over the din, you can hear chefs barking out their orders to the waiters. On my first visit, I stuck mostly to the south, sampling the succulent and spicy fried yard bird, with white mace gravy on a bed of collard greens along with the rich, heartily satisfying oxtails braised in stout and served with plantains. The bar scene is lively and Red Rooster also features live music in its downstairs lounge. Best of all, for this type of quality and scene, the prices are more Harlem-friendly than what you would find for the comparable experience downtown.

310 Lenox Ave. (btw. 125th and 126th sts.). © **212/792-9001.** www.redroosterharlem.com. Reservations recommended. AE, MC, V. Main courses $14–$32. Daily 11:30am–3pm and; 5:30–10:30pm. Subway: 2, 3 to 125th St.

INEXPENSIVE

Also consider **Patsy's Pizzeria,** 2287 First Ave. (btw. 117th and 118th sts.; © **212/ 534-9783**), my favorite pizzeria (and the late Frank Sinatra's, too).

EXPLORING NEW YORK CITY

A word of advice for newcomers: Don't try to tame New York—you can't. Decide on a few must-see attractions, and then let the city take you on its own ride.

The Top Attractions

American Museum of Natural History ★★★   Founded in 1869, this 4-block museum houses the world's greatest natural science collection in a group of buildings made of towers and turrets, pink granite and red brick—a mishmash of architectural styles, but overflowing with neo-Gothic charm. The diversity of the holdings is astounding: some 36 million specimens ranging from microscopic organisms to the world's largest cut gem, the Brazilian Princess Topaz (21,005 carats). If you don't have a lot of time, you can see the best of the best on free **highlights tours** offered daily at 15 minutes after every hour from 10:15am to 3:15pm. **Audio Expeditions,** high-tech audio tours that allow you to access narration in the order you choose, are available to help you make sense of it all.

The museum excels at **special exhibitions,** so check to see what will be on while you're in town in case advance planning is required. The magical **Butterfly Conservatory ★**, a walk-in enclosure housing nearly 500 free-flying tropical butterflies, has developed into a can't-miss fixture from October to May; check to see if it's open while you're in town.

The four-story-tall planetarium sphere in the **Rose Center for Earth and Space ★** hosts the excellent "Cosmic Collisions," possibly the most technologically advanced show on the planet.

Central Park West (btw. 77th and 81st sts.). © **212/769-5100** for information, or 769-5200 for tickets (tickets can also be ordered online for an additional $4 charge). www.amnh.org. Suggested admission $16 adults, $12 seniors and students, $9 children 2–12; Space Show admission $24 adults, $18 seniors and students, $14 children 2–12. Additional charges for IMAX movies and some special exhibitions. Daily 10am–5:45pm; Rose Center also 1st Fri of every month until 8:45pm. Subway: B, C to 81st St.; 1 to 79th St.

Brooklyn Bridge ★★ 📷   Its Gothic-inspired stone pylons and intricate steel-cable webs have moved poets like Walt Whitman and Hart Crane to sing the praises of this great span, the first to cross the East River and connect Manhattan to Brooklyn. Completed in 1883, the beautiful Brooklyn Bridge is now the city's best-known symbol of the age of growth that seized the city during the late 19th century.

Walking the Bridge: Walking the Brooklyn Bridge is one of my all-time favorite New York activities. A wide wood-plank pedestrian walkway is elevated above the traffic, making it a relatively peaceful, and popular, walk. It's a great vantage point from which to contemplate the New York skyline and the East River.

There's a sidewalk entrance on Park Row, just across from City Hall Park (take the 4, 5, or 6 train to Brooklyn Bridge/City Hall). But why take this walk *away* from Manhattan, toward the far-less-impressive Brooklyn skyline? Instead, for Manhattan skyline views, take an A or C train to High Street, one stop into Brooklyn. From there, you'll be on the bridge in no time: Come aboveground, then walk through the little park to Cadman Plaza East and head downslope (left) to the stairwell that will take you up to the footpath. (Following Prospect Place under the bridge, turning right onto Cadman Plaza E., will also take you directly to the stairwell.) It's a 20- to 40-minute stroll over the bridge to Manhattan, depending on your pace, the amount of foot traffic, and the number of stops you make to behold the spectacular views (there are benches along the way). The footpath will deposit you right at City Hall Park.

Subway: A, C to High St.; 4, 5, 6 to Brooklyn Bridge–City Hall.

Ellis Island ★★   One of New York's most moving sights, the restored Ellis Island opened in 1990, slightly north of Liberty Island. Roughly 40% of Americans (myself included) can trace their heritage back to an ancestor who came through here. For the 62 years when it was America's main entry point for immigrants (1892–1954), Ellis Island processed some 12 million people. The statistics can be overwhelming, but the **Immigration Museum** skillfully relates the story of Ellis Island and immigration in America by placing the emphasis on personal experience.

It's difficult to leave the museum unmoved. Today, you enter the Main Building's baggage room, just as the immigrants did, and then climb the stairs to the **Registry Room,** with its dramatic vaulted tiled ceiling, where millions waited anxiously for medical and legal processing. A step-by-step account of the immigrants' voyage is detailed in the exhibit, with haunting photos and touching oral histories. What might be the most poignant exhibit is **"Treasures from Home,"** 1,000 objects and photos donated by descendants of immigrants, including family heirlooms, religious articles, and rare clothing and jewelry. Outside, the **American Immigrant Wall of Honor** commemorates the names of more than 500,000 immigrants and their families, from Myles Standish and George Washington's great-grandfather to the forefathers of John F. Kennedy, Jay Leno, and Barbra Streisand. You can even research your own family's history at the interactive **American Family Immigration History Center.** *Touring tips:* Ferries run daily to Ellis Island and Liberty Island from Battery Park and Liberty State Park at frequent intervals; see the Statue of Liberty listing (p. 116) for details.

In New York Harbor. ✆ **212/363-3200** (general info), or 877/LADY-TIX (523-9849; ticket/ferry info). www.nps.gov/elis/index.htm, www.ellisisland.org, or www.statuecruises.com. Free admission (ferry ticket charge). Daily 9:30am–5pm (last ferry departs around 2pm), with extended hours in the summer. For subway and ferry details, see the Statue of Liberty listing on p. 116 (ferry trip includes stops at both sights).

Empire State Building ★★★   It took 60,000 tons of steel, 10 million bricks, 2.5 million feet of electrical wire, 120 miles of pipe, and 7 million man-hours to build. King Kong climbed it in 1933. A plane slammed into it in 1945. The World Trade Center superseded it in 1972 as the island's tallest building. On that horrific day of September 11, 2001, it once again regained its status as New York City's tallest building, after 29 years of taking second place. Through it all, the Empire State Building has remained one of the city's favorite landmarks, and its signature high-rise. Completed in 1931, the limestone-and-stainless-steel Streamline Deco dazzler climbs 102 stories (1,454 ft.) and now harbors the offices of fashion firms and, in its upper reaches, a jumble of high-tech broadcast equipment.

Always a conversation piece, the Empire State Building glows every night, bathed in colored floodlights to commemorate events of significance (you can find a complete lighting schedule online). The familiar silver spire can be seen from all over the city. But the views that keep nearly three million visitors coming every year are the ones from the 86th- and 102nd-floor **observatories.** The lower one is best—you can walk out on a windy deck and look through coin-operated viewers (bring quarters!) over what, on a clear day, can be as much as an 80-mile visible radius. The citywide panorama is magnificent. Starry nights are pure magic.

350 Fifth Ave. (at 34th St.). ℂ **212/736-3100.** www.esbnyc.com. 86th Floor Observatory admission $20 adults, $18 seniors, $15 children 6–12, free for children 5 and under; Express Pass $41 (ages 6 and over). 86th & 102nd Floor Combination Pass $37 adults, $35 seniors, $31 children 6–12, free for children 5 and under; Express Pass $55 (ages 6 and over). $2 surcharge for tickets purchased online. Daily 8am–2am (last elevator at 1:15am). Subway: B, D, F, M, N, Q, R to 34th St.; 6 to 33rd St.

Grand Central Terminal ★★   Restored in 1998, Grand Central Terminal is one of the most magnificent public spaces in the country. Even if you're not catching one of the subway lines or Metro-North commuter trains that rumble through the bowels of this great place, come and visit. And even if you arrive and leave by subway, be sure to exit the station, walking a couple of blocks south, to about 40th Street, before you turn around to admire Jules-Alexis Coutan's neoclassical sculpture *Transportation* hovering over the south entrance, with a majestically buff Mercury, the Roman god of commerce and travel, as its central figure.

The greatest visual impact comes when you enter the vast **main concourse.** The high windows once again allow sunlight to penetrate the space, glinting off the ½-acre Tennessee marble floor. The brass clock over the central kiosk gleams, as do the gold-and nickel-plated chandeliers piercing the side archways. The masterful **sky ceiling,** again a brilliant greenish blue, depicts the constellations of the winter sky above New York. On the east end of the main concourse is a grand **marble staircase** where there had never been one before, though it had always been in the original plans.

This dramatic Beaux Arts splendor serves as a hub of social activity as well. Excellent-quality retail shops and restaurants have taken over the mezzanine and lower levels. The highlight of the west mezzanine is **Michael Jordan's–The Steak House,** a gorgeous Art Deco space that allows you to dine within view of the sky ceiling. Off the main concourse at street level, there's a nice mix of specialty shops and national retailers, as well as the truly grand **Grand Central Market** for gourmet foods.

42nd St. at Park Ave. ℂ **212/340-2210** (events hot line). www.grandcentralterminal.com. Subway: S, 4, 5, 6, 7 to 42nd St./Grand Central.

Metropolitan Museum of Art ★★★   Home of blockbuster after blockbuster exhibition, the Metropolitan Museum of Art attracts some five million people a year, more than any other spot in New York City. And it's no wonder—this place is magnificent. At 1.6 million square feet, this is the largest museum in the Western Hemisphere. Nearly all the world's cultures are on display through the ages—from Egyptian mummies to ancient Greek statuary to Islamic carvings to Renaissance paintings to Native American masks to 20th-century decorative arts—and masterpieces are the rule. You could go once a week for a lifetime and still find something new on each visit.

So unless you plan on spending your entire vacation in the museum (some people do), you cannot see the entire collection. One good way to get an overview is to take advantage of the little-known **Museum Highlights Tour,** offered every day at

Free Art on Friday

Many museums have free admission (or "pay what you wish") on Friday evenings. They include **The American Folk Art Museum,** 45 W. 53rd St. (🕿 212/265-1040), from 6 to 8pm; the **Asia Society,** 725 Park Ave. (🕿 212/327-9276), from 6 to 9pm; **MoMA** (p. 113), from 4:30 to 8pm; the **Guggenheim** (p. 115), from 6 to 8pm; the **Whitney** (p. 117), from 6 to 9pm; and the **International Center of Photography** (p. 120), 1133 Sixth Ave. (🕿 212/857-0000), from 6:30 to 8pm. Most other museums have late hours on Friday and Saturday, so even if you don't get free admission, you'll likely beat the crowds, which tend to thin out at night.

various times throughout the day (usually 10:15am–3:15pm; tours also offered in Spanish, Italian, German, and Korean). Visit the museum's website for a schedule of this and subject-specific walking tours (Old Master Paintings, American Period Rooms, Arts of China, Islamic Art, and so on); you can also get a schedule of the day's tours at the Visitor Services desk when you arrive. A daily schedule of **Gallery Talks** is available as well.

Highlights include the American Wing's **Garden Court,** with its 19th-century sculpture; the terrific ground-level **Costume Hall;** and the **Frank Lloyd Wright room.** The beautifully renovated **Roman and Greek galleries** are overwhelming, but in a marvelous way, as are the collections of **Byzantine Art** and later **Chinese art.** The highlight of the astounding **Egyptian collection** is the **Temple of Dendur,** in a dramatic, purpose-built glass-walled gallery with Central Park views. The **Greek Galleries,** which at last fully realize McKim, Mead & White's grand neoclassical plans of 1917, and the **Ancient Near East Galleries** are particularly noteworthy.

The Met now offers **podcasts** about current exhibitions at www.metmuseum.org/podcast/index.asp. The speakers can be surprising. For example: *New York Times* food columnist Mark Bittman and restaurateur Danny Meyer discussed John Sloan's painting *Chinese Restaurant* as part of the exhibition "American Stories: Paintings of Everyday Life, 1765–1915."

Fifth Ave. at 82nd St. 🕿 212/535-7710. www.metmuseum.org. Suggested admission (includes same-day entrance to the Cloisters) $20 adults, $15 seniors, $10 students, free for children 11 and under when accompanied by an adult. Sun, holiday Mon (Memorial Day, President's Day, and so forth), and Tues–Thurs 9:30am–5:30pm; Fri–Sat 9:30am–9pm. Strollers are permitted in most areas—inquire at Information Desks for gallery limitations. Oversize and jogging strollers are prohibited. Subway: 4, 5, 6 to 86th St.

Museum of Modern Art ★★   The newer, larger MoMA, after a 2-year renovation, is almost twice the space of the original. The renovation, designed by Yoshio Taniguchi, highlights space and light, with open rooms, high ceilings, and gardens—a beautiful work of architecture and a perfect complement to the art within. This is where you'll find van Gogh's *Starry Night,* Cezanne's *Bather,* Picasso's *Les Demoiselles d'Avignon,* and the great sculpture by Rodin, *Monument to Balzac.* Whenever I visit, I like to browse the fun "Architecture and Design" department, with examples of design for appliances, furniture, and even sports cars. MoMA also features edgy new exhibits and a celebrated film series that attracts serious cinephiles. But the heart of the museum remains the **Abby Aldrich Rockefeller Sculpture Garden,** which has been enlarged; the museum's new design affords additional views of this lovely space from other parts of the museum. And MoMA has installed a museum-wide

Wi-Fi network so that visitors can access a mobile website on handheld devices with HTML browsers (which basically means Apple's iPhone and iPod Touch). They can then load up audio tours and commentary; content is available in eight languages as well as in specialized versions for children, teenagers, and those with visual impairments. MoMA is one of the most expensive museums in New York, but does have a "free" day: Fridays from 4 to 8pm. MoMA has a blog called "Inside/Out," which is a joint effort with its hip affiliate, P.S.1: **www.moma.org/explore/inside_out**.

11 W. 53rd St. (btw. Fifth and Sixth aves.). (C) **212/708-9400.** www.moma.org. Admission $20 adults, $16 seniors, $12 students, free for children 16 and under if accompanied by an adult. Sat–Mon and Wed–Thurs 10:30am–5:30pm; Fri 10:30am–8pm. Subway: E, M to Fifth Ave.; B, D, F to 47th–50th sts./ Rockefeller Center.

Rockefeller Center ★★ ▣ A Streamline Art Deco masterpiece, Rockefeller Center is one of New York's central gathering spots for visitors and New Yorkers alike. Designated a National Historic Landmark in 1988, it's now the world's largest privately owned business-and-entertainment center, with 18 buildings on 21 acres.

For a dramatic approach to the entire complex, start at Fifth Avenue between 49th and 50th streets. The builders purposely created the gentle slope of the Promenade, known here as the **Channel Gardens,** because it's flanked to the south by La Maison Française and to the north by the British Building (the Channel, get it?). The Promenade leads to the **Lower Plaza,** home to the famous ice-skating rink in winter (see next paragraph) and alfresco dining in summer in the shadow of Paul Manship's freshly gilded bronze statue *Prometheus*, more notable for its setting than its magnificence as an artwork. All around, the flags of the United Nations' member countries flap in the breeze. In December and early January, just behind *Prometheus*, towers the city's official and majestic Christmas tree.

The **Rink at Rockefeller Center ★** (*(C)* 212/332-7654; www.rockefellercenter. com) is tiny but positively romantic, especially during December, when the giant Christmas tree's multicolored lights twinkle from above. The rink is open from mid-October to mid-March.

The focal point of this "city within a city" is the **GE Building ★**, at 30 Rockefeller Plaza, a 70-story showpiece towering over the plaza. It's still one of the city's most impressive buildings; walk through for a look at the granite-and-marble lobby, lined with monumental sepia-toned murals by José Maria Sert.

NBC television maintains studios throughout the complex. *Saturday Night Live* and *Late Night with Jimmy Fallon* originate in the GE Building. NBC's *Today* show is broadcast live on weekdays from 7 to 10am from the glass-enclosed studio on the southwest corner of 49th Street and Rockefeller Plaza; come early if you want a visible spot, and bring your HI MOM! sign.

The 70-minute **NBC Studio Tour** (*(C)* 212/664-3700) will take you behind the scenes at the Peacock network. The tour changes daily, but may include the *Today* show, *NBC Nightly News, Dateline NBC, Late Night with Jimmy Fallon,* and/or *Saturday Night Live* sets. Tickets are $18 for adults, $15 for seniors and children 6 to 16. You can reserve your tickets for either tour in advance (reservations are recommended) or buy them right up to tour time at the **NBC Experience** store, on Rockefeller Plaza at 49th Street. They also offer a 75-minute **Rockefeller Center Tour,** hourly every day between 10am and 4pm, costing $12 for adults, $10 for seniors and children 6 to 16; two-tour combination packages are available for $23.

The newly restored **Radio City Music Hall ★**, 1260 Sixth Ave., at 50th Street (*(C)* 212/247-4777; www.radiocity.com), is perhaps the most impressive architectural

HEADING FOR THE TOP OF THE rock

Giving the Empire State Building some friendly competition when it comes to spectacular views is the observation deck of 30 Rockefeller Plaza, known as the **Top of the Rock** ★★. The deck, which comprises floors 67 to 70, which had been closed since 1986, reopened in 2005. The stately deck was constructed in 1933 to resemble the grandeur of a luxury ocean liner, and compared to the Empire State Building, the observation deck here is more spacious and the views, though not quite as high, are just as stunning. You might have just as much fun getting up there as you will on the deck itself; the sky-shuttle elevators with glass ceilings project images from the 1930s to the present day as it zooms its way up. Reserved-time tickets help minimize the lines and are available online. The observation deck is open daily from 8am to midnight; admission rates are $21 for adults, $19 for seniors 62 and older, $14 for children 6 to 12, and free for children 5 and under. For more information, call ✆ **877/NYC-ROCK** (692-7625) or 212/698-2000, or visit **www.topoftherocknyc.com**.

feat of the complex. Designed by Donald Deskey and opened in 1932, it's one of the largest indoor theaters, with 6,200 seats. But its true grandeur derives from its magnificent Art Deco appointments. The crowning touch is the stage's great proscenium arch that, from distant seats, evokes a faraway sun setting on the horizon of the sea. The theater hosts the annual **Christmas Spectacular,** starring the Rockettes. The illuminating 1-hour **Stage Door Tour** is offered Monday through Saturday from 10am to 5pm, Sunday from 11am to 5pm; tickets are $16 for adults, $10 for children 11 and under.

Btw. 48th and 50th sts., from Fifth to Sixth aves. ✆ **212/332-6868.** www.rockefellercenter.com. Subway: B, D, F, M to 47th–50th sts./Rockefeller Center.

Solomon R. Guggenheim Museum ★   It's been called a bun, a snail, a concrete tornado, and even a giant wedding cake; bring your kids, and they'll probably see it as New York's coolest opportunity for skateboarding. Whatever description you choose to apply, Frank Lloyd Wright's only New York building, completed in 1959, is best summed up as a brilliant work of architecture—so consistently brilliant that it competes with the art for your attention. If you're looking for the city's best modern art, head to MoMA or the Whitney first; come to the Guggenheim to see the house.

It's easy to see the bulk of what's on display in 2 to 4 hours. Inside, a spiraling rotunda circles over a slowly inclined ramp that leads you past changing exhibits that, in the past, have ranged from "The Art of the Motorcycle" to "Norman Rockwell: Pictures for the American People," said to be the most comprehensive exhibit ever of the beloved painter's works. Usually the progression is counterintuitive: from the first floor up, rather than from the sixth floor down. If you're not sure, ask a guard before you begin. Permanent exhibits of 19th- and 20th-century art, including strong holdings of Kandinsky, Klee, Picasso, and the French Impressionists, occupy a stark annex called the **Tower Galleries,** an addition accessible at every level, but which some critics claim make the original look like a toilet bowl backed by a water tank (judge for yourself—I think there may be something to that view).

1071 Fifth Ave. (at 89th St.). ✆ **212/423-3500.** www.guggenheim.org. Admission $18 adults, $15 seniors 65 and over and students, free for children 11 and under; pay what you wish Sat 5:45–7:45pm. Sun–Wed and Fri 10am–5:45pm; Sat 10am–7:45pm. Subway: 4, 5, 6 to 86th St.

5

NEW YORK CITY

Exploring New York City

Staten Island Ferry ★ 🛥 Here's New York's best freebie—especially if you just want to glimpse the Statue of Liberty and not climb her steps. You get an enthralling hour-long excursion (round-trip) into the world's biggest harbor. This is not strictly a sightseeing ride, but commuter transportation to and from Staten Island. As a result, during business hours you'll share the boat with working stiffs reading papers and drinking coffee inside, blissfully unaware of the sights outside.

You, however, should go on deck and enjoy the busy harbor traffic. The old orange-and-green boats usually have open decks along the sides or at the bow and stern; try to catch one of these boats if you can, because the newer white boats don't have decks. Grab a seat on the right side of the boat for the best view. On the way out of Manhattan, you'll pass the Statue of Liberty (the boat comes closest to Lady Liberty on the way to Staten Island), Ellis Island, and, from the left side of the boat, Governor's Island; you'll see the Verrazano Narrows Bridge spanning the distance from Brooklyn to Staten Island in the distance.

There's usually another boat waiting to depart for Manhattan. The skyline views are simply awesome on the return trip. It's all well worth the time spent.

Departs from the Whitehall Ferry Terminal at the southern tip of Manhattan. ℂ **718/727-2508.** http://home2.nyc.gov/html/dot/html/ferrybus/statfery.shtml#info. Free admission. 24 hr.; every 20–30 min. weekdays, less frequently during off-peak and weekend hours. Subway: N, R to Whitehall St.; 4, 5 to Bowling Green; 1 to South Ferry (ride in one of the 1st 5 cars).

Statue of Liberty ★★★ ☺ For the millions who first came by ship to America in the last century—either as privileged tourists or needy, hopeful immigrants—Lady Liberty, standing in the Upper Bay, was their first glimpse of America. No monument so embodies the nation's, and the world's, notion of political freedom and economic potential. Even if you don't make it out to Liberty Island, you can get a spine-tingling glimpse from Battery Park, from the New Jersey side of the bay, or during a free ride on the Staten Island Ferry (see above). It's always reassuring to see her torch lighting the way.

Proposed by French statesman Edouard de Laboulaye as a gift from France to the United States, commemorating the two nations' friendship and joint notions of liberty, the statue was designed by sculptor Frédéric-Auguste Bartholdi with the engineering help of Alexandre-Gustave Eiffel (who was responsible for the famed Paris tower) and unveiled on October 28, 1886. *Touring tips:* Ferries leave daily every half-hour to 45 minutes from 9am to about 3:30pm, with more frequent ferries in the morning and extended hours in summer. Try to go early on a weekday to avoid the crowds that swarm in the afternoon, on weekends, and on holidays.

A stop at **Ellis Island** (p. 111) is included in the fare, but if you catch the last ferry, you can visit only the statue or Ellis Island, not both.

Once on Liberty Island, you'll start to get an idea of the statue's immensity: It weighs 225 tons and measures 152 feet from foot to flame. Its nose alone is 4½ feet long, and the index finger is 8 feet long.

After September 11, 2001, access to the top of the statue was prohibited, but as of July 4, 2009, the crown was finally reopened to the public. No more than 10 people are allowed in the crown at a time, and you have to make reservations through the website to have a chance to ascend the statue. Also with advance tickets, you can explore the Statue of Liberty Museum, peer into the inner structure through a glass ceiling near the base of the statue, and enjoy views from the observation deck on top of a 16-story pedestal. *Note:* Without specific entry tickets, you will not be able to enter the statue; ferry tickets only allow access to the island.

You can **buy ferry tickets in advance** via **www.statuecruises.com**, which will allow you to board the boat without standing in the sometimes-long ticket line; however, there is an additional service charge attached. Even if you've already purchased tickets, arrive as much as 30 minutes before your desired ferry time to allow for increased security procedures prior to boarding the ferry. The ferry ride takes about 20 minutes.

On Liberty Island in New York Harbor. (℡ **212/363-3200** (general info), or 877/523-9849 (ticket/ferry info). www.nps.gov/stli or www.statuecruises.com. Free admission; ferry ticket to Statue of Liberty and Ellis Island $12 adults, $10 seniors 62 and over, $5 children 4–12. Daily 9:30am–5pm (last ferry departs around 2pm); extended hours in summer. Subway: 4, 5 to Bowling Green; 1 to South Ferry. Walk south through Battery Park to Castle Clinton, the fort housing the ferry ticket booth.

Times Square 👋 There's no doubting that Times Square has evolved into something much different than it was over a decade ago when it had a deservedly sleazy reputation. Yet there is much debate among New Yorkers about which incarnation was better. Times Square is a place New Yorkers go out of their way to avoid. The crowds, even by New York standards, are stifling; the restaurants, mostly national chains, aren't very good; the shopping, also mostly national chains, is unimaginative; and the attractions, like **Madame Tussaud's New York** wax museum, are kitschy. I suppose it's a little too Vegas for us. Still, you've come all this way—you've got to at least take a peek, if only for the amazing neon spectacle of it all.

Most of the Broadway shows are centered on Times Square, so plan your visit around your show tickets. For your pre-dinner meal, walk 2 blocks west to Ninth Avenue, where you'll find a number of relatively inexpensive, good restaurants. If you are with the kids, the Ferris wheel in the **Toys "R" Us** store makes a visit to Times Square worthwhile.

Subway: A, C, E, N, Q, R, S, 1, 2, 3, 7 to 42nd St./Times Sq.

Wall Street & the New York Stock Exchange Wall Street—it's an iconic name, and the world's prime hub for bulls and bears everywhere (mostly bears recently . . . oww!). There was once an actual wall here hundreds of years ago, hence the name. This narrow 18th-century lane (you'll be surprised at how little it is) is appropriately monumental, lined with neoclassical towers that reach as far skyward as the dreams and greed (never more evident than in 2008) of investors who built it into the world's most famous financial market.

At the heart of the action is the New York Stock Exchange (NYSE), the world's largest securities trader, where billions change hands. The NYSE came into being in 1792, when merchants met daily under a nearby buttonwood tree to try to pass off to each other the U.S. bonds that had been sold to fund the Revolutionary War. By 1903, they were trading stocks of publicly held companies in this Corinthian-columned Beaux Arts "temple" designed by George Post. About 3,000 companies are now listed on the exchange, trading nearly 314 billion shares valued at about $16 trillion. Unfortunately, the NYSE is no longer open to the public for tours.

11 Wall St. (℡ **212/656-3000.** www.nyse.com. Subway: J, Z to Broad St.; 2, 3, 4, 5 to Wall St.

Whitney Museum of American Art ★★ What is arguably the finest collection of 20th-century American art in the world is an imposing presence on Madison Avenue—an inverted three-tiered pyramid of concrete and gray granite with seven seemingly random windows designed by Marcel Breuer, a leader of the Bauhaus movement. The rotating permanent collection consists of an intelligent selection of

WORLD trade center SITE (GROUND ZERO)

Do you call a place where nearly 2,700 people lost their lives an "attraction"? Or do you now call it a shrine? This is the quandary of the World Trade Center site. What had been a big hole for 5 years is a little more than that; construction began in early 2006 on the proposed "Freedom Tower" to be built at the site (now called "One World Trade Center"). But even though there was political bickering over what should rise from that hole, the building is now well underway. The new design retains essential elements of the original—soaring 1,776 feet into the sky, its illuminated mast evoking the Statue of Liberty's torch. From the square base, the Tower will taper into eight tall isosceles triangles, forming an octagon at its center. An observation deck will be located 1,362 feet above ground.

For now, you can see the site through a viewing wall on the Church Street side of the site; on that "Wall of Heroes" are the names of those who lost their lives that day, along with the history of the site, including photos of the construction of the World Trade Center in the late 1960s and how, after it opened in 1972, it changed the New York skyline and downtown. A walk along the Wall of Heroes remains a painfully moving experience. You can also visit the **9/11 Memorial;** go to **www.911memorial. org** for more information.

The site is bounded by Church, Barclay, Liberty, and West streets. Call ⓒ **212/484-1222,** or go to **www.nycgo. com** for viewing information; go to **www.downtownny.com** for lower Manhattan-area information and rebuilding updates. The Tribute Center gives guided tours of the site. Call ⓒ **212/ 422-3520,** or visit **www.tributewtc.org** for more information. Tours are given Sunday to Friday at 11am, noon, and 1 and 3pm; Saturdays at 11am, noon, and 1, 2, 3, and 4pm. The fee is $10 for adults, 11 and under free.

major works by Edward Hopper, Georgia O'Keeffe, Roy Lichtenstein, Jasper Johns, and other significant artists. A pleasing second-floor exhibit space is devoted exclusively to works from its permanent collection from 1900 to 1950, while the rest of the space is dedicated to rotating exhibits.

The springtime **Whitney Biennial** (2010, 2012, and so on) is a major event on the national museum calendar. It serves as the premier launching pad for new American artists working on the vanguard in every media. Free **gallery tours** are offered daily, and music, screenings, and lectures fill the calendar.

945 Madison Ave. (at 75th St.). ⓒ **212/570-3600.** www.whitney.org. Admission $18 adults, $12 seniors, free for full-time students and ages 19–25, free for children 18 and under; pay what you wish Fri 6–9pm. Wed–Thurs and Sat–Sun 11am–6pm; Fri 1–9pm. Subway: 6 to 77th St.

More Manhattan Museums

Cooper-Hewitt National Design Museum ★   Part of the Smithsonian Institution, the Cooper-Hewitt is housed in the Carnegie Mansion, built by steel magnate Andrew Carnegie in 1901 and renovated in 1996. Some 11,000 square feet of gallery space are devoted to changing exhibits that are invariably well conceived, engaging, and educational. Shows are both historic and contemporary in nature, and topics range from Charles and Ray Eames to Russell Wright to Disney theme parks. Many installations are drawn from the museum's own vast collection of industrial design, drawings, textiles, books, and prints.

2 E. 91st St. (at Fifth Ave.). ℂ **212/849-8400.** www.cooperhewitt.org. Admission $15 adults, $10 seniors and students with ID, free for children 11 and under. Mon–Fri 10am–5pm; Sat 10am–6pm; Sun 11am–6pm. Subway: 4, 5, 6 to 86th St.

The Frick Collection ★★
One of the most beautiful mansions remaining on Fifth Avenue is a living testament to New York's vanished Gilded Age, graced with beautiful paintings rather than being a museum. Come here to see the classics by some of the world's most famous painters: Titian, Bellini, Rembrandt, Turner, Vermeer, El Greco, and Goya, to name only a few. A highlight of the collection is the **Fragonard Room,** with the sensual rococo series *The Progress of Love.* The portrait of Montesquieu by Whistler is also stunning. Sculpture, furniture, Chinese vases, and French enamels complement the paintings and round out the collection. Included in the price of admission, the AcousticGuide audio tour is particularly useful because it allows you to follow your own path rather than a prescribed route. In addition to the permanent collection, the Frick regularly mounts small, well-focused temporary exhibitions.

1 E. 70th St. (at Fifth Ave.). ℂ **212/288-0700.** www.frick.org. Admission $18 adults, $12 seniors, $5 students. Children 9 and under not admitted. Tues–Sat 10am–6pm; Sun 11am–5pm. Closed all major holidays. Subway: 6 to 68th St./Hunter College.

USS Intrepid Sea-Air-Space Museum ★★ ☺
The most astonishing thing about the aircraft carrier *Intrepid* is how it can be simultaneously so big and so small. It's a few football fields long, weighs 40,000 tons, holds 40 aircraft, and sometimes doubles as a ballroom for society functions. But stand there and think about landing an A-12 jet on the deck and suddenly it's minuscule. Furthermore, in the narrow passageways below, you'll find it isn't quite the roomiest of vessels. Now a National Historic Landmark, the exhibit also includes the submarine *Growler,* the only intact strategic missile submarine open to the public anywhere in the world, as well as a collection of vintage and modern aircraft, including the A-12 Blackbird, the world's fastest spy plane, and a retired British Airways Concorde jet.

Kids just love this place. They, and you, can climb inside a replica Revolutionary War submarine, sit in an A-6 Intruder cockpit, and follow the progress of America's astronauts as they work in space. There are even Navy flight simulators—including a "Fly with the Blue Angels" program—for educational thrill rides in the Technologies Hall.

The program "All Hands on Deck" teaches children and adults how things work on ships, plus there's an AH-1 Cobra attack helicopter. The action-packed *Intrepid Wings* shows aircraft carrier takeoffs and recoveries in the new Allison and Howard Lutnick Theater; the film runs continuously throughout the day. The grand visitor center makes for an impressive entrance, and the massive museum store is well stocked; goods include NYPD and FDNY logo gear.

Each year, in February, the museum presents **Kids Week,** which takes advantage of so much that New York has to offer for kids. This may include a performance by the Alvin Ailey dance troupe, a kids' fashion show, or some Broadway acts. If you're in town with your family—in 2011 Kids Week was February 19 to 27—come onboard.

Pier 86 (W. 46th St. at Twelfth Ave.). ℂ **877/957-7447** or 212/245-0072. www.intrepidmuseum.org. Admission $22 adults; $18 seniors and students; $17 children 3–17 and veterans; free for active military, retired U.S. military, and children 2 and under. Nov–Mar Tues–Sun 10am–5pm; Apr–Oct Mon–Fri 10am–5pm, Sat–Sun 10am–6pm. Closed Christmas and Thanksgiving. Subway: A, C, E to 42nd St./Port Authority. Bus: M42 Crosstown.

5

NEW YORK CITY

Exploring New York City

International Center of Photography ★ 🎁 The ICP is one of the world's premier educators, collectors, and exhibitors of photographic art. The state-of-the-art gallery space is ideal for viewing rotating exhibitions of the museum's 50,000-plus prints as well as visiting shows. The emphasis is on contemporary photographic works, but historically important photographers aren't ignored. This place is a must on any photography buff's list.

1133 Sixth Ave. (at 43rd St.). © **212/857-0000.** www.icp.org. Admission $12 adults, $8 seniors and students, free for children 11 and under. Tues–Thurs and Sat–Sun 10am–6pm; Fri 10am–8pm. Subway: B, D, F, M to 42nd St.

Morgan Library ★★ 🎁 This New York treasure, boasting one of the world's most important collections of original manuscripts, rare books and bindings, master drawings, and personal writings, has become newly popular since extensive renovations and an addition designed by architect Renzo Piano were completed in 2006. Those renovations include a welcoming entrance on Madison Avenue; new and renovated galleries, so that more of the library's holdings can be exhibited; a modern auditorium; and a new Reading Room with greater capacity and electronic resources and expanded space for collections storage. The permanent collection is nothing but astounding, including not one but *three* Gutenberg Bibles; letters and manuscripts of Jane Austen, Balzac, Byron, Dickens, James Joyce, and Alexander Pope; and a sumptuous, eye-boggling collection of medieval illuminated manuscripts. **Note:** The collection is too vast for it to be all exhibited at one time, and the displays change periodically. Some of the Library's exhibitions have included one on the life of Bob Dylan through music, letters, memorabilia; "On the Money: Cartoons for *The New Yorker*," and "The Modern Stage: Set Designs, 1900–70." You can lunch in the intimate **Morgan Dining Room** as if you were dining in JP's own quarters. **Note:** The museum's website has one of the finest online exhibitions of any museum.

225 Madison Ave. (btw. 36th and 37th sts.). © **212/685-0008.** www.themorgan.org. $12 adults, $8 seniors and students, free for children 11 and under; free for all Fri 7–9pm. Tues–Thurs 10:30am–5pm; Fri 10:30am–9pm; Sat 10am–6pm; Sun 11am–6pm. Subway: 6 to 33rd St.

South Street Seaport & Museum ☺ This landmark historic district on the East River encompasses 11 square blocks of historic buildings, a maritime museum, several piers, shops, and restaurants. The 18th- and 19th-century buildings lining the cobbled streets and alleyways are impeccably restored but nevertheless have a theme park air about them, no doubt due to the mall-familiar shops housed within. The Seaport's biggest tourist attraction is Pier 17, a historic barge converted into a mall, complete with food court and cheap jewelry kiosks.

Despite its rampant commercialism, the Seaport is well worth a look. There's a good amount of history to be discovered here, most of it around the **South Street Seaport Museum,** a fitting tribute to the sea commerce that once thrived here.

In addition to the galleries—which house paintings and prints, ship models, scrimshaw, and nautical designs, as well as frequently changing exhibitions—there are a number of historic ships berthed at the pier to explore, including the 1911 four-masted *Peking* and the 1893 Gloucester fishing schooner *Lettie G. Howard*. A few of the boats are living museums and restoration works in progress; the 1885 cargo schooner *Pioneer* (© **212/748-8786**) offers 2-hour public sails daily from early May to September.

Even **Pier 17** has its merits. Head up to the third-level deck overlooking the East River, where the long wooden chairs will have you thinking about what it was like to cross the Atlantic on the *Normandie*. From this level you can see south to the Statue of Liberty, north to the Gothic majesty of the Brooklyn Bridge, and Brooklyn Heights on the opposite shore.

At the gateway to the Seaport, at Fulton and Water streets, is the **Titanic Memorial Lighthouse,** a monument to those who lost their lives when the ocean liner sank on April 15, 1912. It was erected overlooking the East River in 1913 and moved to this spot in 1968, just after the historic district was so designated.

At Water and South sts.; museum visitor center is at 12 Fulton St. (📞 **212/748-8725** or 212/SEA-PORT (732-7678, for events). www.seany.org. Museum admission $15 adults; $12 students, seniors, and children; free for children 1 and under. Museum Apr–Dec Tues–Sun 10am–6pm; Jan–Mar Thurs–Sun 10am–5pm, ships noon–4pm. Subway: 2, 3, 4, 5 to Fulton St. (walk east, or downslope, on Fulton St. to Water St.).

Skyscrapers & Other Architectural Highlights

Cathedral of St. John the Divine ★   The world's largest Gothic cathedral, St. John the Divine has been a work in progress since 1892. Its sheer size is amazing enough—a nave stretching the length of two football fields and with a seating capacity of 5,000—but keep in mind that there is no steel structural support. The church is being built using traditional Gothic engineering; blocks of granite and limestone are carved out by master masons and their apprentices—which may explain why construction is still ongoing, more than 110 years after it began, with no end in sight. In late 2008, after a $41-million cleaning and repair from a 2001 fire, the church was rededicated, its great nave open and its 8,500-pipe organ playing. You can explore the cathedral on your own, or on the **Public Tour,** offered 6 days a week; also inquire about periodic (usually twice-monthly) **Vertical Tours,** which take you on a hike up the 11-flight circular staircase to the top for spectacular views. To hear the incredible pipe organ in action, attend the weekly **Choral Evensong and Organ Meditation** service, which highlights one of the nation's most treasured pipe organs, Sunday at 6pm.

1047 Amsterdam Ave. (at 112th St.).(📞 **212/316-7490** or 212/932-7347 for tour information and reservations. www.stjohndivine.org. Public Tour $6 adults, $5 seniors and students; Vertical Tour $15 adults, $12 seniors and students. Mon–Sat 7am–6pm; Sun 7am–7pm. Public Tours offered Tues–Sat 11am and 1pm; Sun 1pm. Vertical Tours offered Sat noon and 2pm. Worship services daily 8am (morning prayer), Mon–Sat 5pm (evening prayer), Mon–Sat 8:30am and 12:15pm and Sun 8 and 9am (holy Eucharist), Sun 4pm (choral evensong); AIDS memorial service 4th Sat of the month at 12:15pm. Subway: B, C, 1 to Cathedral Pkwy.

Chrysler Building ★★   Built as Chrysler Corporation headquarters in 1930 (they moved out decades ago), this is perhaps the 20th century's most romantic architectural achievement, especially at night, when the lights in its triangular openings play off its steely crown. As you admire its facade, be sure to note the gargoyles reaching out from the upper floors. The observation deck closed long ago, but you can visit its lavish ground-floor interior, which is Art Deco to the max. The ceiling mural depicting airplanes and other early marvels of the first decades of the 20th century evince the bright promise of technology. The elevators are works of art, masterfully covered in exotic woods (especially note the lotus-shaped marquetry on the doors).

405 Lexington Ave. (at 42nd St.). Subway: S, 4, 5, 6, 7 to 42nd St./Grand Central.

Flatiron Building   This triangular masterpiece, so called for its resemblance to the laundry appliance, was one of the first U.S. skyscrapers. Its knife-blade wedge shape was the only building design possible for the triangular property created by the intersection of Fifth Avenue and Broadway, and that happy coincidence created one of the city's most distinctive landmarks. Built in 1902 and fronted with limestone and terra cotta (not iron), the Flatiron measures only 6 feet across at its narrow end. There's no observation deck, and the building mainly houses publishing offices; but there are a few shops on the ground floor. The building's existence has served to name the neighborhood around it: the Flatiron District, home to a bevy of smart restaurants and shops.

175 Fifth Ave. (at 23rd St.). Subway: R to 23rd St.

New York Public Library ★★   The New York Public Library, designed by Carrère & Hastings (1911), is one of the country's finest examples of Beaux Arts architecture, a majestic structure of white Vermont marble with Corinthian columns and allegorical statues. Before climbing the broad flight of steps to the Fifth Avenue entrance, take note of the famous lion sculptures—*Fortitude* on the right and *Patience* on the left—so dubbed by whip-smart former mayor Fiorello LaGuardia. At Christmastime, they don natty wreaths to keep warm.

This library is actually the **Humanities and Social Sciences Library,** only one of the research libraries in the New York Public Library system. The interior is one of the finest in the city and features **Astor Hall,** with high arched marble ceilings and grand staircases. The stupendous **Main Reading Rooms** have now reopened after a massive restoration and modernization that returned them to their stately glory and moved them into the computer age. In 2008, the Library's facade began a 3-year restoration, to be completed for the building's centennial in 2011. Even if you don't stop in to peruse the periodicals, you may want to check out one of the excellent rotating **exhibitions.** Call or check the site for show schedules.

Fifth Ave. at 42nd St. Ⓒ **212/930-0830** (exhibits and events) or 212/661-7220 (library hours). www.nypl.org. Free admission to all exhibitions. Thurs–Sat 10am–6pm; Tues–Wed 11am–7:30pm; Sun 1–5pm. Subway: B, D, F, M to 42nd St.; S, 4, 5, 6, 7 to Grand Central/42nd St.

St. Patrick's Cathedral   This incredible Gothic white-marble-and-stone structure is the largest Roman Catholic cathedral in the United States, as well as the seat of the Archdiocese of New York. Designed by James Renwick, begun in 1859, and consecrated in 1879, St. Patrick's wasn't completed until 1906. Strangely, Irish Catholics picked one of the city's WASPiest neighborhoods for St. Patrick's. After the death of the beloved John Cardinal O'Connor in 2000, Pope John Paul II installed Bishop Edward Egan, whom he elevated to cardinal in 2001. The vast cathedral seats a congregation of 2,200; if you don't want to come for Mass, you can pop in between services to get a look at the impressive interior.

Fifth Ave. (btw. 50th and 51st sts.). Ⓒ **212/753-2261.** Free admission. Sun–Fri 7am–8:30pm; Sat 8am–8:30pm. Mass Mon–Fri 7, 7:30, 8, and 8:30am, noon, and 12:30, 1, and 5:30pm; Sat 8 and 8:30am, noon, and 12:30 and 5:30pm; Sun 7, 8, 9, and 10:15am (Cardinal's Mass), noon, and 1, 4, and 5:30pm; holy days 7, 7:30, 8, 8:30, 9, 11, and 11:30am, noon, and 12:30, 1, 5:30, and 6:30pm. Subway: B, D, F, M to 47th–50th sts./Rockefeller Center.

United Nations   In the midst of New York City is this working monument to world peace. The U.N. headquarters occupies 18 acres of international territory—neither the city nor the United States has jurisdiction here—along the East River from 42nd to 48th streets. Designed by an international team of architects (led by American Wallace K. Harrison and including Le Corbusier) and finished in 1952, the complex along the East River weds the 39-story glass slab Secretariat with the free-form General Assembly on beautifully landscaped grounds donated by John D. Rockefeller, Jr. A total of 180 nations use the facilities to arbitrate worldwide disputes.

Guided tours leave every half-hour or so and last 45 minutes to an hour.

At First Ave. and 46th St. (C) **212/963-8687.** www.un.org/tours. Guided tours $16 adults, $11 seniors 60 and over and students 13 and over, $9 children 5-12. Children 4 and under not permitted. Weekday tours at 10:30am and 4pm. Guided tours might be canceled with short notice when heads of state and government are meeting. UN weekdays 9:45am–4:45pm, weekends 10–4:15. Subway: S, 4, 5, 6, 7 to 42nd St./Grand Central.

Central Park

Without the miracle of civic planning that is **Central Park ★★★**, Manhattan would be a virtual unbroken block of buildings. Instead, smack in the middle of Gotham, an 843-acre natural retreat provides a daily escape valve and tranquilizer for millions of New Yorkers.

On just about any day, Central Park is crowded with New Yorkers and visitors alike. On nice days, especially weekend days, it's the city's party central. The crowds are part of the appeal—folks come here to peel off their urban armor and relax, and the common goal puts a general feeling of camaraderie in the air. On these days, people-watching is more compelling here than anywhere else in the city. But even on the most crowded days, there's always somewhere to get away from it all, if you just want a little peace and quiet and a moment to commune with nature.

ORIENTATION & GETTING THERE Look at your map—that great green swath in the center of Manhattan is Central Park. It runs from 59th Street (also known as Central Park South) at the south end to 110th Street at the north end, and from Fifth Avenue on the east side to Central Park West (the equivalent of Eighth Ave.) on the west side. A 6-mile rolling road, **Central Park Drive,** circles the park, and has a lane set aside for bikers, joggers, and in-line skaters.

A number of subway stops and lines serve the park, and which one you take depends on where you want to go. To reach the southernmost entrance on the west side, take an A, B, C, D, or 1 train to 59th Street/Columbus Circle. To reach the southeast corner entrance, take the N or R to Fifth Avenue; from this stop, it's an easy walk into the park to the Information Center in the **Dairy** ((C) **212/794-6564;** daily 11am–5pm, to 4pm in winter), midpark at about 65th Street. Here you can ask questions, pick up park information, and purchase a good park map.

If your time for exploring is limited, I suggest entering the park at 72nd or 79th street for maximum exposure (subway: B or C to 72nd St. or 81st St./Museum of Natural History). From here, you can pick up park information at the visitor center at **Belvedere Castle** ((C) **212/772-0210;** Tues–Sun 10am–5pm, to 4pm in winter), midpark at 79th Street. There's also a third visitor center at the **Charles A. Dana Discovery Center** ((C) **212/860-1370;** daily 11am–5pm, to 4pm in winter), at the northeast corner of the park at Harlem Meer, at 110th Street between Fifth and Lenox avenues (subway: 2 or 3 to Central Park North/110th St.). The Dana Center is also an environmental education center hosting workshops, exhibits, music programs, and park tours, and lends fishing poles for fishing in Harlem Meer (park policy is catch-and-release).

Food carts and vendors are set up at all of the park's main gathering points, selling hot dogs, pretzels, and ice cream, so finding a bite to eat is never a problem. You'll also find a fixed food counter at the **Conservatory,** on the east side of the park north of the 72nd Street entrance, and both casual snacks and more sophisticated New American dining at **The Boat House,** on the lake near 72nd Street and Park Drive North ((C) **212/517-2233**).

SAFETY   Even though the park has the lowest crime rate of any of the city's precincts, keep your wits about you, especially in the more remote northern end. It's a good idea to avoid the park entirely after dark, unless you're heading to one of the restaurants for dinner or to **Shakespeare in the Park.**

VISITOR INFORMATION   Call ℂ **212/360-3444** for recorded information, or 212/310-6600 or 212/628-1036 to speak with a person. Call ℂ **888/NY-PARKS** (697-2757) for special-events information. The park also has two comprehensive websites that are worth checking out before you go: the city parks department's site at **www.centralpark.org** and the Central Park Conservancy's site at **www.central parknyc.org**, both of which feature excellent maps and a far more complete rundown of park attractions and activities than there is room to include here. If you have an **emergency** in the park, dial ℂ **800/201-PARK** (7275), which will link you directly to the park rangers.

EXPLORING THE PARK

The best way to see Central Park is to wander along the park's 58 miles of winding pedestrian paths, keeping in mind the following highlights.

The southern part of Central Park is more formally designed and heavily visited than the relatively rugged and remote northern end. Not far from the Dairy is the **Carousel** with 58 hand-carved horses (ℂ **212/879-0244;** daily Apr–Nov 10am–6pm, to 4:30pm in winter; rides are $1); the zoo (see below); and the Wollman Rink for roller- or ice-skating.

The **Mall,** a long, formal walkway lined with elms shading benches and sculptures of sometimes forgotten writers, leads to the focal point of Central Park, **Bethesda Fountain ★** (along the 72nd St. transverse road). **Bethesda Terrace** and its grandly sculpted entryway border a large **lake** where dogs fetch sticks, rowboaters glide by, and dedicated early-morning anglers try their luck at catching carp, perch, catfish, and bass. You can rent a rowboat at or take a gondola ride from **Loeb Boathouse,** on the eastern end of the lake. Boats of another kind are at **Conservatory Water** (on the east side at 73rd St.), a stone-walled pond flanked by statues of both **Hans Christian Andersen** and **Alice in Wonderland.** On Saturday at 10am, die-hard yachtsmen race remote-controlled sailboats in fierce competitions that follow Olympic regulations.

If the action there is too intense, **Sheep Meadow,** on the southwestern side of the park, is a designated quiet zone, where Frisbee throwing and kite flying are as energetic as things get. Another respite is **Strawberry Fields ★**, at 72nd Street on the West Side. This memorial to John Lennon, who was murdered across the street at the Dakota apartment building (72nd St. and Central Park West, northwest corner), is a gorgeous garden area centered on an Italian mosaic bearing the title of the lead Beatle's most famous solo song and his lifelong message: IMAGINE. In keeping with its goal of promoting world peace, the garden has 161 varieties of plants, donated by each of the 161 nations in existence when it was designed in 1985. This is a wonderful place for peaceful contemplation.

Bow Bridge, a graceful lacework of cast iron, designed by Calvert Vaux, crosses over the lake and leads to the most bucolic area of Central Park, the **Ramble.** This dense 38-acre woodland with spiraling paths, rocky outcroppings, and a stream is the best spot for bird-watching and feeling as if you've discovered an unimaginably leafy forest right in the middle of the city.

Central Park

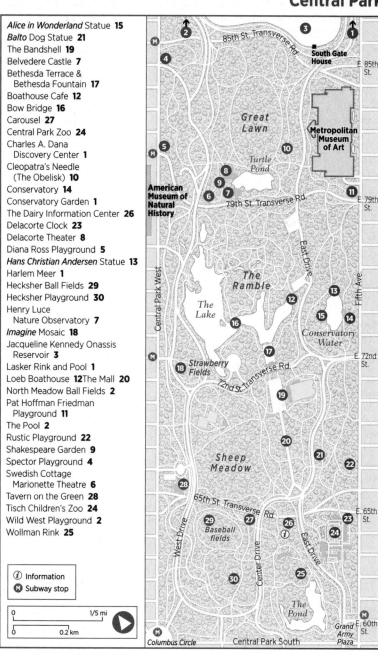

ⓘ Information
Ⓜ Subway stop

0   1/5 mi
0   0.2 km

5

NEW YORK CITY | Exploring New York City

North of the Ramble, **Belvedere Castle** is home to the **Henry Luce Nature Observatory** (© 212/772-0210), worth a visit if you're with children. From the castle, set on Vista Rock (the park's highest point at 135 ft.), you can look down on the **Great Lawn,** where softball players and sun worshipers compete for coveted greenery, and the **Delacorte Theater,** home to Shakespeare in the Park. The small **Shakespeare Garden** south of the theater is scruffy, but it does have plants, herbs, trees, and other bits of greenery mentioned by the playwright. Behind the Belvedere Castle is the **Swedish Cottage Marionette Theatre ★** (© 212/988-9093), hosting various marionette plays for children throughout the year; call to see what's on.

Continue north along the east side of the Great Lawn, parallel to East Drive. Near the glass-enclosed back of the **Metropolitan Museum of Art** (p. 112) is **Cleopatra's Needle,** a 69-foot obelisk originally erected in Heliopolis around 1475 B.C. It was given to the city as a gift from the khedive of Egypt in 1880. (The khedive bestowed a similar obelisk to the city of London, which now sits on the Embankment of the Thames.)

North of the 86th Street Transverse Road is the **Jacqueline Kennedy Onassis Reservoir,** so named after the death of the beloved First Lady, who lived nearby and often enjoyed a run along the 1.5-mile jogging track that circles the reservoir.

North of the reservoir is my favorite part of the park. It's much less traversed and, in some areas, absolutely tranquil. The **North Meadow** (at 96th St.) features 12 baseball and softball fields.

North of the North Meadow, at the northeast end of the park, is the **Conservatory Garden ★** (at 105th St. and Fifth Ave.), Central Park's only formal garden, with a magnificent display of flowers and trees reflected in calm pools of water. **The Lasker Rink and Pool** (© 212/534-7639) is the only swimming pool in Central Park, and, in the winter, it's converted to a skating rink that offers a less hectic alternative to Wollman Rink. **Harlem Meer** and its boathouse have been renovated and look beautiful. The boathouse now berths the **Charles A. Dana Discovery Center,** near 110th Street between Fifth and Lenox avenues (© 212/860-1370), where children learn about the environment and borrow fishing poles for catch-and-release at no charge. **The Pool** (at W. 100th St.), possibly the most idyllic spot in all of Central Park, has been renovated and features willows, grassy banks, and a small pond populated by some very well-fed ducks. You might even spot an egret and a hawk or two lurking around here.

> ### Smoke-Free Parks
>
> In 2011, Mayor Bloomberg and the city of New York passed a controversial bill banning smoking in public parks. As a nonsmoker, I find this to be good news, especially when I'm working out, running, or riding my bike in the park. For others, smokers in particular, it's another blow to their civil liberties.

Central Park Zoo/Tisch Children's Zoo ★ ☺   It has been over a decade since the zoo in Central Park was renovated, making it both more human and more humane. Lithe sea lions frolic in the central pool area with beguiling style. The gigantic but graceful polar bears (one of whom, by the way, made himself a true New Yorker when he began regular visits with a shrink) glide back and forth across a watery pool that has glass walls through which you can observe very large paws doing very smooth strokes.

Because of its small size, the zoo is at its best with the displays of smaller animals. The indoor multilevel Tropic Zone is a real highlight, its steamy rainforest home to everything from black-and-white colobus monkeys to Emerald tree boa constrictors to a leaf-cutter-ant farm; look for the new poison-frog exhibit, which is very cool. The entire zoo is good for short attention spans; you can cover the whole thing in 1½ to 3 hours, depending on the size of the crowds and how long you like to linger. It's also very kid-friendly, with lots of well-written and -illustrated placards that older kids can understand. For the littlest ones, there's the **Tisch Children's Zoo.** With pigs, llamas, potbellied pigs, and more, this petting zoo and playground are a real blast for the 5-and-under set. On the main path leading north from the Tisch Children's Zoo—at East Drive and 67th Street—is one of the most admired statues in the park: the bronze statue of the famous sled dog Balto, which stands on a rock outcropping and is a favorite with kids.

830 Fifth Ave. (at 64th St., just inside Central Park). (C) **212/439-6500.** www.centralparkzoo.com. Admission $12 adults, $9 seniors, $7 children 3–12, free for children 2 and under. Apr–Oct Mon–Fri 10am–5pm, Sat–Sun and holidays 10am–5:30pm; Nov–Mar daily 10am–4:30pm. Last entrance 30 min. before closing. Subway: N, R to Fifth Ave; 6 to 68th St.

ACTIVITIES IN THE PARK

The 6-mile rolling road circling the park, **Central Park Drive,** has a lane set aside for bikers, joggers, and in-line skaters. The best time to use it is when the park is closed to traffic: Monday to Friday 10am to 3pm (except Thanksgiving to New Year's) and 7 to 10pm. It's also closed from 7pm Friday to 6am Monday, but when the weather is nice, the crowds can be hellish.

BIKING Off-road mountain biking isn't permitted; stay on Central Park Drive or your bike may be confiscated by park police.

You can rent 3- and 10-speed bikes as well as tandems in Central Park at the **Loeb Boathouse,** midpark near 74th Street and Park Drive North, just in from Fifth Avenue ((C) **212/517-2233** or 517-3623), for $9 to $20 an hour, with a complete selection of kids' bikes, cruisers, tandems, and the like ($200 deposit required); and at **Metro Bicycles,** 1311 Lexington Ave., at 88th Street ((C) **212/427-4450**). No matter where you rent, be prepared to leave a credit card deposit.

BOATING From March to November, gondola rides and rowboat rentals are available at the **Loeb Boathouse,** midpark near 74th Street and Park Drive North, just in from Fifth Avenue ((C) **212/517-2233** or 517-3623). Rowboats are $10 for the first hour, $2.50 every 15 minutes thereafter, and a $20 deposit is required; reservations are accepted. (Note that rates were not set for the summer season at press time, so these may change.)

HORSE-DRAWN CARRIAGE RIDES Horses belong on city streets as much as chamber pots belong in our homes. You won't need me to tell you how forlorn most of these horses look; if you insist, rides start at the entrance to the park at 59th Street and Central Park South, and cost about $50 for two for a half-hour, but I suggest skipping it.

ICE-SKATING Central Park's **Wollman Rink** ★, on the east side of the park between 62nd and 63rd streets ((C) **212/439-6900;** www.wollmanskatingrink.com), is the city's best outdoor skating spot, more spacious than the tiny rink at Rockefeller Center. It's open for skating from mid-October to mid-April, depending on the weather. Rates are $10 for adults ($14 Fri–Sun), $4.75 for seniors ($8.75 Fri–Sun), and $5.25 for children ($5.50 Sat–Sun), and skate rental is $6; lockers are available (locks are $4.25, $6 Fri–Sun). **Lasker Rink** ((C) **917/492-3857** in winter, 212/534-7639 in summer), on the east side around 106th Street, is a less expensive alternative to the more crowded Wollman Rink. Open November through March. Rates are $6 for adults, $3.50 for kids 11 and under, and skate rental is $2.25.

PLAYGROUNDS   Nineteen Adventure Playgrounds are scattered throughout the park, perfect for jumping, sliding, tottering, swinging, and digging. At Central Park West and 81st Street is the **Diana Ross Playground ★**, voted the city's best by *New York* magazine. Also on the west side is the **Spector Playground,** at 85th Street and Central Park West, and, a little farther north, the **Wild West Playground** at 93rd Street. On the east side is the **Rustic Playground,** at 67th Street and Fifth Avenue, a delightfully landscaped space rife with islands, bridges, and big slides; and the **Pat Hoffman Friedman Playground,** right behind the Metropolitan Museum of Art at East 79th Street, is geared toward older toddlers.

RUNNING   Marathoners and wannabes regularly run in Central Park along the 6-mile **Central Park Drive,** which circles the park (please run toward traffic to avoid being mowed down by wayward cyclists and in-line skaters). The **New York Road Runners** (✆ **212/860-4455;** www.nyrrc.org), organizers of the New York City Marathon, schedule group runs 7 days a week at 6am and 6pm, leaving from the park entrance at 90th Street and Fifth Avenue.

Organized Sightseeing Tours

Circle Line Sightseeing Cruises ★   Circle Line is the only tour company that circumnavigates the entire 35 miles around Manhattan, and I love this ride. The **Full Island** cruise takes 3 hours and passes by the Statue of Liberty, Ellis Island, the Brooklyn Bridge, the United Nations, the George Washington Bridge, and more, including Manhattan's wild northern tip. The panorama is riveting, and the commentary isn't bad. The big boats are basic but fine, with lots of deck room for everybody to enjoy the view. Snacks, soft drinks, coffee, and beer are available onboard for purchase.

If 3 hours is more than you or the kids can handle, go for either the **Semi-Circle** or **Sunset/Harbor Lights** cruises, both of which show you the highlights of the skyline in 1½ hours.

Departing from Pier 83, at W. 42nd St. and Twelfth Ave. ✆ **212/563-3200.** www.circleline42.com. Check the website or call for the most up-to-date schedule. Sightseeing cruises $27–$35 adults, $24–$30 seniors, $19–$22 children 3–12, free for children 2 and under. Subway to Pier 83: A, C, E to 42nd St.

The Attack of the Double-Decker Buses

They are everywhere. There is no escape. They clog up the already over-crowded streets, spewing exhaust, their red or blue exteriors splashed with a garish display of self-promotion and advertising, loudspeakers blaring as the people huddled on the upper deck (swathed in plastic ponchos when it rains) look down at the natives on the streets. I'm talking about double-decker buses. They run in the morning, they run at night, they run all day long.

Can you tell I'm not a fan? I think New York is best appreciated on foot, or on public buses and subways. Sure these double-decker buses have guides, but take the facts they dish out with a grain of salt; they aren't always accurate. If you insist, the top bus tour is **Gray Line New York Tours** (✆ **800/669-0051** or 212/445-0848; www.graylinenewyork. com). Tours depart from various locations. Hop-on, hop-off bus tours start at $49 adults, $39 children 3 to 11.

Especially for Kids

Some of New York's sights and attractions are designed specifically with kids in mind, and I've listed those below. But many of those I've discussed in the rest of this chapter are terrific for kids as well as adults; look for the kids icon next to the attraction.

MUSEUMS

In addition to the museums discussed below, which are designed specifically for kids, also consider the following, discussed elsewhere in this chapter: the **American Museum of Natural History** (p. 110), whose dinosaur displays are guaranteed to wow both you and the kids, and the **South Street Seaport & Museum** (p. 120), which little ones will love for its theme park–like atmosphere and old boats bobbing in the harbor.

Children's Museum of the Arts ☺   Interactive workshop programs for children ages 1 to 12 and their families are the attraction here. Kids dabble in puppet making and computer drawing or join in singalongs and live performances. Also look for rotating exhibitions of the museum's permanent collection featuring WPA work. Call or check the website for the current exhibition and activities schedule.

182 Lafayette St. (btw. Broome and Grand sts.). ✆ **212/274-0986.** www.cmany.org. Admission $10 for ages 1–65, pay what you wish Thurs 4–6pm. Wed–Sun noon–5pm (Thurs to 6pm). Subway: 6 to Spring St.; R to Prince; N to Canal St.

Children's Museum of Manhattan ★ ☺   Here's a great place to take the kids when they're tired of being told not to touch. Designed for ages 2 to 12, this museum is strictly hands-on. Interactive exhibits and activity centers encourage self-discovery—and a recent expansion means that there's now even more to keep the kids busy and learning. The Time Warner Center takes children through the world of animation and helps them produce their own videos. The Body Odyssey is a zany, scientific journey through the human body. This isn't just a museum for the 5-and-up set—there are exhibits especially designed for babies and toddlers, too. The busy schedule also includes daily art classes and storytellers, and a full slate of entertainment on weekends.

212 W. 83rd St. (btw. Broadway and Amsterdam Ave.). ✆ **212/721-1234.** www.cmom.org. Admission $10 children and adults, $7 seniors, free for children 1 and under, free for all on 1st Friday of every month 5–8pm. Tues–Sun 10am–5pm. Subway: 1 to 86th St.

New York Hall of Science ★ ☺   Children of all ages will love this huge hands-on museum, which bills itself as "New York's Only Science Playground." Exhibits allow visitors to be engulfed by a giant soap bubble, float on air in an antigravity mirror, and compose music by dancing in front of light beams. There's a Preschool Discovery Place for the really little ones. But probably best of all is the summertime Outdoor Science Playground for kids 6 and older—ostensibly lessons in physics, but really just a great excuse to laugh, jump, and play on jungle gyms, slides, seesaws, spinners, and more. The museum is located in **Flushing Meadows–Corona Park,** where kids can have even more fun beyond the Hall of Science. Not only are there more than 1,200 acres of park and playgrounds, but there are also a zoo, a carousel, an indoor ice-skating rink, an outdoor pool, and bike and boat rentals.

447-01 111th St., in Flushing Meadows-Corona Park, Queens. ✆ **718/699-0005.** www.nysience.org. Admission $11 adults; $8 seniors, students with college ID, and children 2–17; free for all Fri 2–5pm and Sun 10–11am except for July–Aug. Additional $4 for Science Playground. Rocket Park Mini Golf $6 per person, $5 for children and seniors. Sept–Mar Tues–Thurs 9:30am–2pm, Fri 9:30am–5pm, Sat–Sun 10am–6pm; Apr–Aug Mon–Thurs 9:30am–2pm (till 5pm July–Aug); Fri 9:30am–5pm; Sat–Sun 10am–6pm. Subway: 7 to 111th St.

Spectator Sports

BASEBALL   With two baseball teams in town, you can catch a game almost any day, from Opening Day in April to the beginning of the playoffs in October.

For information on pricing and availability of tickets for the Metropolitans, call the **Mets Ticket Office** at ☏ 718/507-TIXX (8499), or visit http://newyork.mets.mlb.com. Also keep in mind that you can buy game tickets (as well as logo wear and souvenirs, if you want to dress appropriately for the big game) at the **Mets Clubhouse Shop,** which has a midtown Manhattan location.

New Yankee Stadium is across the street from the old one (Subway: C, D, 4 to 161st St./Yankee Stadium). **NY Waterway** offers baseball cruises to games; call ☏ 800/533-3779, or visit www.nywaterway.com for more info. For single-game tickets, contact **Yankee Stadium** (☏ 718/293-6000; http://newyork.yankees.mlb.com) or go to the team's clubhouse shop in Manhattan. Serious baseball fans should check the schedule well in advance for Old Timers' Day, usually held in July, when pinstriped stars of years past return to the stadium to take a bow.

You can also buy Mets and Yankees tickets by contacting **Ticketmaster** (☏ 800/745-3000; www.ticketmaster.com), visiting the stadium on the day of the game, or trying online resale sites such as **StubHub** (www.stubhub.com).

Minor-league baseball ★ coexists with the show in the boroughs, with the **Brooklyn Cyclones,** the New York Mets' minor-league farm team, and the **Staten Island Yankees,** the Yanks' minor leaguers. Boasting their very own waterfront stadium, the Cyclones have been a major factor in the revitalization of Coney Island; KeySpan Park sits right off the boardwalk (subway: D, F, N, Q to Stillwell Ave./Coney Island). The SI Yanks also have their own playing field, the Richmond County Bank Ballpark, just a 5-minute walk from the Staten Island Ferry terminal (subway: N, R to Whitehall St.; 4, 5 to Bowling Green; 1 to South Ferry). What's more, with bargain-basement ticket prices (around the $15 range), this is a great way to experience baseball in the city for a fraction of the major-league hassle and cost. Both teams have a rabidly loyal fan base, so it's a good idea to buy your tickets for the June through September season in advance. For the Cyclones, call ☏ 718/449-8497 or visit **www.brooklyncyclones.com**; to reach the SI Yanks, call ☏ 718/720-9200 or go online to **www.siyanks.com**.

BASKETBALL   There are two pro hoops teams that play in New York at **Madison Square Garden,** Seventh Avenue, between 31st and 33rd streets (☏ 212/465-6741, or 800/745-3000 for tickets; www.thegarden.com or www.ticketmaster.com; subway: A, C, E, 1, 2, 3 to 34th St.). The **New York Knicks** (☏ 877/NYK-DUNK [695-3865] or 212/465-JUMP [5867]; www.nba.com/knicks) are the NBA team from NYC, and their tickets (when bought at the box office) range from $13 to $3,085. The WNBA's **New York Liberty** (☏ 212/564-9622; www.wnba.com/liberty) have vacated MSG for the duration of renovations, which are being done in the summer of 2011 and running through 2013. You can find them at Newark's Prudential Center until then.

Ice Hockey   NHL hockey is represented in Manhattan by the **New York Rangers,** who play at Madison Square Garden, Seventh Avenue between 31st and 33rd streets (☏ 212/465-6741; http://rangers.nhl.com or www.thegarden.com; subway: A, C, E, 1, 2, 3 to 34th St.). Rangers tickets are hard to get, so plan well ahead; call ☏ 800/745-3000, or visit **www.ticketmaster.com** for online orders. Ticket prices range from about $42 to $290.

SHOPPING HIGHLIGHTS

Don't expect to find the purchase of a lifetime on Chinatown's streets, but enjoy the quality browsing. The fish and herbal markets along Canal, Mott, Mulberry, and Elizabeth streets are fun for their bustle and exotica. Dispersed among them (especially along **Canal St.**), you'll find a mind-boggling collection of knockoff sunglasses and watches, cheap backpacks, discount leather goods, and exotic souvenirs. It's a fun daytime browse, but don't expect quality—and be sure to bargain before you buy. (Also, skip the bootleg CDs, video, and software—these are stolen goods, and you *will* be disappointed with the product.) **Mott Street,** between Pell Street and Chatham Square, boasts the most interesting of Chinatown's off-Canal shopping, with an antiques shop or two dispersed among the tiny storefronts selling blue-and-white Chinese dinnerware. If you're out for cool and colorful mementos, duck into **Ting's Gift Shop,** 18 Doyer St. (© **212/962-1081**), one of the oldest operating businesses in Chinatown. Under a vintage pressed-tin ceiling, the shop sells good-quality Chinese toys, kits, and lanterns. Tea lovers should not miss **Ten Ren Tea & Genseng ★**, 75 Mott St. (© **212/349-2286**), where the lovely staff will help you select delectable teas and all the right brewing accessories.

The Lower East Side

The bargains aren't quite what they used to be in the **Historic Orchard Street Shopping District**—which basically runs from Houston to Canal along Allen, Orchard, and Ludlow streets, spreading outward along both sides of Delancey Street—but prices on leather bags, shoes, luggage, and fabrics on the bolt are still quite good. Be aware, though, that the hard sell on Orchard Street can be pretty hard to take. Still, the district is a nice place to discover a part of New York that's disappearing. Come during the week because most stores are Jewish-owned and, therefore, close Friday afternoon and all day Saturday. Sunday tends to be a madhouse.

The artists and other trendsetters who have been turning this neighborhood into a bastion of hip have also added a cutting edge to its shopping scene in recent years. You'll find a growing—and increasingly upscale—crop of alterna-shops south of Houston and north of Grand Street, between Allen and Clinton streets to the east and west, specializing in up-to-the-minute fashions and edgy club clothes, plus funky retro furnishings, Japanese toys, and other offbeat items. Among them are **Reed Space,** 151 Orchard St. (© **212/253-0588**), a cool "lifestyle boutique," home to local and international designers, along with art, music, books, and magazines.

Before you browse, stop into the **Lower East Side Visitor Center,** 70 Orchard St., between Broome and Grand streets (© **866/224-0206** or 212/226-9010; subway: F to Delancey St.), for a shopping guide that includes vendors both old-world and new. Or you can preview the list (and score coupons) online at **www.lowereast sideny.com**.

SoHo

People love to complain about superfashionable SoHo—it's become too trendy, too tony, too Mall of America. True, **J. Crew** is only one of many big names that have supplanted the artists and galleries that inhabited its historic cast-iron buildings. But SoHo is still one of the best shopping 'hoods in the city—and few are more fun to browse. It's the epicenter of cutting-edge fashion and still boasts plenty of unique boutiques. The streets are chock-full of tempting stores, so just come and browse.

SoHo's shopping grid runs from Broadway west to Sixth Avenue, and Houston Street south to Canal Street. **Broadway** is the most commercial strip, with such recognizable names as **Pottery Barn, Banana Republic, Sephora,** and **A/X Armani Exchange. H&M,** the popular Swedish department store with cutting-edge fashions sold at unbelievably low prices, has two stores that face one another on Broadway. **Bloomingdale's** has opened up a downtown branch in the old Canal Jean space. **Prada**'s flagship store, also on Broadway, is worth visiting for its spacious, almost soothing design alone (by Dutch architect Rem Koolhaus). A definite highlight is the two-story **Pearl River** Chinese emporium, which offers everything from silk *cheongsam* (traditional Chinese high-necked dresses) to tea ware.

The 'hood also boasts some fabulous recent additions, like Spain's colorful **Desigual,** 594 Broadway (© **212/343-8206**), Japan's sleek **Uniqlo,** 546 Broadway (© **917/237-8800**), and London's brilliant **Topshop ★,** 478 Broadway (© **212/ 966-9555**), a women's megaclothier. But one long-standing hipster fave, **Yellow Rat Bastard,** 483 Broadway (© **212/925-4377**), is a counterpoint to the big chain stores as a haven for hip-hop/urban/skateboard-style punks.

There also are several hot galleries along West Broadway and peppered throughout SoHo. So whether you're looking to expand your art collection or just see the work of the Next Big Thing, be sure to come to SoHo with plenty of time to wander. You can find a full listing of shops and galleries (most are closed Mon) at **www.artseensoho.com.**

The East Village

The East Village personifies bohemian hip. The easiest subway access is the no. 6 train to Astor Place, and from there, it's just a couple of blocks east.

East 9th Street between Second Avenue and Avenue A is lined with an increasingly smart collection of boutiques, proof that the East Village isn't just for kids anymore. Designers, including **Jill Anderson** (331 E. 9th St.; © **212/253-1747**) and **Huminska** (315 E. 9th St.; © **212/677-3458**) sell excellent-quality and original fashions for women along here.

If it's strange, illegal, or funky, it's probably available on **St. Marks Place,** which takes over for 8th Street, running east from Third Avenue to Avenue A. This skanky strip is a permanent street market, with countless T-shirt and cheap-jewelry stands. The height of the action is between Second and Third avenues, which is prime hunting grounds for used-record collectors.

Greenwich Village

The West Village is great for browsing and gift shopping. Specialty bookstores and record stores, antiques and craft shops, and gourmet food markets dominate. On 8th Street—NYU territory between Broadway and Sixth Avenue—you can find trendy footwear and affordable fashions.

But the biggest shopping boom of late has happened on **Bleecker Street** west of Sixth Avenue. Between Carmine Street and Seventh Avenue, foodies will delight in the strip of boutique food shops, including **Amy's Bread, Wild Edibles,** and **Murray's Cheese ★.** In between are record stores, guitar shops, and a sprinkling of artsy boutiques. On **Christopher Street,** you'll find such wonders as **Aedes De Venustas ★,** a gorgeous little boutique selling fabulous perfumes and scented candles that are difficult to find in the States, and **The Porcelain Room,** 13 Christopher St. (© **212/367-8206**), which is located below street level and offers amazing antique and contemporary porcelains that have to be seen to be believed.

Along Christopher Street you'll also find all manner of LGBT shops, like **Rainbow Greetings** at no. 98 (© **212/638/3310**), for all your pride decor and much more.

Follow Christopher westward, where Bleecker becomes boutique alley, and one jewel box of a shop follows another. Among them: **Intermix, Olive & Bette, Ralph Lauren, Lulu Guinness, Marc Jacobs,** and the new **Michael Kors** emporium.

Those who really love to browse should also wander **west of Seventh Avenue** and along **Hudson Street,** where charming shops such as **House of Cards and Curiosities,** 23 Eighth Ave., between Jane and 12th streets (© **212/675-6178**), the Village's own funky take on an old-fashioned nickel-and-dime, are tucked among the brownstones.

The Flatiron District & Union Square

When 23rd Street was the epitome of New York uptown fashion more than 100 years ago, the major department stores stretched along **Sixth Avenue** for about a mile from 14th Street up. These elegant stores stood in huge cast-iron buildings that were long ago abandoned and left to rust. In the past several years, however, the area has grown into the city's discount shopping center, with superstores and off-pricers filling up the renovated spaces: **Filene's Basement, T.J. Maxx,** and **Bed Bath & Beyond** are all at 620 Sixth Ave., near 18th Street, while **Old Navy** is next door, and **Barnes & Noble** is just a couple of blocks away at Sixth Avenue near 22nd Street.

On Broadway, just a few blocks north of Union Square, is **ABC Carpet & Home** (881 and 888 Broadway, at 19th St.; © **212/473-3000;** www.abccarpet.com), a magnet for aspiring Martha Stewarts, if any of those are still out there. If it's actually a rug you're looking for, a whole slew of imported carpet dealers line Broadway from ABC north to about 25th Street.

Upscale retailers who have rediscovered the architectural majesty of **lower Fifth Avenue** include **Banana Republic, Victoria's Secret,** and **Kenneth Cole.** You won't find much that's new along here, but it's a pleasing stretch nonetheless.

And then, *certo,* there is **Eataly,** at the stately northwest corner of Broadway and Fifth Avenue (© **212/229-2560**). Legendary chef, restaurateur, and Italian-American Mario Batali and partners have splayed seemingly all of Italy's gastronomic delights across 50,000 square feet of prime Flatiron real estate.

Herald Square & the Garment District

Herald Square—where 34th Street, Sixth Avenue, and Broadway converge—is dominated by **Macy's** (W. 34th St. and Broadway; © **212/695-4400;** www.macys.com), the self-proclaimed world's biggest department store. And a few blocks north of Macy's is that dowager of department stores, **Lord & Taylor** (424 Fifth Ave.; © **212/391-3344;** www.lordandtaylor.com).

Times Square & the Theater District

This neighborhood has become increasingly family oriented, hence the fabulous **Toys "R" Us** flagship on Broadway and 44th Street, which even has its own full-scale Ferris wheel; and the mammoth **E-Walk** retail and entertainment complex on 42nd Street between Seventh and Eighth avenues, overflowing with mall-familiar shops like the **Museum Company.**

West 47th Street between Fifth and Sixth avenues is the city's famous **Diamond District.** The street is lined shoulder-to-shoulder with showrooms, and you'll be wheeling and dealing with the mostly Hasidic dealers, who are quite a juxtaposition to the crowds. You'll also notice a wealth of **electronics stores** throughout the neighborhood, many suspiciously trumpeting GOING OUT OF BUSINESS sales. These guys have been going out of business since the Stone Age. That's the bait-and-switch: Pretty soon you've spent too much money for not enough stereo. If you want to check out what they have to offer, find out beforehand the going price on that smartphone or digital camera you're interested in. You can make a good deal if you know exactly what the market is, but these guys will be happy to suck you dry given half a chance.

Fifth Avenue & 57th Street

The heart of Manhattan retail is the corner of Fifth Avenue and 57th Street. There was a time when only the very rich could shop these sacred crossroads. Such is not the case anymore, now that **Tiffany & Co.** (727 Fifth Ave.; ✆ **212/755-8000;** www.tiffany. com), which has long reigned supreme here, sits a stone's throw from **Niketown** (6 E. 57th St.; ✆ **212/891-6453;** www.nike.com) and the **NBA Store** (666 Fifth Ave.; ✆ **212/515-NBA1** [6221]; www.nbastore.com). In addition, a good number of mainstream retailers, like **Banana Republic,** have flagships along Fifth, further democratizing the avenue. Still, you will find a number of big-name, big-ticket designers and jewelers radiating from the crossroads, as well as chichi department stores like **Bergdorf Goodman** (754 Fifth Ave.; ✆ **212/753-7300**), **Henri Bendel** (712 Fifth Ave.; ✆ **212/247-1100**), and **Saks Fifth Avenue** (611 Fifth Ave.; ✆ **212/753-4000;** www.saksfifthavenue.com), all of which help the avenue maintain its classy cachet.

A few blocks east on Lexington is the world's flagship **Bloomingdale's,** 1000 Third Ave. (Lexington Ave. at 59th St.; ✆ **212/705-2000;** www.bloomingdales. com), a great place to shop.

Madison Avenue

Madison Avenue from 57th to 79th streets boasts the most expensive retail real estate in the world. Bring lots of plastic. This ultradeluxe strip—particularly in the high 60s—is home to *the* most luxurious designer boutiques, with **Barneys New York** as the anchor. Don't be intimidated by the glamour or any of the celebrities you're likely to bump into. There are affordable treasures to be had, such as the Ginger Flower room spray at **Shanghai Tang** (714 Madison Ave.; ✆ **212/888-0111**) or a pair of crystal cuff links at the **Lalique** boutique next door at 712 Madison Ave. (✆ **212/355-6550**).

Upper West Side

The Upper West Side's best shopping street is **Columbus Avenue.** Small shops catering to the neighborhood's white-collar mix of young hipsters and families line both sides of the pleasant avenue from 66th Street (where you'll find an excellent branch of **Barnes & Noble**) to about 86th Street. Highlights include **Maxilla & Mandible** for museum-quality natural science–based gifts, and **Harry's Shoes,** but you won't lack for good browsing along here. **The Shops at Columbus Circle,** in the new Time Warner Center, also has a world of upscale choices for shopping.

NEW YORK CITY AFTER DARK

For the latest nightlife listings, check out *Time Out New York* (www.timeoutny. com), a comprehensive weekly magazine of events; the free *Village Voice* (www. villagevoice.com), the city's legendary alternative paper; and *New York Magazine* (www.nymag.com).

GETTING TICKETS   Buying tickets can be simple if the show you want to see isn't sold out. You need only call or surf to **Telecharge** (✆ **212/239-6200;** www.telecharge.com), which handles most Broadway and Off-Broadway shows and some concerts, or **Ticketmaster** (✆ **212/307-4100;** www.ticketmaster.com), which also handles Broadway and Off-Broadway shows and most concerts. You will pay a service fee per ticket, and sometimes a "restoration" fee for a show in an older theater.

The best deal in town on same-day tickets for both Broadway and Off-Broadway shows is at the **Times Square Theatre Centre,** better known as the **TKTS** booth, run by the nonprofit Theatre Development Fund in the heart of the Theater District. Its longtime home at Duffy Square, 47th Street and Broadway, reopened after a major renovation. Now above the ticket-selling windows, you can relax and take in the "crossroads of the world" on the illuminated red stadium seats. The booth is open from 3 to 8pm for evening performances, 10am to 2pm for Wednesday and Saturday matinees, and from 11am to 8pm on Sunday for all performances.

There are separate lines for dramas, which are usually shorter than the lines for musicals. There's often a huge line, so show up early for the best availability and be prepared to wait—but frankly, the crowd is all part of the fun. The shows available change throughout the day, and you might score a ticket to a big hit just before curtain time.

Visit **www.tdf.org** or call **NYC/Onstage** at ✆ **212/768-1818** and press "8" for the latest TKTS information.

The Performing Arts

Apollo Theater ★ 📷   Built in 1914, this legendary Harlem theater launched or abetted the careers of countless musical icons—including Billie Holiday, Duke Ellington, Ella Fitzgerald, Sarah Vaughan, Count Basie, and Aretha Franklin. A major restoration of the Apollo was completed in time for its 75th anniversary. The results are spectacular—from the refurbished terra-cotta facade, to the new box offices, to the high-tech marquee that still shines with 1940s timeless style. The theater remains internationally renowned for hosting African-American performers of all musical genres, from hip-hop acts to Wynton Marsalis's Jazz for Young People events. Since 1934, Wednesday at the Apollo means "Amateur Night"; forget *American Idol*—this rowdy, fun-filled, often hilarious production draws young talents with high hopes of making it big. 253 W. 125th St. (btw. Adam Clayton Powell and Frederick Douglass blvds.). ✆ **212/531-5300** or -5301. www.apollotheater.com. Subway: B or D to 125th St.

Beacon Theatre   This lovely, midsize Upper West Side venue hosts mainly pop-music performances, usually for the over-30 crowd. Originally a 1928 Art Deco movie palace, its impressive lobby, stairway, and auditorium (seating about 2,700) were restored to their gorgeous glory back in 2009. Featured acts have ranged from street-smart pop diva Sheryl Crow to a Hall & Oates reunion to dazzling Rufus Wainwright. There's also an annual early-spring run of sellout Allman Brothers shows here. You'll also find all kinds of special guests and events on the mix-and-match calendar, for kids, comedy fans, and even devout Buddhists—the Dalai Lama and other monks have graced the Beacon. 2124 Broadway (at 74th St.). ✆ **212/465-6500.** www.beacontheatre.com. Subway: 1, 2, or 3 to 72nd St.

Brooklyn Academy of Music 🎭   BAM is the city's most renowned contemporary arts institution, presenting cutting-edge theater, opera, dance, and music. Offerings have included historically informed presentations of baroque opera by William Christie and Les Arts Florissants; pop opera from Lou Reed; Marianne Faithfull singing the music of Kurt Weill; dance by Mark Morris and Mikhail Baryshnikov; the Philip Glass ensemble accompanying screenings of *Koyaanisqatsi* and Lugosi's original *Dracula*; the Royal Dramatic Theater of Sweden directed by Ingmar Bergman; and many more experimental works by both renowned and lesser-known international artists, as well as visiting companies from all over the world. 30 Lafayette Ave. (off Flatbush Ave.), Brooklyn. ℂ **718/636-4100.** www.bam.org. Subway: 2, 3, 4, 5, M, N, Q, or R to Pacific St./Atlantic Ave.

Carnegie Hall ★★ Perhaps the world's most famous performance space, Carnegie Hall offers everything from grand classics to the music of Ravi Shankar. The **Isaac Stern Auditorium,** the 2,804-seat main hall, welcomes visiting orchestras from across the country and the world. Many of the world's premier soloists and ensembles give recitals. The legendary hall is both visually and acoustically brilliant; don't miss an opportunity to experience it if there's something on that interests you.

There's also the intimate 268-seat **Weill Recital Hall,** usually used to showcase chamber music and vocal and instrumental recitals. Carnegie Hall has also, after being occupied by a movie theater for 38 years, reclaimed the ornate underground 650-seat Zankel Concert Hall.

Carnegie ticket prices greatly vary, and are for sale by phone and at the box office, both open 8am to 8pm daily; same-day rush tickets for students and seniors are available, as are $10 partial-view tickets on a first-come, first-served basis. And to answer the famous question, "How do you get to Carnegie Hall?" Either by practice, or by subway. 881 Seventh Ave. (at 57th St.). ℂ **212/247-7800.** www.carnegiehall.org. Subway: N, Q, or R to 57th St.

City Center Modern dance usually takes center stage in this domed, Moorish-revival performing arts palace (and former temple). The companies of Paul Taylor and Alvin Ailey, as well as the American Ballet Theatre, are regularly on the calendar. The dance companies always perform in the pitch-perfect Mainstage Theater, with ticket prices ranging from $10 to $150, or more. Also in the City Center building, plays are presented in Manhattan Theatre Club Stage I and the smaller Stage II, at affordable prices ranging up to $90. 131 W. 55th St. (btw. Sixth and Seventh aves.). ℂ **212/247-0430** or 212/581-1212. www.citycenter.org. Subway: F, N, Q, or R to 57th St.; B, D, or E to Seventh Ave.

Lincoln Center for the Performing Arts New York is the world's premier performing arts city, and Lincoln Center is its premier institution. Lincoln Center's many buildings serve as permanent homes to their own companies as well as major stops for world-class performance troupes from around the globe.

Resident companies include the **Metropolitan Opera** (ℂ **212/362-6000;** www.metopera.org), which ranks first in the world. The opera house also hosts the **American Ballet Theatre** (www.abt.org) each spring, as well as visiting companies such as the Kirov, Royal, and Paris Opera ballets. The **New York State Theater** (ℂ **212/870-5570**) is the home of the **New York City Ballet** (www.nycballet.com), with performances in winter and spring, and the New York City Opera (www.nycopera.com), a superb company with lower prices than the Met.

Symphony-wise, you'd be hard-pressed to do better than the phenomenal **New York Philharmonic ★** (ℂ **212/875-5656;** www.newyorkphilharmonic.org), which performs at Avery Fisher Hall.

Additional resident companies include the **Chamber Music Society of Lincoln Center** (ℂ **212/875-5788;** www.chambermusicsociety.org), which performs at Alice Tully Hall or the Daniel and Joanna S. Rose Rehearsal Studio. The **Film Society of**

Lincoln Center (© 212/875-5600; www.filmlinc.com) screens a daily schedule of movies at the Walter Reade Theater, and it hosts a number of important annual film and video festivals, as well as the Reel to Real program for kids, pairing silent-screen classics with live performances. **Lincoln Center Theater** (© 212/362-7600; www.lct.org) consists of the Vivian Beaumont Theater, a modern and comfortable venue with great sightlines that has been home to much good Broadway drama, and the Mitzi E. Newhouse Theater, a well-respected Off-Broadway house that has also boasted numerous theatrical triumphs.

Check Lincoln Center's website to see what special events will be on while you're in town. **Tickets** for all performances at Avery Fisher and Alice Tully halls can be purchased through **CenterCharge** (© 212/721-6500) or online at www.lincoln-center.org. Tickets for all Lincoln Center Theater performances can be purchased thorough **TeleCharge** (© 212/239-6200; www.telecharge.com). Tickets for New York State Theater productions (New York City Opera and Ballet companies) are available through **Ticketmaster** (© 212/307-4100; www.ticketmaster.com), while tickets for films showing at the Walter Reade Theater can be bought up to 7 days in advance by calling © 212/496-3809.

Offered daily, 1-hour **guided tours** of Lincoln Center tell the story of the great performing arts complex, and even offer glimpses of rehearsals; call © 212/875-5350. 70 Lincoln Center Plaza (at Broadway and 64th St.). © **212/546-2656** or 212/875-5456. www.lincolncenter.org. Subway: 1 to 66th St.

Live Rock, Jazz, Blues & More

In addition to the listings below, you'll find a slew of music clubs on and around Bleecker Street in Greenwich Village, between 6th Avenue and Broadway.

B.B. King Blues Club & Grill   This 550-seat venue is one of the prime anchors of Times Square's "new" 42nd Street. Despite its name, B.B. King's seldom sticks to the blues; what you're likely to find instead is a bill full of pop, funk, and rock names, mainly from the past. The big-ticket talent runs the gamut from George Clinton and the P-Funk All Stars and John Mayall and the Bluesbreakers to Tower of Power to Jimmy Cliff and Delbert McClinton. A few more (relatively) esoteric acts such as Mort Sahl and surf guitarist Dick Dale take the stage on occasion. Tourist-targeted pricing makes for an expensive night on the town, with sometimes-convoluted seating policies—but there's no arguing with the quality of the talent. The Sunday Gospel Bunch is a genuine platter of soul food joy. 237 W. 42nd St. (btw. Seventh and Eighth aves.). © **212/997-4144,** or 212/307-7171 for tickets. www.bbkingblues.com. Subway: A, C, E, Q, 1, 2, 3, or 7 to 42nd St.

Dizzy's Club Coca-Cola ★   This luxurious jazz club is part of the Jazz at Lincoln Center complex in the Time Warner Center on Columbus Circle. You won't find a bad seat at this fifth-floor club, with a stage set in front of a large window with Central Park views. The club attracts an interesting mix of both up-and-coming and established artists. Every Monday the club starts with the student showcase Upstarts! followed by 1-night-only shows from special guest musicians. Covers range from $20 to $35 and $10 for shows after 11pm, with $5 or $10 bar minimums; student discounts are available, and reservations aren't always necessary. Time Warner Center, 60th St. and Broadway. © **212/258-9595.** www.jalc.org/dccc. Subway: A, B, C, D, or 1 to Columbus Circle.

Smoke ★   A relatively young star in the New York jazz scene, Smoke is a welcome throwback to the informal, intimate clubs of the past—the kind of place where on most nights you can just walk in and be amazed. And though it seats only 65, for no more than a $35 cover (not counting bar/table minimums), Smoke manages to attract such talents as the Steve Turre Quartet, Ron Carter, and Eddie Henderson. On Sundays, the club features Latin jazz; every Tuesday, it's B3 grooves and soul jazz, and Wednesdays put the "Sideman in the Spotlight." There are three sets nightly. An affordable menu recently spruced up by a new executive chef sets apart this supper club, and makes for a very happy happy hour. 2751 Broadway (btw. 105th and 106th sts.). © **212/864-6662.** www.smokejazz.com. Subway: 1 to 103rd St.

S.O.B.'s If you like your music hot, hot, hot, visit S.O.B.'s, the city's top world-music venue, specializing in Brazilian, Caribbean, and Latin sounds. The packed house dances and sings along nightly to calypso, samba, mambo, African drums, *bhangra,* and other global grooves, sometimes preceded by free dance lessons. Bookings include top performers from around the globe. Astrud Gilberto, Mighty Sparrow, King Sunny Ade, Eddie Palmieri, Buckwheat Zydeco, BeauSoleil, and Baaba Maal are only a few of the names who added their energy to this lively stage. The room's Tropicana Club style has island pizzazz that carries through to the Caribbean-influenced cooking and extensive (and pricey) tropical-drinks menu. Book ahead if you'd like dinner or a Bossa Nova Brunch. Monday is dedicated to reggae, Friday is salsa, and Saturday is samba night. 204 Varick St. (at Houston St.). © **212/243-4940.** www.sobs.com. Subway: 1 to Houston St.

The Village Vanguard 📷 What CBGB was to punk rock, the Village Vanguard is to jazz. One look at the photos on the walls will show you who's been through since 1935, from Coltrane, Miles, and Monk to recent appearances by Bill Charlap and Roy Hargrove. Expect a mix of established names and high-quality local talent, including the Vanguard's own jazz orchestra on Monday nights. The sound is great, but sightlines aren't, so reserve or come early for a front table; tickets average around $25, with drink minimums. If you are looking for serious jazz, this is the place. 178 Seventh Ave. S. (just below 11th St.). © **212/255-4037.** www.villagevanguard.com. Subway: 1, 2, or 3 to 14th St.

LONG ISLAND & THE HAMPTONS

by Marc Lallanilla

I f there's an island anywhere that has more excitement, variety, and sophistication than Long Island, I haven't heard of it. Stretching about 130 miles from the outer boroughs of New York City to the ocean waves lapping at the shores of Montauk, Long Island defies easy description. Chances are, no matter what you're looking for, you'll find it here. Movie stars and supermodels dancing the night away in velvet-rope nightclubs? Pristine, white-sand beaches with fantastic surf breaks? Gilded Age mansions dripping with crystal chandeliers and priceless artwork? Untrammeled wilderness teeming with rare plants and animals? Check, check, check.

If you hurry out to just one hot spot destination, you'll miss much of what Long Island has to offer. Some of the best farmland on the East Coast is underfoot here, and early settlers created now-historic farms that still produce award-winning wines, heirloom fruits and vegetables, and world-famous Long Island duck. Nature's bounty doesn't stop at land's end, however: Some of America's finest seafood is harvested every day right offshore—and it's probably going to end up on your dinner plate tonight.

When industrial barons of the 19th century were looking for a place near New York City to cool off on hot summer days, they chose Long Island's "Gold Coast": Estates belonging to turn-of-the-20th-century magnates with names like Roosevelt, Astor, and Chrysler abound, and the mansions and gardens that inspired F. Scott Fitzgerald and countless other visitors are still here, waiting for your arrival.

Past these lavish homes, the North Fork contains the majority of Long Island's vineyards, which in short order have begun producing some world-class wines, all in a laid-back setting that was once home to fishing and whaling communities.

Heading south, witness how the other half—or perhaps a smaller fraction than that—vacation, among the eye-popping summer homes of the Hamptons. Here at the far reaches of the largest island to adjoin the continental U.S., you'll find the most exciting surfing in the northeast, some of the best restaurants on the island, with nightlife to match. You might even brush shoulders with fame while dining or sunbathing.

On the southern coast, Jones Beach and Long Beach are time-honored weekend havens for city dwellers, where endless stretches of sand give way to refreshingly clean waters, even when the summer crowds are at

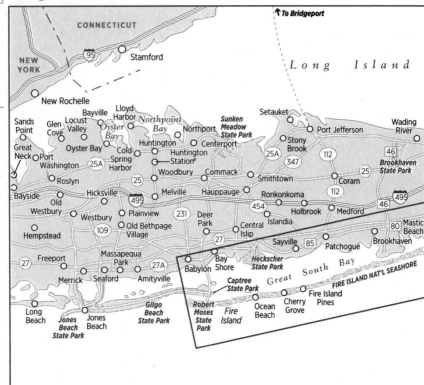

capacity. When you want to escape the masses, there's the car-free paradise of Fire Island, spanning some 30-odd miles along the southern coast of Long Island, and little Shelter Island, tucked away in the crook of the island's forks—a remote and peaceful retreat featuring large swathes of undisturbed nature and wildlife preserves.

THE NORTH SHORE ★

From Great Neck to Wading River

With its graceful bays and breathtaking views of Long Island Sound—not to mention its unbeatable proximity to Gotham—the North Shore is a spectacular stretch of real estate. It's no wonder the country's newly rich industrialists chose to build their mansions here at the turn of the 20th century.

The towns that line this coast have been inhabited by some of America's wealthiest citizens for decades, and this still holds true. During the Roaring Twenties, the **Gold Coast,** as it came to be known, was transformed into a playground of the rich, who built sumptuous homes and gardens, threw lavish parties, groomed racehorses, and indulged in—well, just about everything. Barons of America's Gilded Age bought as

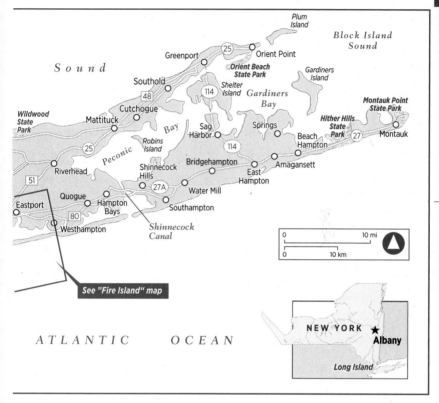

much as 1,000 acres of land and built 100-room mansions modeled on English manor houses and French châteaux.

Yes, this is *Great Gatsby* country—and lucky for you, you can still glimpse some of these estates from the Long Island Expressway, and see others up close, through a tour or a house visit. Drive out from Manhattan, past the densely populated, mall- and car-choked sections closest to the city, and pick up Route 25A in exclusive Great Neck—the inspiration for Fitzgerald's West Egg, by the way. Continuing east, watch as the traffic slowly starts to dissipate, and sit back and take in some of the North Shore's unexpected gems.

Estates like **Old Westbury House and Gardens, Sands Point Preserve,** and **Planting Fields/Coe Hall** are well worth a visit, with gorgeous gardens and grounds that beg you to linger, while **Sagamore Hill**—Theodore Roosevelt's summer home—makes for an excellent stop. But the North Shore's charms go beyond the mansions: There are also impressive art museums and sculpture gardens, sweeping waterfront vistas, hidden Japanese landscapes, and historic villages that only become more charming the farther out you drive onto the island.

141

GETTING THERE

BY CAR   The **Long Island Expressway** (I-495, or the L.I.E.) is your quickest way through here, when it's not packed with traffic. (Avoid rush hour at all costs!) Alternate routes include the Southern State or Northern State parkways, which might be less congested—but don't count on it.

BY TRAIN   More than 85 million people ride the **Long Island Rail Road (LIRR).** For schedule and fare information, call © 516/822-LIRR (5477) or 631/231-LIRR, or visit www.mta.info/lirr. The LIRR services 124 Long Island stations and makes more than 20 stops along the north shore, including Great Neck, Manhasset, Port Washington, Oyster Bay, Locust Valley, Glen Cove, Sea Cliff, Roslyn, Westbury, Hicksville, Syosset, Cold Spring Harbor, Huntington, Northport, St. James, Stony Brook, and Port Jefferson. Cab service is available at all stations, even well past sundown; you can just show up and get a cab or check the LIRR website for cab-company phone numbers.

BY PLANE   LaGuardia and John F. Kennedy airports lie just over the Long Island Border in New York City (p. 58). **Long Island MacArthur Airport,** situated mid-island in Islip (© 631/467-3210; www.macarthurairport.com), is served by **Southwest** (© 800/435-9792; www.southwest.com) and **US Airways Express** (© 800/428-4322; www.usairways.com).

BY FERRY   The **Bridgeport & Port Jefferson Steamboat Company,** 102 W. Broadway, Port Jefferson (© 631/473-0286; www.bpjferry.com), makes the 1¼-hour trip between Port Jefferson and Bridgeport, Connecticut, every 90 minutes from 6am to 9pm Monday through Thursday; Saturday service is similar, with one additional departure at 10pm; Fridays and Sundays have four more departures throughout the day. Car and driver one-way cost is $53, weekends and holidays $95, plus $15 per extra passenger; foot passengers $18; seniors $13; kids 12 and younger free. Reservations are strongly recommended, especially during summer holidays.

VISITOR INFORMATION   The **Long Island Convention & Visitors Bureau** (© 877/FUN-ON-LI (386-6654) or 631/951-3440; www.licvb.com) has an office at 330 Motor Pkwy., Ste. 203, Hauppauge. It's open Monday to Friday from 9am to 5pm; call, visit, or look online for all the info you can handle.

GETTING AROUND   A car is essential on Long Island. **Avis** (© 800/331-1212; www.avis.com) has offices in Massapequa, Huntington Station, Smithtown, Stony Brook, Lynbrook, Roslyn, Hicksville, Carle Place, Melville, New Hyde Park, Port Jefferson, and Port Washington; **Budget** (© 800/527-0700; www.budget.com) has offices in Farmingdale, Garden City, Hicksville, and Huntington Station; and **Hertz** (© 800/654-3131; www.hertz.com) has offices in Roslyn, New Hyde Park, Ronkonkoma, Great Neck, Huntington, West Hempstead, Middle Island, Lynbrook, Centereach, Syosset, East Northport, Farmingdale, and Hicksville.

Sports & Outdoor Pursuits

GOLF   The Red Course at **Eisenhower Park,** East Meadow (© 516/572-0327)—one of three 18-hole courses at Eisenhower Park—was home to the 1926 PGA Championship and was a stop for the PGA Seniors Tour in 2003. But it's a public course—so you can make your own history here, too. Greens fees are $22 to $64. Or bring your clubs to **Bethpage State Park,** 99 Quaker Meeting House Rd.,

Farmingdale (© **516/249-0700**), home to the 2002 and 2009 US Open. Greens fees here range from $18 to $48.

HITTING THE BEACH   Though the north shore shouldn't be your first choice for beaches—they tend to be rocky and rather small—there are a couple of nice ones that allow for swimming in the calm waters of Long Island Sound or for lounging on the sand. The beach in **Governor Alfred E. Smith/Sunken Meadow State Park,** Kings Park (© **631/269-4333**), is 3 miles of sand and surf with tall, glacier-formed bluffs at its western end (the park is also home to the **Sunken Meadow Golf Course**). Farther east, **Wildwood State Park,** in Wading River (© **631/929-4314**), has 2 miles of sandy beach trimmed by a lush hardwood forest.

SPECTATOR SPORTS   Long Island's only major pro sports team is the NHL's **New York Islanders,** who play 40 of their 80 games from October to April at the Nassau Veterans Memorial Coliseum in Uniondale (© **800/882-ISLE** [4753]; islanders.nhl.com).

Shopping

ANTIQUES   Route 25A is dotted with lots of little antiques stores, and you'll find a town full of them when you reach Port Jefferson. Along the way, there are a couple of standout villages.

Cold Spring Harbor is a picturesque little town with some nice places to shop. Of special note is the **Huntington Antiques Center,** 129 Main St. (© **631/549-0105;** huntingtonantiquescenter.com), where you'll find collections from about 20 dealers. There are lots of 18th- and early-19th-century items from England, France, and America, as well as an excellent collection of paintings, prints, and antique Oriental rugs. Farther west is **Giles Antiques** in Port Washington, at 287 Main St. (© **516/883-1104;** www.gilesantiques.com), with an impressive collection of 18th and 19th-century paintings, folk art, estate jewelry, and furniture.

Tiny **Locust Valley,** rarely even plotted on Long Island maps, is a favorite of Long Island antiques hunters in the know. **Oster-Jensen,** 86 Birch Hill Rd. (© **516/676-5454**), carries everything from American country–style antiques to furniture in Federal, English Georgian, and Regency styles. There's a host of smaller items as well. **Locust Valley Antiques,** 94 Forest Ave. (© **516/676-5000;** www.locustvalley antiques.com), boasts two large showrooms of European and Continental artwork and furniture. For a pleasant lunch break, grab one of the best burgers on Long Island at **Buckram Stables Café,** 31 Forest Ave. (© **516/671-3080**).

RETAIL   One of the most renowned shopping strips on the East Coast is the so-called Miracle Mile. The real name is the **Americana Manhasset,** 2060 Northern

 Getaway Trains

From June to October, the LIRR offers 1-day getaways from New York City, which include train fare, connecting bus or ferry fees (if necessary), and entrance fees to attractions. Some are specialty tours of Long Island Wine Country, for example, or the Montauk Lighthouse. Others are beach getaways to places like Fire Island. One caveat: Be sure to return on the same day, or you'll end up paying twice for the return ride. Visit **www.mta.info/lirr/getaways** for details.

Blvd., Manhasset (✆ **800/818-6767** or 516/627-2277; www.americanamanhasset. com), where you'll find such high-end retailers as Brooks Brothers, Tiffany & Co., Louis Vuitton, Burberry, and Prada, as well as the ubiquitous Banana Republic and Gap. Take a break for a fine lunch—salads, panini, and more—at **Cipollini** (✆ **516/ 627-7172;** www.cipollinirestaurant.com).

Gold Coast Mansions

Old Westbury Gardens ★★ Worshipers of formal gardens will be in heaven, and even casual nature lovers will adore the 210 landscaped and blooming acres of the former Phipps estate. Stroll among the wildflower-filled nooks, lilac-laden walkways, wide-open lawns, formal rose gardens, and meticulously maintained ponds—all in a constantly changing display of seasonal colors. Early spring is particularly beautiful, when the tulips and daffodils are in bloom. In summer, concerts, children's crafts, horticultural programs—even yoga and tai chi—can be found on the attraction's calendar of events. Step inside the property's gorgeous, Charles II–style mansion furnished with fine English antiques and decorative arts; except for the outdoor Café in the Woods, it's virtually unchanged from when the Phipps family lived here in the early 20th century.

71 Old Westbury Rd., Old Westbury. ✆ **516/333-0048.** www.oldwestburygardens.org. Admission $10 adults, $8 seniors 62 and over, $5 children 7–12, free for children 6 and under. Mid-Apr to late Oct Wed–Mon 10am–5pm; last vehicle allowed on property at 4pm. Take LIE exit 39 (Glen Cove Rd.). Follow the service road east for 1 mile, turn right onto Old Westbury Rd., and continue ⅔ mile. The gate is on the left. LIRR to Westbury; it's just a 2½-mile taxi ride from there.

Planting Fields Arboretum/Coe Hall ★★ This grand expanse of historic buildings and greenhouses, the former estate of Standard Oil heiress Mai Rogers Coe and insurance king William Robertson Coe, is one of the few Gold Coast properties to remain intact. As in its heyday of the 1920s, the 409 lush acres boast formal gardens, hiking trails, and two greenhouses with unique displays. The main building, Coe Hall, is a showy, 65-room Tudor Revival mansion that has many original pieces and furnishings, along with wood and stone carvings, stained-glass windows, and murals.

1395 Planting Fields Rd., Oyster Bay. ✆ **516/922-9200.** www.plantingfields.org. Grounds daily 9am–5pm; $8 parking fee daily Apr–Oct, other times weekends only. Coe Hall admission $3.50 adults, free for members and children 11 and under. Coe Hall guided tours daily Apr–Oct 12:30 and 2:30pm. LIE to exit 41N. Take Rte. 106 north into Oyster Bay. Left on Lexington Ave., left on Mill River Rd., and follow the signs. LIRR to Oyster Bay; it's a 1½-mile taxi ride.

Sagamore Hill ★★★ Theodore Roosevelt's testosterone-laden tribute to hunting, oak, and all things manly still stands on 100 gorgeous acres overlooking Long Island Sound. His 23-room Victorian estate, the so-called Summer White House from 1902 to 1908, has been preserved just the way he liked it—full of books, animal heads, skins, and exotic treasures—and visiting is a fun experience that also gives you some good historical insight. The home reflects his travels as a Rough Rider in Cuba, big-game hunter in East Africa, and fearless explorer in the Brazilian Amazon. You must take a guided tour, which leaves on the hour and lasts about an hour. On summer weekends, arrive early—tour tickets tend to sell out by afternoon.

Cove Neck Rd., Oyster Bay. ✆ **516/922-4788.** www.nps.gov/sahi. Admission $5 adults, free for children 15 and under. Daily tours of the house on the hour 10am–4pm. Grounds dawn–dusk. Labor Day to Memorial Day Wed–Sun only. LIE to exit 41 north (NY 106 north). Take 106 north to Oyster Bay and follow signs. LIRR to Oyster Bay or Syosset; it's a 3-mile taxi ride from Oyster Bay and 6 miles from Syosset, but it's easier to find cabs at the Syosset station.

Sands Point Preserve ★   You'll think you've died and gone to medieval Europe at this place. The castles on the grounds are a stunning display of extravagance and wealth from a different era. Created by Howard Gould—son of railroad tycoon Jay Gould—the 100,000-square-foot 1904 castle (Castle Gould) and 1912 Tudor-style manor (Hempstead House; residence of second owner, Daniel Guggenheim) sit on a gorgeous piece of property. Also on the 216-acre grounds is an extensive network of nature trails, as well as the beautiful Falaise, a Normandy-style manor house decked out in period furnishings, which was built by Harry F. Guggenheim in 1923.

If you're interested in hiking one of the six nature trails, bring a picnic lunch (you can't miss with a sandwich from **Best Bagels,** 40 Middle Neck Rd., Great Neck; ✆ **516/482-9860**) and make a day of it.

127 Middleneck Rd., Sands Point (Port Washington). ✆ **516/571-7900.** www.sandspointpreserve.org. $5 per car, $2 per walk-in, to visit the preserve Memorial Day to Labor Day (Wed free). Daily 9am–4:30pm. Call for off-season information. Falaise: June–Oct Thurs–Sun noon–3pm. Admission $5 adults and seniors. LIE to exit 36N, go straight 6 miles via Searingtown Rd., Port Washington Blvd., and Middleneck Rd. to entrance.

Vanderbilt Museum and Planetarium ★★ ☺   Judged solely on its name, this would appear to be built for grade-school kids on a science-class road trip. But in reality, the planetarium here was opened by the county merely to help sustain the amazing mansion and museum adjoining it in back. The real reason to come to William K. Vanderbilt II's 43-acre estate is to see the overly extravagant, 24-room Spanish Revival mansion, built in three stages from 1910 to 1936. Rooms exemplify his eclectic taste and amazing worldwide collection from the fields of art and science. Don't miss the Hall of Fish, a collection of aquatic species unknown in this part of the world during Vanderbilt's lifetime. Of course, there is a planetarium here, too—and its shows are great for kids. **Tip:** The installation of a new video and sound system in the planetarium is scheduled for completion in 2012; call to confirm the attraction's reopening.

180 Little Neck Rd., Centerport. ✆ **631/854-5555.** www.vanderbiltmuseum.org. $7 adults, $6 seniors and students, $3 children 11 and under for general admission; planetarium show and mansion tour $5 each. Tues and Fri noon–4pm, Sat 11am–5pm, Sun noon–5pm; call for fall and winter hours and for planetarium schedule. LIE to exit 51, go north on Deer Park Ave., bear left at the fork onto Park Ave. At 3rd light, turn right onto Broadway, continue for 5 miles to Rte. 25A. Cross 25A (to left of Shell gas station), and you're on Little Neck Rd.

More Museums & Attractions

Heckscher Museum of Art ★   This small Beaux Arts museum houses an impressive and wide-ranging collection, which includes more than 1,800 paintings, sculptures, and other works ranging from Egyptian artifacts to Renaissance art to the noted collection from the Hudson River and Long Island landscape schools. Exhibitions have included works by notable photographers like Edward Weston and Ansel Adams, and artists as varied as Robert Rauschenberg, Georgia O'Keeffe, and Fairfield Porter.

2 Prime Ave., Huntington. ✆ **631/351-3250.** www.heckscher.org. Admission $8 adults, $6 seniors, $4 students 10 and over, free for children 9 and under; reduced admission for local residents. Wed–Fri 10am–4pm; Sat–Sun 11am–5pm; 1st Fri of month until 8:30pm. LIE to exit 49N, take Rte. 110N into Huntington, turn right on 25A, make a left at the 1st light. LIRR to Huntington; it's a 3-mile taxi ride.

John P. Humes Japanese Stroll Garden ★★ 📷   This serene Japanese garden is a wonderful refuge from the frenzied world, a truly surprising sanctuary set amid 4 acres of deep woodland. Step through the gate and you'll be awash in *yamazato*—the transcendent feeling of a remote mountain hideout. Follow the trail, a symbolic path to enlightenment that takes you past a lake garden, 40-foot tall Chinese bamboo, ferns, and moss, as well as the shrubs and rocks that are essential to imperial garden design. The garden is the dream child of Ambassador Humes, who was inspired by a 1960 visit to Kyoto, Japan. Make a reservation for a guided tour, which includes a tea ceremony, held just a couple of Saturdays per month; other special events include performances of *shakuhachi* (bamboo flute), ikebana flower-arranging exhibits, and a chrysanthemum show each autumn.

Oyster Bay Rd. and Dogwood Lane, Mill Neck. (ⓒ 516/676-4486. Admission $7 adults, free for children 11 and under; $12 for tour with tea ceremony. Apr to late Oct Sat–Sun 11:30am–4:30pm. LIE to exit 39N to Northern Blvd., turn right and go 3 miles to Wolver Hollow Rd., turn left to end, turn right on Chicken Valley Rd.; go 1¾ miles to Dogwood Lane, turn right.

Nassau County Museum of Art ★★   One of the finest suburban art museums in the nation, this notable collection sits on 145 acres in a Georgian mansion once owned by steel baron Henry Clay Frick. Today, there's a wide variety of artwork to peruse. The permanent collection has more than 600 works of 19th- and 20th-century European and American artists like Edouard Vuillard, Roy Lichtenstein, Frank Stella, and Auguste Rodin. You'll also find an ever-changing schedule of exhibits, along with formal gardens and an outdoor sculpture area that are glorious to walk through on a nice day. The museum's Art Space for Children and their "Family Sundays at the Museum" programs, which feature a wide range of interactive exhibits, highlight their commitment to education.

1 Museum Dr., Roslyn Harbor. (ⓒ **516/484-9337.** www.nassaumuseum.com. Admission $10 adults, $8 seniors, $4 children and students, free for children 3 and under; reduced admissions to Art Space for Children only. Tues–Sun 11am–4:45pm. LIE to exit 39, go north 2 miles to Northern Blvd. (Rte. 25A) and turn left. At the 2nd light turn right. LIRR to Roslyn; it's a 2-mile taxi ride.

Walt Whitman Birthplace   You don't have to be a *Leaves of Grass* fan to enjoy this famous poet's birthplace, a tiny historic home built by Whitman's father in 1810 that looks oddly out of place in the heart of strip mall country. Though Whitman left here at an early age, Long Island was always home for him. An interpretative center has a good collection of his manuscripts and photographs, and a chronology of his career as journalist, editor, and Civil War correspondent, along with recordings of Whitman reading his own work. The home looks much as it did when Whitman was born in 1819, though it has been outfitted with replacement furniture; a barn on the site has been renovated (using its original plank wood) and is now used for meetings, exhibits, and environmental education.

246 Old Walt Whitman Rd., West Hills. (ⓒ **631/427-5240.** www.waltwhitman.org. Admission $5 adults, $4 seniors, free for children 4 and under. Mid-June to Labor Day Mon–Fri 11am–4pm, Sat–Sun 11am–5pm; Labor Day to mid-June Wed–Fri 1–4pm, Sat–Sun 11am–4pm. LIE to exit 49N, north 1¾ miles, turn left on Old Walt Whitman Rd.

Where to Stay

If you are looking to bunk in a place with lots of dining and nightlife options, Port Jefferson (locally known as "Port Jeff") puts you smack in the middle of the action, with restaurants, bars, and shops aplenty, most within walking distance. For chain hotels within easy reach of the Gold Coast, try **Holiday Inn Express,** 3131 Nesconset Hwy., Stony Brook (ⓒ **631/471-8000;** stonybrookny.hiexpress.com); **Hampton Inn,** 680 Commack Rd., Commack (ⓒ **631/462-5700**); and the **Hilton,** 598 Broad Hollow Rd., Melville (ⓒ **631/845-1000**).

SUNDAY driving

Once you get past the traffic-clogged areas close to the city, there are quite a few charming villages sprinkled along the North Shore's many scenic little peninsulas. Not all the towns claim huge Vanderbilt mansions or sprawling gardens, but they still are great places to take a drive. **Sea Cliff** began as a Methodist summer campground in 1871 and now boasts some two dozen homes on the National Register of Historic Places (as well as 900 structures built before World War II). Come to walk the steep streets and admire the Victorian, Queen Anne, and Craftsman homes with their gingerbread porches and Gothic gables. Grab a bite at the charming sidewalk cafe **Once Upon a Moose,** 304 Sea Cliff Ave. (© 516/676-9304), then stop by Memorial Park for spectacular sunsets over the water. **Locust Valley,** named after its towering

locust trees, is a very cute small town (just 1 sq. mile) full of great antiques shops and boutiques and is one of Long Island's best-kept secrets. **Cold Spring Harbor** ★ is another antiques-filled haven right on the water; Route 25A takes you through town and offers some gorgeous water views. Stop in at the **Whaling Museum** ★, Main Street (© 631/367-3418; www.cshwhaling museum.org), then walk the length of Main Street (it's only ¼ mile) and admire some of the structures dating back to the days when whaling was the backbone of industry here. **Port Jefferson** is a bustling town on the water, full of restaurants, antiques shops, marinas, and cute storefronts. It's also a docking point for one of the Connecticut ferries, so it's constantly in motion, especially in the summer.

For a touch of luxury, also consider the stylish **Inn at Great Neck,** 30 Cutter Mill Rd., Great Neck (© **516/773-2000;** www.innatgreatneck.com), a 1920s-themed hotel with modern amenities and a terrific upscale restaurant.

EXPENSIVE

Danfords Hotel & Marina ★★★ A sprawling resort right on Long Island Sound (and conveniently located in happening downtown Port Jeff), Danfords is its own Colonial New England–style village, imbued with a nautical theme. The spacious quarters are done up in navy blue and gold tones and come outfitted with comfy armchairs, mahogany furniture, flatscreen TVs, and granite spa bathrooms. Get a room with a view of the Port Jefferson harbor and it will be filled with light; balcony rooms let you take in the sea air. Wave restaurant serves up New American food, and its cocktail lounge is about as swanky as it gets in Port Jeff—though the crowd still skews older, as in "festive wedding-goers."

25 E. Broadway, Port Jefferson, NY 11777. www.danfords.com. © **800/332-6367** or 631/928-5200. Fax 631/928-9082. 86 units. Apr–Oct $139-$339 double, $359-$559 suite; Nov–Mar $139-$289 double, $329-$499 suite. Weekend packages available. AE, DC, DISC, MC, V. **Amenities:** Restaurant; lounge; exercise room; limited room service; spa. *In room:* A/C, TV, hair dryer, kitchenette (in some rooms), MP3 docking stations, Wi-Fi.

The Three Village Inn ★★ You may have to duck to get through some of the doorways in this charming 1750s country inn, set right on the harbor. That, of course, is just the point. With the exposed beams, narrow hallways, and antiques, you'll feel like you're padding around in your grandmother's attic. The rooms, all smoke-free, aren't huge, but they're comfy and decked out in understated pastels. Cottages give you a bit more space and some have extras you won't find in the inn, such as stone fireplaces and water views. The two excellent on-site restaurants, Mirabelle and the more affordable Mirabelle Tavern—both of which opened here in 2009—serve delicious French bistro–inspired comfort food.

150 Main St., Stony Brook, NY 11790. www.threevillageinn.com. ✆ **631/751-0555.** Fax 631/751-0593. 26 units. $129–$250 double Sun–Thurs; $179–$350 double Fri–Sat. Rates include hot breakfast. AE, DISC, MC, V. LIE to exit 62; north 10 miles to Rte. 25A; left 1½ miles at HISTORIC STONY BROOK sign to Main St.; right ½ mile to the inn. **Amenities:** 2 restaurants; lounge. *In room:* A/C, TV, hair dryer, MP3 docking stations, Wi-Fi.

MODERATE

Swan View Manor   Right across the street from Cold Spring Harbor—and down the road from the restaurants and shops of the pleasant old whaling town—this bed-and-breakfast's main house is a beautiful historic home. However, most of the rooms, all smoke-free, are in the single-story motel section that is oddly furnished with quasi antiques. Though the floral and lace designs and friendly staff make it a welcoming place to stay, the rooms are quite worn, and the traffic rolling by right outside your door means you shouldn't come searching for a quiet getaway. Still, room nos. 17 and 18—in the inn itself—are the quietest.

45 Harbor Rd., Cold Spring Harbor, NY 11724. www.swanview.com. ✆ **631/367-2070.** 19 units. May–Oct weekdays $145–$205 double, weekends $165–$225 double; Nov–Apr weekdays $132–$192 double, weekends $147–$207 double. Rates include continental breakfast. AE, DISC, MC, V. *In room:* A/C, TV.

Where to Eat

The acclaimed **Mirabelle,** which reopened in 2009 at the Three Village Inn, 150 Main St., Stony Brook (✆ **631/751-0555**), continues to serve some of the island's finest upscale French cuisine. The pubby, atmospheric **Canterbury Ales Oyster Bar & Grill,** 46 Audrey Ave., Oyster Bay (✆ **516/922-3614;** www.canterburyales restaurant.com), is the perfect place for a beer and a burger—and, of course, fresh oysters. For friendly roadside dining—and lobster rolls—try **The Shack,** 1 Stony Hollow Rd., Centerport (✆ **631/754-8989;** www.theshack.org).

EXPENSIVE

The Fifth Season ★★★ NEW AMERICAN   Relocated in 2008 from Greenport, Port Jefferson's newest dining destination is also one of Long Island's best. The chef/owners take tremendous pride in selecting only the freshest seasonal ingredients from local farmers and Long Island waters, and their exquisite attention to detail is also evident in the excellent service. Mouthwatering menu standouts include Maryland crab cakes with fennel pollen anglaise, American Kobe beef burger with jicama slaw, and the pan-seared organic salmon with coconut-ginger sauce. Also, the lobster bisque is spot on. Get a table on the porch, order a glass of wine from the well-edited list, and your summer evening will be near perfect.

34 E. Broadway, Port Jefferson. ✆ **631/477-8500.** www.thefifth-season.com. Reservations recommended. Main courses dinner $13–$30, lunch $8–$17. AE, DISC, MC, V. Lunch/brunch daily 11am–4pm, dinner begins at 5pm.

La Plage ★★ 🍴 NEW AMERICAN   This French-inflected New American bistro might be a bit difficult to find, but its out-of-the-way location—at the end of a long road, across the street from the ocean—makes it seem like a secret hideaway. It's hard not to feel romantic here, especially if you dine on the patio while the sun sets, with the salty sea air blowing in from the sandy shore. The appetizers are simple but inspired—try the spring pea and mint ravioli with spicy lamb sausage ragú. The meticulously prepared entrees are equally delicious, including Yukon gold potato–encrusted halibut, or the Long Island duck breast with sour-orange purée. Arrive early to avoid the crowds.

131 Creek Rd., Wading River. © **631/744-9200.** www.laplagerestaurant.net. Reservations requested. Main courses dinner $29–$36; prix-fixe lunch $25. AE, MC, V. Mon–Sat noon–3pm; Mon–Thurs 4–9pm; Fri–Sat 4–10pm; Sun 2–9pm. Labor Day to Memorial Day closed Mon–Tues. LIE to exit 68, go north to Rte. 25A, go east ¾ mile, turn left on Randall Rd., turn right on North Country Rd., at stop sign turn left on Sound Rd., then left onto Creek Rd.

Peter Luger ★★★ STEAKHOUSE "Wow" is the only word that comes to mind when you bite into Luger's porterhouse. This famous steakhouse (the only other location of the Brooklyn landmark) deserves its reputation as one of America's best—they take meat seriously and they do it right. The porterhouse is what you want—dry aged, brushed with a delicious glaze, and served up straightforward, just the way you want it cooked. A word of caution: They don't take credit cards, so bring lots of cash (or a debit card).

255 Northern Blvd., Great Neck. © **516/487-8800.** www.peterluger.com. Reservations recommended. Steak for 2 $85; other entrees $32–$41. No credit cards. Mon–Thurs 11:45am–9:45pm; Fri–Sat 11:45am–10:45pm; Sun 12:45–9:45pm. LIE to exit 33, Lakeville Rd., then left onto Northern Blvd.

MODERATE

Kitchen A Bistro ★★ NEW AMERICAN This much-loved restaurant has attracted a cultlike following, and for good reason; consistently good food is created daily by the innovative chef/owner who takes his fare seriously. Appetizers include a house-made cavatelli with ragú bianco; for dinner, try the sake-braised short rib of beef with French lentils, or the bronzini with eggplant, chorizo, and piquillo peppers. A prix-fixe four-course dinner with wine pairings offers an excellent introduction to this North Shore favorite (lunch is also available prix-fixe). *Tip:* Credit cards not accepted.

404 N. Country Rd., St. James. © **631/862-0151.** http://kitchenabistro.com. Reservations required weekends. Lunch $13–$25; dinner $9–$26. Lunch noon–2pm; dinner 5:30–9:30pm. No credit cards. Located on Rte. 25A/N. Country Rd., just 100 ft. east of Edgewood Ave.

INEXPENSIVE

Tim's Shipwreck Diner ★ DINER For a real down-home vintage diner experience, it doesn't get much better than this. With its classic railroad dining car setting, truly friendly servers (yes, some might call you "hon"), and excellent eggs, pancakes, blintzes, hash browns, and treats like crab-cake eggs Benedict—plus freebies like yummy cornbread and jam, and inventive specials—you'll wonder why all diners can't be exactly like this one. *Tip:* It gets crowded with locals on weekend mornings, so show up early or plan on a brief wait.

46 Main St., Northport. © **631/754-1797.** Lunch $8–$15; breakfast $5–$15. AE, MC, V. Daily 7am–3pm.

The North Shore After Dark

There are a couple of outstanding places for music and other live events. The **Tilles Center,** 720 Northern Blvd., Brookville (© **516/299-3100;** www.tillescenter.org), part of the C. W. Post Campus of Long Island University, boasts a 2,242-seat hall and more than 70 events each season (Sept–June) in music, dance, and theater. Everyone from the Alvin Ailey Dance Theater to James Taylor has performed there. The **NYCB Theatre at Westbury,** 960 Brush Hollow Rd., Westbury (© **516/334-0800;** www. livenation.com), hosts musicians that generally appeal to an older crowd, such as Tom Jones, Pat Benatar, Bobby Vinton, and Frankie Valli. Catch big-name concerts (such as Justin Timberlake, Rihanna, and Britney Spears) and family shows like *Sesame Street Live* at the **Nassau Veterans Memorial Coliseum,** 1255 Hempstead Tpk., Uniondale (✆ **516/794-9300;** nassaucoliseum.com). One bar worth noting: **Chesterfields,** 330 New York Ave., Huntington (✆ **631/425-1457;** chesterfieldsblues.20fr. com), which serves up comedy acts and live music, especially blues and jazz.

THE NORTH FORK ★★

As you head east on Long Island, the land splits in two like a horizontal "V." While the southern fork is dominated by the Hamptons' summer playground, the North Fork is a decidedly different experience. Once you drive past the gateway town of Riverhead, you'll discover a calmer world—one where you can stay right on the beach for less than a king's ransom, while surrounded by some of the finest vineyards in the state.

Most of the tiny, New England–style villages dotting this narrow strip of land are quiet and unpretentious, cheerfully avoiding the bustle—and the attitude—of their southern cousins. Small shops pop up in clusters, farm stands dot the main roads, and a wine tasting is the closest thing to a celebrity drinking binge. The overall pace out here is relaxed and casual: Loll away a lazy afternoon browsing through antiques stores in Southold, or head out to the end of the line at Orient Point for kayaking and birdwatching. Want to spend the day (or a few) just fishing? You've come to the right place.

There isn't nearly the range of lodging, shopping, and dining options here as you'll find elsewhere on Long Island, but activity has been picking up steadily over the past few years. Excellent restaurants like the **North Fork Table & Inn** have created a stir in culinary circles, while places like the **Jedediah Hawkins Inn** now offer more in the way of upscale accommodations. And though it's still no resort destination, the North Fork also boasts summer weekend traffic to compete with the worst of the Hamptons—plan your driving times wisely.

Essentials

GETTING THERE   The **Long Island Expressway** runs to Riverhead; from there, take Route 25 East. The **Long Island Rail Road** (✆ **516/822-LIRR** [5477]) stops in Riverhead, Mattituck, Southold, and Greenport. The **Hampton Jitney** (✆ **631/283-4600;** www.hamptonjitney.com) provides bus service from multiple locations in New York City to 12 stops between Riverhead and Orient Point for $22 one-way, $40 round-trip. **Long Island MacArthur Airport** (✆ **631/467-3210;** www.macarthurairport.com), situated mid–Long Island, is the closest airport and is served by the airlines mentioned in "Getting There," earlier in this chapter. From Connecticut, take the **Cross Sound Ferry** (✆ **631/323-2525;** www.longisland ferry.com), which sails from New London, Connecticut, to Orient Point, New York. Schedules change daily, leaving 8 to 22 times a day—there's also an express passenger-only service (no cars); adult one-way fares range from $15 to $68.

VISITOR INFORMATION   Tourist information booths are located on Main Road in the towns of Laurel (✆ **631/298-5757**) and Greenport (✆ **631/477-1383**), but are open only during summer (scattered hours in other seasons). You can also contact the **Long Island Convention & Visitors Bureau** (✆ **877/FUN-ON-LI** [386-6654] or 631/951-3440; www.licvb.com).

GETTING AROUND   A car is helpful if you plan to shop, visit wineries, hit the beaches, or just explore, but be warned: The traffic in summer can be a nightmare. If you'd prefer to relax, the train is the better option.

Just Ducky

Long Island is famous for its duck, but you won't likely come across any duck farms out here—in fact, the landmark 20-foot-tall Big Duck statue (on Rte. 24 at the Flanders/Hampton Bays border) is probably the only duck you'll see. So what gives? Well, there used to be many farms, but the smell drove residents to shut them down. Now they've been reduced to just a couple of farms, providing ducks to only a few select restaurants. Anyone else who calls it Long Island duck is just a quack (. . . *groan*).

Beaches & Outdoor Pursuits

BEACHES There are lots of beaches out here, but be sure to check for signs, as many are permit-only. With more than 8 miles of sandy shore, **Orient Beach State Park,** Orient Point (✆ 631/323-2440), offers plenty of breathing room, kayak rentals in summer, and a maritime forest of red cedar and prickly-pear cactus. Two permit-only beaches worth checking out are **Norman Klipp Marine Park**—aka Gull Pond Beach—in Greenport, and **Town Beach** in Southold, which is a popular family beach. **South Jamesport Beach** (✆ 631/727-5744; www.riverheadli.com) is another kid-friendly beach, with 3,000 feet of shoreline on Peconic Bay. Pick up your permit from the attendant at either beach (after 10am): It's $10 for a daily nonresident pass.

BIKING With its serene country roads, bucolic surroundings, and flat terrain, the North Fork is great for biking, especially the region around Orient. Rent a bike for $5 an hour at **Orient Beach State Park** (✆ 631/323-2440), and explore the thick forests, marshes, and beautiful beaches of this quiet area on the tip of the North Fork.

BIRDING All the way out at the end of Route 25, **Orient Point County Park** (✆ 631/854-4949) offers 48 acres and a mile of beach, and is home to ospreys, piping plovers, and more. It's also a great place for an early morning or late afternoon hike, or a casual day of beachcombing.

BOATING A fun way to check out Greenport is aboard the *Glory,* a 30-foot fantail launch decked out in varnished mahogany and brass. (Ever proud of its environmental friendliness, this silent, electric-powered boat is the first Coast Guard–inspected tour boat operating by solar power.) It sails all afternoon from Memorial Day to Columbus Day; $18 for adults, $15 for seniors, $5 for kids. Go to Preston's Dock at the foot of Main Street in Greenport, or call ✆ 631/477-2515 (www.greenport launch.com) for details. You can also be your own captain: Canoeing or kayaking on the inlets, creeks, and marshes is a great way to see herons, osprey, hawks, fish, and turtles. Rent from **Eagle's Neck Paddling Company,** 49295 Main Rd., Southold (✆ 631/765-3502; www.eaglesneck.com). Rentals start at $35 for 2 hours; daily and weekly rates are also available.

FARM STANDS You know you've reached the North Fork when the malls fade away and farm stands crop up in their stead. Take advantage of the local bounty: From tomatoes, strawberries, and sweet corn in the summer to pumpkins and apples in the fall, get your produce at **Harbes Family Farms,** 715 Sound Ave., Route 48, Mattituck (✆ 631/298-0800; www.harbesfamilyfarm.com), where pig races, a hedge maze, and other family fun make this a mecca for families with children.

Although Long Island's North Fork is not yet in the same viticultural league as, say, Napa Valley, the region's reputation as a producer of high-quality wines has been steadily growing. Since the first winery set up shop here in the 1970s, this sleepy former potato-farming community has been transformed into a vibrant wine district, producing vintages that appear on world-renowned wine lists.

With Long Island Sound to the north, Peconic Bay to the south, and the Atlantic Ocean to the east, the region benefits from the moderating effects of the surrounding waters. (It's also the sunniest part of New York State.) In fact, the North Fork's maritime climate is often compared to that of Bordeaux, France.

Merlot, the most heavily planted varietal in the region, ripens beautifully and reliably here, but growing conditions are ideal for chardonnay as well. Cabernet franc, cabernet sauvignon, Riesling, and sauvignon blanc have also been performing well.

The North Fork is now home to some 30 vineyards, ranging in size from 2 to 600 acres and yielding a half-million cases annually. While the region does have its fair share of visitors, it still maintains its tranquil, bucolic charms and makes for an excellent day (or more) of wine touring and tasting.

If you plan to make several stops, designate a driver, or opt for the swirl-sniff-sip-spit approach. Better still, schedule one of the services that you can hire for a day of sampling. **Vintage Tours** (*©* **631/765-4689;** www.vintage tour1.com) offers guided wine tours that include lunch, pickup and drop-off service, and transport in a 14-person van ($80 per person weekends, $70 on weekdays). Or tour the vineyards on a trolley with the **North Fork Trolley Company** (*©* **631/369-3031;** www.north forktrolley.com); a three-vineyard tour is $69, including lunch. **Adventure Cycles & Sports** (*©* **516/755-BIKE** [2453]; www.gorideabike.com) runs 5-hour bike tours that include a gourmet picnic lunch, tastings at three vineyards, and 16 miles of gentle cycling ($145 per person).

Wineries are marked with a green and white **wine trail** sign. Here are some highlights (call or visit their websites for more information about tastings, hours, and special events):

o **Bedell Cellars** This includes three vineyards: Bedell Cellars, Corey Creek Vineyard, and Wells Road Vineyard. Known for its excellent merlot, Bedell also produces cabernet franc, chardonnay, Gewürztraminer, viognier, a late-harvest Riesling, and several blends, one of which was recently awarded 91 points by *Wine Spectator*. 36225 Main Rd., Cutchogue (*©* **631/734-7537;** www.bedellcellars.com).

o **Castello di Borghese Vineyard & Winery** The founding vineyard of the Long Island estate wine industry, Castello di Borghese (formerly Hargrave Vineyards, est. 1973), is best known for successfully growing the notoriously finicky pinot noir grape. Special events here include vineyard tours, chocolate and wine-tasting programs—and even a 4-day wine camp for adults. Don't miss the wonderful gift shop. Route 48, Alvah's Lane, Cutchogue (*©* **631/734-5111;** www.castello diborghese.com).

- **The Lenz Winery** One of the oldest wineries on the East End, yielding chardonnays, merlots, Gewürztraminer, and cabernet sauvignon, plus a pinot noir that spends 7 years *sur lie* (French for "on the lees" [or settled yeast cells]), a key element in quality in a traditional method sparkling wine, adding complexity. "Old Vines" merlot is produced here, from some of the oldest merlot vineyards found in North America. Main Road, Peconic (✆ 631/734-6010; www.lenzwine.com).

- **Martha Clara Vineyards** A new kid on the North Fork block, with an inviting barnlike tasting room and patio, friendly staff, and art galleries, this is also an excellent place for families to visit, as there are horse and carriage rides, educational seminars, and dog-friendly tours. A wide variety of reds and whites are produced here, along with sparkling and dessert wines. 6025 Sound Ave., Riverhead (✆ 631/298-0075; www. marthaclaravineyards.com).

- **The Old Field** Amid a shady grove, this 150-year-old family farm makes for a pleasant visit. Taste some of their delightful wines—merlot, cabernet franc, chardonnay, pinot noir blush, the smooth Rooster Tail blend, and sparkling wine—and take a walking tour to learn about their sustainable practices, listen to some live music, or check out their minimuseum. 59600 Main Rd., Southold (✆ 631/765-2465; www.theoldfield.com).

- **Palmer Vineyards** One of the oldest wineries on the North Fork, Palmer has an attractive English-pub-style tasting room and a wooden deck overlooking the 55 acres of their highly acclaimed merlot, chardonnay, cabernet franc, pinot blanc, Gewürztraminer, and cabernet sauvignon varietals. Proprietor tours with a wine-tasting session are also available on seasonal weekends. 108 Sound Ave., Aquebogue (✆ 631/722-9463; www.paumanok.com).

- **Pellegrini Vineyards** Pellegrini's beautiful setting—an inviting tasting room, with high ceilings and exposed beams, and a lovely courtyard—is matched only by their excellent wines. Combining old-world winemaking techniques with state-of-the-art equipment, Pellegrini produces award-winning merlot, chardonnay, cabernet sauvignon, and cabernet franc, along with a rose and ice wine. 23005 Main Rd., Cutchogue (✆ 631/734-4111; www.pellegrinivineyards.com).

- **Shinn Estate Vineyards** Owned by the former proprietors of New York's Home restaurant, Shinn produces 13 delicious wines—including merlot, cabernet sauvignon, cabernet franc, chardonnay, rose, and two delightful blends. Take a tour to learn more about their low-impact farming practices. Better still, reserve one of the sunny, beautiful guest rooms at their on-site bed-and-breakfast. 2000 Oregon Rd., Mattituck (✆ 631/804-0367; www.shinnestate vineyards.com).

Another favorite is historic **Wickham's Fruit Farm,** Route 25, Cutchogue (© **631/734-6441;** www.wickhamsfruitfarm.com), where their cider is the stuff of legend. (*Note:* They're closed Sun.) **Briermere Farms,** 4414 Sound Ave., Riverhead (© **631/722-3931;** www.briermere.com), is also famous for its divine selection of fruit-filled pies, from raspberry cherry to blueberry cream. The rhubarb squares are not to be missed.

FISHING   There is fantastic fishing out here, with many boats geared toward the novice caster. Fluke, bluefish, and enormous sea bass abound, along with flounder, tuna, and shark. The season generally runs from April or May to October, and local captains will set you up with bait and tackle. Good bets are **Captain Bob'**s fleet in Mattituck (© **631/298-5522;** www.captbobfishingfleet.com), or the Peconic Star Fleet with **Capt. Dave Brennan** in Greenport (© **631/289-6899;** www.peconic star.com); expect to pay around $70 to $75 per adult for a full day. If you want to go it alone, contact the **Southold Town Clerk'**s office (© **631/765-1800;** http://southoldtown.northfork.net), **Warren's Bait & Tackle** in Aquebogue (© **631/722-4898**), or **Jamesport Bait & Tackle** in Mattituck (© **631/298-5450**) for beach-fishing permits.

GOLF   While there are several private courses in the North Fork, public links are another story—choices are limited. Try **Cherry Creek Golf Links,** 900 Reeves Ave., Riverhead (© **631/369-6500;** www.cherrycreeklinks.com), which has 18 holes and a driving range; greens fees range from $15 to $65. To work on your chipping and putting, head to 9-hole **Cedars Golf Club,** Cases Lane, Cutchogue (© **631/734-6363**). The semiprivate **Island's End Golf & Country Club,** 5025 Rte. 25, Greenport (© **631/477-0777;** islandsendgolf.com), welcomes public players (if they adhere to their no–T-shirts dress code); greens fees range from $25 to $60.

WINERIES   Long Island's wine industry is young but growing fast. It turns out that the climate—and the well-drained, sandy soil—on the North Fork is ideal for grapes; several vineyards are now producing world-class wines. See box below.

Shopping

The North Fork is an old seafaring world, full of antiques shops, gift stores, and art galleries. Greenport and Southold (and to a lesser extent, Jamesport) have the best selection of stores on the North Fork. You'll find a wealth of stained-glass lamps and handmade furnishings at **Lydia's Antiques and Stained Glass,** 215 Main St., Greenport (© **631/477-1414**). **Jan Davis Antiques,** 45395 Main Rd., Southold (© **631/765-2379**), set in a country store that dates to the 1850s, sells antiques and

---

Custer Observatory

City slickers from New York City, Boston, and elsewhere often forget that night skies near the ocean—where there is no "light pollution"—are often a-twinkle with millions of stars, planets, and other celestial bodies. **Custer Observatory** is Long Island's oldest public observatory (since 1927), and welcomes visitors every Saturday evening from 7pm 'til midnight. Concerts, lectures, film screenings, art exhibits, and other events make this an interesting place to visit even when the weather doesn't cooperate. Call **631/765-2626,** or visit http://custer observatory.org for details.

Family Fun

Looking for a rainy-day activity? See sea lions, clownfish, moray eels, and sharks up close at **Atlantis Marine World**, 431 E. Main St., Riverhead (✆ 631/208-9200; www.atlantis marineworld.com), open year-round 10am to 5pm. The aquarium's daily schedule is jam-packed with feedings, shows, and interactive events, and it's not just about the fish—an Amazon aviary and a penguin petting area are among their attractions. General admission tickets are $23 for adults, $20 seniors and kids ages 3 to 17. Another treat here is the 90-minute boat tour on the *Atlantis Explorer* that highlights the ecological wonders of the Peconic River. Tours depart daily, weather permitting.

collectible dolls. **Three Sisters Antiques,** 1550 Main Rd., Jamesport (✆ 631/722-5980), specializes in linens, postcards, and paper, but you'll also find glass, china, kitchenware, books, and artwork. **Winter Harbor Gallery,** 211 Main St., Greenport (✆ 631/477-0010; www.winterharborgallery.com), is the place for original paintings, hand-turned wood items, and one-of-a-kind photography. And **Jet's Dream,** 212 Main St., Greenport (✆ 631/477-0039; www.jetsdream.com), is the area's premier purveyor of green and sustainable gifts, accessories, and personal care products. Perhaps the single biggest shopping destination in the area—if not the most original—is the enormous **Tanger Outlet Center,** 200 Tanger Mall Dr., Riverhead (✆ 631/369-2732; www.tangeroutlet.com), where you'll find the usual assortment of name-brand shops and outlet stores.

Museums

Horton Point Lighthouse ★   Dating back to 1857, this active lighthouse is now home to a small museum of lighthouse and marine artifacts. The surrounding 8-acre park hugs the coast and offers a broad view of the Long Island Sound. Bring lunch along with you—the tables in the park make for a great picnic spot.

Lighthouse Rd., Southold. ✆ 631/765-5500. www.southoldparkdistrict.com. $5 parking fee. Grounds daily. Museum: Memorial Day to Columbus Day Sat-Sun 11:30am–4pm. From Rte. 48, make a left onto Young Ave., a right onto Old North Rd., then a left onto Lighthouse Rd.

Indian Museum ★   Take an hour on a Sunday afternoon to stop by here and discover some of Long Island's Native American history. The exhibits provide an interesting look into the lives of local tribes, with displays of arrowheads, blades, pipes, tools, toys, fishing tackle, clothing, and other artifacts from the region—including the largest collection of Algonquin pottery you'll likely encounter.

1080 Main Bayview Rd., Southold. ✆ 631/765-5577. www.southoldindianmuseum.org. $4 suggested donation for adults, $2 for kids. Sun 1:30–4:30pm and by appointment.

Where to Stay

Don't expect to see big hotels or resorts on the North Fork. Instead, you'll find many motor inn–style spots dating from the 1950s; thankfully, the increased tourism of recent years has inspired some of these owners to renovate. One of the benefits of this part of the East End: You can actually stay right on the waterfront without remortgaging your own home.

You'll also find some fine B&Bs. In addition to the choices below, consider a stay at the light-drenched **Shinn Estate Farmhouse,** a 19th-century inn with modern decor and amenities, located on the Shinn Estate Vineyard, 2000 Oregon Rd., Mattituck (www.shinnfarmhouse.com; ☎ **631/804-0367**), or the waterfront **Stirling House,** 104 Bay Ave., Greenport (☎ **631/477-0654**). **Freddy's House,** 1535 New Suffolk Rd., Cutchogue (☎ **631/734-4180**), is a fully restored 18th-century farmhouse located on a working family-run farm. If you're in the market for a budget motel, try the old-school roadside **Drosso's Motel,** 69125 Main Rd., Greenport (www.drossosmotel.com; ☎ **631/477-1334**). While it's not on the water, it's a friendly place with an attached miniature golf course and outdoor snack bar.

VERY EXPENSIVE

Jedediah Hawkins Inn ★★★   This 1860s Victorian mansion was saved from the wrecking ball in 2004 and opened as an inn the following year. It has since become the ne plus ultra for luxe accommodations on the North Fork. The place has been beautifully restored, and it comes with a tranquil setting, a fantastic restaurant (reviewed below), and light-drenched, comfortable rooms equipped with flatscreen TVs, gas fireplaces, and Frette linens. The decor is a tasteful blend of modern and antique furnishings, yet each room has its own distinct personality. I love the fresh, airy feel of the Sage Room, but the Belvedere suite on the top floor is the real stunner: exposed brick, angled ceilings, inviting cushions lining the room, and its very own perch up a spiral staircase, where you sit and enjoy a drink, or peer through the telescope off toward the bay.

400 S. Jamesport Ave., Jamesport, NY 11947. www.jedediahhawkinsinn.com. ☎ **631/722-2900.** Fax 631/722-2901. 6 units. $250–$450 double; $600–$695 suite. Rates include hot continental breakfast. 2-night minimum on all weekends. AE, MC, V. **Amenities:** Restaurant, small fitness center, bikes. *In room:* A/C, TV, DVD, hair dryer, Wi-Fi.

EXPENSIVE

Arbor View B&B ★★   Instead of going with the expected antique look, these affable innkeepers opted for a muted decor that leans more toward the sophisticated than the rustic. All rooms are named for grapes, and are decorated to match the color—Champagne, Rose, Merlot. It's located on the main drag, so you'll likely hear some traffic, but not enough to be a deal breaker. The nicest room, the Zinfandel, boasts a gorgeous four-poster bed, but is downstairs right next to the entrance—choose another room if you're sensitive to noise.

8900 Main Rd., East Marion, NY 11939. www.arborviewhouse.com. ☎ **800/963-8777** or 631/477-8440. Call for fax. 4 units. June–Oct $275–$299 double midweek, $285–$315 double weekend; Nov–May $235–$255 double midweek, $255–$275 double weekend. Rates include full breakfast. 2-night minimum on weekends. AE, MC, V. **Amenities:** Spa services available. *In room:* A/C, TV/DVD/CD player, fax, hair dryer, MP3 docking station (in some), no phone, Wi-Fi.

Orient Inn ★★★   We love the look of this turn-of-the-20th-century Arts and Crafts–style shingle house in the tranquil hamlet of Orient. Outside, there's an inviting wraparound porch filled with rocking chairs, while inside, guest rooms are uncluttered and simple, yet utterly elegant. All rooms are spacious and sunlit throughout, done up in a clean white-on-white palette and accented by hardwood floors and dark wood trim—and a beautiful oak four-poster bed in one room. Bathrooms, too, are all-white. Friendly innkeeper Joan Turturro is a French Culinary Institute grad, and prepares a seriously tasty breakfast—as well as dinner, if you make plans in advance. This is an excellent spot, too, for nature lovers, as there are opportunities for birdwatching, biking, beachcombing, and kayaking just a short walk or ride away.

25-500 Main Rd., Orient, NY 11957. www.orientinn-ny.com. © **631/323-2300.** 5 units. June–Oct $200–$245 double midweek, $245–$275 double weekend; call for reduced off-season rates. Rates include full breakfast. AE, MC, V. **Amenities:** Dinner upon request. *In room:* A/C, no phone, Wi-Fi.

MODERATE

Bayview Inn ★   Close to the water but not exactly on it, you'll only have a "bay view" here if you brought binoculars. Still, it's nice and quiet, and the beach is just a short walk away. The rooms in the inn are cozy, but with smallish bathrooms—snag room no. 8, which is a bit bigger. The cottage is a separate house next door with two efficiency units; they're nice and modern, but sparsely furnished and quite sterile. The owners also run **Motel on the Bay,** across the street, which really is on the bay.

10 Front St., South Jamesport, NY 11970. www.northforkmotels.com. © **631/722-2659.** 27 units. Memorial Day to Labor Day $175–$195 double inn rooms, $200–$250 double cottage rooms; early Sept to late May $125–$155 double inn rooms, $175–$225 double cottages. 2-night minimum for inn rooms on summer weekends, 3-night minimum for cottage rooms. AE, DISC, MC, V. From Rte. 25, turn south on S. Jamesport Ave. to Front St. **Amenities:** Restaurant; lounge. *In room:* A/C, TV/VCR, full kitchens (cottage rooms), no phone, Wi-Fi.

Silver Sands ★   Set back a ways from the road, this motel stretches over a quarter-mile of private beach, which is *the* reason to stay here. Motel rooms have microwaves and fridges, but are otherwise pretty simple, with linoleum floors and dated furniture. Family-run for over 50 years, the Silver Sands has expanded steadily, acquiring neighboring properties as they were vacated, so no two of the cottages are alike, though furnishings are in the same vein as the motel. The affable, down-to-earth owners have a webcam set up to view a nearby osprey's nest, and they've also been quietly building a reputation for harvesting some of the finest oysters around, right out of the bay here.

Silvermere Rd., Greenport, NY 11944. www.silversands-motel.com. © **631/477-0011.** 40 units. Mid-June to Labor Day motel rooms $150–$200 double; early Sept to mid-June motel rooms $100–$150 double, cottages $150–$200 double with 3-night minimum; cottages only by the week. Motel rates include breakfast. AE, DC, DISC, MC, V. Head east on Rte. 25 out of Southold; at the 1st right after passing the Lutheran church, you'll see the sign for the motel on the right. **Amenities:** Outdoor heated pool. *In room:* A/C, TV, kitchenette or microwave and fridge (motel rooms), kitchens (cottages only).

Where to Eat

Restaurants on the North Fork operate according to their own timetables: They close when people stop coming in, their "in season" starts up whenever the traffic warrants, and they may shut down at a moment's notice for a month's vacation. It's best to call first.

   VINe, 100 South St., Greenport (© **631/477-6238;** www.vinewinebar.com), is an appealing little wine bar serving exquisite small plates showcasing local and artisanal foods. More than 50 wines are available by the taste, glass, or bottle. For waterfront dining, try the consistently top-quality **Seafood Barge,** 62980 Main Rd., Southold (© **631/765-3010**). Stock up on picnic provisions at the **Village Cheese Shop,** 105 Love Lane, Mattituck (© **631/298-8556**), which has an excellent cheese selection (or eat on-site, where they serve scrumptious fondues and raclette). For fresh seafood plates to go, head straight for **Brauns Seafood,** 30840 Main Rd., Cutchogue (© **631/734-5550;** www.braunseafood.com).

EXPENSIVE

Frisky Oyster ★★★ CONTINENTAL   The granddaddy of the North Fork fine-dining scene, this modern restaurant with a Manhattan ambience sits in an unassuming storefront in bustling Greenport. Step inside and you'll find a candlelit space, house music, walls lined with colorful banquettes, and even more colorful wall coverings. You may not actually find oysters on the menu (it changes often), but you will discover an inventive cuisine that's often tweaked with Asian, French, or Mexican touches. Choose from a selection of excellent starters, like prosciutto-wrapped black mission figs with blue cheese. Entrees won't disappoint either, with such choices as garganelli with fresh lobster, baby arugula, and Meyer lemon vodka cream. And be sure to finish off with "The Best Key Lime Pie"—it has sufficient cause to boast. For a slightly more casual experience, check out their new offshoot, **F.O.B.'s** (Frisky's Oyster Bar) at 136 Front St. (📞 **631/477-4265**), which opens at noon for lunch.

27 Front St., Greenport. 📞 **631/477-4265.** www.thefriskyoyster.com. Reservations recommended. Main courses $27–$44. AE, DC, DISC, MC, V. Sun, Wed, Thurs 5–10pm, Fri–Sat until 11pm.

Luce & Hawkins ★★★ NEW AMERICAN Part of the luxurious Jedediah Hawkins Inn, this restaurant has raised the North Fork's culinary ante by turning out top-tier New American cuisine that takes full advantage of the region's bounty (and their own kitchen garden). The dining area, spread over a few rooms, is beautifully appointed, with comfortable banquettes, marble fireplace mantels, and flowery curtains, yet modern art and down-to-earth service keep it from crossing over into stuffiness. Luce & Hawkins now offers a lighter, slightly more affordable lunch, and there's a prix-fixe brunch on Sundays, too. Chef Keith Luce is also behind the eatery next door at **Luce's Landing,** a more casual, tavern-style affair that serves breakfast, lunch, and dinner.

400 S. Jamesport Ave., Jamesport (in the Jedediah Hawkins Inn). 📞 **631/722-2900.** www.jedediah hawkinsinn.com. Reservations recommended. Main courses $28–$45. AE, MC, V. Dinner Thurs–Mon 5:30–10pm; lunch Fri–Mon 11am–2:30pm; Tues–Wed noon–8pm.

North Fork Table & Inn ★★★ NEW AMERICAN This excellent restaurant has become the standard bearer in the area for the meticulous preparation of creative, locally sourced meals. The bright space has a romantic country-inn feel, with wood-plank floors and ceiling beams. Cozy alcoves add a dash of romance to the atmosphere as well. But the food, of course—from a kitchen led by Gerard Hayden, formerly of Aureole in New York City—is the reason to come here. Using only the freshest seasonal ingredients, dishes are given a simple, yet artful presentation with a perfect melding of flavors. The 10-spice glazed Colorado lamb loin, for example, comes with smoked lamb sausage, curried couscous, and roasted sweet peppers. The desserts, too, like the strawberry-rhubarb shortcake and warm sugar-and-spice donuts, are out of this world. This place books up far in advance, so reservations might be very hard to come by.

57225 Main Rd. (Rte. 25), Southold. 📞 **631/765-0177.** www.northforktableandinn.com. Reservations recommended. Main courses dinner $32–$45, lunch $28–$42. AE, DISC, MC, V. Thurs and Sun–Mon 5–9pm; Fri–Sat 5–10pm; lunch Sat–Sun noon–2:30pm.

MODERATE

Legends ★ AMERICAN With its location across the street from the bay, you'd expect fresh fish here—and you'd be right. Decked out in casual mariner garb, the bar area can get rowdy, with 22 TVs and a stone fireplace, and serving some 200 beers to complement inventive dishes that range from red Incan quinoa with shiitake mushrooms, asparagus, and haricot vert to spicy oysters Miguel with tequila and chipotle. For a quieter experience, step into the dining room, where the only thing resembling noise is light Muzak. The menu changes seasonally, offering starters such as tuna Napoleon with avocado and miso-ginger vinaigrette, followed by entrees like Egyptian-style pecan crusted shrimp with roasted eggplant.

835 First St., New Suffolk. ✆ **631/734-5123.** www.legends-restaurant.com. Reservations accepted in the dining room. Main courses $15–$39; pub $9–$18. AE, DC, DISC, MC, V. Summer daily noon–10pm; off season Sun–Thurs noon–9pm, Fri–Sat noon–10pm. From Cutchogue, turn left at the light (New Suffolk), go 1½ miles to the blinking lights, turn left onto New Suffolk Ave., then left onto First St.

Love Lane Kitchen ★★ NEW AMERICAN This pretty, tiled, whitewashed eatery on appealing little Love Lane opens right out onto a courtyard, making for a casual and welcoming atmosphere, but the kitchen here takes its food very seriously. The dinner menu changes weekly, offering satisfying bistro-style fare that includes steak frites and more adventurous creations like duck tagine with Israeli couscous, but the farm-fresh breakfasts and lunches are what put this place on the North Fork map. Stop by for morning treats like eggs rancheros and homemade granola, or a special like homemade pastrami hash; for lunch, go with the mouthwatering Cuban sandwich with house-roasted pork loin or the exceptional fish and chips. Takeout is also available.

240 Love Lane, Mattituck. ✆ **631/298-8989.** www.lovelanekitchen.com. Lunch $5–$15; dinner $14–$42. AE, MC, V. Breakfast daily 7am–2pm; lunch daily until 6pm; dinner Wed–Sun 5–9:30pm.

Modern Snack Bar AMERICAN When this '50s-style eatery opens its doors for the season in April—as it has done for over 60 years—people flock here for mom-knows-best dishes like meatloaf and fried chicken, along with their famous mashed turnips (really, they're delicious). Originally just offering burgers 'n' such, the menu now includes lobster salad, roast Long Island duckling, and a hearty fisherman's seafood plate. Definitely save room for pie.

628 Main Rd., Aquebogue. ✆ **631/722-3655.** www.modernsnackbar.com. Main courses $9–$23. AE, DISC, MC, V. Early Apr to mid-Dec Tues–Thurs 11am–9pm; Fri–Sat 11am–10pm; Sun noon–9pm.

INEXPENSIVE

Bruce's Cheese Emporium and Café ★ CAFE Step into this Greenport market and you're immediately hit with the aromas of coffee and cheese mingled together. Tables are set in the middle of the market and surrounded by old-time photos and antiques. It's a great place to come for a morning omelet or a lunchtime sandwich, or just to buy bread and cheese to take to the waterfront.

208 Main St., Greenport. ✆ **631/477-0023.** www.brucescheeseemp.com. Omelets and sandwiches $7–$18. AE, MC, V. July–Aug daily 8am–5pm; Sept–Dec and Apr–June Sun–Mon and Thurs–Fri 9am–4pm, Sat 9am–5pm; Jan–Mar Fri–Sun 9am–4pm.

The North Fork After Dark

While the North Fork nightlife scene is nothing like the Hamptons, you can still find some happening places on weekend nights, primarily in Greenport. If you want to stand elbow to elbow with tons of revelers on an outdoor wharf with the music blasting till the wee hours, check out **Claudio's Clam Bar,** 111 Main St., Greenport (✆ **631/477-1889;** www.claudios.com), open May to October. **Bay & Main,** 300 Main St. (✆ **631/477-1442**), right in the heart of town, also comes alive at night. The pub at **Legends,** 835 First St., New Suffolk (✆ **631/734-5123**), is welcoming and lively, with some fine brews on tap (and hundreds by the bottle) to satisfy your late-night thirst. For a taste of old Greenport, hang with the locals at the **Whiskey Wind Tavern,** 30–32 Front St. (✆ **631/477-6179**), where many a nor'easter has blown fishermen and their friends (as well as their dogs) for an evening of darts, pool, and, of course, a glass or two of whiskey.

6 SOUTH SHORE BEACHES: LONG BEACH, JONES BEACH & ROBERT MOSES STATE PARK ★★

Standing in the heart of Manhattan—especially on a steamy summer afternoon—it's hard to believe that sea breezes and white-sand beaches are only an hour away. While Jones Beach, Long Beach, and Robert Moses State Park are the biggest stretches of sand, there are some smaller (and sometimes less crowded) beaches you may want to check out as well. Just watch your head while swimming at these beaches—they also tend to be surfer haunts. **Tobay Beach** is a half-mile of sand just east of Jones Beach, and **Gilgo Beach** is another gorgeous stretch 6 miles west of Robert Moses.

Jones Beach

For nearly 100 years, Jones Beach has been a seaside haven for thousands of city-weary New Yorkers. With more than 6 miles of ocean beach and a half-mile of bay beach, it can get crowded, but the water is surprisingly clean. There are also some swimming pools available (and locker rooms); call ✆ **516/785-1600** for updates on fees and hours. *Tip:* To escape the crushing crowds and the tourists promenading along the park's 2-mile boardwalk, head to the beach's west end—there you'll find quiet, undeveloped areas that are home to a variety of migratory birds and native plants.

With a summertime stadium, Jones Beach is also a fun setting to take in a concert by some of music's biggest names. The beach and stadium are set out over a causeway and are not accessible by train. In fact, when Jones Beach opened in the 1920s, it was socially exclusionary; buses couldn't negotiate the low underpasses, and less wealthy people didn't own cars. Today, beach- and concertgoers travel the causeway by car and bus to walk the Jones Beach boardwalk.

ESSENTIALS

GETTING THERE From New York City, the **Long Island Rail Road** (✆ **516/822-LIRR** [5477]; www.mta.info/lirr) offers a Jones Beach Package in summer, which includes round-trip rail fare to Freeport plus round-trip Long Island Bus connections to the beach. By car, take the Long Island Expressway east or Grand Central Parkway east to Northern State Parkway east, to Wantagh Parkway south, to Jones Beach State Park or Belt/Southern State Parkway east, to Wantagh Parkway south, to the state park. It's $10 to park in summer.

VISITOR INFORMATION The main number for **Jones Beach State Park** is ✆ **516/785-1600.**

ACTIVITIES & ATTRACTIONS

CONCERTS From June to August, the **Nikon at Jones Beach Theater** (✆ **888/706-7600** or 516/221-1000; www.jonesbeach.com) hosts the hottest outdoor music events around: The Goo Goo Dolls, Jill Scott, Stevie Nicks, Maroon 5, Bob Dylan, and Journey all played here in 2011.

GOLF A fun way to pass some time with a great view of the ocean is at the **Pitch & Putt** (✆ **516/785-1600**; Apr–Nov), a par-3 course that's right next to the boardwalk and the Atlantic Ocean. Park in field 4 or 5. Cost is $7 per 18 holes ($4 seniors); club rental is $2.

NATURE The **Theodore Roosevelt Nature Center,** at the west end of Jones Beach Park (**✆ 516/679-7254**), houses educational exhibits, stargazing parties, art classes, interactive activities, environmental displays, and video programs. Children can dig in a mystery bone discovery area, explore a section of a shipwreck, and see a butterfly garden, along with exhibits on the dunes and endangered species. It's open from 10am to 4pm on weekends year-round and Wednesday to Sunday from Memorial Day to Labor Day.

Robert Moses State Park

Technically part of Fire Island because it sits at the island's western end, this beautiful stretch of beach is in a different world because you can actually drive here. Motor over to the eastern end of the park and you'll see the barriers that prevent access to the car-free area of Fire Island. So park and take a stroll on the 5 sandy miles, try your hand at surf fishing, or take in a game of 18-hole pitch-and-putt.

ESSENTIALS

GETTING THERE Take the Southern State Parkway to Robert Moses Causeway (exit 40) and go south to the western end of Fire Island. Parking fee is $10 in summer.

VISITOR INFORMATION The main number for **Robert Moses State Park** is **✆ 631/669-0470.**

Long Beach

In the past, Long Beach—with miles of surprisingly clean beach and water, along with a lengthy boardwalk—was best experienced as a day trip from the city because it wasn't set up for overnighters. But now, thanks to the 2009 opening of the **Allegria Hotel & Spa,** 80 W. Broadway, Long Beach (www.allegriahotel.com; **✆ 888/ON-BEACH** [662-3224] or 516/889-1300), visitors can spend the night—or make a weekend of it—here at the City by the Sea. With seven stories, 143 rooms, a beach-front location, a full-service rooftop spa, an infinity-edge pool, and an excellent restaurant (the Atlantica), the Allegria also rents bikes and surfboards, and provides guests access to the beach via a tunnel. Really, what more could you possibly need?

Still, if you're not in the market for an overnight, a day trip (it's less than an hourlong train ride from Manhattan) is a great option. Just be prepared: The beaches get supercrowded on summer weekends, and the skies are even more crowded with planes on their way into and out of New York.

To actually get onto the beach, you have to purchase a beach pass ($10) on the weekends from late May to late June and then daily until early September. You can buy them from the cabanas on the boardwalk or with your train ticket from New York City. When you tire of the sand, take a bike ride on the boardwalk; the center lane is reserved for bikes, and the salty air is exhilarating. For rentals, try **Buddy's,** 907 W. Beech St. (**✆ 516/431-0804**); they'll set you up with a 3-hour rental for $15.

ESSENTIALS

GETTING THERE The **Long Island Rail Road** (**✆ 516/822-LIRR** [5477]; www.mta.info/lirr) goes straight to Long Beach in about 40 minutes from Penn Station. Driving? Take Route 27 to Route 878. If street parking proves difficult—and it probably will—your best bet is the train station lot, which is just a couple of blocks from the ocean.

Contact the **Long Beach Chamber of Commerce,** 350 National Blvd. (✆ **516/432-6000;** www.lbchamber.com), or the **Long Island Convention & Visitors Bureau** (✆ **877/FUN-ON-LI** [386-6654] or 631/951-3440; www.discoverlongisland.com).

WHERE TO EAT

There are a few worthwhile restaurants, congregated on Park Avenue just west of the train station, or on Beech Street, west of where the beach ends. **Billy's Beach Cafe,** 222 Park Ave. (✆ **516/889-2233;** www.billysbeachcafe.com), has good half-pound burgers and wings, and the kitchen stays open until 2am. **Fresco Creperie,** 150A E. Park Ave. (✆ **516/897-8097;** frescocreperie.com), serves delicious, affordable savory and sweet—you guessed it!—crepes, while right next door **John Henry's,** 150 E. Park Ave. (✆ **516/897-9551**), is a good old-fashioned pub with traditional pub fare. Both the cuisine and the decor at **Duke Falcon's,** 36 W. Park Ave. (✆ **516/897-7000;** www.dukefalcons.com), span the globe, and it takes a while to sift through the zillions of entrees that include everything from Italian and Japanese dishes to a delicious Chilean sea bass. Finally, you'll find creative Italian cuisine at the intimate **Caffe Laguna,** 960 W. Beech St. (✆ **516/432-2717;** www.caffelaguna.com).

FIRE ISLAND ★★★

A half-mile-wide, 32-mile-long, car-free island—laid-back Fire Island feels about as far away in spirit from the Big Apple as you can possibly get on a day trip. A patchwork of federally protected national seashore and private property, the island has few formal addresses; folks ride beat-up bicycles barefoot, and regulars talk of "the mainland" as if it were a distant continent rather than right across the bay. Here on the island, informality rules the day, and most areas are refreshingly attitude free. With punishing winters, Fire Island is strictly a summertime getaway. When Memorial Day hits, the small hamlets fill with warm-weather revelers, while other parts of the island see only congregations of deer. And after September's over, almost everything shuts down.

Because cars are off-limits and the water taxi is expensive, it's best to decide what kind of experience you're after before you arrive here. **Ocean Beach** is the hub of island activity, where you'll find most of the island's hotels and restaurants, along with most of the party-hearty weekend visitors. The small hamlets of **Kismet** and **Ocean Bay Park** are mostly residential and great for crowd escape, but have few hotels or restaurants. **Cherry Grove** and **Fire Island Pines** are popular gay communities. And to get away from everyone, head to **Watch Hill** and points east—the area boasts a fantastic wildlife preserve, but no facilities other than camping. Walk the beach at night and it'll be just you, the surf, and the moonlight. Out here (and on the western end), beaches are clothing-optional, though going topless is tolerated everywhere.

Essentials

GETTING THERE Unless you're a world-class swimmer, the ferry is your only other option for getting out here. Though some boats operate year-round, they mostly run from May to October a few times daily, with very frequent service in July and August. Take the **Long Island Rail Road** (✆ **516/822-LIRR** [5477]; www.mta.info/lirr) to one of three stops: Bay Shore, Sayville, or Patchogue. Van taxis will be waiting to whisk you to a ferry for only a few dollars per person. If you're planning on spending only a day, purchase one of the LIRR's packages and you'll save some

Although all of Fire Island has a reputation as a hangout for gays and lesbians, the action is mostly in The Pines (for men) and Cherry Grove (for women and men). Both are small communities: Cherry Grove, especially, gets the party going . . . and keeps it going every summer night, while The Pines tends to be quieter. The beaches are gorgeous; in fine weather don't be surprised to find people walking around in their birthday suits. The biggest day of the year out here is the Invasion of The Pines on July 4, when boatloads of drag queens from Cherry Grove come and "terrorize" the posh Pines. You'll find a few places to stay. In The Pines, the most popular is **Hotel Ciel** (© 631/597-6500, ext. 26). Or look for a place to rent with **Pines Harbor Realty** (© 631/597-7575; www. pinesharborrealty.com), though be aware that real estate here is some of the most expensive on Fire Island. Over in Cherry Grove, shack up at the **Grove Hotel** (© 631/597-6600; www.grove hotel.com), or check into the **Belvedere Guest House** (© 631/597-6448; belvederefireisland.com). Nightclubs hop in these two towns until all hours of the night and morning. In The Pines, kick the party off with colorful concoctions during Low Tea (otherwise known as the "Tea Dance") from 5 to 8pm at the **Blue Whale** (© 631/597-6500, ext. 22). Then move on to High Tea from 7 to 10pm at the View Deck above **The Pavilion** (© 631/597-6500, ext. 28), where you get the added benefit of checking out anyone coming off the ferries; you can also head to Middle Tea at The Pavilion itself from 8 to 10pm. But the party really gets going at the Pavilion at midnight, where you can dance until dawn.

In Cherry Grove the **Grove Hotel** (© 631/597-6600; www.grovehotel. com) is the hottest spot, with drag shows, live bands, and theme parties throughout the summer. For the best people-watching, snag a table overlooking the main walk. Another popular gathering place is **Cherry's Pit** (© 631/597-6820); you can catch a great view of the sunset over on the bayside deck. They also serve food. Eat with a view of the ocean at **Jumping Jack's** (© 631/597-4174). Or go grab a great pie at **Cherry Grove Pizza** (© 631/597-6766).

Note that you may see some interesting scenes as you pass through the woods between Cherry Grove and The Pines, affectionately known as the "Meat Rack."

Look online for more gay listings and news for the area. The most comprehensive site is **www.fireislandqnews.com**, which also has a calendar of area events. Also try **www.asthegroveturns. net** and **www.fipines.com**.

money. **Fire Island Ferries** (© 631/665-3600; www.fireislandferries.com) gets you from Bay Shore to Ocean Beach, Kismet, Ocean Bay Park, and a few other communities from the Fire Island Ferry Terminal; **Sayville Ferry** (© 631/589-8980; www.sayvilleferry.com) takes you from Sayville to Cherry Grove, The Pines, and Sunken Forest from the Sailors Haven Ferry Terminal; and **Davis Park Ferry** (© 631/475-1665; www.davisparkferry.com) gets you from Patchogue to Watch Hill from the Watch Hill Ferry Terminal. Most ferries are $7 to $10 for the 20- to 30-minute jaunt across the bay.

GETTING AROUND   Cars are off-limits. You can walk from town to town, but distances are deceptively long; so consider calling **Fire Island Water Taxi** (© 631/665-8885; www.fireislandwatertaxi.com), and they'll come and collect you

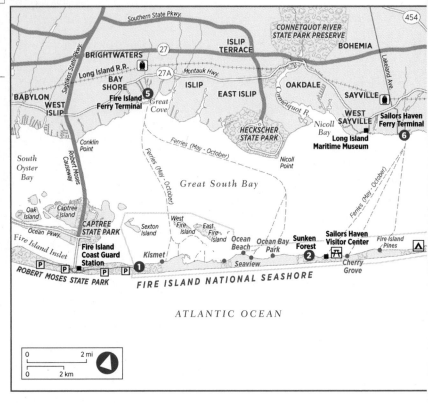

from any pier. Rates range from $7 to $30 for pier-to-pier service (children and seniors are half-price), plus additional fees for bikes and dogs.

Besides expensive water taxis and hoofing it, **bikes** are the only way to get around. Rent them from **Ocean Beach Hardware,** 482 Bayberry Walk, Ocean Beach (© **631/583-5826**), for $25 per day. (**Note:** On weekends, Ocean Beach forbids bike riding; just walk your bike to Seaview, and ride from there.)

VISITOR INFORMATION There's no tourist office here, but the **Long Island Convention & Visitors Bureau** (© **877/FUN-ON-LI** [386-6654]) may provide some info, as does the updated website www.fireisland.com.

Shopping

While tacky T-shirt shops and home-decor stores dominate the streets of Ocean Beach, you can find real art at the **Kenny Goodman Gallery,** 325 Denhoff Walk, Ocean Beach (© **631/583-8207**), open weekends only in May, June, September, and October, daily in July and August. Since 1968, Kenny has made beautiful wooden walking sticks and eerily disturbing wooden heads, along with gorgeous silver jewelry. For fashions and accessories without a touristy theme, head to **Flair House** on Bay Walk near the ferry landing (© **631/583-5025**).

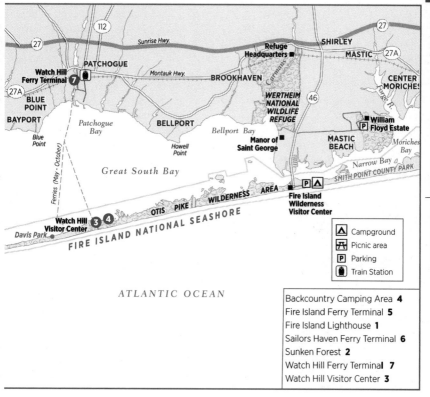

Campground
Picnic area
Parking
Train Station

Backcountry Camping Area **4**
Fire Island Ferry Terminal **5**
Fire Island Lighthouse **1**
Sailors Haven Ferry Terminal **6**
Sunken Forest **2**
Watch Hill Ferry Terminal **7**
Watch Hill Visitor Center **3**

Exploring Fire Island

For killer 360-degree views of island, bay, and ocean—you can even see Manhattan on a superclear day—climb the 156 steps to the top of the **Fire Island Lighthouse** (© **631/661-4876;** www.fireislandlighthouse.com), near Kismet at the island's western end. The light has been guiding ships since 1825. It's open 9:30am to 5pm daily from April to June and Labor Day to mid-December, 9:30am to 6pm daily July to Labor Day, and January to March weekdays 10am to 4pm and weekends noon to 4pm (in winter call ahead to confirm). Tours are offered daily in summer, and on weekends in the off season; admission is $6 for adults, $4 for seniors and children 12 and under. Farther east, the **Sunken Forest** (© **631/597-6183**) is a gorgeous nature preserve and a great walkabout that's free and always open. Set behind the dunes, this 250-year-old forest is a crowded collection of American holly and sassafras that twists and tangles to create a shady canopy. The dense growth has withstood the punishment of constant salt spray better than most of the homes. The marked boardwalk trail will help you sort out what's what.

Where to Stay

With demand for accommodations far outweighing supply, it's decidedly a seller's market. Even tiny, moldy rooms without A/C get away with charging more than $100 a night. An exception: **The Palms Hotel,** 168 Cottage Walk, Ocean Beach (www.palmshotelfireisland.com; ✆ **631/583-8870**). Rooms are small, but you get comfy beds, flatscreen TVs, and even outdoor showers. If you have money to burn, consider the boutique-y, gay- (and straight-) friendly **Madison Fire Island Pines,** 22 Atlantic Walk, Fire Island Pines (www.themadisonfi.com; ✆ **631/597-6061**).

Clegg's Hotel ★   The owners of this hotel, family-run since the 1940s, actually care about cleanliness. Plus, Clegg's occupies a prime position just steps from the ferry, in the middle of the Ocean Beach action. Standard rooms are closet-size and sparsely furnished with either a full bed or two twins. You'll have to share a bathroom with several other rooms. A better choice? One of the studio apartments with a bay view: You'll also get a small private bathroom and a kitchenette.

478 Bayberry Walk, Ocean Beach, Fire Island, NY 11770. www.cleggshotel.com. ✆ **631/583-5399.** 20 units. May–Oct Sun–Thurs $160 double, $235 suite; Fri and Sat package $395 double, $450 suite. Off-season rates available upon request. Rates include continental breakfast. 2-night minimum on weekends. AE, MC, V. **Amenities:** Complimentary use of bikes and beach chairs. *In room:* A/C, kitchenette in suites, no phone.

CAMPGROUNDS

Unless you know someone, camping at **Watch Hill** is the only way to sleep for free out here, and while it's far removed from any facilities or action, it's super quiet and in the island's most beautiful area. The official campground, which is not free (sites are $25 a night), has 26 tent sites and one group site. It also books up a year in advance; get the rules and tips at www.watchhillfi.com, or call ✆ **631/597-6664.** Last-minute campers, however, can try for a free backcountry pass from the **Watch Hill Visitor Center** (✆ **631/597-6455**) and walk ¼ mile east on the beach into the Otis Pike Wilderness Area. Pop your tent anywhere behind the dunes. But be aware that passes are available on a first-come, first-served basis.

RENTALS

Most people rent a home for their Fire Island vacations. For a place in Ocean Beach, Seaview, Robbins Rest, or other points on the island's western end, call **Red Wagon Realty,** 471 Denhoff, Ocean Beach (✆ **631/583-8158**). For The Pines, call **Pines Harbor Realty** (www.pinesharborrealty.com; ✆ **631/597-7575**); In Cherry Grove, call **A Summer Place** (www.asummerplacerealty.com; ✆ **631/597-6140**).

Where to Eat

Bring plenty of cash. Restaurateurs have only a couple of months to make money, so it's not cheap to eat out here. For great sunsets and good eats, also consider the **Hideaway at Houser's Hotel,** 785 Evergreen Walk, Ocean Beach (✆ **631/583-8900**).

Matthew's Seafood House ★★ SEAFOOD   Get past the hokey fishnet decor and you'll find Fire Island's best seafood here. You can sit on a wooden patio overlooking the bay, the cornbread is warm, and portions are supersized, making the high prices more tolerable. Stick with the fish: Shrimp and scallops are excellent, and tuna or swordfish steaks are prepared many ways. Come on Sunday (3–6pm) for the weekly party that includes deals on drinks, as well as clams, wings, and other bar food.

Rachel's Bake Shop ★ 🍴 DINER   This centrally located eatery has been dishing up breakfast, lunch, and dinner for more than 30 years, and the fan-cooled, skylight-filled building is the town's closest thing to a reasonably priced diner. Breakfast is served from 7am to 4pm, and the blueberry pancakes are a great way to start the morning or afternoon. Dinners are fair; your best bet is to have breakfast or lunch here. Want something to go? Hit the bakery next door.

325 Bay Walk, Ocean Beach. © **631/583-9552.** Breakfasts and burgers $6–$12; dinner entrees $12–$19.
AE, MC, V. Memorial Day to mid-Oct daily 6am–4am.

Fire Island After Dark

Drinkers love the down-at-the-heels feel of **Housers,** 781 Evergreen Walk, Ocean Beach (© **631/583-8900;** www.housersbar.com); it's one of the biggest indoor scenes in town. To party on the water, head to **Casino Café and Bar,** on the ocean in Davis Park (© **631/597-6150;** www.casinocafefireisland.com), with its huge deck where DJs spin on the weekends. The food here is good, too.

THE SOUTH FORK: THE HAMPTONS ★★★

With picturesque towns, long stretches of some of the most beautiful beaches in the world, and bucolic landscapes, it only makes sense that the rich and famous would spend their summers here. Where else can you wake up to a fresh-from-the-farm breakfast, have a magnificent day at the beach, shop at some of the chicest stores in the country, dine at a top-tier restaurant, and party with celebrities all night long? Generally referred to as simply "the Hamptons," the South Fork actually consists of a group of towns, not all of which actually end in "hampton," and each one has its own flavor. Ever since the railroad was built out to Southampton in 1870, people have been hooked on the South Fork.

While winters are relatively quiet, the summer season brings crushing crowds and a flashy nightclub scene. A drive along Route 27 requires immense patience, so it's worthwhile figuring out what kind of experience you seek so that there's not a lot of backtracking. **Eastport** is a tiny hamlet filled with antiques shops; **Westhampton** has tree-lined streets and Victorian mansions; **Southampton** boasts old money, huge estates, and chic stores; **East Hampton** is the trendy, new-money capital of Long Island (Jerry Seinfeld, Billy Joel, and Martha Stewart have homes here); **Sag Harbor** is a gorgeous town on the water where even the dry cleaner has antique irons in the window; **Amagansett** and **Bridgehampton** are cute little towns; and laid-back **Montauk** relishes its position at the island's tip—set apart from the more exclusive villages, it's also a big draw for fishermen, surfers, and outdoors types.

Summers are indeed fun here, but I recommend a visit in the fall, when the days are cooler, the crowds are thinner, the attitude and the paparazzi head back to Manhattan, and farm stands overflow with colorful produce. It's an excellent season for beachcombing, too.

To locate the towns in this section, please see the map on p. 140.

Essentials

GETTING THERE   The **Long Island Rail Road** (© **516/822-LIRR** [5477]; www.mta.info/lirr) makes stops in Westhampton, Hampton Bays, Southampton, Bridgehampton, East Hampton, Amagansett, and Montauk. By car, take the **Long Island Expressway** to Riverhead (where it ends) and head south to Route 27, which takes you all the way out to Montauk. The **Hampton Jitney** (© **800/936-0440** or 631/283-4600; www.hamptonjitney.com) buses run daily. Pickup locations include Manhattan, LaGuardia, JFK, and Islip airports and several stops in the Hamptons. The complete route takes around 3½ hours, but allow for traffic delays at peak travel times, especially on summer weekends and holidays. Count on round-trip fares of about $50 (discounts for seniors and children). The buses run by **Hampton Luxury Liner** (© **631/537-5800;** www.hamptonluxuryliner.com) have more room than other bus lines, with just 33 reclining leather captain's seats for $40 each way. But if money is no object, hop on an airplane and skip the traffic: **MacArthur Airport** (© **631/467-3210;** www.macarthurairport.com), situated mid–Long Island, is the closest airport (see section 1 of this chapter). **Viking Ferry** (462 W. Lake Dr., Montauk; © **631/668-5700;** www.vikingfleet.com) runs a passengers-only, high-speed service between Montauk and Block Island, as well as New London, Connecticut, and Martha's Vineyard, Massachusetts. Round-trip adult tickets range from $70 to $120; discounts for children; added fees for bikes and surfboards.

VISITOR INFORMATION   The **Southampton Chamber of Commerce** is at 76 Main St., Southampton (© **631/283-0402;** www.southamptonchamber.com), or contact the **Long Island Convention and Visitors Bureau** (© **877/FUN-ON-LI** [386-6654] or 631/951-3440; www.licvb.com).

GETTING AROUND   Cars are your best option out here. Rent from **Hertz** (© **800/654-3131**) in Riverhead or **Avis** (© **800/331-1212**), which has an office in Southampton. For a taxi in Southampton, call **Jr's Four-Ones Taxi** (© **631/283-1900**). In Montauk, call **Lindy's Taxi** (© **631/668-2468;** www.lindystaxi.com).

Beaches & Active Pursuits

BEACHES   Hamptons beaches are world-class for a reason: Not only are the grains of gold perfectly maintained, but they also stretch on forever. Unlike some beaches that are interrupted by cliffs or rocks, these sandy stretches allow you to walk for hours, just getting lost in the grandness of the ocean—and if you look to the other side, the grandness of the homes. There's only one problem when it comes to enjoying these beaches: parking. Walk, ride a bike, take a taxi—do anything but drive to the beach. Nonresident parking permit fees run up to $350 and daily parking fees can be $40—if a spot's even available.

Your best option? Stay at a hotel that has beach rights. Hotels like Gurney's Inn are right on the water, so you'll have no problems. Some off-beach places like the Southampton Inn will shuttle you to the water for free.

So where do you go? There are too many great beaches in the area to list here, but a few favorites are worth mentioning. In Southampton, **Cooper's Beach** is the main public beach; it's beautifully maintained and you'll find a concession stand; but it can get crowded, and parking costs as much as $40. **Old Town Beach** is much less crowded and there's no parking permit required; but it has only 30 spaces, so get there early. **Main Beach** in East Hampton is gorgeous and in view of some giant mansions. A weekday parking pass is $20, but there are no nonresident parking permits on weekends. **Westhampton Beach Village** has some of the best beaches on Long Island, but forget about parking—even walking onto the beach requires a permit (✆ 631/288-1654).

If you want to tote your lunch along, pick up sandwiches to go at **Hampton Bagels;** there's one in East Hampton, 74 N. Main (✆ 631/324-5411), and another in Hampton Bays, 252 W. Montauk Hwy. (✆ 631/728-7893). For something fancier, check out the staggering cheese selection at **Cavaniola's Gourmet,** 89B Division St., Sag Harbor (✆ 631/725-0095; http://cavaniola.com), or the huge salad bar at **Schmidt's Market,** 120 N. Sea Rd., Southampton (✆ 631/283-5777).

BIKING   Biking is a great idea in this land of gently rolling hills and parking-permit hell. Rent or purchase one at **Bermuda Bikes Plus,** 36 Gingerbread Lane, East Hampton (✆ 631/324-6688; bermudabikes.com), starting at $25 for a 7-hour day. The folks at **Montauk Bike Shop,** 725A Montauk Hwy., Montauk (✆ 631/668-8975; www.montaukbikeshop.com), are full of information about some terrific trails in the area, including **Hither Hills** and **Camp Hero** state parks. As luck would have it, they also rent bikes, starting at $15 an hour or $55 a day.

BOATING   Go exploring on the water by kayak. **Mill Creek Kayaks,** 3253 Noyac Rd., Sag Harbor (✆ 631/725-4712), will take you out for lessons ($30 per hour) or rent you a kayak or a stand-up paddleboard ($16–$20 per hour). They also offer a wetlands wildlife tour and a children's tour ($45). Open May to October. You can also rent kayaks—as well as bicycles, mopeds, wet suits, and just about any beach accessory—from **Plaza Surf & Sports,** 716 Main St., Montauk (✆ 631/668-9300; www.plazasurfnsports.net).

FISHING   Montauk is renowned as one of the nation's best places for surf-casting. Start working out now: 40- and 50-pound bass migrate through these waters in the fall, and gigantic fluke, porgies, sea bass, and stripers can be caught in the summer as well. Go with **Viking Fleet,** Montauk Harbor (✆ 631/668-5700; www.viking fleet.com); a half-day's fishing is $50 for adults, $30 for kids 5 to 12. Six hours of night fishing—a very cool experience—goes for $85 per person.

GOLF   **Montauk Downs State Park,** on Fairview Avenue east of **Montauk** (✆ 631/668-5000), has a beautiful 18-hole, par-72 course. For New York State residents, it's $24 to $46 for 18 holes ($48–$92 for out-of-staters). A great-value course is the 9-hole **Sag Harbor State Golf Course,** off Route 114 between East Hampton and Sag Harbor (✆ 631/725-2503). It's just $18 on weekdays, $24 on weekends. The famed **Shinnecock Hills,** 200 Tuckahoe Rd., Southampton, was home to the US Open in 2004, but it's a private course, so you'll have to make friends with a member to play here.

HIKING   **Shadmoor State Park,** east of Montauk (✆ 631/668-3781 or 668-5000), has 99 open acres of rugged and hilly terrain, where you can hike on trails leading to high bluffs with magnificent ocean views. Bring your binoculars to take advantage of some world-class bird-watching. Though it's better known for its beautiful shoreline, **Hither Hills State Park,** on Old Montauk Highway (✆ 631/668-2554), has miles of hiking and biking trails, as does **Elizabeth A. Morton National Wildlife Refuge,** 784 Noyack Rd., Sag Harbor (✆ 631/286-0485).

SPAS   An ocean of spa treatments are available at Gurney's Inn from their **Seawater Spa,** 290 Old Montauk Hwy., Montauk (✆ 631/668-2345; www.gurneysinn. com). If you're up for a splurge, go for the $220 90-minute Marine Kur therapy, which

Mills were once a fixture in every early-American village, but most have fallen into rubble. The stone mill that gave its name to the town of Water Mill, built by English settler Edward Howell shortly after his arrival in 1640, was hand-hewn from boulders found near the site. Ownership of the mill passed through several families over the centuries until it eventually fell into disuse. Local residents rallied to restore the landmark, and Water Mill is now the oldest town in America with a still-functioning water mill. Learn more at the **Water Mill Museum,** 41 Old Mill Rd. (© 631/726-4625; www.watermillmuseum.org).

includes exfoliation, a seaweed wrap, and a hydrotherapy massage (in a tub of heated seawater!). Or pay $30 for access to the huge indoor heated seawater pool, steam room, and the Roman baths.

SURFING   Surfers, get ye to Montauk. Just below the Lighthouse, you'll find some of the biggest waves on Long Island—along with the boarders who come out here to catch them. The currents are very tricky where the ocean meets the sound, but experienced riders will have a blast. **Ditch Plains,** as you may already know, is the most popular spot on the East End for longboarders and paddle surfers. *Tip:* A parking permit or sticker is needed. Pick up or rent your supplies at **Plaza Surf & Sports,** 716 Main St., Montauk (© 631/668-9300; www.plazasurfnsports.net).

U-PICK FARMS   Have fun picking your own fruit. **Hank Kraszewski Farms** has a couple of outlets: For strawberries, head out to Route 39, Southampton Bypass, Southampton (© 631/726-4667), and for pumpkins, take Route 27, to Water Mill (same number).

WINERIES   While you won't find a winery every mile like on the North Fork, the South Fork does boast three fine wineries: **Wölffer Estate,** 139 Sagg Rd., Sagaponack (© 631/537-5106; www.wolffer.com); **Duckwalk Vineyards,** 231 Montauk Hwy., Water Mill (© 631/726-7555; www.duckwalk.com); and **Channing Daughters,** 1927 Scuttlehole Rd., Bridgehampton (© 631/537-7224; www.channingdaughters.com). All three of these wineries have tasting rooms and tours—call ahead for seasonal hours of operation.

Shopping

Walk along Main Street in Southampton, where you'll find the country homes of upscale Manhattan shops like **Saks Fifth Avenue,** 50 Main St. (© 631/283-3500), and the clothing and furnishings at **Edward Archer,** 85 Main St. (© 631/283-2668). Gallery-wise, don't miss the collection of artists at the **Chrysalis Gallery,** 2 Main St. (© 631/287-1883).

East Hampton also boasts loads of upscale and chic shops like the **Coach Factory Stores,** 60 Newtown Lane (© 631/329-1777), and **Tory Burch,** 47 Newtown Lane (© 631/907-9150), plus many art galleries showing the work of highly regarded artists.

For antiques, head to Bridgehampton. Try **Hampton Briggs Antiques,** 2462 Main St. (© 631/537-6286; www.hamptonbriggsantiques.com), for Asian pieces, and **English Country Antiques,** 26 Snake Hollow Rd. (© 631/537-0606;

www.ecantiques.com), for French and English Country furniture. Check out the **Shinnecock Trading Post,** Old Montauk Highway, Southampton (© **631/287-2460;** www.shinnecocktradingpost.com), for Native American arts and crafts.

Museums & Attractions

Art lovers will want to see the impressive collection at the **Parrish Art Museum,** 25 Job's Lane, Southampton (© **631/283-2118;** www.parrishart.org), which focuses on artists who have lived in the East End, including the impressionist William Merritt Chase, along with Jackson Pollack, Lee Krasner, William de Kooning, and Dan Flavin. From May to October, you can take a guided tour of the **Pollock-Krasner House & Studio,** 830 Fireplace Rd., where Pollack and Krasner lived and worked since 1945, in the hamlet of Springs in East Hampton (© **631/324-4929;** http://sb.cc.stonybrook.edu/pkhouse). Call for an appointment and information on hours.

Montauk Point Lighthouse Museum ★★ Up on a hill, overlooking the rocky coastline of Long Island's easternmost point, this museum boasts a bevy of artifacts and a glorious view. Commissioned by Congress under George Washington in 1792 and completed in 1796, the first lighthouse in New York State has old exhibits of historical documents and depictions of the lonely life of a lighthouse keeper. There's also a 110-foot tower that you can climb for a stunning view of the ocean, the coastline, and the dense scrub lining the road from the town of Montauk.

Located at the very end of Rte. 27. © **888/MTK-POIN** (685-7646) or 631/668-2544. www.montauk lighthouse.com. Admission $9 adults, $7 seniors, $4 children. Mid-May to mid-Oct daily, usually 10:30am–4:30 or 5:30pm; scattered hours in the off season, mostly weekends only.

Guild Hall ★ One of East Hampton's hidden treasures, this museum and cultural center is home to an impressive art gallery with rotating exhibits, political and cultural lectures, art classes, theater and dance performances, and children's activities—even movie screenings of local favorites like—believe it or not—*Jaws.* Their art museum houses works by local luminaries like Jackson Pollack, Andy Warhol, and Ross Belckner.

158 Main St., East Hampton. © **631/324-0806.** www.guildhall.org. Hours and admission vary by event; call box office at 631/324-4050 for details.

Whaling Museum ★ Housed in a gorgeous 1845 Greek Revival mansion built by whaling-ship magnate Benjamin Huntting, the home is as cool as the collection inside, devoted to the industry that put this part of the world on the map. Highlights include 100-year-old genuine whale jawbones, a reconstructed 18th-century kitchen, tools and weapons of whalers, and samples of whale oil.

200 Main St. (at Garden St.), Sag Harbor. © **631/725-0770.** www.sagharborwhalingmuseum.org. Admission $5 adults, $4 seniors and students, $1 children 3–11. Mid-May to Oct Mon–Sat 10am–5pm, Sun 1–5pm.

Children's Museum of the East End ★ Perfect for the little ones on a cold or rainy day, this Bridgehampton center keeps younger children busy (older kids might be bored) with hands-on exhibits, workshops and displays including replicas of fire engines and sailing ships, a noise-making musical forest, a turn-of-the-century soda fountain, art, dance and drawing classes, Lego activities, and waffle-making events (mmmm . . . waffles).

376 Bridgehampton/Sag Harbor Tpk., Bridgehampton. © **631/537-8250.** http://cmee.org. $9 admission for nonmembers. Mon–Sat 9am–5pm; Sun 10am–5pm.

Where to Stay

Accommodations range from small motels to extravagant resorts to tiny historical inns. Check out sleepy Amagansett's **Reform Club Inn,** 23 Windmill Lane (http://reformclubinn.com; ℭ 631/267-8500), which combines a modern, design-y aesthetic with a laid-back beach-house feel; rooms start at $750 per night and climb rapidly from there. Another splurge-worthy option: the elegant Arts and Crafts–style **Baker House 1650,** 181 Main St., East Hampton (ℭ 631/324-4081; www.bakerhouse1650.com), where rates range from $275 up to $950. The more affordable (and decidedly hipper) **Solé East,** 90 Second House Rd., Montauk (ℭ 631/668-2105; www.soleeast.com), offers recently renovated bungalow-style rooms in a low-key Zen-like setting, while **East Deck,** right next to Ditch Plains, Montauk (ℭ 631/668-2334; www.eastdeckmotel.com), is a simple but clean and friendly option beloved by surfers and relaxed families ($90 up to $1,000 for a one-bedroom apartment). Another high-end choice: The **Inn at Baron's Cove,** 31 West Water St., Sag Harbor (ℭ 631/725-2100; www.baronscove.com).

EXPENSIVE

c/o The Maidstone ★★★
Some recent renovations to this gorgeous Greek Revival Inn (formerly the Maidstone Arms) overlooking East Hampton's town pond updated the place from top to bottom, imbuing it with a sophisticated, modern, and distinctly Scandinavian sensibility. The common areas explode with color and Nordic style—vibrant Josef Frank pillows, whimsical upholstery, and original contemporary photography—while cozy rooms and cottages are kitted out with Swedish antiques, flatscreen TVs, iPod docks, and even PlayStations. The hotel is also dedicated to going completely green: Drinking water is filtered on-site, linens are organic, toiletries are all-natural, and bikes are available for guests' use. Finally, the on-site restaurant, the Living Room, serves Scandinavian-inflected new American cuisine, following the tenets of the slow-food philosophy; they'll even fix a box lunch for you to take to the beach.

207 Main St., East Hampton, NY 11937. www.themaidstone.com. ℭ 631/324-5006. 19 units. Mid-May to mid-Sept $450–$1,200 double; off-season weekends $325–$725 double, off-season weekdays $265–$575 double. 3-night minimum July–Aug weekends, 2-night minimum on weekends off season. AE, MC, V. Pets allowed with $25 daily fee. **Amenities:** Restaurant; lounge; babysitting; complimentary bikes; concierge; beach parking permit. In room: A/C, TV/DVD, minibar, MP3 docking station, PlayStation 3, Wi-Fi.

Gurney's Inn Resort & Spa ★★★
With an idyllic setting on a bluff over a gorgeous stretch of private ocean beach, the friendly and unpretentious Gurney's sprawls across several building and has a great European-style spa. Only some of the buildings are right on the ocean, and the range of rates reflects your view. Although the nautical theme and cruise ship vibe of the place scream 1970s, most of the recently renovated rooms are spacious and modern inside. The marble-and-glass interiors may not be overly charming, but a beige-and-green color scheme gives them some warmth, and they are comfortable and generally get plenty of light. Head to the full-service spa if you have a vision of getting a massage on the beach; this is the place to make it a reality.

290 Old Montauk Hwy., Montauk, NY 11954. www.gurneysinn.com. ℭ 631/668-2345. Fax 631/668-3576. 109 units. Late May to Labor Day midweek $325–$735 double, weekend $350–$795 double, $735 and way up suite and cottages; Labor Day to mid-Oct and mid-Apr to late May midweek $240–$510 double, weekend $285–$540 double, $510 and way up suite and cottages; mid-Oct to mid-Apr

midweek $199–$390 double, weekend $254–$465 double, $390 and way up suite and cottage. Packages available. Rates include $26 dinner credit and $15 breakfast credit per person. 2-night minimum in June, 3-night minimum July–Aug, 2-night weekend minimum off season. AE, DC, DISC, MC, V. Free valet parking. **Amenities:** 3 restaurants; lounge; children's programs in summer; concierge; big exercise room overlooking ocean; heated indoor seawater pool; limited room service; spa. *In room:* A/C, TV w/pay movies, fridge, hair dryer, kitchenette in cottages, Wi-Fi.

1708 House ★★★ This cozy Colonial bed-and-breakfast actually does date from 1708, and you can stay in the original 18th-century rooms. The inn has just four rooms (nos. 1–4) in this style: They're not the world's largest, but they have original wood floors and exposed-beam ceilings, along with beautiful four-poster beds and claw-foot tubs. The other rooms were added in 1996, and are also decked out in gorgeous furniture and wood floors, but they're more modern. The three cottages, with porches and exposed wood ceilings, are beachy and contemporary. The atmospheric cellar, possibly the oldest one of its kind in New York, has a fireplace and a low-timbered ceiling—it's a wonderful place to share a bottle of local wine.

126 Main St., Southampton, NY 11968. www.1708house.com. ✆ **631/287-1708.** Fax 631/287-3593. 15 units. May–Oct weekdays $225–$550 double, weekends $325–$675 double; Nov–Apr weekdays $145–$255 double, weekends $175–$325 double. Rates include continental breakfast. 2-night minimum on weekends May–June and Sept–Oct; 3-night minimum on weekends July–Aug; 4-night minimum on holidays. AE, MC, V. **Amenities:** Wine cellar. *In room:* A/C, TV (some w/DVD), hair dryer, kitchens in 2 cottages, Wi-Fi.

MODERATE

Inn at Quogue ★★ 🛏 A combination of quaint country inn and pool-centered resort, this 200-year-old, 67-unit inn stretches across several different buildings off the beaten path of the eponymous town. It offers cheap, small, poolside rooms as well as the more formal, but much nicer inn rooms. Some are tiny but all are bright and nicely decorated. If you can, grab room no. 1 in the main house, a bright, big split-level room with original floors from 1785; I'm also partial to cheery no. 13. The large cottage features contemporary furnishings, three bedrooms, and an outdoor deck with a fireplace.

47–52 Quogue St., Quogue, NY 11959. www.innatquogue.com. ✆ **631/653-6560.** Fax 631/653-6580. 67 units. Fall and spring $215–$275 double, winter $125–$190 double, summer $325–$450 double; cottage $300–$700. 2-night minimum on weekends July–Aug and holidays. AE, DISC, MC, V. **Amenities:** Restaurant; lounge; bike rental; outdoor pool; Wi-Fi in common areas. *In room:* A/C, TV, hair dryer and kitchenette in some rooms.

Seatuck Cove House ★★★ If you've ever dreamed of staying in one of the enormous waterfront homes that dot the shoreline, then this bed-and-breakfast in mellow Eastport is for you. Its country-furnished look gives it a laid-back feel, and you're just a stone's throw from the inn's small private beach. The rooms are painted white and, with one exception, they're spacious and bright, with separate sitting areas. The Dune Road room is amazing—huge with great water views, a temperature-controlled whirlpool tub, flatscreen digital TV with DVD player, stone fireplace, and high ceilings.

61 S. Bay Ave., Eastport, NY 11941. www.seatuckcovehouse.com. ✆ **631/325-3300.** Fax 631/325-8443. 5 units. May–Oct weekdays $175–$400 double, weekends $200–$475 double; Nov–Apr weekdays $100–$225 double, weekends $150–$325 double. Rates include full breakfast. 2-night minimum on weekends May–Oct. AE, DISC, MC, V. Go east through village of Eastport, turn right onto S. Bay Ave., travel to end of road. Children not permitted. **Amenities:** Heated outdoor pool. *In room:* A/C, 4 units w/ TV, hair dryer, Wi-Fi.

Southampton Inn ★★ ☺ Set on extensive grounds with a conference center, pool, tennis court, children's play area, game room, and other fun activities for kids, this Tudor-style inn is more of a resort destination, but it's just around the corner from the town's chic shops and restaurants. And with the inn's free shuttle to the beach in summer, the nightmare of parking near Southampton sand vanishes. It's the kind of place that caters to everyone—families, groups, couples, even pet lovers—and does a good job making everyone happy. Standard rooms are very comfortable (Tempur-Pedic mattresses!) and spacious, and come loaded with amenities, making for a good value even in the heart of summer. Try to reserve one of the stylish "Designer queens" if possible. The restaurant, OSO, specializes in steak, seafood, and locally grown produce—and, believe it or not, it's reasonably priced.

91 Hill St., Southampton, NY 11968. www.southamptoninn.com. ✆ **800/832-6500** or 631/283-6500. Fax 631/283-6559. 90 units. July–Sept $299–$499 double, May–June $229–$429 double; Oct $199–$349 double; Nov–Apr $179–$309 double. Packages available. 2-night minimum on weekends May–Sept; 3-night minimum on summer holiday weekends. AE, DC, DISC, MC, V. Pets allowed with $39 fee. **Amenities:** Restaurant; concierge; outdoor heated pool; outdoor tennis court; complimentary beach shuttle. *In room:* A/C, TV, fridge, hair dryer, Wi-Fi.

INEXPENSIVE

Harborside Resort Motel A solid, affordable option that's just 3 blocks from the sound and one of its beaches, this small L-shaped motel provides decent rooms in a quiet locale. Rooms are nothing extravagant and some are a tight fit; some are a little heavy on the wood paneling, while others are painted white. Still, when you need to get out, there's a pool and tennis court on the premises—and, of course, the beach nearby.

371 W. Lake Dr., Montauk, NY 11954. www.montaukharborside.com. ✆ **631/668-2511.** 28 units. Early summer midweek $110–$180 double, weekend $135–$198 double, $260 and up apt; peak summer midweek $120–$190, weekend $150–$210, $275 and up apt; spring and fall midweek $75–$118 double, weekend $95–$135 double, $170 and up apt; winter midweek $58–$78 double, weekend $68–$88 double. 3-night weekend minimum in summer; 2-night weekend minimum in spring and fall. AE, DC, DISC, MC, V. 1 mile east of Montauk, turn left onto W. Lake Dr. (C.R. 77). **Amenities:** Outdoor pool; tennis court. *In room:* A/C, TV, fridge, kitchenettes (in some apts), Wi-Fi.

Sunrise Guest House ★★ 📋 Now *this* is my idea of a romantic, low-key beach getaway. A true guesthouse, the charming 1920s-era Sunrise feels like your own private retreat, with a pleasant flower-filled porch overlooking the ocean right across the street, and a very chilled-out and welcoming atmosphere. There's a living room with a fireplace, a breakfast area, and even an outdoor hot tub in the back for guests to use. All four comfortable rooms come with a private bathroom, hardwood floors, and tasteful antique furnishings, and three of these are two-room suites with a gas fireplace and a separate sitting area. Best of all: You're mere steps away from miles of pristine beach. It's an excellent place for couples—I'd recommend a visit in the off season.

681 Old Montauk Hwy., Montauk, NY 11954. www.sunrisebnb.com. ✆ **631/668-7286.** 4 units. Late June to early Sept $155–$295 double; May to late June and Sept to mid-Oct $120–$225 double; winter $95–$175 double. Ask about off-season specials. Rates include continental breakfast in summer and on weekends. 2-night weekend minimum, 3-night holiday weekend minimum. MC, V. Children 11 and under not permitted. **Amenities:** Wi-Fi. *In room:* A/C, TV.

CAMPGROUNDS

Hither Hills State Park, Montauk (✆ **631/668-2554**), is a gem of a beach park without the pretension of the Hamptons. It also has a rarity: camping just steps from the 2-mile-long white-sand beach. A campground in chic East Hampton seems like an anomaly (and it is), but 607-acre **Cedar Point County Park** (✆ **631/852-7620**) is set in a densely wooded area of East Hampton overlooking Gardiner's Bay. The 190 campsites, which are a few minutes' walk from the water, can be used for tents and campers, though none has an electric hookup. The proprietors of the Cedar Point General Store show summer movies on the lawn on Saturdays; they also offer free use of recreational equipment.

Where to Eat

Restaurants in the super-fashionable South Fork come and go pretty quickly—even landmarks like The Laundry and Tierra Mar are now shuttered—so it pays to stay up-to-date by picking up the ubiquitous *Dan's Papers.* Three upscale, celeb faves that have stood the test of time are **Nick & Toni's,** 136 N. Main St., East Hampton (𝒞 631/324-3550; www.nickand tonis.com); **Della Femina,** 99 N. Main St., East Hampton (𝒞 631/329-6666; www.dellafemina.com); and **Mirko's,** Water Mill Square, Water Mill (𝒞 631/726-4444). Keep in mind that reservations at many of these and other see-and-be-seen dining establishments can be very hard to come by, unless you know someone. But give it a try—you might get lucky. For top-quality Thai, try **Phao Thai Kitchen,** 29 Main St., Sag Harbor (𝒞 631/725-0101). **Turtle Crossing,** 221 Pantigo Rd., East Hampton (𝒞 631/324-7166; www.turtlecrossing.com), serves up satisfying Southwestern fare and barbecue. In Montauk, head straight to **Inlet Seafood,** 541 East Lake Dr. (𝒞 631/668-4272; inletseafood.com), owned by six local green-minded fishermen, or **Duryea's Lobster Deck,** 65 Tuthill Rd. (𝒞 631/668-2410), for views and amazingly fresh seafood.

Dress Code

While you'll always find the well dressed (and well heeled) in Hamptons restaurants, you won't feel out of place in casual attire unless you're dining at a very formal place like East Hampton's **The Palm** (an outpost of the NYC steakhouse). Servers at celebrity hangout Almond and other bold-face venues are typically clad in blue jeans. If you're in doubt, call ahead and ask.

EXPENSIVE

Almond ★★★ FRENCH BISTRO   This is one of the Hamptons' hottest dining destinations. It might be a challenge to score a reservation here, but if you do, ask for a table in the back for a more relaxed atmosphere. The menu offers traditional French bistro fare that is as simple as the decor, with only a few selections each night. Steak frites is an excellent choice, while the flounder and salmon are always tender; the macaroni and cheese is wonderfully over-the-top, flavored with chopped truffles and prosciutto.

1970 Montauk Hwy., Bridgehampton. 𝒞 **631/537-8885.** www.almondrestaurant.com. Reservations recommended. Main courses $19–$45. AE, DC, DISC, MC, V. Memorial Day to Labor Day Mon–Tues and Thurs 6–11pm, Fri–Sat 6pm–midnight, Sun 6–10pm; early Sept to late May Mon and Thurs 6–10pm, Fri–Sat 6–11pm, Sun 6–9pm.

MODERATE

Estia's Little Kitchen ★ MEXICAN/NEW AMERICAN   This teeny little roadside eatery, located a mile west of Sag Harbor Village, serves up extremely fresh and simple, yet carefully prepared, Mexican-accented food in a cheerful, cozy setting. We love the chocolate-chip pancakes and the breakfast burrito with andouille sausage; the

No trip to the East End is complete without a stop at the roadside mainstay **Lobster Roll**, 1980 Montauk Hwy., Amagansett (✆ **631/267-3740; www. lobsterroll.com**), which is credited with inventing the sandwich that has come to define summer on the Northeast coast. Load up on rich lobster bisque, crab cakes, or their signature dish. Down the road a piece, you'll find another much-loved clam shack, **Cyril's Fish House**, 2167 Montauk Hwy. (✆ **631/267-7993**), serving Caribbean-inflected seafood and colorful tropical drinks. At the aptly named **Clam Bar**, 2025 Montauk Hwy. (✆ **631/267-6348; www.clambar online.com**), grab a stool at the outdoor bar and suck down briny clams and oysters, straight-from-the-sea fish and chips, or their famous tuna bits.

"over-under" frittata comes with arugula, bacon, and sweet potato. The dinner menu, while small, is inspired: Recent offerings included paella with andouille, shrimp, chicken, and local fish; tender crab cakes; and a sweet corn risotto with sea scallops.

1615 Bridgehampton-Sag Harbor Tpk., Sag Harbor ✆ **631/725-1045**. www.eatshampton.com. Reservations recommended for dinner. Lunch salads and sandwiches $11–$17; dinner main courses $18–$30. AE, MC, V. Mon and Wed-Thurs 8am-2:30pm; Fri-Sun 8am-9pm. Call to confirm dinner hours in the off season.

Rowdy Hall ★ AMERICAN   The acclaimed burger at this English pub–style restaurant lives up to its hype: Stacked high with all the fixin's, it's also well worth the $14. Even if you're not a burger fan, this place, tucked back among the shops of tony East Hampton, serves a good selection of upscale pub food (yellowtail tuna, pork paillard) and great imported and domestic beer and wine, which makes it perfect for lunch or dinner.

10 Main St., East Hampton. ✆ **631/324-8555**. www.rowdyhall.com. Reservations not accepted. Main courses $14–$23. AE, MC, V. Daily noon-11pm.

Southampton Publick House ★★ 🎁 PUB   This bustling pub is the only microbrewery out here, so come by for a meal or just for the party that rages continuously. You'll find summer wheat beers and winter stouts on their inventive beer menu—formulas that have won them all kinds of awards. The menu covers the basics, but they're done well—from lager-battered fish and chips to great baby back ribs and roast Long Island duck. Come on a Tuesday for two-for-one dinner entrees.

40 Bowden Sq., Southampton. ✆ **631/283-2800**. www.publick.com. AE, DC, DISC, MC, V. Main courses $9–$25. Mon-Thurs 11:30am-10pm; Fri 11:30am-11pm; Sat noon-11pm; Sun noon-9pm.

INEXPENSIVE

Golden Pear COFFEE SHOP   With great coffee, fresh-baked muffins, and fluffy omelets, the four small Golden Pears are quaint but consistently good. While you wish the prices were just a little more reasonable, they're the perfect place to grab a morning coffee with your copy of the *New York Times*. Or come by later in the day for lunch, when you'll find soups, salads, and the delicious Santa Fe Lasagna, with layers of corn tortillas, roasted chicken, black beans, and cheese.

Locations: 99 Main St., Southampton; ✆ **631/283-8900**. 34 Newtown Lane, East Hampton; ✆ **631/329-1600**. 2426 Montauk Hwy., Bridgehampton; ✆ **631/537-1100**. 111 Main St., Sag Harbor; ✆ **631/725-2270**. www.goldenpearcafe.com. Sandwiches and entrees $11–$19. AE, MC, V. Daily 6:45am-5:30pm.

Sip 'n Soda ★★ ☺ 🖋 DINER   This old-fashioned soda fountain dates from 1958 and is a fun place for kids and adults alike. It also boasts prices that haven't hit the new millennium yet, making for some of the cheapest eats in Southampton.

40 Hampton St., Southampton. ℂ **631/283-9752.** Entrees from $5. No credit cards. July–Aug Thurs–Mon 7:30am–10pm, Tues–Wed 7:30am–6pm; rest of year daily 7:30am–5pm.

Townline BBQ ★ BARBECUE   This order-from-the-counter Southern barbecue joint, brought to you by the owners of Nick & Toni's and Rowdy Hall, has long wood tables inside and a few picnic tables outside—the perfect, low-key setting to chow down on swoon-worthy fried mac and cheese, corn bread, and, of course, slow-smoked meats. The pulled pork, on a fluffy potato bun with mounds of coleslaw, is excellent; order it with some spicy bread and butter pickles. Don't miss the desserts, especially the banana pudding and warm and flaky fried cherry pie, both of which are fantastically decadent.

Corner of Townline Rd. and Montauk Hwy., Sagaponack. ℂ **631/537-2271.** www.townlinebbq.com. Sandwiches and platters $6–$16. MC, V. Daily 11:30am–10pm.

The Hamptons After Dark

As you might imagine, Hamptons nightlife can be quite the scene. Bars can fill up quickly and some even roll out the velvet rope to restrict their clientele to models and people with movie deals. You'll never be lacking for nightlife, though; just wander around Southampton or East Hampton and you may well mistake it for ancient Rome right before its decline. Grab a copy of *Dan's Papers* or pick up the *East Hampton Star* or the *Southampton Press* for listings. Two current A-list clubs: **Pink Elephant,** 281 C.R. 39A, Southampton (ℂ **631/287-9888**), and **Dune,** 1181 North Sea Rd., Southampton (ℂ **631/283-0808**). Dress the part to increase your chances of getting past the door.

Year-round live music draws folks in droves to Amagansett's **Stephen Talkhouse,** 161 Main St. (ℂ **631/267-3117;** www.stephentalkhouse.com), for events that are often standing-room-only. Acts range from local blues acts to bigger names like Suzanne Vega or Todd Rundgren, and folks like Billy Joel and Paul McCartney have been known to show up unannounced and party with the band. One newer venue, the **Southampton Social Club,** 256 Elm St. (ℂ **631/287-1400;** www.southampton socialclub.com), has a speak-easy cachet and enough buzz to give other celebrity-studded clubs a run for their money.

Two of the better dive bars in the area are the **Montauket,** 88 Firestone Rd., Montauk (ℂ **631/668-5992**)—come here for the sunset—and **Murf's Backstreet Tavern,** 64 Division St., Sag Harbor (ℂ **631/725-8355**). For margaritas, check out the **Blue Parrot,** 33A Main St., East Hampton (ℂ **631/329-2583;** www.blue parroteasthampton.com), a well-established Mexican restaurant and bar where locals and power brokers alike rub elbows.

SHELTER ISLAND ★

Nestled between Long Island's two forks, tiny Shelter Island has served as a secluded getaway spot for centuries. Relaxed and barely developed, it has some nice beaches, protected coves great for boating and swimming, and an atmosphere unlike anything on the North or South forks. While most of the island's neighborhoods are filled with picturesque Victorian-era homes, more than one-third of the island is owned by the

Nature Conservancy and maintained as a preserve, and there's lots of lush greenery and dense woods all across the island. The only "townlike" area is around Shelter Island Heights on the island's northwest corner, where you'll find a couple of restaurants and antiques shops, and the north ferry.

Essentials

GETTING THERE Shelter Island is accessible only by boat; it's about a 10-minute ferry trip from the mainland. If you're driving, take the **LIE** out to Riverhead, then head north to Greenport or south to Sag Harbor—the distance is roughly the same. From Greenport on the North Fork, the **North Ferry Co. (✆ 631/749-0139;** www.north ferry.com) runs every 15 to 30 minutes from 6am to midnight (hours are extended during the summer). The round-trip price is $13 per car and driver, $5 for bicycles and riders, $4 per extra person or for walk-ons. From Sag Harbor, the **South Ferry (✆ 631/749-1200;** www.southferry.com) runs every 10 to 12 minutes from 5:40am to 11:45pm year-round, with extended hours in the summer and extended weekend hours the rest of the year. The round-trip price is $15 per car, $6 for bicycles, and $2 per person for walk-ons. *Tip:* Bring cash; the ferries don't take credit or debit cards. Because Shelter Island is so small, it doesn't matter which ferry you take, but if you don't want to bother with a car, you can take the **Long Island Rail Road (✆ 516/822-LIRR** [5477]; www.mta. info/lirr) to Greenport; the ferry is right next to the train station.

VISITOR INFORMATION Contact the **Long Island Convention & Visitors Bureau** at ✆ **877/FUN-ON-LI** (386-6654) or 631/951-3440, or at www.licvb.com. Alternatively, try the (somewhat limited) listings found on the **Shelter Island Chamber of Commerce** website at www.shelterislandchamber.com.

GETTING AROUND While the island is small, if you really want to explore, you'll need a car. Check out the South Fork section of this chapter for information on rentals. If you just want to relax at your hotel, you can arrange for a pickup at the ferry, or get a taxi by calling **Shelter Island Go'fors (✆ 631/749-4252).**

Beaches & Outdoor Pursuits

BEACHES The beaches here tend to be narrow strips of sand, but protected by the North and South forks, the waters are calm and perfect for swimming. Head to **Crescent Beach** and **Silver Beach,** both along the southwestern area of the island.

FISHING From May to July, the striped bass and bluefish are biting just off the island; from August to October, they migrate east toward Montauk. In either season, you can head out to the hot spots with Captain Jim Hull at **Light Tackle Challenge,** 91 W. Neck Rd. (✆ **631/749-1906).**

HIKING The **Mashomack Preserve,** Route 114 (near the South Ferry office; ✆ **631/749-1001),** stretches over 2,000 acres in southeastern Shelter Island—more than a third of the island. The Nature Conservancy purchased this ex–hunting club territory in 1980 and has protected its marshes, freshwater ponds, tidal creeks, and oak and beech woodlands ever since. Car free, it's a great place to go on easy hikes and look for osprey, ibis, hummingbirds, muskrats, deer, foxes, harbor seals, and terrapins (aka turtles). It's open daily April to September from 9am to 5pm; from October to March, the hours are 9am to 4pm, and it's closed Tuesdays. Admission is free, with a suggested donation of $2. Park just inside the preserve entrance and pick up a trail map to hike the four well-marked trails of varying lengths and difficulty (up to 11 miles), or call the office for a guided hike. *Tip:* To minimize disturbance to plants and animals, bicycles and even jogging are prohibited here.

KAYAKING The "sheltered" waters of the island's bays make for a perfect place to slice through on a kayak, and you'll likely see deer, osprey, and other wildlife on and off the shore. Go with **Shelter Island Kayak Tours,** Route 114 and Duvall Road (✆ **631/749-1990;** www.kayaksi.com). Rent a kayak ($30 per hr., 2-hr. minimum) or take a 2-hour tour ($60). The **Nature Conservancy** (✆ **631/749-1001**) also runs a few kayaking trips around Mashomack Preserve in the summer.

Where to Stay

EXPENSIVE

Sunset Beach ★★★ Designed by celebrity hotelier André Balazs, this waterside hotel oozes hipness from every corner. The minimalist rooms are done all in white, with contemporary aluminum lamps and splashes of color (like bold orange sinks). But the real highlight of these rooms is outside: enormous balconies on all of them, looking out onto the water, which more than makes up for the teeny bathrooms and small kitchenettes. The restaurant here attracts a crowd of people watchers who are willing to endure coma-inducing service for the chance to see and be seen (in other words, don't bother).

35 Shore Rd., Shelter Island, NY 11965. www.sunsetbeachli.com. ✆ **631/749-2001.** Fax 631/749-1843. 20 units. Weekday $345 and up double, weekend $565 and up double. 2-night weekend minimum, 3-night minimum summer holiday weekends. AE, DC, DISC, MC, V. Closed mid-Sept to mid-May. From the North Ferry, take Rte. 114 south to W. Neck Rd., which becomes Shore Rd. Pets allowed with $150 fee. **Amenities:** Restaurant; free use of mountain bikes and kayaks; room service, Wi-Fi (in lobby). *In room:* A/C, TV/DVD, hair dryer, kitchenettes (some units), minibar.

MODERATE

The Pridwin ★ ☺ At the other end of the same stretch of beach as the Sunset Beach hotel (see above), the Pridwin is decidedly less hip while offering good value. With one big inn and several small cottages, the grounds are fairly extensive—including three tennis courts. The smallish, carpeted hotel rooms are simple; get one with a water view, which is spectacular. Cottages vary from beach-y designer studios with a large deck (and great view of the bay) to a small, two-bedroom house up the hill—where there's plenty of space for an entire family, but no water in sight.

81 Shore Rd., Crescent Beach, Shelter Island, NY 11964. www.pridwin.com. ✆ **800/273-2497** or 631/749-0476. Fax 631/749-2071. 49 units. Late June to early Sept $227-$297 double, $307-$367 cottages; May–June and Sept–Oct Sun–Thurs $197-$237 double, $277-$297 cottages. Off-season rates include continental breakfast on weekends only; daily buffet breakfast in season. AE, MC, V. From the North Ferry, take 114 south to West Neck Rd.; it becomes Shore Rd., and the hotel is on the left. **Amenities:** Restaurant; lounge; bike rentals; outdoor saltwater pool; 3 tennis courts; extensive watersports rentals; Wi-Fi (in public areas). *In room:* A/C, TV, hair dryer, kitchenette (in cottages).

Ram's Head Inn ★★ Hidden away at the end of a peninsula off the east side of the island, this is truly a getaway, and one of the island's most luxurious inns. Accommodations range from two-room suites to small individual rooms with shared bathrooms; you'll find comfortable wicker furniture, lacy table coverings, and nice touches like pedestal sinks throughout. Grab no. 1 or nos. 2&3 (a suite) and have access to a shared balcony. Outside, the grounds are gorgeous, with Adirondack chairs, hammocks, and free use of the hotel's boats at their private beach.

108 Rams Island Dr., Shelter Island, NY 11965. www.shelterislandinns.com. ✆ **631/749-0811.** 17 units, 5 with private bathroom. May–Oct $75-$175 double with shared bathroom, $165-$375 suite with semi-private bathroom, $135-$295 double with private bathroom. Special discount midweek rates available. AE, MC, V. Closed Nov–Apr. From North Ferry take 114 north, bear right onto Cartwright Rd., turn right at stop sign to Ram Island Rd., turn right onto Ram Island Dr. **Amenities:** Restaurant; lounge; tiny fitness room; limited room service; sauna; tennis court; complimentary watersports equipment. *In room:* A/C.

Where to Eat

For reasonably priced comfort food (think meatloaf, shrimp dumplings, fried chicken, and so on) with terrific views, head to **Uncle Buck's,** 26 Sunnyside Ave. (© **631/749-0416**), new in 2009, at the Shelter Island Country Club.

EXPENSIVE

Ram's Head ★★★ AMERICAN   Shelter Island's best restaurant is in the flowery and formal dining room of the Ram's Head Inn. The seafood plates offer a delectable blend of flavors: Dig into the sautéed sweet pepper crab cake or the grilled Moroccan-spiced swordfish. Meat dishes also won't disappoint, with options like the *pot-au-feu*, and the roasted pork tenderloin with caramel-citrus sauce. Topping it off with excellent service, a well-chosen wine list, and an inviting bar area for a drink before or after dinner, it's worth the short trip to this remote part of the island.

108 Rams Island Dr. © **631/749-0811.** www.shelterislandinns.com. Reservations recommended. Main courses $19–$35. AE, MC, V. May–Oct Wed–Mon 6–10pm, Sat–Sun 11:30am–2pm. From South Ferry take 114 north, bear right onto Cartwright Rd., turn right at stop sign to Ram Island Rd., turn right onto Ram Island Dr.

Vine Street Café ★★★ 🍴 AMERICAN   This cafe's interior couldn't be more basic: wood floors, simple wooden tables and chairs, white walls, exposed beams. But the brief, seasonal menu—relying on local, organic ingredients—presents intensively complex flavors, such as the miso-glazed salmon. A range of steaks—from filet to a 42-ounce dry aged porterhouse—are offered, and the seafood options only get better, with ceviches and a seasonal raw bar.

41 South Ferry Rd. © **631/749-3210.** www.vinestreetcafe.com. Reservations preferred. Main courses $21–$107. AE, DISC, MC, V. Memorial Day to mid-Sept Sun–Thurs 5–10pm, Fri–Sat 5–11pm; mid-Sept to Memorial Day Thurs and Mon 5–9:30pm, Fri 5–10pm, Sat 5–10:30pm, Sun 5–9pm.

MODERATE

Sweet Tomato's ★★ AMERICAN   This eatery in the tiny town of Shelter Island Heights makes for a good dinner stop after antiquing. The Northern Italian menu doesn't present any surprises, but in the bright, cheery restaurant with hardwood floors, the classics are served up nicely. Try the chicken Antonio: chicken breast chunks with sautéed onions and peas in a pink, cognac cream sauce with rigatoni.

15 Grand Ave. © **631/749-4114.** Main courses $14–$29. AE, DC, DISC, MC, V. July to Labor Day Mon–Fri from 5pm, Sat–Sun from noon; rest of the year Tues–Sun from 5pm.

INEXPENSIVE

Pat & Steve's Family Restaurant ★ ☺ DINER   With a friendly staff and some of the most affordable food on the island, it's no wonder this family favorite fills up for breakfast, lunch, and dinner. But don't worry—with the quick service you won't be waiting long for a table. The menu covers the diner standards; we're partial to the pancakes at any time of day.

63 North Ferry Rd. (Rte. 114). © **631/749-1998.** Sandwiches $5–$9. No credit cards. Sun–Tues 6am–3pm; Fri–Sat 6am–8pm.

THE HUDSON RIVER VALLEY

by Neil Edward Schlecht

The Mississippi may be the longest and most famous river in the United States, but no river commands a larger place in American history than the Hudson. America's first great waterway flows from the Adirondacks down to New York City and the open sea. The rise of the United States from renegade colony to great nation is intrinsically linked at every stage to the mighty Hudson River. Recently celebrating 400 years since it was first sailed by Henry Hudson in 1609, the Hudson became the principal avenue of transportation for the emergent colonies in the 17th and 18th centuries and strategic territory during the war for American independence. As the young nation evolved, the Hudson became the axis along which some of America's most legendary families—among them, the Livingstons, Vanderbilts, Roosevelts, and Rockefellers—shaped the face of American industry and politics, leaving legacies of grand country estates and the towns that grew up around them.

Just over 300 miles long, the river is less mighty in size than stature. The Hudson River Valley spans eight counties along the east and west banks of the river, extending from Albany down to Yonkers. Divided into manageable thirds, the Lower, Middle, and Upper Hudson together compose a National Heritage Area and one of the most beautiful regions in the eastern United States. The river valley's extraordinary landscapes gave birth to America's first art school, the Hudson River school of painters, and writers like Edith Wharton and Washington Irving set their stories and novels along the banks of the Hudson. Though a place of immense historical importance and beauty, the river valley also has an impressive roster of sights and activities. The Hudson is lined with stunning country manor houses open to the public, unique museums, splendid historic sites, and easygoing Victorian hamlets. You can hike, kayak, fish, boat, golf, and even ski within easy reach of any of the towns along the Hudson. The valley—flush with organic farms and orchards, artisanal cheese makers, farmers' markets, and a growing number of wineries and small restaurants with Culinary Institute chefs at the helm—is fast becoming a real destination for gastronomes. For lovers of culture, history, the arts, the outdoors, and good food, the Hudson River Valley has few rivals anywhere in the country.

ORIENTATION

Arriving

BY PLANE   Most visitors traveling by air will probably fly into one of three major airports in the New York City area. For information on those, see chapter 5. Other possibilities include **Albany International Airport** (ALB), 737 Albany-Shaker Rd. (✆ **518/242-2222;** www.albanyairport.com), at the north end of the Upper Hudson Valley, and Newburgh's **Stewart International Airport** (SWF), Route 207, New Windsor (✆ **845/564-2100;** www.stewartintlairport.com), which handles daily flights from major U.S. cities such as Atlanta, Chicago, Philadelphia, Raleigh/Durham, and Washington, D.C.

BY CAR   Most visitors embark on tours of the Hudson Valley by private automobile. Major car-rental companies, including Avis, Budget, Enterprise, Hertz, National, and Thrifty, have representatives at all the major airports. The Lower Hudson Valley begins just north of New York City, on either side of the river; take either I-87 (New York State Thruway) north or the Taconic State Parkway. From Albany south, take I-87 south to 9W or I-90 south to Route 9. Heading either east or west, the most direct route is along I-84.

BY TRAIN   Amtrak (✆ **800/USA-RAIL** [872-7245]; www.amtrak.com) has service to the Hudson Valley from New York City, Syracuse, Buffalo, Montreal, and Boston, with stops in Albany, Rensselaer, Poughkeepsie, Rhinecliff, New Rochelle, Yonkers, Croton Harmon, and Hudson.

The **Metro-North Railroad** (✆ **800/638-7646;** www.mta.nyc.ny.us/mnr) travels up and down the Hudson. The trip along the river on the east side is one of the most scenic train trips in the U.S. The commuter line runs from Grand Central Station in New York City and services Westchester, Orange, Rockland, Putnam, and Dutchess counties (with stops in Beacon, Chappaqua, Cold Spring, Garrison, Katonah, Poughkeepsie, Tarrytown, and Yonkers, among others). Some packages include round-trip train travel and admission to sights, such as the 1-day getaway to Dia:Beacon and the Rockefeller estate, Kykuit.

BY BUS   Bus service throughout the Hudson Valley is available on **Adirondack/ Pine Hills Trailways** (✆ **800/776-7548;** www.trailwaysny.com), with service to New York City, New Paltz, Kingston, and Albany; **Greyhound Bus Lines** (✆ **800/231-2222;** www.greyhound.com); and **Shortline Coach USA** (✆ **800/ 631-8405;** www.shortlinebus.com), with local service from New York City and throughout Orange, Rockland, and Dutchess counties.

Visitor Information

General tourist information is available by calling **Hudson Valley Tourism, Inc.** (✆ **800/232-4782**) or by visiting the organization's website, www.travelhudson valley.org, for links to the very informative sites maintained by each of the eight counties that touch upon the Hudson River Valley. Tourist information offices or kiosks (and even cabooses) are found in a number of towns and at many historic sites, often operated in season only.

Many good free publications are widely available at hotels, restaurants, and other sites; look for *Hudson Valley Guide, Hooked on the Hudson River Valley, About Town, The Valley Table,* and *Chronogram.* These all contain information on arts, entertainment, and dining.

Area Layout

The Hudson Valley extends from the banks of the river to the foothills of the Catskill Mountains in the west and approaches the Connecticut border in the east (and the Massachusetts border in the Upper Hudson Valley). This chapter is in an order contrary to the current of the Hudson River: from Lower to Upper. For the purposes of this chapter, the **Lower Hudson** includes the area from Yonkers and Nyack to Newburgh and Beacon (comprising Rockland, Orange, Westchester, and Putnam counties); the **Mid-Hudson,** from Newburgh to Rhinebeck (Ulster and Dutchess counties); and the **Upper Hudson,** west of the river and north to Chatham (Columbia County). These dividing lines are somewhat arbitrary, with occasional county overlap; if you're intending to explore only a single section of the Hudson Valley, be aware that attractions and lodgings in one part of the valley may be only minutes by car from those categorized in another. Towns that could certainly be considered part of the Hudson Valley, such as Saugerties and Catskill, are discussed instead in chapter 8, "The Catskill Mountain Region."

 When to Go

Many of the great Hudson River estates and other attractions in the region are closed during the long winter months. In **spring** and **summer,** a number of the estates have extensive formal gardens and are absolutely glorious in May and June, and many have special events like concerts. In **autumn,** the leaves are ablaze with color and gorgeously set off against the backdrop of the river.

The Hudson River Valley is packed with sights from one end to the other, but the area is pretty manageable in size and easy to get around, especially if you have your own transportation. From the town of Hudson in the north to Yonkers, just outside New York City, is a distance of under 120 miles and just 2 hours by car. You could spend a couple of days or a couple of weeks making your way up the river. For this reason, note that in the sections that follow, attractions are grouped geographically, rather than alphabetically.

Getting Around

BY CAR   By far the easiest way to get around the Hudson Valley is by car. Public transportation, especially where it concerns county bus systems, is unduly complicated. Your best bet if not traveling by private automobile is one of the major bus carriers (see above), the train, or a tour operator. The main roads traversing the length of the Hudson Valley are I-87 and Route 9W on the west side of the river and Route 9 and the Taconic Parkway on the east.

All the major car-rental agencies have outlets at the area's airports and at several addresses throughout the region, including **Avis, Budget, Dollar, Enterprise,** and **Hertz.**

BY BUS OR TRAIN   See "Arriving," above.

BY TAXI   Local taxis are available at all the major train and bus stations, and in larger towns. Among taxi services throughout the Hudson Valley are **Yellow Cab Company** in Poughkeepsie (© **845/471-1100**); **Rhinebeck Taxi** (© **845/876-5466**); and **Howard's Taxi** in Hudson (© **518/828-7673**).

BY ORGANIZED TOUR   **Shortline Coach USA** (© **800/631-8405;** www.shortlinebus.com) offers Hudson Valley day trips and overnight packages and tours.

River Valley Tours (☎ **239/395-2191;** www.rivervalleytours.com) organizes week-long, inn-to-inn, and boat and bus trips along the Hudson. They're not offered often and are a little pricey (at just under $2,000 per person), but they allow visitors to really experience the grandeur and history of the Hudson River. **New York Water-way** (☎ **800/53-FERRY** [533-3779]; www.nywaterway.com) offers tours by boat (including Sleepy Hollow, Autumn on the Hudson, and Kykuit cruises) from Pier 78 in Manhattan (weekends and Mon holidays May–Oct). **Metro-North Railroad** (☎ **800/METRO-INFO** [638-7646]; http://mta.info/mnr/html/outbound.htm) has a series of "One-Day Getaways" to such places as West Point and Cold Spring, Dia:Beacon, Philipsburg Manor and Kykuit, and Woodbury Commons Outlet Mall, as well as organized cruises and 1-day hiking and biking tours.

THE LOWER HUDSON VALLEY

The Lower Hudson Valley, just north of New York City, claims some of the region's most popular sights, including the literary legends and grand estates of Sleepy Hollow, West Point Military Academy, and important Revolutionary War sites. Two of the valley's most picturesque and enjoyable villages, Cold Spring and Nyack, cling to either side of the river, and the scenery, with the rocky Palisades framing the wide expanses of the river, is stunning.

Exploring the Lower Hudson Valley
EAST SIDE OF THE HUDSON

Washington Irving's Sunnyside ★ Washington Irving—man of letters, diplomat, architectural historian, gentleman farmer, and first true international celebrity—designed an eclectic cottage in the country in 1835. Before he wrote *The Legend of Sleepy Hollow* and introduced the world to the Headless Horseman and Rip Van Winkle, Irving lived in England and was minister to Spain, where he rediscovered the Alhambra palace and reawakened its mystical architecture and aura with his *Tales of the Alhambra*. Sunnyside, with its mélange of historic and architectural styles, including a Dutch stepped-gable roofline, a Spanish tower, and master bedroom modeled after a Paris apartment, was Irving's personal romantic retreat. Today the pastoral villa, swathed in vines and wisteria and nestled into the grounds along the Hudson, remains as he left it, with his books and writing papers in the study. The train rumbles by the riverfront property, as it did toward the end of Irving's life (he died here in 1859). During the holidays, Sunnyside is festooned with Victorian Christmas decorations, and there are singalongs and storytelling. The 45-minute tours are led by guides in 19th-century costume.

W. Sunnyside Lane, off Rte. 9, Tarrytown. ☎ **914/631-8200** Mon–Fri, or 591-8763 on weekends. www.hudsonvalley.org. Admission $12 adults, $10 seniors, $8 students 5–17, free for children 4 and under. Grounds-only admission $5 adults and seniors, $3 students 5–17, free for children 4 and under. Apr–Oct Wed–Mon 10am–5pm (last tour at 4pm); Nov–Dec Sat–Sun (and last Fri in Nov) 10am–4pm (last tour at 3pm). Closed Jan–Mar. Metro-North to Tarrytown.

Lyndhurst ★★ ☺ One of the most impressive estates along the Lower Hudson, this handsomely restored Gothic Revival mansion, the finest of its style in the U.S., was designed by A. J. Davis in 1838 for a former New York City mayor. Later purchased by the railroad magnate and financier Jay Gould, the villa features an asymmetrical structure and grand Gothic interiors (including lots of faux stone and marble and stained-glass windows). The 67-acre estate features a massive glass and

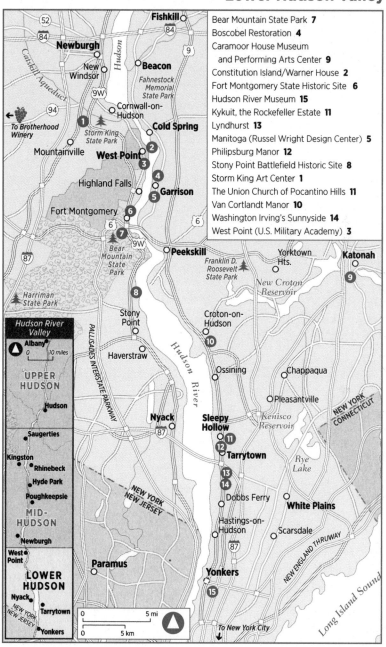

Bear Mountain State Park **7**
Boscobel Restoration **4**
Caramoor House Museum
 and Performing Arts Center **9**
Constitution Island/Warner House **2**
Fort Montgomery State Historic Site **6**
Hudson River Museum **15**
Kykuit, the Rockefeller Estate **11**
Lyndhurst **13**
Manitoga (Russel Wright Design Center) **5**
Philipsburg Manor **12**
Stony Point Battlefield Historic Site **8**
Storm King Art Center **1**
The Union Church of Pocantino Hills **11**
Van Cortlandt Manor **10**
Washington Irving's Sunnyside **14**
West Point (U.S. Military Academy) **3**

Sleepy Hollow Cemetery

Near Philipsburg Manor, in a gorgeous natural setting, is **Sleepy Hollow Cemetery ★★**, 85 peaceful acres where several famous former residents of the Lower Hudson River Valley, including Andrew Carnegie, William Rockefeller, and Washington Irving, are buried. (Alas, you won't find either the Headless Horseman or Ichabod Crane, both fictional characters, entombed here.)

The cemetery, on the east side of Route 9 just north of Tarrytown and the town of Sleepy Hollow, is open to the public and offers themed walking tours on select dates; call ℂ **914/631-0081** or visit www.sleepyhollowcemetery.org for more information. It's open Monday through Friday from 8am to 4:30pm and weekends from 8:30am to 4:30pm.

steel-framed conservatory (the largest of its day), rose garden, and arboretum. Today the mansion, a National Trust Historic Site, is decorated with many original furnishings and decorative objects culled from the three families who inhabited the estate over 123 years. Lectures and other activities, including vintage "base ball" games staged on the front lawn and candlelight Christmas evenings, are held at Lyndhurst. The self-guided audio tour, included in the price of admission, covers the entire property and Hudson Valley history; a children's version tunes kids into history and architecture. Plan on at least an hour or two here, several to explore the grounds.

635 S. Broadway, Tarrytown. ℂ **914/631-4481.** lyndhurst.wordpress.com. Admission $12 adults, $11 seniors, $6 students 12–17, free for children 11 and under; grounds-only pass $4. Mid-Apr to Oct Tues–Sun and holiday Mon 10am–5pm (last admission 4:15pm); Nov to mid-Apr weekends and holiday Mon 10am–4pm (last tour 3:30pm). Guided tours at 10:30am, 11:45am, and 2:15, 3:30, and 4:15pm Tues–Fri, more frequently on weekends. Metro-North to Tarrytown.

Philipsburg Manor ★★ ☺ Just a half-hour upriver from the 21st-century pace of New York City, this eye-opening agricultural estate is a jarring retreat to the late 17th and early 18th centuries. The bridge across the millpond of this Colonial farm and water-powered gristmill transports visitors to a complicated time in history, when this estate functioned as one of the largest slave plantations in the North—a shock to those who associate slavery only with the South. Organizers use that history to educate and place the estate, the entire Hudson Valley, and the influence of African culture in a historical context. Live demonstrations and scripted vignettes by interpreters in period dress bring to life the Colonial period, re-creating the lives of the single caretaker and 23 skilled slaves who lived and worked at this provision plantation. Frederick Philipse made his fortune in shipping and export to the West Indies, commerce that included the human slave trade. The large original manor house dates from 1685, when Philipse's landholdings in the area totaled more than 50,000 acres. When he died a bachelor, he left a 50-page inventory of his belongings, including the names of all his slaves, testimony to his extraordinary wealth. The site still functions as a working farm, with horses and sheep, wool spinning, milling of flour, and harvesting of rye. A great, educational outing for families (children will especially enjoy the special "Hands on the House" tours, featuring interactive "touch rooms," held on weekends at 11:30am and 2:30 and 4pm); allow a couple of hours.

Rte. 9, Sleepy Hollow. ℂ **914/631-8200** Mon–Fri, or 631-3992 on weekends. www.hudsonvalley.org. Admission $12 adults, $10 seniors, $8 students 5–17, free for children 4 and under. Apr–Oct Wed–Mon 11am–5pm (last tour at 4pm); Nov–Dec Sat–Sun (and last Fri in Nov) 10am–4pm (last tour at 3pm). Closed Jan–Mar. Metro-North to Tarrytown.

Kykuit, the Rockefeller Estate ★★★ The Hudson River is lined from one end to the other with grand manor houses, but none compares to Kykuit (pronounced "*Kye*-cut"). It's not the oldest or even the largest of the estates, but many people find it the most spectacular. When John D. Rockefeller, founder of Standard Oil, built Kykuit in its present classical Greek-Roman style in 1913, he was the richest man in the world. The estate, which became home to four generations of one of America's most famous business and philanthropic families, is architecturally grand and spectacularly sited and landscaped, with lovely stone terraces, fountains, and extensive Italianate formal gardens. Kykuit also houses Governor (and later Vice President) Nelson Rockefeller's incredible collection of 20th-century modern art, which graces the gardens and fills the entire lower level of the house. The sculpture collection includes important works by Alexander Calder, Henry Moore, Constantin Brancusi, and David Smith among its 70 works, all placed with great care to take maximum advantage of the gardens and their sweeping views of the Hudson (both perhaps unequaled by any of the great river estates). Outstanding among the pieces in the very 60s art gallery in the house is a unique series of giant and shockingly vibrant tapestries commissioned from Pablo Picasso.

Visits to Kykuit begin at Philipsburg Manor (see above); coaches shuttle visitors to Kykuit. Tours of Kykuit last between 2 and 3 hours. Choose from among several different tours depending on your interest: Classic Tour (main floor, inner gardens, and outdoor sculpture); in-depth Grand Tour; Selected Highlights Tour; and Timesaver Tour. In high season, tours often sell out by midday; advance reservations for individuals are suggested, especially for the Grand Tour.

Pocantico Hills, Sleepy Hollow (Rte. 9, 2 miles north of the Tappan Zee Bridge). ℂ **914/631-8200** Mon–Fri, or 631-3992 on weekends. www.hudsonvalley.org. Admission, Classic Tour, Timesaver, or Selected Highlights Tour $23 adults, $21 seniors and children; Grand Tour $40; indoor tours not recommended for children 9 and under. Second week of May to Nov 1, Wed–Mon: Classic Tour 10am–3pm (until 4pm on weekends and during daylight saving time); Grand Tour 9:45am and 1:45pm, also 2:15, 3, and 3:15pm weekends; Selected Highlights Tour 11am and 1:15pm; Time Saver Tour 12:50 and 3:50pm. Visitor center at Philipsburg Manor opens 9am to sell Kykuit tickets for that day only; tickets available by phone and online. Metro-North to Tarrytown.

Boscobel Restoration ★★ Two things about this magnificent mansion on the Hudson stand out: its splendid setting, among the finest in the entire Hudson Valley, and its incredible history. The house, an early-19th-century neoclassical Georgian mansion, was rescued from government destruction (it was sold at auction for $35 in the 1950s), moved piece by piece to its current location, and meticulously restored thanks to the generosity of the co-founder of *Reader's Digest*. The decorative arts of the Federal period that fill the house are indeed impressive, but they have a difficult time competing with the extraordinary river and gorge views afforded from the lawns, gardens, and orchards. No estate site along the river is more dramatic. Many activities are held here and should not be missed, including the Hudson Valley Shakespeare Festival (advance reservations required; www.hvshakespeare.org) in the summer, dancing to big-band music in the fall, and pre-Victorian Christmas Candlelight tours.

1601 Rte. 9D, Garrison. ℂ **845/265-3638.** www.boscobel.org. Admission $16 adults, $13 seniors, $8 children 6–14, free for children 5 and under, $40 family of 4; grounds only, $9 adults, $8 seniors, $5 children ages 6–14, free for children 5 and under, $25 family of 4. Apr–Oct Wed–Mon 9:30am–5pm (last tour at 4pm); Nov–Dec Wed–Mon 9:30am–4pm (last tour at 3pm). Closed Jan–Mar. Metro-North to Tarrytown.

WEST SIDE OF THE HUDSON

West Point (U.S. Military Academy) ★   West Point, the nation's oldest and foremost military college—it's more than 200 years old and also the oldest continually used military post in the U.S.—has produced some of the greatest generals and leaders this country has known, including Robert E. Lee, Ulysses S. Grant, Douglas MacArthur, George Patton, and Dwight D. Eisenhower. (Edgar Allan Poe, however, dropped out!) West Point is one of the nation's most esteemed and rigorous science and engineering colleges. The most popular attraction in the entire Hudson Valley, West Point is no longer as visitor-friendly as it once was, however, due to heightened security concerns. In fact, whereas visitors once were free to roam the campus among the orderly cadets in their dress blues, today the only way to visit is by organized 1- or 2-hour (June–Oct only) tours on a bus. It makes stops at the famous Cadet Chapel, which possesses stained-glass windows that were gifts of graduating classes and contains the largest church organ in the world, with more than 21,000 pipes; the Cadet Cemetery; and Trophy Point, where cannons captured from five wars are gathered in remembrance. The massive campus (home to 4,000 student soldiers), with its Gothic Revival buildings perched on the west side above the Hudson River, is undeniably handsome, especially in fall. Tickets for all tours must be purchased at the visitor center. Call ahead to confirm the tour schedule. Behind the visitor center, the West Point Museum is the oldest and largest collection of war memorabilia and war trophies in the U.S. See an atomic bomb, the cannon that fired the first American shot in World War I, Hitler's Lilliputian presentation pistol, and uniforms and artifacts that trace the history of warfare. For war and history buffs, it will be fascinating; for others, considerably less so. Allow 2 to 3 hours for the entire visit.

Rte. 218, Highland Falls. © **845/446-4724.** www.usma.edu or www.westpointtours.com. West Point 2-hr. tours admission $14 adults, $12 children 11 and under; museum free; 1-hr. tours admission $12 adults, $9 children 11 and under. 1-hr. tours Apr–Oct Mon–Sat 9:45am–3:30pm, Sun 11am–3:30pm; Nov Mon–Fri 10am–2:30pm, Sat 10am–3:30pm, Sun 11am–3:30pm; Dec Mon–Fri 11:30am and 1:30pm, Sat–Sun 11am–2:45pm; Dec 24 and Dec 31 11:30am. 2-hr. tours June–Oct daily 11:15am and 1:45pm; Nov 1:45pm only. Advance reservations for groups of 10 or more only. No tours on Sat of home football games or during graduation, 3rd week in May. Museum daily 10:30am–4:15pm.

Storm King Art Center ★★★ ☺   A most unusual museum, this fabulous collection of modern, monumental sculpture benefits from one of the most stunning outdoor settings modern art has ever seen: 500 acres of rolling hills, meadows, and woodlands that, especially in autumn, are capable of converting contemporary-art doubters into passionate enthusiasts. Storm King's interplay between nature and human creativity is extraordinary. On view are nearly 100 large-scale works by some of the greatest American and European sculptors of the postwar 20th century, including Mark di Suvero, Isamu Noguchi, Alexander Calder, Richard Serra, Andy Goldsworthy, and, forming the nucleus of the collection, 13 works by David Smith (with the outdoor placement echoing Smith's studio in the Adirondacks). One of the most recent installations is Maya Lin's monumental 11-acre, undulating, and oceanlike *Storm King Wavefield* (with "waves" reaching as high as 15 ft.). Every year Storm King presents a temporary exhibition of a couple of dozen works by a major sculptor. Though a warm, sunny day may be nicest to enjoy Storm King, the sculptures look and feel different under different conditions and in different seasons, so there is really no bad time to visit. Storm King, which celebrated its 50th anniversary in 2010, is a great place to spend an entire day, and perfect for introducing children to art;

constitution island/WARNER HOUSE

From the end of June to the beginning of October, visitors to West Point can take a ferry out to **Constitution Island,** nearly forgotten in the middle of the Hudson River, 900 feet east of the military academy. The tiny island (287 acres) is home to the 1836 Warner mansion, the fully furnished Victorian home of the writers Susan and Anna Warner (Susan was the author of the million-selling *Wide, Wide World*), and Revolutionary War ruins of Fort Constitution (chains were floated across the Hudson here to delay advancing British troops). The sisters, who never married, lived on the island until their deaths (they are buried at West Point Cemetery). Costumed docents lead visitors on a most unexpected view of American history from the middle of one of its most historic rivers, and kids love it. Reservations are essential, as tours are limited to 40 people; ferries leave from the South Dock at West Point. Tours are given Wednesday and Thursday from the last week in June to October 1 at 1 and 2pm; www.constitutionisland.org. Admission is $10 adults, $9 seniors and children ages 6 to 16, free for children 5 and under. Tours last 2 hours, 15 minutes. For reservations and information, call ✆ **845/446-8676.**

bring a picnic lunch (no food concessions are on the grounds). Guided tram tours make it easier on elderly and visitors with disabilities. You'll need several hours to see Storm King; you could easily spend an entire day here.

Old Pleasant Hill Rd., Mountainville. ✆ **845/534-3115.** www.stormking.org. Admission $12 adults, $10 seniors, $8 college students and children grades K-12, free for children 4 and under; Acoustiguide audio tours $5; free admission last Thurs June-Aug. Apr-early Nov Wed-Sun and holiday Mon 10am-5:30pm (on Sat Memorial Day to Labor Day, grounds remain open until 8pm and trams until 7pm); second week of Nov Wed-Sun 10am-5pm. Closed mid-Nov through Mar. Free docent-guided "Highlights of the Collection" tours daily (check website for schedule); free self-guided trams (hop on and off) daily noon-4:30pm.

More to See & Do
EAST SIDE OF THE HUDSON

In addition to the listings below, don't miss **Cold Spring,** one of the Hudson's most adorable waterfront towns located in Putnam County about an hour north of New York City. You'll find inviting views of the river, and a main street chockablock with antiques dealers, inns, cafes, and restaurants in Victorian cottages. Head 9 miles north on Route 9D, after the Bear Mountain Bridge.

Hudson River Museum ★ ☺ This large cultural complex in Yonkers, just north of New York City, covers several bases, including fine art, science, and history. It features six modern-art galleries (showing the works of George Segal and Andy Warhol, among others) and a high-tech planetarium. Also on the premises is a handsome restored 19th-century Victorian mansion overlooking the Hudson River and Palisades. The museum hosts a variety of interesting temporary exhibits as well as lectures, concerts, creative workshops, special seniors and family programs, and outdoors activities, such as kayaking on the Hudson.

511 Warburton Ave., Yonkers. ✆ **914/963-4550.** www.hrm.org. Admission $5 adults, $3 seniors and children. Planetarium admission $2 adults, $2 seniors and children. Wed-Sun noon-5pm; Fri noon-8pm.

The Union Church of Pocantico Hills ★★ 🎁 A short jaunt from the Rocke-fellers' Kykuit Estate is this tiny country chapel, remarkable not for its architecture per se but for its unique collection of stained-glass windows by Marc Chagall and Henri Matisse, two masters of modern art better known for their works on canvas. The collection, commissioned by the Rockefeller family, features a large rose window by Matisse—the final work of his life—and a series of nine side windows by Cha-gall—his only cycle of church windows in the U.S.—that illustrate biblical passages. One, at the back right-hand corner, is a memorial to the son of Nelson Rockefeller, who died on an expedition to New Guinea in the early 1960s. Matisse's rose window is very soothing, while Chagall's painterly images swirl with brilliant color; try to visit on a sunny day, when it is ablaze with dramatic light and color.

Rte. 448 (Bedford Rd.), Sleepy Hollow. ✆ **914/631-8200** Mon–Fri, or 914/332-6659. www.hudson valley.org. Admission $5. Guided tours (30 min.) available. Apr–Oct Mon and Wed–Fri 11am–5pm, Sat 10am–5pm, Sun 2–5pm; Nov–Dec Mon and Wed–Fri 11am–4pm, Sat 10am–4pm, Sun 2–4pm. Closed Jan–Mar.

Van Cortlandt Manor Although superficially the least spectacular of the seven Historic Hudson Valley properties, this working estate and Revolutionary War–era country manor house is a living-history museum that reveals much about the life and activities of the 18th century. Guides don Federal period dress, and the massive open-hearth kitchen and grounds play host to cooking, blacksmithing, weaving, and brick-making demonstrations. The tavern on the premises served customers of a ferry business that carried people back and forth across the Croton River.

S. Riverside Ave. (off Rte. 9; Croton Point Ave. exit), Croton-on-Hudson. ✆ **914/631-8200** Mon–Fri, or 914/271-8981 on weekends. www.hudsonvalley.org. Guided tours admission $12 adults, $10 seniors, $8 children 5–17, free for children 4 and under; grounds-only pass $5 adults, $3 children 5–17. Late May to 1st week of Sept Thurs–Sun 11am–5pm (last tour 4pm); Nov–Dec weekends only 10am–4pm (last tour 3pm). Closed Jan to late May.

Caramoor House Museum and Performing Arts Center ★ 🎁 A little off the beaten track for most Hudson Valley visitors, this surprising mansion and per-forming arts center is well worth a visit for a summer concert or a view of the unusual Mediterranean villa constructed by a wealthy New York couple. Walter and Lucie Rosen purchased entire rooms from European palaces, churches, and country homes, then brought them to the U.S. to incorporate into their sprawling mansion. It's hard to believe that the mansion and its bewildering array of Eastern, medieval, and Renaissance art and antiques were assembled on-site in the late 1930s. Caramoor is best known as a center of music and arts, and in particular for its summer outdoor Music Festival, which grew out of the Rosens' love for hosting concerts for their large circle of friends. The heart of the Rosen house is the extraordinary Music Room, a small palace unto itself, where chamber concerts are held throughout the year. For-mal afternoon tea (house tour included) is served on the family's original china in the Summer Dining Room, Thursday and Friday afternoons from 1:30 to 4pm ($30). Tours of the house last 1 hour.

149 Girdle Ridge Rd. (off Rte. 22), Katonah. ✆ **914/232-5035.** www.caramoor.org. Admission (Rosen house museum) adults $10, free for children 15 and under. May–Dec guided tours Wed–Sun 1–4pm (last tour 3pm). Metro-North to Katonah.

Manitoga/The Russel Wright Design Center ★ 🎁 Russel Wright, a preemi-nent midcentury American designer, tucked a unique country home into the woods and blurred the lines between interior and exterior, combining natural materials with industrial design. The only 20th-century modern home open to the public in New York, the 1962 house is very Zen-like, with abundant vegetation nearly camouflaging its simple lines. The house is sliced into a cliff above a dramatic waterfall and pond carved out of an abandoned quarry. Wright named the site Manitoga, which means "place of the great spirit," but he called the house "Dragon Rock," after his daughter's description of the massive rock that dips into the pond. In addition to the house, open for guided 90-minute tours, there are more than 4 miles of wooded hiking trails on the property.

Rte. 9D, Garrison. (C) **845/424-3812.** www.russelwrightcenter.org. House tour admission $15 adults, $13 seniors, $5 children 12 and under; hiking trails suggested contribution $5 adults, $3 seniors and children. May–Oct guided tours Mon–Fri (select days only; contact/see website for schedule) 11am, weekends 11am and 1:30pm; woodland garden paths weekdays year-round 9am–4pm, weekends Apr–Oct 10am–6pm; reservations recommended.

WEST SIDE OF THE HUDSON

Nyack ★ One of the more charmingly "lived-in" river villages along the Lower Hudson, Nyack is a bedroom community of New York with a laid-back life all its own. The town has a smattering of antiques shops, cafes, booksellers, and restaurants. The American realist painter Edward Hopper was born and went to high school in Nyack, and his mid-19th-century Queen Anne childhood home, today the **Hopper House Art Center** (82 N. Broadway; (C) **845/358-0774;** www.yearofedwardhopper.com; $5 adults, $3 seniors, free for children and students; Thurs–Sun 1–5pm), is preserved as a small museum of the artist's life and career and gallery space for temporary exhibitions. The **Runcible Spoon** (37–9 N. Broadway; (C) **845/358-9398**) is a great little bakery and favorite rest stop for cyclists who make the 50-mile round-trip from New York City.

Stony Point Battlefield State Historic Site This site commemorates the historic 1779 Battle of Stony Point, during which American forces led by Brigadier General Anthony Wayne stormed a British stronghold at midnight and caught the enemy by surprise. The victory was the last major battle in the North and is credited with boosting American morale. Visitors can walk the battlefield and see an audiovisual presentation at the on-site museum. Stony Point Lighthouse, built on the site in 1826, is the oldest on the Hudson; lantern walks and lighthouse cruises are offered several times a year (check the website for schedules).

Battlefield Rd. (off Rte. 9W), Stony Point. (C) **845/786-2521.** http://nysparks.state.ny.us. Free admission to grounds (but $5 parking fee); museum $2 adults, $1 seniors and children 5–12; audio tours $4 adults, $3 children 12 and under. Grounds mid-Apr to Oct Mon–Sat 10am–5pm; Sun noon–5pm; Nov to mid-Apr Mon–Fri 10am–4pm. Museum Wed–Sat 10am–4:30pm, Sun noon–4:30pm.

Fort Montgomery State Historic Site Fort Montgomery was the site of a brave 1777 Revolutionary War battle to control the Hudson River. Patriot troops effectively stalled the British march to aid Burgoyne's army at Saratoga—which may have made the difference in the war. Visitors can view ruins of the fortifications and listen to an audio tour that explains the battle and importance of the Hudson to the Patriot and British war plans. A visitor center and trails are now open.

Rte. 9G, 1/4 miles north of Bear Mountain State Park, Bear Mountain. (C) **845/446-2134.** http://nysparks. state.ny.us. Free admission; audio tours $4 adults, $3 children 12 and under. Wed–Sun 9am–4pm.

Especially for Kids

The Lower Hudson Valley has a number of great activities for families and kids. Tops is **Bear Mountain State Park:** In addition to its zoo, swimming lake and pool, ice-skating rink, and hiking trails, it has added an incredible $3-million carousel; the carved animals aren't just horses, but bobcats, rabbits, and bears—animals found in the park. The **Hudson River Museum** in Yonkers is a favorite of kids for its state-of-the-art planetarium. Although contemporary sculpture might not sound like most kids' idea of fun, the **Storm King Art Center,** with 100 monumental pieces spread over 500 beautiful acres, is a blast for children, who may have a more intuitive under-standing of the works than their parents! Several of the historic houses and estates along the river are entertaining for children. Interpreters in period dress at **Sunny-side, Van Cortland Manor,** and **Philipsburg Manor** are entertaining and educa-tional; the latter, a working farm that aims to present history lessons through actors and demonstrations, is particularly eye-opening. Occasional activities at **Lyndhurst,** such as vintage "base ball" games, should also delight kids.

Sports & Outdoor Pursuits

The Lower Hudson Valley abounds in outdoor sports, from hiking and biking to cross-country skiing to kayaking and sailing.

BOATING & SAILING Hudson Highlands Cruises (✆ 845/534-7245; www.commanderboat.com) embarks on 3-hour narrated cruises through the Hudson Highlands ($18 adults, $16 seniors and children 12 and under) departing from West Point, as well as cruises from Haverstraw and Peekskill ($25–$35 adults, $20–$30 seniors, $15–$20 children 12 and under). See "Boating & Sailing," in the "Mid-Hudson Valley" section (p. 208), as well.

CYCLING & MOUNTAIN BIKING Bike rentals are available from **Bikeway,** 692 Rte. 6, in Mahopac (✆ **845/621-2800;** bikeway.com), and 1581 Rte. 376, Wappingers Falls (✆ **845/463-7433**).

FISHING The Hudson, which flows from the Adirondacks to the open sea, is excellent for striped bass from mid-March to the end of May. There is also good trout fishing. For more information, visit www.hudsonriver.com. For guided fishing tours, check out the roster of Hudson River guides and charter boats on http://nyfisherman. net/hudsonriverguides.html.

GOLF Garrison Golf Club ★★, 2015 Rte. 9, Garrison (✆ **845/424-4747;** www.thegarrison.com), is a stunning course in the Hudson Highlands 800 feet above the river; the views are so pretty you may not care how you hit 'em. Rates are $45 to $90. There are more than 150 other golf courses in the Hudson River Valley; for specific information and course previews, see **www.hudsonrivergolf.com** and **www.golfhudsonvalley.com**.

HIKING There are too many great hiking spots in state parks in the Lower Hudson Valley to mention. Near Cold Spring, **Hudson Highlands State Park** has a number of great day trails. Recommended hikes in the vicinity of Cold Spring include Breakneck Ridge and Bull Hill; in the southern highlands south of Garrison, popular trails include those to Anthony's Nose and White Rock. Pick up a map at **Hudson Valley Outfitters,** 63 Main St., Cold Spring (✆ **845/265-0221;** www.hudsonvalleyoutfitters.com), which also offers guided hikes in the area, or contact the New York–New Jersey Trail Confer-ence (p. 55). **Bear Mountain and Harriman state parks** ★★ make up the majority of the Palisades Interstate Park and afford dozens of splendid hiking opportunities, including a section of the Appalachian Trail. For trail maps and more information, visit the Palisades Interstate Park Commission at Bear Mountain (© 845/786-2701). See "Hiking," in the "Mid-Hudson Valley" section (p. 209), as well.

KAYAKING & RAFTING   **Hudson Valley Outfitters** ★ (see "Hiking," above) is tops in the region for kayak rentals and guided tours. Its major competitor is **Pack & Paddle Adventures,** 45 Beekman St., Beacon (© **845/831-1300**), which also handles kayak and canoe rentals and instruction.

SWIMMING   **Bear Mountain State Park,** 3006 Seven Lakes Dr., Bear Mountain, NY (© **845/786-2701;** http://nysparks.state.ny.us/parks/13/details.aspx), allows for swimming in both Hessian Lake and the Bear Mountain pool, open in summer. There is also a public pool at Tallman State Park (Palisades Interstate Park Commission; © **845/359-0544**), just south of Nyack on Route 9W.

WINTER SPORTS   For snowshoe and cross-country ski packages, contact Cold Spring's **Hudson Valley Outfitters** (see "Hiking," above). **Bear Mountain State Park** has cross-country ski trails, ski jumps, and an outdoor skating rink open late October through mid-March. **Croton Point Park,** 1A Croton Point Ave., Croton-on-Hudson, NY (© **914/862-5290;** http://parks.westchestergov.com).

Shopping

The biggest draw by far among shopaholics is **Woodbury Commons Premium Outlets** ★, about an hour north of New York City in Central Valley, just south of Newburgh (498 Red Apple Court; © **845/928-4000;** www.premiumoutlets.com; Mon–Sat 10am–9pm, Sun 10am–8pm). There are more than 220 purveyors of clothing, home furnishings, jewelry, luggage, leather, and gift items, including Barneys New York, Burberry, Calvin Klein, Chanel, Coach, Dolce & Gabbana, Giorgio Armani, Gucci, Neiman Marcus Last Call, Saks Fifth Avenue, Versace, and Williams-Sonoma. By car, take exit 16 off the New York State Thruway, or I-87. You can also hop a Gray Line bus from the Port Authority Bus Terminal at 42nd Street and Eighth Avenue in New York City. The bus leaves daily beginning at 8:30am and the last departs at 2:45pm (© **800/472-9546;** www.grayline.com/New_York/Woodbury_Common_Premium_Outlets_Shopping_Tour; $37 adults, $19 children 5–11 round-trip). **Cold Spring** is the top antiques center in the Lower Hudson Valley. Main Street is lined with more than a dozen small antiques dealers and cute home-furnishings shops. **Taca-Tiques Antiques,** 109 Main St. (© **845/265-2655**), specializes in Victorian and estate sterling silver and beveled mirrors. **Nyack** is another town with a number of antiquing possibilities. Elsewhere, **Boscobel Restoration** in Garrison has one of the best gift shops attached to a historic site.

Though it's a bit removed from the Hudson Valley per se, lots of folks make the trip west to the **Sugar Loaf Art & Craft Village,** a hamlet in Orange County (north of Warwick, off Rte. 17) that features more than 50 shops and galleries dealing in jewelry, stained glass, and metalsmithing, among others. Sugar Loaf is open Tuesday to Sunday from 11am to 5pm; call © **914/469-9181** for events and more information.

Where to Stay

The Lower Hudson Valley's proximity to New York City makes it popular as a day trip, but there is so much to see and do that it is fortunate to have the widest and most plentiful array of accommodations in the valley. There's a good mix of historic inns, modern hotels, and small B&Bs, as well as motel and hotel chains that are hard to come by farther up the Hudson.

EAST SIDE OF THE HUDSON
Very Expensive

Castle on the Hudson ★★   This small, exclusive hotel, in a grand 45-room castle built in 1910 on a bluff overlooking the river, offers some of the most extravagant accommodations in the Hudson Valley. If you're willing and able to live like a prince, this is the place. Reminiscent of castles in Scotland and Wales, it comes equipped with the requisite stone walls, turrets, and heavy medieval touches, though the property has been endowed with every possible luxury for guests. Rooms (the entire property is smoke free) are elegant and extremely plush, but not over the top, with fine carpets, flowing drapes, and stylish linens on four-poster and canopied beds. The landscaped grounds don't skimp on fantastic views of the Hudson River. The Castle's fancy Equus restaurant is one of the most highly touted in the Lower Hudson Valley.

400 Benedict Ave., Tarrytown, NY 10591. www.castleonthehudson.com. **© 800/616-4487** or 914/631-1980. Fax 914/631-4612. 31 units. $275–$360 double; $385–$800 suite. AE, DC, DISC, MC, V. Free parking. **Amenities:** Restaurant; bar; concierge; fitness center; large outdoor pool; limited room service; tennis court. *In room:* A/C, TV/VCR, CD player, high-speed Internet.

Expensive

The Bird & Bottle Inn ★   Make a detour right into the Revolutionary War era at this charming inn, one of the oldest in New York State. The Bird & Bottle began its business life on the Old Albany Post Road in 1761 as Warren's Tavern, and the wide floorboards, dark beams, and rustic flavor of the place bow very little to modernity. For anyone looking for a dose of history, this is it. Rooms are not fussy, as indeed they shouldn't be, but are very comfortable and inviting, with luxurious four-poster and canopied beds and working fireplaces stocked with wood. For maximum privacy, check out The Cottage, located 50 feet from the main building. The restaurant reeks of Early American flavor. The cozy first-floor bar, affectionately known as the Drinking Room, is a great place for exactly that.

1123 Old Albany Post Rd. (off Rte. 9D), Garrison, NY 10524. www.thebirdandbottleinn.com. **© 845/424-2333.** Fax 845/424-2358. 4 units. $165–$230 double. Rates include breakfast. Weekend 2-night minimum. AE, MC, V. Free parking. **Amenities:** Restaurant; tavern. *In room:* A/C, no phone.

Inn at the Garrison ★★   A tiny inn (just four rooms) ensconced within a golf club that's best known for its greens, distant Hudson River views and excellent restaurant, this is a luxurious little place if you can get it when a wedding party isn't renting it out. Rooms are soothing and contemporary, with superb linens, bedding, and products. On the second floor, they have terrific views over the golf course and of the Hudson. There are yoga classes, spa treatments, and a gym, as well as golf, of course, and the splendid Valley Restaurant, but very little in terms of service (there's no reception service, and you'll be carrying your own bags upstairs). This is more like a hands-off B&B in unique surroundings—and where you'll also have to fetch your own breakfast at the grill and bar.

1123 Old Albany Post Rd. (off Rte. 9D), Garrison, NY 10524. www.thegarrison.com/the-inn/overview. html. **© 845/424-2333.** Fax 845/424-2358. 4 units. Apr–Oct $150–$175 double, $150 weekends (call for off-season rates). AE, MC, V. Free parking. **Amenities:** Restaurant; tavern; gym, yoga. *In room:* A/C, TV, Wi-Fi.

Moderate

Pig Hill Inn 📷   Right on Cold Spring's antiques shop–filled Main Street, this friendly and rustic little B&B is tucked behind a little antiques-and-gift shop of its own. In the cozy public rooms are plenty of decorative pigs on display, of course, while guest rooms are attractively done with Chippendale pieces, chinoiserie, and other antiques. Rooms have four-poster beds and comfortable quilts; many are equipped with fireplaces. Some rooms are very light and airy, while others are considerably darker and more masculine (and a few rooms have private bathrooms located in the hallway rather than the room itself). A gourmet breakfast is served in the Victorian conservatory, out back in the cute terraced garden area, in the main dining area, or even in bed.

73 Main St., Cold Spring, NY 10516. www.pighillinn.com. © **845/265-9247.** Fax 845/265-4614. 9 units, 5 with private bathroom. $150–$230 double; Fri–Sun $170–$250 double. Rates include full breakfast. Weekend and holiday 2-night minimum in high season. AE, DC, DISC, MC, V. Free parking. *In room:* A/C, Wi-Fi.

Tarrytown House Estate & Conference Center ★ ☺   A sprawling hotel complex and conference estate, with one 1840s mansion and six or seven outpost buildings on the property, is tucked serenely behind gates just up the road from Washington Irving's Sunnyside home on the river. Loaded with amenities and sports facilities, this is a perfect place for both business and leisure travelers, including families. Rooms are quite large and comfortable; they were recently renovated in attractive contemporary style (brightly colored and flowered, but unfussy, bedcovers). The best rooms by far are those in the Georgian-style King House mansion: They have antiques, fireplaces, and large, nicely appointed bathrooms—some even have terrific wraparound terraces.

E. Sunnyside Lane, Tarrytown, NY 10591. www.tarrytownhouseestate.com. © **800/553-8118** or 914/591-8200. Fax 914/591-0059. 212 units. $169–$259 double. AE, DC, DISC, MC, V. Free parking. **Amenities:** Restaurant; bar; concierge; fitness center w/sauna; large indoor and outdoor pools; limited room service; 3 tennis courts; basketball court; racquetball. *In room:* A/C, TV/VCR, Wi-Fi.

WEST SIDE OF THE HUDSON
Expensive

The Thayer Hotel at Westpoint ★   Ensconced within the grounds of the West Point campus, this landmark hotel is the best bet for anyone who always wanted to attend the military academy. A fine, large old hotel (constructed in 1926), built in a similar style to the Gothic campus and named for General Thayer, the "father of the academy," it has decent-size rooms with large, firm beds. Although one side looks over the beautiful campus and the other over the Hudson River, light sleepers should know that the train rumbles by right below on the river side, both late at night and early in the morning. You'll miss the river views, but the campus side is much quieter. The medieval-style restaurant in the basement is the best restaurant in the immediate area; Sunday brunch is especially popular.

674 Thayer Rd., West Point, NY 10996. www.thethayerhotel.com. © **800/247-5047** or 845/446-4731. Fax 845/446-0338. 127 units. $235–$299 double. AE, DC, DISC, MC, V. Free parking. **Amenities:** Restaurant; concierge; fitness center; limited room service. *In room:* A/C, TV w/pay movies.

Moderate

Bear Mountain Inn ★ ☺   This sturdy wood-and-stone lodge hotel, opened in 1915 on a spectacular site within the Bear Mountain State Park, is still (!) putting the finishing touches on its extensive renovation (years in the making) that will bring this landmark of park architecture back to its rustic glory. The interior of the main lodge features original chestnut log posts and beams, massive stone fireplaces, timber framing, birch and iron light fixtures, and plenty of animal trophies. All of the accommodations—including the Overlook Lodge and Stone cottages a mile from the main inn across Hessian Lake—are getting a makeover, but at press time those in the main inn have been undergoing renovation for more than 5 years and are still in the process of being transformed into luxury suites, with new furnishings and top-quality linens. Kids will love all the activities just outside the door, including the Wildlife Center, swimming in the lake, and hopping on the fantastic carousel; the inn is also pet-friendly. Because the renovation has gone on interminably, you may wish to verify that the main lodge is again open before reserving.

Bear Mountain State Park, Bear Mountain. www.visitbearmountain.com. ✆ **845/786-2731.** Fax 845/786-2543. 78 units. Prices for newly renovated rooms and suites TBD. AE, DC, DISC, MC, V. Free parking. **Amenities:** Restaurant; bar; outdoor pool; spa; skating rink. *In room:* A/C, TV, kitchenette, Wi-Fi.

Caldwell House ★★ 🛏
A classic, New England–style B&B in a historic Colonial home built in the early 19th century, this friendly and intimate inn is a perfect base for exploring the west side of the lower Hudson. The four rooms are lovingly decorated with period furnishings. The spacious Catherine Caldwell room is the choice for honeymooners, with its step-up Jacuzzi tub, antique sink, and gorgeous four-poster bed. The three-course breakfasts dreamed up by owner Carmela—who has published her own cookbook—are something to write home about, especially the crème brûlée French toast, ginger scones, and pumpkin pancakes. Carmela even sells her hand-knitted items in the gift shop. Clearly, this is the kind of place for people who genuinely enjoy staying at B&Bs. Look online for "getaway specials."

25 Orrs Mills Rd., Salisbury Mills, NY 12577. www.caldwellhouse.com. ✆ **800/210-5565.** Fax 845/496-5924. 4 units. Mon–Thurs $165–$225 double; Fri–Sun $185–$260 double. Rates include full gourmet breakfast. AE, MC, V. Free parking. *In room:* A/C, TV/VCR, Wi-Fi.

Cromwell Manor ★
This sophisticated inn, in an imposing, historic house with white pillars, sits on 7 acres and is just minutes from Storm King Art Center and 5 miles from West Point. Well managed and decorated in period style (rooms are elegant, but a few touches and bathrooms may strike some as a little modern and functional), it is one of the best B&Bs in the Hudson Valley. It faces a 4,000-acre nature preserve, spectacular in autumn. The Cromwell Suite has a private entrance and a bathroom so large that the owners have stuck a StairMaster in it (kid you not!). The separate Chimneys Cottage, the oldest part of the house (1764), is the most charming; it has four guest rooms, one of which has an enormous sitting room. The hands-on owners host a number of special events, such as weekend chef dinners and cooking classes.

174 Angola Rd., Cornwall, NY 12518. www.cromwellmanor.com. ✆ **845/534-7136.** Fax 845/534-0354. 13 units. $145–$380 double. Rates include full gourmet breakfast. AE, MC, V. Free parking. *In room:* A/C, Wi-Fi.

Storm King Lodge ★ 🛏
Just down the road from the splendid Storm King Art Center, this charming, family-run, year-round B&B is a relaxing place to stay. It's also ideal for art lovers and outdoorsy sorts; innkeeper Gay is a kayaker and can help organize outings on the Hudson. The home, once a carriage house on a 19th-century farm, is quiet and comfortable, with a high-ceilinged and cozy wood-paneled great room and a serene, covered back deck, with stunning views past Storm King (including views of Andrew Goldsworthy's *The Wall That Went for a Walk*) to the Hudson Hills. The four guest rooms, three of which are upstairs off the great room, are very

clean and spacious, with nice private bathrooms; two rooms (Pine and Lavender) have working fireplaces. Families or couples should check out the Guest Cottage, with two bedrooms (that can be rented separately) and a full kitchen next to the large swimming pool.

100 Pleasant Hill Rd., Mountainville, NY 10953. www.stormkinglodge.com. ✆ **845/534-9421.** Fax 845/534-9416. 5 units. $160–$200 weeknights, $175–$250 weekends double. Rates include buffet breakfast. MC, V. Free parking. **Amenities:** Outdoor pool. In room: A/C.

CAMPGROUNDS

There are many campgrounds around the Hudson Valley. Among them are **Croton Point,** Route 9, Croton (✆ **914/271-3293;** year-round; 180 sites, 48 with electricity); **Mills-Norrie State Park,** Old Post Road, Staatsburg (✆ **800/456-CAMP;** mid-May to late Oct; 55 sites); **Harriman State Park: Beaver Pond,** Route 106, Bear Mountain (✆ **800/456-CAMP** [2267]; mid-Apr to early Oct; 200 sites); and **Fahnestock State Park,** Route 301, Carmel (✆ **80/456-CAMP** [2267]; Memorial Day weekend to Labor Day weekend; 86 sites).

Where to Eat

Whether it's pizza for kids tired of touring grand estates, a romantic dinner in a historic inn, or a casual meal in a riverfront restaurant, you'll find a good mix of dining options in the Lower Hudson Valley.

EAST SIDE OF THE HUDSON
Expensive

The Bird & Bottle Inn ★ AMERICAN/CONTINENTAL A tavern and inn since Colonial times, when travelers stopped along the Old Post Road to Albany for fortification, this inn, recently renovated and reopened with a new owner and chef, remains one of the most atmospheric places to dine in the Hudson Valley. The three separate dining rooms with fireplaces are models of rustic elegance. Dinner features a seasonal three-course prix-fixe tasting menu. Your appetizer might be salmon tartare, followed by roasted rack of lamb or a grilled Trinidadian-spiced pork chop. The wine list has a number of surprisingly affordable choices. The Sunday champagne brunch is also quite an affair, though more casual.

1123 Old Albany Post Rd. (off Rte. 9D), Garrison. ✆ **845/424-2333.** www.thebirdandbottleinn.com. Reservations recommended weekends and holidays. Main courses $16–$45; dinner prix-fixe $54; brunch $32. AE, MC, V. Thurs–Sat 6–10pm; Sun 4–8pm; Sat–Sun brunch 11:30am–3pm.

Blue Hill at Stone Barns ★★★ NEW AMERICAN This offshoot of the classic NYC restaurant, Blue Hill, run by acclaimed chef Dan Barber, is one of the finest restaurants in the state. For farm-to-table foodies, this place is paradise: There is no menu per se, just a presentation of 100-plus of the freshest daily ingredients from this working, nonprofit farm and other local farms and purveyors, which diners and chefs craft into a pre-fixe "farmer's feast" of four, five, or eight courses (mains might include Blue Hill Farm pigs, soft-shell crabs, or Cornish Cross chickens). The sleek dining room within the massive-stone former cow barn is elegant but relaxed (still, shorts are not permitted, and jackets are preferred for men). It's not cheap, but for a special occasion it would be hard to recommend a better meal outside of New York City.

630 Bedford Rd., Pocantico Hills. ✆ **914/366-9600.** http://bluehillfarm.com. Reservations essential. Prix-fixe menus $88 (Sun only), $108, and $148. AE, DC, MC, V. Sun and Wed–Thurs 5–10pm; Fri–Sat 5–11pm; Sun 11:30am–2pm.

Valley ★★★ 🍴 NEW AMERICAN   One of the most sophisticated restaurants in the Hudson Valley, this serene spot, specializing in seasonal, "farm-to-table" American cuisine, is unexpectedly tucked in among the perfect green lawns of the Garrison, a golf club and spa. High on the eastern bank of the Hudson is this smallish restaurant, a handsome contemporary dining room with rustic touches, pale woods, and a striking glass wine wall. The focus is on fresh ingredients and organic meats and poultry from its own Garrison farm as well as other nearby Hudson Valley farms. The seasonal menu is expertly prepared, but for most people this will be a special night out (the "Eat Local" small plates menu on Thurs nights is more casual). In warm weather, the outdoor deck is a coveted spot, though I'm still partial to the elegantly understated dining room.

2015 Rte. 9, Garrison. ℂ **845/424-2339** or 424-3604. www.thegarrison.com/restaurants/valley.html. Reservations recommended. Main courses $28–$36. AE, DC, MC, V. Mar–Sept Thurs–Sat 5:30–9:30pm, Sun 11:30am–2pm.

Moderate

Brasserie Le Bouchon ★ FRENCH BISTRO   This French restaurant stands out in laid-back, antiques-mad Cold Spring: It's sexy and chic, with deep-bordello-red walls and ceilings, red banquettes, glittering mirrors, and bistro lighting. For the most part, it emphasizes home-cooked French comfort food like mussels, slow-braised pork tenderloin, and steak frites. Appetizers include foie gras. Desserts, such as Grand Marnier double-dark chocolate mousse, are similarly sinful. The restaurant is late-night cool, and it has a little bar at the back, a good spot to have a drink. If it's nice outside, you can dine on the patio, though it pales in comparison to the interior.

76 Main St., Cold Spring. ℂ **845/265-7676.** Reservations recommended weekends and holidays. Main courses $15–$29. AE, MC, V. Daily noon–10pm.

Lanterna Tuscan Bistro TUSCAN   Nyack is a delightful little town, and in Lanterna it gets what it deserves, a charming restaurant with flair but few pretensions. A small and mostly minimalist space with wood tables, white tablecloths, white walls, and slow-moving ceiling fans, it has one long corridor and two small sitting areas—one up front and the other back by the kitchen. The chef, Rossano Giannini, turns out authentic Tuscan dishes and also gives cooking classes, demonstrations, and wine tastings. Lunch might be a simple affair of homemade pasta and soup or salad, while the dinner menu features risotto, fresh fish (halibut sautéed with white wine and herbs is a good one), and hearty meat dishes such as filet mignon topped with Gorgonzola and a Barolo reduction. As you would hope, the wine list has some good Italian selections. On a nice day, a few tables are set up on the sidewalk for alfresco dining.

3 S. Broadway, Nyack. ℂ **845/353-8361.** www.lanternausa.com. Reservations recommended weekends and holidays. Main courses $16–$29. AE, DC, MC, V. Mon–Thurs 11am–10pm; Fri–Sat 11am–11pm; Sun 11am–9pm.

Sushi Mike's ★★ 🍴 SUSHI   Locals claim the sushi here is every bit as good as what you'll find in New York City, and it's hard to disagree. My wife is a sushi snob, and she loves to detour off the Saw Mill River Parkway on the way out of the city to dip into Sushi Mike's, a friendly and fun little spot with excellent and creative rolls, sushi, and sashimi, as well as daily seafood specials. The owner, Mike, is a gregarious sort who greets regulars and newcomers at the door and comes around to the tables to make sure his diners are happy. There is sometimes live jazz on weekend and

Monday nights, when a vocalist and keyboard player are crammed in next to the sushi bar; if you're not interested in being serenaded, sit in the lower dining room, or, in warm weather, at one of the handful of tables on the street corner.

146 Main St., Dobbs Ferry, NY. ☎ **914/591-0054.** www.sushimikes.com. Reservations recommended. Main courses $17–$28. AE, DC, MC, V. Mon–Fri 11:30am–3pm; Mon–Thurs 4:30–10pm; Fri 4:30–11pm; Sat noon–11pm; Sun 3–10pm.

Tavern at Highlands Country Club ★★ 🍽️ ☺ AMERICAN   Focusing on a farm-to-table approach of local providers, this intimate, cozy little restaurant on the premises of a golf club is surprisingly ambitious. Inside a vintage brick playhouse, with rustic, tavernlike tables and a larger garden room, the restaurant is sophisticated but approachable. I'm a fan of the herb-and-citrus-crusted hake, but there are also comfort items like the tavern burger and buttermilk fried chicken. There's even a $6 children's menu. The well-chosen wine list is all-American (with a nod to New York wineries), while the specialty beer list is totally New York–centric.

955 Rte. 9D, Garrison. ☎ **845/424-3254.** www.highlandscountryclub.net. Reservations recommended. Main courses $19–$23. AE, MC, V. Wed–Thurs noon–9pm; Fri–Sat noon–10pm; Sun 11am–9pm; July–Aug also Tues noon–9pm.

WEST SIDE OF THE HUDSON
Moderate

MacArthur's Restaurant (at The Thayer Hotel) ★ AMERICAN   Eat where the parents of West Point cadets do, in this 1920s hotel on the campus of the famous military academy. The Thayer Hotel's restaurant, now nicely renovated, has a vaguely medieval feel, like dining in the workers' mess hall in a Gothic castle. Even if you're not staying here, it's worth passing through two or three security checkpoints for a meal. Entrees include pan-seared red snapper, baked stuffed shrimp with crabmeat, and rack of lamb with mint demi-glace. Sunday's champagne brunch is very popular, as are special events like comedy and dinner and dancing on Friday and Saturday evenings. A good spot for a predinner drink, adjacent to the main dining room and overlooking the Hudson, is General Patton's Tavern (no one ever said the West Point connection was subtle).

674 Thayer Rd., West Point. ☎ **845/446-4731.** Reservations recommended. Main courses $16–$30; Sun brunch $28. AE, DC, DISC, MC, V. Daily 7–10:30am and 5:30–9pm; Mon–Sat 11am–2pm; Sun brunch 10am–2pm.

Inexpensive

Prima Pizza ☺ PIZZA   A family-owned, old-fashioned New York pizza joint, Prima has been in the same family since 1954. It's friendly and cozy, with bar stools at the counter and about 10 tables under hanging plants. The fresh dough is made daily, and sauces and meatballs are made on the premises. Besides some very creative brick-oven pizzas, including lemon chicken and health-conscious no-fat and low-fat, it serves a mean hot meatball sub and more substantial dishes like lasagna and eggplant parmigiana.

252 Main St., Cornwall. ☎ **800/22-NY-PIE** (226-9743). www.pizzaofnewyork.com. Reservations not accepted. Main courses $13–$19. AE, DISC, MC, V. Tues–Thurs 10am–9pm; Fri 10am–10pm; Sat 11am–10pm; Sun noon–9pm.

The Lower Hudson Valley After Dark

The small towns along the Hudson River Valley provide just a few alternatives for evening entertainment; the biggest offering is of summertime concerts. In Katonah, **Caramoor Performing Arts Center** ★★, 149 Girdle Ridge Rd. (off Rte. 22;

© 914/232-5035; www.caramoor.org), features the popular Summer Music Festival, with outdoor classical music concerts, as well as indoor chamber and cabaret performances in the spring and fall. **Boscobel Restoration** in Garrison, 1601 Rte. 9D (© 845/265-3638; www.boscobel.org), is home to the **Hudson Valley Shakespeare Festival ★★★** (www.hvshakespeare.org) on the lawn in the summer and dancing to big-band music in the fall. In Tarrytown, **The Music Hall Theatre,** 13 Main St. (© 914/631-1000; www.tarrytownmusichall.org), a terrific 1885 theater and National Historic Landmark that was saved from destruction, is a great place to see a theater production or music performance. Events range from *Sleeping Beauty,* the ballet, to Eddie Palmieri, the Latin jazz giant.

THE MID-HUDSON VALLEY

The Mid-Hudson Valley is the historic Great Estates region, a stretch of the river valley where families like the Vanderbilts and the Mills built truly spectacular spreads that epitomized the fantastic wealth and lofty aspirations of the Gilded Age. The region was also home to Franklin and Eleanor Roosevelt, pivotal 20th-century American figures who remained vitally connected to their roots here. The region received an unexpected overdose of media attention in 2010, when Chelsea Clinton had her wedding in easygoing Rhinebeck. Parts of the Mid-Hudson are slowly undergoing greatly needed revitalization, especially on the west side of the river, with towns like Kingston and Newburgh taking advantage of their waterfront locations for development, spawning lively bar and restaurant scenes, and Beacon catapulting to life with the arrival of a stunning contemporary-art museum and new art galleries. Though within easy reach of many towns on both sides of the Hudson, several places near the river but also at the edge of the Catskill Mountains, including New Paltz, High Falls, and the Minnewaska Preserve (and the Mohonk Mountain House), are covered in chapter 8.

Exploring the Mid-Hudson Valley
EAST SIDE OF THE HUDSON

Dia:Beacon ★★★   In a 1929 Nabisco box-printing factory on the banks of the Hudson, the Dia Art Foundation has created the world's largest contemporary-art museum, an institution that adheres to the foundation's single-minded purpose. The new museum houses Dia's rarely seen permanent collection of pivotal conceptual, minimalist, and Earth artists, mostly men who came of age in the 1960s and 1970s. Nearly 250,000 square feet of gallery space—illuminated almost entirely by natural light that streams in through the factory's original skylights—were designed to exhibit the works of single artists. Works include sculptures by Richard Serra (whose long gallery, the former train shed, is devoted to three of his massive *Torqued Ellipse* pieces), the fluorescent-light sculptures of Dan Flavin, Andy Warhol's work *Shadows,* and mixed-media installations by Joseph Beuys. Other noted artists include Gerhardt Richter, Louise Bourgeois, Sol LeWitt, Walter De Maria, and Bruce Nauman (whose creepy installation documenting the nocturnal comings and goings of rats in his studio is perfectly suited to the basement). These are challenging artists across the board, and their minimalist works will surely strike some viewers as head scratchers; but even visitors who aren't great fans of contemporary art are likely to find the museum space and the site on the river quite extraordinary. Check online for schedules of free gallery talks the last Saturday of each month at 2pm.

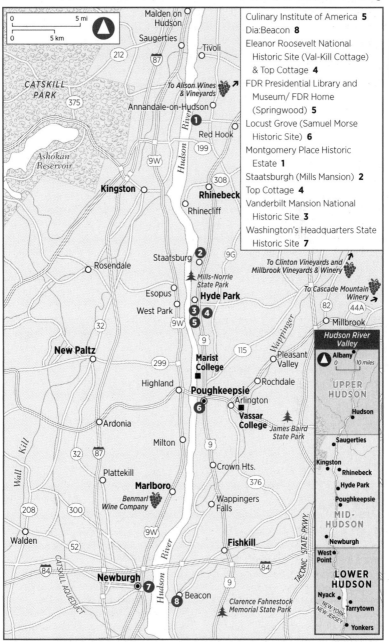

Culinary Institute of America **5**
Dia:Beacon **8**
Eleanor Roosevelt National
   Historic Site (Val-Kill Cottage)
   & Top Cottage **4**
FDR Presidential Library and
   Museum/ FDR Home
   (Springwood) **5**
Locust Grove (Samuel Morse
   Historic Site) **6**
Montgomery Place Historic
   Estate **1**
Staatsburgh (Mills Mansion) **2**
Top Cottage **4**
Vanderbilt Mansion National
   Historic Site **3**
Washington's Headquarters State
   Historic Site **7**

Note: Metro-North Railroad offers a "1-day getaway" fare that includes round-trip train fare from New York City and discounted admission to Dia:Beacon. See www.mta.info/mnr/html/getaways/outbound_diabeacon.htm for prices and additional information.

3 Beekman St., Beacon. © **845/440-0100.** www.diabeacon.org. Admission $10 adults, $7 seniors and students, free for children 11 and under. Mid-Apr to mid-Oct Thurs–Mon 11am–6pm; mid-Oct to mid-Apr Fri–Mon 11am–4pm. Metro-North to Beacon.

Vanderbilt Mansion National Historic Site ★★★   One of the finest and most intact of the lavish estates built by wealthy 19th-century industrialists along the Hudson, Frederick William Vanderbilt's 54-room country palace in Hyde Park, built in 1898, is a no-holds-barred gem. One of the first steel-framed houses in the U.S., at 55,000 square feet (on 670 acres), it was the smallest and least expensive of the famed Vanderbilt mansions (others were in Newport, Bar Harbor, and Asheville), but it still epitomized the Gilded Age's nouveau riche. French in every respect, from Louise's Versailles-like bedroom to the grand dining room and Frederick's glittering master bedroom, it was decorated in impressively grand style. Yet the house, where the Vanderbilts spent only a few weeks each year in the spring and fall, functioned as a kind of spa retreat. Guests were encouraged to enjoy the outdoors: the majestic views of the Hudson and Catskills in the distance and the wonderful gardens and woodlands surrounding the house.

Rte. 9, Hyde Park. © **845/229-9115.** www.nps.gov/vama. Admission (guided 45-min. tour) $8 adults, free for children 15 and under. Daily 9am–5pm (by guided tour only, the last at 4pm). Closed Thanksgiving, Christmas, and New Year's Day. Grounds daily year-round 7am–sunset (free admission). Metro-North and Amtrak to Poughkeepsie.

Franklin Delano Roosevelt Presidential Library and Museum/FDR Home (Springwood) ★★★   Franklin Delano Roosevelt, the four-term president of the United States who was faced with not only the Great Depression and World War II, but living with polio, loved the Hudson River Valley. FDR designed his own presidential library, the nation's first, while still in his second term and built it next to his lifelong home in Hyde Park. He actually used the study while president and often would be in residence while the library was open to the public; it is the only presidential library to have been used by a sitting president. See his cluttered White House desk (left as it was the last day of his presidency), exhibits on the FDR presidency and times, and FDR's beloved 1936 Ford Phaeton, with the original hand controls that allowed him to travel all over the estate. Two wings added in memory of

---

Take the Trolley

After your visit to Dia:Beacon, hop aboard Beacon's Main Street Trolley (Fri–Sun) for a spin through town and check out the city's self-described "Renaissance on the Hudson." The trolley makes several stops along Main Street (hop on and off all afternoon for $2), but be sure to check out the charming East End antiques district and the contemporary galleries that dot Main Street. Highlights include **Open Space** (510 Main), **Collaborative Concepts** (348 Main), **Concentric Gallery** (174 Main), and **Hudson Beach Glass,** housed in a restored firehouse (162 Main). *Note:* If the trolley isn't running during your visit, it's just a 1-mile drive to downtown from Dia:Beacon.

These historic sites in Hyde Park belong to the extensive network of national parks. Several new discount passes are available to visitors, including the National Parks and Federal Recreation Lands Annual Pass, $80 (individuals; good for 1 year), and Interagency Senior Pass, $10 (for seniors only; lifetime membership). Older passes, including National Parks Passes, Golden Eagle, Golden Eagle Hologram, Golden Access, and Golden Age Passports, will continue to be honored according to the provisions of the pass. All park passes, good for free entry to any Vanderbilt-Roosevelt historic site tour, can be purchased at the national park sites in Hyde Park. For more information, see www.nps.gov or http://store.usgs.gov/pass.

his wife, Eleanor Roosevelt, make this the only presidential library to have a section devoted to a first lady. Springwood, the house next door, was built by FDR's father; FDR expanded the modest farmhouse in an eclectic Dutch Colonial style. The home isn't grand by the standard of the great river estates, but FDR entertained Churchill, the king and queen of England, and other dignitaries here. FDR and Eleanor are buried in the rose garden on the grounds. The Wallace Center, an impressive new visitor center at the entrance to the library (where tickets for all FDR sites are purchased), presents a short film on FDR and Eleanor. Advance reservations during the popular fall foliage season are a good idea (© **877/444-6777;** www.nps.gov/hofr/planyourvisit/feesandreservations.htm), and reservations are accepted up to 5 months in advance.

4079 Albany Post Rd. (off Rte. 9), Hyde Park. © **800/FDR-VISIT** (337-8474) or 845/229-5320. www.nps.gov/hofr or www.fdrlibrary.marist.edu. Admission (museum and guided tour of the Springwood home, good for 2 days) $14 adults, free for children 15 and under. Buildings daily 9am–5pm (last tour 4pm); grounds daily 7am–sunset. Metro-North and Amtrak to Poughkeepsie.

Eleanor Roosevelt National Historic Site (Val-Kill Cottage) & Top Cottage ★ Both Eleanor Roosevelt—who, like her husband, grew up in the Hudson River Valley—and FDR maintained serene and simple private country retreats away from Springwood. When FDR was away, and after his death, Eleanor—one of the most admired and influential women in American history—lived and worked out of Val-Kill Cottage, the only home she ever owned. A simple, rustic, cabinlike home, Val-Kill is where Eleanor received world leaders and made her mark on civil rights legislation and international humanitarian issues (as a U.N. delegate, she chaired the committee that drafted the U.N. Human Rights Universal Declaration). The grounds were also the headquarters of Val-Kill Industries, which Eleanor and several other women established to teach trades to rural workers and produce Colonial Revival furniture and crafts.

FDR's retreat on a hilltop, which he christened Top Cottage, was more rustic still. He built it on Dutchess Hill in the 1930s as an informal place to get away from it all and think about issues confronting his presidency. FDR was at his most relaxed here, even allowing himself to be photographed in his wheelchair. Restored but unfurnished, Top Cottage has recently been opened to visitors who come to see FDR's cherished views of the Catskill and Shawangunk mountains from the famous porch, where he entertained guests such as Winston Churchill and King George VI and

Queen Elizabeth II of England (guests at his "scandalous" 1939 hot dog dinner). A wooded trail leads from Springwood to Val-Kill and Top Cottage. Visits to both cottages are by guided tour only (tickets are available at the visitor center at the FDR Presidential Library and Museum).

Rte. 9G, Hyde Park. ℂ **845/229-9115** or 229-9422. www.nps.gov/elro. Admission (45-min. guided tour) to either, $8 adults, free for children 15 and under. May–Oct daily 9am–5pm; Nov–Apr Thurs–Mon 9am–5pm (last tour 4pm); grounds year-round daily sunrise–sunset. Metro-North and Amtrak to Poughkeepsie.

Staatsburgh (Mills Mansion) ★★   One of the most opulent and elegant of the Hudson River estates, Staatsburgh, an 1896, 65-room Beaux Arts mansion on 1,600 acres (now the Mills-Norrie State Park), was the country home of Ogden and Ruth Livingston Mills. Mrs. Mills, a member of the prominent Livingston clan, inherited the simpler original home—one of five Mills family mansions—in 1890. She and her husband renovated it in grand European style, combining her aristocratic lineage with the big new money of the era, and the result is pure Gilded Age: 18-foot ceilings, a massive Louis XIV–style dining room with green Italian marble on the walls, sumptuous library, dramatic central staircase crowned by a ceiling mural, and 14 bathrooms. The house, the first in the area to have electricity, is outfitted with all original furnishings. Staatsburgh is thought to have been the model for the Bellomont estate in Edith Wharton's *The House of Mirth*. A number of special events (with special admission prices) are held here, including summer concerts, "Celtic Day in the Park" (Sept), "Scarborough Fair" (June), "Gilded Age Christmas," and an antique-car show in October. Note that the mansion continues to undergo extensive exterior and interior restoration (expected to last several years). Visits are by guided tour only.

Old Post Rd. (off Rte. 9), Staatsburgh. ℂ **845/889-8851.** www.hvnet.com/houses/mills. Admission $5 adults, $4 seniors and students, $1 children 5–12, free for children 4 and under. Apr to Labor Day Wed–Sat 10am–5pm, Sun noon–5pm (last tour 4:30pm); Labor Day to last Sun in Oct Wed–Sun noon–5pm; Dec special extended hours for holiday program; Jan–Mar Sun 11am–4pm. Closed Nov. Metro-North and Amtrak to Poughkeepsie.

Montgomery Place Historic Estate ★   Montgomery Place, reopened after a restoration, is one of the most lovingly sited and best preserved estates along the Hudson. This 434-acre, early-19th-century country Federal-style home enjoys splendid lawns and gardens and outstanding views overlooking the Hudson River and the distant Catskill Mountains. The most prominent designers of the day, the architect A. J. Davis and landscape designer Andrew Jackson Downing, built the home in fieldstone and stucco for the widow of Revolutionary War hero General Richard Montgomery. Inside are family possessions from the late 1700s all the way to the second half of the 20th century. The house exhibits a very strong French influence, with hand-painted wallpaper and a formal parlor fashioned after Dolley Madison's White House parlor, though the massive kitchen in the basement and its original hearth are very Dutch in style. Many of the gardens were created in the 1930s, and they are some of the most beautiful of any estate along the Hudson. Montgomery Place is a great place to bring a picnic lunch and walk among the orchards, gardens, and woodland trails that lead to Sawkill Falls.

Annandale Rd. (River Rd., off Rte. 9G), Annandale-on-Hudson. ℂ **914/631-8200** or 845/758-5461. www.hudsonvalley.org. Admission (by 45-min. guided tour only) Mid-May to Oct Thurs–Sun 11am–4pm, Sun noon–5pm (last tour 3pm); grounds daily 9am–4pm. Metro-North and Amtrak to Rhinecliff.

Walk Across the Hudson

Claiming to be the longest pedestrian bridge in the world, the landmark 1888 Poughkeepsie Railroad Bridge (✆ 845/454-9649; www.walkway.org), now known as **Walkway Over the Hudson,** had its grand reopening in October 2009. The 6,767-foot (1¼-mile) bridge, the longest in the world when it was inaugurated, is now a "linear park," open to walkers, cyclists, joggers, people with disabilities, and pets on leashes connecting to rail trails and parks on both sides of the river. The views up and down the river are spectacular, especially at sunset and in autumn. It stretches from Poughkeepsie, on the east side of the Hudson, to the town of Lloyd on the west side.

WEST SIDE OF THE HUDSON

Washington's Headquarters State Historic Site ★ General George Washington established his military headquarters on the banks of the Hudson in Newburgh in 1782 and 1783, during the final years of the Revolutionary War. He, his wife, Martha, and his principal aides and their servants occupied a 1750 farmhouse donated to the army by a prosperous family, the Hasbroucks. Washington stayed here 16 months (and Martha 12 months), longer than at any other headquarters during the war. In 1850, the property was declared the nation's first public historic site. The farmhouse displays Washington's office (where he wrote the famous "circular letter" and Newburgh addresses) and the original tables and chairs of the general's aides-de-camp. A museum, opened in 1910, across the lawn displays memorabilia such as medals of honor (including a 1783 original badge of military merit), locks of Washington's hair, and Martha's pocket watch from her first marriage. Revolutionary War buffs may also wish to visit the **New Windsor Cantonment** (✆ **845/561-1765**), a few miles away on Route 300. The staff at Washington's Headquarters can give directions to reach this site where Washington's 7,500 troops and their families camped during the winter of 1782 and 1783. There are living-history presentations and military demonstrations in season.

84 Liberty St., Newburgh. ✆ **914/562-1195.** www.nysparks.com/historic-sites/17/details.aspx. Admission $4 adults, $3 seniors and students, $1 children 5–12, free for children 4 and under. Mid-Apr to Oct Wed–Sat 10am–5pm, Sun 1–5pm; Nov to mid-Apr by appointment.

Other Attractions
EAST SIDE OF THE HUDSON

Culinary Institute of America ★★ This lovely 150-acre riverside campus (a former Jesuit seminary) looks every bit the part of prestigious northeastern college—except the students are decked out in chef's whites and the professors wield knives. The nation's oldest culinary-arts school and only residential college in the world dedicated to culinary training, the CIA (chefs, not spies) is open for tours (not to mention culinary "boot camps" for serious nonprofessionals). The institute has trained thousands of chefs and food-service-industry professionals, including some of the most prominent chefs in the country, since its founding in 1946. You'll see and smell what's cooking in the 41 kitchens and bake shops. If you're a foodie, a tour of this culinary temple is a must; others, with perhaps less interest in the behind-the-scenes of cooking school, may just want to have lunch or dinner at one of the excellent restaurants. CIA also operates four restaurants and a bakery cafe, all staffed by students, open to the public (see "Where to Eat," later in this chapter), and a culinary bookstore and gift shop. *Note:* All restaurants are closed when school is not in session; see the website for dates of closing (most of the month of July, plus selected dates throughout the year).

1946 Campus Dr., Hyde Park. ℰ **845/285-4627.** www.ciachef.edu. Admission $6. Tours (reservation required) Mon 10am and 4pm; Wed–Fri 4pm (when classes in session only). Closed July.

Rhinebeck ★★   Briefly famous in 2010 as the host of Chelsea Clinton's secretive wedding, this historic, gracious small town marked by the oldest inn in America, the Beekman Arms is one of the most visitor-friendly spots along the Hudson. It has an expanding number of inns, sophisticated restaurants (including a tavern where George Washington dined), diverse furnishings and antiques shops, and even an art house movie theater. It's a perfect town to walk around and enjoy at a leisurely pace. Chief among its attractions are the **Old Rhinebeck Aerodrome,** a museum of antique airplanes with 30 annual air shows, and **Wilderstein,** an elegant 19th-century Queen Anne mansion once occupied by Daisy Suckley, FDR's distant cousin and close confidant. The house, which features a five-story tower, a massive veranda, and reams of family documents and belongings, has ongoing renovation, but is fascinating for the contrast it provides to the grander and somewhat more buttoned-up estates up and down the Hudson.

Old Rhinebeck Aerodrome: Stone Church Rd. and Norton Rd., Rhinebeck. ℰ **845/752-3200.** www.oldrhinebeck.org. Admission Mon–Fri (museum) $10 adults, $8 seniors, military, and students 13–17, $3 children 6–12, free for children 5 and under; Sat–Sun (museum and air show) $20 adults, $15 seniors, military, and students 13–17, $5 children 6–12, free for children 5 and under. June to mid-Oct daily 10am–5pm; air shows every Sat–Sun mid-June to mid-Oct 2pm. **Wilderstein:** 330 Morton Rd., Rhinebeck. ℰ **845/876-4818.** www.wilderstein.org. Admission $10 adults, $9 seniors and students, free for children 11 and under; May–Oct Thurs–Sun noon–4pm and Dec holiday weekends noon–4pm.

Locust Grove (Samuel Morse Historic Site)   Locust Grove, a 150-acre estate and Tuscan-style villa, was purchased by Samuel Morse, painter-turned-inventor. The 19th-century artist invented the electric telegraph and Morse code and made a fortune that his paintings—though respected—never brought him. Morse purchased the 1830 Georgian estate from the Young family (today the art, furnishings, and decorative arts primarily recall their stay here) and brought in the noted architect A. J. Davis (designer of Lyndhurst and Montgomery Place) to expand and remodel it. The property has a man-made lake, waterfall, and lovely gardens. A recent addition to the estate is a small but well-done museum dedicated to the life, art, and inventions of Morse, and an excellent visitor center that shows a film on the estate and Morse's life.

2683 South Rd. (Rte. 9), Poughkeepsie. ℰ **845/454-4500.** www.lgny.org. Admission $10 adults, $6 students 6–18, free for children 5 and under. Tours May–Nov daily 10am–4pm (last tour 3:15pm); Apr and Dec Sat–Sun 10am–4pm (last tour 3:15pm). Grounds year-round daily 8am–dusk (free admission).

WEST SIDE OF THE HUDSON

Kingston ★   New York State's first capital, the old Dutch town of Kingston, on the west bank of the Hudson, has two distinct historic areas of great interest to visitors. In uptown Kingston is the historic **Stockade District,** a pleasant commercial area marked by the presence of 21 pre-Revolutionary, Dutch-style stone houses (all four corners at the intersection of John and Cross sts. are occupied by 18th-century stone houses, unique in the U.S.). Chief among the historic landmarks is the **Senate House,** which housed the first New York State Senate in 1777 after the adoption of the first constitution, until British troops burned Kingston later that same year. The Senate House Museum contains Colonial artifacts and the paintings of John Vanderlyn. Along North Front and Wall streets is a pretty 2-block area of buildings with turn-of-the-20th-century-style canopied sidewalks, called the Pike Plan, home to a number of shops, galleries, restaurants, and cafes. The Old Town Stockade Farmers' Market is held Saturday, June through September. Opposite the Old Dutch Church is the **Fred J. Johnston Museum,** an 1812 Federal-style house with an excellent collection of American decorative arts. At the other end of town, Kingston's historic waterfront area, the **Rondout,** reached its pinnacle in the days of the D & H Canal in the early 19th century, but declined with the advent of the railroad. Today, it's a nicely revitalized commercial area with a burgeoning number of restaurants and bars. It is also home to the **Hudson River Maritime Museum and Lighthouse** (an old boat shop with exhibits on the history of boating and ships), weekend vintage trolley rides out to the Hudson (which begin in front of the Maritime Museum), Sampson opera house, and a handsome new visitor center. Boats leave from the Maritime Museum to go out along Rondout Creek to the 1913 Rondout Lighthouse (call © **845/336-8145** for information). The Rondout is also the spot to catch the larger **Hudson River Cruises** on the *Rip Van Winkle* ship (for more information, see p. 208).

Senate House: 296 Fair St., Kingston. © **914/338-2786.** www.nps.gov/nr/travel/kingston/k2.htm. Admission $3 adults, $2 seniors, $1 children 5-12. Apr 15-Oct Wed-Sat 10am-5pm, Sun 1-5pm. **Fred J. Johnston Museum:** 63 Main St., Kingston.© **845/339-0720.** Admission $3. May-Oct Sat-Sun 1-4pm. **Hudson River Maritime Museum:** 1 Rondout Landing, Kingston. © **845/338-0071.** www.hrmm.org. Admission museum only, $5 adults, $4 seniors and children 6-12, free for children 5 and under; boat to lighthouse $15 adults, $12 seniors and children ($3 discount with admission to museum). Museum Apr-Oct daily 11am-5pm (July-Aug Wed until 8pm); boat rides May-Oct weekends and holiday Mon noon-3pm.

Especially for Kids

Kids will love the **Rhinebeck Aerodrome,** with its vintage airplanes and cool air shows. In Kingston, families can take a **Hudson River cruise** out to the lighthouse or hop aboard a vintage trolley car. Some of the great estates have extraordinary grounds and gardens with trails through the property; check out the **Vanderbilt Mansion, Staatsburgh,** and **Montgomery Place.** And finally, as an educational supplement to history classes, take the kids to **Washington's Headquarters** in Newburgh and the **FDR Presidential Library and Museum** in Hyde Park.

Shopping

In the Mid-Hudson Valley, **Beacon, Red Hook,** and **Rhinebeck** are the best towns for antiquing. Each has a couple of streets lined with good and interesting shops. In Beacon, now home to an exploding roster of antiques shops, gift stores, and galleries, **Relic,** 484 Main St. (© **845/440-0248**), is the place for vintage housewares. **Beacon Hill Antiques** (474 Main St.; © **845/831-4577**) peddles fine antiques while **Past Tense Antiques,** across the street at 457 Main (© **845/838-4255**), offers well-priced antique and vintage pieces. **Hoffman's Barn Sale** in Red Hook, 19 Old Farm Rd. (© **845/758-5668**), is an old barn with thousands of old, used, and antique items of varying quality. A particularly fine store in Rhinebeck is **Asher House Antiques,** 6380 Mill St. (© **845/876-1796**), which deals in both elegant and country-rustic English and French pieces. Behind the Beekman Arms Hotel on Mill Street is the **Beekman Arms Antique Market,** with several dealers in an old barn (© **845/876-3477**). **Gold Goat,** 6119 Rte. 9 (© **845/876-1582**), is a small gallery with some cool pieces of American folk art. Rhinebeck hosts the **Rhinebeck Antiques Fair,** with three big shows annually featuring more than 200 dealers at the Dutchess County Fairgrounds, Route 9 (✆ **845/876-1989;** www.rhinebeck antiquesfair.com). In Hyde Park, the **Hyde Park Antiques Center,** 4192 Albany Post Rd. (✆ **845/229-8200**), has 45 dealers and is open daily.

Those with a specific interest in arts and crafts should pick up the free *Explore Dutchess County Crafts and Arts Trail* brochure (available at many hotels, shops, and tourist information offices), which details more than two dozen crafts shops and galleries on the east side of the Hudson, as well as crafts shows.

Sports & Outdoor Pursuits

The Mid-Hudson Valley is rich in outdoor activities, including river cruises, hiking and biking, and cross-country skiing. Besides more traditional outdoor sports, thrill seekers may want to check out barnstorming flights on biplanes over the Hudson Valley at the Old Rhinebeck Aerodrome (p. 206). Flights take off before and after air shows (15 min.; $40 per person).

BOATING & SAILING **Hudson River Cruises,** Rondout Landing at the end of Broadway, in Kingston (✆ **800/843-7472;** www.hudsonrivercruises.com), sets sail aboard the *Rip Van Winkle,* a modern 300-passenger vessel. The standard 2-hour cruises ($21 adults, $19 seniors, $13 children 4–11) visit the Mid-Hudson Valley in spring, summer, and fall; there are also specialty live-music, murder-mystery, and kiddie cruises. In Newburgh, **Hudson River Adventures** (Newburgh Landing; ✆ **845/220-2120;** www.prideofthehudson.com) operates 2-hour sightseeing cruises ($20 adults, $18 seniors and children 4–11) Wednesday to Sunday from May to October on the *Pride of the Hudson,* a 130-passenger boat.

The *Hudson River Sloop Clearwater* ★★, part of an environmental project to clean up the Hudson River, is a 75-foot, single-masted replica of a 19th-century ship, which embarks on 3-, 6-, and occasional 8-hour cruises along the Hudson from April to mid-November. It sets sail from Saugerties, Kingston, and New York City's 79th Street Boat Basin, among other ports of call along the river. Sail prices on the *Sloop* or its sister ship, *Mystic Whaler,* range from $35 to $50 for adults, with discounts available for children, students, and seniors. For schedules and more information, call ✆ **800/67-SLOOP** (677-5667, ext. 107) or visit www.clearwater.org.

GOLF There are more than 150 golf courses in the Hudson River Valley. **Dinsmore Golf Course** ★, Old Post Road (Rte. 9), Staatsburgh (✆ **845/889-4071;** http://nysparks.state.ny.us/golf-courses/21/details.aspx; greens fees $17–$26), the second-oldest golf course in the United States, is part of the 1,000-acre Mills-Norrie State Park, which includes the Mills Mansion State Historic Site. With panoramic views of the Hudson River and majestic Catskill Mountains, it was named "Best Public Golf Course in the Hudson Valley" by *Hudson Valley Magazine.* Putnam County's **Centennial Golf Club** ★★, Simpson Road, Carmel (✆ **845/225-5700;** www. centennialgolf.com; greens fees $30–$135), a hilly 1999 design by Larry Nelson, is one of the most picturesque in the Hudson Valley. **The Garrison Golf Club** ★, 2015 Rte. 9, Garrison (✆ **845/424-3604;** www.thegarrison.com/golf.html; greens fees $35–$95), is a classic old 18-hole course with spectacular views from 800 feet above the Hudson across from West Point. It has a yoga and spa center and distinguished restaurant on the premises.

For additional course information, course previews, and discount pass books, see **www.hudsonvalleygolf.com**.

HIKING Four miles north of Cold Spring on Route 9D, an excellent trail leads to **South Beacon Mountain,** the highest point in the East Hudson Highlands (a 6-mile round-trip). The 5-mile **Breakneck Ridge Trail,** also in Beacon, with views of the Hudson and Shawangunk and Catskill mountains, was voted the top hiking trail in New York State on www.trails.com. **Clarence Fahnestock Memorial State Park,** a 7,000-acre park southwest of Beacon (Rte. 301, Carmel; © 914/225-7207), is also a terrific place for hiking, with a number of trails and loops (suggested hikes include Three Lakes Trail and East Mountain–Round Hill). Less strenuous trails can also be found in **Mills-Norrie State Park** (© 914/889-4100), the site of the Staatsburgh Mills Mansion. On the other side of the Hudson, **Bear Mountain Loop** near Newburgh is a popular trail.

SPA/WELLNESS The Rhinebeck campus and Wellness Center at **Omega Institute for Holistic Studies ★★** (150 Lake Dr., Rhinebeck, NY; © 877/944-2002; www.eomega.org), on 185 acres with a lake, gardens, and rolling hills, offers retreats and wellness, spiritual growth and environmental workshops, yoga, hiking trails, tennis and basketball, and more.

SWIMMING Canopus Lake in **Clarence Fahnestock Memorial State Park,** southwest of Beacon (Rte. 301, Carmel; © 914/225-7207), has an attractive beach and swimming area open to the public.

WINTER SPORTS **Fahnestock Winter Park** (Rte. 301, Carmel), part of Clarence Fahnestock Memorial State Park between Cold Spring and Beacon, is one of the best spots for Nordic skiing, snowshoeing, and sledding. Besides tons of trails, it also offers equipment rentals and lessons. For information and condition reports, call © 845/225-3998.

Where to Stay

The Mid-Hudson isn't loaded with accommodations options—there is little in the way of national chain hotels and motels—but the few it does have are quite special.

EAST SIDE OF THE HUDSON
Expensive/Moderate

Belvedere Mansion ★★ For unrestrained luxury—and fantasy—in a country inn, none comes close to the Belvedere. The 1900 neoclassical mansion, with its pillared facade perched above the Hudson just south of Rhinebeck, features a carriage house, pond, and lodge on the property, and a bewildering choice of accommodations. The seven main-house rooms are the biggest and most expensive; several have fantastic river views and details like claw-foot tubs and canopied beds. The Henry Hudson Suite is a cool trio of rooms on the top floor, all sharing a bathroom—perfect for a genteel family or group of friends. A nice bargain are the four small rooms called "cozies," which adequately describes their charm. The Belvedere Restaurant, in the mansion, is sumptuous, a place for a fancy meal.

10 Old Rte. 9, Staatsburgh, NY 12561. www.belvederemansion.com. © **845/889-8000.** 22 units. "Cozies" $105–$125 double; Zen Lodge $125–$175; Carriage House $150–$195 double; Mansion Rooms $225–$275; Hunt Lodge $250–$450 suite. All rates include gourmet breakfast. 2-night minimum stay weekends; 3-night minimum some holidays. AE, DC, DISC, MC, V. Free parking. **Amenities:** Restaurant; tavern. *In room:* A/C, Wi-Fi.

Beekman Arms/Delamater Inn ★ The Beekman Arms claims the distinction of being America's oldest continually operating inn; it's been around since 1761, and very much looks the part. How's this for pedigree? George Washington, Benedict

Arnold, and Alexander Hamilton all drank, ate, and slept here. And the Colonial Tap Room (tavern) and lobby look like they could still welcome them, with their wide-plank floors, stone hearth, and hand-hewn beams. The upstairs rooms in the main inn are nicely decorated and perfectly comfortable, if not quite as special as the public rooms might lead you to expect. The Delamater Inn, just up the street on Mill Street/ Route 9, is the relative new kid on the block; the noted architect A. J. Davis built the main American Gothic house in 1844. The oldest rooms are in the main house, carriage house, and gables; Courtyard and Townsend House rooms are the newest but blandest rooms, although they have working fireplaces and four have kitchenettes. A new addition is the one-bedroom suite in the 19th-century Stone House.

6387 Mill St./Montgomery St. (Rte. 9), Rhinebeck, NY 12572. www.beekmandelamaterinn.com. 🕐 **845/876-7077.** Fax 845/876-7080. 73 units. Beekman Arms $110–$185 double; Delamater Inn $125–$300 double; Carriage House $155–$195. Rates include breakfast. 2-night minimum stay on weekends May–Oct and all holiday weekends. AE, DC, DISC, MC, V. Free parking. **Amenities:** Restaurant; tavern. In room: A/C, kitchens (in some Delamater courtyard rooms), fireplaces (in some rooms).

Journey Inn ★ 🍴　A contemporary inn run by two sisters who've named rooms after favorite sojourns and stocked them with souvenirs, this exceedingly friendly and very comfortable B&B has one exclusive advantage going for it: It is literally right across the street from the gate of the Vanderbilt mansion and just minutes from all the FDR attractions in Hyde Park (as well as the Culinary Institute of America). While the inn isn't old and decorated with period furniture, for many travelers that will be a blessing: Instead, it has new, excellent bathrooms, great big comfortable beds, central air-conditioning, and no creaky floors. The sisters, Diane and Michele, wow visitors with their gourmet breakfast creations in the breakfast wing (one is the baker, the other the cook).

1 Sherwood Place, Hyde Park, NY 12538. www.journeyinn.com. 🕐 **845/229-8972.** 7 units. $150–$185 double; $200–$225 suite. Rates include full breakfast. Weekend and weekday (May–Nov) 2-night minimum. MC, V. Free parking. In room: A/C, Wi-Fi.

Mt. Beacon Bed & Breakfast ★★ 🛏　This 1911 Colonial revival, a three-story manor house at the foot of Mount Beacon, will charm any B&B lover but seems particularly suited for picky New Yorkers making the trip here for Dia:Beacon. For one, the manor's delightful proprietor, Lauren, is adamant about their "no teddy bears" decorating policy. Instead, you'll get antique furniture, oriental rugs, wood-burning fireplaces, beautiful heart-of-pine floors, and three gorgeous, custom-upholstered rooms. The smallest, the "Toile Room," is done in a French yellow-and-black palette and has a separate, private bathroom with a vintage claw-foot tub and amazing modern shower head. (All other rooms have in-room bathrooms.) In the morning, you're treated to a full, homemade breakfast (including an egg soufflé on our visit) and complimentary copies of *The New York Times*. The outdoor pool is a draw in the summer.

829 Walcott Ave. 9D, Beacon, NY 12508. www.mtbeaconbedandbreakfast.com. 🕐 **845/831-0737.** Fax 845/831-0801. 3 units (1 with separate, private bathroom). $165–$175 double; $195 suite. Extra person $30. Rates include gourmet breakfast. 2-night minimum required most weekends, holidays, and peak season. AE, DISC, MC, V. Free parking. **Amenities:** Outdoor pool, smoke-free rooms. In-room: A/C, TV/DVD (in some rooms), Wi-Fi, fireplace.

WEST SIDE OF THE HUDSON
Expensive

Buttermilk Falls Inn + Spa ★★★　Nestled in among 70 acres of wooded, river-hugging land fronting the Hudson, this spectacular inn is a real find in the Mid-Hudson Valley. Though small and friendly, with the feel of a hideaway, it provides the amenities of a much larger hotel. Guest rooms are elegantly designed, with antique touches and period furnishings. Whirlpool tubs and plush linens are found in all. The Foxglove Room on the first floor of the main house is equipped for visitors with disabilities. More private options, great for families, are Carriage House rooms: the cliff-top "North Cottage," the two-story cottage "Pony's Pad," and the modern, three-bedroom "Riverknoll Downs," with a massive deck overlooking the Hudson. Meander among the stunning grounds and you'll discover wooded trails, an art gallery housed in a barn, waterfalls and ponds, a riverfront esplanade, and more. The expertly staffed spa occupies a gorgeous facility that includes a glass-enclosed indoor-outdoor saltwater pool, and a Jacuzzi. The newest addition to the property is the gourmet restaurant, Henry's Farm to Table (below).

220 North Rd., Milton-on-Hudson, NY 12547. www.buttermilkfallsinn.com. (C) **845/795-1310.** 16 units. $225–$350 double; $300–$975 suite, cottage, and house. Special packages available online. All rates include gourmet breakfast. AE, DC, DISC, MC, V. Free parking. **Amenities:** Restaurant; free high-speed Internet access; day spa; 1 room for those w/limited mobility. *In room:* A/C, TV, Wi-Fi (some guest house suites).

Moderate

Inn at Twaalfskill ★ 🎁 Tucked into a leafy residential neighborhood, this sweet little B&B has flowering gardens, old oak trees, a flowing brook (that lends the inn its name), and a very relaxed attitude. The handsomely renovated 1902 house has just three guest rooms, but they are tastefully and luxuriously decorated with plush bedding and linens and high-quality bath products. The fresh-baked breakfast is served in the conservatory, and the Adirondack chairs on the wide porch are a great spot to relax with a book. Best of all, the inn is less than a mile from the Hudson River, and just across the bridge to Poughkeepsie, placing it within very easy reach of the great estates on the other side of the river.

144 Vineyard Ave., Highland, NY 12528. www.innattwaalfskill.com. (C) **845/691-3605.** 3 units. Fri–Sun $165–$185 double; Mon–Thurs $155–$175 double. Rates include full breakfast. 2-night minimum stay required holiday weekends. AE, MC, V. Free parking. *In room:* A/C, TV, hair dryer.

Where to Eat

With the Culinary Institute of America on the east bank of the Hudson, it's not surprising that there's some great eating in this section of the valley. In addition to the restaurants below, visitors on the West side of the Hudson should drop in on **Henry's Farm to Table** ★★, the excellent, warm, and pretty reasonably priced new restaurant overlooking the river at Buttermilk Falls Inn + Spa (p. 210), for local produce, meats, and fish (from a CIA grad chef). Also, a great stop in Rhinebeck for breakfast, lunch, coffee, and desserts is **Bread Alone** ★, 45 E. Market St. ((C) **845/876-3108;** www.breadalone.com), a cute cafe that features scrumptious artisanal breads and does lunches to go.

EAST SIDE OF THE HUDSON
Expensive

Culinary Institute of America (CIA) ★★★ AMERICAN/FRENCH/ITALIAN/ BAKED GOODS   The nation's foremost culinary-arts college has four on-campus restaurants and a bakery cafe, which are open to the public. They're staffed by students of CIA, but they hardly seem like training grounds. All are extremely professional, which is why it can be so hard to get a reservation (they're accepted 3 months in advance, and for some weekends in season, you may need that much of a cushion). The three main restaurants are the elegant **Escoffier Restaurant,** serving classic and contemporary French fare; **Ristorante Caterina de Medici,** a handsome Tuscan-styled villa with a regionally varied Italian menu; and **American Bounty Restaurant,** which focuses on regional American specialties and ingredients from the Hudson River Valley. Casual **St. Andrew's Café** offers wood-fired pizzas and vegetarian dishes, while the newest addition to the roster is the Apple Pie Bakery Café, an informal place for baked goods and a simple lunch or early dinner. The three main restaurants request business or "country club casual" (collared shirt and slacks or khakis) attire and no jeans, sneakers, or sandals. *Note:* All restaurants are closed when school is not in session; see the website for dates of closing (most of July, plus selected dates throughout the year).

1946 Campus Dr. (off Rte. 9), Hyde Park. ℭ **845/471-6608.** www.ciachef.edu/restaurants/default.asp. Reservations essential (may be made online). Main courses $14–$34. AE, DC, DISC, MC, V. American Bounty Tues–Sat 11:30am–1pm and 6:30–8:30pm; Apple Pie Bakery Café Mon–Fri 8am–6:30pm; Escoffier Tues–Sat 11:30am–1pm and 6:30–8:30pm; Ristorante Caterina de Medici Mon–Fri 11:30am–1pm and 6:30–8:30pm (selected menu items available in Al Forno Room Mon–Fri 11:30am–6pm); St. Andrew's Café Mon–Fri 11:30am–1pm and 6:30–8:30pm.

The Local ★★ NEW AMERICAN   One of the newest additions to the fine-dining scene in the mid-Hudson Valley is this handsome little restaurant in a country-chic two-story little house (an erstwhile blacksmith's shop) just off Rhinebeck's main drag. With black-and-white-striped floors, a nice little bar area, and an interesting menu of small plates and inventive seasonal dishes, it's become quite the local draw. The CIA-trained chef, Wesley Dier, sources from local farms and purveyors; the eclectic menu is like sophisticated comfort food. Start with a snack jar of roasted almonds or marinated olives, and try sharing some of the creative small plates, such as soy cola-glazed pork belly or beef sliders. The Normandy Duck "two ways" main course is outstanding. The small restaurant can get busy; the most coveted seats are those on the second-floor balcony, overlooking the spotless open kitchen.

38 W. Market St., Rhinebeck. ℭ **845/876-2214.** www.thelocalrestaurantandbar.com. Reservations recommended. Main courses $22–$29. AE, DC, DISC, MC, V. Tues–Sat 5:30–10pm; Sun 10:30am–3pm.

Terrapin Restaurant ★★ AMERICAN/INTERNATIONAL   Housed in an 1825 church, with soaring ceilings, this fine-dining restaurant and next-door bistro aims high. If you're in the mood for a sandwich or funky quesadilla, especially for lunch, try the Red Bistro/Bar (which is also open very late on weekends). Otherwise, check out the elegant main dining room, where chef/owner Josh Kroner cooks up imaginative takes on American cuisine—adding Mexican and Asian twists—with the freshest of local ingredients. Start out with a selection of tapas, such as grilled lamb chop with chimichurri sauce, and proceed to an appetizer like potato gnocchi with sautéed duck livers, shiitake mushrooms, and leeks. Terrapin's extensive and well-priced wine list is one of the Valley's best.

6426 Montgomery St., Rhinebeck. ℭ **845/876-3330.** www.terrapinrestaurant.com. Reservations recommended on weekends. Main courses $20–$36. AE, DC, DISC, MC, V. Bistro Sun–Thurs 11:30am–11pm, Fri–Sat noon–2am; dining room Sun–Thurs 5–9:30pm, Fri–Sat 5–10:30pm.

Moderate

The Tavern at Beekman Arms ★ AMERICAN/CONTINENTAL   In Rhine-beck, a stop at the restaurant and tavern of America's oldest continually operating inn is almost obligatory. The Colonial Tap Room especially exudes Revolutionary War–era flavor, with its wide-plank floorboards and wood posts, paneling, and beams. It's a great place for a mug of ale and hearty soup—probably just what George Washington and his fellow war planners did when they dined here in the 1780s. I always eat in the Tap Room, just for the ambience, but the connected restaurant serves the same high-quality menu. Main courses include appropriately hearty items like boneless, coffee-braised beef short ribs, cast-iron seared hangar steak, and Long Island duck. Slightly less macho dishes, such as crabmeat-stuffed shrimp, also make appearances. Sunday brunch is a popular outing for locals and visitors alike.

6387 Mill St. (Rte. 9), Rhinebeck. (© **845/876-1766.** www.beekmandelamaterinn.com. Reservations recommended on weekends. Main courses $14–$30. AE, DC, DISC, MC, V. Mon–Sat 11:30am–3pm; Mon–Thurs 5:30–9pm; Fri–Sat 5:30–10pm; Sun 4–9pm; Sun brunch 10:30am–2pm.

Inexpensive

Foster's Coach House ☺ 🍴 PUB FARE A homey, historic restaurant with family-friendly prices, Foster's has been in operation since just after World War I. An old tavern was converted into a full-scale restaurant, with horse stalls as dining booths. It is dark and cool but incredibly relaxed. The bar is a favorite watering hole for locals when there's a game on. The Kid's Menu items, just $6, should keep the little ones content. Foster's is a perfect place to drop in for lunch or an informal dinner, and the outdoor terrace in summer months is particularly inviting. Basics are best: chopped sirloin with onions and mushroom gravy, turkey with stuffing and gravy, shrimp scampi, and sandwiches and burgers for lunch. Beer is cheap, and so is the wine list.

6411 Montgomery St., Rhinebeck. (© **845/876-8052.** www.fosterscoachhouse.com. Main courses $7–$21. AE, DC, DISC, MC, V. Tues–Sat 11am–11pm; Sun noon–11pm.

Poppy's ☺ BURGERS A good stop in Beacon after visiting Dia is this hipster hamburger joint, which takes pains to use the finest natural and local beef and ingredients. The BBQ bacon burger is a treat, as are the hand-cut fries and sweet potato chips. On burgers, you can get a fried egg on top, or hickory-smoked bacon. There are also a veggie burger, chili, and a "sloppy Joseph." It's a simple place, with just a handful of tables inside and a couple on the sidewalk, and burgers are served in plain paper bags, but you're not paying for ambience; you're paying for the quality of humanely raised, grass-fed, organic local meat. And don't miss the "Mexican Coca-Cola," made with real sugar.

184 Main St., Beacon. (© **845/765-2121.** www.poppyburger.com. Reservations not accepted. Main courses $6–$9. MC, V. Wed–Sat noon–8pm; Sun noon–6pm.

WEST SIDE OF THE HUDSON
Expensive

Ship to Shore ★ AMERICAN/STEAKHOUSE This cool, jazzy spot, one of the new arrivals in the revitalized Kingston waterfront district known as the Rondout, is a hip take on the classic New York steakhouse. The chef, a graduate of the Culinary Institute of America, prepares an extensive menu of steaks and chops as well as seafood and pastas, always augmented by a long list of fresh daily specials. Meat eaters can dive into a 32-ounce bone-in rib-eye or cast-iron seared flank steak, while seafood lovers can try dishes like pan-seared bronzini or a seafood mac & cheese (with lobster tail, shrimp, and scallops). For lunch, there are some great, creative sandwiches and an array of salads. Back past the bar are a couple of more intimate dining areas if the front gets too loud. There's live jazz on Friday and Saturday nights, and Wednesday is half-price wine night.

15 W. Strand (Rondout District), Kingston. (© **845/334-8887.** www.shiptoshorehudsonvalley.com. Reservations recommended on weekends. Main courses $14–$32. AE, DISC, MC, V. Daily 11am–11pm; brunch Sun 10am–3pm.

WINE TRAILS & FARMERS' markets

The Hudson Valley, the nation's oldest winemaking region, is today home to about three dozen wineries. Though few of the area's wineries have yet attained national followings, a number of them offer tours and tastings, and several are blessed with outstandingly scenic locations. If you'd like to visit a winery or two during your stay, all you have to do is follow the trail—either the **Dutchess Wine Trail** (✆ 845/266-5372; www. dutchesswinetrail.com), on the east side of the Hudson, or the **Shawangunk Wine Trail** (✆ 845/255-2494; www. shawangunkwinetrail.com), on the west side of the river. More than a dozen are open to regular visits. The following is merely a selection of my favorites: The Dutchess (Country) Trail consists of **Cascade Mountain Winery,** 835 Cascade Mountain Rd., Amenia (✆ 845/373-9021; www.cascademt.com), which has a lovely setting and a very nice little restaurant with outdoor seating; **Clinton Vineyards,** Schultzville Road, Clinton Corners (✆ 845/266-5372; www. clintonvineyards.com), makers of a pretty nice white, a Seyval blanc; and **Millbrook Vineyards & Winery ★**, 26 Wing Rd., Millbrook (✆ 800/662-WINE [9463]; www.millbrookwine.com), the largest and one of the best of the lot. Millbrook makes a good pinot noir reserve, offers a full tour, features art exhibits and live music on Saturday nights in summer, and is worth the visit for the views over the rolling hillsides and horse farms alone.

Several of the nine family-owned wineries of the Shawangunk Trail, all sandwiched between the Shawangunk Mountains and the Hudson River in Ulster County, are easily visited on a Hudson Valley trip. Among them are **Brotherhood Winery,** 35 North St., Washingtonville (✆ 845/496-9101; www.brotherhood-winery.com), the oldest winery in the United States, in operation since 1839. Though the winery doesn't grow its own grapes (instead importing them from Long Island, the Finger Lakes, and California), its grounds constitute a well-stocked campus, with vast underground vaulted cellars and a whole host of shops and activities on-site. Claiming to be the oldest continuously operating vineyard in the U.S. is **Benmarl Wine Company,** 156 Highland Ave., Marlboro-on-Hudson (✆ 845/236-4265; www.benmarl.com), a small, family-owned independent with awe-inspiring views from a hilltop location on the west side of the Hudson (btw. Newburgh and New Paltz).

Farmers' markets and **pick-your-own farm stands** are everywhere in this beautiful, bucolic region. There are dozens and dozens, so here are just a few: **Mead Orchards and Farm Stand,** 25 Scism Rd., Tivoli (9 miles north of Rhinebeck; ✆ 914/756-5641), with pick-your-own apples and pumpkins; **Greig Farm,** Pitcher Lane, Red Hook (✆ 914/758-1234), which has pick-your-own fruits and vegetables and a farm market; **Millbrook Farmers' Market,** Franklin Avenue at Front Street, Millbrook village, every Saturday from 9am to 1pm; and **Tarrytown Farmers' Market,** Patriot's Park, Route 9, Tarrytown (✆ 914/923-4837). Ask around and locals will come up with many more.

Moderate

Raccoon Saloon ★ 🍴 NEW AMERICAN   This unassuming, family-owned and -operated restaurant and bar is one of the most charming spots along the Hudson. It has a relaxed bar with a couple of separate, vintage dining rooms and a small terrace with tables and stunning views high above a rushing waterfall and the mighty Hudson

River. The Raccoon usually walks away with top honors in the poll that names the Hudson Valley's best burgers (and they are truly fantastic: large and juicy, served with homemade ketchup and extras like guacamole, mushrooms, and bacon). Try the more sophisticated black truffle chicken-liver pâté, or seared filet of salmon with mandarin orange sauce. Desserts are all homemade, and ice creams are imaginative and delicious: Flavors include basil, lavender, and honey.

Rte. 9W, Marlboro-on-Hudson. (© **845/236-7872.** Reservations recommended weekends. Main courses $9-$23. AE, DISC, MC, V. Sun-Thurs 11am-9:30pm; Fri-Sat 11:30am-10:30pm.

The Mid-Hudson Valley After Dark

The spectacular **Richard B. Fisher Center for the Performing Arts ★★★**, on the campus of Bard College in Annandale-on-Hudson (© 845/758-7900; www.bard.edu/fishercenter), is the work of the innovative architect Frank Gehry (designer of the Guggenheim Bilbao and Disney auditorium in L.A.). This distinctive and intimate theater, which seats just 900 in the main hall, has featured performances by Elvis Costello, Merce Cunningham, the American Symphony Orchestra, and Ballet Hispanico, but it remains primarily a teaching space. If any public performances are scheduled, it's very much worth the trek. Poughkeepsie's legendary **Bardavon Opera House ★**, 35 Market St. (© 845/473-2072; www.bardavon.org), which has hosted a variety of classical music, opera, and other musical and theatrical performances since 1869, is one of the top spots in the valley. Programs include music, dance, film, and theater; the schedule ranges from the Hudson Valley Philharmonic and Itzhak Perlman to Lily Tomlin and screenings of *King Kong*. An unexpected treasure on the west side of the Hudson, in Marlboro, is **The Falcon ★★★**, 1348 9E (© 845/236-7970; www.liveatthefalcon.com), a very cool and intimate jazz club (that also plays host to blues, R & B, and rock acts) with very good food as well as art exhibits. It draws some excellent bands to its barnlike space, making it a draw for people from the Hudson Valley, Catskills, and even Manhattan.

Beacon, basking in the attention of the Dia:Beacon Art Center, has initiated a program called **"Second Saturdays,"** in which trolleys pick up passengers at the train station and ferry them down Main Street, where art galleries and shops stay open until 9pm on the second Saturday of every month and a number of bars and restaurants feature live music. For more information on scheduling, call © 845/838-4243. Newburgh and Kingston's **revitalized waterfronts** are loaded with bars and restaurants. Both have become real scenes in the past couple of years. A Newburgh-Beacon commuter ferry is in the works, which will make it very easy to cross the Hudson and check out the restaurants and bars on either side. Rhinebeck has a number of congenial local bars, but its cool local art house theater, **Upstate Films ★**, 6415 Montgomery St. (© 845/876-2515; www.upstatefilms.org), is unique in these parts. One of the last of its kind, the 1950s-era **Hyde Park Drive-In Movie Theater**, Route 9 (across from the FDR Presidential Library and Springwood; © 845/229-4738), schedules first-run movies in summer ($7 adults, $4 children ages 4–11; Tues is $5 night).

THE UPPER HUDSON VALLEY

The great estates are also part of the fabric in the Upper Hudson Valley, the most pastoral segment of the region. The simple beauty of the landscape was a perfect complement to the Hudson River school of painters and the Shakers, who established one of their largest communities in the area east of the Hudson, near

Chatham; today, there's an excellent museum and library dedicated to the Shaker legacy in this part of the valley. Revitalization of towns in this once-grand and later run-down region has been a struggle, but has now taken root in several villages along the Upper Hudson. Best known is the small city of Hudson, which has exploded as an art and antiques (and dining) destination, but Red Hook and tiny and unassuming Tivoli, tucked into the east bank of the river, have developed their own lively restaurant scenes. The west side of the Upper Hudson Valley, including the attractive town of Saugerties, is covered in chapter 8, as populations west of the Hudson tend to identify even more with the nearby Catskill Mountains than the river.

Exploring the Upper Hudson Valley

Though the predominantly rural Upper Hudson Valley isn't as loaded with the must-see attractions that are in the Mid- and Lower Hudson Valley, it is distinguished by two splendid estates; the town of Hudson, home to the area's best antiques and design shops; and the fascinating traditions of the Shaker community. Just to the south are the charming historic villages of Tivoli and Red Hook, which despite their small size have a surprising number of shops and restaurants.

Clermont State Historic Site ★   The oldest of the great estates on the Hudson, this 1750 Georgian manor house was home to seven successive generations of one of New York State's most prominent families, the Livingstons. Philip Livingston was one of the signatories of the Declaration of Independence, and Robert Livingston possessed one of the largest private libraries in the U.S., a large portion of which survives at Clermont. The family's important role in Revolutionary activities led the British to burn Clermont in 1777. The nearly 500-acre estate, on a 45-foot-high bluff with great views of the river below and the Catskill Mountains in the distance, has excellent woodland hiking trails out past the formal gardens, bar, and gardener's cottages. The house today for the most part evokes the 1920s, when the house was remodeled as a Colonial Revival, though it contains furnishings and belongings from more than 200 years of Livingstons at Clermont. The visitor center plays a short film that interviews the last resident of the house, Alice Livingston.

1 Clermont Ave. (off Rte. 9G), Germantown. ⓒ **518/537-4240.** www.friendsofclermont.org. Admission $5 adults, $4 seniors and students, $1 children 5–12, free for children 4 and under ($5 vehicle fee for special events). Apr–Oct Tues–Sun 11am–4pm; Nov–Dec Sat–Sun 11am–3pm (last tour 30 min. before closing). Grounds year-round daily 8:30am–sunset.

Olana State Historic Site ★★★ ☺   Olana, though not as massively grand as some of the homes built by the 19th-century industrialists, is surely the most unique of all the great Hudson Valley estates. A Persian fantasy perched on a hill high above the river, with stunning panoramic views, it was the home of the accomplished Hudson River school painter Frederick Church (1826–1900). Well traveled in the Middle East, Europe, and South America, Church made his home perhaps his most important work of art, an indoor and outdoor museum incorporating artifacts, design elements, and furnishings of his favorite places. He was particularly taken with Moorish-style architecture and design, which is reflected in the mansion's windows, courtyards, thick carpets, and decorative tile motifs; sumptuous parlors look like opium dens. The landscaping on the 336-acre estate grew out of Church's romantic, painterly affection for the Hudson Valley. Inaugurated in 2009, the **Evelyn & Maurice Sharp Gallery,** a second-floor exhibition space, focuses on the Hudson River school and landscape painting of the Valley. Guided tours last 45 minutes; in high

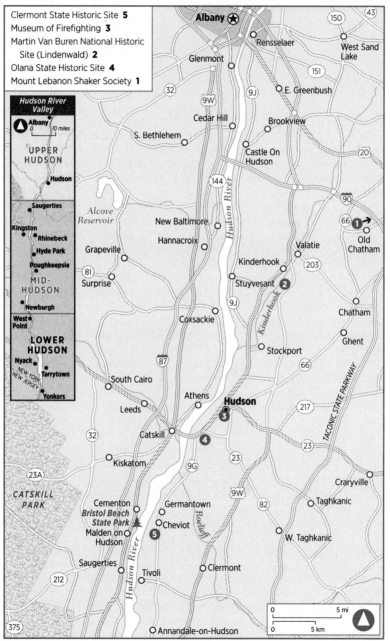

Clermont State Historic Site **5**
Museum of Firefighting **3**
Martin Van Buren National Historic
Site (Lindenwald) **2**
Olana State Historic Site **4**
Mount Lebanon Shaker Society **1**

Hudson River Valley

Albany
0   10 miles

UPPER
HUDSON

Hudson

Saugerties

Kingston   Rhinebeck
          Hyde Park
Poughkeepsie
MID-
HUDSON
          Newburgh

West
Point
LOWER
HUDSON

Nyack
          Tarrytown
NEW YORK
NEW JERSEY
          Yonkers

Albany

Rensselaer

West Sand
Lake

Glenmont

E. Greenbush

Cedar Hill

Brookview

S. Bethlehem

Castle On
Hudson

Hudson River

Alcove
Reservoir

New Baltimore

Hannacroix

Valatie

Old
Chatham

Grapeville

Kinderhook

Surprise

Stuyvesant

Chatham

Coxsackie

Stockport

Ghent

Kinderhook

South Cairo

Athens

Hudson

Leeds

Catskill

Kiskatom

Craryville

CATSKILL
PARK

Cementon
Bristol Beach
State Park
Malden on
Hudson

Germantown

Cheviot

Taghkanic

W. Taghkanic

Roeleff

TACONIC STATE PARKWAY

Saugerties

Tivoli

Clermont

Hudson River

Annandale-on-Hudson

0   5 mi
0   5 km

season, tours (maximum 12 people) often sell out early in the day, and reservations are suggested on weekends.

Rte. 9G, Hudson. ✆ **518/828-0135.** www.olana.org. Admission to house (by tour only) and second floor Sharp gallery tours are each $9 adults, $8 seniors and students, free for children 11 and under; combined house and gallery tours $12 adults, $10 seniors and students, free for children 11 and under; grounds $5 vehicle fee on weekends and holidays. Apr–Oct Tues–Sun 10am–5pm; Nov–Mar Fri–Sun 10am–4pm (gallery closed). Last tour 1 hr. before closing.

Hudson ★★   Only a decade or so ago, Hudson was a small upstate town with very little going for it save a setting near the river and good bones in its run-down architecture. However, an influx of antiques dealers and part-time residents from New York City has given it a remarkable makeover, resulting in a premier upstate shopping destination. Today it is *the* antiquing destination of the Hudson Valley and full of enjoyable shops, restaurants, and bars. Most of the development and refurbishing is restricted to a single street, the long and charming **Warren Street,** which is packed end-to-end with antiques shops, several catering to those with an interest in contemporary and midcentury modern aesthetics. Also worth checking out in Hudson is the surprisingly engaging **FASNY Museum of Firefighting** (117 Harry Howard Ave.; ✆ **518/828-7695;** donation suggested; daily 9am–4:30pm). Hudson, home to the oldest volunteer fire department in the U.S., is also the site of this large and very well-organized museum, which has been around since 1925. It contains more than 80 fire apparatus, ranging from a 1725 Newsham wooden cart, the first fire "engine" in New York City, to wonderfully ornate, mid-19th-century carriages. A small 9/11 exhibit in the front reminds visitors of the importance and bravery of firefighters. For current information on gallery exhibits and other Hudson happenings, visit **www. warrenstreet.com**.

Martin Van Buren National Historic Site (Lindenwald)   The eighth president of the U.S.—admittedly, not one of the best-remembered presidents in American history—Martin Van Buren (1782–1862) grew up in the Upper Hudson Valley in the town of Kinderhook (it's said that "okay" comes from his references to Old Kinderhook by its initials). Van Buren bought the estate in 1839 during his presidency as a place to retire. He named the 226-acre farm Lindenwald and built a Georgian-style mansion here, where he lived out the final 21 years of his life.

Old Post Rd. (Rte. 9H), Kinderhook. ✆ **518/758-9689.** www.nps.gov/mava. Admission (good for 1 week) $5 adults, $12 families (up to 4 adults and accompanying children ages 15 and under). Mid-May to Oct 31 daily 9am–4pm (tours hourly).

Mount Lebanon Shaker Society ★★★ ☺ 🏛   The Shaker Museum and Library that, until recently, had been housed in Old Chatham has relocated its galleries and programs to the "North Family" of the Mount Lebanon Shaker Society site, in New Lebanon, about 13 miles northeast along Rte. 20. Mount Lebanon, home to the Shakers' Great Stone Barn (a stunning building gutted by fire in 1972 and the largest stone barn in America), was the largest Shaker community and principal settlement from 1785 to the mid–20th century; it comprised 6,000 acres and more than 100 buildings. Shakers, the Early American religious group known for not only their religious devotion and sexual abstinence, but also their exquisite craftsmanship and ingenious architectural simplicity that influenced legions of designers, established communities in upstate New York and New England at the end of the 18th century. The Shakers believed that every living act was an act of devotion, and they pursued their work like prayer. This rustic museum of nearly 20,000 objects and repository of books, journals, and photographs contains one of the largest collections of the community's heavenly round baskets, furniture, and machinery.

Darrow Rd. (at Shaker Rd.), New Lebanon. © **518/794-9500.** www.shakermuseumandlibrary.org/ mtlebanon.html. Admission $8 adults, $4 children 8–17, free for children 7 and under. Late May to late Oct Wed–Mon 10am–5pm.

Especially for Kids

The **Museum of Firefighting** in Hudson is sure to delight kids—especially little boys—with its fantastic collection of vintage fire trucks. The grounds at the **Clermont** and **Olana** estates are great for exploring, with plenty of beautiful trails, and for having a picnic.

Sports & Outdoor Pursuits

HIKING Nice and easy hiking trails can be found at the state historic sites **Clermont** (Clermont; © 518/537-4240), **Olana** (Greenport; © 518/828-0135), and **Martin Van Buren Park** (Kinderhook; © 800/724-1846).

WINTER SPORTS For downhill skiing, try **Catamount,** Route 23, Hillsdale (© 800/342-1840; www.catamountski.com), on the Massachusetts border in the southern Berkshires. There are good cross-country ski trails at the state historic sites **Clermont** (Clermont; © 518/537-4240), **Olana** (Greenport; © 518/828-0135), and **Martin Van Buren Park** (Kinderhook; © 800/724-1846).

Shopping

Antiquing is a huge business and pastime in the Upper Hudson Valley. In the past decade, **Hudson ★★★** has been transformed from a sleepy and fairly run-down upstate town into one of the premier antiques destinations in New York State, with more than 75 shops and galleries spread out along 6 blocks of Warren Street and, to a much lesser degree, a few streets that fan out from there. Pieces range from Egyptian to fine French and midcentury modern. There are far too many to mention, but among the nicest shops (in walking order along Warren St.) are **Hudson Supermarket Antiques,** 310 Warren St. (© 518/822-0028); **Vincent R. Mulford Antiques,** 419 Warren St. (© 518/828-5489); **Skalar Antiques,** 438½ Warrant St. (© 518/828-1170); **Eustace & Zamus,** 513 Warren St. (© 518/822-9200); **Gottlieb Gallery,** 524 Warren St. (© 518/822-1761); **Historical Materialism,** 601 Warren St. (© 518/671-6151); and **Neven and Neven Moderne,** 618 Warren St. (© 518/828-4214). If those are too precious or pricey, check out **Fern,** 610½ Warren St. (© 518/828-2886) and, above all, **The Armory Art & Antique Gallery,** at 5th and State (© 518/822-1477), an eclectic and lower-priced assembly of some 60 dealers. For a full list of shops and galleries (and websites), visit **Hudson Antique Dealers Association** (HADA) at www.hudsonantiques.net. A cool art gallery dealing in contemporary photography is **Carrie Haddad Photographs,** 318 Warren St. (© 518/828-7655). Other non-antiques shops of interest, selling mostly housewares and gift items, include **Shop Naked,** 608 Warren St. (© 518/671-6336); **Pieces,** 609 Warren St. (© 518/822-8131); **Rural Residence,** 316 Warren St. (© 518/822-1061); and the unique jewelry store **Ornamentum,** 506½ Warren St. (© 518/671-6770). **Hudson City Books,** 553 Warren St. (© 518/671-6020), is a fantastic local bookshop.

The **Mount Lebanon Shaker Society**—which recently merged with the Shaker Museum & Library that was in Old Chatham—in New Lebanon (Darrow Rd.;

$\mathcal{C}$ **518/794-9500**) expects to continue the tradition of a gift shop with an excellent selection of high-quality crafts based on Shaker traditions (such as splendid oval boxes, furniture, and baskets), as well as books about the Shakers. Shaker crafts aren't cheap, but they're extremely well-made and make great gifts.

Where to Stay

Options in the Upper Hudson Valley are largely limited to small but charming and intimate inns and bed-and-breakfasts, but they are some of the nicest in the entire region. The area is close enough to other sections of the valley that you might also consider basing yourself farther downriver.

EXPENSIVE

Madalin Hotel ★★ A beautiful old hotel, originally built in 1909 and painstakingly restored in 2006, this inn and restaurant have quickly become the anchor of a lively scene in tiny Tivoli, a lovely little town tucked into the hills of the Upper Hudson Valley. The 11 rooms in the three-story building are spacious and understated, tastefully outfitted with Eastlake period pieces. The inn is even better known for its excellent restaurant downstairs, Madalin's Table (see review below), which features a wraparound porch, a popular spot to be on warm evenings. The centerpiece of the restaurant is the gorgeously carved 19-foot bar in the tavern.

53 Broadway, Tivoli, NY 12583. www.madalinhotel.com. $\mathcal{C}$ **845/757-2100.** 11 units. $199–$299 double. High season 2-night minimum. AE, DC, MC, V. Free parking on street. **Amenities:** Restaurant, bar. *In room:* A/C, flatscreen TV, Wi-Fi.

Mount Merino Manor ★★★ 🎁 Occupying an 1870 manor house built by the private physician of Frederick Church, Dr. Gustavus Sabine, on the outskirts of Hudson, this is one of the grandest hotels along the river. Ensconced on 100 bucolic acres, it is a luxury B&B that's more like a boutique retreat hotel. The seven rooms and suites come equipped with luxurious linens, elegant period furnishings, and sumptuous, impeccable bathrooms (some with incredible two-person soaking tubs). Lovely breakfasts are served in an elegant dining room, and a guest kitchen is open round-the-clock for nibbles and beverages. The result is a romantic, serene retreat, perfect to unwind and get away from it all, but also close enough to Hudson to get your fill of antiques shopping and restaurants. There is also easy access to hiking, biking, and cross-country skiing.

4317 Rte. 23, Hudson 12534. mountmerinomanor.com. $\mathcal{C}$ **518/828-5583.** Fax 518/828-4292. 7 units. Midweek and weekends Dec–May $175–$295 double; weekends Nov–Apr $195–$375 double. High season 2-night minimum. Children 11 and older. AE, DC, MC, V. Free parking on street. *In room:* A/C, flatscreen TV, Wi-Fi.

MODERATE

The Country Squire B&B ★★ This stylish B&B, in the heart of Hudson and 2 blocks from the burgeoning expanse of shops and restaurants along Warren Street, is the perfect place to stay if you're an art and antiques hound. A well-designed and clutter-free but very comfortable Queen Anne Victorian, the sensitively restored home, built in 1900, features a wealth of interesting architectural details, such as parquet floors, leaded and stained-glass windows, pocket doors, and five fireplaces. The inn's five guest rooms are sedately and elegantly decorated with a nice mix of handsome antique pieces and a few cool modern furnishings and accents. The most contemporary of the rooms has a private deck. The spacious private bathrooms, with

Staying Out on the Farm

A great option for families, just a short drive north of Hudson, is a farm stay at **Kinderhook Farm** ★★★ (© 505/603-1815; www.kinderhookfarmstay.com), Route 21, Ghent. At this artistically decorated 18th-century farmhouse, which sits on a 1,200-acre working farm, guests have their own kitchen garden to pick items for cooking their own dinner (farm-fresh eggs and produce are included), and they can visit the FarmStore for organic meat.

Accommodations in the loftlike, semi-private barn are rustic chic, with two stylishly decorated sleeping areas (each with its own sitting area), great views, a large bathroom sheathed in pine, and an outdoor dining space. Activities include gathering eggs, hanging out with lambs, and feeding baby chicks, horses, and Ginny the donkey. Rates (for up to four adults and two children) are $285 per night, 2-night minimum, or $1,800 for a week.

wainscoting and claw-foot tubs, are particularly inviting, and bedding and linens are first-rate.

251 Allen St., Hudson, NY 12534. www.countrysquireny.com. © **518/822-9229.** 5 units. May–Oct Sun–Thurs $165–$180 double, Fri–Sat $175–$195 double; Nov–Apr Sun–Thurs $125–$145 double, Fri–Sat $135–$155 double. Rates include breakfast. AE, MC, V. Free parking on street. *In room:* Seasonal A/C, TV, fax (1 room), Wi-Fi.

The Inn at Green River ★★ 📖 A luxurious B&B set in a serene residential area of Hillsdale, as accessible to the Hudson River Valley as it is to the Berkshires, this inn is steeped in romance and relaxation. Rooms in the 1830s Federal-style farmhouse are exquisitely decorated with local antiques and art; most have fireplaces and soaking or Jacuzzi tubs. The property is surrounded by lovingly tended gardens overlooking a creek that flows into Green River. The proprietor Deborah Bowen is known for her sumptuous breakfasts, served in the candlelit dining room and featuring such delectables as lemon-ricotta hot cakes and fresh-baked scones. Deborah recently added a beautiful enclosed porch and deck.

9 Nobletown Rd., Hillsdale, NY 12529. © **518/325-7248.** 7 units. July–Aug $159–$289 double; Sept–Oct $149–$269 double; Nov–Apr $139–$239 double; May–June $149–$269 double. Rates include breakfast. 2-night minimum stay required on weekends; 3- or 4-night minimum on holidays and some weekends July–Aug. AE, DC, MC, V. Free parking on street. *In room:* A/C, Wi-Fi.

The Inn at Hudson ★★ 🗡 Just a few blocks from Hudson's main drag, teeming with antiques shops, is this elegant 1906 brick Dutch and Jacobean mansion, the Morgan Jones House. All rooms are named for their dominant decorative colors; three are especially spacious and handsomely decorated with antiques from local dealers. As impressive as they are, the carved woodwork of the dining room, library, and foyer is even more so. If you're planning to stay several days in the area, the inn rate policies make it a very good deal. And families will appreciate the Yellow & Blue Suite, which has two bedrooms with a connecting bathroom, available for the same price as the other rooms.

317 Allen St., Hudson, NY 12534. www.theinnathudson.com. © **518/822-9322.** 5 units. $200–$225 double 1st night, $100–$125 double additional nights. Rates include breakfast. AE, DISC, MC, V. Free parking. *In room:* A/C, cable TV, Wi-Fi.

Red Hook Local Treats Along the Side of the Road

The Hudson River Valley may be all about organic farm-to-table cuisine and the CIA, but if you'd rather sit at a picnic table and wolf down some inexpensive comfort food, don't miss some local favorites, sure to be a hit with kids. **Bubby's Burritos** (summer only) is a tiny roadside trailer dispensing fresh vegetarian burritos and quesadillas (there are just four items on the menu) in a little park area next to Montgomery Place Orchards on Rte. 9 (at Rte. 199) 2 miles outside Red Hook on the way to Tivoli. **Gigi Market** at Greig Farm, 227 Pitcher Lane, Red Hook

(© **845/758-1999**), is an indoor farmers' market and cafe with local cheeses, salads and panini, and prepared foods (Wed–Sun 8am–6pm). And for dessert, you've got to make a stop at **Holy Cow Ice Cream**, 7270 S. Broadway (© **845/758-5959**; daily 11am–10pm), an old-school ice-cream shop and local institution with picnic tables outside. I'm a sucker for the milkshakes and Brownie Sundae made with coffee ice cream, salted peanuts, and hot fudge—just $3 for much more ice cream than anyone should eat in one sitting.

Inn at Silver Maple Farm ★ 💼   A large converted barn complex on the outskirts of Chatham, on the New York side of the Berkshire foothills, this picturesque 10-acre estate nestled into a hillside is a relaxing retreat. Rooms are varied, with a number of different views and designs. In all, you'll find comfortable beds, handsome linens, and down comforters, with other touches like antique trunks and hand-painted murals. The Pines suite has a downstairs living room, fireplace, and upstairs loft with a cathedral ceiling. The Lodge rooms are rustic and sedately decorated, without the frills of a few others. Breakfast is generous and includes items like French toast, apple-pie pancakes, and fresh-baked muffins.

Rte. 295, Canaan, NY 12029. www.silvermaplefarm.com. © **518/781-3600.** Fax 518/781-3883. 11 units. May–Oct weekends $130–$225 double, $275–$295 suite; May–Oct midweek $120–$190 double, $255–$275 suite; Nov–Apr $120–$180 double, $235–$255 suite. Rates include full breakfast. AE, DISC, MC, V. Free parking. *In room:* A/C, TV, Wi-Fi.

Where to Eat

You may have to search out a restaurant in the northern section of the valley because its best dining is quite spread out, but the restaurants below are every bit as good as those in the Mid- and Lower Hudson Valley. Also worth a visit, especially for live-music fans, is the new **Club Helsinki** ★★ in Hudson (p. 224), with a great bar and very nice, Southern/Low Country menu in a handsome space (Thurs–Tues 5–10pm).

EXPENSIVE

DA/BA Restaurant ★★   MODERN SCANDINAVIAN   A vaunted dining newcomer to Hudson that is the city's first destination restaurant, DA/BA is ambitious but not pretentious; instead, it's sedate and friendly. Rarified haute cuisine like golden whitefish roe coexists comfortably next to such pub fare as dirt-cheap classics like BLTs and burgers. The candlelit, earth-tone dining room appeals equally to foodie hipsters, visiting families, and locals. The young guns behind this restaurant, including a young Swedish chef, take pains to say DA/BA isn't a Swedish restaurant, but the creative, contemporary mains do include Swedish meatballs and Päron chicken in a cognac thyme sauce.

225 Warren St., Hudson. ℂ **518/249-4631.** www.dabahudson.com. Reservations recommended. Main courses $21–$28. AE, DISC, MC, V. Mon–Sat 6–10pm.

Mercato Osteria & Enoteca ★★ ITALIAN   On the ground floor of a sweet Victorian house in the tranquil village of Red Hook, this congenial, airy, and good-looking neighborhood restaurant has rustic wooden tables and floors, a long zinc bar, and very good authentic *osteria* (country Italian) dishes, based on market-fresh, local ingredients. Run by a husband-and-wife team, the Roman chef-owner comes from a very long line of pasta makers in Italy. Not surprisingly, his homemade pastas are a standout, from gnocchi to rigatoni sorrentina with tomato basil sauce and fresh bufala. There's usually a risotto special, and main courses like quail saltimbocca should tempt the adventurous diner. The all-Italian wine list, unusual in these parts, has some very nice regional finds (the chef has also worked in the wine industry and as a sommelier).

61 E. Market St., Red Hook. ℂ **518/758-5879.** www.mercatoredhook.com. Reservations recommended. Main courses $21–$26. AE, DISC, MC, V. Wed–Thurs 5:30–9:30pm; Fri–Sat 5:30–10pm; Sun 5–9pm.

Swoon Kitchenbar ★★ CREATIVE BISTRO   At this comfortable locals' favorite in Hudson, the ever-growing antiques destination of the Upper Valley, the creative menu is impeccably prepared, using fresh, quality local ingredients. The long rectangular dining room is accented with green plants and flowers and a wonderful pressed-tin ceiling, marble tables, and an antique tile floor. The inventive menu includes a homemade charcuterie plate, with meats that come from local farms, and mains like braised pork belly and crispy monkfish cheeks. Swoon's surprisingly long wine list has several excellent and accessibly priced choices, and the homemade pastries and desserts—one of the owners is the pastry chef—are memorable. The restaurant earns its boastful name.

340 Warren St., Hudson. ℂ **518/822-8938.** www.swoonkitchenbar.com. Reservations recommended weekends. Main courses $23–$35. AE, MC, V. Fri–Sat 11:30am–11pm; Thurs and Sun–Mon 5–10pm.

MODERATE

Madalin's Table ★★ AMERICAN   Part of the renovated Madalin Hotel (see above), this new restaurant is a welcome addition to the burgeoning scene in out-of-the-way, but hip, Tivoli. The chef, Brian Kaywork, is a CIA grad, and he works with fresh local ingredients to prepare a seasonal menu that may not be particularly inventive, yet is certainly rewarding. Sample the straightforward tavern fare, such as a yummy burger or fish and chips, or excellently prepared fresh seafood, and local meats, including molasses-brined pork tenderloin, and seasonal specials. The wine list isn't massive, but wines are very well chosen, with a few unexpected choices. The main dining room is an elegant turn-of-the-20th-century space tucked behind the foyer and outfitted with crisp white tablecloths. But on warm summer nights, it seems that everyone clamors for a table on the sweeping wraparound veranda, from which one can survey the local scene, made up of professors and students from nearby Bard College, weekenders, and a handful of celebrities who hide out in these parts.

53 Broadway, Tivoli, NY 12583. ℂ **845/757-2100.** www.madalinhotel.com. Reservations recommended weekends. Main courses $14–$24. AE, MC, V. Wed–Sun 5–9:30pm; Sun brunch 10am–2:30pm.

Osaka ★★ 🍴 SUSHI/JAPANESE   In these parts, along the upper stretches of the Hudson, good sushi is probably less common than in your hometown. But this small and friendly little place, in a cute little slate-colored house on the adorable main street of Tivoli, is a most welcome find. People come from neighboring towns for the sushi, tempura, and teriyaki dishes. The interior is simple and contemporary, done up in pale woods; the sushi bar, though, is the place to be. The lunch specials, served Monday through Saturday from 11:30am to 2:30pm, are an excellent deal, though those with a big appetite might find themselves still hungry. Another branch of the restaurant can be found at 22 Garden St. in nearby Rhinebeck.

74 Broadway, Tivoli. © **845/757-5055.** www.osakasushi.net. Reservations recommended weekends. Main courses $12–$26; sushi $4–$11. AE, MC, V. Mon and Wed–Thurs 11:30am–2:30pm and 4:30–9:30pm; Fri–Sat 11:30am–2:30pm and 4:30–10:30pm; Sun 3–9:30pm.

Red Dot 🍴 CREATIVE BISTRO   As much bar as bistro, this groovy, dark two-room space is a popular watering hole for locals and visitors to Hudson, and though it's a fun spot for an early or late-night drink, it's also a good spot for easygoing comfort food for dinner or brunch. Check out the generous salads, mussels marinière, braised short ribs, and specials like a salmon BLT. In summer, a seat on the lovely outdoor patio out back, swathed in ivy and featuring a stone waterfall, is a nice little retreat. When I'm in Hudson hitting the antiques shops, I rarely fail to duck in for an Old Speckled Hen—a rarity, on tap—and some superb frites with Belgian mayonnaise.

321 Warren St., Hudson. © **518/828-3657.** Reservations recommended weekends. Main courses $8–$24. MC, V. Wed–Sat 5–10pm; Sat–Sun 11am–3pm; Sun 5–9pm.

The Upper Hudson Valley After Dark

The nightlife is pretty quiet in the largely rural Upper Hudson Valley. When you tire from all the antiques shops and galleries in Hudson, pay a visit to the **Hudson Opera House ★★**, housed in the Old City Hall, 327 Warren St. (© **518/822-1438;** www.hudsonoperahouse.org). It hosts a variety of events, including concerts, theater productions, workshops, lectures, and poetry readings. Check out theater productions, including children's theater, at **Stageworks/Hudson,** 41 Cross St., Hudson (© **518/822-9667**), and **Walking the Dog Theater,** 110 Front St. (© **518/755-1716**). Productions have included Tony Kushner's *The Illusion.* Tickets are $22 to $27 for adults, $20 to $25 for seniors, and $11 to $13 for students. In Tivoli, **Kaatsbaan International Dance Center,** 120 Broadway (© **845/757-5106**), hosts a wide array of performances and events, from ballet to stage readings.

Hudson is home to the greatest number of cafes and lively bar/restaurants in the area. **Club Helsinki ★★★**, 405 Columbia St. (© **518/828-4800;** http://helsinki hudson.com), a legendary live-music club that relocated to Hudson from Great Barrington, Massachusetts, is no longer as intimate and quirky, but it may be better off in its handsome new home, a one-time 19th-century door factory. The lineup of eclectic national acts is impressive, with everything from jazz, alternative rock, and country to swing, Cajun, and Celtic. There are also swing and tango dance lessons, and a chic bar and very good restaurant featuring Low-Country and Southern cooking. My longtime favorite place for a pint on Warren Street is **Red Dot,** 321 Warren St. (© **518/828-3657;** see restaurant review above), although a chic wine bar **(p.m.) ★**, 119 Warren St. (© **518/828-2833;** www.pmwinebar.com), which serves tapas and wine flights and has a well-chosen wine list (with an emphasis on Spain and Portugal), is equally cool, and quieter. For a pint of northeastern microbrew and a good read, park yourself at the bar at **The Spotty Dog Books & Ale,** 440 Warren St. (© **518/671-6006**).

THE CATSKILL MOUNTAIN REGION

by Neil Edward Schlecht

The groundbreaking American conservation movement originated in the Catskill Mountains, 6,000 square miles of mountains, rivers, forests, and parkland considered America's First Wilderness. Though just 100 miles north of New York City, the region's natural state has been remarkably preserved, thanks to the state constitution that designated a quarter of a million acres of "forever wild" forest and the region's importance as the watershed for New York City and almost half the state.

Famous (or infamous) to many Americans through Hollywood movies like *Dirty Dancing* and *A Walk on the Moon,* the Catskill Mountain region is an area in transition. For most of a century, it was *the* summer vacation area for New Yorkers, beginning in the late 19th century, when steam trains deposited elegantly dressed vacationers at stations for their horse-drawn carriage rides to massive mountain lodges and boarding houses. That trend continued through the 1960s, when it became popular for the kind of resorts—many of them ethnic enclaves where family men from the city joined their wives, kids, and neighbors on weekends in the mountains and engaged in 9-to-5 schedules of planned activities—that earned it a perhaps unwelcome sobriquet, the "Borscht Belt."

Today, that type of vacationing has fallen out of favor. The region, still boldly beautiful, if less remote, is being transformed into a different kind of Catskills, open to younger and new types of visitors and residents, and new forms of leisure activities. The new Catskill Mountain Region has set about recapturing its essence, the great outdoors, while holding onto an easygoing, rural lifestyle.

The spiritual and natural heart of the region remains the 700,000-acre Catskill Park and Forest Preserve, a dense area with 35 peaks soaring to elevations of 3,500 feet. This scenic area overflows with lush hills and valleys, forests, farmland, waterfalls, trout streams, reservoirs, and six major river systems. It is regarded as one of the world's greatest fly-fishing areas, and anglers make pilgrimages from across the globe to wade in its trout streams. The Catskill Mountains practically beg for outdoors enthusiasts to sample the incredible variety of hiking and biking trails, sheer cliffs for rock climbing, and peaks for skiing. But you don't have to be a fleece-clad extreme-sports fan to enjoy the region, which is also home to a great number of historic homesteads, out-of-the-way antiques shops, pick-your-own co-ops and dairy farms, and nostalgic attractions like old trains and vintage "base ball" (yes, it was two words originally) teams.

Amazingly, a few old-school resorts hang on, in what can only be described as a nostalgic time warp, charmingly resistant to change. If you want a trip down a musty memory lane, you can still find a megaresort where you play shuffleboard at 11:30am, attend pool games at 1pm, and get your hair set before a bland buffet dinner and the night's entertainment of Rocco singing Italian love songs.

ORIENTATION

Arriving

BY PLANE   Most visitors traveling by air will probably fly into one of the three major airports in the New York City area. For information on those, see chapter 5. Other visitors traveling by air will arrive via **Albany International Airport** (ALB), 737 Albany-Shaker Rd. (© **518/242-2299;** www.albanyairport.com), or **Stewart International Airport** (SWF), Route 207, New Windsor (© **845/564-2100;** www.stewartintl airport.com), near Newburgh, which handles 50 daily flights from major U.S. cities such as Atlanta, Chicago, Philadelphia, Raleigh/Durham, and Washington, D.C.

BY CAR   Most visitors tour the Catskill Mountain Region by car (or motorcycle); it's certainly the most convenient way of getting around. The region begins about 90 miles, or about 2 hours, north of New York City; there is easy access via exits 16 through 21B of the New York State Thruway (I-87). From the south, Route I-81 and Route 17 (future I-86) also provide direct access. From New England, I-84 and I-90 connect with I-88, I-87, and Route 17 (future I-86).

Major car-rental companies, including **Avis, Budget, Enterprise, Hertz, National,** and **Thrifty,** have representatives at all the major airports.

BY TRAIN   **Amtrak** will get you as close as Poughkeepsie, Schenectady, Albany, or Syracuse. For more information and reservations, contact Amtrak at © **800/USA-RAIL** (872-7245), or visit www.amtrak.com.

BY BUS   **Greyhound** (© **800/231-2222;** www.greyhound.com) travels to Andes, Arkville, Bearsville, Catskill, Fleischmanns, Hensonville, Kerhonkson, Liberty, Livingston Manor, Monticello, Mountainville, New Paltz, Phoenicia, Rock Hill, Roscoe, Tannersville, Windham, and Woodstock, among other towns. **Adirondack, New York & Pine Hill Trailways** (© **800/776-7548;** www.trailwaysny.com) serves most of the Catskill region, including New Paltz, Woodstock, Phoenicia, Margaretville, Andes, Windham, Hunter, Cairo, Saugerties, Catskill, and more. **Shortline Coach USA** (© **800/631-8405;** www.coachusa.com/shortline) covers the western section, from New York City to Ellenville, Hancock, Livingston Manor, Monticello, and Roscoe.

Visitor Information

Get additional information before you go from the **Catskill Association for Tourism Services** (© **800/NYS-CATS** [697-2287]; www.visitthecatskills.com) or from one of the four counties that make up the Catskill Mountain region: **Ulster County Tourism Office,** 10 Westbrook Lane, Kingston (© **800/342-5826;** www.ulster tourism.info); **Green County Promotion Department,** P.O. Box 527, Catskill

The Catskill Mountain Region

Bronck Museum **6**
Catskill Fly Fishing Center
 & Museum **11**
Delaware & Ulster Railride **3**
Five State Lookout **4**
Hanford Mills Museum **2**
Healing Waters Farm **1**
Huguenot Street Stone
 Houses **9**
Kaaterskill Falls **5**
Minnewaska State Park
 Preserve **10**
Mohonk Mountain House **10**
North-South Lake **5**
Thomas Cole National
 Historic Site **7**
Opus 40 and the Quarryman's
 Museum **12**
Tibetan Buddhist Monastery **8**

Weathering the Storm

The heavy storms of late August and early September 2011—Hurricane Irene (responsible for 40 deaths in 11 states) and Tropical Storm Lee—were, in contrast to projections, unexpectedly kind to New York City and Long Island, saving their worst damage for the eastern half of upstate New York, particularly the Catskill Mountain Region. The region, dotted with lakes, rivers, and reservoirs that form a watershed for New York City, was devastated by flood waters. Many residents called the flooding the worst in their lifetimes. Hardest hit were the small Catskills towns of Margaretville, Fleischmanns, Prattsville, Arkville, and Windham; in all, homes and central business districts were under as much as 16 feet of water. The main streets of Margaretville and Windham became raging rivers, and the whole of Prattsville was very nearly wiped off the map. Many bridges and roads were damaged and even destroyed; farms were particularly ravaged, suffering at least $45 million in losses and damages. Also hard hit was Central New York, especially the areas around Binghamton and Cooperstown. Governor Andrew Cuomo estimated the damage to New York State to be as high as $1 billion.

At this writing, it's still too early to fully assess damages or know with certainty which businesses will not be able to make a comeback—but it's a safe bet that there will be a number of them. State parks in affected areas were reopened to the public less than a month after the storms, although many hiking trails in the Catskills and Adirondacks suffered great damage, and it might be a year or more before they are fully restored. If you travel to the Catskills or Adirondacks in 2012, it's best to call ahead to hotels, inns, and restaurants in the most severely affected areas. For up-to-date information on flooding, aid, and other weather-related issues in upstate New York, visit www.watershedpost.com.

(© **800/355-2287;** www.greenetourism.com); **Delaware County Chamber of Commerce,** 5½ Main St., Delhi (© **866/746-2281;** www.delawarecounty.org); and **Sullivan County Visitors Association,** 100 North St., Monticello (© **800/882-2287;** www.scva.net).

SOUTHEASTERN CATSKILL REGION (ULSTER COUNTY)

The southeastern section of the Catskill Mountains, centered in Ulster County and the closest to New York City (many parts are 2 hr. or less by car), is one of the most historic, sophisticated, and beautiful parts of the Catskill region. It's an area of bucolic farmlands and original settlers' stone houses belonging to French, Dutch, and English immigrants. The area straddles the easily blurred divide between the Catskill Mountains and the Mid-Hudson Valley and is thus easy to combine with tours of the west bank of the river valley. Some of the most legendary names are contained in this section that skirts the southern edge of the Catskill Forest Preserve: Mohonk Mountain House, Woodstock, and New Paltz, as well as small but increasingly happening up-and-comer towns such as Saugerties and Phoenicia. This section is so close to the western portion of the Mid-Hudson River Valley that you might also consider attractions, lodging, and dining options in chapter 7.

Essentials

GETTING THERE   From north and south, direct access by car is via exits 18 to 20 of the New York State Thruway (I-87).

VISITOR INFORMATION   Contact the **Ulster County Tourism Office,** 10 Westbrook Lane, Kingston (© **800/342-5826;** www.ulstertourism.info). The **Woodstock Chamber of Commerce** operates an information kiosk, 10 Rock City Rd., Woodstock (© **845/679-6234;** Thurs–Sun 11am–6pm), which dispenses town and area maps.

New Paltz & Environs ★★

The largest historical attraction in the southeastern Catskills is in New Paltz, a likable college town (SUNY–New Paltz) founded in 1678. The **Huguenot Street Stone Houses ★★,** 18 Broadhead Ave. (© **845/255-1660;** www.huguenotstreet.org), represent some of the oldest remaining architecture in the region. This collection of a half-dozen Colonial-era stone houses was built by a small group of French religious refugees, the Protestant Huguenots. A National Historic Landmark, the Huguenot district once occupied 40,000 acres at the edge of the Wallkill River. The original stone houses, the earliest of which was built in 1692, have been restored with period furnishings and heirlooms and operate as house museums. Also on-site are the bright-yellow **1705 DuBois Fort** (now a visitor center and museum shop, where tours begin) and the **French Church,** a reconstruction of the 1717 original. Guided tours are the only way to see the interiors of the stone house museums. A deluxe (90-min.) tour includes three period houses and the French Church and costs $12 adults, $11 seniors, $5 students ages 6 to 17, free for children 5 and under; a standard (60-min.) tour, which visits two period houses, is $9 adults, $8 seniors, $3 students 6 to 17, free for children 5 and under; a self-guided cellphone tour (60 min.; $6) is also available. Tours are offered May Saturday to Sunday 10:30am to 5pm; June to October Thursday to Tuesday 10:30am to 5pm; November to December Saturday to Sunday 11am to 3pm. Walk-in guided tours are offered at 11am and 2pm any day the visitor center is open. Consult the website for a healthy calendar of special events. If visiting out of season, you can still stroll along the street and view the exterior of the houses (and maybe peek in a window or two), but you can also call in advance to see if a special tour might be arranged. Tours are also available of **Locust Lawn Estate,** a 19th-century "American Homestead Farm," 400 Rte. 32 S., outside of New Paltz (© **845/255-6070;** 1-hr. tour $8 adults, $7 seniors, $4 ages 6–17, free for children 5 and under; June–Oct Sat–Sun 2pm).

In the tiny, charming village of **High Falls,** which backs up to the waters that flowed through what was once the Delaware and Hudson Canal, the **D & H Canal Museum,** in an 1885 church on Mohonk Road (© **845/687-9311;** www.canal museum.org; $4 adults, $2 children; May–Oct Sat–Sun 11am–5pm), displays original locks and vignettes relating to life along the 19th-century canal. A great spot for easy hikes is the **D & H Canal Heritage Corridor** in Rosendale (© **845/331-2100**), which runs 35 miles along the D & H towpaths and the Ontario & Western Railway from Ellenville to Kingston. The village of **Rosendale** is on the upswing, with a cinema in the old town theater and lively new bars and restaurants that belie its small size. The newly renovated **Five Locks Walk,** an enjoyable, easy half-hour hike in the woods, covers the ground between locks 16 and 20 alongside the canal.

The **Mohonk Preserve ★★★** is more than 6,000 acres of fabulously wild forests, fields, ponds, and streams, all part of the northern Shawangunk Mountains, with more than 60 miles of fantastic trails through dense woodlands and up bleached-white mountain crags. It is the largest privately held preserve (it's owned by a non-profit environmental organization) in New York State. Not to be missed are the unmatched, breathtaking views from the climb to the tower at **Skytop**—at this spot, 1,500 feet above sea level, you can see into six states on a clear day. Day passes and more information are available at the Mohonk Preserve Visitor Center, Route 44/55 (© **845/255-0919;** www.mohonkpreserve.org). The legendary **Mohonk Mountain House** ★★★, a fantasylike Victorian castle perched on a ridge within the preserve, is worth a visit even if you're not staying there—and it really has to be seen to be believed (see "Where to Stay," later in this chapter). Day guests can hike the trails ($13), eat at the imposing lodge restaurant, and ice-skate at the beautiful outdoor pavilion.

Minnewaska State Park Preserve ★★, Route 44/55 in Gardiner, is 12,000 acres ripe for hiking, biking, cross-country skiing, and lake swimming. There are 30 miles of footpaths and carriageways, as well as two lakes, waterfalls, and great mountain viewpoints. The panoramic views of the **Rondout Valley** from an overlook off Route 44/55, just beyond the Minnewaska Preserve, are breathtaking. A park preserve information office (© **845/255-0752**), which issues climbing permits, can be found along Route 44/55 as you climb on the road above Gardiner. The incredibly sheer white cliffs of the **Shawangunk Mountains** ★★ (www.gunks.com or www.mohonkpreserve.org) allow for some of the best rock climbing on the East Coast. The Eastern Mountain Sports shop next door to the Minnewaska Lodge provides guides and equipment. The **Wallkill Valley Rail Trail** (www.gorailtrail.org), which extends from New Paltz to Gardiner, is 12 miles of linear park, perfect for low-impact cycling, hiking, and skiing.

An up-and-coming boutique winery, with gorgeous views of the Shawangunk cliffs, is **Whitecliff Vineyard and Winery** ★, 331 McKinstry Rd., Gardiner (© **845/255-4613;** www.whitecliffwine.com); it's a member of the Shawangunk Wine Trail (www.shawangunkwinetrail.com). Run by a husband-and-wife team, Whitecliff (June–Oct Sun–Fri 11:30am–5:30pm and Sat 11am–6pm; Feb–May and Nov–Dec Thurs–Mon 11:30am–5pm; Jan Sat 11am–6pm) produces nice European-style reds and whites (tastings $11). Also in Gardiner, and recently opened to the public, is **Tuthilltown Spirits** ★★, 14 Gristmill Lane (© **845/633-8734;** www.tuthilltown.com), New York state's first whiskey distillery since Prohibition and a maker of superb artisanal whiskey, bourbon, and rye, set in a 220-year-old gristmill. Tours of the distillery are available by reservation only (tour with tasting $15; Sat–Sun noon and 3pm, Mar–Sept noon, 2, and 4pm; tastings at the tasting room $10, Thurs–Mon 11am–6pm, Sun noon–6pm, no reservation necessary). Another area winery open for visits is **Adair Vineyards,** 52 Allhusen Rd., New Paltz (© **845/255-1377;** www.adairwine.com; May–Oct Fri–Sun; 11am–6pm and Nov to mid-Dec; Fri–Sun 11am–5pm), set in a 200-year-old dairy barn.

Though perhaps not as pristine as historic Huguenot Street in New Paltz, the two dozen stone houses that populate the downtown area of **Hurley** ★, off Route 209 (about 15 miles north of New Palz, about equidistant from Woodstock), are also among the oldest and largest grouping of lived-in stone houses in the country. Main Street, a National Historic Landmark District, is lined with 10 of them, dating from the first half of the 18th century, in a quarter-mile. Your only real opportunity to peek inside some of them is on **Hurley Stone House Day,** held the second Saturday in July, when guided tours are held ($15 adults, $12 students and seniors, $2 children

12 and under, free for children 4 and under) and Levon Helm, former member of The Band, has played free concerts. For more information, call ✆ **845/331-4121,** or visit www.stonehouseday.org.

Woodstock ★ & Saugerties ★★

Woodstock has a name recognition any tourist town would die for, even if it's rather unearned. The watershed 1969 rock concert that took its name and defined a generation didn't actually happen here, but in an open field some 60 miles southwest of here, in Bethel (where there's now a terrific museum about the Woodstock era and superb live-music venue; see p. 254). Still, Woodstock, a longtime artists' community (beginning with the Byrdcliffe Arts Colony in 1902), had a vibe and creativity that fueled the '60s counterculture. In recent years, the village has been transformed by high-end boutiques as well as a smattering of T-shirt and hippie shops feeding off the concert legacy. Though touristy and disappointingly commercial, it's still a pretty and enjoyable place, perfect for strolling, and the top shopping destination in this part of the Catskill Mountains (hands down, the place to satisfy your inner hippie with tie-dye tees and peace-sign art). The long main street, stuffed with shops and galleries, is Mill Hill Road, which becomes Tinker Street. **Byrdcliffe Arts Colony ★**, 34 Tinker St. (✆ **845/679-2079;** www.woodstockguild.org), offers self-guided walking tours of the legendary Arts and Crafts colony (the largest surviving colony of its kind), as well as artists-in-residence programs and a gallery open to the public. The **Woodstock Artists Association and Museum,** 28 Tinker St. (✆ **845/679-2940**), is a long-standing cooperative with a large gallery space exhibiting work of local and nonlocal artists. The **Center for Photography at Woodstock,** 59 Tinker St. (✆ **845/679-6337**), has excellent photography exhibits by well-known artists, along with workshops. Other galleries worth a look include the **Fletcher Gallery,** 40 Mill Hill Rd. (✆ **845/679-4411**); **Art Forms,** 32 Mill Hill Rd. (✆ **845/679-1100**); **Fleur de Lis Gallery,** 34 Tinker St. (✆ **845/679-2688**); and **Clouds Gallery,** 1 Mill Hill Rd. (✆ **845/679-8155**). Cool quilting classes are available at **Woodstock Quilt Supply,** 79 Tinker St. (✆ **845/679-0733;** www.quiltstock.com).

Woodstock may not have been the site of the legendary concert, but it has plenty of year-round live-music concerts, poetry readings, and theater performances. The **Maverick concert series ★**, founded in 1916, is the oldest summer chamber music series in the U.S. Check the events schedule at **www.maverickconcerts.org** and get information and tickets by calling ✆ **845/679-8217. The Woodstock Playhouse** has performances of theater, music, and dance in the summer season (✆ **845/679-4101;** www.woodstockplayhouse.org). With a main stage, bar, and lounge, the **Bearsville Theater,** Route 212, Bearsville (✆ **845/679-4406;** www.bearsvilletheater.com), hosts diverse music groups, dancing, and arts performances year-round.

A worthwhile detour is to the **Karma Triyana Dharmachakra Tibetan Buddhist Monastery,** 335 Meads Mountain Rd. (which begins as Rock City Rd.; ✆ **845/679-5906;** www.kagyu.org), high above Woodstock—a must, not just for Buddhists, but for anyone with an interest in eclectic architecture. Free guided tours are held for individuals on Saturdays and Sundays at 1pm.

Appealing **Saugerties** has been officially discovered. A little town upriver from Kingston, just 10 miles northeast of Woodstock, it has a sweet main drag called Partition Street, lined with good restaurants and suddenly teeming with art galleries, antiques dealers, and shops; it appears to be busily transforming itself into a mini-Hudson, the antiquing destination of the Upper Hudson River Valley. Still a peaceful and charming place, it makes a good base for exploring both the Catskills and the Upper and Mid-Hudson Valley. Not to be missed is the enjoyable .5-mile-long walking trail through woodlands and freshwater tidal wetlands out to the river and **Saugerties Lighthouse** ★ (off Rte. 9W), built in 1838 (you can even sleep here, as it's a fully functioning B&B; see "Unique Lodging in Saugerties," later in this chapter). In summer, there's a picnic deck overlooking the river, where locals come to swim, and weekend tours of the lighthouse interior that include a documentary (Sat–Sun noon–3pm; donations accepted; call © **845/247-0656** for more information). **Opus 40 and the Quarryman's Museum** ★★, 50 Fite Rd. (© **845/246-3400;** www.opus40.org), is a wild and curious work of land/environmental art (which *Architectural Digest* called "one of the largest and most beguiling works of art on the entire continent"). It's a massive (6-acre) artwork of stones fitted tightly together, forming ramps and terraces in an abandoned bluestone quarry. A single self-taught sculptor, Harvey Fite, constructed the piece with traditional tools over nearly 4 decades of his life. The site is open Memorial Day to Columbus Day, 11:30am to 5pm ($10 adults, $7 students and seniors, $3 school-age children, free for children 5 and under). In summer, Saugerties gives itself over to an elite influx of equestrian fans with their fancy horses and trailers. The **HITS-on-the-Hudson National Show Jumping Championships,** 319 Main St. (© **845/246-8833;** www.hitsshows.com), are held in Saugerties from late May to mid-September. Admission is free weekdays and $5 on weekends.

Mount Tremper & Phoenicia ★

The busy main road to Mount Tremper, Route 28, skirts the northern shore of **Ashokan Reservoir** ★★, a beautiful 12-square-mile lake. Follow **Route 28A** around the 40 miles of shoreline for spectacular views of mountains rising in all directions; it's especially scenic in the fall. A little farther on, in Mount Tremper, **Emerson Place** (5340 Rte 28; www.emersonplace.com) is a surprising empire of refined goods and services at the southern edge of the Catskill Forest Preserve purposely built as a tourist destination. **Emerson Country Store,** inhabiting a mid-19th-century dairy barn, comprises a surprising array of upscale shops; see "Shopping," below. But the major attraction in these parts is the **Kaleidoscope at Emerson Place** ★ (© **877/688-5800;** www.kaleidostore.com/largest.htm). Like a planetarium, only trippier, the 60-foot kaleidoscope inside the old barn silo—according to the *Guinness Book of World Records,* the world's largest—gives visitors an opportunity to climb inside the tube of a superhuman kaleidoscope. The psychedelic shows (Sun–Thurs 10am–5pm and Fri–Sat 10am–6pm; $5, free for children 11 and under) are a blast, with different programs seasonally.

Tiny **Phoenicia** is an example of the revived Catskills. Only a few years ago, this was just another forgotten little town with gorgeous mountain views. Today it's a symbol, like Rosendale and especially Andes, of the revitalization going on in the region. Though still a little rough around the edges, its perfectly unassuming Main Street now has a handful of creative, stylish shops and an excellent restaurant, all of which cohabit nicely with the longtime local bars. **The Town Tinker** ★, Bridge Street (© **845/688-5553;** www.towntinker.com), in a barn at the edge of town, rents inner tubes for floating down a 5-mile stretch of the Esopus River, something no kid could refuse. Tubes are $15 per day, and the Tinker even provides tube taxi transportation ($5).

The **Catskill Mountain Railroad ★**, Route 28, Mount Pleasant (© **845/688-7400;** www.catskillmtrailroad.com), operates the **Esopus Scenic Train** ($14 adults, $8 children 4–11, free for children 3 and under), a 12-mile round-trip between Phoenicia and Cold Brook Station (Boiceville); after departing the Mount Pleasant depot, the train travels along the Esopus Creek. Departures are Saturday to Sunday, late May to mid-June and mid- to late Sept; and Friday, late June to early September. An added bonus on the shuttle is that you can tube down the river from Phoenicia to Mount Pleasant, and then take the train back. If you're lucky enough to be in the area in autumn, check out the Leaf Peeper Special. There's also a **Kingston City Shuttle,** a 45-minute ride through Kingston that's part of a long-term plan to restore train service to Ashokan and Phoenicia.

Sports & Outdoor Activities

BIKING & HIKING   For the best hiking (certainly some of the finest in the state), check out the **Mohonk** and **Minnewaska preserves ★★★** near New Paltz (see above). The **Wallkill Valley Rail Trail** stretches 12 miles from the New Paltz/ Rosendale town line to Gardiner. The widely available free brochure *Hiking Ulster County* has details of plenty of trails in the Catskill Forest Preserve and Overlook Mountain Wild Forest, near Woodstock; see also www.co.ulster.ny.us. *Bicycling Magazine* has details of a great (100-mile-plus) reservoir loop for hard-core road cyclists, starting in New Paltz (http://bicycling.trimbleoutdoors.com/ ViewTrip/355113), as well as a mountain-biking route through Minnewaska State Preserve. Bike rentals are available from **Favata's Table Rock Tours and Bicycle Shop,** 386 Main St., Rosendale (© **845/658-7832;** www.trtbicycles.com); **Bicycle Depot,** 15 Main St., New Paltz (© **845/255-3859;** www.bicycledepot.blogspot. com); **Overlook Mountain Bikes,** 93 Tinker St., Woodstock (© **845/679-2122;** www.overlookmountainbikes.com); and **Revolution Bicycles,** 196 Main St., Saugerties (© **845/687-3570;** www.revolutionbicycles.webs.com).

KAYAKING/TUBING   **Atlantic Kayak Tours,** 320 W. Saugerties Rd., Saugerties (© **845/246-2187;** www.atlantickayaktours.com), guides experts and novices on 40 different tours along the Hudson. Rent a kayak at **Bernetta's Kayaks,** 12 Calderone Dr., Wallkill (© **845/464-5106**). **The Town Tinker,** Bridge Street, Phoenicia (© **845/688-5553;** www.towntinker.com), does inner tube rentals for floating down a 5-mile stretch of the Esopus River (including a course with rapids and flumes). Tubes are $15 per day, tube taxi transportation $5.

ROCK CLIMBING   The **Gunks** (Shawangunk Mountains) are one of the greatest rock-climbing destinations in the northeast, if not the entire country. **EMS,** 3124 Rte. 44/55, Gardiner (© **800/310-4504**), has equipment and climbing lessons.

SKIING   Northwest of Phoenicia, **Belleayre Mountain,** Route 28, Highmount (© **845/254-5600;** www.belleayre.com), has the highest skiable peak and longest trail in the Catskills, with 36 other trails and eight lifts, but also a lower mountain that's perfect for beginners and intermediates.

Shopping

Woodstock ★★ is the pinnacle among shoppers' destinations in the Catskill Mountains. It has everything from antiques and modern clothing to Tibetan crafts and tribal rugs. A neat little antiques shop is **Treasure Chest Antiques,** a tiny cottage down Waterfall Way (off Tinker St.). **The Golden Notebook,** 25–29 Tinker St.

(© **845/679-8000**), is a great little bookshop, a real readers' hangout. You'll find unique quilts at **Woodstock Quilt Supply,** 79 Tinker St. (© **845/679-0733;** www.quiltstock.com).

Saugerties ★ is on the upswing, and its main drag, Partition Street, is a smaller cousin of Hudson's Warren Street across the river. Worth a look are **Saugerties Antiques Gallery,** 104 Partition St. (© **845/246-2323**); **Partition Street Antiques,** 114 Partition St. (© **845/247-0932**), full of antique wicker and Stickley and Arts and Crafts furniture. **Arcadia,** 78 Partition St. (© **845/246-7321**), is a cute housewares shop with nice ceramic pieces. A great bookshop and cafe is **The Inquiring Mind** ★★, 200 Main St. (© **845/255-8300**), and I'm dying to get a haircut or hot shave at the old-fashioned **Hot Towel Barbers,** 72 Partition St. (© **845/246-3610**).

New Paltz has a number of Woodstock-like stores overflowing with tie-dye and incense, but it also has a few good antiques shops. One is **Medusa,** 2 Church St. (© **845/255-6000**). Also take a look at **Water Street Market,** 10 Main St. (www.waterstreetmarket.com), which contains several specialty crafts shops, art galleries, restaurants, an excellent cheese shop, the Catskills photography of G. Steve Jordan, and The Antique Barn.

If you're traveling on Route 28, it's hard to miss the bevy of polished, upscale specialty shops at **Emerson Country Store** ★, 5340 Rte. 28, Mount Tremper (© **845/688-5800**). From fine women's apparel, a bath-and-spa emporium, and Simon Pearce glassware to country furnishings and gardening shops, and the amazing Kaleidostore, specializing in hundreds of fine-art kaleidoscopes, this is one shopping experience that will entertain you before making off with your wallet. Tiny **Phoenicia,** just down the road, has a handful of interesting home furnishings and gift shops, including **The Tender Land,** 45 Main St. (© **845/688-2001**); **The Nest Egg,** 84 Main St. (© **845/688-5851**); and **Tender Land Home,** 64 Main St. (© **845/688-7213**).

Where to Stay

VERY EXPENSIVE

Emerson Resort & Spa ★   This sleek inn and spa hotel has rebounded from a 2005 devastating fire, but in most people's estimation, it's not half the hotel it once was. It may be a bit stylized and self-consciously chic (not to mention very pricey) for the Catskills, but it's definitely one of the most luxurious spots in the region. Suites all have gas fireplaces and private decks overlooking the river. The inn caters to sybarites with a desire for big-city pampering in the country, with a top-notch Asian-inspired spa, with wellness classes and a full roster of spa services. Service is not quite as five-star as prices and amenities might indicate, and the former top-flight restaurant has closed, now only offering breakfast. The inn and resort are adults-only. For less precious and more economical accommodations, check out the woodsier **Emerson Lodge** next door.

5340 Rte. 28, Mt. Tremper, NY 12457. www.emersonresort.com. © **877/688-2828.** 25 units. $366–$526 double. AE, DC, DISC, MC, V. Free parking. **Amenities:** Restaurant; concierge; fitness center & spa. *In room:* A/C, flatscreen TV/DVD, fireplace, Wi-Fi, stocked 18-bottle wine cooler.

Mohonk Mountain House ★★★ ☺   This landmark Victorian castle is one of the country's great old mountaintop resorts, on a 2,200-acre rocky ridge overlooking a glacial lake, pristine gardens, and the 7,000-acre Mohonk Forest Preserve. The fanciful seven-story lodge is tricked out with turrets, towers, porches, parlors, and cozy hearthside dens. Rooms vary in size and overlook the gardens, mountains, or lake, but all are done in Edwardian, Victorian, and Arts and Crafts furnishings; many have fireplaces and balconies. If it brings to mind the Stanley Hotel in *The Shining*, it's no coincidence; Stephen King is a repeat guest, though the overall feel at Mohonk is soothingly old-fashioned rather than creepy. Activities abound, with ice-skating in the beautiful open-air pavilion, snowshoeing and cross-country skiing in winter, 85 miles of woodland trails, boating, tennis, golf, rock climbing, and plenty of live entertainment and children's programs. This is a pricey vacation endeavor, admittedly, but a wholly unique and beautiful, even regal, option that has few real rivals anywhere.

1000 Mountain Rest Rd., Lake Mohonk, New Paltz, NY 12561. www.mohonk.com. © **800/772-6646** or 845/255-1000. Fax 845/256-2100. 265 units. $540–$840 double; $750–$2,500 suite. $175 children 13 and over; $99 children 4–12; free for children 3 and under. Rates include 3 meals plus afternoon tea and many complimentary activities and entertainment. Jackets suggested for men at dinner. 2-night minimum stay most weekends. AE, DC, DISC, MC, V. Free valet parking. **Amenities:** Restaurant; bike rental $30/half-day; concierge; croquet; 9-hole golf course; guest services; health club; horseback riding; ice-skating pavilion; library; swimming and boating lake; indoor heated pool; on-site guided rock climbing; cross-country skiing facilities; full-service spa; 6 clay and Har-Tru tennis courts. *In room:* A/C, Wi-Fi.

EXPENSIVE

Kate's Lazy Meadow Motel ★ 📫 If someone told you a member of the New Wave band The B-52s bought and renovated a 1950s motel in the Catskills, you might imagine it would look . . . exactly like this. Kate is Kate Pierson of that famously buoyant band from Athens, Georgia, and she and a team of hip designers from New York City have created a quirky, retro-kitsch retreat, a Love Shack in the mountains, for those cool enough to appreciate it. The funky motel rooms all burst with bright colors, paneled walls, and hip, Jetsons-esque mid-20th-century furnishings. Several rooms have kitchenettes. One unit is pet-friendly (as long as your mutt doesn't weigh more than 25 lb.). Kate's Lazy Meadow certainly achieves what it sets out to do, even if you do get the feeling you're paying a premium for the name recognition and novelty. For an extra dose of '50s style, there's also a stable of a half-dozen whimsically named Airstream trailers down by the creek. If you're traveling with kids, check out the family-friendly cabins. This place is for a certain type of traveler who gets it—and doesn't mind paying the tab for its unique appeal.

5191 Rte. 28, Mt. Tremper, NY 12457. www.lazymeadow.com. © **845/688-7200.** 18 units. Mon–Thurs $175–$250 double; Fri–Sat $180–$280 double; cabins $300–$600; Airstreams $175–$200. 2-night minimum on summer weekends. MC, V. Free parking. **Amenities:** Outdoor Jacuzzi. *In room:* A/C, TV, DVD/CD players, high-speed Internet access.

MODERATE

Audrey's Farmhouse 📫 Dog lovers who don't dream of traveling without their loyal companions will be in dog heaven at this friendly, laid-back B&B in a cozy, 1740 farmhouse, run by a couple who's passionate about animals. Dogs are so welcome that those without four-legged friends may feel left out, or even annoyed because the only time dogs have to stay in their rooms is during breakfast (though you can have breakfast in bed, if you can't bear to leave your pet out). Other than that, dogs have free reign of the place. It's also a great spot for hikers. The emphasis in rooms is more on comfort than on luxury; my favorite is the Cathedral room, with its peaked ceiling.

2188 Bruynswick Rd., Wallkill, NY 12589. www.audreysfarmhouse.com. © **800/501-3872** or 845/895-3440. 5 units. $135–$195 double; $215 suite. Rates include full breakfast. 2-night minimum stay on weekends; 3-night minimum on holiday weekends. AE, MC, V. Free parking. **Amenities:** Outdoor swimming pool. *In room:* A/C, Wi-Fi.

UNIQUE lodging IN SAUGERTIES

Saugerties, fast becoming one of the hippest little spots between the Upper Hudson Valley and the Catskill Mountains, is still being discovered. Two "inns" offer unique and "in the know" small-scale accommodations. **The Inn at Café Tamayo** ★, 89 Partition St., Saugerties, NY 12477 (© **845/246-9371;** http://saugertiesbnb.com; four units; $110–$150 double, $160–$190 suite; rates include full breakfast), a great value and one of the best restaurants in the region, is housed in an 1864 building on the main drag; upstairs are two simple but well-appointed, good-value rooms and one suite with queen-size brass beds, comfortable reading chairs, and TVs.

Even more unexpected and special is **Saugerties Lighthouse** ★★, off 9W and Mynderse Street, Saugerties, NY 12477 (© **845/247-0656;** www.saugertieslighthouse.com; two units; $225 double; rate includes breakfast). Not just a poetic name for an inn, it's an actual B&B within an 1869 lighthouse at water's edge. It may not be the most conveniently located B&B you'll ever stay at—access is by a .5-mile-long trail through wood- and wetlands—but it surely will be one of the most interesting: How often do you get to sleep in the upstairs of a historic lighthouse overlooking the Hudson River? Inside the lighthouse are a small museum, keeper's quarters, two bedrooms, a kitchen, and a living room. Rooms are nicely furnished. Linens, towels, and soap are provided, but it's suggested that you take only a few belongings in a backpack. A single downstairs bathroom, with a sink, shower with hot water, and composting toilet, is shared by everyone staying in the lighthouse. Area restaurants will deliver to the lighthouse; guests can also make use of the kitchen, refrigerator, and gas grill. Pets are allowed if guests rent both rooms.

Minnewaska Lodge ★   Outdoors enthusiasts especially will appreciate this 3-year-old small lodge built at the base of the 1,200-foot Shawangunk cliffs on 17 acres. The area, adjacent to the Mohonk Preserve and a short distance from Minnewaska State Park (and just 6 miles from New Paltz), is a favorite of hikers and rock climbers. The lodge is woodsy and rustic, like a comfortable mountain inn, with high ceilings and lots of windows in common rooms. The terrific outdoor deck looks out onto the 'Gunks (cliffs), and some rooms have private decks (the suite has a private patio). Rooms on the second floor are handsomely decorated in a contemporary style and have cathedral ceilings and either cliff or forest views.

3116 Rte. 44/55, Gardiner (outside New Paltz), NY 12525. www.minnewaskalodge.com. © **845/255-1110.** 26 units. $135–$259 double; $245–$359 suite. Rates include continental breakfast. 2-night minimum stay on weekends, 3-night minimum stay on holiday weekends. AE, DC, DISC, MC, V. Free parking. **Amenities:** Restaurant; fitness center; gift shop. *In room:* A/C, TV, free high-speed Internet.

The Stone House Bed & Breakfast ★★★ 🎁   In a charming, 300-year-old stone house in Hurley, one of the Catskills towns with old Dutch roots, this lovely property pays tribute to the area's heritage by naming its rooms for paintings by Johannes Vermeer, the 17th-century Dutch master. And they're suitably aesthetically minded, with four-poster beds and luxurious Frette sheets. It's nearly impossible to choose a favorite room, but "The Girl with the Pearl Earring" seems to be the consensus pick. This is the type of elegance and historic character not often (ever?) seen in

B&Bs, and the husband-and-wife team, Sam and Nadia, run it with aplomb and great attention to detail, serving terrific breakfasts and orienting guests to the Catskills' great offerings. The grounds and views overlooking the Esopus Creek are outstanding. Look online for great package deals, such as 3 nights for the price of 2.

476 Old Rte. 209, Hurley, NY 12443. http://hurleystonehouse.com. © **845/339-4041.** 5 units. Weekdays $129–$225 double; weekends $$169–$275 double. Rates include full breakfast. 2-night minimum stay on weekends May–Dec. AE, DC, MC, V. Free parking. *In room:* A/C, Wi-Fi.

The Woodbine Inn & Arts Center 🎁   This quirky inn is a good deal for families or groups who want to rent the whole place. Within easy reach of Saugerties and Woodstock, in a residential neighborhood in a small hamlet, this funky place has a vintage speak-easy bar; arts center with yoga, dance and cooking classes, and arts workshops; clean and comfortably decorated rooms; a full kitchen and BBQ patio; and even a ballroom. Pets are welcome too, making the kind of easy, relaxed country getaway that the Catskills are all about. Individual rooms are available on nights the entire inn is not rented out.

144 Malden Ave., Palenville, NY 12463. www.thewoodbine.com. © **518/947-6787** or 845/679-5549. 4 units. $145–$185 double; $750 per night entire inn (2-night minimum). Rates include full breakfast. AE, DISC, MC, V. Free parking. **Amenities:** Lounge/bar. *In room:* A/C, Wi-Fi.

INEXPENSIVE

Twin Gables 🗝   A former boardinghouse for artists, this charming and easygoing old guesthouse on Woodstock's main drag has the perfect feel of the town and is a good option if you're looking for something affordable. Rooms are colorful, clean, and very sweetly decorated; most feature pretty quilts and hooked rugs. Quite a variety of accommodations are available. Some have shared bathrooms, others large private ones. A couple have twin beds, and there's even a single, which is becoming harder and harder to find. My favorite would have to be room no. 11, which is lavender with a large private bathroom. The young couple that owns and operates Twin Gables has ensured that it maintains a very high quality-to-price ratio.

73 Tinker St., Woodstock, NY 12498. www.twingableswoodstockny.com. © **845/679-9479.** 9 units. $89–$144 double; $174 suite. Rates include continental breakfast. DISC, MC, V. Free parking. *In room:* A/C.

CAMPGROUNDS

Blue Mountain Campground, 3783 Rte. 32, Saugerties (© **845/246-7564;** www.bluemountaincampground.com), has 50 sites with electricity.

Where to Eat

In addition to the restaurants described below, an excellent place for breakfast or lunch is the superb bakery **Bread Alone ★**, which has branches in Boiceville (Rte. 28; © **914/657-3328**), just east of Mount Tremper, and Woodstock, 22 Mill Hill Rd. (© **845/679-2108**); it features splendid artisanal breads, creative panini and other sandwiches, and homemade soups and salads. Fans of craft beers should check out **HopHeads Craft Beer Market & Tasting Bar ★**, 2303 Lucas Turnpike in High Falls (© **845/687-4750;** www.hopheadscafe.com). Not only does it have an awesome selection of rotating microbrews from the U.S. and Belgium, but it has some tasty (and locally sourced) tidbits to go with them, such as charcuterie and cheeses, beer-friendly sandwiches, and fish tacos.

Bear Café ★★ NEW AMERICAN   In a theater complex that was the original playground of the founder of Bearsville Records (and manager of Dylan, Joplin, and

The Band), this excellent restaurant with a rock-'n'-roll pedigree is a sophisticated but refreshingly casual eatery a couple of miles from Woodstock. The decor is charmingly rustic and warm, with peaked old-wood ceilings overlooking a flowing brook (the outdoor deck in season if a personal favorite). Although you could opt for something simple like a half-pound burger, this is a place to indulge; meat eaters should try the signature dish, filet mignon with port garlic sauce and Stilton blue cheese, a French classic of sweet and sharp tastes. Service is excellent, as are the delectable home-made desserts.

Rte. 212 (Bearsville Theatre Complex), Bearsville. ✆ **845/679-5555.** www.bearcafe.com. Reservations recommended. Main courses $12–$34. AE, MC, V. Sun-Mon and Wed-Thurs 5–10pm; Fri-Sat 5–10:30pm.

Bywater Bistro ☺ AMERICAN BISTRO   This restaurant took the reins from the Rosendale Cement Co., the former restaurant in a house that was once a bordello in the 1860s. The restaurant, popular with locals, remains stylishly relaxed and warmly contemporary, although with some new Southwestern accents. Chef Sam Ullman's menu uses the best of local ingredients, but looks to Asia, France, and the Americas for inspiration. Entrees change weekly and might include Jamaican-jerked pork tenderloin with mint raita, teriyaki grilled sea scallops, and ale-braised short ribs. All bistro dinners are available in either half or full plates, a nice option for those with smaller appetites or kids in tow, and the wine list includes more wines by the glass than are available in bottles, a rarity. Out back is a relaxed garden terrace for alfresco dining.

419 Main St., Rosendale. ✆ **845/658-3210.** www.bywaterbistro.com. Reservations recommended on weekends. Main courses $9–$27. MC, V. Thurs-Fri 3–10pm; Sat-Sun 11am-11pm.

Café Tamayo ★★ NEW AMERICAN   A saloonlike, romantic, and even modestly sexy spot in an original 1864 tavern with several spectacular features—including a gorgeous old carved mahogany bar with antique mirrors and slow-moving ceiling fans powered by a cool original pulley system—this is one of the most attractive restaurants in the region. Run by a husband-and-wife team, the restaurant focuses on local produce and organic meats and poultry, and the chef, a Culinary Institute of America (CIA) grad, puts a creative twist on American fare. There are good daily specials and dishes such as braised beef brisket and shell steak au poivre with Madeira sauce. The menu changes daily and is a great value: three courses for $30 or four courses for $35 (a la carte is frequently available, too). The wine list is remarkably affordable and includes a large number of New York State wines.

89 Partition St., Saugerties. ✆ **845/246-9371.** www.cafetamayo.com. Reservations recommended weekends. Main courses $21–$28. MC, V. Wed-Sun 5–10pm; Sun 11:30am-3pm.

Cucina ★★★ CONTEMPORARY ITALIAN   The newest addition to the Woodstock area dining scene, this modern Italian trattoria in a yellow Victorian farmhouse is a winner. There's a long communal table that seats 24 down the middle of the minimalist but warm dining room, with fireside dining in winter and tables on the pretty wraparound porch in summer. Chef Gianni Scappin's menu starts with excellent pastas and thin-crust pizzas, always based on local ingredients, but doesn't shy away from more unusual items (such as kale salad and unique pizza toppings), elaborate main dishes (short-rib stew), and creative nightly specials. Look for seasonal prix-fixe, three-course menus that are a steal (Sun–Thurs).

109 Mill Hill Rd. ✆ **845/679-9800.** www.cucinawoodstock.com. Reservations recommended. Main courses $13–$32. MC, V. Mon-Sat 5–10pm; Sun 11am-9pm.

Oriole 9 ★ 🍴 BISTRO/BREAKFAST CAFE   This popular restaurant—open for breakfast and lunch only—is cool and casual, using only all-natural and organic products (it has its own organic farm). The owners are a chef trained in Holland and a woman whose parents once ran Café Espresso in Woodstock in the '60s (where Dylan and Joan Baez hung out). Lunch is informal, with great salads and super sandwiches; breakfast is yummy, with scrumptious omelets and creative fare like artichokes with truffled scrambled eggs.

17 Tinker St., Woodstock. 𝄞 **845/679-5763.** www.oriole9.com. Reservations not accepted. Main courses $7–$14. MC, V. Daily 8:30am–4:30pm (occasional dinners Sat).

Peekamoose Restaurant & Tap Room ★★ ☺ 🍴 NEW AMERICAN   The owners and chef of this stylishly rustic eatery, with a high, barnlike ceiling a few miles west of Phoenicia, come with the pedigree of associations with some of New York City's most ballyhooed restaurants (Picholine, Le Bernadin, Remi), and they bring an uncommon gastronomic excitement to the Catskills. The menu, based on fresh and organic offerings from the Catskills and Hudson Valley, isn't highly adventurous, but it changes daily; some of the highlights include homemade goat-cheese gnocchi, caramelized sea scallops, and slow-braised beef short ribs. There's a substantial kids' menu; tasty comfort food in the tavern; and extensive, superbly chosen beer and wine lists.

8373 Rte. 28, Big Indian. 𝄞 **845/254-6500.** www.peekamooserestaurant.com. Reservations recommended. Main courses $15–$28. AE, DISC, MC, V. Thurs–Mon 4–10pm.

Sweet Sue's ★★ 🍴 BISTRO/BREAKFAST CAFE   Plenty of locals will tell you that Sue's is the stuff of legend. That's big praise for an informal, bustling, and noisy breakfast-and-lunch place, but Sue's is still the real deal, a terrific neighborhood cafe. Breakfast is extraordinary, with pecan-crusted French toast, 25 kinds of huge pancakes (including Hawaiian—coconut and pineapple—and seasonal varieties like pumpkin and peach), and amazing home fries. The lunch menu changes weekly but always makes use of the finest handpicked produce and locals meats, with vegetarian specials. You'll almost surely have to wait for a table, but you will be happy you did. On warm days, the tables outside are most coveted.

Main St., Phoenicia. 𝄞 **845/688-7852.** Reservations not accepted. Main courses $5–$14. No credit cards. Thurs–Mon 7am–3pm.

Tuthill House at the Mill ★★ 🍴 AMERICAN   Within a 1788 gristmill, a National Historic Landmark situated over a waterfall, this secluded restaurant looks great, with romantic old beams, plank floors, and chandeliers. But it's not content to rest on historic laurels and a privileged setting. The menu, ranging from eggplant Parmesan and homemade lasagna to veal saltimbocca and juicy angus steaks, is a nice cut above comfort food. Blow off the skimpy wine list and opt for a cocktail that takes advantage of the artisanal spirits produced by Tuthilltown distillery, just a few paces away; the small tavern in the front of the house is a great spot to have a drink before dinner (as is the terrace outdoors overlooking the river).

20 Gristmill Lane, Gardiner. 𝄞 **845/246-9371.** www.tuthillhouse.com. Reservations recommended weekends. Main courses $10–$32. MC, V. Thurs–Tues noon–9:30pm.

NORTHEASTERN CATSKILL REGION (GREENE COUNTY)

The upper reaches of Ulster County extend along the Upper Hudson Valley, where, in the glory days of train travel from New York City in the late 19th century, steam trains brought thousands of people seeking country refuge at grand hotels like the Catskill Mountain House and Mohonk Mountain House to the station at Catskill. There they were met by horse-drawn carriages for their long rides up into the mountains. But most of the northeastern section of the Catskills is decidedly rural Greene County, the biggest ski destination in the Catskill Mountains. Though for years much of the region lived off of ski tourism and little else, today several of the sleepy little towns in Greene County are receiving new injections of life in the form of inns, restaurants, and cultural organizations and are welcoming new visitors to the area.

Essentials

GETTING THERE   By car, there is easy access via exits 21 through 21B of the New York State Thruway (I-87).

VISITOR INFORMATION   The **Greene County Promotion Department,** P.O. Box 527, Catskill (*©* **800/355-2287;** www.greenetourism.com), operates a visitor center at exit 21 of the New York State Thruway (I-87) on the right after the tollbooth.

Exploring the Northeastern Catskill Region

Catskill, a historic town across the river from Hudson, frankly has seen better days—and may again, as it is pinning its hopes on a rebound and trickle-down effect from nearby Hudson and Saugerties. Its riverfront zone and marina are slowly being developed, and, in addition to a restaurant and public boat dock, there's a small museum and interpretation center of the area's history in the old freight master's building on **The Point** overlooking Catskill Creek and the Hudson River. A Saturday farmers' market and concerts are held here in summer, including the Catskill Jazz Festival the first week of August. The most important historic sight in Catskill is the **Thomas Cole National Historic Site (Cedar Grove) ★**, 218 Spring St. (*©* **518/943-7465;** www.thomascole.org; admission $9 adults, $7 students and seniors; by guided tour only, May–Oct Thurs–Sun 10am–4pm, with last tour at 3pm). Worth a brief peek in downtown Catskill is the **Greene County Council on the Arts,** 398 Main St., with two floors of exhibit area for local artists.

Farther north along Route 9W in Coxsackie, the **Bronck Museum ★★**, 90 County Rte. 42 (*©* **518/731-6490;** www.gchistory.org; guided tours $5 adults, $3 students ages 12–15, $2 children 5–11, free for children 4 and under; Memorial Day to mid-Oct Wed–Fri noon–4pm, Sat 10am–4pm, Sun and holidays 1–4pm), is distinguished by a real rarity, the oldest surviving home in upstate New York. This beautifully solid stone Dutch medieval house was built in 1663, predating the Constitution by 113 years. The museum is actually an entire complex of architecturally significant buildings. The original house has massive beams, wide floorboards, a cellar hatchway, and an early Dutch door; rooms feature Federal, Empire, and Victorian furniture. Also on the premises are a 1785 Federal brick house and three barns (including the unique 1835 "13-Sided Barn," the oldest multisided barn in New York). If your surname begins with O' and you want to get your Irish up, you might pop in to see a couple of sights in East Durham. The **Our Lady of Knock Shrine,** Route 145, features stained-glass and mahogany carvings from County Mayo, Ireland. The **Irish American Heritage Museum,** 2267 Rte. 145 (© **518/634-7497;** www.irishamerican heritagemuseum.org), has exhibits and educational programs about the Irish experience in America. On the agenda in East Durham is a future Irish Village. More interesting for most is the **Five State Lookout ★★**, a spectacular overlook with distant views of—of course—five states, on Route 23 (the Mohican Trail) in East Windham. The village of **Freehold** is yet another small town emblematic of the revitalization going on in the Catskill Mountain region; this unassuming place has a couple of restaurants, a country store, and a pub, a regional hangout. On Route 23A in Jewett is another ethnic contribution to the area, one of interest to architects: **St. John the Baptist Ukrainian Catholic Church and Grazhda** (© **518/734-5330;** www.brama.com/stjohn), a small, wonderfully crafted, rustic wooden basilica, built without nails or cement. You may have to get the non-English-speaking priest to open it up so you can see the wooden chandelier, but it's worth a look.

Several of the small towns in this region get their biggest jolt from winter downhill skiing and snowboarding at **Windham and Hunter mountains** (see "Sports & Outdoor Activities," below), though the areas, with their golf courses and summer music and arts festivals, are also good year-round destinations. The village of **Hunter** has a newly thriving arts scene due to the efforts of the **Catskill Mountain Foundation,** Route 23A (© **518/263-4908**), which operates an arts center, a farm market, an excellent bookstore, and a cool movie theater. The town hosts an impressive roster of music festivals and summer concerts; see p. 245. In Tannersville, next door to Hunter, is a sight for naturalists: the **Mountain Top Arboretum,** Route 23C (© **518/589-3903;** www.mtarbor.org), a pretty 10-acre spot surrounded by mountains and containing nice woodland walking trails and flowering trees, evergreens, wildflowers, and shrubs; it's especially beautiful in summer.

Tip: The **Kaaterskill Trolley** (© **518/589-6150;** $1, free for children 4 and under) runs from the village of Hunter to Tannersville and South and North Lake beaches, between noon and 9:30pm; the weekend schedule begins Friday at 5:30pm.

Besides the mountains, the natural highlight of the area is **Kaaterskill Falls ★★**, Route 23A, Haines Falls (© **518/589-5058**), the highest waterfall in New York State (higher even than Niagara). There's a beautiful and easy .5-mile hike along a path from the bottom that wends along the creek, though you have to park in a small lot on Route 23A, cross the road, and walk along it to the beginning of the path. You can also see the falls from the top by taking Route 23A to North Lake Road and turning right on Laurel House Lane. A short path there takes you right to the edge of the precipitous drop; some folks are brave enough to sit on the flat rocks dangling their feet over the edge of the falls. Nearby is **North-South Lake,** the former site of the famed Catskill Mountain House, the first great mountain resort in the U.S. If you have time, I suggest you take both paths to see the falls from both ends.

Shopping

The **Bookstore,** run by the Catskill Mountain Foundation, Main Street, Hunter (© **518/263-5157**), is the only—yes, only—new-edition bookstore in Greene County. **The Barn,** Route 23 West at Jewett Road, Windham (© **888/883-0444**), is a restored barn full of antique furnishings, clothing, toys, and other collectibles. **Ulla Darni at the Blue Pearl,** 7751 Rte. 23, East Windham (© **518/734-6525**), features the fanciful lamps, sconces, and chandeliers of renowned lighting artist Ulla

Darni. Her colorful, handcrafted lamps fetch huge prices. **Windham Fine Arts,** in a 19th-century house at 5380 Main St., Windham (☎ **518/734-6850;** www.windham finearts.com), focuses mostly on regional painters and sculptors. The **Windham Mini Mall,** 5359 Main St., Windham (☎ **518/734-5050**), is a general store with gourmet foods, a tempting candy display, books, jewelry, and camping and fishing supplies. **Village Candle, Pottery & Gifts,** Main Street, Tannersville (☎ **518/589-6002**), has an outstanding collection of scented candles and outdoors goods. **The Snowy Owl,** Main Street, Tannersville (☎ **518/589-9939**), is a cool home-furnishings and gift store with a decidedly mountain look.

Sports & Outdoor Activities

GOLF   There are nearly a dozen golf courses in the northeastern Catskills. Call ☎ **866/840-GOLF** (4653), or check out the website www.greenecountygolf.com for additional information. The finest is **Windham Country Club,** South Street, Windham (☎ **518/734-9910;** www.windhamcountryclub.com), a championship course highly rated by *Golf Digest.*

WINTER SPORTS   Skiing is the big draw in these parts. **Hunter Mountain ★,** Route 23A West, Hunter (☎ **888/HUNTER-MTN** [486-8376]; www.huntermtn. com), is a skier's (and boarder's) mountain—the closest "big mountain" to New York City, its management likes to say—that's long been popular with hard-core, rowdy singles who party it up afterward at the bars in Tannersville. A couple of years ago, the mountain added The Learning Center, a huge and superb beginner's ski facility that's doing much to attract families. It features excellent learners' packages. In off season, there is a host of festivals, such as Oktoberfest and Celtic, German Alps, and Microbrew festivals. **Mountain Trails Cross-Country Ski Center,** Route 23A, Tannersville (☎ **518/589-5361**), has 20 miles of groomed trails, along with instruction, rentals, and a warming hut. Bike rentals are available at **Twilight Mountain Sports,** North Lake Road and Route 23A, Haines Falls (☎ **518/589-6480**).

   Windham Mountain, C.D. Lane Road, Windham (☎ **518/734-4300;** www. skiwindham.com), has a nice variety of trails and facilities. If you're not into the singles scene and, perhaps, less of a hard-core skier, Windham is an excellent choice. Both Windham and Hunter mountains feature mountain biking on trails in the off season and chairlifts up for the views (a great idea in fall foliage season). Check out **Windham Mountain Outfitters,** Route 296 and South Street, Windham (☎ **518/734-4700**), for ski and snowboard rentals and other equipment, including bicycle and kayak rentals.

Where to Stay

The northeastern section of the Catskill Mountains is home to a number of the classic old resorts and attractions that have been here for years. The area around Cairo and Round Top, tucked in the fold of the Catskill Forest Preserve, has a number of small, family-run resorts.

Albergo Allegria ★★ 🔥   This stellar family-owned and -operated midsize inn is top-of-the-line all the way, and it couldn't be any friendlier. The building has 19th-century heritage, though it's been nicely updated. Rooms in the main house are all uniquely decorated and different in size, offering something for just about everybody and every budget; many have excellent mountain views. Even the cheapest, called the "cozy rooms," are pretty spacious. The large "requested rooms," named for months of the year, are probably the best value. Carriage House Suites are new construction within the old carriage house; they have cathedral ceilings and separate entrances, perfect for skiers and anyone wanting a bit of privacy. Check online for Internet "last-minute" specials and other packages. Families should inquire about sister properties: the Farmhouse and the Mountain Streams Cottage.

Rte. 296, Windham, NY 12442. www.albergousa.com. ℂ **518/734-5560.** Fax 518/734-5570. 21 units. $93–$229 double; $169–$299 suite. Rates include full breakfast. AE, DC, DISC, MC, V. Free parking. *In room:* A/C, TV.

The Kaaterskill ★ 🎁   This unusual and peaceful lodging, on 40 country acres with superlative Catskill Mountains views, is a place to really get away from it all. It's a retreat to nature, with wooded walking trails, a pond, and secluded picnic area, all surrounded by the wide Kaaterskill Creek, as well as horses, wild Canadian geese, chickens, and rabbits (and the inn is pet-friendly). The four rooms, in a restored Dutch barn, are spacious and stylishly outfitted, with good bedding, fireplaces, private patios, Jacuzzi bathtubs, and small kitchenettes. However, service is scant, and the breakfast is really skimpy for the prices (it's not truly a B&B). But if you are mostly looking for a quiet and relaxing stay, in a tucked-away location that's still close to Hudson River Valley and Catskills highlights, this could be your ticket.

424 High Falls Rd. Extension, Catskill, NY. www.thekaaterskill.com. ℂ **518/678-0026.** 4 units. $180–$195 double. 2-night minimum stay on weekends (3 nights on holiday weekends). AE, DC, MC, V. Free parking. *In room:* A/C, TV/DVD, high-speed Internet, kitchenette.

Washington Irving Lodge ★★   A charming Victorian ambience pervades this lovely 1890 house, outfitted with nice antiques, modern bathrooms, a fantastic reading room and parlor, fully equipped cocktail lounge, and large dining room. Some rooms on the third floor are very large, while those in the original tower (my favorite) are very cozy and rustic, with paneled walls and tower windows. All are very warmly decorated and have a 19th-century feel. The house sits on 8 acres and has an outdoor pool and a tennis court, rarities for an inn of this size. The friendly owner, Stephanie, is sometimes helped out by her equally gregarious son Nick, whom you may find tending bar. Midweek ski packages are available.

Rte. 23A, Hunter, NY 12442. www.washingtonirving.com. ℂ **518/589-5560.** Fax 518/589-5775. 15 units. $140–$175 double. Rates include full breakfast. 2-night minimum stay on weekends in season. AE, DC, DISC, MC, V. Free parking. **Amenities:** Bar; outdoor pool; tennis court. *In room:* A/C, TV.

Where to Eat

The Catskill Mountain Country Store and Restaurant ★ 🎁 ☺ BREAKFAST/CAFE   This cute and casual gourmet country store hides one of the best places for breakfast in the Catskills. The morning menu is as impressively creative as it is long, and portions are gigantic. The eight kinds of signature pancakes are outstanding, as are items like banana pecan French toast and the slightly spicy Italian wrap. Breakfast is served all day. The lunch menu features mostly healthy and organic-based items, using the store's own farm-fresh produce, such as spicy arugula salad, homemade soups, great wraps, chili, and burgers, with a few Tex-Mex offerings as well. Children will love the minizoo and gardens out back, where they'll find the pigs Priscilla and Daisy, as well as chickens, roosters, and more.

5510 Rte. 23, Windham. ℂ **518/734-3387.** www.catskillmtncountrystore.com. Reservations not accepted. Main courses $6–$12. DC, MC, V. Mon–Fri 9am–3pm; Sat 8am–4pm; Sun 8am–3pm.

Cave Mountain Brewing Company TAVERN/PUB   This lively spot is popular as an après-ski joint. It brews about a dozen of its own good craft beers, ranging from blonde ale to rye IPA (you can try a sampler of six). And while it serves a decent menu of pub food, with items like pulled pork and burgers, the place can get rowdy when there's a game on the big-screen TV or during a big ski weekend. It has cheapo nightly specials ranging from $1 tacos on Mondays to $5 fish and chips on Wednesdays (as well as beer and shot specials).

5359 Rte. 23/Main St., Windham. ✆ **518/734-9222.** www.cavemountainbrewingcompany.com. Reservations not accepted. Main courses $9–$15. AE, MC, V. Mon–Fri 4pm–midnight; Sat–Sun noon–midnight.

Last Chance Cheese & Antiques ★ ☺ AMERICAN   The name doesn't lie: This casual spot, with a country-store ambience, is part restaurant, part antiques, gifts, and gourmet-foods shop. It's decorated with hanging musical instruments and antiques, and it has a deli with a few tables and an enclosed patio dining area. The menu is surprisingly diverse. Start with a homemade soup, the excellent cheese fondue or a nice, large salad, followed by specialty sandwiches, or light fare like quiches, or go whole-hog with substantial entrees, such as St. Louis ribs, meatloaf, or stuffed filet of sole. An even bigger surprise is that this little place has a phenomenal beer list to go with 100 imported cheeses: Choose from among 300 imported beers, including several very select Belgian ales.

Main St., Tannersville. ✆ **518/589-6424.** http://lastchanceonline.com. Reservations not accepted. Main courses $10–$19. AE, MC, V. Daily 11am–7pm.

Maggie's Krooked Café & Juice Bar ★ 🎒 BREAKFAST/CAFE   Named for the crooked floor, if not the exuberant personality of the eponymous chef and owner, this friendly and cool little two-room bohemian cafe is done up in funky colors. Maggie's does an amazing breakfast (which she serves all day), with a long list of egg dishes and omelets and great buckwheat and potato pancakes. Lunch—the cafe menu—is mainly burgers and simple items like veggie melts, salads, and grilled-chicken sandwiches. I recently had a delicious veggie melt at Maggie's. The home-baked muffins and cakes are incredible; get 'em to go.

Main St., Tannersville. ✆ **518/589-6101.** www.krookedcafe.com. Reservations not accepted. Main courses $11–$15. AE, MC, V. Daily 7am–7pm.

Ruby's Hotel & Restaurant ★★ 🎒 NEW AMERICAN   A converted 19th-century hotel in the village of Freehold, a town on the upswing, Ruby's is a funky venture by a dynamic former New York City chef, Ana Sporer, who has inhabited the cool space with a light hand but tons of vigor. Unassuming from the street, the restaurant features an amazing Deco bar, a classic 1938 soda fountain, hand-blocked Victorian wallpaper, and the original tables and chairs found in the place. Fortunately, the menu and execution are anything but afterthoughts. Though the menu changes frequently according to the whims of the chef and seasonal ingredients, you'll also find standards such as coq au vin, braised lamb shank with saffron Israeli couscous, and homey favorites like turkey chili, chicken potpie, and a Cuban sandwich. A few rooms upstairs have been renovated for overnight stays, and there's also an art gallery upstairs, open during dining hours.

3689 Rte. 67, Freehold. ✆ **518/634-7790.** www.rubyshotel.com. Reservations recommended. Main courses $10–$29. AE, MC, V. Summer (June–Aug) Thurs 5–9pm and Fri–Sat 5–10pm; winter Fri–Sat 5–10pm.

Vesuvio NORTHERN ITALIAN   This romantic and surprisingly formal, family-owned restaurant—with the same chef, Joseph Baglio, for more than 25 years—has two large dining rooms and an outdoor space. Pastas, such as fettuccine *matriciana* (with prosciutto, pancetta, and more), are very good, as are traditional items like veal chops, rack of lamb, and filet mignon. The children's menu (cheese ravioli or penne with meatballs, followed by ice cream) should keep the kids happy. Vesuvio features a nice wine list and superb service.

Goshen Rd., Hensonville. (℆ **518/734-3663.** Reservations recommended. Main courses $16–$29. AE, DC, DISC, MC, V. Mon–Thurs 4–10pm; Fri–Sat 4–11pm; Sun 3–10pm.

Special Events & Hunter/Windham After Dark

The summertime **Shakespeare on the Hudson Festival** (℆ 877/2-MCDUFF [262-3833]; www.shakespeareonthehudson.com), with actors from New York City and elsewhere, is held in a great space along the river in Athens, 1 mile north of the Rip Van Winkle Bridge on Route 385. The **Windham Chamber Music Festival,** 740 Rte. 32C, Windham (℆ **518/738-3852;** www.windhammusic.com), features a sophisticated lineup of chamber-music concerts from January to Labor Day at the Historic Windham Civic Center on Main Street. The renovated **Catskill Mountain Foundation Movie Theater,** Main Street, Hunter (℆ **518/263-4702**), features first-run Hollywood and foreign and independent films in two great theaters. A wide array of classical music, theater, dance, and popular music performances are held across the street at the foundation's red-barn **Performing Arts Center and Gallery,** Main Street, Hunter (℆ **518/263-4908;** www.catskillmtn. org). Nostalgia buffs may want to catch a flick at the **Drive-In Movie Theater** (℆ **877/742-7675**) on Route 296 between Hunter and Jewett; it's open seasonally, from May to September. A handful of bars and clubs on Main Street in Tannersville (just east of Hunter) cater to après-ski buffs in search of singles and dance action, though they've been a little more sophisticated and less rowdy in recent years.

NORTHWESTERN CATSKILL REGION (DELAWARE COUNTY)

The intensely rural Catskill region gets even more rural and remote in Delaware County, home to just 25,000 New Yorkers—but to 700 miles of fishing streams and 11,000 acres of reservoirs and other waterways. This sector of the Catskills is a land of long uninterrupted vistas, deep green valleys, rivers, streams, and isolated dairy farms, with a handful of covered bridges and historic towns tossed in. Though just over 3 hours from New York City, it's one of the best places in the state to get away from it all and get outdoors to hike, mountain-bike, kayak, or ski. How rural is it? Well, you can pick up a brochure from the **Catskill Center for Conservation and Development** in Arkville (℆ **845/586-2611;** www.catskillcenter.org) and spend several days doing a self-guided tour of the *Barns of Delaware County.* Hmm. Sounds like a movie.

However, young weekenders from the City, a mix of artists and hipsters, have also migrated here, principally around Andes, and are busy transforming the area, mixing cool with country.

Essentials

GETTING THERE   Route 28 is a 110-mile corridor running west from Kingston to Cooperstown, bisecting Delaware County and providing easy access to the entire county.

VISITOR INFORMATION   **Delaware County Chamber of Commerce,** 5½ Main St., Delhi (© 866/775-4425; www.delawarecounty.org or www.greatwestern catskills.com).

Exploring the Northwestern Catskill Region

Roxbury today is a graceful and fairly somnolent burg, but it wasn't always that way. Its Main Street is lined with impressive Tudor and Victorian homes and maple shade trees. Helen Gould Shepard, daughter of the famous financier and railroad magnate—and Roxbury native—Jay Gould, was the town benefactor in the late 1800s. She was responsible for the **Gould Memorial Church** ★ (Main St./Rte. 30), built in 1894 by the same architect who designed the state capitol and the famous Dakota apartment building in New York City. Inside are four Tiffany stained-glass windows and a monumental pipe organ. Behind the church is pretty **Kirkside Park,** formerly Helen Gould's estate. The site has been cleaned up and restored in recent years, with rustic bridges built over the stream and trails and walkways added. A **vintage "base ball"** team, the Roxbury Nine, plays its games (according to strict 1864 rules and uniforms) here May through August (admission is free). On Labor Day, the town celebrates "Turn of the Century Day": Locals dress in period costume, and the opposing team is brought in by vintage train. (Look for additional costumed ca.-1898 "railrides into yesteryear" in May and July; check the schedule at www.roxburyny. com.) The **John Burroughs Homestead and Woodchuck Lodge,** John Burroughs Memorial Road (© 607/326-372; www.roxburyny.com; open occasionally in summer), was the rustic summer retreat of the renowned naturalist and essayist. The 1860s farmhouse, a National Historic Landmark, remains as it was when Burroughs lived and wrote here. To get to it, turn west off of Route 30 heading north to Grand Gorge from Roxbury; the house is several miles up on the right.

The **Hanford Mills Museum,** Routes 10 and 12, East Meredith (© 800/295-4992; www.hanfordmills.org; mid-May to mid-Oct Wed–Sun 10am–5pm; admission $8.50 adults and children 13 and over, $6.50 seniors, $4.25 active and retired military, free for children 12 and under; last tour at 4pm), is a restored farmstead with 16 historic buildings, including a working, water-powered sawmill, an antique boxcar, a woodworking shop, and special events like an Old-Fashioned 4th of July, Quilt Show, and Lumberjack Festival.

The Penn Central Railroad arrived in these parts in 1872. The **Delaware & Ulster Railride** ★, 43510 Rte. 28, in Arkville (© 800/225-4132; www.durr.org), south of Roxbury, is a tourist excursion train that takes visitors through the Catskill Mountains in a historic train or open-air flat car, departing from the old depot, a must for train fans. The Ulster & Delaware Railroad was one of the most scenic of the day, traversing dramatic mountain scenery from the Hudson to Oneonta. Special events include train runs with staging of a "Great Train Robbery" and "Twilight on the Rails," a slow-moving party excursion with live music and food onboard. From the end of May to the end of October, trains depart for the trip to Roxbury's 1872 depot at 11am and 2pm on weekends and July through September at 11am and 2pm Thursdays and Fridays; admission is $12 adults, $9 seniors, and $7 children 3 to 12. The Rip Van

THE CATSKILL MOUNTAIN REGION | Northwestern Catskill Region (Delaware County)

TAKE ME OUT TO LAST century

Vintage "base ball"—America's pastime as it was played pre-Ruth, when it was spelled "base ball"—has taken off as the ultimate in retro sporting style. Players wear thick period woolen uniforms and for the most part use no gloves; balls and bats are constructed strictly according to regulations of the day. There are about 100 teams in the U.S., and quite a number in New York State and the Northeast. Roxbury's opponents are the New York Gothams, Brooklyn Atlantics, Providence Grays, and Hartford Senators, among others. What no one seems able to agree on is which era should be faithfully reproduced. Some teams play by 1860 rules, while others adopt 1864 rules, and still others prefer to live in 1872, 1887, or 1898. The Roxbury Nine—which counts Mrs. Gould Shepard's grandson on its roster—is one of the most active in the Northeast, playing 16 to 20 games every summer and drawing as many as 3,000 people in attendance. Turn-of-the-Century Days are celebrated on Labor Day weekend. For more information on vintage "base ball," visit www.roxburyny.com and www.vbba.org.

Winkle Flyer Dinner Train runs on selected dates ($50–$130 adults, including dinner and train fare). Check the website or call for current schedules and special-event trains.

Margaretville is one of the most commercially developed of the small rural towns in Delaware County, with a cute Main Street (where the indie flick *You Can Count On Me*, with Laura Linney and Matthew Broderick, was filmed) lined with several antiques shops, a village pub, and a couple of restaurants. **Andes** ★ (http://andesnewyork.com) is a historic village that is perhaps the epitome of the new Catskills, undergoing a true style makeover, with dozens of new shops and art galleries going in on Main Street. It has attracted an active community of artists, who are giving the town a brighter future, but its past is especially colorful. During the Anti-Rent War of the 1840s in New York, the local sheriff and his deputies arrived at the Moses Earle farm to collect overdue rents. Locals disguised themselves as Indians, killing the sheriff and resulting in the arrest of 100 men and two death sentences. The **Hunting Tavern Museum,** Main Street (✆ 845/676-3775; Memorial Day to Columbus Day Sat 10am–3pm), is housed in one of the oldest buildings in Andes and tells the story of village life in the 19th century.

Shopping

As rural as Delaware County is, it's not exactly a shopper's mecca. However, a number of tourist-oriented shops are in old barns, which makes it fun. **Pakatakan Farmer's Market** is held Saturday from May to October in a fantastic 1899 Round Barn, one of the oldest such structures, on Route 30 in Halcottsville. In season, you'll see dozens of farms selling produce across the region.

If you must shop for man-made things, Margaretville is your place. The **Margaretville Antique Center,** Main Street (✆ 845/586-2424), has several dealers under one room, while **The Commons in Margaretville,** Main Street, has antiques, clothing, kitchenware, flowers, and Internet hookups. Walton's **Country Emporium,** 134 Delaware St. (✆ 607/865-8440; www.cntryempproducts.com), is a marketplace in a historic building with lots of gourmet foods, antiques, and crafts.

A funky flea market is held Saturday and Sunday in summer, along Route 28 in Arkville. Andes has a couple of interesting antiques shops and several cool new art galleries on Main Street, including **Blink,** 454 Lower Main St. (© **845/676-3900**), which features contemporary art and jewelry designs. In Arkville, **Robert's Auction House,** 43311 State Hwy. 28 across from the train depot on Route 28 (© **845/586-6070;** www.robertsauctiononline.com), holds entertaining auctions well attended by locals and visitors to the area every Saturday at 6pm. It's a lot of fun, like a yard sale, except with an auctioneer at the helm.

Sports & Outdoor Activities

CANOEING & KAYAKING With all the water around, **canoeing** and **kayaking** are big, especially along the east and west branches of the Delaware River. Rentals, and in some cases canoe and kayak tours, are available from **Al's Sport Store,** routes 30 and 206 in Downsville (© **607/363-7740;** www.alssportstore.com); **Catskill Outfitters,** Delaware and North Street, Walton (© **800/631-0105;** www.catskill outfitters.com); and **Susan's Pleasant Pheasant Farm,** 1 Bragg Hollow Rd., Halcottsville (© **607/326-4266;** www.pleasantpheasantfarm.com).

FISHING The western Catskills are one of North America's top fishing destinations. You'll find great tailwater, still-water, and freestone fishing. Fly-fishing is huge in the east and west branches of the Delaware River, Beaverkill River, and Willowemoc. The junction pool at Hancock, where the east and west branches join to form the main stem of the Delaware River, is legendary for large brown and rainbow trout. **Pepacton Reservoir** is a great open-water brown-trout fishery. **Al's Sport Store,** routes 30 and 206 in Downsville (© **607/363-7740;** www.alssportstore.com), is the best resource in the area for equipment and knowledge. Al knows everything about fishing the Catskills. For more information on fishing in the northern Catskills, request a **Delaware County Chamber Fishing Guide** (© **800/642-4443;** www. delawarecounty.org) or an **I Love NY Fishing Map** (© **607/652-7366**). The **West Branch Angler & Sportsman's Resort** in Deposit is a terrific upscale cabin resort targeting anglers (see "Where to Stay," below).

Remember, state licenses are required for fishing (p. 54).

GOLF For golf, check out the sweet and hilly **Shepard Hills Golf & Tennis Club,** Golf Course Road (1 mile off Rte. 30), Roxbury (© **607/326-7121;** www. shepardhills.com). The 9-hole course dates from 1916.

HIKING & BIKING The **Catskill Scenic Trail** ★ (© **607/652-2821;** http:// catskillscenictrail.org) is 26 gentle miles of Rails-to-Trails (hard-packed rail paths on top of the former trail bed of the Ulster & Delaware Railroad) that run from Grand Gorge to Bloomville; it's terrific for hiking, biking, and cross-country skiing (in winter, watch out for snowmobiles roaring by). The best spot to pick up the trail is Railroad Avenue in Stamford; a section runs through Roxbury. Within 15 miles of Margaretville, there are 12 peaks above 3,000 feet; **Balsam Lake Mountain** has nice marked trails. **Dry Brook Trail** begins at a trail head in Margaretville and passes Pakatakan Mountain, Dry Brook Ridge, and Balsam Lake Mountain. In **Andes,** a nice hike is around the Pepacton Reservoir to Big Pond and Little Pond; from the trail heads, you can hike to the summits of **Cabot or Touchmenot mountains.** The **Catskill Center for Conservation and Development,** Route 28, Arkville (© **845/586-2611;** www.catskillcenter.org), offers guided hikes, snowshoe excursions, and bird walks.

Mountain bikers have lots to choose from, but **Plattekill Mountain** ★ (✆ 800/ **GOTTA-BIKE** [468-8224]; www.plattekill.com) is one of the top-five mountain-biking destinations in North America; it's very popular with extreme downhill crazies in head-to-toe gear and caked in mud, but there are also trails for novices and intermediates.

WINTER SPORTS Skiers and boarders have two good options: **Belleayre Mountain** (p. 233) and **Plattekill Mountain** (✆ 800/NEED-2-SKI [633-3275]; www.plattekill.com), a small, laid-back 1950s-era resort that's good for families and novice-to-intermediate skiers.

Special Events

One of the big annual events in the area is the **Great County Fair** (✆ 607/865-4763; www.delawarecountyfair.org), held in mid-August in Walton (closing in on 120 years of tradition). You'll find live music, tractor pulls, midway rides, goat shows, livestock auctions, and more. The **Belleayre Music Festival** ★★ (✆ 800/942-6904; www.belleayremusic.org) in July and August brings big-name musicians, such as Wynton Marsalis and the Neville Brothers, to the mountain in Highmount. See also the information above about vintage "base ball" and Turn-of-the-Century Day in Roxbury.

Where to Stay

Andes Hotel ★ 🎣 Although best known for its restaurant and tavern—despite the name—this congenial spot has 10 renovated and cheery, modern motel rooms that are perfectly located if you want to stay in Andes and not have to drive anywhere after dinner or drinks at Andes Hotel. They're not in the historic (1850) building, but a '70s-style motel wing out back—perfect stumbling distance. The rooms are equipped with two full-size beds and a sofa sleeper and feature colorful accents and wall colors.

110 Main St., Andes. www.andeshotel.com. ✆ **845/676-3980.** 10 units. $100 double. AE, DISC, MC, V. Free parking. *In room:* A/C, TV.

Margaretville Mountain Inn An 1866 Queen Anne, slate-roofed Victorian, up a long road from downtown Margaretville, this comfortable and informal, if a tad dowdy, inn has stupendous mountain views on its side. The panoramic view from the porch, overlooking Catskill Mountain State Park, is worth the price of a night's stay. Rooms have some period antiques and modern bathrooms; the Emerald Room inhabits the turret, but I prefer the cozy Birch Room. The owners also have a property right in Margaretville, with two two-bedroom "village suites" with full kitchens, fireplaces, and a private yard (each sleeps as many as six—a real bargain for close-knit families).

Margaretville Mountain Rd., Margaretville, NY 12455. www.margaretvilleinn.com. ✆ **845/586-3933.** Fax 845/586-1699. 6 units. $95–$135 double; $120–$165 suite; $125–$165 2-bedroom village suite. AE, DISC, MC, V. Free parking. *In room:* A/C, TV, VCR (in village suites), kitchen (in village suites), Wi-Fi (free).

The Roxbury ★★★ 🏨 This hugely appealing, uniquely conceived lodging is all about fun, contemporary design—as unexpected as it is welcome in these rural parts. Just 1 block back from Main Street, it's a large Colonial home with an attached wing, a 1960s motor lodge, updated with colorful, hipster styling. There are motel units, boundary-pushing and whimsically named studio theme rooms, and swanky suites, occupying the upstairs of the main house. Most accommodations feature full kitchenettes. Rooms are sleek and modern, with Day-Glo colors, chrome accents, and tastefully modern furnishings: The Genie's Bottle and Shagadelic suites are delightfully

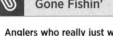

Gone Fishin'

Anglers who really just want to concentrate on the fish and don't want anything fancy or expensive should check out the **Downsville Motel,** routes 30 and 206, Downsville (www.downsville motel.com; ✆ **607/363-7575;** $70 double, $120 two-bedroom apartment). The eight rooms are standard motel rooms, but they have private balconies overlooking the east branch of the Delaware River, and they're just paces from Al's Sports Store, which dispenses just about anything a fisherman could need.

over-the-top. Terrific additions include **Public Lounge** (http://publiclounge.net), a cool spot for cocktails just across the street (which can deliver to your room), and the two-part **Shimmer Spa** (just $20 for general access), with touches of glam and a hot tub, sauna, fireplace, and shower made of river rock. For many guests, this funky spot is a destination.

2258 County Hwy. 41, Roxbury, NY 12474. www.theroxburymotel.com. ✆ **607/326-7200.** 18 units. $90–$125 studio room; $125–$170 kitchenette room; $165–$335 suite. Rates include breakfast. AE, DC, DISC, MC, V. Free parking. **Amenities:** Cocktail lounge; spa; Wi-Fi; DVD library. *In room:* A/C, TV, DVD player.

Scott's Oquaga Lake House ☺   This family-owned resort, incredibly, has been in the same family since 1869 and continues with oddball stubbornness. But that's not even the most notable fact about it: What's really unique is that several generations of the "singing Scott family" continue to perform in nightly cabaret revues for their guests all summer. The shows have to be seen to be believed. For some guests, it will be like time travel to another, gentler planet: planet 1940s Americana. Their literature says it best: "the excitement of a cruise; the friendliness of a bed & breakfast." The resort's accommodations are pretty modest, but the place is ensconced on 1,100 lakefront acres, and spring-fed Oquaga Lake is stunning, making it a family favorite. All recreational activities, meals, and, best of all, cabaret shows are included in the price, and the family is strict about enforcing a "no tipping" policy. You can take free ballroom- or square-dancing lessons, water-ski, or play tennis, golf, or volleyball; the possibilities for fun are endless.

Oquaga Lake Rd., Deposit, NY 13754. www.scottsfamilyresort.com. ✆ **607/467-3094.** 135 units. $280–$324 double; $412 2-bedroom suite (children staying in parent's room, $63). Weekly rates available. Rates include 3 meals daily and all activities and entertainment. AE, MC, V. Free parking. **Amenities:** Restaurant; bar; 9-hole golf course; 3 outdoor and 1 indoor tennis courts; sail- and rowboats; cabaret shows. *In room:* A/C, TV.

West Branch Angler & Sportsman's Resort ★ ☺   Though this great setup of very well-outfitted cabins on the banks of the west branch of the Delaware River—one of the world's most famous tailwater trout fisheries—is all about fly-fishing, you don't have to come with your waders and rods to enjoy the place. If you want something out of the ordinary, with good amenities and services but lots of contact with nature, this is the place. It sits on 300 acres of mountain forests, with lots of hiking and biking trails, and has a very nice restaurant and bar, swings, and a playground overlooking the river, as well as miniature golf and a large outdoor pool. The one- and two-bedroom cabins are upscale rustic, with porches facing the river, picnic areas, and nice kitchens; some have fireplaces. If fishing is what your stay in the Catskills is all about, this is really your kind of place. There's a full-service fly shop, expert instruction, and guides. Grandview cabins with river views have one bedroom but can accommodate up to four people, making them more economical than the executive cabins. As expected from such an outdoorsy place, the hotel is dog-friendly (two maximum per cabin).

Faulkner Rd., Deposit, NY 13754. www.westbranchresort.com. (C) **800/201-2557.** Fax 607/467-2215. 36 units. $180–$232 1-bedroom cabin; $242–$262 2-bedroom executive cabin, $113 lodge apartment (all rates based on double occupancy). Rates include breakfast. 2-night minimum stay on weekends in season. AE, MC, V. Free parking. Dogs welcome. **Amenities:** Restaurant; bar; miniature golf; exercise room; pool. *In room:* A/C, TV, Wi-Fi.

Where to Eat

In addition to the restaurants below, **Public Lounge** ★, 2318 County Hwy. 41 (Bridge St.; *C* **607/326-4026;** http://publiclounge.net), a funky cocktail lounge tucked into a nondescript barn across the street from The Roxbury (p. 249), serves great cocktails as well as fairly priced thin-crust pizzas, quesadillas, and steak and fish dishes Wednesday to Sunday nights.

The Andes Hotel ★★ *❡* CREATIVE AMERICAN   Sally and Ed O'Neill bought and restored this classic 1850 inn, with a massive front porch, in the center of Andes. Ed is a Culinary Institute grad, and the restaurant strikes a nice balance between creative impulses and down-to-earth good food and good value. The decor is simple, with reddish brown paneling and simple white tablecloths and drop ceilings. Appetizers include an excellent warm wild-mushroom salad. A nightly special (on Mon it's baby-back ribs) complements the unpretentious but consistently well-prepared menu, which features items like a grilled pork loin, roasted brook trout, and bacon-wrapped sea scallops. Lunch menu items are simpler, such as pulled-pork barbecue, and a good value. The friendly tavern next door, where there's a great beer selection (10 beers on tap, 70 in bottle) and live music on Saturday night, serves bar comfort food, like popcorn chicken and Texas beef chili. Despite the name, this place is better known for its restaurant than accommodations, though the 10 motel-style accommodations are pretty stylish after a refurbishment.

110 Main St., Andes. *C* **845/676-3980.** www.andeshotel.com. Reservations recommended. Main courses $16–$24. AE, MC, V. Mon–Sat noon–3pm and 4:30–9pm; Sun 10am–3pm and 4:30–9pm.

The Old Schoolhouse Inn & Restaurant 🍴☺ AMERICAN   A hunter's paradise, this restaurant, although in a 1903 schoolhouse (on the National Register of Historical Places), looks more like a hunting lodge. It is crammed to the rafters with taxidermy and hunting trophies of all shapes, sizes, and species. The Sunday brunch is a big local affair, with a huge spread under the watchful eyes of moose and elk in the front room and a shrimp-and-salad bar. Entrees are upscale and sophisticated, with a large array of fresh trout preparations, steaks, "Texas Longhorn burgers," and pastas. There's a pretty extensive kids' menu too. Vegetarians and animals-rights activists beware: This may not be your kind of place!

Main St., Downsville. *C* **607/363-7814.** www.oldschoolhouseinn.com. Reservations recommended on weekends. Main courses $12–$31. AE, MC, V. Tues–Sun 11:30–3pm and 5–10pm.

River Run Restaurant & Trout Skeller Pub ★ AMERICAN/GRILL   Tucked into the riverfront acreage of the West Branch Angler & Sportsman's Resort, this nice restaurant is a perfect place to unwind (and, if you're staying in one of the cabins, easy to get to) after a long day of—what else?—fishing. It's got the requisite masculine lodge feel; and the tavern downstairs has a fancy, huge plasma TV behind the bar,

Dining Down on the Farm

For a one-of-a-kind dining experience in Delaware County, head to **Stone & Thistle Farm** and its weekend-only farm restaurant, **Fable ★★** [find]. Farm-to-table informs not only the name and provisions, but the entire ethos behind this eco-foodie initiative (1211 Kelso Rd., East Meredith, NY 13757; ℰ **607/278-5800**; www.stoneand thistlefarm.com/fable.htm). A gourmet, five-course, prix-fixe dinner ($50 per person, excluding tax, service, wine, and beer) on Saturday night only follows a 6:30pm farm tour. Diners sit down to a meal of local organic produce and grass-fed meats at a communal table in a modern addition to the 1860 Greek Revival farmhouse. There's New York beer and wine available, but you can bring your own for a $10 corkage fee. Fable also serves a terrific

buffet brunch ($20 per person) on Sunday morning, which includes an 11am tour of the farm. To complete the eco-agro experience, stay at **Stone Tavern Farm**, 2080 Upper Meeker Hollow Rd., Roxbury, NY 12474 (www.stonetavern farm.com/LODGING.html; ℰ **607/326-3600**; $239 per night double occupancy), an 1803 farmhouse on 400 acres of a working family farm (the house is the oldest in Roxbury, and there are horseback riding and lessons and camping, too). Breakfast incorporates eggs, bacon, and sausage right from the farm. Or stay at a nearby treehouse yurt (how often do you get the chance to sleep in a yurt?) at **Harmony Hill Retreat**, 694 McKee Hill Rd., East Meredith, NY 13757 (www.harmonyhill retreat.com; ℰ **877/278-6609**; May–Oct $115–$135 per night).

so you can kick back with a beer and watch big-screen sports. The restaurant is the spot for fine dining. It features a number of nice pastas, including spinach ravioli, and shrimp and scallop carbonara, and entrees are pretty evenly divided between meat and fish, with a grilled burgundy filet, veal tenderloin, and grilled scarlet-red snapper among the well-prepared options. The tavern menu at the Trout Skeller Pub includes items like club sandwiches and big, juicy burgers.

At the West Branch Angler & Sportsman's Resort, 150 Faulkner Rd., Hancock. ℰ **607/467-5533**. www. westbranchresort.com. Reservations recommended. Main courses $14–$28. AE, MC, V. Daily 5–11pm; Sun brunch 10am–3pm; bar menu only in Trout Skeller lounge daily 5–10pm. Closed Oct–Apr.

SOUTHWESTERN CATSKILL REGION (SULLIVAN COUNTY)

Rivers, even more than mountains, are the defining characteristic of Sullivan County, in the southwestern quadrant of the Catskills. The Upper Delaware River paints the southwestern border of Sullivan County, separating New York State from Pennsylvania and running about 75 miles, all the way from Hancock to Sparrowbush. In addition to the Delaware, considered one of the top-10 fishing rivers in the world, the county boasts Beaverkill and Willowemoc creeks, making it one of the most important destinations in North America for trout fly-fishing. River sports like canoeing and kayaking, are also huge. Beyond the area's natural bounty, Sullivan County is a picturesque region of covered bridges, scattered historic sights, and a sprinkling of towns undergoing revitalization and positioned to take advantage of growing outdoors and cultural tourism, like Narrowsburg, Livingston Manor, and Roscoe.

Although many know that the legendary (or infamous, I suppose, depending upon your viewpoint) 1969 Woodstock concert took place in the Catskills, few are aware that all those hippies descended on an open field near Bethel, not the town whose name the festival adopted (which is 60 miles northeast). The biggest news of the past couple years in the region is the great new museum (and concert pavilion) on the original site, summoning the legacy of Woodstock's countercultural moment in the sun (actually, it was in the rain and mud, wasn't it?).

Essentials

GETTING THERE   Route 17 (future I-86 "Quickway") cuts northwest across Sullivan County, running from the New York State Thruway (I-87) and passing through Rock Hill on the way west to Deposit.

VISITOR INFORMATION   Contact **Sullivan County Visitors Association,** 100 North St., Monticello (© **800/882-CATS** [2287]; www.scva.net), or the **National Park Service Upper Delaware Scenic and Recreational River** information center, Narrowsburg (© **570/685-4871;** www.nps.gov/upde), for more information.

Exploring the Southwestern Catskill Region

Roscoe ★, which bills itself as "Trout Town, USA," is a pleasant, laid-back town with an attractive downtown that's lined with shops set up to capitalize on the tourist trade, which consists almost wholly of outdoors enthusiasts and fishermen. Roscoe is one of the primary base camps in the Catskill region for anglers; it's perched at the edge of one of the most famous fishing spots in the country, **Junction Pool** ★—the confluence of the renowned trout-fishing streams, Beaverkill and Willowemoc creeks. The kickoff of fly-fishing season is celebrated here every April 1. Legend holds that the fish are detained long enough at this crossroads, unsure of which direction to swim, that they grow exponentially in size and then offer themselves up as catch-and-release trophies. The **Roscoe O&W Railway Museum,** Railroad Avenue (© **607/498-4346;** www.nyow.org; Memorial Day to Columbus Day Sat–Sun 11am–3pm; free admission), across from the red car, is a minor museum that contains artifacts and memorabilia from the old O&W railway line, a scale-model railroad, and exhibits on the area's major attractions and industry. However, after a 15-year wait, the Beaverkill Trout Car, a 1927 Lackawanna passenger car that is outfitted with live trout tanks and displays on railroading and fishing, has joined the red NY O&W caboose across from the museum. Train fanatics should check out the series of self-guided tours of O&W sites in and around Roscoe, detailed on the website.

Anglers have their own cultural institution to celebrate: the **Catskill Fly Fishing Center & Museum** ★★, 1031 Old Rte. 17 (btw. exits 94 and 96 off Rte. 17), Livingston Manor (© **845/439-4810;** www.cffcm.net; Apr–Oct daily 10am–4pm, Nov–Mar Tues–Fri 10am–1pm, Sat 10am–4pm; $3 adults and students, $1 children 11 and under), is a handsomely built and displayed exhibit touting the achievements, art, science, and folklore of fly-fishing. Especially interesting are the numerous displays of wet, dry, nymph, and streamer flies and the actual tying tables of several of the most renowned tiers in the business. A stuffed doll of a 6-pound fish gives kids an idea of what it would be like to catch a big one. Expert fly-fishers conduct demonstrations on Saturday from April to October, and there's a gift shop with all kinds of fishing paraphernalia and novelty items.

Fans of **historic covered bridges** have a number to choose from in Sullivan County, including ones in **Willowemoc** (built in 1860, 2 miles west of town);

Beaverkill (1865, in Beaverkill State Campground); and **Livingston Manor** (1860, just north of town). All are signed. A different type of bridge, but well worth seeking out, is the centerpiece of the **Stone Arch Bridge Historical Park,** Route 52 near Kenoza Lake. The three-arched stone bridge was built in 1880 by Swiss-German immigrants.

Down Route 17 from Livingston Manor, the town of **Liberty** is distinguished by an attractive historic district with classic Gothic Revival, Romanesque, and Greek Revival buildings. Revitalization efforts seemed to get an unlikely boost from the relocation of the historic (1948) **Munson Diner**—featured on *Seinfeld* and *Law & Order,* and once frequented by Andy Warhol—which was uprooted from Hell's Kitchen in Manhattan and transplanted in Liberty (but after a couple of go-rounds, it's now gone under, most likely for good). The **Apple Pond Farm and Renewable Energy Education Center** (© 845/482-4674; www.applepond farm.com; Tues–Sun 10am–5pm), Hahn Road, in Callicoon Center, is a traditional horse-powered organic farm that offers demonstrations of milking, work and sport horses, and border collies, as well as goat-cheese-making classes and horse-drawn wagon rides and an opportunity to learn about turbine and solar renewable energy. It's a great spot for families.

Gay-Friendly Sullivan County

Sullivan County is one of the few predominantly rural counties around that openly court gay visitors and promote gay-friendly establishments. Look for the "Out in the Catskills" rack card that highlights certain gay-friendly businesses and other informational brochures with a gay and lesbian rainbow symbol on them.

Bethel, on Route 178 west of Route 17, is the actual site of the 1969 Woodstock Festival, the famous rock-'n'-roll party where Jimi Hendrix, Janis Joplin, and others jammed for a seriously mind-altered audience. Despite the name, the concerts didn't go down in Woodstock, where most people logically assume they did. **Bethel Woods Center for the Arts ★★★**, 200 Hurd Rd., Bethel (© 866/781-2922; www. bethelwoodscenter.org), now occupies the hallowed grounds with a beautiful pavilion that seats 4,800 for pop, jazz, rock, and classical concerts. The stunning new **Museum at Bethel Woods ★★** (Apr–May and Labor Day to Dec 31 Thurs–Sun 10am–5pm; Memorial Day to Labor Day daily 10am–7pm; adults $15, seniors $13, children 8–17 $11, and 3–7 $6, free for children 2 and under) contains interactive exhibits on the 1960s political and social transformation and the legendary Woodstock concert, including performance clips, as well as special exhibits such as one on John Lennon's and Yoko Ono's "Bed-In for Peace" protest. There's a museum cafe on the premises serving sandwiches, quiches, salads, and picnic baskets to go.

Farther south, the surprising village of **Narrowsburg ★**, perched on the Upper Delaware River and nestled between the Catskills and Pennsylvania's Poconos, is on the upswing, with a number of galleries and restaurants now populating its main street and a rich cultural life for such a small town, with an opera company in summer residence at the Tusten Theater, a film series, and chamber music concerts. Its biggest attraction, aside from its picturesque location at the edge of Big Eddy, is the **Fort Delaware Museum of Colonial History ★**, 6615 Rte. 97 (© 845/252-6660 or 845/807-0261; www.co.sullivan.ny.us; Memorial Day to Labor Day Fri–Sat and Mon 10am–5pm [last tour 4pm], Sun noon–5pm [last tour 4pm]; admission $7 adults, $5 seniors, $4 children 5–14, $20 families up to two adults and three children), a fascinating living-history museum. Originally established as a museum in

1959, Fort Delaware was a stockaded settlement of the Connecticut Yankees in the Delaware Valley in the mid–18th century. Interpreters in 18th-century period dress reenact the work habits and traditions of the day, including candle making, spinning and weaving, woodworking, blacksmithing, and cooking over open fire pits. Interactive exhibits and children's workshops are intelligently designed and really involve kids in history; children can even be a part of daylong apprentice programs, craft days, and 3-day camps in which they learn an 18th-century skill. The **Delaware Arts Center,** 37 Main St. (© **845/252-7576**), is an active cultural center with art exhibits and concerts held in the historic Arlington Hotel.

Minisink Battleground Park (© **845/807-0261;** www.co.sullivan.ny.us; daily 8am–dusk; free admission), County Road 168 near Route 97 in Minisink Ford, is a 57-acre park on the site of a 1779 Revolutionary War battle, the only one that took place along the Upper Delaware. A tiny Colonial militia took on Tories and Native Americans who were aligned with the British. On-site are self-guided trails and an interpretive history center.

Shopping

There are a number of good antiques stores in Sullivan County; pick up a copy of the "Antiques Trail Map," available at many hotels and restaurants, as well as antiques shops. Among the best are **Ferndale Marketplace Antiques & Gardens,** 52 Ferndale Rd., Ferndale (© **845/292-8701**), a very large, 120-year-old country general store with seven dealers; **Antiques of Callicoon,** 26 Upper Main St., Callicoon (© **845/887-5918**), in a 19th-century building across from the train station; **Artisans Gallery,** 110 Mill St., Liberty (© **845/295-9278**); **Memories,** Route 17 Quickway, Parksville (© **845/292-4270**), a massive gallery between Livingston Manor and Liberty; **Town & Country Antiques,** 1 N. Main St., Liberty (© **845/292-1363**), distinguished by its fabulous storefront; and **Hamilton's Antique Shoppe,** Route 55/Main Street, Neversink (© **845/985-2671**). Roscoe has a number of cute shops (in addition to all the fishing gear and tackle stores), including **Annie's Place,** Stewart Avenue, Roscoe (© **607/498-4139**), with contemporary country gifts; and the perfectly named **The Fisherman's Wife,** Stewart Avenue, Roscoe (© **607/498-6055**), a purveyor of antiques and collectibles.

Narrowsburg has a nice art gallery, **River Gallery,** Main Street (© **845/252-3230**), showing contemporary artists and photographers, while its **Delaware Arts Alliance,** 37 Main St. (© **845/252-7576**), shows local artists.

Sports & Outdoor Activities

FISHING Anglers will be in heaven in this part of the Catskill Mountains. Sullivan County possesses several of the best trout streams in North America; the Delaware River and Beaverkill and Willowemoc creeks are among the most storied trout-fishing rivers in the world, and the famed fly fisher Lee Wulff established a fly-fishing school here. The fishing season, which attracts anglers from across the globe, begins in April. Pick up a copy of the *Sullivan County Visitors Guide* for a full listing of lakes, streams, and fishing preserves in the county. The **Catskill Fish Hatchery,** 402 Mongaup Rd., Livingston Manor (© **845/439-4328**), open year-round, is the site of more than one million brown trout raised annually. For instruction and guided incursions into the world of fly-fishing, try **Catskill Flies & Fishing Adventures,** Roscoe (© **607/498-6146**); **Baxter House River Outfitters & Guide Services,** Old Route 17, Roscoe (© **800/905-5095** or 607/498-5811); or **Tite-Line Fly Fishing School,** 563 Gulf Rd., Roscoe (© **607/498-5866**). **Gone Fishing Guide Service,** 20 Lake St.,

Narrowsburg (© **845/252-3657**), also offers half- and full-day float fishing trips. Among the many providers of equipment and tackle are **Beaverkill Angler,** Stewart Avenue, Roscoe (© **607/498-5194**), and **The Little Store,** 26 Broad St., Roscoe (© **607/498-5553**).

GOLF Golf fans can tee it up at some fine courses in scenic locales. Try the championship courses at **Grossinger Country Club,** 26 Rte. 52 E., Liberty (© **914/292-9000;** www.grossingergolf.net; greens fees $45–$85), whose "Big G," which features an island green on hole 13, is considered one of the most beautiful and difficult in the Northeast; **Concord Resort & Golf Club,** Route 17/Concord Road, Kiamesha Lake (© **888/448-9686** or 845/794-4000; www.concordresort.com; greens fees $35–$65), which has two championship courses, one called "the Monster," a *Golf Digest* top-100 course for more than 25 years; and **Villa Roma Country Club,** 356 Villa Roma Rd., Callicoon (© **800/727-8455** or 845/887-5080; www.villaroma. com; greens fees $30–$70; Apr–Nov).

HIKING In Sullivan County, there's very good hiking along the **Tusten Mountain Trail,** a moderately difficult but immensely scenic 3-mile round-trip trail maintained by the National Park Service. The trail head is near the Ten Mile River access site off Route 97 between Barryville and Narrowsburg, and the trail climbs to an elevation of more than 1,100 feet. For more information, call © **570/685-4871,** or visit www. nps.gov/upde. A nice easy trail with great distant views is **Walnut Mountain Park** (© **845/292-7690**), in Liberty, open May through September.

RAFTING & KAYAKING The rivers of Sullivan County, lacing the foothills of the Catskills and Pocono Mountains, are ideal for rafting, canoeing, tubing, and kayaking. The most experienced operator for boat rentals of all sorts is **Lander's River Trips** in Narrowsburg (© **800/252-3925**); it has campgrounds along the Delaware River and rents mountain bikes (and offers combined canoeing or rafting plus camping trips).

WILDLIFE Sullivan County plays host to more **bald eagles** than any other spot on the East Coast, and the state set aside more than 1,200 acres specifically for the protection of the migrant eagle population of about 100 that return every winter. **The Eagle Institute,** Barryville (© **845/557-6162;** www.eagleinstitute.org; weekends Dec–Mar), offers interpretative programs and guided eagle watches on weekends during the winter migrating season. Along Route 55A is a bald eagle observation site on the **Neversink Reservoir,** just outside the village of Neversink. Guided bald eagle habitat trails are found in **Pond Eddy,** with the Upper Delaware Scenic and Recreational River National Park Services; the best times to see bald eagles are December and early March (call © **570/729-8251** for additional information).

Where to Stay
EXPENSIVE
Ecce Bed & Breakfast ★★ 🏠 For sublime views and setting, this B&B can't be beat. High above the Delaware River, in the southwesternmost extreme of the Catskills, this small, personal inn is all about serenity and the stupendous, unending views, which make guests feel like they're sleeping in the clouds (the view from the deck is stunning, breathtaking, and every other cliché you can think of). Situated on a bluff 300 feet above the river and on 60 acres of private woods, this is truly a place to escape and unwind. Take hikes, spot bald eagles, and enjoy some downtime. Although it may seem that you're miles from anywhere, you're just a short drive from

the new museum and concert pavilion at Bethel Woods. Gourmet country breakfasts can be enjoyed on the deck (one of several) overlooking the river. If it's views you're after, settle into the turret of the Sunrise Room. Rooms are spacious and nicely appointed, but not fussy (and admittedly less of a selling point than the views and grounds), and the two hosts are extremely gracious and helpful.

19 Silverfish Rd., Barryville, NY 12719. www.eccebedandbreakfast.com. ℂ **888/557-8562** or 845/557-8562. 5 units. May–Oct $200–$285 double; Nov–Apr $175–$245 double. $50 additional for 3rd person in room. Rates include full breakfast. AE, DC, DISC, MC, V. Free parking. *In room:* A/C, TV, DVD/VCR/CD player.

Inn at Lake Joseph ★★ This professionally run, luxury country inn, secluded on a 20-acre estate and surrounded by forest and down a wooded path from beautiful Lake Joseph, may be just the place for a relaxing and pampering getaway. Formerly a summer residence and then a retreat for two Catholic cardinals, the 140-year-old Victorian estate exudes elegance and tranquillity. Rooms are divided among the main house, the carriage house, and the mountain lodge–like cottage; rooms in the outbuildings are nicely secluded, and though they're more modern and rustic than the manor house, they're more special. Several of those rooms are plain gigantic, with cathedral ceilings; many have private sun decks and a couple have full kitchens. All but one room has a gas fireplace, and a guest kitchen is open around the clock. Pets are welcome in the carriage house and cottage rooms as well as on the grounds, and non–dog lovers should note that plenty of guests here love to travel with their pets. The inn overflows with relaxing spots, from the pool to hammocks strewn in the woods, but some guests will find the inn overpriced and fancy for this section of the Catskills.

400 Saint Joseph Rd., Forestburgh, NY 12777. www.lakejoseph.com. ℂ **845/791-9506.** Fax 845/794-1948. 15 units. $185–$320 double; $255–$640 carriage house and cottage room/suite. Rates include full breakfast. 2-night minimum required on weekends and July-Aug and some holiday weeks. AE, DC, DISC, MC, V. Free parking. **Amenities:** Bikes; boating facilities; outdoor pool; tennis court. *In room:* A/C, TV/VCR, fridge (in some rooms), Jacuzzi, microwave.

New Age Health Spa ★ 🍴 A country-style, intimate, all-inclusive destination spa tucked away in the hills at the edge of the Catskills State Forest Preserve, this is the perfect place for a relaxing retreat without the factory feel of some larger, more institutional spas. All kinds of treatments and classes, including tai chi, aqua aerobics, yoga, and meditation, are available; classes are included in the price. Guest rooms are located in five lodges and are very comfortable but not overly fancy; healthful spa-cuisine meals are served in the rustic dining room, which has a nice deck area for eating outdoors. Beautiful hiking trails wind through the 280-acre property (guided hikes are scheduled), and horses roam down by the stable. Lots of outdoor activities are programmed, as are frequent mind-and-body lectures. Guests are not allowed nicotine, caffeine, or alcohol, and guests caught smoking or drinking will be asked to leave. Check the website for specials, such as the "Bring a Friend for Free" promotion.

658 Rte. 55, Neversink, NY 12765. www.newagehealthspa.com. ℂ **800/682-4348** or 845/985-7600. Fax 845/985-2467. 37 units. $418–$838 double. Rates include 3 meals daily, classes, and activities (spa treatments extra). 2-night minimum required. AE, DC, DISC, MC, V. Free parking. **Amenities:** Restaurant; full spa facilities; 2 outdoor tennis courts; TV & computer lounge. *In room:* A/C.

MODERATE

Hancock House Hotel 🗝 In downtown Hancock, but within walking distance of the Delaware River, this new hotel is designed to look and feel considerably older: It's fashioned after a 19th-century hotel of the same name that once stood in town (and where FDR once gave a speech from the balcony in 1929 as governor of New York). They're good-sized and tastefully appointed with Mission furniture and top-quality linens—and are quite a good deal. The hotel has extra features, such as Honest Eddie's Tap Room and the '50s-style Fannie's Café (serving breakfast and lunch) that make it especially appealing to groups and families who don't necessarily want to venture out for meals.

137 E. Front St., Hancock, NY 13783. www.newhancockhouse.com. (© **607/637-7100.** Fax 607/637-4859. 29 units. Sun–Thurs 125 double, $170–$175 suite; Fri–Sat $145 double, $190–$200 suite. AE, DISC, MC, V. Free parking. **Amenities:** Restaurant, bar. *In room:* A/C, TV, DVD/VCR/CD player.

The Lodge at Rock Hill   This surprising hotel, on 65 acres facing a major road, was an old Howard Johnson, but you'd never know it once inside. Renovated with sedate colors, warm tones, and excellent furnishings, rooms are very large and impeccably clean. Out back, there are hiking trails through the entire property. Take my word for it: Behind a boring facade, which reveals its HoJo origins, is a good-value hotel. The indoor pool with a deck and a nice big Jacuzzi is a huge bonus, as is the fact that the hotel is pet-friendly.

283 Rock Hill Dr., Rock Hill, NY 12775. www.lodgeatrockhill.com. (© **866/RH-LODGE** (745-6343) or 845/796-3100. Fax 845/796-3130. 73 units. $139–$189 double; $159–$239 suite. Rates include continental breakfast. AE, DC, DISC, MC, V. Free parking. Pets accepted. **Amenities:** Jacuzzi; indoor pool. *In room:* A/C, TV, Wi-Fi (free).

INEXPENSIVE

The Reynolds House Inn and Motel   The oldest operational B&B in the county, this welcoming inn was built in 1902 as a "tourist home," or boardinghouse. John D. Rockefeller, a fishing fanatic, used to stay here, and "his" room, the largest and with a claw-foot tub, retains his name. The rooms are cozy and very attractively decorated, though bathrooms are on the small side. Today a charming Irishman and his wife run the inn, which also has inexpensive motel rooms and a cottage out back—perfect for long-term fishermen.

1934 Old Rte. 17 S., Roscoe, NY 12776. www.reynoldshouseinn.com. (© **607/498-4422.** Fax 607/498-5808. 7 units (in main house); 8 motel rooms. Main house $95–$240 double; motel rooms $80–$180 double. Rates include full breakfast. 2-night minimum on weekends May–Oct. AE, DC, DISC, MC, V. Free parking. *In room:* A/C, TV.

Where to Eat

The restaurant and tap room at **Hancock House Hotel** in Hancock (p. 257) are also very good options for well-priced comfort food.

EXPENSIVE

The 1906 Restaurant ★ AMERICAN/GRILL   This upscale restaurant, a favorite of visitors and second-home owners in the area, has one of the best reputations in Sullivan County. The interior is almost homey, with tin ceilings and lots of pine paneling, exposed brick, and ceiling fans, as well as an odd overdose of pink tablecloths.

A Fine Catch

Folks with fishing on their minds, but who prefer stocked ponds to world-class trout streams, might check out **Eldred Preserve**, Route 55, Eldred, NY 12732 (www.eldredpreserve.com; (© **800/557-FISH** [3474]; $75–$95 double). The motel complex—rooms are simple but large—is built around a fishing preserve and ponds stocked with trout and catfish for either catch-and-release or catch-and-keep. An outdoor pool and a restaurant are on the premises.

The menu is also a bit of a surprise, featuring anything but comfort food; it includes several exotic meats, such as ostrich and buffalo. Other signature dishes include steak au poivre, baby rack of lamb, and the 1906 burger, prepared with sautéed onions and mushrooms, Swiss cheese, and bourbon or chili corn sauce (it tries hard to prove its worth at $14). Specials exhibit some flair: They include Cajun shrimp over fettuccine with jalapeño sauce, and veal rollatini with mushrooms and Marsala sauce. The wine list, with more than 175 selections, is one of the most extensive in the Catskills, and it's been continually recognized by *Wine Spectator*.

41 Lower Main St., Callicoon. ☎ **845/887-1906.** www.1906restaurant.com. Reservations recommended. Main courses $15–$34. AE, MC, V. Mon–Sat 5–10pm.

MODERATE

Cobblers AMERICAN   A casual, genial spot, this is exactly the kind of neighborhood restaurant you'd expect to find in a transitional but historic town like Liberty. It has a *Cheers*-like bar of regulars and a simple attached dining room, with black leather-backed booths, and it's known for its home-cooked dishes that are a cut above the norm. Known far and wide (or at least throughout Liberty) for its mandarin-orange salad with sliced almonds and scallions (they even sell the vinaigrette by the bottle), it also serves a nice variety of soups, pastas, and hearty meat dishes.

77 N. Main St., Liberty. ☎ **845/292-2970.** Reservations recommended on weekends. Main courses $11–$21. MC, V. Daily 11:30am–10pm.

Main Street Café ★ ☺ AMERICAN/BREAKFAST   Its name screams small-town Americana, an apt descriptor for this tasty neighborhood restaurant in the quaint town of Narrowsburg. Primarily open for breakfast and lunch—but also for tapas "from 4pm 'til late" Thursday to Sunday, on the deck overlooking the Delaware River—this simple but good-looking place serves the kind of straightforward, satisfying comfort food that appeals to just about everyone, from a meatloaf sandwich and grass-fed local beef burgers to baked mac and cheese (as well as a few outliers, like Thai-inspired massaman curry). Breakfasts and desserts are outstanding, and there's a nice cocktail and wine list, too.

40 Main St., Narrowsburg. ☎ **845/252-7222.** www.mainstreetcafenarrowsburg.com. Reservations recommended. Main courses $10–$15. AE, MC, V. Mon and Wed 8am–4pm; Thurs–Sun 8am–10pm.

After Dark

The Bethel Woods Center for the Arts ★★★, 200 Hurd Rd., Bethel (☎ **866/781-2922;** www.bethelwoodscenter.org), an outstanding concert pavilion (partially covered with lawn seating) on the grounds of the 1969 Woodstock concert—attended by an astonishing 400,000 people—plays host to a wide range of mainstream rock, pop, jazz, and classical concerts, including Bob Dylan, the Boston Pops, Lynyrd Skynyrd, and B.B. King. The pavilion seats 4,800, with room for another 12,000 on the lawn. **Callicoon Theater,** 30 Olympia St., Callicoon (☎ **845/887-4460;** www.artsalliancesite.org), is a cool single-screen 1948 "post-Deco" theater still in use, showing first-run and art and independent films. **Tusten Theater** ★★, 210 Bridge St., Narrowsburg (☎ **845/252-7272;** www.artsalliancesite.org), is a fantastic, nicely renovated 1926 Deco-style theater that seats 160 for live music, including blues, jazz, chamber, and theater performances; the Delaware Valley Opera is in residence at the theater during the summer. The annual summer **Jazzfest** at the theater produces a great lineup of bands in May and June; call ☎ **845/252-7272** for schedules.

THE CAPITAL REGION: SARATOGA SPRINGS & ALBANY

by Neil Edward Schlecht

9

S andwiched between the gentility of the Upper Hudson River Valley and the wilds of the Adirondack Mountains are two upstate towns at polar opposites. The oft-maligned capital city of the Empire State, Albany is an everyman's working city, home to lobbyists, bickering state legislators, and banking and insurance industry workers. Just a half-hour but worlds away, charming Saratoga Springs is all about leisure: Its relaxed pace and cultural refinement override such prosaic matters as work.

Virtually equidistant from New York City, Boston, and Montreal, Albany is ideally placed for a state capital—if you don't mind often severe winters. On the banks of the Upper Hudson, Albany, now 350 years old, lays claim to being the oldest chartered city in the United States. The original Dutch settlement Beverwyck is today a city dominated by government business, one much more accustomed to lobbyists than tourists, but it can claim a surprisingly full slate of cultural and architectural offerings sufficient to entertain anyone visiting without an official government or business agenda.

Saratoga Springs, a graceful and historic resort town just north of the state capital, has become one of the state's most popular vacation destinations. The site of the tide-turning 1777 Battle of Saratoga, Saratoga by the mid–19th century had earned the moniker "Queen of the Spas." It is still renowned for its therapeutic mineral springs, as well as its expansive urban parks and a beautiful downtown dominated by Victorian architecture. Saratoga Springs especially thrives in warm months, when its elegant Race Course hosts one of the nation's most prestigious thoroughbred-racing seasons and the city simmers with a rich platter of cultural events, including prestigious ballet and music companies in residence.

ARRIVING

BY PLANE Most visitors traveling by air will arrive via **Albany International Airport (ALB),** 737 Albany-Shaker Rd. (*©* **518/242-2222;** www.albanyairport. com), located about 10 minutes from downtown Albany and about a half-hour from Saratoga Springs. The airport is served by most major domestic and several international airlines. The information desk can provide details on getting to Albany or Saratoga Springs, as well as basic lodging and tourist information.

Ground transportation to Albany or Saratoga Springs is by bus, airport shuttle, private car, charter limo, courtesy car, or taxi. To Albany, the Capital District Transit Authority (CDTA) operates **ShuttleFly** buses that depart the airport Monday through Friday several times each hour between 6am and 11pm (on weekends, service begins about a half-hour earlier). For additional information, call CDTA at *©* **518/482-8822.** Taxis are also on hand at airport arrival gates. You can make airport transportation reservations by calling **Albany Yellow Taxi** (*©* **518/869-2258**), **Saratoga Taxi** (*©* **518/584-2700**), or **Saratoga Capitaland Taxi** (*©* **518/583-3131**) among taxis, and **Premiere Limo** (*©* **800/515-6123** or 518/459-6123) or **A Destiny Limousine of Saratoga** (*©* **518/587-5221**) among limousine services. From the airport, taxi fares to Albany and Saratoga Springs are about $15 and $45, respectively; a limo should cost about $50 to Albany and $100 to Saratoga.

DRIVING FROM ALBANY INTERNATIONAL AIRPORT To downtown Albany, you can either take Albany-Shaker Road south, which will put you close to the visitor center and Broadway, or take I-87 south to I-90 west. The highways that ring Albany are notoriously confusing, though, and if you go the wrong way, you may end up circling around for a seemingly interminable length of time.

The fastest way to reach Saratoga Springs is to take I-87 north to exit 13N. Follow Route 9 north about 5 miles to downtown Saratoga Springs.

BY CAR Most major car-rental companies have representatives at Albany International Airport. See the appendix for company names and their respective Web addresses.

To get to Albany from points north, take the Adirondack Northway (I-87) south to I-90 east to I-787 south. From points south, take the New York State Thruway (I-87) to exit 23 to I-787 north. From the western part of the state, take the New York State Thruway (I-87) to exit 24 and follow I-90 to I-787 south. To Saratoga Springs from points south, take I-87 to exit 13 south and Route 9 right into town; from the north, take I-87 south to exit 15 and Route 50 south. Saratoga Springs is about 3 hours by car from New York City. From Albany, the drive to Saratoga Springs is about a half-hour.

BY TRAIN The **Albany-Rensselaer Rail Station,** 525 East St., Rensselaer (*©* **518/462-5763**), receives Amtrak trains from western New York (Empire Service), the Midwestern U.S. and Massachusetts (Lake Shore Limited), Canada (Maple Leaf), and points north and south of the capital (Adirondack and Ethan Allen Express Lines). Taxis are available for travel to downtown Albany.

To Saratoga Springs, there is daily service on Amtrak's Adirondack (originating in NYC and Montreal) and Ethan Allen Express (traveling from NYC to Vermont) lines. The Saratoga station is located at West Avenue and Station Lane; there are taxis as well as Enterprise and Thrifty car-rental agencies at the station. For more information and reservations, contact Amtrak at *©* **800/USA-RAIL** (872-7245), or visit www. amtrak.com.

BY BUS Greyhound (© 518/434-8095 or 800/231-2222; www.greyhound.com) and **Adirondack Trailways** (© 800/776-7548; www.trailways.com) travel to both Albany and Saratoga Springs. **Upstate Transit** (© 518/584-5252; www.upstatetours.com) travels between Albany and Saratoga.

SARATOGA SPRINGS ★★★

35 miles N of Albany; 190 miles N of New York City; 290 miles E of Buffalo; 200 miles NW of Boston

A historic and stately town that saw its fortunes rise with the explosion of casino and thoroughbred-racing tourism in the late 19th century, Saratoga has confidently bounced back from its postwar, 20th-century malaise (when corruption and scandals led to a gambling prohibition, the closing of the racecourse, and widespread urban decline). Today, Saratoga is again proudly strutting its stuff as a resort hot spot in upstate New York. In warm months, Saratoga hits high stride with the advent of 6 weeks of horse racing at one of the world's prettiest tracks, public parks in full bloom, and an enviable offering of culture, with both the New York City Ballet and the Philadelphia Orchestra in summer residence. Horse-mad, cigar-smoking track bettors mingle with urban sophisticates in designer outfits at outdoor cocktail parties, while families hit the trails in Saratoga State Spa Park and soak up classical music concerts and outdoor picnics.

Saratoga today is indistinguishable from summer culture, horse racing, and its attendant galas, but its historic importance is well established. Nearby is the site of the most famous battle of the Revolutionary War, the 1777 Battle of Saratoga, which marked the turning point in favor of General Washington's American forces. At the end of the 1800s, Saratoga was touted for the healing properties of its naturally carbonated mineral springs; at its apex, the small town counted two of the largest hotels in the world, each with more than 1,000 rooms. Saratoga lost many of its famous hotels to postwar razing, but this graceful town retains an outstanding collection of predominantly Victorian architecture.

Visitor Information

Saratoga has one of New York's best-organized tourism information offices. The **Heritage Area Visitors Center,** 297 Broadway (© 518/587-3241; www.saratogaspringsvisitorcenter.org), has a wealth of helpful information, on not only Saratoga Springs but also upstate New York. It also has regional displays, videos, and memorabilia, and offers walking tours in season. From May to October, it's open daily from 9am to 4pm; from November to April, it's open Monday through Saturday from 9am to 4pm. The Saratoga County Chamber of Commerce also operates an **Information Booth** (© 518/584-3255), Broadway at Congress Park, open July and August from 9am to 5pm daily. You can also visit the chamber's website at **www.saratoga.org**. Free area maps are available at both the visitor center and the information booth.

City Layout

Saratoga Springs is relatively small, compact, and easy to navigate. Everything revolves around the main axis, Broadway, which is the name for Route 9 once you come into town. Most restaurants and shops are located on the small streets off Broadway (though there are plenty on Broadway, too), such as Phila, Caroline, and Spring streets. Saratoga Spa State Park is just a mile southwest of downtown on Broadway, while Union Avenue, site of grand Victorian homes and the Saratoga Race

Downtown Saratoga Springs

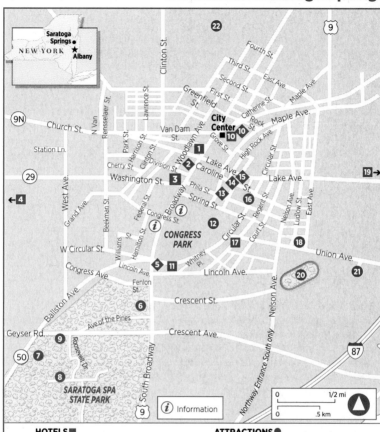

Saratoga Springs •
NEW YORK ★ Albany

9

ⓘ Information

0 ——— 1/2 mi
0 ——— .5 km

HOTELS ■
Adelphi Hotel **3**
Bacon Hill Inn **13**
Batcheller Mansion Inn **11**
Circular Manor B&B **17**
The Mansion Inn of Saratoga **4**
Saratoga Arms **1**
The Saratoga Hilton at City Lake **10**

RESTAURANTS ◆
Beverly's **13**
Chianti II Ristorante **5**
Forno Bistro **10**
Sperry's Restaurant **14**
Tiznaw Restaurant **15**
The Wine Bar **2**

ATTRACTIONS ●
The Children's Museum
  at Saratoga **16**
The Gardens at Yaddo **21**
National Museum of Dance
  & Hall of Fame **6**
National Museum of Racing
  and Hall of Fame **18**
Roosevelt Baths and Spa **8**
Saratoga Automobile Museum **9**
Saratoga Performing Arts Center **7**
Saratoga Race Course **20**
Saratoga Spa State Park **7**
Saratoga Springs History Museum **12**
The Tang Teaching
  Museum and Art Gallery **22**

Course, is a couple of blocks due west of Broadway. Skidmore College is a couple of miles straight up North Broadway.

Getting Around

BY PUBLIC TRANSPORTATION Most of Saratoga is easily walked, but in summer (late June to Labor Day) a **Saratoga Springs Visitor Trolley** (© 518/584-3255) operates a Broadway loop ($1 round-trip).

BY CAR Car-rental agencies in and around Saratoga Springs include **Enterprise Rent-A-Car,** 180 S. Broadway (© 518/587-0687); **New Country Saratoga Auto Park,** Route 50 (© 518/584-7272); and **Saratoga Car Rental, Inc.,** 360 Maple Ave. (© 518/583-4448).

BY TAXI Taxi services include **Saratoga Taxi,** 15 W. Harrison St. (© 518/584-2700); **A Destiny Limousine,** 80 Church Ave., Ballston Spa (© 518/587-5221); and **Saratoga Capitaland Taxi,** 285 Broadway (© 518/583-3131).

Exploring Saratoga Springs

Saratoga is a delight to explore on foot, whether through its plentiful parks and gardens or its historic streets that are graced with fine examples of late-19th and early-20th-century architecture. But exploring Saratoga also means doing what visitors have come to this resort town to do for many decades: see a horse race at the internationally renowned Saratoga Race Course, walk or ski in Saratoga Spa State Park, and take advantage of some of the best summer cultural life any city has to offer.

THE "MANE" ATTRACTIONS ★★★

Saratogians like to say that their town isn't just about horses, but during the race season, everything else definitely takes a back seat to the track. Saratoga's race season lasts 6 weeks, from late July to Labor Day. The Saratoga Race Course, built in 1864, is the oldest thoroughbred track in the nation, acclaimed as perhaps the most beautiful in the country; its fans are legion. If you're in Saratoga during the meet, it's an obligatory visit to join the socialites and the hard-core race fans and bettors. Races are held Wednesday through Monday, with the first race post time at 1pm. **The Saratoga Race Course** (© 518/584-6200), a 350-acre, 1⅛-mile track, is located at 267 Union Ave. General (grandstand) admission is $3 ($5 on Travers Day, the last Sat in Aug) and Clubhouse admission is $5 ($10 on Travers Day). Reserved seats in the Clubhouse are $8, grandstand $5. For advance ticket purchase, contact the **New York Racing Association** at © 718/641-4700, or during race season at © 518/584-6200, ext. 360. You can also visit their website, **www.nyra.com/index_saratoga.html**, or call © 800/814-7846 for tickets, schedules, and additional information.

Race fans may also enjoy a bit of harness racing, which you can witness year-round at the **Saratoga Casino & Raceway,** 342 Jefferson St. (© 518/584-2110). Races generally start at 7:40pm, but see http://saratogacasino.com/Racing.aspx for the exact schedule. Polo, anyone? From June to September, **Saratoga Polo** organizes matches

Rewards for Early Risers

Early morning before races is a great time to come out to the track; expert commentary accompanies the thoroughbreds as they go through their morning workouts, and a buffet breakfast is served each racing day on the Clubhouse Porch from 7 to 9:30am.

at historic Whitney Field (corner of Bloomfield and Denton roads), every Friday and Sunday evening at 5:30pm. For more information, call ✆ **518/584-8108,** or visit **www.saratogapolo.com**. Clubhouse admission is $25, while tailgate tickets are $25 per car.

MORE TO SEE & DO

The Children's Museum at Saratoga ☺ Less a museum than a terrific playground, the space includes adorable areas meant to create a little person's Main Street around 1920: There are a bank, a general store, a diner, a schoolhouse, and a fire station (complete with a sliding pole). Kids will be entertained for at least an hour or 2.

69 Caroline St. ✆ **518/584-5540.** www.childrensmuseumatsaratoga.org. Admission $6, free for children under 1. July to Labor Day Mon–Sat 9:30am–4:30pm; early Sept to June Tues–Sat 9:30am–4:30pm, Sun noon–4:30pm.

National Museum of Dance & Hall of Fame ★ ☺ Housed in the old Washington Bath House, a handsome European-style mineral spa built in 1918, this is the only museum in the country dedicated to American professional dance. Its archives, photographs, and exhibits of sets and costumes chronicle a century of dance. The museum is also a place that makes new contributions to the field; on-site are three full-size dance studios modeled after those of the New York City Ballet, which, not coincidentally, takes up residence in Saratoga Springs every July. Visitors have the opportunity to view rehearsals as well as participate in workshops, classes, and lectures. For children or adults interested in dance, the museum's programs are excellent learning tools. Plan on about a half-hour, unless there are rehearsals or workshops.

99 S. Broadway (Rte. 9). ✆ **518/584-2225.** www.dancemuseum.org. Admission $6.50 adults, $5 seniors and students, $3 children 11 and under. Group tours (by appt. only) $5 adults, $4 seniors and students, $2 children 11 and under. Tues–Sun 10am–4:30pm (summer months only).

National Museum of Racing and Hall of Fame ☺ Across the road from the famous Saratoga Race Course, this midsize museum pays tribute to 3 centuries of thoroughbred racing in the U.S. Trophies, memorabilia, artwork, and film tell the story of the sport that grips the attention of so many in Saratoga during summer race season. The Hall of Fame celebrates the greatest names, both jockeys and horses, in the sport's history. Uniforms and artifacts are on display, and interactive screens allow visitors to relive great moments in racing. The museum is mostly for true fans, though even those without much interest in horse racing can pick up some interesting tidbits (including facts that kids are likely to enjoy and ponder). For example, did you know that the average racehorse weighs 1,000 pounds? And whereas a Ferrari can go from zero to 60 mph in 5.5 seconds, a racehorse can accelerate to 42 mph in just 2.5 seconds. The museum is unlikely to detain you for more than 45 minutes.

191 Union Ave. ✆ **800/562-5394** or 518/584-0400. www.racingmuseum.net. Admission $7 adults, $5 seniors and students, free for children 4 and under. Jan to mid-Apr Wed–Sat 10am–4pm; mid-Apr to Dec Mon–Sat 10am–4pm, Sun noon–4pm (during the Saratoga racing meet, museum daily 9am–5pm).

Saratoga Automobile Museum ★ ☺ Housed in an old bottling plant in the middle of Saratoga Spa State Park, this surprising museum will delight car lovers. On view are some interesting classic automobiles representing the once-vital New York State auto industry, such as Charles A. Lindbergh's 1928 Franklin, made in Syracuse, and an extraordinary 1931 Pierce Arrow, manufactured in Buffalo. The top floor is devoted to race cars, and there are curiosities like the 1957 BMW Isetta 300, called the "Rolling Egg." Kids into cars will love the tables set up with pads of paper and crayons and an invitation to draw and display their "dream car." A recent exhibit was

"Forza Italia!" full of Italian sporting vehicles. A spin through the museum should take about 45 minutes.

110 Ave. of the Pines (Saratoga Spa State Park). ⒸＴ **518/587-1935.** www.saratogaautomuseum.org. Admission $8 adults, $5 seniors, $3.50 children 6-16, free for children 5 and under. June-Oct daily 10am-5pm; Nov-May Tues-Sun 10am-5pm.

Saratoga National Historical Park ★   Saratoga was no less than the turning point in the American Revolution. In 1777, American troops defeated the British army—considered to be one of the most significant military victories in history—and forced its surrender on October 17, prompting France to recognize American independence and sign on as its ally. Today, this historical area is a national park, which comprises the 4-square-mile battlefield in Stillwater, the General Philip Schuyler House, and the Saratoga Monument in the nearby village of Victory. A 9½-mile battlefield tour road traces American defensive positions, battle sites, and British defensive positions, with a series of 10 interpretive stops along the way. Also on the grounds is the 4-mile Wilkinson Trail for hiking and cross-country skiing. Living-history demonstrations are presented in summer months.

The Schuyler House, located 8 miles north in Schuylerville, was the residence of General Philip Schuyler. Burned by the British, the present reconstruction was built after the American victory. The Saratoga Monument is a 155-foot memorial that marks Burgoyne's surrender. Plan on several hours if you go to all the sites.

648 Rte. 32 (at Rte. 4), Stillwater (15 miles southeast of Saratoga Springs). ⒸＴ **518/664-9821.** www.nps. gov/sara. Admission $5 private vehicle, $3 individual (on foot, bike, or horse) or by National Parks Annual or Senior Pass (p. 49). Visitor center year-round daily 9am-5pm; Tour Rd. Apr-Nov daily 9am-7pm; The Schuyler House Memorial Day to Labor Day Wed-Sun 9:30am-4:30pm (after Labor Day, weekends only 9:30am-4:30pm).

Saratoga Spa State Park ★ ☺   Saratoga Springs rose to prominence in the mid–19th century as a spa town, on the strengths of mineral springs and baths that drew wealthy patrons to exercise and "take the waters." Now a National Historic Landmark—and certainly one of the prettiest urban parks in the country—Saratoga Spa State Park is still a relaxing place to escape from daily pressures. The 2,200-acre park ("the public's resort") is a pine forest with natural geysers; it's home to a swimming pool complex, two golf courses, endless trails for walking and cross-country skiing in winter, picnic pavilions, a skating rink, tennis courts, and two restored bathhouses, designed in the classical European spa tradition. Also tucked into the park are a large historic hotel, three restaurants, the renowned Saratoga Performing Arts Center, and two small museums. You could easily spend all day in the park, depending on the diversions you choose. Special events, great for families, include the wildflower walk spring tour and trail races.

19 Roosevelt Dr. ⒸＴ **518/584-2535.** www.saratogaspastatepark.org. Admission charged for some activities. Year-round dawn-dusk.

Saratoga Museums Pass

The Saratoga Museums Pass allows visitors to buy one and get one free admission at any of 10 participating museums, including the National Museum of Racing, National Museum of Dance, Saratoga Automobile Museum, and Tang Teaching Museum and Art Gallery. Visit www.saratoga.org/ museumspass for more information and to download and print the pass.

hyde COLLECTION ART MUSEUM

Saratoga Springs' charms can make the resort town difficult to leave, but art fans may be pried loose by the presence of a splendid collection of old and modern masters just 20 minutes north of town in Glens Falls. The **Hyde Collection Art Museum ★★**, housed in a gorgeous renovated mansion, is reminiscent of New York City's Frick Collection in its breadth and beautiful setting. Among the treasures assembled in the 1912, neo-Renaissance Florentine-style villa are works by Raphael, da Vinci, Van Dyck, Tiepolo, El Greco, Rubens, Tintoretto, Homer, Whistler, Turner, Degas, Seurat, Renoir, Picasso, and van Gogh. The most remarkable works are Rembrandt's unusual *Portrait of Christ* (1655–57), purchased from the Russian government in 1934, and Botticelli's small *Annunciation* (1492). You'll need at least an hour here, more for art aficionados. The museum is located about 8 miles north of Saratoga Springs at 16 Warren St. in Glens Falls (② **518/792-1761;** www.hydecollection.org). Admission is free, but donations are accepted (suggested donation is $8 per person); special exhibits are $12 adults, $8 seniors and students. The museum's open Tuesday through Friday from 11am to 4pm; and Saturday and Sunday from noon to 5pm. Docent-led tours ($6 per person) of the museum and tours of Hyde House are also available (see the website for a schedule).

Saratoga Springs History Museum In its heyday in the late 19th century, Saratoga was the elegant refuge of high-society high rollers. The Canfield Casino, built in 1870 in Congress Park, is a stately red-brick Victorian that today is home only to the ghosts of gamblers past and a museum and historical collection that chronicles Saratoga Springs' era as a resort known the world over. The original casino was built by John Morrissey, a heavyweight champion boxer turned entrepreneur, and later made over in haute style by a wealthy gambler, Richard Canfield, at the turn of the 20th century. Canfield's lavish decor included marble tables, massive mirrors, grand chandeliers, and the world's largest seamless rug. In the casino's parlors, Amelia Earhart was feted and grand balls and teas attracted the Gilded Age's fabulous wealthy. The Historical Society's exhibitions of photography depict Saratoga Springs in all its splendor, and on the second floor is a re-creation of the high-stakes room and parlors with an original collection of handcrafted John Henry Belter furnishings. On the top floor, eight rooms re-create Pine Grove, the prominent Walworth family's Victorian home that was demolished in the 1950s. Allow about an hour to tour the museum.

Congress Park (off Broadway). ② **518/584-6920.** www.saratogasprings-historymuseum.org. Admission $5 adults, $4 seniors and students, free for children 11 and under. Memorial Day to Labor Day Mon–Sat 10am–4pm and Sun 1–4pm; rest of year Wed–Sat 10am–4pm, Sun 1–4pm. Free guided casino tours, summer Tues 1pm and Wed–Thurs 11am.

The Tang Teaching Museum and Art Gallery ★ 📷 The first art museum in Saratoga Springs, on the campus of Skidmore College, the Tang is most notable for its striking modern architecture. A visit here is a must for any fan of modern architecture. The stunning building in stone, concrete, and stainless steel by Antoine Predock slopes gently out of the ground and is surrounded by white pines, tucked neatly into the landscape; two large exterior staircases ascend and effectively create a shortcut across campus that goes over the top of the building. The irregularly shaped galleries inside the 39,000-foot museum host often challenging contemporary art and

SARATOGA'S spas & SPRINGS

Native Americans believed the waters of Saratoga Springs had natural therapeutic properties, and so did early Americans such as George Washington and Alexander Hamilton. Saratoga Springs became a famous spa town in the 19th century, and was known as "Queen of the Spas," with hotels hosting visitors seeking the local mineral waters for drinking and mineral baths. A geological fault line runs through Saratoga Springs and a solid layer of shale produces naturally carbonated waters from deep limestone beds. Saratoga Springs' heritage as a mineral spa resort town lives on, if on a smaller scale. **Roosevelt Baths and Spa ★**, 39 Roosevelt Dr., in Saratoga Spa State Park (*②* **800/452-7275;** www.gideonputnam.com/spa.aspx), makes the most of the town's heritage with a full-service spa in one of the old classic spa buildings, built in 1935. It's been gussied up, but it retains old steam cubicles and instruments. Services include mineral baths, massages, reflexology, body wraps, facials, and hot stone therapy. More modern is **The Crystal Spa** (at the Grand Union Motel), 120 S. Broadway (*②* **518/584-2556;** www.grandunionmotel.com/spa.htm), also offering clay and mud wraps, facials, and "pamper packages." You can also take a **self-guided tour** of Saratoga's mineral springs. There are 16 spots in and around the city, in Congress Park, Saratoga Spa State Park, and High Rock Park. Pick up the tour brochure *Tasting Tour of Saratoga's Springs* at the Saratoga Springs Visitor Center.

cross-disciplinary exhibits focusing on fields like music and physics (highlighting its role as a teaching institution). Allow about an hour to explore.

815 N. Broadway. *②* **518/580-8080.** http://tang.skidmore.edu. Free admission (suggested donation $5 adults, $2 seniors, $3 students). Tues–Fri noon–5pm (Thurs until 9pm).

ESPECIALLY FOR KIDS

Saratoga Springs is a nice and relaxed place for families, with plenty of parks and sights that should entertain children of all ages. Most kids would love to attend a thoroughbred horse race at the **Saratoga Race Course,** one of the most famous and beautiful tracks in the world (p. 264). There are great features for kids at the track, including free walking tours of the stable area, a tram ride, and a starting gate demonstration. An interactive exhibit, the Discovery Paddock and Horse Play! Gallery, teaches children how horses and jockeys prepare for races, and kids can even ride the "Equipony" and dress up like a jockey, "weigh in" on a scale, and hammer a shoe on a mock-horse hoof. Open every racing day from 11am to 4pm.in season.

The **Saratoga Children's Museum,** with its cute play areas, is a no-brainer for tots, and the **Saratoga Automobile Museum** (p. 265) is also a fun outing. Older children, especially those budding ballerinas, will enjoy the **National Museum of Dance & Hall of Fame. Saratoga Spa State Park** is a delightful urban park with miles of hiking trails, two swimming pools, and a skating rink, fun in any season. The Heritage Area Visitors Center publishes a brochure called *Things to Do with Kids!*

ORGANIZED TOURS

Saratoga Race Course, Union Avenue (*②* **518/584-6200;** www.nyra.com), offers free walking tours of the stable area and a tram ride and starting gate demonstration daily from 7:30 to 9am in season. The **Upper Hudson River Railroad ★**, 3 Railroad Place, North Creek (*②* **518/251-5334;** www.uhrr.com), is a scenic passenger-train ride (2½ hours round-trip) that departs from the North Creek depot and runs along the Hudson up into the Adirondacks (May–Oct Thurs–Sun; $18 adults, $12 children 3–12). For guided hiking, cycling, rock climbing, and snowshoeing adventures, as well as equipment rentals, contact **All Outdoors,** 35 Van Dam St. (© **518/587-0455**).

OUTDOOR PURSUITS

For additional information on outdoor activities in Saratoga Springs, consult the website **www.saratoga.org** and click on "Things to Do."

BIKING, IN-LINE SKATING & JOGGING   The 2,200-acre Saratoga Spa State Park is by far the best place in town, with tons of trails in a gorgeous park just minutes from downtown—in fact, within walking or jogging distance. For bikes and bike rentals, try **Blue Sky Bicycles,** 71 Church St. (© **518/583-0600;** www.blueskybicycles.com), or **Elevate Cycles,** 35 Van Dam St. (© **518/587-0455;** www.elevatecycles.com).

BOATING & FISHING   Saratoga Lake, on the outskirts of town, is the place for boating and fishing enthusiasts. **Lake Lonely Boat Livery,** 378 Crescent Ave., Saratoga Springs (© **518/587-1721**), has a tackle shop and rowboat and canoe rentals; there are largemouth bass, northern pike, and panfish in the lake. **Point Breeze Marina,** 1459 Rte. 9P, Saratoga Lake (© **518/587-3397**), is the largest marina in town and rents boats, canoes, and pontoons. **Saratoga Boatworks,** 549 Union Ave., Route 9P, Saratoga Lake (© **518/584-2628**), rents ski boats, pontoons, and fishing boats. **Saratoga Rowing Center,** 251 County Rte. 67, Saratoga Springs (© **518/584-7844**), is a sports shop dedicated solely to rowing, with rentals and instruction.

GARDENS   Garden and horticultural enthusiasts should visit the **Gardens at Yaddo ★** (© **518/584-0746;** www.yaddo.org), handsome turn-of-the-20th-century gardens and a working artists' community created by a philanthropic couple. A rose garden with a fountain, terraces, and a pergola was inspired by Italian Renaissance gardens, while the rock garden features ponds and fountains. The Yaddo Gardens, on Union Avenue (near exit 14 of I-87), are open to the public free of charge, with guided tours ($5 per person) on weekends at 11am, from mid-June to Labor Day and also Tuesday during racing season. **Congress Park,** off Broadway, was developed beginning in 1826. It has nature walks and ponds, and a wealth of tree species; the visitor center even publishes a free guide for easy identification. **Saratoga Spa State Park** comprises 2,200 acres of woodlands and trails featuring naturally carbonated mineral springs.

GOLF   **Saratoga Lake Golf Club,** 35 Grace Moore Rd. (off Lake Rd.), Saratoga Springs (© **518/581-6616;** www.saratogalakegolf.com), is a public 18-hole course, opened in 2001 on 200 acres near the lake. Greens fees are $26 to $48. **Saratoga Spa Championship & Executive Golf,** 60 Roosevelt Dr. (© **518/584-2006;** www.saratogaspagolf.com), is an 18-hole course in the pine forests of Saratoga Spa State Park. Greens fees are $26 to $42 (discounts for New York State residents). **Saratoga National Golf Club ★★**, 458 Union Ave., Saratoga Springs (© **518/583-4653;** www.golfsaratoga.com), sits on 400 acres of rolling hills in wetlands within pitching range of the Race Course and gets all kinds of accolades. It was named Golf Course of the Year (2005) by the National Golf Course Owners Association, named the no. 2 Best Public Access Course in New York by *Golfweek,* and ranked no. 5 among Best New Upscale Public Courses in the U.S. in 2001 by *Golf Digest.* You'll pay for the privilege of playing at such a noteworthy course, of course: Greens fees are $100 to $185.

architectural TOURS

Saratoga Springs is awash in splendid examples of Victorian and other diverse styles of architecture, from Queen Anne and Colonial Revival to early Federal, Greek Revival, and English Gothic. To get a feel for the array of styles, simply stroll down Union Avenue, Circular Street, and others in the historic district, or take a more systematic approach by following the self-guided walking tours laid out in brochures of Saratoga's Historic West and East Sides, available at the visitor center. Each highlights about two dozen buildings in a manageable walking area.

The small town of **Ballston Spa,** about 5 miles south of Saratoga Springs off Church Avenue (Rte. 50), is a Victorian village with about 20 or so notable houses and churches. Pamphlets for self-guided tours of Ballston Spa are also available at the visitor center.

HORSE RACING See "The 'Mane' Attractions," earlier in this chapter.

TENNIS Use of the eight hard-court and clay tennis courts in **Saratoga Spa State Park** is free to park visitors.

WINTER SPORTS Saratoga Spa State Park (© 518/584-2535; www.saratogaspastatepark.org) is the place for ice-skating, snowshoeing, and cross-country skiing, with several miles of groomed and ungroomed trails for the latter two sports. Winter-use trail maps are available at the Park Office.

Shopping

Until recently, Saratoga Springs had no national chain stores in its historic downtown. Today, inevitably, local independent shops mingle with a small number of chains, such as Gap, Eddie Bauer, and Banana Republic. In the heart of downtown, there are also about a half-dozen antiques dealers, mostly on Broadway and Regent Street, including **Forty Caroline Antiques,** 454 Broadway, in the Downstreet Marketplace (© 518/584-4017; www.fortycaroline.com); and **Regent Street Antique Center,** 153 Regent St. (© 518/584-0107), with 30 dealers under its historic roof. A good antiquarian bookseller is **Lyrical Ballad Bookstore,** 7–9 Phila St. (© 518/584-8779), and a popular antiques shop is **Saratoga Collectible Closet,** 474 Maple Ave. (5 min. north of Saratoga on Rte. 9; © 518/682-2002). Nearby in Ballston Spa, there are several antiques dealers, including **Stone Soup Antiques Gallery,** 19 Low St. (© 518/885-5232; www.stonesoupantiquesgallery.com); and **Daisy Dry Goods,** 28 Front St. (© 518/885-2782; www.daisydrygoodsballstonspa.com). Jewelry, clothing, home furnishings and accessories, and gift shops line Broadway and dot other streets in historic downtown Saratoga Springs. A particularly interesting shop, specializing in contemporary American glass, is **Symmetry Gallery,** 348 Broadway (© 518/584-5090; www.symmetrygallery.com). Check out **deJonghe Original Jewelry,** 470 Broadway (© 518/587-6422; www.djoriginals.com), for elaborate original designs by Dennis deJonghe.

SARATOGA'S FARMS

The Saratoga area is blessed with a surfeit of farms, including dairy and horse farms, orchards, and farm stands. **Saratoga Farmers' Market,** 110 Spring St. (© 518/638-8530; www.saratogafarmersmarket.org), is located in High Rock Park and open May to October, Wednesday 3 to 6pm and Saturday 9am to 1pm. **Saratoga Apple,** 1174

Rte. 29, Schuylerville (📞 **518/695-3131**), is a year-round farmers' market and pick-your-own apple orchard with wagon rides in autumn. **Weber's Farm,** 115 King Rd., Saratoga Springs, has a pick-your-own vegetable operation from May to December. **Hanehan's Pumpkins,** 223 County Rte. 67, Saratoga Springs, is a farm stand that sells pumpkins, squash, and corn in season. **Clark Dahlia Garden & Greenhouses,** 139 Hop City Rd., Ballston Spa (📞 **518/885-7356**), has homemade jams, seasonal produce, and fruit and flowers. **Bliss Glad Farm,** 129 Hop City Rd., Ballston Spa (📞 **518/885-9314**), specializes in gladiolus bulbs and has cut flowers and perennials. There are many others in easy reach of Saratoga Springs; pick up a brochure of Saratoga farms at the visitor center.

Where to Stay

Many of the city's most charming Victorian homes have been converted into welcoming bed-and-breakfast inns, making Saratoga a great place for those who prefer staying in a character-filled old house rather than a generic hotel. Hotel rates rise meteorically (doubling or even tripling) when most in demand during racing season. But they also climb considerably during Skidmore College's graduation in May, the Jazz Festival in late June, and other special events, when many hotels and inns require at least 2-night stays. In general, weekend rates are higher than midweek rates; be sure to confirm rates when booking. In addition, not all hotels and inns are open year-round. For race season, depending on the type of accommodations you want, I'd recommend booking 6 months to 1 year in advance. The Saratoga Chamber of Commerce and the visitor center (see "Visitor Information," earlier in this chapter) can help with reservations in high season; their website, **www.saratoga.org**, may be useful for finding additional hotels.

EXPENSIVE

Saratoga Arms ★★   Perfectly situated on the main drag in the heart of the historic district, this family-owned small hotel is like a grown-up B&B, elegant but very relaxed. A one-time boardinghouse converted to a luxury inn in 1999, it's in a beautiful 1870 "Second Empire" red-brick building with a terrific wraparound porch; from its antique wicker chairs, you can watch the world go by. Rooms are a good size and nicely appointed, with period antiques, handsome ornamental molding, and nice details like luxury robes and towels. Several rooms have electric fireplaces, and a number have claw-foot bathtubs. Prices vary according to season, as well as bed and room types; the highest prices are for rooms with king beds, fireplaces, and whirlpool tubs.

495–497 Broadway, Saratoga Springs, NY 12866. www.saratogaarms.com. 📞 **518/584-1775.** Fax 518/581-4064. 31 units. $195–$495 double; $375–$625 suite. Rates include breakfast. AE, DC, DISC, MC, V. Free parking. *In room:* A/C, TV, CD player, hair dryer, minibar.

The Saratoga Hilton at City Center ★★ ☺   A large and unmistakable presence right on Broadway downtown, this revamped and remodeled business hotel presents something no others do in Saratoga: chic, modern, and luxurious rooms with all the big-city amenities. Anyone living in fear of Saratoga's (perhaps overused) Victorian decor should make a beeline here. Rooms are sleek, spacious, and uncluttered, decorated with warm, soothing colors. Kids will appreciate the indoor pool. Check online for specials, packages, and getaway deals, as low as $139 per night (and a racing-season package beginning at $231 a night).

534 Broadway, Saratoga Springs, NY 12866. www.thesaratogahotel.com. 📞 **888/866-3591** or 518/584-4000. Fax 518/584-7430. 240 units. $219–$339 double; $239–$529 suite. AE, DC, DISC, MC, V. **Amenities:** Restaurant; concierge; fitness center; indoor pool. *In room:* A/C, TV, Wi-Fi.

MODERATE

Adelphi Hotel ★★   In a world of homogenized hotels, it's a treat to discover an eclectic and eccentric midsize lodging that wears its exuberant personality on its sleeve. Behind an 1877 brick facade is one of the funkier places you're likely to stay, with just the right touch of high Victorian decadence. The Adelphi survived the demolitions of most of Saratoga Springs' great old hotels from the town's tourism heyday; its atmosphere is born of old-world touches and Victorian clutter. Period antiques, old engravings and photographs, lacy curtains, and charming print wallpaper adorn rooms, which are all uniquely decorated; styles range from English country house, French provincial, and high Victorian to Adirondack, Arts and Crafts, and folk art. The second-floor piazza is ideal for people-watching, and there's a charming pool with leafy landscaping and a lovely pergola out back.

365 Broadway, Saratoga Springs, NY 12866. www.adelphihotel.com. © **518/587-4688.** Fax 518/587-0851. 39 units. $130–$350 double; $170–$550 suite. Rates include continental breakfast. Some weekends 2-night minimum stay; during race weekends 3-night minimum stay. Closed the second week of Oct to the third week of Mar. AE, DC, DISC, MC, V. Free parking. **Amenities:** 2 cafes; outdoor pool. *In room:* A/C, TV, Wi-Fi.

Bacon Hill Inn ★★ 📖   Located 10 miles east of Saratoga Springs, this handsome country farmhouse is a special retreat with easy access to town. The Italianate Victorian home was built in 1862 by a state senator and is still surrounded by hundreds of acres of farmland and preserves many of its original details and outbuildings. Rooms are handsome, with Victorian wallpaper and authentic details, but less fussy than some period-obsessed inns in the area. One large suite with a beautiful sleigh bed is named for the 1903 grand piano in the bay window. The innkeeper is a practicing massage therapist, so it's no surprise that a full massage menu is part of the relaxing attractions here. Contact the inn for off-season discounts and special events.

359 Wall Street Rd., Schuylerville, NY 12871. www.baconhillinn.com. © **518/695-3693.** 4 units. $175 double; $275 suite. Rates include breakfast. See website for special packages. AE, DISC, MC, V. Free parking. *In room:* A/C, TV.

Batcheller Mansion Inn ★   This castlelike 1873 Victorian is extraordinary from the outside: A riot of turrets and minarets, it looks like something hatched from the fertile imagination of Walt Disney or Antoni Gaudí. Inside, the grand home is quirky and rambling (its plans were considered so unique they were actually copyrighted), with loads of interesting parlors and Victorian furnishings. That said, some of the accommodations are slightly disappointing given the prices, with heavy executive-style desks and dated furnishings that aren't quite period. But special features abound: The raspberry-colored Trask Room has its own grand balcony, and the Brady Room, for those of you looking for something out of the ordinary, has a regulation-size billiard table as well as a massive Jacuzzi tub.

20 Circular St. (at Whitney), Saratoga Springs, NY 12866. www.batchellermansioninn.com. © **800/616-7012** or 518/584-7012. Fax 518/581-7746. 9 units. Nov–Mar Sun–Thurs $165–$220 double, Fri–Sat $185–$265 double; Apr–Oct Sun–Thurs $170–$255 double, Fri–Sat $210–$295 double; racing season $345–$475 double. Rates include breakfast. 2-night minimum stay on weekends. AE, MC, V. Free parking. *In room:* A/C, Wi-Fi.

Circular Manor B&B ★★ 📖   A warm and stately 1903 Colonial Revival, on a quiet street in the historic district within walking distance of both downtown and the Race Course, this small B&B owned by Dieter and Michele Funicello is gracious and friendly. The large and marvelously restored home has Victorian flourishes, including a welcoming Queen Anne circular porch and quartersawn oak staircase banisters, floors, and pocket doors. All the rooms are handsomely decorated; most bathrooms have marble floors and antique fixtures, including claw-foot tubs and Deco sinks. The sun-filled Hydrangea Suite, with a sitting room and French doors, is one of the better rooms you'll find at a B&B. Breakfast is a gourmet repast. May through October only.

120 Circular St., Saratoga Springs, NY 12866. www.circularmanor.com. © **518/585-6393.** 5 units. $170–$205 double, $220 suite; racing season $265–$295 double, $340 suite. Rates include full breakfast. MC, V. Free parking on street. *In room:* A/C.

The Mansion Inn of Saratoga ★★★ 🍴   Seven miles west of downtown Saratoga Springs is one of the finest places to stay in the area, a magnificently restored 1866 Victorian on 4 acres. The period details in the house—impressively carved wood and marble mantelpieces, a Tiffany chandelier, etched-glass doors, and a gracious parlor with a grand piano—make this a very romantic and sophisticated place for a getaway. Each unique room is sumptuously decorated with bold colors and inviting large beds dressed with top-of-the-line linens. Groups of two couples or families should check out the two-bedroom, two-bathroom private house, The Cottage, located just behind the inn. The gourmet breakfast is taken in the handsome dining room in front of a massive fireplace. In the early evening, complimentary cocktails are served in the parlor. Given the level of luxury in the rooms and general pampering, room rates are surprisingly reasonable. Open year-round.

801 Rte. 29, Rock City Falls, NY 12863. www.themansionsaratoga.com. © **888/996-9977** or 518/885-1607. 10 units. May–Oct (excluding racing season) Sun–Thurs $135–$155 double, $200 suite and Fri–Sat $160–$175 double, $225 suite; racing season Sun–Thurs $240–$285 double, $350 suite and Fri–Sat $250–$295 double, $399 suite; Nov–Apr Sun–Thurs $125–$140 double, $160 suite and Fri–Sat $140–$155 double, $180 suite. Cottage Sun–Thurs $300 and Fri–Sat $350; racing season $450–$499. See website for special packages and multinight deals. Rates include breakfast. AE, DISC, MC, V. Free parking. *In room:* A/C, TV.

CAMPGROUNDS

Whispering Pines Campsites & RV Park, 560 Sand Hill Rd., Greenfield Center (www.saratogacamping.com; © **518/893-0416**), is 8 miles northwest of Saratoga Springs and set on 75 acres of pines with a new outdoor pool and restroom facility.

Where to Eat

Saratoga Springs has a very nice little roster of fine dining and laid-back eateries, with something to appeal to even picky gourmands and fussy families. Like the majority of inns, almost all are independently and locally owned, and most are within easy walking distance of the main drag downtown.

EXPENSIVE

Chianti Il Ristorante ★★★ 🍴   NORTHERN ITALIAN   Ask Saratogians for their favorite restaurant in town and they're almost sure to tell you Chianti. It's now located in new, larger, and more self-consciously upscale digs, with a bronze door that's a copy of the St. Peter's Holy Door at the Vatican. What remains the same is flickering candlelight, a warm welcome from your Italian host and owner, and prices that are as accessible as ever. And the kitchen doesn't disappoint, with dishes such as porcini risotto in a light cream sauce, *filetto al Gorgonzola* (beef filet prepared with Gorgonzola cheese), dry-aged filet mignon, and grilled homemade sausage. There are also many good-value pastas such as *scarola e salsiccia* (fusilli with beans, escarole, and sausage), and the salads are huge and excellently prepared. The extensive wine list includes many well-chosen Brunellos and Super Tuscans, and some impressive high-priced options as well as plenty of affordable options. Be prepared for a wait, as no reservations are accepted.

18 Division St. ✆ **518/580-0025.** www.chiantiristorante.com. Reservations not accepted. Main courses $18–$25. AE, MC, V. Mon–Thurs 5–9:30pm; Fri–Sat 5–10:30pm; Sun 5–9pm.

Sperry's Restaurant ★ AMERICAN BISTRO Sperry's, known for its grilled seafood and crab cakes, is a dependable local favorite that's been around since 1932, and it rarely disappoints. It's an attractive bistro with black-and-white tile floors, a few high-backed booths, and a welcoming bar on one of Saratoga Springs' cutest streets. The restaurant has a long list of daily specials, and entrees such as crispy skin brook trout, a Cajun-spiced, grilled rib-eye, and caramelized diver sea scallops in orange saffron sauce; lunch specialties include jambalaya and a Cuban sandwich. There's outdoor seating on the back patio.

30½ Caroline St. ✆ **518/584-9618.** www.sperrysrestaurant.com. Reservations recommended on week-ends for dinner. Main courses $18–$34. AE, MC, V. Mon–Thurs 5–9:30pm; Fri–Sat 5–10:30pm; Sun 5–9pm.

Tiznow Restaurant ★★ FRENCH/ASIAN With leather booths, large mirrors, ocher walls, and white tablecloths, this warm bistro—smart and romantic but still casual—is a local favorite and one of the top choices in Saratoga. The menu is an eclectic mix of French and Asian dishes, complemented by an outstanding, unusual selection of Belgian beers (both on draft and in bottle) and a soundtrack of Latin jazz. There are plenty of interesting flavors and accents, such as Thai mussels (steamed in sambal, coconut milk, and lemongrass), Moroccan-spiced duck breast, and grilled lamb steak (with cinnamon, clove, cumin, orange zest, and mint couscous).

84 Henry St. ✆ **518/226-0655.** www.tiznowrestaurant.com. Reservations recommended. Main courses $21–$25. AE, DC, MC, V. Wed–Sun 5–10pm.

MODERATE

Forno Bistro ★ 🍴 TUSCAN/ITALIAN This casual, stylish Tuscan bistro in an old firehouse is operated by the same folks behind Chianti Il Ristorante. It's a dependable spot for a rustic Italian menu focusing on straightforward dishes, from antipasti to wood-fired thin-crust pizzas to main courses like *Milanese di maiale* (breaded pork chop) and *bistecca Toscana* (an 18-oz. New York Angus strip steak). The wine list is fairly broad for a casual eatery, with a nice selection of both Tuscan and northern Italian varietals with some New York and Californian vintages. Don't miss the fantastic cannoli and tiramisu for dessert.

541 Broadway. ✆ **518/581-2401.** www.fornobistro.com. Reservations not accepted. Main courses $14–$25. AE, MC, V. Daily 5–11pm.

The Wine Bar ★ CREATIVE AMERICAN With 50 wines by the glass and a ventilated smoking lounge where cigars are welcomed, this is the joint for would-be high rollers to celebrate their winnings at the track (or drown their sorrows in a good glass of wine and a nice meal). Trendy but moderately priced, with an upstairs bar and attractively modern and clean decor, it features a menu that will appeal to both wine-and-cigar guys and fashionable sorts. Dishes are available in both small-plate (tapas) and entree portions, and they change seasonally; among recent offerings were lobster poached in truffle butter with roasted beet and citrus salad; rare ahi crusted with Asian spices and served with a calamari stir-fry; and a beef filet with braised vegetables, forest mushrooms, and a foie gras sauce. On Friday and Saturday nights, there's live piano music.

417 Broadway. $\textcircled{C}$ **518/584-8777.** www.thewinebarofsaratoga.com. Reservations recommended. Main courses $14–$30. AE, DISC, MC, V. Mon–Sat 4–10pm.

INEXPENSIVE

Beverly's ★ 🍴 🍷 BREAKFAST/AMERICAN   This slender cafe should be your first stop in the morning if your hotel doesn't include breakfast. The morning menu is extraordinary, with both creative dishes and traditional fresh-baked comfort foods and great coffee. The standard menu includes baguette French toast, eggs Benedict, and pancakes with a touch of wheat germ. Daily breakfast specials include whimsical dishes like poached eggs on roasted eggplant with dill hollandaise, or banana-and-walnut pancakes. Beverly's is also open for lunch, which might be a chicken teriyaki salad, grilled chicken breast with roasted peppers and pesto, or the quiche of the day. In summer, there's outdoor garden patio seating.

47 Phila St. $\textcircled{C}$ **518/583-2755.** Reservations not accepted. Main courses $4–$11. AE, MC, V. Daily 7am–3pm.

Saratoga Springs After Dark

The **Saratoga Performing Arts Center** ★★★, or SPAC, is in a class by itself and one of the country's most distinguished arts venues. From June to September, this is *the* place to be in Saratoga Springs (after you've already been to the Race Course, of course) to see the amazing roster of high-culture talent that takes up summer residence, including the New York City Ballet and the Philadelphia Orchestra. SPAC is also the host of the Saratoga Chamber Music Festival, Freihofer's Jazz Festival in late June (which has been hosting top-flight jazz talent for over 30 years), the Lake George Opera, the 3-day Saratoga Wine & Food Festival, and modern dance recitals, as well as a series of pop and rock concerts (with acts ranging from Kings of Leon to Motley Crüe). Set within the Saratoga Spa State Park grounds, perfect for walks and picnics, the center has a sheltered amphitheater and an intimate Spa Little Theatre. The box office opens in early May, but preseason discounts are available (up to 50% off ticket prices). The "tickets" section of SPAC's website offers a number of other discount ticket options. Call the box office at $\textcircled{C}$ **518/584-9330,** or check the website, **www. spac.org**, for schedules and tickets.

Opera Saratoga ★ (formerly Lake George Opera) celebrated its 50th anniversary season in 2011. It stages classic operas, including *Cosi Fan Tutte* and *La Bohème* in the Spa Little Theatre, its home of 14 years on the grounds of the Saratoga Spa State Park. For current schedule information, visit their website at http://operasaratoga.org, or call $\textcircled{C}$ **518/584-6018;** visit **www.spac.org** to purchase tickets.

Caffè Lena ★★, 47 Phila St. ($\textcircled{C}$ **518/583-0022;** www.caffelena.org), is a small and legendary upstairs folk-music coffeehouse that's a little tattered but still reeks of all the folkies who have played here since 1960 (making it the oldest continually operating coffeehouse in the U.S.). There's mostly live acoustic music (and some blues, jazz, and poetry) Thursday to Sunday nights, and some relatively big names, like Tish Hinojosa, still drop by. Reservations are recommended; covers are generally $10 to $15. **9 Maple Avenue** ★, named for its address ($\textcircled{C}$ **518/583-CLUB** [2582]; www.9mapleavenue.com), is a cool little jazz bar with live music on Friday and Saturday nights, as well as a huge selection of single-malt scotches and bourbons, a martini menu, and great cocktails. The oldest saloon in downtown Saratoga, **Tin 'n' Lint,** 2 Caroline St. ($\textcircled{C}$ **518/587-5897**), known locally as TNL, has been around since the 1930s and remains popular with Skidmore students; it's where Don McLean, a former waiter, wrote the '70s pop anthem "American Pie" on a cocktail napkin. **The Wine Bar ★**, 417 Broadway (© **518/584-8777**), has a cigar lounge, an upstairs bar, loads of wine by the glass, and live piano music on weekends. (See restaurant review above.) The local movie theater, **Saratoga Film Forum,** 320 Broadway (© **518/584-FILM**), shows first-run films. For a romantic end to the evening (or a nice afternoon activity), **Saratoga Horse & Carriage Company** (© **800/320-6211** or 518/584-8820; www.saratogahorseandcarriage.com) provides horse-drawn carriage rides through Saratoga Springs. For contracted private rides, they'll pick you up at your hotel or inn in Saratoga. But if you'd rather your night go late, check out **Vapor Night Club,** at Saratoga Casino and Raceway, Crescent Avenue (© **518/581-5722;** www.vapornightclub.com), a slick dance club that has swank VIP lounges, theme nights, and live music featuring regional party bands (with no cover charge, with doors opening at 8pm on Fri and Sat).

ALBANY

The local author William Kennedy famously chronicled the state capital with his cycle of Albany novels, including *Legs* and *Ironweed,* which summoned not only the politics and grime of the city, but also its ghosts. Kennedy's depiction was of a city that has long been a little raw and rough around the edges—a reality Albany struggles to escape. Recent political infighting in the State Senate hasn't helped the city's reputation.

The capital of New York State, Albany is a manageable, medium-size city dominated by government and banking—and a firm wish for greater respect. Locals are proud of their city's great history in the Upper Hudson Valley, its culture, and continued efforts at urban renewal, but the city has had a somewhat difficult time convincing many from around the state of its charms. Beyond school groups on civics-class field trips, Albany attracts many more visitors for government and business trips than for leisure travel. The latter, though, are likely to find a fascinating dose of history, a full roster of summer festivals, user-friendly public spaces, and a few surprises that may just win the city some newfound respect.

Two monumental building projects have distinguished the city's physical evolution. The New York State Capitol, a stunning pile of native stone, took more than 30 years and the efforts of five architects to build, finally exhausting the patience of the governor, Theodore Roosevelt, in 1899. In the 1970s, another governor, Nelson Rockefeller, left his imprint on the capital by building the dramatic Empire State Plaza and remaking downtown as one of the most starkly modern government headquarters this side of Brasilia. Rockefeller's ambition was to make Albany the country's most beautiful capital city; whether that was accomplished or not is a matter of debate, but the modern-art collection he amassed in the name of the capital is the largest publicly owned and displayed in the country.

Visitor Information

The **Albany Heritage Area Visitors Center,** 25 Quackenbush Sq. (© **800/258-3582** or 518/434-1217; www.albany.org), is open Monday through Friday from 9am to 4pm, Saturday from 10am to 3pm, and Sunday and weekends from 11am to 3pm. In addition to the tourist information center, there are a small history gallery, a planetarium, and a gift shop. Trolley tours leave from here in summer (see "Organized Tours," later in this chapter). For pretrip information, consult the website www.albany.org.

Downtown Albany

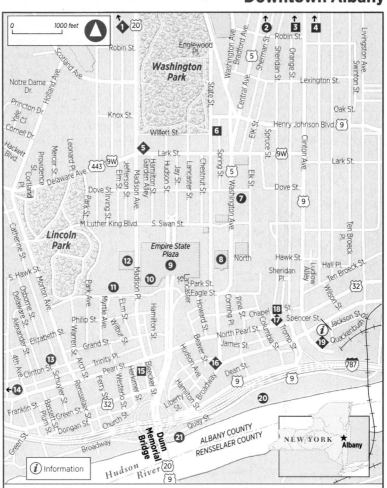

HOTELS ■
Angels Bed and Breakfast **15**
The Desmond **3**
Hampton Inn & Suites Albany **18**
Homewood Suites **4**
The Morgan State House **6**

RESTAURANTS ◆
Albany Pump Station **19**
Creó **1**
Jack's Oyster House **16**
Justin's on Lark **5**
Yono's **17**

ATTRACTIONS ●
Albany Institute of History & Art **7**
Corning Tower Observation Deck **10**
Empire State Plaza/The Egg **9**
Historic Cherry Hill **14**
Hudson River Way **20**
New York State Capitol **8**
New York State Executive Mansion **11**
New York State Museum **12**
Schuyler Mansion State Historic Site **13**
Shaker Heritage Society **2**
USS Slater **21**

City Layout

Downtown Albany is compact and easy enough to get around, by foot, by bus, or by trolley. However, much of the city's hotel accommodations and dining establishments lie beyond the major highways that ring the city, I-787 and I-90, in suburbs like Colonie (north of Albany). Central Avenue is the main thoroughfare that leads all the way from downtown to Colonie, and is often referred to as "Restaurant Row." The major highways around Albany are notoriously difficult for newcomers to navigate; one frequently circles and circles, unable to determine which way one actually wants to go. Map out destinations in advance if you're staying on the outskirts of town, and ask locals for directions.

Getting Around

BY PUBLIC TRANSPORTATION The **Downtown Albany Circulator** (bus nos. 16 and 20; $1.50 base fare or $4 unlimited day card) runs between Empire State Plaza and Broadway on weekdays from 6:30am to 6pm. there is also an **Albany City Trolley** (© 518/462-3825; www.albanyaquaducks.com) downtown, which also offers all-day/on-off historic tours on the "Albany Aqua Ducks" ($15 adults, $12 seniors, and $8 children ages 4–12). For schedules and additional route information, contact the Capital District Authority (© 518/482-3371; www.cdta.org).

BY CAR Car-rental agencies in Albany include **Enterprise Rent-A-Car,** Pepsi Arena, 51 S. Pearl St. (© 518/383-3444), and **Hertz Rent-A-Car** in the Crowne Plaza Hotel (© 518/434-6911). You'll find representatives of **Avis, Budget, Enterprise, Hertz, National,** and **Thrifty** at Albany International Airport (see "Arriving," p. 261).

BY TAXI Taxi services include **Yellow Cab,** 137 Lark St. (© 518/426-4609); **Advantage Limousine & Car Service** (© 518/433-0100); and **Premiere Transportation,** 456 N. Pearl St. (© 800/515-6123 or 518/459-6123).

BY TRAIN See "Arriving," p. 261.

BY BUS **Adirondack Trailways,** 34 Hamilton St. (© 800/776-7548 or 518/527-7060; www.trailways.com), and **Greyhound Bus,** 34 Hamilton St. (© 518/434-8095), travel to Albany and other destinations in upstate New York.

Exploring Albany

Albany has just a handful of must-see sights, including two excellent museums and the State Capitol building, almost all conveniently located downtown. The best idea is probably to start at the unmistakable Empire State Plaza, where several of the top sights are located.

THE TOP ATTRACTIONS

Albany Institute of History & Art ★ ☺ Albany's top art museum is the second-oldest museum in the United States—older even than the Smithsonian and Louvre. Restored and sensitively expanded about a decade ago—two turn-of-the-20th-century buildings were linked by a modern glass lobby—the museum presents the history of the Hudson River and Albany through the works of local artists and artisans. The permanent collection includes decorative arts, furniture, and nearly 5 centuries of paintings and sculpture. Among the most important are paintings by artists such as Thomas Cole, from the Hudson River School, the first American school of art. In the

Colonial Albany gallery are furnishings, paintings, and artifacts that tell the story of the ancient Dutch settlement in this area 350 years ago. Ancient Egypt galleries feature a pair of mummies, a priest, and a priestess, from 304 B.C. and 966 B.C. The museum presents special exhibits that are among the best in upstate New York, and there are plenty of lectures and activities geared toward children. An hour or two should be sufficient here.

125 Washington Ave. $\mathcal{C}$ **518/463-4478.** www.albanyinstitute.org. Admission $10 adults, $8 seniors and students, $6 children 6-12, free for children 5 and under. Wed-Sat 10am-5pm; Sun noon-5pm.

Empire State Plaza ★ ☺   This dramatic public plaza is Albany's most distinctive urban feature. Its official name is Governor Nelson A. Rockefeller State Plaza, after the man who undertook the massive project in 1962 (it wasn't finished until 1978). Rockefeller envisioned a kind of starkly modern Brasília in upstate New York. Fiercely controversial at the time, for not only its daring aesthetics but also the fact that an entire residential neighborhood was wiped out to install it, the plaza and its unique buildings have since grown on most locals and visitors. The centerpiece of the plaza is the spherical Performing Arts Center, known to all as "The Egg." One glance and you'll know why. The plaza is flanked by the New York State Museum, the New York State Capitol (alongside legislative and justice buildings), four tall state agency buildings, and the tallest structure in Albany, the 42-story Corning Tower. War and other memorials share the open air with an important 92-piece collection of large-scale modern sculpture, most by artists associated with the New York School, including Tony Smith, Alexander Calder, David Smith, and Claes Oldenburg. The Empire Plaza might be cold and off-putting, but the city schedules events such as concerts, festivals, ice-skating, fireworks, and other activities that draw Albany residents, rather than keeping them away. Free public 1-hour tours are given by reservation only, but free self-guided audio tours are available Monday through Friday, 9am to 3pm.

Bordered by State St., South St., and Madison Ave. $\mathcal{C}$ **518/474-2418.** www.ogs.state.ny.us. Free admission. Concourse and Plaza, daily 6am-6pm.

New York State Capitol ★★   This impressive building, seat of New York State government since the 1880s and a jarring contrast with the starkly modern Empire Plaza and agency buildings that rise around it, was the first massive and problematic project in the area. It took more than 3 decades (beginning at the end of the 19th c.) and five architects to build, and cost more than $25 million, making it the most expensive government building of its time. One of the last load-bearing structures to be built with no steel reinforcements until the top floor, and constructed of solid granite masonry, it was to have been crowned by a cupola, but the governor at the time, Theodore Roosevelt, had had enough and proclaimed it finished in 1899. Its grandest features are the Great Western Staircase—the so-called "$1-million staircase," a riot of elaborate stonework that contains more than 1,000 carved small faces (most are anonymous, but there are 77 "famous" visages, such as Andrew Jackson and Henry Hudson)—and the vibrant William de Leftwich Dodge ceiling murals of battle depictions in the Governor's Reception Room. Free walk-in tours last about 45 minutes; it's wise to phone ahead to confirm the schedule. Free self-guided audio tours are available Monday through Friday, 9am to 3pm.

Plaza Visitor Center, Room 106 Concourse, Empire State Plaza. $\mathcal{C}$ **518/474-2418.** www.ogs.state.ny.us. Free admission. Guided tours Mon-Fri 10am, noon, and 2, 3, and 3:45pm; Sat 11am and 1 and 3pm. No parking (paid parking on the street or next to the New York State Museum).

New York State Museum ★★ ☺ This massive museum, which from the exterior looks like a giant monolith, is the largest museum of its kind in the country. It aims to tell the story of New York State, both natural and cultural. Several new galleries have really enlivened this war horse. Among the permanent galleries, "The World Trade Center: Rescue, Recovery, Response," was the first major museum exhibit of artifacts from the September 11, 2001, terrorist attacks. It documents the 24-hour aftermath of the disaster with giant fragments of the towers, a destroyed fire engine (one of the first on the scene), and the stunning video shot by two French brothers. Elsewhere, New York City is traced from early port to metropolis, with a recent gallery addition devoted to Harlem. A large and accurate depiction of a Mohawk Iroquois village longhouse is a visitor favorite. Of great interest to visitors who can't visit New York City is the hall of rotating great art from the city's major museums (including the Metropolitan, Guggenheim, and MoMA). On the top floor is the new Café Terrace, with great views of the Empire State Plaza and creative regional displays, along with something that kids run screaming toward: a historic, functioning 36-horse carousel, hand-carved in the 1890s in Brooklyn. Allow at least a couple of hours (and check the website for current exhibitions).

Madison Ave. (btw. Eagle and Swan sts.). ✆ **518/474-5877.** www.nysm.nysed.gov. Free admission to museum and carousel (donation suggested). Mon–Sat 9:30am–5pm. Paid parking on the street or next to the museum.

MORE TO SEE & DO

Historic Cherry Hill This stately home, a big yellow clapboard Georgian Colonial that once looked over gentle lands to the edge of the Hudson River, is today in the middle of a bad neighborhood and the din of the highway. But no matter, it still presents an interesting history lesson, told through the story of Catherine Putnam and the Van Rensselaer family, whose descendants occupied the house for 200 years, until 1963. The house is overflowing with original furnishings, documents, and artifacts, and is most interesting for the way organizers present it as a reflection of Albany history. Cherry Hill was closed in 2009 for restoration, which is ongoing; check the website for news of its reopening and for hours and admission prices. Currently offered is a behind-the-scenes restoration tour, Wednesdays at 1, 2, and 3pm, and Saturdays at 2 and 3pm.

523½ S. Pearl St. (off I-787). ✆ **518/434-4791.** www.historiccherryhill.org. Behind-the-scenes tour admission $5 adults, $4 seniors and college students, $2 children 12–18. Architecture Hunt admission $2 adults and $1 children 6–11.

Hudson River Way ☺ This cool pedestrian bridge connects downtown to Corning Preserve Park on the banks of the Hudson. It is lined with 30 *trompe l'oeil* paintings on lampposts that depict the city's history and heritage, from prehistoric times and early Dutch merchants to the present. There are also two large murals on staircase landings.

Maiden Lane/Corning Preserve Park. ✆ **518/434-2032.** www.albanyny.org. Free admission.

New York State Executive Mansion The Governor's Mansion, built in 1856 as a banker's home, was totally remodeled in the 1860s. The first governor to live (and rent) here was in 1875; in 1877 the state purchased it, and it was given its third major makeover in 1885, to its current Queen Anne style. Famous inhabitants include Theodore Roosevelt and Franklin Delano Roosevelt (whose wheelchair you can see in the exhibit space on the second floor). The house, which isn't overly large or grand,

ALBANY'S highs & LOWS

It takes just 28 seconds to reach the 42nd-floor **Corning Tower Observation Deck,** which makes this the tallest building between New York City and Montreal. On a clear day, you can see the Catskills, the Green Mountains of Vermont, and the Hudson River. The observation deck is open Monday through Saturday from 10am to 2:30pm; admission is free. At the other extreme, underground in the Concourse passageway that travels beneath the Empire State Plaza, is a most unexpected art gallery—the largest publicly owned and displayed **art collection** in the U.S., purchased at the behest of Gov. Nelson A. Rockefeller, who strongly believed that art was a fundamental component of a capital city. Mixed in with fast-food shops and government offices are dozens of works by some of the most important artists of the 20th century, almost all of whom were identified with the New York School, including Isamu Noguchi, Robert Motherwell, Ellsworth Kelly, Franz Kline, Mark Rothko, and Donald Judd, among many others. Note that many large sculptures are also placed outside, on and around the plaza. The Concourse is open Monday through Friday from 6am to 11pm and on weekends from 10am to 2:30pm; free admission.

is still the official residence of the current governor, David Paterson. Tours last about an hour.

138 Eagle St. © **518/473-7521.** www.governor.ny.gov. Free admission. Guided tours Thurs 10 and 11am, noon, and 1 and 2pm (by appt. only; reservations required at least 2 weeks in advance). No parking (paid parking on the street or next to the New York State Museum).

Shaker Heritage Society ★ ☺ America's first Shaker settlement, the 1776 Watervliet Church Community, retains its 1848 Meeting House and seven other buildings and is on the National Registry of Historical Places. The Shakers (the United Society of Believers), an Early American religious group, were known for their remarkable craftsmanship as well as their religious devotion. Work was a way of devoting oneself to God, and they sought to create heaven on earth with a communitarian social structure and celibacy; they adopted needy children and brought them into the "family," to work on the 770-acre estate; on Sunday, outsiders came to see their mesmerizing church services. The Shakers, who at their peak numbered about 350 here, abandoned the site in 1924. Mother Ann Lee and more than 400 other Shakers are buried on the grounds. In addition to the fine architecture, the craft workshops held on the premises should appeal to older kids. There is a gift shop selling books and the famous Shaker-style baskets. Allow about an hour to tour the site.

25 Meeting House Rd (across from Albany International Airport), Colonie. © **518/456-7890.** www. shakerheritage.org. http://shakerheritage.blogspot.com. Free admission (donations accepted). Feb-Oct Tues–Sat 9:30am–4pm; Nov–Dec Mon–Sat 10am–4pm. Closed Jan. Guided tours for groups of 8 or more only; $3 per person.

Schuyler Mansion State Historic Site This large, English-style 1762 estate, the home of Philip Schuyler, one of the first four generals under Washington during the first 2 years of the Revolutionary War, is more interesting for what it represents than what there actually is to see. The house is only partially restored, but it was essentially a military outpost during the war, with visits by George Washington, Benedict Arnold, and Alexander Hamilton, who married Schuyler's daughter at the mansion. Incredibly,

Schuyler had the British general John Burgoyne and his retinue under house arrest here after their defeat at the Battle of Saratoga, and Loyalists raided the house in an attempt to kidnap Burgoyne in 1781.

32 Catherine St. ☎ **518/434-0834.** www.nysparks.com/historic-sites/33/details.aspx. Admission $5 adults, $4 seniors and students, free for children 12 and under. Mid-May to Oct Wed–Sun 11am–5pm; Nov to mid-May Mon–Fri tours by appt. only.

USS Slater ☺   A World War I destroyer escort ship, one of three remaining, sits docked on the banks of the Hudson, open to tours of the crew's quarters, galley, and main guns.

Snow Dock, adjacent to Dunn Memorial Bridge (off I-787). ☎ **518/431-1943.** www.ussslater.org. Admission $7 adults, $6 students 12–16, $5 children 6–11, free for children 5 and under. Apr–Nov Wed–Sun 10am–4pm. Closed Dec–Mar.

Especially for Kids

As the state capital, Albany plays host to tons of school visits, of course, even though at first glance it might not appear the best place to travel with kids. Actually, it's got plenty for children of all ages. Starting with the Albany Visitors Center, the **Henry Hudson Planetarium** (☎ **518/434-0405** for tickets and information) has shows every Saturday at 11:30am and 12:30pm. The **Albany Institute of History & Art** schedules a bevy of special children's programs. The **New York State Museum** has interesting exhibits that will appeal to both younger and older children, including one on 9/11, another on the Adirondacks, and a Native American longhouse that kids can enter and play around with using a nifty interactive feature. But best of all is the antique carousel on the museum's top floor. Older kids may appreciate the architecture and crafts workshops at the **Shaker Heritage Society.** The **Hudson River Way** is a pedestrian bridge with lampposts marked by paintings that trick the eye and tell the story of Albany's history. And young soldiers will surely find it cool to board a World War I destroyer, the **USS Slater,** docked on the Hudson.

Organized Tours

The **Albany Area Visitors Center** (☎ **800/258-3582** or 518/434-1217; www.albany.org) offers a variety of seasonal tours, including Hudson River walking tours, guided horse-drawn carriage tours, mansion garden tours, and guided trolley tours of downtown. Some are free, while others charge a fee of around $10; most are offered from July to the end of August. Guided trolley tours of downtown, historic homes, and historic churches are offered from July to the end of August. They begin at the visitor center at Quackenbush Square (corner of Clinton and Broadway). For more information, call ☎ **518/434-0405;** advance reservations are recommended. You can also download a free audio walking tour of downtown (there are two routes, a full-length and abbreviated version), at www.albany.org/VisitorCenter/walking-tourofalbany.aspx to your MP3 player or iPhone, or print out a walking-tour brochure with map. **Albany Remembered Tours,** 100 State St. (☎ **518/427-0401**), offers guided walking tours of historic sights. The **Upper Hudson River Railroad,**

> ### 💬 Rack 'Em Up
>
> The modern billiard ball was created in Albany in 1868, using celluloid as a substitute for ivory (of which there was a shortage), by John Wesley Hyatt. The Albany Billiard Ball Company on Delaware Avenue produced billiard balls until it went out of business in 1986.

3 Railroad Place, North Creek (© **518/251-5334;** www.uhrr.com), runs seasonal 2-hour train trips along a gorgeous section of the Upper Hudson River, spring, summer, and fall; $13 adults, $12 seniors, $9 children 3 to 11. **Dutch Apple Cruises,** corner of Quay and Madison avenues (© **518/463-0220;** www.dutchapplecruises. com), cruises the Hudson with narrated lunch and dinner trips with entertainment. **Canal Pilot,** Waterford (© **518/928-1863**), does custom boat tours of the Hudson River as well as Lake Erie and Champlain canals. **Hart Tours,** 1 Becker Terrace, Delmar (© **800/724-4225** or 518/439-6095), is a tour operator that has 1-, 2-, and 3-day area itineraries, including tours of the Adirondacks and the Capital District.

Outdoor Pursuits

BIKING & JOGGING The **Hudson-Mohawk Bikeway** is a 41-mile path along the Hudson and Mohawk rivers, connecting Albany with Schenectady and Troy, with smaller, more manageable paths. It begins in Island Creek Park and continues through Corning Preserve Park (at the end of the Hudson River Way bridge). **State Bike Route 9** runs to Hudson Shores Park, near Watervliet. For more information, call © **518/458-2161** or pick up a copy of *Capital District Regional Bike-Hike Map* at the visitor center.

FESTIVALS Especially in summer, Albany thrives with public outdoor festivals, many held at the Empire State Plaza. Visit www.albanyevents.org and www.albany.org for more information, as dates and specifics change. Here's a sampling:

o **Albany Tulip Festival ★**. Washington Park (early to mid-May; © **518/434-2032;** www.albany.com/news/tulip-festival.cfm). The city and park bloom with tens of thousands of tulips, a 60-year-old tradition and reflection of the city's Dutch ancestry.
o **Albany Alive at Five.** Thursday-night free outdoor summer concerts in Albany Riverfront Park (June–Aug; © **518/434-2032**).
o **Price Chopper Fourth of July.** Empire State Plaza: fireworks, music, and more.
o **Classic Rock, Swing, and Oldies concerts.** Empire State Plaza (Wed July–Aug; © **518/473-0559;** www.ogs.state.ny.us).
o **African-American Family Day.** Empire State Plaza (first week of Aug; © **518/473-0559;** www.ogs.state.ny.us).
o **Food Festival.** Empire State Plaza (mid-Aug; © **518/473-0559;** www.ogs.state. ny.us).
o **Albany LatinFest.** Washington Park (late Aug; © **518/434-2032**).
o **Albany Riverfront Jazz Festival.** Albany Riverfront Park: outdoor jazz followed by fireworks (early Sept; © **518/434-2032**).
o **Columbus Parade and Italian Festival.** Albany Riverfront Park (early to mid-Oct; © **518/434-2032**).

GOLF **Orchard Creek Golf Club,** 6700 Dunnsville Rd., Altamont (© **518/861-5000;** www.orchardcreek.com), an 18-hole public course, has won accolades from *Golf Digest* among others for its great course and reasonable fees (greens fees $27–$59). Family-owned **Stadium Golf Club,** 333 Jackson Ave., Schenectady (© **518/374-9104;** www.stadiumgolfclub.com), is another 18-hole course, just north of Albany. Greens fees are $27 to $37.

PARKS & GARDENS **Washington Park,** at State and Willett streets, is where the annual springtime Tulip Festival is held. **Corning Riverfront Park** is at the west bank of the Hudson, at the end of the **Hudson River Way** pedestrian bridge.

WINTER SPORTS You can **ice-skate** outdoors at Empire State Plaza (✆ **518/474-2418**) and Swinburne Rink (✆ **518/438-2406**). The closest down-hill skiing is at **Ski Windham,** Windham (✆ **800/729-7549;** www.skiwindham.com), and **Catamount,** Route 23, Hillsdale (✆ **800/342-1840;** www.catamountski.com), on the Massachusetts border in the southern Berkshires.

SPECTATOR SPORTS

The Class A minor-league baseball team, the **Tri-City Valley Cats,** an affiliate of the Houston Astros (✆ **518/629-CATS** [2287]; www.tcvalleycats.com), plays at the 4,500-capacity Joseph L. Bruno Stadium in North Greenbush, on the campus of Hudson Valley Community College. Tickets are $5 to $20.

FARMERS' MARKETS

The largest weekly market in the area is the **Troy Waterfront Farmers Market** (www.troymarket.org), held Saturday from 9am to 1pm at Riverfront Park in Troy. (In winter, the market moves to Uncle Sam Atrium, at Broadway and 3rd sts.) You'll find meat, dairy, produce, and flower vendors, as well as potters, vintners, and local pro-ducers of soap, cheese, honey, wine, yarns, and possibly the best homemade pesto on the planet, from Woodstock-based Buddha Pesto. **Goold Orchards,** 1297 Brookview Station Rd., Castleton (✆ **518/732-7317**), south of Albany on Route 9J along the Hudson, features an apple orchard, a farm store, a cider mill, and a bake shop. It offers pick-your-own apples, strawberries, and pumpkins in season, as well as an apple festival in October and a corn maze. City versions of farmers' markets in town are Wallenberg Park, Clinton Avenue and North Pearl (Mon 10am–1pm); SUNY Plaza, corner of Broadway and State (Thurs 11am–2pm); and Empire State Plaza (Wed and Fri 11am–2pm).

Where to Stay

The supply of good downtown hotels in Albany is woefully limited for a state capital. By far the best choice is one of the small B&B/boutique inns that have cropped up to take the place of larger hotels. Most decent hotels of any size, which tend to be standard hotel and motel chains, are on the outskirts of town, in a suburb called Colonie.

Angels Bed and Breakfast ★ ▮▮ An intimate urban B&B in the heart of down-town Albany—within convenient walking distance of major capital sights like the capitol and The Egg performing arts center—this nicely restored home was the John Stafford House when it began life in 1811. Transformed into an attractive small inn, the architecturally significant residence provides just three cleanly decorated and comfortable rooms, all with a private bathroom, on the second floor; on the ground floor is a cute little cafe, and the third floor is where the innkeeper lives. An outdoor roof deck is a fine place to relax.

96 Madison Ave., Albany, NY 12202. www.angelsbedandbreakfast.com. ✆ **518/426-4104.** Fax 518/426-4109. 3 units. $99–$179 double. Rates include full breakfast. AE, DISC, MC, V. Free parking on street. *In room:* A/C.

The Desmond ◢ This large hotel and conference center is designed to look like a village of sorts, which it succeeds at in a Disneyesque kind of way. Bellboys are even dressed in faux-Colonial get-ups. But it's actually a pretty good place to stay, with good-size and comfortable rooms with four-poster canopy beds, 18th-century replica furnishings, and lots of floral prints. The entirely nonsmoking hotel is close to the airport and has all the facilities you're likely to need.

660 Albany-Shaker Rd., Albany, NY 12211 (in Colonie; I-87, exit 4). www.desmondhotelsalbany.com.
© **800/448-3500** or 518/869-8100. Fax 518/869-7659. 324 units. $139–$219 double. AE, DC, DISC, MC, V. Free parking. **Amenities:** 2 restaurants; fitness center; indoor & outdoor pools; limited room service. *In room:* A/C, TV, Wi-Fi (free).

Hampton Inn & Suites Albany–Downtown ★ ☺   This is the most welcoming of Albany's few downtown chain hotels, within walking distance of the State Capitol and surrounding sights. Standard rooms can be a bit compact and are pretty standard in style, but the beds are plush and comfortable. Traditional Hampton Inn amenities such as free in-room broadband and a substantial Continental breakfast make this a good choice for families; it's also pet-friendly ($75 fee). Check the hotel's website for constantly updated specials—you'll almost always catch a bargain. Yono's, the upscale restaurant (p. 286) on-site, is one of Albany's finest dining experiences.

25 Chapel St. (at Sheridan Ave.), Albany, NY 12210. http://hamptoninn1.hilton.com. © **518/432-7000.** Fax 518/432-1113. 165 units. $109–$189 double; $229–$319 suite. Rates include continental breakfast. AE, DC, DISC, MC, V. Self-parking $13. **Amenities:** 2 restaurants (including Yono's, p. 286), exercise room, sauna. *In room:* A/C, TV, kitchenette (in suites), Wi-Fi (free).

Homewood Suites by Hilton Albany ★ ☺   A couple miles from the airport, this comfortable and very professionally run chain hotel has a large indoor pool and is ideal for either families or those in Albany on business and longer stays. Rooms—divided among studios and one- and two-bedroom suites with kitchenettes—are large, with contemporary decor and quality linens and a cut above your standard midrange hotel. Best of all, everything is impeccably maintained, and management is very responsive to guests' needs. Public areas include a lounge with large fireplace, attractive patio, and covered BBQ area, and an outdoor basketball court. Reasonable rates, as well as the complimentary breakfast and nightly "Welcome Home" reception (Mon–Thurs) with light meals and beer and wine, make this a very attractive deal.

216 Wolf Rd., Albany, NY 12205. http://hamptoninn1.hilton.com. © **518/438-4300.** Fax 518/435-9064. 133 units. $139–$179 double; $319 2-bedroom suite. Rates include breakfast. AE, DC, DISC, MC, V. Free parking. **Amenities:** Restaurant, indoor pool, exercise room, basketball court. *In room:* A/C, TV, kitchenette (in suites), Wi-Fi (free).

The Morgan State House ★★★ ✦   One of the finest urban B&Bs you're likely to stumble unexpectedly upon, the elegant and professionally run Morgan State House is really a European-style boutique hotel. Its rooms are huge and gorgeously decorated, with 19th-century period detailing and furnishings, tile bathrooms, and some of the best down and feather bedding and linens you'll ever rest your head on. The town house, on "Mansion Row" just a few blocks from the Empire State Plaza and across the street from peaceful Washington Park, was built in 1888 by the same architect who designed the cathedral in Albany. You can also land one of the 10 "corporate suites," or apartments with kitchenettes, at **The Washington Park State House,** in a condo building a couple of doors down at 399 State St. They're a touch more modern, and are ideal for business travelers. Guests at Washington Park also have breakfast at the Morgan State House (which you can have in the charming interior garden courtyard). No children 15 and under are accepted at either place.

393 State St., Albany, NY 12210. www.statehouse.com. © **888/427-6063** or 518/427-6063. Fax 518/463-1316. 16 units. Morgan State House $135–$224 double; $224–$286 suite. Washington Park State House $135–$175 apt. Rates include full breakfast. AE, DISC, MC, V. Free parking. *In room:* A/C, TV, kitchenettes (in Washington Park State House rooms), Wi-Fi.

Where to Eat

Lark Street downtown is home to a number of small neighborhood eateries with cuisine from around the world, while the majority of chain and fast-food restaurants are located on Central Avenue, also known as "Restaurant Row."

EXPENSIVE

Jack's Oyster House ★ ✋ CLASSIC AMERICAN Known locally simply as "Jack's," this Albany classic has been around since 1913, and it still has the kind of clubby insider ambience associated with another era. The menu for the most part stubbornly resists trendiness. Classic appetizers include Jack's Famous 1913 Manhattan clam chowder, clams casino, shrimp cocktail, and oysters Rockefeller. Main courses (all served with complimentary salad, seasonal vegetables, starch, and oven-baked bread) include steak Diane, calf's liver, and jumbo lobster tail. In fact, there's an entire 1913 traditional dinner menu (at current prices, alas). There's little worry about being trendy at Jack's, though it's overpriced and service and quality can be uneven.

42-44 State St. ✆ **518/465-8854.** www.jacksoysterhouse.com. Reservations recommended. Main courses $22–$50. AE, DISC, MC, V. Daily 11:30am–10pm.

Yono's ★★ ASIAN/INDONESIAN This white-gloved Indonesian fine dining establishment is probably not what you'd expect to find in Albany and especially within a Hampton Inn & Suites hotel. Elegant, in a slightly ostentatious way, the restaurant still features the creations of acclaimed chef Yono Purnomo, whose sophisticated (and pricey) menu focuses on delicious Indonesian specialties, though a full roster of well-prepared Continental dishes is also available, "if you're feeling less adventurous." The wine list is outstanding, with more than 500 bottles (though pairing wines with spicy Indonesian dishes is a bit of an art; try a Riesling or even a Belgian-style beer). Multicourse tasting menus ($55–$89) focusing on either Indonesian cuisine or the season may be the way to go for the uninitiated. For casual and inexpensive dining, check out Yono's other restaurant at the same location, **dp,** a high-ceilinged brasserie, for lunch, dinner, and cocktails.

25 Chapel St. (in Hampton Inn & Suites). ✆ **518/436-7747.** www.yonosrestaurant.com and www.dpbrasserie.com. Reservations recommended. Main courses $21–$36. AE, DISC, MC, V. Wed–Sat 5:30–11pm.

MODERATE

Albany Pump Station (C.H. Evans Brewing Co.) ☺ 🍴 AMERICAN/PUB FARE Housed in a cavernous 19th-century former pump station (the original brewery dates to 1786 in nearby Hudson, NY), this fun place is part microbrewery and part restaurant. It gets crowded at happy hour with downtown office workers, then begins to fill up with individual and family diners as the evening progresses. The menu is surprisingly diverse, with plenty of salads, pastas, burgers, sandwiches, and other pub grub, but also pretty decent entrees that go a bit beyond: old-fashioned meatloaf, French Quarter gumbo, and eggplant lasagna. The house beers are quite good; check out the award-winning Kick-Ass Brown Ale, Quackenbush Blonde, and Pump Station Pale, or the cask ales available on Fridays. A late-night menu kicks in after 10pm (11pm Fri–Sat), and there's a special (and cheap) kids' menu.

19 Quackenbush Sq. ✆ **518/447-9000.** www.evansale.com. Reservations recommended on weekends. Main courses $9–$19. AE, DISC, MC, V. Mon–Thurs 11:30am–10pm; Fri–Sat 11:30am–midnight; Sun noon–9pm.

Lark Street Dining & Drinking

The small stretch of Lark Street just west of the Capitol buildings is home to a number of neighborhood eateries as well as a couple of notably creative ventures. In addition to **Justin's on Lark** (see below), **The Wine Bar & Bistro on Lark ★★**, 200 Lark St. (© 518/463-2881; www.winebaronlark.com), is an intimate warren of brick-walled rooms that feels both cozy and a little crunched (narrow tables barely support the generous wine glasses). But you'll find a steadily improving bistro menu of small plates (and more elaborate tasting menus), a very impressive and adventurous wine list (probably the best in the city), and outdoor patio dining. Don't miss a stop at **Crisan Bakery ★★**, 197 Lark St. (© 518/445-2727; crisanbakery.com), which calls itself an "edible art gallery." And with good reason: husband and wife Claudia and Ignatius craft spectacular cakes and pastries with the precision of sculptors working in butter cream, génoise, and ganache, as well as homemade gelato and even edible jewelry (for a special occasion, I suppose).

Creó ★ MEDITERRANEAN/INTERNATIONAL   Chic and trendy for Albany, and striving for cool with an attractive modern interior, open kitchen, sleek outdoor terrace dining area, and grass-topped roof (!), this pleasant spot might fool you into thinking you're in Florida or Southern California—making it a nice addition to the capitol-region dining scene. You're unlikely to get the most mind-blowing meal of your life, but the menu is eclectic and on the whole dependable. Best bets are wood-fired pizzas (with some interesting combos), fresh salads, and rotisserie rosemary chicken, all well priced (some main courses get a little pricey). Locals frequent the bar for cocktail specials and half-priced appetizers during happy hour from 4 to 6pm, and many claim that Sunday brunch (with specialties like bananas foster pancakes and breakfast pizza) is the best in Albany. The restaurant is out near SUNY—Albany University, northwest of downtown.

1475 Western Ave. (Stuyvesant Plaza). © **518/482-8000.** www.creorestaurant.com. Reservations recommended. Main courses $15–$38. AE, DC, MC, V. Mon 11:30am–9pm; Tues-Sat 11:30am–10pm; Sun 10am–9pm.

Justin's on Lark AMERICAN/INTERNATIONAL   This longtime anchor of the Lark Street dining scene received a much-needed makeover a few years back, with menu and chef changes. The result is a pretty hip but relaxed joint that serves up comfort food such as a grilled, center-cut pork chop or something with a Latino, Asian, or Caribbean twist (like the Jamaican jerk chicken) and nightly live jazz, making it an excellent neighborhood hangout. For night owls, the good news is that it's open late (until 1am), and you can even get a plate of Cuban *ropa vieja* at that hour. For those with a lighter meal in mind, there's a cafe menu of salads, soups, and sandwiches. A local favorite is the Sunday brunch.

301 Lark St. © **518/436-7008.** www.justinsonlark.com. Reservations recommended on weekends. Main courses $16–$22. AE, MC, V. Daily 11:30am–1am.

Albany After Dark

The Egg ★★★, Empire State Plaza Concourse Level (© **518/473-1845;** www.theegg.org), is the funky spherical half-egg on the plaza; its two theaters inside are nearly as cool as the exterior. It hosts a diverse range of entertainment, from the modern dance of Mark Morris and classical music to comedy, theater, international performers including Cesária Évora, and the guitar riffs of rock bands like Cheap Trick. **The Palace Performing Arts Center** ★, 19 Clinton Ave. (© **518/465-3664;** www.palacealbany.com), is a gorgeously restored, grand 1931 movie theater that now hosts top-level talent, including pop concerts (such as Billy Joel and Sum 41), comedy (Jerry Seinfeld), and the Albany Symphony Orchestra and the Albany Berkshire Ballet. It also handles a number of children's theater performances during the school year. The **Times Union Center,** 51 S. Pearl St. (© **866/308-3394** or 518/487-2100; www.timesunioncenter-albany.com), is the big place in town for large rock and country-music concerts (such as Keith Urban) in addition to sporting events. The **Capital Repertory Theatre,** 111 N. Pearl St. (© **518/445-7469;** http://capitalrep.org), features Broadway and Off-Broadway touring musicals and dramatic theater. Outside of town, the **Troy Savings Bank Music Hall** ★★, 7 State St., Troy (© **518/273-0038;** www.troymusichall.org), a wonderfully preserved concert hall in a former 1823 bank, hosts some of the area's best jazz concerts as well as chamber music and other performances; there's almost always something interesting scheduled, and it's just 8 miles from downtown Albany. Its heritage includes performances by such musical eminences as Ella Fitzgerald and Yo-Yo Ma.

Bars and pubs worth visiting include **Wolff's Biergarten** ★, 895 Broadway (© **518/427-2461;** www.wolffsbiergarten.com), in North Albany (also known as the Warehouse District, Albany's best impersonation of NYC's Meat-Packing District), a modern and stylish take on a German beer garden that's housed in an old firehouse (they have a great selection of German, Belgian, and Czech beers); **Albany Pump Station,** 19 Quackenbush Sq. (© **518/447-9000**), a brewpub within a historic pump station; **Riverfront Bar & Grill,** Corning Riverfront Park (© **518/426-4738**), which you can access by crossing the Hudson River Way pedestrian bridge; and the **Waterworks Pub,** 76 Central Ave. (© **518/465-9079**), with a large dance floor and DJs spinning tunes. Movie theaters include **Hoyt's** at Crossgates Mall (© **518/452-6440**) and **Spectrum 7 Theaters,** 290 Delaware Ave. (© **518/449-8995**).

CENTRAL NEW YORK

by Marc Lallanilla

One of the joys of travel is discovering hidden gems, and Central New York is practically brimming over with them. As the "middle child" of Upstate New York, its charms may be more subtle, but there's no shortage of must-see attractions with international appeal, as well as smaller destinations that are perfect for travelers looking for a quiet but beautiful getaway. The Baseball Hall of Fame in Cooperstown draws a fervent coterie of fans from around the world, but the Leatherstocking region—named for stories like Last of the Mohicans, written by local legend James Fenimore Cooper—isn't really about big, exciting tourist traps. Come, like Cooper did centuries ago, with an explorer's spirit, and you'll be rewarded in kind.

History runs deep here: The fertile Mohawk Valley carved a route west to the Great Lakes for the Algonquin and Iroquois, and later for the German, Dutch, Welsh, and other immigrants who settled in the area. Conflict on this frontier helped set the stage for the French and Indian War, and later the American Revolution. When the Erie Canal opened in 1825, it provided an unprecedented commercial link to the west and helped make New York the wealthiest trading center in North America, if not the world. The 20th century, which brought agricultural disease, the Great Depression, and Rust Belt economic decline, had a devastating effect on what was once a thriving expanse of canal cities, factory towns, and local farms.

Today, however, these towns celebrate their heritage at the **Erie Canal Village** and the **Fort Stanwix National Monument.** Oneida Lake and Otsego Lake attract happy throngs eager for outdoor recreation, while Utica provides such cultural attractions as the Stanley Center for the Arts and the Munson-Williams-Proctor Arts Institute. Of course, when it's time to move on, you'll have an easy ride to the Adirondacks, the Catskills, the Thousand Islands, or the Finger Lakes regions.

COOPERSTOWN ★★★

77 miles W of Albany; 141 miles E of Rochester; 213 miles NW of New York City

If the name "Cooperstown" makes you think of one thing and one thing only—baseball—you're not alone. Foremost among Cooperstown's attractions is, of course, the **Baseball Hall of Fame,** even though almost everybody—including Abner Doubleday himself, allegedly—agrees that he didn't invent the sport here. Nonetheless, the town has long been associated with the heart and soul of America's national pastime.

But if you limit your visit to baseball-themed attractions, you'll miss the charms of one of America's sweetest small towns. Set along the shores of tranquil Otsego Lake, the village of Cooperstown boasts an almost ridiculous amount of history and culture for its size. Locals are understandably proud of James Fenimore Cooper, author of the *Leatherstocking Tales* and son of town namesake William Cooper. The **Fenimore Art Museum** and the **Glimmerglass Opera** are world-class arts institutions. And despite the influx of summer tourists, Cooperstown maintains an easy friendliness, giving the impression of a small community of folks who all seem to know one another. A sense of nostalgia permeates this place, with its tree-lined streets and beautiful Victorian-era houses. Its main street feels almost like a movie set—wholesome, all-American, and ready for a small-town Fourth of July parade. Spend some time on or around the lake, browse through mom-and-pop stores, and eventually you'll get the feeling that you've just stepped back in time. But don't linger too long, or you'll miss dinner: Restaurants—and most places in the town—shut down as early as 9pm.

Essentials

GETTING THERE   Cooperstown is easiest to get to by car. From the New York State Thruway (I-90), take exit 30 at Herkimer and go south on State Highway 28 or State Highway 80—both will take you to Cooperstown. By bus, **Trailways** (© **800/776-7548;** www.trailwaysny.com) provides service between Cooperstown and other towns both big and small. The closest airport, **Albany International Airport** (© **518/242-2200;** www.albanyairport.com), is about 75 miles east (chapter 9).

VISITOR INFORMATION   The helpful **Cooperstown Chamber of Commerce** (31 Chestnut St.; © **607/547-9983;** www.cooperstownchamber.org) is open most days from 9am; closing times vary by day and by season. For an updated calendar of events, brochures, and other promotional stuff, call **Cooperstown Getaway** (© **888/875-2969;** www.cooperstowngetaway.org).

GETTING AROUND   Parking spots are as rare as hen's teeth in summer and on weekends, and parking regulations are strictly enforced, so unless you're staying right in town, leave your car parked and take the **trolley,** which runs from the public parking lots to all major attractions. Look for the blue PARK AND TAKE THE TROLLEY signs as you approach Cooperstown. Parking is free in the outer lots at the following locations: off Route 28 just south of Cooperstown (traveling north from Oneonta); off Route 28 (Glen Ave.) at Maple Street (traveling south on Rte. 28 from Rte. 20); and on Route 80 at the upper parking lot of Fenimore Art Museum (traveling south on Rte. 80 from Rte. 20). An unlimited daily trolley pass, which you can purchase onboard, is $2, and the trolley stops at the museums, Main Street shopping, and other points of interest. In spring and fall, the trolley runs only on weekends from 9am to 5pm; summer hours are extended until 9pm every day. There is also a limited amount of paid parking at **Doubleday Field,** accessible from Chestnut Street (south of the Cooperstown Chamber of Commerce), or from Main Street (next to Key Bank), for $2 hourly or $10 per day July through Labor Day, and half that in June.

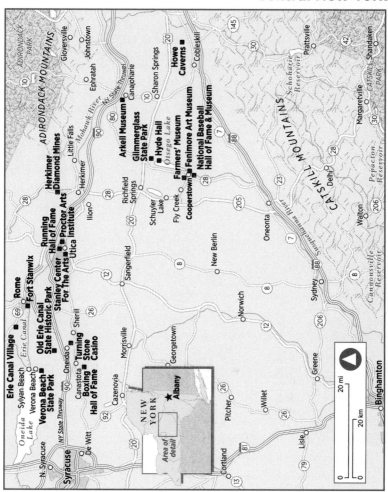

Exploring Cooperstown

Baseball Hall of Fame ★★★   Die-hard fans enter the hallowed Hall with high expectations, and the museum—with some 38,000 exhibited items—both delivers and surprises. Even stoic, just-along-for-the-ride types will find plenty to see and do here. The well-curated museum effectively and poignantly demonstrates how important this sport has been to America's past and present. You'll learn about the Negro Leagues and the integration of baseball—check out the hate mail sent to Jackie Robinson. The Diamond Dreams exhibit tells the story of women in baseball. There's a whole room devoted to Babe Ruth, complete with his bat and his locker, and even a section exploring the history of "Take Me Out to the Ballgame." And, of course, you'll see artifacts from the greatest moments in the game's history: the 1903 baseball from the first World Series, Roberto Clemente's bat from his 3,000th hit, "Shoeless" Joe Jackson's shoes, even Curt Schilling's bloody sock from the 2004 World Series, as well as over 135,000 baseball cards, including rarities like the T206 Honus Wagner card. The museum's Sandlot Kids Clubhouse exhibit will keep younger children entertained. Depending on how big a fan you are, you could spend anywhere from 2 hours to a full day (or more) browsing, learning, and loving the game.

25 Main St. © **888/HALL-OF-FAME** (425-5633) or 607/547-7200. www.baseballhall.org. Admission $20 adults, $12 seniors, $7 children 7–12, free for children 6 and under. Memorial Day to Labor Day daily 9am–9pm; Labor Day to Memorial Day daily 9am–5pm. Closed Thanksgiving, Christmas, and New Year's Day.

Brewery Ommegang ★★   Come here to pay tribute to Central New York's rich hops farming heritage—indeed, the region was the leading producer of hops in the United States in the 1800s. But this isn't your typical American microbrewery; at Ommegang, the brewers are committed to creating authentic Belgian ales, using their own strain of yeast, high-temperature open fermentation, warm cellaring, and incorporating such spices as star anise, cardamom, orange peel, and coriander. The resulting award-winning beers (now distributed nationwide) are robust, hoppy, and well worth the trip. While tours are brief, they are interesting, and run by friendly staff who are passionate about their beer and their craft. The brewery, housed in an elegant old white building on 136 acres of picnic-ready grounds, now houses a new cafe featuring classic Belgian dishes like stews, crepes, waffles, and, of course, beer-steamed *moules* and frites (mussels and fries).

656 County Hwy. 33. © **800/544-1809** or 607/544-1800. www.ommegang.com. Free 25-min. tours include beer tasting. Memorial Day to Labor Day daily 11am–6pm, until 7pm Thurs–Fri; Labor Day to Memorial Day daily noon–5pm. From Main St. in Cooperstown, turn left onto Chestnut St./NY-28, then turn left on Rte. 11C. Turn right on County Hwy. 33.

Farmers' Museum ★ ☺   This living-history museum with over 23,000 collected pieces of Americana, from butter molds to horse carriages, is a fun, compelling look at rural village life around 1845, and you'll want to set aside at least an hour for a visit. The 26 historic buildings were moved to this site, a working farm since 1790, to re-create a 19th-century village. Kids will love seeing the different breeds of sheep, cows, chicken, and ducks on the farm. Village workers in period costumes look and fully act the part: The blacksmith bangs out horseshoes, the affable pharmacist gives a demonstration on herbal remedies, and the museum offers daily mini-workshops on farm crafts during the summer. (Take time to talk to the workers, as they really know their stuff.) And don't miss a ride on the carousel: The hand-carved wooden sculptures—all animals indigenous to New York State—are remarkable. Check the website for workshop schedules and prices.

Value Pass

If you're planning on visiting the **Baseball Hall of Fame,** the **Farmers' Museum,** and the **Fenimore Art Museum,** buy a multiple-entry pass at the first one you visit. Entrance to all three costs $37 for adults, $11 for kids. Entry to the Hall of Fame plus one other museum costs $28 for adults, $11 for kids 7 to 10.

5775 State Hwy. 80 (Lake Rd.), 1½ miles north of Cooperstown. © **888/547-1450** or 607/547-1450. www.farmersmuseum.org. Admission mid-May to mid-Oct $12 adults, $11 seniors, $6 children 7–12;

HOTELS ■
American Hotel **15**
Cooperstown Shadowbrook
Campground **13**
Inn at Cooperstown **5**
Lake Front Motel **12**
The Otesaga **4**

RESTAURANTS ◆
Alex & Ika **6**
Blue Mingo Grill **1**
Brooks House of BBQ **19**
Danny's Market **9**
Nicoletta's Italian Café **8**
T.J.'s Place **7**

To Fly Creek
and Richfield
Springs

To Route 166,
Middlefield
and Cherry Valley

To Oneonta and

ATTRACTIONS ●
Baseball Hall of Fame **11**
Brewery Ommegang **18**
Doubleday Field **10**
Farmer's Museum **2**
Fenimore Art Museum **3**
Glimmerglass Opera **16**
Glimmerglass State Park **17**
Hyde Hall **14**

Otsego Lake

Cooperstown
NEW YORK ★ Albany

other times $10 adults, $9 seniors, $5.50 children; always free for children 6 and under. Apr to mid-May and mid- to late Oct Tues–Sun 10am–4pm; mid-May to mid-Oct daily 10am–5pm. Closed Nov–Mar except for special events.

Fenimore Art Museum ★   This elegant 1930s mansion overlooking Otsego Lake, built on the site of James Fenimore Cooper's home, houses a world-class art collection and hosts exhibitions of renowned artists like Edward Hopper, John Singer Sargent, Jackson Pollack, and Mark Rothko. You'll also find a revolving collection depicting local life, portraits of Cooper, a great collection of folk art, and examples of Hudson River School paintings, such as Thomas Cole's *Scene from the Last of the Mohicans* (1827). Fans of Native American art will marvel at the impressive displays of masks, bows and arrows, headdresses, moccasins, and gorgeous beadwork from tribes all over America. But our favorite pieces here are the life masks by sculptor John Henri Isaac Browere: They were cast in bronze from the subjects' actual faces, and include depictions of Thomas Jefferson and Dolley Madison.

5798 State Hwy. 80 (Lake Rd.). ℂ **888/547-1450** or 607/547-1400. www.fenimoreartmuseum.org. Admission $12 adults, $11 seniors, free for children 12 and under. Mid-May to mid-Oct daily 10am–5pm; mid-Oct to Dec and Apr to mid-May Tues–Sun 10am–4pm. Closed Jan–Mar.

Hyde Hall ★ An enormous neoclassic mansion and museum, Hyde Hall was built by George Clarke between 1817 and 1834 to be a showplace at the center of his vast agricultural empire. It's considered one of the nation's major private architectural undertakings from the years between the Revolutionary and the Civil wars, and it provides a distinct contrast to the Farmers' Museum in showing how the other half lived. Today, in addition to witnessing the ongoing restoration work, you'll explore great rooms, a chapel, servants' quarters, and even one of the first interior flush toilets in upstate New York. With four structures on the property, and a lovely view of Otsego Lake, you'll want to spend some time beyond the hour-long tour. Bring a picnic lunch, or take advantage of the reimbursement voucher that entitles you to $7 off admission to adjacent **Glimmerglass State Park** (see below).

1527 Co. Hwy. 31 ℂ **607/547-5098.** www.hydehall.org. Tours are on the hour from 10am to 4pm; $10 adults, $8 seniors and children 5–12. Mid-May to Oct 31. From Cooperstown, go east on Main St. over the bridge and up E. Lake Rd. (Rte. 31) about 8 miles, past Glimmerglass State Park. Turn left on Mill Rd., and follow it for about ½ mile. Turn left.

Outdoor Activities

BOATING Between Memorial Day and Columbus Day in October, take a 1-hour, partially narrated historic tour of pretty Otsego Lake aboard the double-decker *Glimmerglass Queen,* 10 Fair St. at the Lake Front Motel (ℂ 607/547-9511). Or do it yourself without the chattering by renting a canoe, kayak, or pontoon boat from **Sam Smith's Boatyard,** 6098 State Hwy. 80 (ℂ **607/547-2543;** samsmithsboatyard. com), for $10 to $25 an hour.

GOLF If you're a duffer and you're in the area, chances are you already know about the scenic **Leatherstocking Golf Course** at The Otesaga, 60 Lake St. (ℂ **800/348-6222** or 607/547-9931; www.otesaga.com), one of the nation's most elite resort courses. The traditional-style links, which hug the western shore of Otsego Lake, offer many challenges, but it's the 18th tee that is most intimidating: Starting on an island, you have to hit back over the water toward the hotel. Greens fees are $89 for guests and $99 for nonguests; save almost $30 by teeing off after 3pm.

HIKING & BIKING A wide, sandy beach, over 5 miles of biking lush green hiking and biking trails, picnic spots, and playgrounds combine to make **Glimmerglass State Park** (1527 Co. Hwy. 31; ℂ **607/547-8662**), 8 miles outside of Cooperstown, a favorite destination for families and nature lovers. Take a bike ride to the scenic covered bridge, enjoy winter sports like ice-skating and cross-country skiing, or simply let the beauty of Otsego Lake wash over you.

Shopping

In his novel *Independence Day,* Richard Ford describes Cooperstown's main street thus: "Shops on both sides are selling baseball everything: uniforms, cards, posters, bumper stickers, no doubt hubcaps and condoms." I can't vouch for the last two items, but it's true that the main drag is almost entirely devoted to trinkets of the trade. From autographed baseball cards and inscribed bats to baseball bracelets, you'll find it here. Get your wooden bat personalized at **Cooperstown Bat Co.,** 118 Main St. (*(C)* **888/547-2415;** www.cooperstownbat.com). **Pioneer Sports Cards,** 106 Main St. (*(C)* **607/547-2323**), has an excellent selection for collectors to admire. **Riverwood,** 88 Main St. (*(C)* **607/547-4403;** riverwoodgifts.com), stocks an impressive assortment of games, toys, artwork, and handicrafts by local artisans. At family-owned **Davidson's Jewelry & Augur's Books,** 73 Main St. (*(C)* **607/547-5099;** www.davidsonsjewelry.com), you'll find an eclectic collection of gifts, art, books, and jewelry including—you guessed it—baseball-themed jewelry. Outside of the baseball realm and 3 miles from town, **Fly Creek Cider Mill & Orchard,** 288 Goose St., Fly Creek (*(C)* **800/505-6455;** www.flycreekcidermill.com; Apr–Dec), offers samples of cider, salsa, fudge, and tasty cheddar cheese, and a chance to tour the 150-year-old water-powered cider mill.

Where to Stay

There are some reliable bed-and-breakfasts in the area, such as the stately Italianate-Victorian **Landmark Inn,** 64 Chestnut St. (www.landmarkinncooperstown.com; *(C)* **866/384-3466**), or the charming and cozy **Cooperstown Bed & Breakfast,** 88 Chestnut St. (www.cooperstownbandb.com; *(C)* **607/547-2532**). Also consider the **Cooper Inn,** 15 Chestnut St. (www.cooperinn.com; *(C)* **800/348-6222**), the Otesaga's (more affordable) sister property. One chain option in the city limits is the **Best Western,** 50 Commons Dr. (www.bwcooperstown.com; *(C)* **607/547-7100**). In Oneonta, 25 miles away, you'll also find a **Holiday Inn,** 5206 State Hwy. 23 (www.hioneonta.com; *(C)* **607/433-2250**). Families on a budget might also look to the **Lake 'N Pines Motel,** 7102 State Hwy. 80 (www.lakenpinesmotel.com; *(C)* **800/615-5253**), on Otsego Lake and near the Glimmerglass Opera.

VERY EXPENSIVE

The Otesaga ★★★ Celebrating its 100th anniversary in 2009—after $45 million in renovations since the early '90s—Central New York's grande dame is still going strong, and today you can experience it from mid-April to the end of November. Located on the shores of the gloriously undeveloped Otsego Lake, this majestic Federal-style hotel boasts grounds and interiors as impressive as the 30-foot pillars that grace the classic portico fronting the building. Luxuriously furnished and very comfortable guest rooms are done in creamy tones and floral patterns. All have high ceilings, lots of space, and bathrooms with pedestal sinks; some, like no. 245, are huge. There's a refined elegance about the place; step out onto one of the numerous verandas and you'll find serenity as well, along with some great views of the lake and the challenging golf course. While the look and feel of the hotel is decidedly old-world—jackets are required at dinner for gentlemen—the Otesaga has an infrastructure that is thoroughly modern and includes Wi-Fi. One caveat: You must stay on the Modified American Plan (MAP), which means breakfast, dinner, and afternoon tea and cookies are included.

60 Lake St., Cooperstown, NY 13326. www.otesaga.com. *(C)* **800/348-6222** or 607/547-9931. Fax 607/547-9675. 135 units. $340–$455 single occupancy; $420–$535 double occupancy; $550–$820 2-bedroom; $470–$670 suites. Rates include breakfast buffet and 5-course dinner. 2-night minimum on weekends. AE, MC, V. Free valet parking. **Amenities:** 2 restaurants; 2 lounges; babysitting; concierge; golf course; exercise room; heated outdoor pool; limited room service; 2 tennis courts. *In room:* A/C, TV, hair dryer, Wi-Fi.

EXPENSIVE

Inn at Cooperstown ★★ This gorgeous, yellow Victorian inn dates from 1874, and with no TVs or phones in the rooms, it remains a great place to get away from it all. A classic inn without a trace of pretension (and with amazingly affable innkeepers), it's right off of Main Street and just a short walk from the Hall of Fame. The hotel was the first designed by Henry J. Hardenbergh, who went on to design New York City's Plaza Hotel. The grand dreams he had are more apparent outside of the inn, with its extravagant facade and sweeping veranda (where guests can often be found relaxing in rocking chairs in the afternoon, sipping complimentary iced tea or lemonade). The inside has a very cozy feel: Rooms are by no means enormous but they're comfortable (though some have quite small showers). Upgrade to the premium rooms, which have been beautifully redone with four-poster beds and plush furnishings, or to the two-bedroom luxury suite, which is on two floors, with a fireplace, a flatscreen television, and a private entrance.

16 Chestnut St., Cooperstown, NY 13326. www.innatcooperstown.com. ⓒ **607/547-5756.** 18 units. $110–$199 standard rooms; $125–$235 premium rooms; $190–$305 premium suite; $280–$495 luxury suite. Rates include continental breakfast. 2-night minimum on weekends Apr–Oct. AE, DISC, MC, V. *In room:* A/C, CD player, hair dryer, no phone, Wi-Fi.

MODERATE

American Hotel ★★ 🎁 It's hard to say which is more impressive about this restored 1847 Greek Revival–style inn: the charming and cheerful owners or the care the pair put into the gorgeous renovation. Located in tiny Sharon Springs—an old hot-springs resort just 25 miles from Cooperstown—the building was saved from ruin when the current owners bought it in 1996, reopening in 2002 after extensive renovations. The rooms are on the small side, but they are bright and tastefully appointed with subtle colors and eclectic decor. Room no. 1, on the ground floor, is more spacious and sunny, with access to the front porch and double doors to keep out noise. The hallways are decorated with folk art, while vintage postcards and signs from the town's heyday adorn the cozy sitting area. There are two porches for lounging, and a peaceful backyard and patio. The tiny pub (check out the black walnut bar, made of a tree from the driveway) is a lovely place to have a midafternoon drink, and the award-winning restaurant—serving exquisite yet simple twists on traditional comfort food, with an emphasis on local ingredients—is a destination in itself.

192 Main St. (P.O. Box 121), Sharon Springs, NY 13459. www.americanhotelny.com. ⓒ **518/284-2105.** 9 units. $200 double weeknights; $225 double weekends. Rates include full breakfast. 2-night minimum on weekends July–Aug. AE, DC, DISC, MC, V. Btw. I-88 and I-90 at the crossroads of routes 10 and 20. The hotel is on the east side of Main St./Rte. 10, 3 blocks north of Rte. 20. **Amenities:** Restaurant; lounge. *In room:* A/C, TV, hair dryer, Wi-Fi.

Lake Front Motel and Restaurant If your priorities are affordability and proximity to town, you can't beat the Lake Front, which has an excellent location right on Otsego Lake. While rooms have little to offer in the way of charm, they are clean and well maintained, and most of them come with lake views. Pay a bit more and you can upgrade to a room that sits practically on the water and comes with a private porch.

10 Fair St., Cooperstown, NY 13326. www.lakefrontmotelandrestaurant.com. ⓒ **607/547-9511.** Fax 607/547-2792. 45 units. June–Aug $148–$220 double; Sept–Oct $99–$220 double; Nov–Apr $95–$149 double; May $95–$220 double. MC, V. From the traffic light, follow Rte. 80 (Chestnut St.) 1 block north, turn right on Lake St., and continue 2 blocks to Fair St.; turn left. **Amenities:** Restaurant. *In room:* A/C, TV, hair dryer.

CAMPGROUNDS

Cooperstown Shadow Brook Campground, 2149 County Hwy. 31 (© **607/264-8431**), has a pool, playground, stocked fishing pond, and theme weekends; it's a great spot for families. **Glimmerglass State Park,** overlooking Otsego Lake, has 42 campsites available for $12 per night, $84 per week (see above).

Where to Eat

Cooperstown is many good things, but a foodie destination isn't one of them. Luckily, there are exceptions—the places listed below, and the wonderful restaurant at the **American Hotel** (see above). For an early-morning or late-afternoon treat, grab a doughnut at **Schneider's Bakery,** 157 Main St. (© **607/547-9631**), and don't forget to sample the apple dumplings and other yummy things at the **Fly Creek Cider Mill & Orchard,** 288 Goose St., Fly Creek (© **800/505-6455;** www.fly creekcidermill.com).

EXPENSIVE

Alex & Ika ★★★ ECLECTIC AMERICAN   Make no mistake: This is *the* most innovative restaurant in Central New York, offering some of the finest cuisine in all of upstate in a comfortable, casual setting. Formerly located in an old bowling alley in tiny Cherry Valley, this house of culinary masterpieces is now right in downtown Cooperstown—a welcome respite from ball-town's food scene. The kitchen serves up consistently excellent dishes, like the mouthwatering star anise roast duck with Thai coconut curry, as well as simpler fare like their fingerling potato fries, reportedly beloved by Rachel Ray. While desserts are tasty, not all are as inspired as the starters and main courses, so there's no need to save room. Good news: The restaurant has added some more affordable options at dinner, and now serves lunch—an excellent bang for your buck—so if you're on a budget, you can still join the party.

149 Main St., Cooperstown. © **607/547-4070.** www.alexandika.com. Reservations suggested. Main courses $9–$32; lunch $9–$12. AE, MC, V. Daily 11am–10pm.

MODERATE

Blue Mingo Grill ★★ SEAFOOD   Located near **Sam Smith's Boatyard** (see above), this is the place to go in Cooperstown for seafood. Casual and comfortable, the Blue Mingo's evening blackboard menu changes daily, but the accent on fresh fish and local produce never wavers. Crab cakes with an orange-wasabi sauce consistently get rave reviews, as do their waterfront views of Otsego Lake (many diners, in fact, choose to arrive by boat).

6098 State Hwy. 80. © **607/547-7496.** http://bluemingogrill.com. Reservations recommended. Lunch $5–$16; main courses $19–$30. AE, MC, V. Memorial Day to Labor Day 11:30am–10pm; Labor Day to Columbus Day 11:30am–9pm.

Nicoletta's Italian Café ★ SOUTHERN ITALIAN   Locals and tourists alike flock to this intimate, romantic Main Street restaurant, where the delightful aroma of roasted garlic perfumes the air and Sinatra is likely to be playing in the background. But even when it gets crowded here, it's never too loud for conversation. And once your meal arrives, you may not want to talk anyway (portions are huge). Nicoletta's covers all the basics and does them well—one house favorite is the *frutti di mare,* a full platter of shrimp, scallops, mussels, and clams served in a light tomato broth.

96 Main St. © **607/547-7499.** www.nicolettasitaliancafe.com. Reservations recommended. Main courses and pastas $11–$22. AE, MC, V. Daily 4–9pm.

INEXPENSIVE

Brooks House of BBQ ★ 🍖 BARBECUE   If you know people who grew up in Central New York, chances are they have eaten—and continue to crave—this famous barbecued bird. The Brooks family has been serving up their perfectly charred, succulent chicken since the mid-1950s, and the restaurant, in nearby Oneonta, is indeed an institution in these parts. (They even claim to have the largest indoor charcoal pit in the East.) While there are also burgers, seafood, and sandwiches on the menu, it's really all about the chicken. I recommend forgoing the wait for a table and digging into your meal at the long S-shaped counter instead.

5560 State Hwy. 7, Oneonta. © **800/498-2445.** www.brooksbbq.com. Meals $7–$16; sandwiches and burgers $4–$6. AE, DISC, MC, V. Tues–Sun 11am–9pm. Take I-88 West to exit 16. Turn left at stop sign at end of ramp, then left at light onto Rte. 7. Go straight for about ¼ mile; restaurant is on the left.

Danny's Market ★ 🍖 DELI   One of Main Street's busiest storefronts, this popular deli packs 'em in for a good reason: great sandwiches served on excellent homemade fresh-baked bagels and bread. It's the best place in town to stock up on provisions for a summer lakeside picnic. Try the "Chicken Dilemma," which comes with homemade mozzarella and roasted red peppers, or "the Phil"—rare roast beef with cheddar, bacon, and chipotle mayo. Danny's gets crowded and it has a small seating area, so expect to wait for a table or plan on eating outside.

92 Main St. © **607/547-4053.** Sandwiches $7–$8. DISC, MC, V. Mon–Sat 7:30am–8pm; Sun 10am–5pm; closes earlier in the winter.

T.J.'s Place ☺ AMERICAN   If you're looking for a family-style restaurant with an atmosphere that ranges from lively to loud, this is a good bet. With vintage Coca-Cola signs, plasma-screen TVs, wall-to-wall baseball memorabilia, and the attached Homeplate gift shop, T.J.'s has plenty for the kids to look at, and the extensive menu includes all the crowd pleasers—burgers, BLTs, lasagna, and ribs, plus an ample selection of salads.

124 Main St. © **800/860-5670** or 607/547-4040. Reservations not accepted. Main courses $10–$17; lunch $9–$15. DISC, MC, V. June–Aug daily 7:30am–10pm; rest of year daily 7:30am–8pm.

Cooperstown After Dark

PERFORMING ARTS   Glimmerglass Opera, north of Cooperstown on Route 80 (© **607/547-5704;** www.glimmerglass.org), has evolved from performances in the auditorium of Cooperstown High School in 1975 to an internationally acclaimed summer opera house. The 900-seat theater sits on 43 acres of farmland with splendid views of the countryside and Otsego Lake. The grounds are picnic-ready, too—wine, sandwiches, and pre-ordered gourmet picnics, delivered fresh daily, are available. Before each performance is a 1-hour preview of the performance that's free for ticket holders; backstage tours and a Young Artists Program round out the company's offerings. For a fun and easy way to get there, take the Cooperstown Trolley from the Otesaga hotel—round-trip tickets are $5. *Tip:* Plan on arriving at least 35 minutes early, and dress for the weather.

UTICA & ENVIRONS

96 miles NE of Albany; 203 miles E of Buffalo

When the Erie Canal opened in 1825, Utica and the entire Mohawk Valley went from being a land of verdant farms and forests to one of America's greatest industrial and cultural areas. Even the founders of the Oneida community—a utopian society responsible for some of the country's finest flatware—chose to settle in these parts; the legacy of their industry can be found at the **Oneida Outlet Store,** 606 Sherrill Rd., Sherrill (© **315/361-3662**). While the Mohawk Valley's boomtown days are long gone, a drive around some of the old Erie Canal towns will yield some pleasant surprises. Little Falls and Canajoharie are two villages with considerable charm, and they deserve a look-see. The surrounding area, too, is home to plenty of year-round outdoor activity—from the beaches of **Lake Oneida** to the spectacular hidden worlds of **Howe Caverns**—while reopenings and expansions of cultural and historic landmarks promise good things for the future.

Essentials

GETTING THERE The New York State Thruway (I-90) passes through the heart of it all. **Amtrak** (© **315/797-8962;** www.amtrak.com), **Greyhound** (© **315/734-4471;** www.greyhound.com), and **Adirondack Trailways** (© **800/776-7548;** www.trailwaysny.com) all arrive at **Union Station,** 321 Main St., Utica. (With its marble columns and vaulted ceilings, the beautifully restored Italianate-style train station is a destination in itself.) The major airport in the area is **Syracuse Hancock International** (p. 392).

VISITOR INFORMATION For the most detailed info, visit or call the **Oneida County Convention & Visitors Bureau,** literally right off I-90 exit 31 (© **800/426-3132;** www.oneidacountycvb.com; Mon–Thurs 9am–7pm, Fri–Sun 9am–6pm). For general information, contact the **Central Leatherstocking Region** tourist office (© **800/233-8778**). And for tips on exploring this stretch of the Erie Canal, contact the **Erie Canalway National Heritage Corridor** (© **518/237-7000;** www.erie canalway.org).

GETTING AROUND A car is more than a little helpful. And while half the fun is in winding along smaller local roads, I-90 provides the quickest route between major points; just be aware that it's a toll road. If you need a taxi, try **City Cab** (© **315/724-5454**) or **Courtesy Cab Co.** (© **315/797-7272**).

Area Attractions

One of Utica's treasures is the Philip Johnson–designed **Munson Williams Proctor Arts Institute,** 310 Genesee St. (© **315/797-0000;** www.mwpai.org), with more than 20,000 works of art, including paintings by Picasso, Kandinsky, Dalí, Mondrian, and Thomas Cole. The museum's original 1850 mansion, connected to Johnson's modern addition by an education center, houses opulent furnishings and decorative pieces. Art and history buffs alike will be pleasantly surprised by the collection at the **Arkell Museum,** 2 Erie Blvd. in Canajoharie (© **518/673-2314;** www.arkell museum.org). Opposite the old Beech-Nut factory, the Arkell features artwork by Winslow Homer, Andrew Wyeth, and Georgia O'Keeffe, along with some exhibits on Mohawk Valley history.

Erie Canal Village ★★ ☺ This reconstructed 18th-century settlement makes for an enjoyable half-day outing for the family. Built on the site where the first shovelful of earth was turned for the Erie Canal on July 4, 1817, there's now an entire village full of exhibits and buildings staffed by costumed players. Tour the Erie Canal Museum, stroll through the Harden Museum of horse-drawn carriages, and thrill to the history of cheese making at the New York State Museum of Cheese. You can also take a relaxing

40-minute boat ride on the bucolic Erie Canal and visit an original 1800s-era tavern, ice house, church, blacksmith shop, train station, school, and print shop.

5789 Rome New London Rd., Rome. © **315/337-3999.** www.eriecanalvillage.net. Admission $10 adults, $7 seniors, $5 children 5–17, free for children 4 and under. Memorial Day to Labor Day Tues–Sat 10am–5pm. Take I-90 to exit 32, turn right on 233N to 49W.

Fort Stanwix ★ ☺ Surrounded by an imposing palisade, this hard-to-miss landmark is a fun stop for history buffs and families alike. Built in 1758, the fort protected the region back when it was an essential link between the waterways to the Atlantic Ocean and the Great Lakes. Later, this militia outpost became an important base of protection during the French and Indian War and the Revolutionary War. Today it has been almost completely reconstructed, while the attached Willet Center provides an expanded home for other exhibits and artifacts. Guided tours are available, or spend some time exploring the fort on your own.

100 N. James St., Rome. © **315/338-7730.** www.nps.gov/fost. Free admission. Visitors Center daily 9am–5pm; Fort Apr to late Nov daily 9:15am–4:45pm, Dec–Mar tours daily at 10:30am and 12:30 and 2:30pm, weather permitting. I-90 to exit 32, 233N to 49W into downtown Rome.

Howe Caverns ★ Step out of the elevator that plunges you 156 feet below the earth's surface, and you'll walk into an underground marvel of colorful rock grottoes, softly curved flowstone, and gleaming stalactites and stalagmites. Ancient Indian legends spoke of a mysterious place named "Otsgaragee, or "Cave of the Great Galleries," but it wasn't until 1842 that farmer Lester Howe discovered this passage to New York's underworld. Today you can't miss the ads on billboards for miles around; Howe Caverns comes in second only to Niagara Falls for the state's top natural attraction. Three tours are available: the Traditional Tour with a quarter-mile ride on the underground Lake of Venus, a 2-hour Lantern Tour that re-creates Howe's early lamp-lit discovery, and an adrenaline-packed Adventure Tour for amateur spelunkers that includes lighted helmets and other protective gear.

255 Discovery Dr., Howes Cave. © **518/296-8900.** www.howecaverns.com. Admission $23 adults, $20 seniors, $19 children 12–15, $12 children 5–11, free for children 4 and under. Apr–Oct daily 9am–6pm; Nov–Mar daily 9am–5pm. I-90 to exit 25A; I-88 west to exit 22.

Matt Brewing Company ★ Best known for its fine selection of Saranac brews, the Matt Brewing Company is worth a visit for the excellent tour—and tasting, of course—of beer and soft drinks like root beer and ginger beer. Founded in 1888, the brewery is now run by the third and fourth generations of the Matt family. In addition to good beer, they are also dedicated to energy-efficient production, recycling everything from packaging materials and grains to CO_2 recovered during fermentation. Summer visitors can also hit the brewery for their annual series of concerts and for Thursday night happy hour events.

830 Varick St., Utica. © **800/765-6288** or 315/624-2434. www.saranac.com. Tours $5 adults, free for children 12 and under. June–Aug tours Mon–Sat 1 and 3pm; Sept–May tours Fri–Sat 1 and 3pm. Tours run 1 hr. plus; call in advance to make reservations. New York State Thruway exit 31, take Genesee St. south through downtown Utica to Court St. and take a right.

Beaches & Outdoor Activities

BIKING This part of the state offers some nice cycling paths, particularly the old Erie Canal trails. The 36-mile **Old Erie Canal State Park Trail** (www.nyscanals.gov/exvac/trail) and the 60-mile Mohawk-Hudson Bikeway (www.mhbht.org) are two good options.

Jocks of the World, Unite!

Sports fans who just didn't get their fill at the Baseball Hall of Fame have plenty of other options to choose from in this sports-crazed region. In addition to Cooperstown's number one attraction, there's Utica's **National Distance Running Hall of Fame** (114 Genesee St.; © 315/724-4525; www.distance running.com), home of the annual Boilermaker 15K race. The "sweet science" gets its due at the **International Boxing Hall of Fame** in Canastota (1 Hall of Fame Dr.; © 315/697-7095; www.ibhof.com).

HITTING THE BEACH   Lined with restaurants and an amusement park, **Sylvan Beach** is a nice stretch of sand on the eastern shore of Oneida Lake—one that gets absolutely packed with sunbathers in the summertime. Parking is tight, so if you're planning to soak up the sun, come early or lodge within walking distance. Farther north, **Sandy Island Beach State Park,** off Route 3 on County Route 15 in Pulaski (© 315/387-2657), is part of the Eastern Lake Ontario Dune and Wetland Area, a 17-mile stretch of shoreline on Lake Ontario. This state park includes the only significant freshwater dune site in the northeastern U.S.—good news for wildlife lovers. The dunes are home to several species of migratory birds and waterfowl, including sandpipers, plovers, killdeer, gulls, and terns. You may also see foxes, deer, beavers, and turtles moving among the wetland and shore areas.

GOLF   Hit the links in Rome at the 9-hole **Delta Knolls Golf Course,** 8388 Elmer Hill Rd. (© 315/339-1280; greens fees $7). In Utica, line up your shots at the **Valley View Golf Course,** 620 Memorial Pkwy., Utica (© 315/732-8755; www.valleyviewgolf.com; greens fees $35).

PROSPECTING   While a visit to the **Herkimer Diamond Mines,** 4601 State Rte. 28 in Herkimer (© 315/717-0175; www.herkimerdiamond.com; $10 adults and teens, $8 children 5–12, free for children 4 and under), isn't likely to make you a millionaire, the sparkling quartz crystals found here (they're not actual diamonds) make one-of-a-kind souvenirs. Your admission fee includes a hammer, but you may want to bring your own chisels, shovels, and protective eyewear.

Especially for Kids

Right on the shores of Oneida Lake is **Sylvan Beach Amusement Park,** on Route 13 in Sylvan Beach (© 315/762-5212; May–Sept), home of central New York's largest roller coaster and The Screamer, a high-performance 40-passenger speedboat. This is a fun little park, especially for younger kids, with bumper cars and boats, a slide, and plenty of games. Best of all, admission is free—you just pay for your activities. A smaller spot for summer fun is the **Peterpaul Recreation Park,** 5615 Rome New London Rd., Rome (© 315/339-2666; www.peterpaulrecreation.com), with batting cages, bumper boats, and kiddie karts. At the **Fort Rickey Children's Discovery Zoo,** 5135 Rome New London Rd. (© 315/336-1930; www.fortrickey. com), kids can touch a python or a porcupine—check their website for discount admission coupons. Speaking of zoos, Utica has the popular **Utica Zoo,** 99 Steele Hill Rd. (© 315/738-0472; www.uticazoo.org), along with the well-regarded **Children's Museum,** 311 Main St. (© 315/724-6129; www.museum4kids.net).

Where to Stay

The **Radisson,** 200 Genesee St., Utica (☎ **888/201-1718** or 315/797-8010), and the brand-new **Wingate,** 90 Dart Circle, Rome (☎ **315/334-4244**), are top chain choices in the area. For B&B lovers, the Italianate Victorian **Rosemont Inn,** 1423 Genesee St., Utica (http://rosemontinnbb.com; ☎ **866/353-4907**), and the **Window Box Guest House,** 29 Front St., Canajoharie (www.windowboxguesthouse.com; ☎ **518/673-3131**), are good bets.

MODERATE

Hotel Utica ★★ 💼 This historic hotel in downtown Utica reopened to considerable fanfare in 2001 after a nearly 30-year hiatus, upgrading to a four-star classification in 2009. Dating back to 1912, it boasts some notable history: FDR campaigned here in the '20s, Lionel Hampton played here in 1939, Judy Garland sang here around 1950, and Bobby Kennedy stayed here on a campaign trip. The renovations have stayed true to the grand style of the original hotel, notably in the enormous, two-story lobby, exuding old-world elegance with stately faux-marble pillars, crystal chandeliers, and a grand piano. While the rooms aren't quite so jaw-dropping, they are large and comfortable, with mahogany wood furnishings, and many come with views of the Mohawk Valley. If you need even more space, suites are available on every floor.

102 Lafayette St., Utica, NY 13502. www.hotelutica.com. ☎ **877/906-1912** or 315/724-7829. Fax 315/733-7663. 112 units. $119–$139 double; $149–$179 suite. AE, DC, DISC, MC, V. **Amenities:** Restaurant; lounge; small exercise room; limited room service. *In room:* A/C, TV w/pay movies (suites have VCRs), fridge (in most rooms), hair dryer, Wi-Fi.

Sunset Cottages ★ Located right on the beach at the edge of Lake Oneida, expect to be close to a nonstop party here, though inside the rooms you'll find it surprisingly quiet. The 1-, 2-, 3-, and 4-bedroom cottages themselves are nothing fancy, though they are spacious. With full kitchens, barbecue grills, and picnic tables, they're nicer than any of the lakefront motels. When you book, confirm that they will provide linens, and reserve one of the newer cottages, which are bright and airy.

Park Ave. (P.O. Box 134), Sylvan Beach, NY 13157. www.sylvanbeach.com/sunset. ☎ **315/762-4093.** 28 units. Apr–Sept $130–$200 double; Oct–Mar $100–$125 double. 2-night minimum stay; 7-night minimum stay in summer. MC, V. From I-90 take exit 34 at Canastota. Turn right on Rte. 13 N. for 7 miles. Turn right after crossing the bridge; it loops around to become Park Ave. *In room:* A/C (in the newer units), TV, kitchen, Wi-Fi.

Turning Stone Resort & Casino ★★ A sprawling, 737-room resort with lots of restaurants, three 18-hole golf courses (plus two par 9s), three pools, and two spas to complement the ringing slot machines, the Oneida Indian–run Turning Stone has accommodations for every price point and type of traveler. The casino hotel has standard rooms that are basic, but suites are large and come with upgraded amenities. The Tower has dramatic, contemporary rooms and amenities such as balconies and fireplaces, not to mention great views of the rolling countryside from the upper floors. The Hotel is a sleek, modern building that's centrally located to all the resort's amenities. Most luxe is The Lodge, which feels like a separate resort. Heavy on wood and modern decor, the spacious suites here boast balconies, and some even have outdoor Jacuzzis. The most affordable options are down the road in The Inn, a clean, comfortable, converted motel that recently completed an extensive renovation; a free shuttle transports guests to the casino complex. Book a massage in the **Skaná Spa**—it's a soothing environment with several treatment rooms, along with mineral baths and Jacuzzis.

5218 Patrick Rd., Verona, NY 13478. www.turningstone.com. © **800/771-7711** or 315/361-7711. 737 units. Prices vary widely based on availability, season, and lodging option. As a result, room rates can range from $80 to $1,700. Packages available. AE, DC, DISC, MC, V. Free valet parking. From I-90 take exit 33. **Amenities:** 13 restaurants, from carryout to formal dining; airport transfer ($75); 3 18-hole golf courses, 2 9-hole courses; 2 large exercise rooms; 2 Jacuzzis; 3 indoor pools; room service (in most of hotel); 2 spas; 8 tennis courts (4 indoor, 4 outdoor); massage. *In room:* A/C, TV w/pay movies, hair dryer, minibar (in some rooms), Wi-Fi.

CAMPGROUNDS

To pitch your tent with a great view of Lake Oneida, set up at **Verona Beach State Park,** Route 13, Verona Beach (© **315/762-4463**). For another waterview campground, check out the 101 campsites available at **Delta Lake State Park,** 8797 State Rte. 46, Rome (© **315/337-4670**).

Where to Eat

The Utica/Rome area has a notable food heritage, due in large part to the waves of Italian immigrants who settled in the area in the late 19th century. **Teddy's,** 851 Black River Blvd., Rome (© **315/336-7839;** www.teddysrestaurantny.com), is a good place to try the regional specialty known as riggies (rigatoni with sweet peppers, olives, onions, mushrooms, and hot cherry peppers), while the **Florentine Pastry Shop,** 667 Bleecker St., Utica (© **315/724-8032**), serves up mouthwatering pastries and pusties (custard-filled tarts).

Another Utica mainstay is **Dominique's Chesterfield,** 1713 Bleecker St. (© **315/732-9356;** www. chesterfield1713.com), famous for traditional Italian-American cooking, and offering a decent wine list. Also consider **Ancora!** at 261 Genesee St., Utica (© **315/724-4815**), next to the Stanley Center for the Arts (see below), for tapas-style plates and crepes served with a contemporary flair.

> ### A Good Read
>
> We can't think of a better accompaniment to a drive around the Mohawk Valley than one of Richard Russo's hilarious, big-hearted, character-driven novels. Russo, who grew up in Gloversville, set *The Risk Pool, Mohawk, and Bridge of Sighs* in fictional towns very closely based on his hometown.

EXPENSIVE

Wildflowers ★★★ CONTINENTAL Turning Stone's signature restaurant in its upscale Lodge is one of the area's best places to eat. The space is contemporary, with wood floors and angled banquettes, but be sure to get a table in the brighter front room; you can also sit outside. Service is friendly, and the dishes are dramatically presented, like the Steak Diane, flambéed in a mushroom red-wine sauce. Fortunately, the food delivers. Try the foie gras torchon with champagne sauce, the pan-seared red albacore with roasted fennel and orange, and the Australian grass-fed Wagyu beef strip loin.

5218 Patrick Rd., Verona (in Turning Stone Resort). © **800/771-7711.** www.turningstone.com. Reservations recommended. Main courses $28–$54. AE, DC, DISC, MC, V. Sun–Thurs 6am–2pm and 5–10pm; Fri–Sat 6am–2pm and 5–11pm.

MODERATE

Savoy ★ AMERICAN   The Savoy is a friendly neighborhood spot that starts filling up fast the moment it opens—and it's been doing that for over 100 years. The menu features a good selection of soups, salads, and pizzas, along with heaping portions of chicken, steak, and fish—and prime rib on Friday and Saturday nights. You'll also find pastas, like linguine shrimp scampi and a rigatoni with vodka sauce. Parties of four or more might like the family-style dining option for $19 per person ($8 for kids 12 and under).

225 E. Dominick St., Rome. ✆ **315/339-3166.** www.romesavoy.com. Main courses $8–$26. AE, DC, DISC, MC, V. Mon–Thurs 11:30am–9pm; Fri 11:30am–10pm; Sat 5–10pm; Sun 4–9pm.

INEXPENSIVE

Harpoon Eddie's ★ AMERICAN   Since this restaurant is set right on the beach, there's always a party happening here. In fact, it's probably the area's best place to sit outside and have a cold drink while checking out all the beach activity. If you want a bite, there are burgers, pizzas, and wings plus some nice fish dishes like mahimahi, grouper, and haddock sandwiches.

611 Park Ave., Sylvan Beach. ✆ **315/762-5238.** www.sylvanbeach.com/harpoons. Main courses $8–$17. MC, V. Spring Mon–Thurs 4–10:30pm, Fri–Sat noon–11:30pm, Sun noon–9:30pm; summer Thurs–Sat noon–11:30pm, Sun–Wed noon–10:30pm (season changes when the owner says it does).

Saltsman's Hotel ★★ 🍴 AMERICAN   It's no longer a hotel, and it really is in the middle of nowhere, but if you're in the market for authentic old New York country cooking—and a unique time warp of an eating experience—this place is the real deal. Built in 1813, Saltsman's claims to be one of the oldest continually operating restaurants in the state, and their approach to dining seems pretty much the same as it was when the restaurant opened. Arrive starving—this meal will be an event. Hearty dishes like fried chicken and sweet ham come with coleslaw, bread, a vegetable, and an appetizer, along with a delicious, rich baked onion casserole *and* corn fritters with syrup. The building heaves with history, from the tin ceiling in the Victorian parlor to the beautiful, old-world bar. Bonus: In early June, they even serve milkweed, a regional specialty and a real rarity. *Note:* Although credit cards are not accepted, you can use a debit card.

Junction of Routes 67 and 10, Ephratah. ✆ **518/993-4412.** www.saltsmans.com. Reservations recommended. Meals $11–$20. No credit cards. Call for hours. Open Easter–Halloween Wed–Sun.

SeaShell Inn ★ AMERICAN   A good alternative to the party-hearty beachfront bars that line Lake Oneida, this laid-back waterfront restaurant is a trusted choice for locals, too. Inside, you'll find knotty pine walls, ceiling fans, and glass-covered tables filled with sand and shells, while outside on the lawn, the patio tables have a peaceful view of the lake. Besides fried frogs' legs, you won't find anything wildly different on the menu, but it's mostly done well, with emphasis on Italian-style seafood and pastas. Don't fixate on the appetizers: Dinners come with plenty of extras.

6297 Lake Shore Rd. S., Verona Beach. ✆ **315/762-4606.** www.seashellonthelake.com. Main courses $9–$26. AE, DISC, MC, V. Apr–Oct Sun from noon, Tues–Sat from 4pm.

Utica & Environs After Dark

While Utica is not exactly brimming over with nightlife, there are some decent options for drinks or entertainment. The historic **Stanley Center for the Arts,** 261 Genesee St., Utica (✆ **315/725/1113;** www.cnyarts.com), stages everything from

Broadway to hip-hop shows. Lavishly restored to its "Mexican Baroque" splendor, the theater boasts the largest free-hanging chandelier in the world, lit entirely with LEDs. The Brewery District is home to some decent bars and occasional live music—**The Electric Company,** 700 Varick St., Utica (© **315/792-9271;** www.electricco.net), displays the work of local artists, hosts local bands, and serves up local (and national) brews. For a homey bar that's been around forever, head to **Griffin's Pub,** 226 Genesee St., Utica (© **315/724-5792**), or for more upscale drinks at a more upscale spot, where artisanal cocktails are made to order, try **Space 26,** 26 Bank Place, Utica (© **315/735-4407**). Had enough booze? Check out the **Tramontane Cafe,** 1105 Lincoln Ave., Utica (© **315/732-8257**), for live music in a coffeehouse setting. And, of course, there's **Turning Stone Casino,** just off I-90's exit 33 (© **800/771-7711;** www.turningstone.com), with slots, tables, restaurants, cocktail lounges, and some of the biggest comedy and music acts to be found in this part of New York State.

THE FINGER LAKES REGION

by Neil Edward Schlecht

On a map of New York, 11 skinny blue streaks snake across the middle of the state. These curious parallel formations are the Finger Lakes, carved by glaciers receding at the end of the last ice age and named for their obvious resemblance to the slender, crooked digits of a human hand. The lakes are deep cobalt, glossy-surfaced, and as narrow as rivers. The vast Finger Lakes region beyond them is a pastoral patchwork of storybook waterfront villages, grand Victorian homes, dairy farms, forests, and wineries amid sloped vineyards. But the lakes run through it all.

The principal "fingers" are the five major lakes that stripe the region. These unique bodies of water, which range in length from 3 to 40 miles and are as narrow as ⅓ of a mile across, are framed by a gentle rise of vineyard-covered banks and rolling hills. The region is one of mesmerizing beauty, like a dream marriage of Scotland and Napa Valley. The lakes have created unique conditions and microclimates that are ideal for grape growing, and this is one of the most notable winemaking regions in the country; an ever-growing roster of nearly 100 wineries dot the banks of the lakes. In contrast to the massive operations of decades past, several are boutique and family-owned wineries that have made great strides in challenging the accepted supremacy of West Coast winemakers. In addition, chef-driven restaurants are fast taking root to take advantage of the local wines and farm-fresh products.

Quite remarkably, though, the Finger Lakes region remains unknown to many Americans—and even many New Yorkers. Anchored by medium-size upstate cities on either side—Syracuse and Rochester—the Finger Lakes are largely about outdoor recreation and small-town life. Yet the area packs a few surprises, such as the magnificent, family-friendly Corning Museum of Glass, in the town made famous by CorningWare; the progressive charms of Ithaca, home to Cornell University and a quintessential college town; the summer haunts of Mark Twain; delightful, picturesque villages like Skaneateles and Aurora; the legacies of the Underground Railroad that carried slaves to freedom; and the origins of the women's suffrage and civil rights movements, American aviation, and the modern Mormon Church.

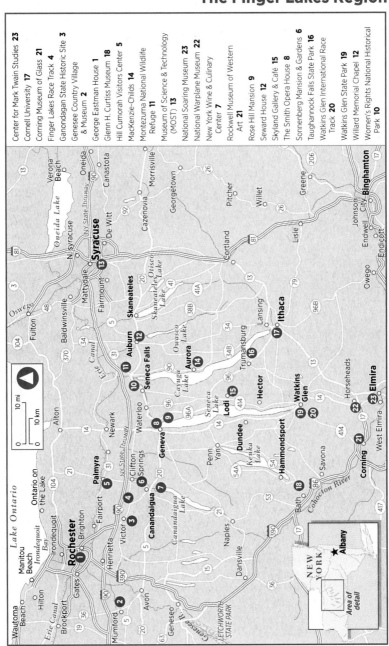

Center for Mark Twain Studies **23**
Cornell University **17**
Corning Museum of Glass **21**
Finger Lakes Race Track **4**
Ganondagan State Historic Site **3**
Genesee Country Village & Museum **2**
George Eastman House **1**
Glenn H. Curtiss Museum **18**
Hill Cumorah Visitors Center **5**
MacKenzie-Childs **14**
Montezuma National Wildlife Refuge **11**
Museum of Science & Technology (MOST) **13**
National Soaring Museum **23**
National Warplane Museum **22**
New York Wine & Culinary Center **7**
Rockwell Museum of Western Art **21**
Rose Hill Mansion **9**
Seward House **12**
Skyland Gallery & Café **15**
The Smith Opera House **8**
Sonnenberg Mansion & Gardens **6**
Taughannock Falls State Park **16**
Watkins Glen International Race Track **20**
Watkins Glen State Park **19**
Willard Memorial Chapel **12**
Women's Rights National Historical Park **10**

In warm months, the Finger Lakes region comes alive with boaters, cyclists, and wine tourists. Though the area is most often thought of as a summer destination, the ideal time to visit extends from spring to late fall. It can be gorgeous even in winter—which is actually milder than most parts of upstate New York—but perhaps most stunning in autumn, when the brilliant blue lake waters are framed by an earthy palette of reds and yellows and sun-kissed, golden vineyards.

ORIENTATION
Arriving

BY PLANE   Most visitors traveling by air will fly into either the **Greater Rochester International Airport** (ROC), 1200 Brooks Ave., Rochester (📞 **716/464-6000;** www.rochesterintlairport.com), or Syracuse's **Hancock International Airport** (SYR), 1000 Colonel Eileen Collins Blvd., Syracuse (📞 **315/454-4330;** www.syrairport.org); both are serviced by most major airlines. Smaller regional airports are **Elmira/Corning Regional Airport** (ELM), 276 Sing Sing Rd., Horse-heads (📞 **607/795-0402;** www.ecairport.com), and small **Ithaca/Tompkins County Airport** (ITH), 72 Brown Rd., Ithaca (📞 **607/257-0456;** www.ithaca-airport.com).

BY CAR   The Finger Lakes region is within a day's drive of most major metropolitan areas in the northeastern U.S. and eastern Canada; Seneca Lake is about 300 miles from New York City, 400 miles from Boston, 230 miles from Toronto, and 275 miles from Philadelphia. The New York State Thruway (I-90) travels across the top of the region, from Albany all the way to Rochester and beyond. From Binghamton and Pennsylvania, I-81 travels north to Syracuse, and Route 17 west to Corning.

BY TRAIN   Amtrak (📞 **800/USA-RAIL** [872-7245]; www.amtrak.com) has service to the Finger Lakes region and heads to Syracuse and Rochester from New York City, Buffalo, Boston, and other cities.

BY BUS   Bus service to the Finger Lakes is available on **Greyhound Bus Lines** (📞 **800/231-2222;** www.greyhound.com), with stations in Ithaca, Syracuse, Geneva, and Rochester, and **Trailways** (📞 **800/343-9999;** www.trailways.com), which travels to Elmira, Geneva, Rochester, and Syracuse.

Visitor Information

For general tourist information before your trip, contact the **Finger Lakes Association,** 309 Lake St., Penn Yan, NY 14527 (📞 **800/530-7488;** www.fingerlakes.org). Its Web page has contact information and links to each of the region's individual

---

 Say What?

The Finger Lakes take their names from Native American languages of the original inhabitants of the region. Lake and place names can work a real number on your tongue; here's a guide to meanings and pronunciations:

Skaneateles	"long lake"	Skinny-atlas
Cayuga	"boat landing"	Kah-*yoo*-gah
Seneca	"place of the stone"	*Sen*-uh-kah
Keuka	"canoe landing"	*Kyoo*-kah
Canandaigua	"chosen place"	Can-uhn-*day*-gwuh

The Finger Lakes region, with nearly 100 wineries and some 10,000 acres of vineyards, is one of the nation's great wine-producing regions. The region is continually growing in name recognition and estimation among wine aficionados, and many visitors compare it to the Napa Valley of 2 decades ago. A cool-climate viticultural region—comparable to the Burgundy and Champagne regions in France—the Finger Lakes are ideal for growing vinifera, or noble (European), grapes. The region produces excellent Riesling, chardonnay, cabernet franc, and sparkling ice wines. It's also a terrific place to try more unusual wines, such as Gewürztraminer, Rkatsiteli, and rare ice wines.

The wine country is centered on four main lakes: Cayuga, Seneca, Keuka, and, to a lesser degree, Canandaigua. Pick up brochures on the individual trails in the region as well as the *Free Map & Guide* of all the wineries in the Finger Lakes, and see the listings and sidebars on each wine trail below. An indispensable stop for anyone either prior to winery visits or without the time or inclination

to attack a wine trail is the new **New York Wine & Culinary Center** in Canandaigua (p. 339), and while there are events held at wineries throughout the warm months, one of the best times—or at least one of the most hedonistic—is the **Finger Lakes Wine Festival** (© 866/461-7223; www.flwinefest. com), held in late July at the Watkins Glen International racetrack.

You may want to think about someone else doing the driving; limo and bus wine tours are quite popular in season. For organized wine tours in limousines and other multipassenger vehicles, contact one of the following wine transportation and tour specialists: **Finger Lakes Winery Tours & Transportation** (© 315/828-6289; www.fingerlakes winerytours.com), **Quality Winery Tours** (© 877/424-7004; www.qualitywine tours.com), **VRA Imperial Limousine, Inc.** (© 800/303-6100; www.implimo. com), **Park Place Limousine and Transportation Services** (© 585/223-7780; www.rochesterlimousine.com), and **Grapevine Country Tours** (© 800/536-8123; www.grapevinecountrytours.com).

county websites. Another very helpful tourism organization is **Finger Lakes Wine Country** (© 800/813-2958; www.fingerlakeswinecountry.com), which focuses on the southwestern quadrant of the region, where most of the best wineries are located.

Many good free publications are widely available across the region, at hotels, restaurants, and other sites, with tons of information on wine routes, outdoor activities, accommodations, festivals, and more.

Area Layout

Stretching from Lake Ontario in the north and almost to the Pennsylvania border in the south, about midway between New York City and Niagara Falls, the Finger Lakes region covers some 9,000 square miles and touches upon 14 counties, occupying a huge chunk of central-western New York. The region is roughly equidistant between Albany and Buffalo.

The region is covered below in a clockwise direction, beginning with the southeast region around Ithaca. Many of the major towns and attractions in the area tend to be clustered at the top or bottom ends of lakes. When you're traveling by car, it's probably easiest to move in one direction from east to west or west to east, rather than circling entire lakes that, though not wide, are certainly long.

Getting Around

BY CAR   A car is virtually indispensable for any kind of traveling in the Finger Lakes region. There is very little public transportation in the area, except between major cities. The major car-rental companies have outlets at both Rochester International Airport and Syracuse's Hancock International Airport.

BY ORGANIZED TOUR   **Finger Lakes Tours, Ltd.,** Drawer 9, Jasper, NY 14855 (© **607/792-3663;** www.finger-lakes-tours.com), offers all-inclusive family, hunting, fishing, biking and hiking, wine festival, and even "women only" organized tours of the region, in a variety of price ranges. Geneva-based **Grapevine Country Tours** (© **877/536-8123;** www.grapevinecountrytours.com) organizes Finger Lakes Wine Trail tours.

ITHACA & SOUTHERN CAYUGA LAKE ★★

240 miles NW of New York City; 40 miles E of Corning

Ithaca, home to Cornell University and Ithaca College, may be best known as a laid-back college town, but given its stunning setting on the south shore of 40-mile-long Cayuga Lake, and sandwiched between two incredible gorges, it perhaps deserves to be even better known for its natural beauty. Certainly that's not lost on residents, many of whom cruise around town with T-shirts or bumper stickers that read, ITHACA IS GORGES. Ithaca is a cosmopolitan town with many of the amenities of a bigger city, such as good restaurants, bars, and theaters, but few of the hassles—all of which contributed to its once being ranked as the number one "emerging city" in the U.S., by *Cities Ranked & Rated.* The city and surrounding Tompkins County abound in beautiful natural areas ripe for hiking, biking, and other outdoor activities, while wine fans can follow the Cayuga Wine Trail. Some 15 wineries line the southern (and mostly western) section of the lake, where they are easily accessible from Ithaca.

Essentials

GETTING THERE

BY PLANE   The regional **Ithaca/Tompkins County Airport** (ITH), 72 Brown Rd., Ithaca (© **607/257-0456;** www.ithaca-airport.com or www.flyithaca.com), is serviced by US Airways and Northwest Airlines. It's less than 10 miles north of town on Route 13.

BY CAR   Ithaca is about a 4-hour drive from New York City. The nearest major highways are I-81, which travels north to Syracuse, and Route 17, which heads west to Corning. Routes 13 and 96B head directly into Ithaca.

BY BUS   **Greyhound** stops in Ithaca at the Brenda Wallace Bus Terminal, 710 W. State St. (© **800/231-2222** or 607/272-7930); **Shortline Bus** (© **800/631-8405** or 607/277-8800; www.shortlinebus.com) travels to Ithaca, also stopping at 710 W. State St., as well as Elmira, from New York City.

VISITOR INFORMATION   The **Ithaca/Tompkins County Convention & Visitors Bureau** is located at 904 E. Shore Dr., Ithaca (© **800/284-8422** or 607/272-1313; www.visitithaca.com). A new downtown **Visitors Center and Ticket Center,** opened in June 2009, is located at 171 The Commons (© **607/273-7482**).

Exploring Ithaca & Southern Cayuga Lake

The top attraction in town, apart from nearby Cayuga Lake, is **Cornell University** ★★, a handsome Ivy League school on 745 acres. It sits high on a hill in so-called "Collegetown," from which it surveys the rest of Ithaca and the splendid stripe of Cayuga Lake that stretches northward. On campus, the top draw is the **Herbert F. Johnson Museum of Art** ★★ (University Ave.; ✆ 607/255-6464; www.museum.cornell.edu; Tues–Sun 10am–5pm; free admission), a modern cement structure designed by I. M. Pei (1973). The museum counts more than 30,000 pieces in its collection, with particular strengths in Asian art (ranging from antiquity to contemporary artists from Japan, China, India, and the Himalayas and Middle East), as well as prints and photographs. The museum hosts interesting traveling exhibitions, but even visitors without strong interests in art shouldn't miss the unsurpassed fifth-floor views of Cayuga Lake and the gentle hillsides surrounding Ithaca. Across the street from the museum is a path that leads down to a suspension bridge over **Fall Creek Gorge** ★, one of two beautiful and deep gorges that frame the Cornell campus, and Beebe Lake. The trails around the gorge and lake are popular with sunbathing students who make their way down to the water. Find your way to **Ithaca Falls** and stand near the cascading falls that rush down tiers of stone 100 feet high and 175 feet wide. The most visible building on campus, McGraw Tower, is known for the **Cornell Chimes,** an old school tradition played daily by students and alumni (for information about chimes concerts, call ✆ 607/255-5330). **Cornell campus tours** are available by calling ✆ 670/254-INFO (4636).

East of Beebe Lake is the university's museum of living plants, **Cornell Plantations** ★ (1 Plantations Rd., Cornell University; ✆ 607/255-2400; www.plantations.cornell.edu; Tues–Sat 10am–5pm, Sun noon–4pm; free admission), a real find and well worth a visit for garden lovers or anyone seeking a bit of solace. The public is welcome to visit the botanical garden, wildflower garden, and Newman Arboretum, which specializes in New York State trees and shrubs, as well as any of the 3,000 acres of natural areas in and around the campus (which contains more than 9 miles of walking trails). Of particular interest are the orderly herb garden with raised theme beds (herbs are grouped according to usage) and a quiet knoll area that contains more than 300 species of rhododendrons. Free "drop-in tours" are offered on Wednesdays and Saturdays, and there are other walks and classes available; check the schedule online for events. Part of the **Cornell Lab of Ornithology** is the Sapsucker Woods Bird Sanctuary ★ (159 Sapsucker Woods Rd., off Rte. 13, Ithaca; ✆ 800/843-BIRD [2473]; www.birds.cornell.edu; Mon–Thurs 8am–5pm, Fri 8am–4pm, Sat 9:30am–4pm, Sun 11am–4pm; trails open daily; free admission), home to 200 species of birds. An observatory, a bird-feeding garden, trails, and a multimedia theater that allows visitors to hear birds in surround sound will appeal to hard-core birders.

Just 7 miles north of Ithaca, in Trumansburg along the west side of Cayuga Lake, is one of the region's most beautiful sights. Tucked in **Taughannock Falls State Park** ★★ (Taughannock Park Rd./Rte. 89 N.; ✆ 607/387-6739) is the highest free-falling waterfall in the eastern U.S.; at 215 feet, it is higher even than Niagara Falls. You can drive up to a lookout or hike in from the entrance to the park (the hike is an easy, flat .75-mile walk). The falls are best viewed in spring and fall; in summer there is often very little water and visitors are inevitably disappointed. Summer concerts are held in the park.

cayuga WINE TRAIL

The **Cayuga Wine Trail** ★ (✆ **800/ 684-5217;** www.cayugawinetrail.com) comprises a grouping of 16 small wineries clustered around Cayuga Lake. As the first wine trail in New York State, it has served as the model for the three other Finger Lakes wine trails. A tour of the wineries on the west side of Cayuga (all but two on the trail) could easily be combined with visits to wineries on the east side of Seneca Lake (p. 322). Among those welcoming visitors for tours and tastings are (listed in order from south to north on each bank of the lake) the following:

EAST BANK

Long Point Winery ★ 1485 Lake Rd., Aurora (✆ **315/364-6990;** www.long pointwinery.com). This is one of the few Finger Lakes wineries that might make better dry reds—including merlot, cabernet franc, and Syrah—than whites. The farmhouse tasting room has great long views of Cayuga Lake (Mon–Thurs 10am–5pm, Fri–Sat 10am–6pm, Sun 11am–5:30pm; closed Jan).

WEST BANK

Lucas Vineyards ★ 3862 C.R. 150, Interlaken (✆ **800/682-WINE** [9463]; www.lucasvineyards.com). Cayuga Lake's oldest winery is a family-owned operation with a farmhouse tasting room and attractively landscaped gardens with great water views. Don't mind some wines' cutesy names ("Miss Behavin'," "Miss Chevious—a Nautie white"; Jan–Apr Mon–Sat 10:30am–5pm, Sun noon–5pm; May–Dec Mon–Sat 10:30am–5:30pm, Sun noon–5:30pm).

Sheldrake Point Vineyard & Simply Red Lakeside Bistro ★★ 7448 C.R. 153, Ovid (off Rte. 89; ✆ **866/ 743-5372** or 607/532-9401; www.sheldrake point.com). One of the more appealing

compounds in the region sits on a mid-19th-century farmstead, with an excellent lakeside restaurant serving lunch and dinner (May–Oct; see p. 318), outdoor seating, and a professionally run tasting shop. I quite like their dry Riesling and cabernet franc (Jan–Mar daily noon–5pm; Apr–Dec daily 11am–5:30pm).

Hosmer Winery ★★ 6999 Rte. 89, Ovid (✆ **607/869-3393;** www.hosmer winery.com). Some of the finest dry Rieslings in the region are produced here. The tasting room and gift shop are the antithesis of slick, but fans of cool-climate whites are in for a treat. Try the Vintner's Reserve Riesling, the award-winning dry and semidry Riesling, and the dry rosé (Apr–Dec Mon–Sat 10am–5pm, Sun noon–5pm; Jan–Mar Fri–Sun noon–4pm, Mon–Thurs by appointment).

Goose Watch Winery ★ 5480 Rte. 89, Romulus (✆ **315/549-2599;** www. goosewatch.com). Goose Watch Winery has a relaxed tasting room in an old barn and excellent views of the lake, a picnic deck, and boat docking—not to mention an interesting selection of premium wines, including a number of unusual varietals you may never have heard of, like Diamond, Chambourcin, Lemberger, Villard Blanc, Melody, Rosé of Isabella, and Traminette, as well as pinot gris, viognier, and white port (year-round daily 10am–6pm).

Swedish Hill Vineyard 4565 Rte. 414, Romulus (✆ **888/549-WINE** [9463] or 315/549-8326; www.swedishhill.com). This family-owned operation offers a very large selection of wines, including chardonnay, Riesling, port, and brandy (year-round daily 9am–6pm; guided tours May–Oct weekdays 1 and 3pm, weekends noon, 2, and 4pm).

If you're lucky enough to find yourself in Ithaca the first weekend after Memorial Day, you'll stumble upon an event that reveals the community-based soul of this college town, during the lively and friendly annual **Ithaca Festival**, which has been put on in charming low-key fashion since the late 1970s.

The opening parade on Friday is a wacky classic, including adults parading as dancing tofu, kids dressed up like compost piles, and the hilarious Volvo Ballet, complete with tutus wrapped around boxy station wagons. Call *©* 607/273-3646, or visit www.ithaca festival.org for information.

Especially for Kids

Families will enjoy a visit to **Sciencenter** ★, 601 First St. (*©* **607/272-0600;** www. sciencenter.org), a hands-on science museum with a walk-in camera, an outdoor playground, "piano stairs," and other exhibits that will entertain children. It's open Tuesday to Saturday from 10am to 5pm, Sunday from noon to 5pm (July–Aug, also Mon 10am–5pm; admission $7 adults, $6 seniors, $5 children 3–17, free for children 2 and under). The museum's **Sagan Planet Walk** is an outdoor scale model of the sun and nine planets, built as a memorial to Cornell astronomer Carl Sagan. The walk starts at The Commons in downtown, goes along Willow Avenue and Cayuga Street, and ends at Sciencenter, about ¼ mile away; kids can get a passport to the solar system stamped at stations along the way and earn free admission to Sciencenter.

The **Museum of the Earth** (at the Paleontological Research Institution), 1259 Trumansburg Rd. (*©* **607/273-6623;** www.museumoftheearth.org), is an 18,000-square-foot interactive exhibit and education facility dedicated to the 3.5-billion-year history of life on Earth. It displays one of the country's largest fossil collections, including the skeleton of the Hyde Park Mastodon and a 500-foot mural, "The Rock of Ages, Sands of Time." It's open Memorial Day to Labor Day, Monday to Saturday 10am to 5pm and Sunday 11am to 5pm; the rest of the year, Monday and Thursday to Saturday 10am to 5pm and Sunday 11am to 5pm. Admission is $8 for adults and teens, $5 for seniors, and $3 for children 4 to 17 (free for children 3 and under).

Children will enjoy the opportunity to climb high into the forest canopy on the TreeTops observation tower at **The Cayuga Nature Center,** 1420 Taughannock Blvd. (Rte. 89; *©* **607/273-6260**). The falls, trails, and swimming at **Taughannock Falls State Park** are also popular with kids of all ages.

Sports & Outdoor Pursuits

Tompkins County, and specifically the area around Ithaca and Cayuga Lake, replete with gorges, glens, and state parks, is one of the best in the Finger Lakes for all manner of outdoor sports, from hiking and biking to golf and sailing. Locals are a very outdoorsy lot, so you'll have plenty of company.

Outdoors outfitters, with backpacking, canoeing, and skiing equipment, include **Cornell Outdoor Education,** Bartels Hall, Campus Road, Cornell University (*©* **607/255-1807**); **The Outdoor Store,** 206 The Commons (*©* **607/273-3891**); and **Eastern Mountain Sports,** 722 Meadow St. (*©* **607/272-1935**).

BOATING & SAILING Cayuga Lake Cruises' **Dinner Cruise** aboard the 1915 M/V *Manhattan* is a great way to see Cayuga Lake. The boat sets sail mid-April to late October from the waterfront (M/V *Manhattan* Pier), 708 W. Buffalo St. (© **607/256-0898;** cayugalakecruises.com). The company offers dinner, lunch, and brunch cruises. Lake charters for sightseeing and fishing on Cayuga Lake are available from **Tiohero Tours** (© **866/846-4376;** www.tioherotours.com), which offers 1- and 2-hour narrated lake tours.

Private boat rentals are available from **Taughannock Boat Rentals,** Taughannock Park Road (Rte. 89; © **607/387-4439**), and **Puddledockers,** 704 W. Buffalo St. (© **888/273-0096;** www.puddledockers.com), for nonmotorized boat rentals.

CAMPING   **Taughannock Falls State Park,** Taughannock Park Road/Route 89 in Trumansburg, allows camping; call © **800/456-CAMP** (2267) or 607/387-6739 or visit www.reserveamerica.com for more information. For private campgrounds, check out **Spruce Row Campsite & RV Resort,** 2271 Kraft Rd. (© **607/387-9225**), near Taughannock Falls State Park, which has a pool and plenty of family recreation.

HIKING & BIKING   Excellent trails for hiking and biking exist all over the Ithaca area. On the Cornell University campus, there are more than 9 miles of trails operated by **Cornell Plantations** (© **607/255-2400**). **Six Mile Creek Gorge,** on Hudson Street across from the South Hill School, is an old Native American trail that passes a former mill and a wildflower preserve. The beautiful **Cascadilla Creek Gorge ★**, at University Avenue and Court Street, is a greenway connecting downtown Ithaca to the colleges on the hills (Cornell and Ithaca College). The gorge walk, past gently cascading waterfalls, is just over a mile long with plenty of stairs for a good workout. The **South Hill Recreation Way,** off Hudson Street, is a gravel trail built on a railroad track, and it's very popular with local joggers, cyclists, and cross-country skiers. You can enter near Crescent Place, where there's a self-guided interpretative nature tour. Trails in and around **Ithaca Falls,** off Lake Street, are among the most scenic in the area, as are those that lead to the falls in **Taughannock Falls State Park,** off Route 89 in Trumansburg. The **Cayuga Waterfront Trail,** when completed over the next few years, will be a 6-mile linear park along the southern tip of Cayuga Lake.

The **Cayuga Nature Center,** 1420 Taughannock Blvd. (Rte. 89; © **607/273-6260**), has 5 miles of hiking trails and the TreeTops observation tower. The **Circle Greenway,** 108 E. Green St. (© **607/272-1313**), is a 10-mile walk that passes the waterfront, gorges, the Cornell campus, and The Commons downtown.

Robert H. Treman State Park, 105 Enfield Falls Rd. (© **607/273-3440;** http://nysparks.state.ny.us/parks/135/details.aspx), has trails that wend their way past a dozen waterfalls, including the 115-foot Lucifer Falls, with distant views down the wooded gorge. In **Buttermilk Falls State Park,** Route 13 South (© **670/273-5761;** http://nyfalls.com/buttermilk-falls-state-park.html), you can hike the gorge trail and see 10 waterfalls (and end with a swim in the wake of the falls).

Trail maps for many of these hikes are available at the tourism information office or local sports shops.

Bike rentals are available from **The Outdoor Store,** 206 The Commons (© **607/273-3891**), and **Cayuga Mountain Bike Shop,** 138 W. State St. (© **607/277-6821**). Check with these outfitters to see which trails allow mountain bikers.

GOLF   There are half a dozen golf courses in the area; one of the best is **Hillendale Golf Course,** 218 N. Applegate Rd. (© **607/273-2363;** www.hillendale.com). Greens fees are $19 during the week, $21 on weekends; discounts for seniors and juniors (17 and under) are available.

SWIMMING   **Buttermilk Falls State Park** (see above) has a fantastic natural pool at the base of the falls. Another swimming treat in the area is dipping into the natural, stream-fed basin at the lower falls of **Robert H. Treman State Park** (see above). There is also swimming in **Taughannock Falls State Park,** off Route 89 in Trumansburg, though areas close to the falls are off-limits. **Cass Park,** 701 Taughannock Blvd. (Rte. 89 N.; ℭ **607/273-9211**), has an Olympic-size pool that's open to the public.

WINTER SPORTS   Cross-country skiers should head to **Taughannock Falls State Park** (ℭ **607/387-6739**), off Route 89 in Trumansburg, or the terrifically named **Podunk Cross-Country Ski Center,** Podunk Road, Trumansburg (ℭ **607/387-3093**), which has 7 miles of trails, with rental and instruction available. Most of the state parks in the area allow Nordic skiing. The closest downhill skiing is in Cortland, at **Greek Peak Mountain,** 200 Rte. 392 (ℭ **800/955-2-SKI** [2754]; www.greekpeak.net). Ice-skating is found at **Cass Park Rink & Pool,** 701 Taughannock Blvd., Route 89 (ℭ **607/273-9211**).

Shopping

Downtown Ithaca Commons, or simply "The Commons," at the corner of West State and Cayuga streets, is a pleasant area of shops and restaurants along a wide pedestrian boulevard. It's packed with gift shops, clothing stores, bookstores, and art galleries. If you're interested in touring art studios and galleries, pick up a copy of *Greater Ithaca Art Trail* (www.arttrail.com), a guide to the studios of 49 local artists; open studio weekends are held in October. For a good sense of the region's agricultural and artsy roots, visit the **Ithaca Farmers Market,** Route 13 at Steamboat Landing (Third St.); it's open April through December on Saturday from 9am to 3pm, and June through October, Sunday from 10am to 3pm (ℭ **607/273-7109;** www.ithacamarket.com). A cooperative with more than 125 local members, the market, in a covered pavilion on the waterfront, delivers a fabulous and entertaining array of produce, food vendors, music, art, and crafts. Cheeseheads and others interested in local farm products should make the short trek to **Bronson Hill Cheesery,** 5491 Bergen Rd., Mecklenburg (on the west side of Cayuga Lake; ℭ **607/387-3108**), a family farm that specializes in fresh, handcrafted cow-milk cheeses.

Where to Stay

Hotel rooms are at a premium (both impossible to find and expensive) during Cornell and Ithaca College graduations (end of May) and Finger Lakes region festivals and events (including NASCAR); high season lasts from April to November. Rates at inns are generally also higher on weekends. Visitors might also want to consider staying in Aurora at the spectacular **Aurora Inn** (35 min. north along Cayuga Lake's east bank); see the sidebar on p. 320.

EXPENSIVE

Hilton Garden Inn ★ ☺   Ideally located on Ithaca's Downtown Commons, the latest addition to the Ithaca hotel scene fills a needed niche: a good value, well located, comfortable, and dependable hotel for business and leisure travelers who desire a full range of services, including a heated indoor pool, as well as the anonymity that comes from staying in a larger hotel. And the beauty of the area can be appreciated from the top floors of the nine-story tower, with commanding views of

Cayuga Lake. Rooms are nicely decorated, if a tad bland, but guests who need to work will be pleasantly surprised by the work areas with ergonomic Aeron desk chairs.

130 E. Seneca St., Ithaca, NY 14853. www.hiltongardeninn.com.© **1-877-STAY-HGI** (782-9444) or 607/277-8900. Fax 607/277-8910. 104 units. $199–$299 double. AE, DC, MC, V. Free parking. **Amenities:** 2 restaurants; pub; fitness center; indoor pool; room service. *In room:* A/C, TV w/pay movies, hair dryer, Wi-Fi (free).

The Statler Hotel ★

On the campus of Cornell, this large and well-run hotel is associated with the university's well-regarded Hotel Management School and the staff includes student workers whose very grades may depend on the service they give you; as a result, you can expect A+ attitudes all around. Rooms are good-size, standard modern hotel rooms, though they have Four Seasons pillow-top bedding and nice linens. Bathrooms are small, but have nice marble countertops. Many rooms have excellent views of the campus extending all the way to Cayuga Lake.

11 East Ave., Cornell University, Ithaca, NY 14853. www.statlerhotel.cornell.edu.© **800/541-2501** or 607/257-2500. Fax 607/254-2504. 153 units. $250–$320 double; $375–$580 suite. AE, DC, MC, V. Free parking. **Amenities:** 3 restaurants; complimentary shuttle from airport and bus station; 24-hr. fitness center; limited room service. *In room:* A/C, TV w/pay movies, high-speed Internet access.

MODERATE

Inn on Columbia ★★ 🏨

Less B&B than European-style boutique hotel (albeit with just three rooms), this completely revamped 1832 Greek Revival house on South Hill, near Ithaca College and Cornell, is a swank and stylish place to stay. It's owned by a married couple, the husband an architect (he did the revamping) and the wife a chef who cooks up Asian-fusion dishes and inventive breakfasts "when guests allow her to." Choose the room in the main house, with vaulted ceilings and skylights; the carriage house, with an outdoor deck, full kitchen, and living room; or the hexagonal gazebo room. No architectural detail has been overlooked, from automatic lights to custom furniture; the overall aesthetic is cool and modern. If you're pulling into town with no reservations, check out the "Procrastinator's Special"—any unoccupied room is just $125 (suite $185) for that night.

228 Columbia St., Ithaca, NY 14850. www.columbiabb.com.© **607/272-0204.** 3 units. $165–$225 main house double; $250–$275 carriage house and gazebo. Rates include full breakfast. DC, MC, V. Free parking. *In room:* A/C, TV, stereo, Wi-Fi.

La Tourelle Resort & Spa ★

A fine country inn in a peaceful location on the outskirts of Ithaca, this small hotel is a good choice for those who like the amenities of large hotels but some of the intimacies of smaller inns. Rooms are large but fall just short of being luxurious, decorated with either light wood furnishings and salmon-colored floral designs or darker Mexican, handcrafted furniture and more masculine decor. Though their appeal may be limited, two incongruous tower rooms are circular and have kitschy sunken round beds, mirror-paneled ceilings, and even a disco ball—perfect for that retro anniversary weekend! Tennis aficionados can stay at the tennis cottage near the courts. For dining there's also **John Thomas Steakhouse,** in an 1800s farmhouse and serving dinner nightly and featuring dry-aged beef.

1150 Danby Rd. (Rte. 96B), Ithaca, NY 14850. www.latourelle.com.© **800/765-1492** or 607/273-2734. Fax 607/300-1500. 54 units. $169–$299 double. AE, DC, MC, V. Free parking. **Amenities:** 2 restaurants; spa; 4 tennis courts (2 lighted for night play). *In room:* A/C, TV w/pay movies, hair dryer, high-speed Internet.

Taughannock Farms Inn ★★ 🍴

Well known for its restaurant (p. 318), this large inn, on a beautiful location at the edge of Taughannock State Park overlooking

Cayuga Lakeside Inns

Ithaca may overlook the southern tip of Cayuga Lake, but if you want a real lakeside room, the **Silver Strand at Sheldrake**, a Victorian B&B on the west bank, is about as close as you can get to being on the lake without sleeping on a boat. Come for the stupendous views; the inn sits on a quiet road on Sheldrake Point, which opens to expansive, distant vistas of the lake. All five of its simply decorated rooms have lake views as well as private decks. The inn, in a large mid-19th-century manse at 7398 Wyers Point Rd., Ovid, NY 14521 (ℂ 800/283-5253; www.silverstrand. net), is about 20 miles north of Ithaca on the west side of Cayuga Lake (and only minutes from about a half-dozen wineries). Silver Strand offers guests the use of bikes, boats, and a private beach and sun deck. Rates are $170 to $215 double, including breakfast.

Cayuga Lake, is a compound, occupying an exquisite 1873 mansion and three more modern guesthouses. The main house has five rooms, with either lake or forest views; though guests have to contend with the restaurant's popularity, those rooms have a bit more character than the more private and generally modern guesthouse rooms. Rooms are decorated with some Victorian antiques and bold wallpapers and floral decor. The guesthouses are particularly good for families and friends traveling together. The inn is open from May to November only. The 10-room guesthouse across the property has great lake views, but the modern decor is a bit lacking in personality.

2030 Gorge Rd. (Rte. 89 at Taughannock State Park), Trumansburg, NY 14886. www.t-farms.com. ℂ888/387-7711 or 607/387-7711. 22 units. $90–$195 main inn double; $95–$225 guesthouse double. Rates include full breakfast. AE, DC, MC, V. Free parking. **Amenities:** Restaurant; small bar. *In room:* A/C, TV (guesthouse rooms only), hair dryer, high-speed Internet access.

William Henry Miller Inn ★★★ 🛏️ The top B&B in Ithaca—and one of the most beautiful private homes in town—has an enviable downtown location: just paces from The Commons. An 1880 Victorian built by Cornell's first architecture student and owned by just two families before becoming an inn, the house combines rich details like stained-glass windows and custom chestnut woodwork. Seven rooms are in two floors of the main house, and there are a two-room suite and another room in the carriage house. My favorite may be the soothing Library guest room. The charming and considerate owner, Lynette, has added ramps and a wheelchair elevator, making a couple of rooms completely accessible, a real rarity at a B&B. She and assistant innkeeper Katie also put out home-baked dessert items in the evening and serve a lovely breakfast.

303 N. Aurora St., Ithaca, NY 14850. www.millerinn.com. ℂ877/256-4553 or 607/256-4553. Fax 607/256-0092. 9 units. $165–$230-double; $215–$250 suite. Rates include full breakfast. AE, DC, MC, V. Free parking. **Amenities:** Wheelchair elevator; rooms for those w/limited mobility. *In room:* A/C, TV, CD player, Jacuzzi (some rooms), Wi-Fi.

Where to Eat

Ithaca is quite cosmopolitan for a small city, and its roster of diverse restaurants of various nationalities and persuasions, everything from Greek to barbecue and cutting-edge vegetarian, reflects its widespread tastes and personality. You can choose to dine on the waterfront, at a college hangout, or out in the country at an elegant inn.

EXPENSIVE

Simply Red Lakeside Bistro ★★ 🎒 CREATIVE AMERICAN BISTRO On the premises of Sheldrake Point Winery on the west bank of Cayuga Lake, Simply Red is the work of the South Africa–born chef Samantha Buyskes at the helm (the restaurant is named for her flaming locks). This terrific bistro was once more bohemian chic, but today it presents a tidy, uptown look. It's still one of the best restaurants in the Finger Lakes. Its fresh menu, best sampled in the "chef's table" prix-fixe menu that changes every week, is all about locally grown produce and regionally raised, free-range, grain-fed meats. Monday nights are "Southern Nights," featuring live music and Southern standards such as fried green tomatoes, shrimp and grits, and cornmeal-crusted, Cajun-spiced catfish, while Friday nights feature tapas, wine, and live tunes. There's another branch of the restaurant at **La Tourelle Resort** (p. 316), and it serves lunch Monday to Friday and brunch Saturday to Sunday.

7448 C.R. 153, Ovid.🄫 **607/532-9401.** www.simplyredbistro.com. Reservations recommended. Main courses $12–$32. DC, MC, V. Apr–June Thurs–Mon 11am–4pm, Mon and Fri 5–9pm.

Taughannock Farms Inn ★ 🍴 AMERICAN This large Victorian inn and estate has an elegant dining room overlooking Cayuga Lake. It has been an inn since 1945, and its four-course meals—for which diners pay a single entree price—are a local favorite. Diners start with an appetizer, which might be roasted almond-and-mushroom pâté; move on to a salad; and then tuck into a timeless entree: New York strip, rack of lamb, prime rib, or the catch of the day. Vegetarians have a single choice: portobello Wellington. Save room for dessert; the menu lists more than a dozen homemade options.

2030 Gorge Rd., Trumansburg.🄫 **607/387-7711.** www.t-farms.com/dining.php. Reservations recommended. Main courses (including 3 additional courses) $25–$39. AE, MC, V. May–Oct Mon–Sat 5–9pm, Sun 3–8pm; Apr and Nov Thurs–Sat 5–9pm, Sun 3–7pm.

MODERATE

Just a Taste Wine & Tapas Bar ★ SPANISH/TAPAS The tantalizingly long list of authentic Spanish tapas and the casual menu of salads, pastas, and creative sandwiches at this popular spot take a back seat to its locally nonpareil wine lists. Choose from among 40 wines by the glass (or taste or half-liter) and many more by the bottle, or check out the interesting international wine flights of five to six wines (on my last visit, there were seven different flights and a few very hard-to-find bottles on offer). If you're not sure about a wine, your server will even give you a "sip," just like getting a taste at the local ice-cream parlor. The main restaurant is a little nondescript, but the backyard garden patio is a very pleasant place to dine—or, let's face it, just drink—in warmer months.

116 N. Aurora St., Ithaca.🄫 **607/277-9463.** Reservations recommended on weekends. Main courses $9–$18; tapas $3–$9. AE, DC, MC, V. Sun–Thurs 5:30–10pm; Fri–Sat 5:30–11pm.

Maxie's Supper Club and Oyster Bar ★★ 🍴 CAJUN/SEAFOOD A lively local late-night favorite, this New Orleans–style restaurant in a former Union hall is a taste of Cajun country in upstate New York. It's a great place to kick back and enjoy some Jambalaya "me-oh-my-ho," po' boy sandwiches, "Jumbo Gumbo," and fresh seafood from the raw bar, as well as good daily specials like fried-fish tacos. I'm happy to report that Maxie's now features a healthy roster of Finger Lakes wines among its wide-ranging list of boutique wines, and a semidry Riesling or Gewürztraminer goes well with Cajun fare. Oyster junkies should check out Happy Hour's half-priced raw oysters and clams every day from 4 to 6pm; on "Chicken-Fried Tuesdays," there are fried-chicken dinners for $12 and live Americana roots music. On Sunday, there's brunch from 11am to 3pm, and live music at night ranges from jazz, blues, and bluegrass to neo-hippie jams.

635 W. State St. (corner of State St. and Rte. 13S), Ithaca. © **607/272-4136.** www.maxies.com. Reservations not accepted. Main courses $11–$23. AE, MC, V. Sun–Thurs 4pm–11pm; Fri–Sat 4pm–midnight.

INEXPENSIVE

Moosewood Restaurant 🍴 😊 GOURMET VEGETARIAN/INTERNATIONAL   Vegetarians and innovative chefs around the world revere the restaurant's recipes (the original *Moosewood Cookbook* is one of the top 10 best-selling cookbooks of all time)—and here is where it all began. This informal restaurant—now in its 4th decade—located in a converted school-building-turned-alternative-mall, is run by a cooperative (or "collective," as they call it) that delivers imaginative vegetarian and healthy cooking. *Bon Appétit* magazine named the Moosewood one of the 13 most influential restaurants of the 20th century. Although the restaurant is by most accounts past its prime, the menu continues to feature fresh, locally grown (and usually organic) produce and whole grains, beans, and soy. Nonvegetarians will be delighted to find fresh fish on the menu, as will parents who can order simple and very cheap kids' plates.

215 N. Cayuga St. (in the DeWitt Building), Ithaca. © **607/273-9610.** www.moosewoodrestaurant.com. Reservations not accepted. Main courses $15–$19. AE, DISC, MC, V. Lunch Mon–Sat 11:30am–3pm; dinner Sun–Thurs 5:30–8:30pm, Fri–Sat 5:30–9pm. Bar and cafe year-round Mon–Thurs 11:30am–8:30pm; Fri–Sat 11:30am–9pm; Sun 5–8:30pm.

Ithaca After Dark

Ithaca has quite a lot of theater and music programs, especially in summer. The **Kitchen Theater,** 116 N. Cayuga St. (© **607/273-4497**), in the historic Greek Revival Clinton House, is a top spot for year-round classic and contemporary theater. In summer, the **Hangar Theatre** ★, just north of downtown, on Taughannock Boulevard/Route 89 (© **607/273-8588**), offers professional, children's, and experimental theater in a renovated municipal airport hangar near Lake Cayuga, and the concessions are from the Simply Red restaurant (p. 318). The **State Theatre** ★★, 111 W. State St. (© **607/277-6633;** www.stateofithaca.com), a historic theater that had been condemned, is still in the process of being fully refurbished; it hosts a wide array of programs from rock and progressive country (Broken Social Scene; Lucinda Williams) to silent movies and plays like *The Vagina Monologues.* **Summer outdoor concert series** are held at The Commons, Taughannock Falls State Park, and the Cornell University quad. For more information on music and performing arts, see **www.ithacaevents.com.** The annual 4-day **Ithaca Festival,** held the first weekend after Memorial Day, features several stages and performances by musicians, painters, dance groups, and more. Visit **www.ithacafestival.org** for more information, or call © **607/273-4646.**

Just a Taste Wine & Tapas Bar (see above) makes a good stop for flights of wine and appetizers before moving on for dinner or a show. Another restaurant with a great bar and a late-night crowd is **Maxie's Supper Club** (see above). **Chanticleer,** 101 W. State St. (© **607/272-9678**)—famous for its neon rooster sign on the corner—is a low-key watering hole with a bit of a gritty feel to go with its pool tables and jukebox. Also near The Commons is **Micawber's Tavern,** 118 N. Aurora (© **607/273-9243**), a lively bar with live pop and rock music and "Happy 15 Minutes" starting at

aurora's AMAZING MAKEOVER

Until recently, the diminutive but picturesque village of Aurora was just a little-known town speck in the Finger Lakes, albeit one with million-dollar views from the east shore of Cayuga Lake. In the past few years, though, it has undergone a startling makeover. For a while, whispers could be heard all over the Finger Lakes: "Did you hear about the town that rich woman bought?" As it turns out, Pleasant Rowland, who attended Wells College in Aurora and made a fortune with her American Girl dolls (which she sold to Mattel), didn't exactly purchase the town. Rather, she decided to direct her philanthropy toward her alma mater, bestowing both the college and the town with a series of gifts, including multimillion-dollar restorations of historic buildings owned by the college. She also bailed out MacKenzie-Childs, a whimsical but previously bankrupt ceramics maker.

Rowland's Aurora Foundation gutted and resurrected the **Aurora Inn** ★★★, 391 Main St., Aurora, NY 13026 (www.aurora-inn.com; ✆ **866/364-8808** or 315/364-8888; fax 315/364-8887; $150–$350 double, $225–$400 suite; May–Oct daily, Nov–Apr Thurs–Sun), owned by the college and overlooking the lake. The foundation completely transformed the 1833 inn into a boutique hotel of rich, though restrained, style. It is now one of the most exquisite country inns in the Finger Lakes region, with gorgeously decorated rooms (several with decks overlooking the lake), a luxurious restaurant (May–Oct), and services to match a much larger hotel (the Aurora Inn has just 10 rooms). Check out special packages and summer events (such as a lake wine cruise) online.

A couple of miles north of town, **MacKenzie-Childs** ★★★, 3260 Rte. 90 (✆ **888/665-1999** or 315/364-6118; www.mackenzie-childs.com), makes uniquely fanciful and brightly colored

handmade ceramics, glassware, and furniture that might be called modern baroque. You'll either love it or hate it (picture chairs with large fishes forming the backs painted with clouds and swirling pastels or fringed, tufted stools with circus-tent stripes). The visitor center presents behind-the-scenes studio tours daily from 9am to 5pm. Visitors can tour the utterly incredible, dreamlike 19th-century **Farmhouse,** done up in high MacKenzie-Childs Victorian style, with four rooms (40 min.; daily 10am–4pm; free admission). For now, the equally spectacular, but even more mind-bending, **Restaurant MacKenzie-Childs** is no longer open for meals or tea. (Hopefully, they'll find a way to make it operational again, because it looks as though it was decorated by someone dreaming of Alice in Wonderland while on acid, and it's not currently visited on the tour.)

The daughter and son-in-law of the original creators and owners of MacKenzie-Childs have opened a fanciful homestead in nearby Kings Ferry as a small and decidedly funky inn and shop. If you like their dinnerware, you'll love staying at **Home Again** ★, 1671 Rte. 90, King Ferry (www.homeagainshop.com/stay-home; ✆ **315/688-8626**), decorated in full-on MacKenzie-Childs style. The six idiosyncratic rooms range from $100 for a childlike space to $200 for the master bedroom suite, which occupies the entire third floor of the house. Breakfast is DIY (do-it-yourself). For reservations, e-mail heatherandnils@gmail.com.

For breakfast or lunch in Aurora, check out the counter or back deck at **Dorie's,** 283 Main St. (✆ **315/364-8818**), a nostalgic ice-cream and soda fountain (Sun–Thurs 7am–8pm; Fri–Sat 7am–9pm), or yummy **Pizza Aurora,** a cute and brightly colored artisanal pie maker across the street in a 1940s garage (Mon–Thurs 11am–8pm; Fri–Sat 11am–10pm; Sun noon–8pm).

5:15pm. If it's a more relaxed drink you're after, **The Baggage Room,** 806 W. Buffalo St. (*C* **607/2721-2609**), a small but atmospheric lounge set in the luggage room of Ithaca's former train station, is a real throwback. Up on the hill in Collegetown near Cornell, **Stella's Martini Bar,** 403 College Ave. (*C* **607/277-1490**), is one of the coolest spots, with live music on weekends.

Ten miles north (on Rte. 96) of Ithaca, in Trumansburg ("T-Burg"), is a handful of bars, including the curiously named live-music pub **Rongovian Embassy to the U.S.** (known to local barflies as the Rongo). Its stage featuring local rock bands and a good selection of beers is located at 1 Main St. (*C* **607/387-3334;** www.rongo. com). It's open until 1am Tuesday to Sunday.

WATKINS GLEN & SOUTHERN/ EASTERN SENECA LAKE ★

28 miles W of Ithaca; 21 miles N of Corning

At the southern tip of Seneca Lake, the deepest and second-longest of the Finger Lakes and the one with the most wineries clustered around it, Watkins Glen is a small town that looms large on the tourism landscape in summer. It is home to Watkins Glen State Park, site of a spectacular gorge and thundering waterfalls—perhaps the single most beautiful natural area in the entire region—as well as the annual NASCAR rally at "The Glen" and Finger Lakes Wine Festival. But even those heavily attended events have a hard time competing with the town's peaceful, picturesque location on the waterfront of Seneca Lake.

The southeast bank of Seneca Lake, which local winemakers only somewhat facetiously call the "Banana Belt," due to its warmer microclimate, is home to several of the Finger Lakes' best wineries and most notable farm-fresh, chef-driven restaurants, as well as a growing number of small inns. In fact, Route 414, which skirts the eastern edge of the lake, is emerging as the restaurant row of the Finger Lakes.

Essentials

GETTING THERE   From the north, take exit 42 off the New York State Thruway (I-90); from the south, take Route 17 (I-86) to Route 14 North.

VISITOR INFORMATION   The **Schuyler County Chamber of Commerce Visitors Center** is at 100 N. Franklin St. (at First St.) in Watkins Glen (*C* **800/607-4552;** www.watkinsglenchamber.com). It's open Monday to Friday from 9am to 5pm.

Exploring Watkins Glen & Southern Seneca Lake

If you can look past the off-putting old salt factory, cluster of low-end retail shops, and trailer campground that mar the southern end of the lake, otherwise-lovely **Seneca Harbor ★★** is a perfect picture. It consists of a marina full of bobbing sailboats and fishing boats, a New England–style red schoolhouse at the end of the public fishing pier, and vineyard-laced hillsides rising from the lake. The boardwalk provides some of the most beautiful views of any vantage point in the Finger Lakes. This part of Seneca Lake is the perfect place to get out on the water on a yacht or sailboat. Most chartered boats set sail from May to the end of October. Check out **Seneca Sailing Adventures,** which sails the 38-foot *Lea Sea Anne I* for private and nonprivate cruises on the lake (ranging from $80 per person to $600 for a full-day private

seneca LAKE WINE TRAIL

The **Seneca Lake Wine Trail** ★★★ (© **877/536-2717**; www.senecalake wine.com) is the biggest in the region, including 35 wineries dotting the shores of Seneca Lake and producing some of the best wines in New York State. Visits to those on the east side of Seneca Lake might easily be combined with a tour of wineries dotting the west bank of Cayuga Lake (p. 312), while those on the west bank of Seneca could be combined with visits to Keuka Lake wineries (p. 336). If you're planning on visiting a number of wineries, consider purchasing "A Riesling to Visit" passport ($12), which gets you a flight of wine samples at each participating winery (one per visit) from May to August. Among the wineries worth visiting for tastings and/ or touring are the following:

EAST BANK
Atwater Estate Vineyards ★
5055 Rte. 414, Hector (© **800/331-7323**; www.atwatervineyards.com). This relatively new winery is situated among some of the area's oldest vineyards. It has a handsome yellow tasting room and gift shop attached to a barn, and a deck with views of Seneca Lake. The wines, with colorful, distinctive labels, have become among those to contend with in the region; try the Gewürztraminer and dry Riesling. In summer, Simply Red Bistro creates "Vine Dining," multicourse dinners that combine wine and local ingredients at the winery (call for schedule). Open May to December Monday to Saturday 10am to 5pm and Sunday from 11am to 5pm; January to April Sunday to Friday noon to 5pm and Saturday 10am to 5pm.

Red Newt Cellars ★★
3675 Tichenor Rd., Hector (© **607/546-4100**; www.rednewt.com). Red Newt Cellars is as much a winery as a restaurant (p. 326). The winery is directed by David Whiting and the restaurant by his wife, the chef Debra Whiting. Red Newt's wines, including a top Riesling reserve and very nice cabernet franc (and even an unexpectedly good Syrah), are recognized as some of the finest in the region, though the winery produces no estate wines (all fruit is purchased). If you've grown tired of small sips of wine, the restaurant's outdoor terrace overlooking vineyards is a terrific place for a more substantial wine flight, glass, or bottle. Open Monday to Saturday 10am to 5pm and Sunday from noon to 5pm.

Hazlitt 1852 Vineyards ★
5712 Rte. 414, Hector (© **888/750-0492** or 607/546-9463; www.hazlitt1852.com). Best known for its party atmosphere, rock-'n'- roll music, and mass-market "Red Cat" wines, this is the place if you just want to have fun and taste some wines. No intimidating wine-snob atmosphere here. It's not

cruise). Call © **607/742-5100** or visit www.senecasailingadventures.com for more information. **Captain Bill's** larger *Seneca Legacy* offers 1-hour sightseeing as well as dinner, lunch, and moonlight cocktail cruises—even a teen cruise with "loud music" ($13–$43 adults, $6–$16 children). A smaller vintage motor vessel, the *Stroller IV*, is also available. Call © **607/535-4541,** or visit www.senecaharborstation.com for reservations and information.

Watkins Glen State Park ★★★, off Route 14 at the south end of the village, is one of the certain highlights of the Finger Lakes. Opened in 1863, the 776-acre park contains a spectacular gorge sculpted in slate, formed more than 12,000 years ago at the end of the last ice age and carved by the flow of Glen Creek ever since, and 19 separate waterfalls. The walking trails in and around the gorge are splendid and just grape juice, though; some wines, for example the 2004 Riesling, are quite fine indeed. Open November to May Monday to Saturday from 10am to 5pm and Sunday from 11am to 5pm; June through October Monday to Saturday 10am to 5:30pm and Sunday from 11am to 5:30pm.

Wagner Vineyards ★ 9322 Rte. 414, Lodi (ⓒ **866/924-6378;** www.wagner vineyards.com). Operating in an unusual octagonal winery, Wagner Vineyards produces 30 wines and a full slate of micro-brew beers, has a gift shop, and offers nice guided tours and full tastings. Open year-round daily 10am to 5pm. There's a pleasant restaurant, Ginny Lee Café, that serves lunch daily from 11am to 4pm; on Friday nights in the summer, live music plays on the terrace overlooking Seneca Lake, and dinner (fish fry or barbecued chicken) is served from 7 to 9pm. It's one of the best evening spots around, popular with both locals and visitors.

Lamoreaux Landing Wine Cellars ★★ 9224 Rte. 414, Lodi (ⓒ **607/582-6011;** www.lamoreauxwine.com). This Napa-style building has floor-to-ceiling windows and views of surrounding vineyards. It has won numerous awards for its serious vinifera wines, including its cabernet franc, Gewürztraminer, chardonnay, and a sparkling blanc de blanc. Open year-round for tastings, Monday to Saturday 10am to 5pm and Sunday noon to 5pm.

WEST BANK

Lakewood Vineyards ★ 4024 Rte. 14, Watkins Glen (ⓒ **607/535-9252;** www. lakewoodvineyards.com). Lakewood Vineyards is a family-run, friendly, low-key winery with beautiful views, good Rieslings and chardonnays, and a surprising pinot noir. Open year-round Monday through Saturday from 10am to 5pm and Sunday from noon to 5pm.

Glenora Wine Cellars ★ 5435 Rte. 14, Dundee (ⓒ **800/243-5513** or 607/243-5511; www.glenora.com). A great variety of wines are made here. It has terrific views of Seneca Lake and vineyards as well as a picnic area and large tasting and gift shop. The winery operates a very nice restaurant and inn overlooking vines and the lake. Open year-round daily from 10am to 5pm (extended hours in summer).

Anthony Road Wine Company ★★ 1020 Anthony Rd., Penn Yan (ⓒ **800/559-2182** or 607/243-5511; www.anthonyroadwine.com). This has quickly become one of Seneca's finest producers. In a large, airy space overlooking the lake, it shows off its wide range of serious wines, including a delicious dry Riesling and rosé. The select, low-production Martini-Reinhardt wines are standouts—especially the Riesling and trockenbeeren. Open year-round Monday through Saturday from 10am to 5pm and Sunday from noon to 5pm.

accessible to almost all walkers; you can walk right in behind the 60-foot drop of Central Cascade. It takes about an hour to walk the gorge trail, with a steep climb at the end. Shuttle buses ($3) return walkers to the entrance, or you can walk back along the Indian trail, which is parallel to the gorge but flatter. Hikers should wear appropriate hiking shoes because the trails can be wet and slick. Park entrance is $6 per vehicle. Call ⓒ **607/535-4511,** or visit www.nysparks.state.ny.us for more information.

The **Watkins Glen International Race Track** ★★, 2790 County Rte. 16 (ⓒ **866/461-RACE** [7223] or 607/535-2481; www.theglen.com), opens up with car-club events and races in June and July, including the SCCA Glen Nationals, but it really heats up at the end of the first week of August with the NASCAR Nextel Cup

Among wineries along the Lake that are not official members of the Seneca Lake Wine Trail, but are still very much worth visiting, are these:

EAST BANK

Damiani Wine Cellars ★ 4704 Rte. 414, Burdett (✆ **607/546-5557**; www.damianiwinecellars.com). This tiny operation has crafted some very good wines since its first vintage in 2004. I particularly liked the cabernet franc and meritage (a Bordeaux-style blend). Open daily 11am to 5pm.

Standing Stone ★ 9934 Rte. 414, Hector (✆ **607/582-6051**; www.standingstonewines.com). This small, hands-on family winery includes a pretty yellow farmhouse, gardens, and a cheese room with gorgeous lake views from the deck. Standing Stone makes nice whites, including the Riesling and reserve chardonnay, and an outstanding Vidal ("ice") dessert wine. Open year-round daily 11:30am to 5pm (until 6pm Sat).

Shalestone Vineyards ★★ 9681 Rte. 414, Lodi (✆ **607/582-6600**; www.shalestonevineyards.com). In these parts known for their Rieslings and chardonnays, winemaker Rob Thomas and his wife make only reds. "Red is all we do" is their slogan. Their small-batch, handcrafted reds are surprisingly excellent; try the Harmony, a cabernet franc/merlot blend, and the cabernet franc. Open June through September Thursday to Monday noon to 5pm; April Saturday noon to 5pm; May Friday to Sunday noon to 5pm.; October Friday 1 to 5pm.

Silver Thread Vineyard ★★ 1401 Caywood Rd., Lodi (✆ **607/582-6116**; www.silverthreadwine.com). Though tiny and easy to overlook, this is a winery to watch. The owner is committed to organic, artisanal winemaking, and he produces six very nice wines, including a dry Riesling, Gewürztraminer, and even a burgundy-style pinot noir. Look for signs indicating the long gravel road that wends toward the lake. Open May through November Saturday and Sunday from noon to 5pm; other times by appointment only.

WEST BANK

Hermann J. Wiemer Vineyard ★★★ 3962 Rte. 14, Dundee (✆ **800/371-7971** or 607/243-7971; www.wiemer.com). This is one of the Finger Lakes' standout wineries (and my personal favorite), headed by a dedicated German transplant who produces very serious, elegant white wines in the European cool-climate tradition. His dry Johannisberg Riesling, Gewürztraminer, and semidry Riesling go toe-to-toe with my other favorite winery, Dr. Frank's (on Keuka). Also not to be missed are the late-harvest Rieslings, which make excellent dessert wines. Tastings here are intimate; if you're serious about wine, this is a must-stop. Open year-round Monday through Saturday 10am to 5pm and Sunday 11am to 5pm.

series, a race that draws many thousands and fills every hotel and inn and campsite for hundreds of miles in New York State's largest sporting weekend. Other racing events are held in summer, including the Vintage Grand Prix in September, but none comes close to NASCAR. The new IRL IndyCar Series is held at the end of September. The other huge event in town, also held at the WGI, is the annual **Finger Lakes Wine Festival** ★★★ (✆ **866/461-7223** or 607/535-2481; www.flwinefest.com), held in mid-July. Most of the local 80-plus wineries are on hand, along with musicians, craft vendors, exhibits from the Corning Museum of Glass, food and wine seminars, and even a toga party. As you can imagine, plenty of wine is consumed and people get pretty festive. Advance tickets (and accommodations) are a must for most of the events at WGI, so plan ahead (way in advance for NASCAR, as much as a year or more). Tickets ($30; $40 for 2 days) for the wine festival are available at many of the local wineries. The largest concentration of wineries in the region is clustered about Seneca Lake, and many of the wineries on the **Seneca Lake Wine Trail** are just a cork's throw from Watkins Glen; for more on that collective and wine tours, see the sidebar on p. 322.

On the east side of Seneca Lake is **Skyland Gallery & Café** ★, Route 414, Lodi (© **607/546-5050;** www.skylandfarm.net), which owner Barbara Hummel describes as a "fantasy land of high art, exquisite craft, joy, and dessert." The large gallery space shows off the unique works, including pottery, jewelry, and wood toys, of 300 local and regional artisans, all part of a compound that consists of a renovated barn (with a two-story tree soaring through the cafe), gardens, and animal pens. It's the kind of place that will entertain both kids and parents for at least a couple of hours, and the cafe makes an excellent lunch pit stop, with nice sandwiches, salads, and incredible gelato and other desserts.

Where to Stay

Watkins Glen proper isn't loaded with great lodgings, though options near the lake include sleeping at a winery right on the lake's west bank or at one of the growing number of small inns along the east bank. If you're arriving for NASCAR or the Finger Lakes Wine Festival, you may have to look far and wide for accommodations, so be sure to look at hotels and inns listed in other sections of this chapter; those in and near Geneva, Corning, Elmira, Ithaca, and Hammondsport are all easy drives from Watkins Glen. See www.schuylerny.com, or call © **800/607-4552** for assistance in getting a room. If you want to camp, check out the sites at **Watkins Glen State Park** (© **607/535-4511**), **Clute Memorial Park** (© **607/535-4438**), or the "kutely" spelled **KOA Kampground & Kabins,** located on Route 414 (www.watkinsglenkoa. com; © **800/562-7430**), which has a heated pool and good bathrooms.

The Fox and the Grapes 🍇 Young and friendly James Pellegrini—who may not seem like the stereotype of Victorian innkeeper—oversees this homey B&B. It's ideally located, just up from the east bank of Seneca Lake, near plenty of the area's best wineries and restaurants. The house is a large white 1885 Victorian manor with great lake views from the terrace and back room (the deck is the place to be for sunset). Accommodations are elegant, but not overly fussy, with relatively sedate colors and furnishings, but bedding could stand to be upgraded. Those who might otherwise be disinclined to check into a Victorian B&B will be happy to see the huge-screen TV and collection of DVDs in the massive living room (there are no TVs in rooms) that boasts a fireplace and an entire floor of Persian rugs.

9496 State Rte. 414, Lodi, NY 14860. www.thefoxandthegrapes.com. © **607/582-7528.** 5 units. $110–$175 double. Rates include full breakfast. AE, DC, MC, V. Free parking. *In room:* A/C, Wi-Fi.

Idlwilde Inn ★ 🛏 This sprawling, 18-room, 1892 Victorian mansion features a great veranda, attractive gardens, and stupendous lake views. There's an interesting mix of rooms, from the impressively grand to small, affordable, and simply furnished (the cheapest share a bathroom); note that some furnishings and linens are a bit worn, in need of updating. The master bedroom, no. 6, is stunningly large, like an absolutely palatial New York City apartment, with its own deck, two fireplaces, and two sitting rooms, while no. 10 has a sitting room in a circular turret and a private deck with excellent lake views. Two new rooms with cathedral ceilings have been added upstairs in the carriage house. The inn, run by a charming European couple and her in-laws, is open seasonally from the end of April to November.

1 Lakeview Ave., Watkins Glen, NY 14891. www.idlwildeinn.com.© **607/535-3081.** 5 units. $105–$265 double. Rates include full breakfast. AE, DC, MC, V. Free parking. *In room:* A/C.

The Inn at Glenora Wine Cellars ★   At Glenora, perched on the west bank of Seneca Lake and just 8 miles north of Watkins Glen, wine lovers are in for a treat: They can sleep at a winery. This modern hostelry is set amid acres of vineyards and only steps from the tasting room. The location is by far the hotel's biggest selling point: All the comfortable, if somewhat plain rooms—large and equipped with Stickley furniture—have expansive, unimpeded views of the water from either private terraces or patios, the real reason for staying here. "Vintner's select" rooms have king-size beds, Jacuzzi tubs, and electric fireplaces. The inn also has an excellent restaurant and easy access to other Seneca Lake wineries and major attractions. Families and vacationing couples may wish to inquire about the two-bedroom vineyard cottage, with a fully equipped kitchen and vineyard and lake views.

5435 Rte. 14, Dundee, NY 14837. www.glenora.com/Inn.© **800/243-5513.** 30 units. Sun–Thurs $159–$259 double; Fri–Sat $209–$289. Rates include full breakfast. AE, DC, MC, V. Free parking. **Amenities:** Restaurant; bar. *In room:* A/C, TV.

The Pearl of Seneca Lake B&B ★★★   This large country home is perched on 14 acres (with 385 ft. of lake frontage) on the west side of Seneca Lake, just outside of Dundee. The secluded location, with a long nature trail through meadows and woods, is the perfect place to get away from it all but still be close enough to hit the Finger Lakes wineries. Rooms are spacious and airy, with clean decor, furniture crafted by local Mennonite craftsmen, and an abundance of natural light. All have access to either private decks or a long porch. The owners, Mary and Peter Muller, are gracious hosts, and they provide great amenities, such as refrigerators stocked with waters and sodas, and afternoon baked goods. Breakfast is all-you-can-eat (and Mary is a baker who makes all her own breads, scones, and cookies). There's great swimming from the lovely, long dock, and a canoe and rowboat. The Merlot Room, the only one on the first floor, is fully handicapped-accessible, with ramps at both entrances.

4827 Red Cedar Lane, Dundee, NY 14837. www.thepearlofsenecalake.com.© **866/507-3275.** 4 units. Nov–Mar weekdays $130, weekends $150 double; Apr–Oct weekdays $170, weekends $180 double. Rates include full breakfast. AE, DC, MC, V. Free parking. *In room:* A/C, fridge, Wi-Fi, microwave.

Where to Eat

Some of the finest dining in the Finger Lakes is found around the edges of Seneca Lake, with a handful of unique, personal restaurants overlooking the shores. The restaurants do a good job of pairing their menus with local wines.

EXPENSIVE

The Bistro at Red Newt Cellars ★★★ ☺ AMERICAN BISTRO   On the premises of one of the region's top wineries, this appetizing bistro restaurant is an excellent place to match food and wine. It's a family affair at Red Newt: The chef and winemaker are a husband-wife team, Debra and David Whiting. The restaurant's covered terrace overlooks vineyards and farmland and is a particularly fine spot for lunch. Debra makes creative entrees like lamb chops with mint-and-macadamia-nut crust in red-wine sauce; grilled bacon-wrapped pork tenderloin stuffed with chèvre, pork sausage, and chard; and comfort food like white lasagna. Sample from eight different Finger Lakes wine flights, and a comprehensive list of local wines by the bottle. You'll find live acoustic music during the Winelovers' night (Wed May–Oct, and Thurs Feb–Apr and Nov–Dec), when there's an extensive selection of wines by the glass and half-priced bottles. Lunch is casual, but still delicious, featuring incredibly fresh salads and sandwiches. There's even a "Little Newts" menu for the kids.

3675 Tichenor Rd., Hector.© **607/546-4100.** www.rednewt.com. Reservations recommended for dinner. Main courses $21–$32; prix-fixe "chef's menu" $60. AE, MC, V. Daily noon–4pm and Wed–Sun 5–9pm.

Suzanne Fine Regional Cuisine ★★★ 🏫 NEW AMERICAN   To my mind, it fits the bill for what this wine region cries out for: uncomplicated, fresh, perfectly prepared dishes, in an elegant, even romantic, country atmosphere. Run by Chef Suzanne and her husband, Bob, the restaurant inhabits the first floor of a handsome 1903 farmhouse, in a peaceful spot with pristine views of Seneca Lake from the veranda and front tables (it's not uncommon to see guests get up from their tables with glasses of wine in hand to inspect the sunset). The menu is small, and changes frequently, but you can't go wrong with items like wild Alaskan king salmon with corn salsa, or a perfectly cooked filet mignon with potato purée and chanterelle ragout. The terrific homemade desserts—or cheese plate—pair perfectly with a Finger Lakes Riesling or ice wine from a winery just down the road (there are 40-odd local wines on the list). Open seasonally, from the end of April to mid-November.

9013 Rte. 414, Hector.© **607/582-7545.** www.suzannefrc.com. Reservations required. Main courses $23–$33. MC, V. Apr–May Thurs–Sun 5–9pm; June to mid-Nov Wed–Sun 5–9pm.

MODERATE

Dano's Heuriger ★★★ 🍴 AUSTRIAN   The newest addition to the dining scene is a modern take on the traditional Viennese wine garden or tavern (known as a *heuriger*). The Austrian chef Dano Hutnik and his wife, Karen Gilman, have created a challenging but relaxed, hip eatery, where patrons can sample small plates of Austrian specialties, such as charcuterie, sausages, smoked and poached fish, and roasted meats, all of which can be easily paired with either Finger Lakes or Austrian wines. The modern minimalist architecture of the restaurant—something akin to a contemporary bunker with massive overhead lamps and large windows—is fairly radical in these parts. Desserts are emphatically traditional, including strudel, Linzer torte, and *rigo jansci*—but I'll let the waiter describe the last item.

9564 Rte. 414, Lodi.© **607/582-7555.** www.danosonseneca.com. Reservations recommended. Main courses $8–$20. MC, V. Sun–Mon and Wed–Thurs noon–8:30pm; Fri–Sat noon–9pm; call for winter hours.

Seneca Harbor Station AMERICAN/SEAFOOD   This spot, in a former 19th-century train station, has the distinct advantage of fantastic views of the marina at the southern end of Seneca Lake. A casual bar and restaurant, it's a good stop for an informal lunch, like chicken Florentine, and classic dinner items such as seafood pastas, grilled meats, and fresh-fish dishes and platters (such as rainbow trout Florentine). Nothing fancy, but reliable, and with those dockside views, it's a place to linger.

3 N. Franklin St., Watkins Glen.© **607/535-6101.** Reservations not accepted. Main courses $10–$35. AE, MC, V. Daily 11:30am–3:30pm and 4:30–9pm.

Stonecat Café ★★ 🏫 ☺ REGIONAL ORGANIC/BISTRO   Housed in a former roadside fruit stand, this cool, relaxed restaurant is not only the hippest joint in the area, but also one of the best. The renovated interior has just the right touch of shabby chic, but the deck overlooking vineyards and with distant views toward Seneca Lake is my favorite place to watch early evening turn into night. The menu

11

THE FINGER LAKES REGION

Watkins Glen & Southern/Eastern Seneca Lake

features organic local produce and meats, with a specialty of house-smoked meats and fish. I'm a huge fan of the pulled-pork barbecue, slow-cooked for 8 hours on grape and apple wood, and the cornmeal-crusted catfish. There's a Wednesday pub-night menu and a kids' menu too. The wine and beer lists are exclusively from New York State. Sunday is jazz brunch, a great time to linger over the views of the vineyards. Open seasonally, from the end of April to October.

5315 Rte. 414, Hector. © **607/546-5000.** www.stonecatcafe.com. Reservations recommended. Main courses $15–$24. AE, MC, V. Apr–Oct Wed 5–9pm; Thurs–Sat noon–4:30pm and 5–9pm; Sun 10:30am–3pm and 5–9pm.

Veraisons Restaurant CONTINENTAL   On-site at the Glenora winery (and inn), this handsome, modern space not only is in the midst of vineyards, but also boasts cathedral ceilings, a large stone fireplace, and panoramic views of Seneca Lake. If the weather is good, dining on the outdoor terrace is essential. The menu combines traditional French cooking with regional ingredients. On one visit, I had a very nice roasted-pork roulade, stuffed with mushrooms and served with roasted garlic-cheddar mashed potatoes. Many of the dishes are, appropriately, prepared with wine, and the wine list focuses on the house and other Finger Lakes wines. But on Friday nights, it's time for a fish fry and microbrews.

5435 Rte. 14, Dundee. © **607/243-9500.** www.glenora.com. Reservations recommended. Main courses $16–$32. AE, MC, V. Daily 11:30am–3:30pm; Mon–Thurs 5–9pm; Fri–Sat 5–10pm; Sun 4–9pm.

Watkins Glen & Seneca Lake After Dark

Perhaps the best option in Watkins Glen is to hang with locals at **The Crooked Rooster Brewpub** ★, 29 N. Franklin St. (© **607/535-9797**), which serves up its own Rooster Fish craft ales, plus a good list of Finger Lakes wines, live music, and pub grub. Around the bend of the east bank of Seneca Lake, though, there are three surprising options about 10 miles from town. One is the live music on Friday and Saturday nights (from jazz and blues to folk) at **Stonecat Café** ★★, a cool restaurant near Hector (recommended above). Another is **Big Johnsons,** 800 Rte. 414, Hector (© **607/546-5800**), a congenial roadside bar that's not so far removed from a Texas honky-tonk or roadhouse blues bar. It's got stuffed moose heads and other taxidermy, and a large and rocking bar, with tables out front where the regulars tend to gather. Big Johnsons is the big draw for locals, who come to knock back beers and listen to live rock and country bands on weekends. The crowd isn't just kids—there are plenty of older "friendly folks," as the sign outside says. Wagner Vineyards features live music outdoors on Friday evenings at **Ginny Lee Café,** 9322 Rte. 414, Lodi (© **866/924-6378**), a fun spot that's a big draw for locals and visitors alike.

CORNING ★ & ELMIRA

250 miles NW of New York City; 150 miles E of Niagara Falls; 90 miles SE of Rochester

Two towns just south of the Finger Lakes proper give travelers a taste of something different in this region known for its unique bodies of water and pastoral charms. Corning is a small town of just 12,000 people, but as the headquarters of the Fortune 500 Company Corning Inc., it's a very big deal in the Finger Lakes region. Quite literally, it's the town that Corning built; the company, the original makers of Corning-Ware, Pyrex, and now high-tech materials like fiber optics, has employed as much as half the town's population. Corning was once known as "crystal city" for its concentration of glassworks, and today glass remains the town's calling card. One of the Finger Lakes' biggest attractions is the world-renowned Corning Museum of Glass.

Elmira, just to the east, is a largely blue-collar town, and though it serves as a southern gateway to the Finger Lakes, it doesn't figure as a stop on many itineraries. However, it offers a handful of nice surprises. Home to Elmira College, the town is known in select circles as the "soaring capital of the United States," a reference to its important place in aviation history. It also makes much of its association with the legendary writer and humorist Mark Twain, who wrote many of his most famous works while summering in Elmira. Fans of late-19th-century architecture will also delight in the surprising concentration of Victorian homes; Elmira is said to have more per capita than any other area in North America.

Essentials

GETTING THERE

BY PLANE   **Elmira-Corning Regional Airport** (ELM), 276 Sing Sing Rd., Horseheads (© **607/795-0402;** www.ecairport.com), serviced by Northwest and US Airways, is 12 miles from downtown Corning.

BY CAR   Corning is directly off Route 17/I-86 and a straight shot along Route 414 south of Watkins Glen; from the south, take Route 15. Elmira is off Route 17/I-86, just 20 minutes east of Corning.

BY BUS   Trailways (© **607/734-2001;** www.trailways.com) travels to Elmira and its terminal at 100 E. Church St.

VISITOR INFORMATION   The **Steuben County Conference & Visitors Bureau** is located at 1 W. Market St., Corning (© **866/946-3386** or 607/936-6544; www.corningfingerlakes.com). The **Chemung County Chamber of Commerce** is located at 400 E. Church St., Elmira (© **800/MARK-TWAIN** [627-5892]; www. chemungchamber.org).

GETTING AROUND   The Corning Museum of Glass operates a **free shuttle service** daily from 8am to 6pm, from the museum along Cedar Street to Market Street and the Rockwell Museum, and back, allowing visitors to park for free at either museum.

Exploring Corning

Corning Inc.'s major gift to the city, the **Corning Museum of Glass ★★★** (I-86, exit 46; © **800/732-6845** or 607/937-5371; www.cmog.org) is the premier and most comprehensive collection of historic and art glass in the world. Anyone with an interest in glass (even if that doesn't describe you, you're almost certain to be surprised and engaged) could spend many hours or even days here; it is quite literally dazzling. On view are 35,000 glass pieces representing 35 centuries of glass craftsmanship, beginning with a piece dating from 1411 B.C. There are also a gallery of glass sculpture and a glass innovation center, with ingeniously designed interactive exhibits that depict the use of glass in technology. The museum, now entering its 6th decade, is anything but static: It offers indoor and outdoor hot-glass demonstrations, glassmaking workshops, and some of the best shopping to be found, with a sprawling array of shops dealing in glass, crystal, and jewelry. Crystal fans familiar with Steuben glass (which originated in Corning), and particularly the work of glass artist Frederick Carder, will delight in finding a huge gallery of his works.

The museum is especially well designed for children, who usually can't get enough of the interactive science exhibits and opportunities to handle telescopes and peer through a periscope that "sees" out the roof of the building. A walk-in glass workshop allows visitors to make their very own glass souvenirs. The museum is open daily from 9am to 5pm; May through Labor Day it's open daily until 8pm. Admission is $14 for adults, $12 for seniors and military, $13 for students, and free for children 18 and under. Audio (iPod touch) guides are $3. With one paid admission, you are allowed to visit again one time in the same calendar year for free. A combination ticket ($18 for adults, $16 for seniors and military, $17 for students, free for kids and teens 19 and under) includes admission to CMoG and the Rockwell Museum (see below). The museum also operates a free shuttle service from the museum to Market Street, downtown. Plan on spending about 3 hours at the Corning Museum of Glass, and more if you plan to take part in workshops.

The **Rockwell Museum of Western Art ★★**, 111 Cedar St. (© **607/937-5386;** www.rockwellmuseum.org), which occupies the former City Hall, maintains an excellent collection of both historic and contemporary western and Native American art, as well as one of the best-designed small museums in the Northeast. An inviting design of bold colors and gorgeous woods inside the shell of a neo-Romanesque building, the museum features daring juxtapositions that work surprisingly well, including a number of fantastic pieces by Native Americans. The second floor has a lodge room with a fireplace, couches, and chairs, and feels like it's been ripped from a classic western lodge. A neat idea for children: the color-coded "art backpacks" that come equipped with games and lesson and drawing books, making the museum an especially interactive place. Museum hours are as follows: July through Labor Day daily from 9am to 8pm; September through June Monday to Saturday 9am to 5pm and Sunday 11am to 5pm. Admission is $6.50 for adults, $5.50 for seniors and students, and free for children and teens 19 and under. See the discount combination admissions to the Corning Museum of Glass and the Rockwell above. Allow an hour or two.

Those hungry to get outdoors south of the lakes can get up in the air. **Balloons Over Corning,** 352 Brewster St., Painted Post (© **607/937-3910**), has organized hot-air balloons with beautiful views over Corning and the Finger Lakes area for the past 15 years. Flights take off 2 hours before sunset in summer. And spectacular **glider flights** are available at the Harris Hill Soaring Center in Elmira; see the sidebar on p. 56.

Shopping

Corning, devastated by floods in 1972, rebuilt the picturesque centerpiece of its downtown, Market Street, which, today, retains a 19th-century appearance and is alive with glass galleries, gift shops, and restaurants and bars. **Vitrix Hot Glass Studio,** 77 W. Market St. (© **607/936-2488**); **Lost Angel Glass,** 79 W. Market St. (© **607/937-3578**); and **West End Gallery,** 12 W. Market St. (© **607/936-2011**), are three of the best galleries representing the American studio glass movement, though a number of others are easily discovered as you walk about town. The two major museums in town, the Rockwell Museum of Western Art and the Corning Museum of Glass, both have excellent on-site shops. The latter is a must for anyone with the slightest interest in glass; items range from inexpensive glass souvenirs to one-of-a-kind glass art and Steuben crystal pieces.

Where to Stay

Corning can get pretty crowded, both with business travelers and when big events occur, such as the Corning Classic LPGA golf tournament, the NASCAR race, the Finger Lakes Wine Festival in nearby Watkins Glen, and even Cornell University's graduation. In addition to the chain motels below, you might check out one of these in town: **Comfort Inn** (66 W. Pulteney St.; ℂ **607/962-1515**), **Days Inn** (23 Riverside Dr.; www.comfortinn.com; ℂ **607/936-9370**), and **Staybridge Suites** (201 Townley Ave.; www.staybridge.com/sbscorningny; ℂ **877/238-8889** or 607/936-7800). For campers, there is the **Hickory Hill Family Camping Resort,** Route 17/I-86, exit 38 (www.hickoryhillcampresort.com; ℂ **800/760-0947**).

Hillcrest Manor ★★★ 🍴 One of the finest B&Bs in the Finger Lakes, this 1890 Greek Revival mansion, an impressively grand structure of massive pillars, porches, and terraces, sits in a quiet residential neighborhood up the hill from downtown Corning. Rooms are huge and decorated with great, luxurious taste by two gentlemen, art-glass and antiques collectors who moved to Corning from Seattle. The house has stately parlors, an elegant candlelit dining room, and a palatial cedar stairway. Two of the rooms, the Master Bedroom and the Honeymoon Suite, are almost ridiculously large; I can envision myself relaxing here for days on end. Don't be put off by the inn's website, which is as amateur as the house is elegant. Children 11 and under are not generally permitted.

227 Cedar St., Corning, NY 14830. www.corninghillcrestmanor.com. ℂ **607/936-4548.** 5 units. $165 double; $200 suite. Rates include full breakfast. MC, V. Free parking. *In room:* A/C, TV, dataport.

Radisson Hotel Corning 🍴 This large and well-run hotel has an excellent location: tucked into a small campus of sorts at the east end of Market Street, just steps from all the restaurants, bars, and shops. It is the only full-service hotel in downtown Corning, a reason for its popularity with business travelers, though with its indoor pool and on-site restaurant, it's also a good place for families and other leisure travelers. Rooms are spacious and attractively appointed, with nice bedding, large work desks, and high-speed Internet access, and there are pet-friendly rooms.

125 Denison Pkwy. E., Corning, NY 14830. www.radisson.com/corningny. ℂ **800/395-7046** or 607/962-5000. Fax 607/962-4166. 173 units. $154–$209 double; $235 suite. AE, DC, DISC, MC, V. Free parking. **Amenities:** Restaurant; bar; fitness center; outdoor Jacuzzi; indoor heated pool. *In room:* A/C, TV, Wi-Fi.

Where to Eat

Virtually all the places to eat out in town are on Market Street, which makes it easy to stroll up and down the blocks while shopping and choose one of about a half-dozen restaurants. In addition to the restaurants below, you might also consider **The Cantina,** 111 Cedar St. (ℂ **607/974-8226**), a Tex-Mex/Southwestern restaurant on the premises of the Rockwell Museum, and the microbrewery **Market Street Brewing Co.,** 63 Market St. (ℂ **607/936-2337**), which offers tavern fare as well as live music on Friday nights to go along with its craft beers.

The Cellar ★ TAPAS/WINE BAR This vibrantly colored, contemporary-looking, loungelike space is dedicated to wines (including 40 by the glass), martinis, and small plates. House specialties include ahi tuna ribbons in a kaffir lime ginger marinade, and a summer lobster roll, but you can also go big with paella or a dry-aged New York strip. There's live music every Friday night and happy hours Monday to Saturday from 4 to 7pm, when the small joint can get quite noisy.

21 W. Market St. ℂ **607/377-5552.** www.corningwinebar.com. Reservations recommended. Main courses $10–$31. AE, DISC, MC, V. Mon–Sat 4–11pm.

The Gaffer Grille and Taproom ☺ INTERNATIONAL/GRILLED MEATS
This casual eatery and bar, with some nice, cozy booths set against exposed-brick walls,
is one of the most popular among Corning residents. It features a pretty standard menu,
with lots of steaks, ribs, and chicken, along with other items like crushed peppercorn
yellowfin tuna and cheese tortellini with vodka sauce, but dishes are consistently well
prepared, and the ambience is very agreeable. The taproom, with a more casual menu,
serves dinner until 11pm. The half-dozen items on the kids' menu should be just the
thing to revive most children after a tiring day at the Corning Museum of Glass.

58 W. Market St. ✆ **607/962-4649.** www.gaffergrilleandtaproom.com. Reservations recommended on
weekends. Main courses $10–$30. AE, DISC, MC, V. Mon–Fri 11:30am–10pm; Sat 4:30–10pm. Taproom
Mon–Sat 11:30am–11pm.

Three Birds Restaurant ★★ AMERICAN BISTRO   This upscale restaurant,
run by a husband-wife team on Corning's historic Market Street, is tops for dining in
this agreeable town and is popular with locals for a special night out. On its creative
American menu, signature dishes include excellent salads; crispy Chesapeake crab
and corn cakes; and honey-roasted, pecan-crusted pork tenderloin. Lots of Finger
Lakes wines make the nice but manageable list. Early diners and bargain hunters
should check out the Early Bird specials from 4 to 6pm, which feature half-priced
"smaller portion" entrees. One side of the high-ceilinged restaurant is a lively bar
known for its excellent martinis, with a special bar menu (and free Mediterranean
olive bar on Thurs evenings).

73 E. Market St. ✆ **607/936-8862.** www.threebirdsrestaurant.com. Reservations recommended. Main
courses $16–$42. AE, DISC, MC, V. Mon–Sat 4–10pm.

Corning After Dark

There's not a whole lot going on in Corning after dark, though a couple of bars on
Market Street—once a long lineup of bars in the blue-collar, pre–great flood of
1972—draw locals and visitors alike. **Market Street Brewing Co.,** 63 Market St.
(✆ **607/936-2337**), and **Glory Hole Pub,** 74 Market St. (✆ **607/962-1474**), are
both watering-hole-cum-restaurants. **Palace Theatre** ★, 17 W. Market St. (✆ **607/
936-3844;** www.corningpalacetheatre.com), is a historic movie theater showing current independent and art house releases.

Exploring Elmira

Although Elmira's most famous son currently is Tommy Hilfiger, the designer who
co-opted red, white, and blue from Ralph Lauren and successfully marketed his clothing to the hip-hop and rock-'n'-roll communities, the city was once home to a more
important cultural figure. Mark Twain, born Samuel Clemens, met and married his
wife, Olivia Langdon, in Elmira, and he spent 20 summers in the area. From his study
at Quarry Farm, he composed some of his most famous works, including *The Adventures of Huckleberry Finn* and *The Adventures of Tom Sawyer*. On the pretty campus of
Elmira College, 1 Park Place (btw. Fifth St. and Washington Ave.), is the Center for
Mark Twain Studies (closed to the public) as well as **Twain's original study** from
1874, now a literary landmark, with several original artifacts, including his chair, photographs taken at the farm, and some documents. The study, located next to the pond,
is open to visitors mid-June through August Monday to Saturday from 9am to 5pm
(✆ **607/735-1941;** free admission). Twain, his wife, and their children are buried at
Elmira's **Woodlawn Cemetery** (Walnut St.; ✆ **607/732-0151;** daily 8am–9pm).
Twain himself wrote many of the epitaphs on the tombstones. Nearby, **Woodlawn**

National Cemetery hides a little-known secret: the graves of some 3,000 Confederate soldiers, making it the northernmost Confederate grave site (at one time, there were about 12,000 POWs in Elmira, which earned it the sobriquet "Hellmira," at least down south).

Architecture buffs may be amazed by the collection of Victorian, Greek, Tudor, and Georgian Revival houses, built in the mid-to-late 19th and early-20th centuries. Pick up a copy of *A Walking Tour of the History Near Westside* (available at the Tourism Information Office and several inns and hotels), which spotlights and describes a few dozen homes along West Church and West Water streets, and to a lesser degree, Gray, Walnut, and Grove streets, all just north of the Chemung River.

Women Make the Grade

Founded in 1855, **Elmira College**, off exit 56 of Route 17/I-86, was the first exclusive women's college and the first institution of higher learning to grant women degrees that were equal in stature to those awarded men.

About 5 miles north of Elmira, the **National Warplane Museum ★**, 17 Aviation Dr., Horseheads (© **607/739-8200;** www.wingsofeagles.com), is the place to see 37 original military flying machines from World War I to the Gulf War. Even better than seeing the planes up close, though, is the opportunity to go up in a vintage aircraft—whether a PT-17 or a B-17 bomber, known as "Fuddy Duddy." Flights at the **Elmira Soaring School** aren't cheap (starting at $350 per person; Apr–Nov only; reservations required), but they can be the thrill of a lifetime. The museum is open Tuesday through Saturday from 10am to 4pm; admission is $7 for adults, $5.50 for seniors, and $4.50 for children 6 to 17.

The **National Soaring Museum ★**, Harris Hill, 51 Soaring Hill Dr. (just south of Rte. 17, exit 49, 50, or 51; © **607/734-3128;** www.soaringmuseum.org), has the country's largest collection of gliders and sailplanes, which takes visitors through the history of motorless flight. Next door, the **Harris Hill Soaring Center** (© **607/734-0641;** www.harrishillsoaring.org) offers graceful **sailplane rides ★★★** in either a Schweizer 2-33 trainer or a Schleicher ASK-21 high-performance sailplane ($75–$85; late June to Aug daily 10am–6pm and Apr to late June and Sept–Oct Sat–Sun 10am–6pm), a unique and mesmerizing experience (see "Soaring Over the Finger Lakes," below). Flights soar after takeoff from Harris Hill, providing stunning views of the valley. The Soaring Center has one of the most active youth clubs in the country, and several of the pilots are teenagers and college kids. The museum is open daily from 10am to 5pm (closed weekends Jan–Feb). Admission is $7.50 for adults, $6 for seniors, $4.50 for children 7 to 17, free for children 6 and under, and $209 for families of four.

Tip: One of the best ways to see a lot of Elmira in a short time is to hop aboard **The Elmiran,** a green trolley car that makes daily runs July and August, with a narrated history of the town, Mark Twain, and more. Catch it at the Holiday Inn Riverview, 760 E. Water St. (© **607/734-4211;** $2 adults, free for children 11 and under).

Where to Stay & Eat

Elmira is largely home to generic hotels and motels. By far the best place to stay in Elmira is **The Painted Lady B&B ★**, 520 W. Water St., Elmira, NY 14905 (www.thepaintedlady.net; © **607/846-3500;** fax 607/732-7515), a very large and meticulously decorated 1875 Victorian mansion in the heart of the historic district. Accommodations are massive, are big on frills, and have luxurious bedding and bathrooms for $165 to $195 for a double or $230 for a suite. The home-cooked breakfasts are

Soaring Over the Finger Lakes

Taking to the sky in a motorless glider plane, or sailplane, is a singular experience, especially in a region as pretty as the Finger Lakes. Flights are available to visitors (Apr–Oct, weather permitting) at the **Harris Hill Soaring Center** (© 607/734-0641; www.harrishill soaring.org), located between Elmira and Corning, just south of Interstate 86. I recently took to the air with a young pilot who'd been flying since he was 13 (er, yes, don't expect to fly it yourself!). While it's a thrill to glide silently above the patchwork quilt of farms and small towns along the Chemung River, it's really a trip if your pilot decides to "pull some Gs" and do some fancy maneuvers, suddenly plummeting the sailplane toward the Earth and then pulling up, yanking the bottom out of your stomach. Moves like that aren't for those with a fear of flying or heights, but anyone with a predilection for roller coasters will be in heaven. Visitors can opt for either relatively clunky Schweizer 2-33 trainers or ultrasleek Schleicher ASK-21 high-performance sailplanes. I highly recommend the latter, which can sail higher and are more silent (and are only $10 more, $85 for a 40-min. ride). See soaring details on p. 56.

delicious, and there's a fantastic billiards room. For a bite, check out **Charlie's Café,** 205 Hoffman St. (© 607/733-0440; www.charliescafeelmira.com/old/index.html, a neighborhood restaurant that is rather surprisingly staffed by formally dressed waiters and which has a homey, almost Old World ambience. It serves a bit of everything, but is strongest for grilled meats and fish, and is open for lunch and dinner Monday to Saturday and brunch on Sunday (and can do to-go lunches).

KEUKA LAKE ★★★

30 miles NW of Corning; 40 miles SW of Geneva

The far southwest quadrant of the Finger Lakes region contains but a single Finger Lake, the small and curiously Y-shaped Keuka Lake. To many locals, Keuka is the most beautiful of all the Finger Lakes—an assessment I'm inclined to agree with. It's something about the deep blue of the water, the way the narrow lake splits in two, and how vineyards blanket the gentle rise of the banks. Two of the more charming small villages in the Finger Lakes, Hammondsport and Naples, are located near the lake, and the Keuka Lake Wine Trail includes some of the most interesting and best-sited wineries in the Finger Lakes region.

Essentials
GETTING THERE
BY CAR Hammondsport, at the southern end of Keuka Lake, is off Route 54, which intersects with Route 17/I-86. Routes 54 and 54A travel north along the east and west sides of Keuka Lake toward Geneva.

VISITOR INFORMATION The **Finger Lakes Association,** which oversees promotion for the entire region, is located at 309 Lake St. in Penn Yan (© 800/548-4386; www.fingerlakes.org). There are also tourist information offices relatively nearby in Watkins Glen and Corning (see earlier in this chapter).

The Fairest of the Finger Lakes?

Uniquely shaped **Keuka Lake** may be the prettiest and most pristine of all the Finger Lakes—though you'll undoubtedly get arguments from natives with preferences for Skaneateles, Seneca, or Cayuga. The word *keuka* in the original Native American language is thought to have meant "crooked"—a quality reflected in the lake's Y shape. **Keuka Lake State Park** has a nice public beach for swimming, a boat launch, fishing, picnic facilities, and a children's playground. The park is located along the north shore of the West Branch of Keuka Lake, 6 miles south of Penn Yan on Route 54A.

For further exploration of the lake, **North Country Kayak & Canoe,** 16878 W. Lake Rd., Hammondsport (☎ 607/868-7456), offers kayak and canoe rentals from June to September. If fishing is your thing, serene Keuka Lake has rainbow trout, lake trout, largemouth bass, and more. Check **www.corningfingerlakes.com/visitors/hunting-fishing** for details on fishing and lodging packages and equipment and tackle shops.

Another way to enjoy the water is to take a cruise on the lake. Esperanza Mansion (see below) operates *The Esperanza Rose* ★, a 65-foot vintage wooden sailing vessel (☎ 315/595-6618; www.esperanzaboat.com). It offers lunch, sightseeing, and dinner cruises Tuesday through Sunday, Memorial Day to October ($21–$44 per person).

Another spectacular way to see Keuka Lake is to drive (or cycle) around its 20-mile perimeter. **Route 54A ★★**, which travels south of Penn Yan between the two upper prongs of the lake and then traverses its western length, is a mesmerizing scenic drive, hands-down one of the prettiest in the entire state. If you're planning to visit some wineries, you can take Route 54A to High Road.

Exploring Hammondsport

Tiny **Hammondsport ★**, at the southern end of Keuka Lake, is a postcard-perfect small town built around an attractive village square. Though tiny, it bustles with a disproportionate number of antiques and gifts shops, an ice-cream parlor, and a couple of restaurants and inns. If you'd like a bit of small-town life to complement your Finger Lakes experience, it makes a good base.

Besides the lake and wineries (see the "Keuka Lake Wine Trail" box, below), the biggest attraction in the immediate area is the **Glenn H. Curtiss Museum ★**, 8419 Rte. 54, Hammondsport (☎ 607/569-2160; www.glennhcurtissmuseum.org; May–Oct Mon–Sat 9am–5pm, Sun 10am–5pm; Nov–Apr daily 10am–4pm; $7.50 adults, $6 seniors, $4.50 students 7–18, $20 families, and free for children 6 and under), devoted to one of the true pioneers of American aviation, who was also a Hammondsport native. In the early 20th century, Curtiss began designing motorcycles and moved on to dirigibles, airplanes, and hydroaeroplanes ("flying boats"). His first flight, in 1908, was the first advertised public flight of aircraft (the Wright Brothers had already been aloft, but in total secrecy). The museum displays a fine collection of historical aircraft and antique Curtiss motorcycles (including a reproduction of the one he used to achieve the world speed record of 136 mph). The museum also presents dioramas on turn-of-the-20th-century life and winemaking, as well as an interactive children's gallery.

Shoppers in Hammondsport should check out **Opera House Antiques,** 61–63 Shethar St. (☎ 607/569-3525), a multidealer shop featuring silver, linens, and

keuka LAKE WINE TRAIL

Fifteen wineries are within easy reach of the banks of beautiful Keuka Lake. The **Keuka Lake Wine Trail ★★** (© 800/440-4898; www.keukawine trail.com; brochure widely available in the area) is smaller than the Cayuga or Seneca trails, but it comprises eight independent wineries located on or near the lake, including one of the standouts of the entire Finger Lakes region. Check the trail's website for special scheduled events throughout the year. Visits to Keuka Lake wineries can easily be combined with a tour of those along the west (and even east) bank of nearby Seneca Lake; see p. 322 for details on the Seneca Lake Wine Trail. **Heron Hill Winery ★★**, 9249 County Rte. 76, Hammondsport (© 800/441-4241; www.heronhill.com), has a gorgeous setting high above Keuka Lake, as well as frequent music events, a cafe with an outdoor terrace, and a good gift shop. It's open year-round Monday through Saturday from 10am to 5pm and Sunday from noon to 5pm.

Perhaps the most distinguished winery in the entire region and a favorite of connoisseurs is **Dr. Konstantin Frank's Vinifera Wine Cellars ★★★**, 9749 Middle Rd., Hammondsport (© 800/320-0735; www.drfrankwines.com). Dr. Frank, as it's known, produces outstanding perennial, international award-winning wines, including a splendid dry Riesling and Gewürztraminer. Though the Finger Lakes aren't yet well known for their reds, Dr. Frank's cabernet sauvignon, cabernet franc, and pinot noir are quite excellent, and the rare Rkatsiteli and Chateau Frank sparkling wines are surprisingly good. The setting on the slopes of Keuka Lake is lovely, and the full tasting, while serious about the wines, is conducted by a lively group of folks who make it educational but not stuffy. Dr. Frank's remains a family-owned operation, now run by Frank's grandson. It's open year-round Monday through Saturday from 9am to 5pm and Sunday from noon to 5pm.

Not officially part of the Keuka Lake Wine Trail, but very near those that are, **Bully Hill Vineyards**, 8843 Greyton H. Taylor Memorial Dr., Hammondsport (© 607/868-3610; www.bullyhill.com), has a reputation as one of the zaniest wineries in the region, a reflection of its original owner, a gadfly who left the Taylor winery and repeatedly battled Coca-Cola (for the rights to use the

period furniture. Across the street is **Scandia House,** 64 Shethar St. (© 607/569-2667), a shop specializing in women's clothing, Scandinavian sweaters, and housewares. **Mud Lust Pottery,** 59 Shethar St. (© 607/569-3068), features locally crafted fine pottery. Chocoholics should check out **The Chocolatier of Hammondsport,** 69 Shethar St. (© 607/569-2157), a new shop that deals in high-end chocolates and confections.

If you're sore from driving around the lakes or boating or cycling, pay a visit to the family-run **Finger Lakes Wellness Center & Health Spa,** 7531 County Rte. 13, Bath (© 607/776-3737; www.fingerlakeswellness.com), just south of Hammondsport, for a massage.

Where to Stay

If you're looking to explore Keuka Lake and its wineries, or even nearby attractions in Watkins Glen and Corning, Hammondsport makes an excellent base, and its

Taylor name) after it purchased his family's business. Tours and tastings aim to inject fun into the sometimes-formal wine world. Also on the premises are a restaurant and the **Greyton H. Taylor Wine Museum,** with antique winemaking implements and artwork (much of which found its way onto Bully Hill labels) of the owner. Open Monday to Saturday from 9am to 5pm and Sunday from 11:30am to 5pm for tours and tastings ($2); restaurant and wine museum open daily mid-May through October (restaurant for lunch daily, dinner Fri–Sat).

On the east side of Keuka Lake, **Ravines Wine Cellars,** 14630 Rte. 54, Hammondsport (✆ **607/292-7007;** www.ravineswinecellars.com), is a boutique winery with a tasting bar inside an attractive new Tuscan-style villa. Ravines makes quality, European-style vinifera wines, including Riesling, pinot noir, and meritage, a bordeaux-style blend. Open Monday to Saturday from 10am to 5pm and Sunday from noon to 5pm, April through November (plus weekends in Mar and Dec). Tucked away on a quiet country road a mile or so from Keuka is **McGregor Vineyard ★,** 5503 Dutch St., Dundee (✆ **800/272-0192;** www.mcgregorwinery.com). The family-run

winery, in a cool space that looks more like a beer hall than a tasting room, has developed a cult following for its oddball varietals from Eastern Europe. Chief among them is the coveted, powerful, and age-worthy Black Russian, a blend of Saperavi and Sereksiya Charni. It sells out quickly every year, though, so it may be tough to get a taste of it. Open year-round daily 10am to 6pm (until 5pm Dec–Mar), but July and August, until 8pm on Friday and Saturday.

For a taste of old-school Finger Lakes wineries and a time when the region concentrated more on jugs of sweet wine than on low-yield noble grapes, visit **Pleasant Valley Wine Company ★,** Route 88, Hammondsport (✆ **607/569-6111;** www.pleasantvalleywine.com). Established in 1860, it's the oldest bonded winery in the Finger Lakes region, holder of U.S. Bond No. 1, in fact. Physically, it is the most atmospheric winery in the entire region—it retains original buildings carved out of the rocky hillside. Full guided tours ($5) include an introductory film. It's open April to December daily from 10am to 5pm, and January to March Tuesday through Saturday from 10am to 4pm.

small-town attributes are attracting more and more travelers. But it remains strictly a place for small inns rather than hotels.

Black Sheep Inn ★★★ ♦   This carefully curated inn, inhabiting a historic and immaculate 1859 octagon house—one of only about 100 that remain in New York State—is among the small number of top-tier inns in the region. Helpful owners Debbie Meritsky and Marc Rotman have created a handsome and stately, but completely relaxing, inn. The five rooms are built around a formal spiral staircase and are wonderful oases, with top-quality linens and bedding, well-chosen antique furnishings, period-specific wallpapers, and luxurious bathrooms. Debbie's breakfasts, cooked in a restaurant-worthy kitchen, are gourmet, and she will also prepare boxed lunches and even a catered gourmet picnic dinner. Although the Black Sheep isn't inexpensive, it's so well done and offers such impeccable service that it represents a very good value.

8329 Pleasant Valley Rd., Hammondsport, NY 14840. www.stayblacksheepinn.com. ⓒ**877/274-6286** or 607/569-3767. 5 units. $149–$269 double. Rates include full breakfast. 2-night minimum stay required. AE, DC, MC, V. Free parking. **Amenities:** Spa services (36-hr. notice required). *In room:* A/C, Wi-Fi.

Esperanza Mansion Spectacularly set high on a bluff overlooking one of the upper prongs of Keuka Lake, this imposing, completely restored 1838 Greek Revival manse has rooms in the main house and simpler, motel-style rooms attached, in addition to two restaurants. The setting is absolutely stunning; at a minimum, it merits a visit for lunch or a glass of wine on the terrace for the dreamy distant views of the lake—perhaps the finest in all the Finger Lakes. The nine mansion rooms are spacious and appointed with nouveau antiques, but don't feel special. About half of the rooms have stunning lake views (the real reason for staying here). The main house seems overly restored; I actually prefer the inn rooms, which are less self-conscious. Guests should also know that it's frequently the site of weddings and other large celebrations, which can be a hindrance.

3465 Rte. 54A, Bluff Point, NY 14478. www.esperanzamansion.com. ⓒ **866/927-4400** or 315/536-4400. 30 units. Mansion rooms $179–$275 double; Inn rooms $119–$190. Rates include full breakfast. AE, DC, MC, V. Free parking. **Amenities:** 2 restaurants; bar. *In room:* A/C, TV.

Village Tavern Restaurant & Inn 🍷 Above one of the most distinguished restaurants in this section of the Finger Lakes, and right on the Village Square and just a block from Keuka Lake, this good-value small inn has four simple, rather dated but comfortable rooms with a private entrance and kitchenette or full kitchen. Room no. 1 is a two-bedroom suite, a good value for families or couples traveling (closely) together. Dining and then staying at the Tavern is like having a nice dinner (and perhaps too many glasses of wine) at a friend's place and then conveniently stumbling upstairs to crash.

30 Mechanic St., Hammondsport, NY 14840. www.villagetaverninn.com. ⓒ **607/569-2528.** 4 units. Weekdays $69–$119 double; weekends $79–$129 double. 2-night minimum stay on weekends May–Nov. Rates include full breakfast. AE, DC, MC, V. Free parking. *In room:* A/C, TV, Wi-Fi.

Where to Eat

In addition to Hammondsport's one very good restaurant, below, **Union Block Café,** on the village square at 31 Shethar St. (ⓒ **607/569-2244**), is a good spot for coffee, panini, wraps, and pizzas, as well as Wi-Fi access.

Village Tavern Restaurant & Inn ★ ☺SEAFOOD/INTERNATIONAL Though it is virtually the only place in town to dine, that hardly matters: This cozy, family-owned restaurant would be a winner even with plenty of competition. It looks more like a comfortable neighborhood joint than a haven for gastronomes, so its encyclopedic wine and beer lists are completely unexpected. The menu features many good seafood specialties, such as crayfish étouffée, catfish Creole, and fried seafood platters; there are also homemade soups, roast prime rib, and the "famous Friday fish fry." The restaurant, which has a small kids' menu, is popular with local families, and the long bar is a friendly regional hangout and occasionally features live music. In fact, the tavern is much cooler, with a hip staff and hip music, than the dated wood paneling and pink tablecloths under glass would lead any reasonable person to expect.

30 Mechanic St., Hammondsport. ⓒ **607/569-2528.** Reservations recommended. Main courses $14–$43. AE, DISC, MC, V. Memorial Day to Oct daily 11:30am–9:30pm (Sun brunch 10am–3pm); Nov–Dec and Feb–Mar Thurs–Sun 11:30am–9:30pm; Apr to Memorial Day Wed–Sun 11:30am–9:30pm. Taproom same days as restaurant 11:30am–1am. Closed Jan.

CANANDAIGUA LAKE ★

30 miles SE of Rochester; 19 miles W of Geneva

Canandaigua, which lies at the northern end of the lake of the same name, is the kind of laid-back small town that epitomizes the Finger Lakes region. Canandaigua Lake, the birthplace of the Seneca Nation that ruled this area in pre-Colonial days, is the area's principal attraction, but there are a number of unique sights and experiences in this part of what is rather redundantly called Lake Country. (Ontario County is home to 5 of the 11 Finger Lakes.) With the presence of the splendid **New York Wine & Culinary Center,** Canandaigua is looking to become an important gateway to the Finger Lakes.

Essentials

GETTING THERE

BY CAR Canandaigua is reached along either Route 21 or 332 south from I-90.

VISITOR INFORMATION The **Finger Lakes Visitors Connection** (✆ **877-FUN-IN-NY** [386-4669] or 585/394-3915; www.visitfingerlakes.com) is located at 25 Gorham St.

Exploring Canandaigua Lake

The Finger Lakes region is increasingly focused on its fast-improving wineries and the local gastronomy tied to the wines. And there is no better expression of this newfound interest than the massive **New York Wine & Culinary Center ★★★**, 800 S. Main St. (✆ **585/394-7070;** www.nywcc.com). Just removed from the north shore of Canandaigua Lake, this sparkling center offers a window onto the best local food and wine products. Of greatest interest to most visitors who are in the region to explore the Finger Lakes wine country will be the Tasting Room, where tasting flights of New York State wines change frequently. It's a great place to learn about the local vintages before embarking on your own wine trail—or, if you don't have time for that, a decent substitute. The center also has a great hands-on kitchen, where short-term cooking and wine-pairing classes are offered (look for CIA-type boot camps in the future). Finally, head upstairs to the excellent restaurant and bar for lunch or dinner. The menu, naturally, focuses on local products and New York wines and craft beers. There's live music and a terrific wraparound deck (and on Thurs you can bring your own wine for no corkage fee). The restaurant is open Memorial Day to mid-October daily 11:30am to 9pm; mid-October to May Tuesday and Wednesday 11:30am to 3pm, Thursday to Saturday 11:30am to 9pm, and Sunday 11:30am to 3pm; reservations recommended. For a special treat, check out the schedule of winemaker dinners, held in the sumptuous, medieval-style wine and spirits room.

Naturalists and garden enthusiasts should not miss the **Sonnenberg Mansion & Gardens ★★**, 151 Charlotte St. (✆ **585/394-4922;** www.sonnenberg.org). The 50-acre estate and 1887 Queen Anne Victorian mansion, which once belonged to the founder of what is today Citibank, possesses some of the loveliest formal gardens and landscaping you're likely to encounter in New York State, including Italian, Japanese, and rock gardens. The grounds also maintain an impressive conservatory and Finger Lakes Wine Center, which conducts tastings on the premises. Special events, such as the "Haunted Gardens" in October and "Festival of Lights" in November and December, are truly special. The Sonnenberg is open daily Memorial Day to Labor Day from 9:30am to 5:30pm and from May 2 to the day before Memorial Day and the day after Labor Day to October 31 daily from 9:30am to 4:30pm. Admission is $10 for adults, $9 for seniors, $5 students 13 to 17, and free for children 12 and under.

Nearby Attractions

The Church of Jesus Christ of Latter-day Saints, better known to the rest of the world as the Mormon religion, got its start in the northwest region of the Finger Lakes before moving out west to Utah. Near Palmyra (17 miles northeast of Canandaigua), according to Mormon texts, Joseph Smith received golden plates, later translated into the Book of Mormon, from an angel in 1827. North of Canandaigua, along Route 21, is the **Hill Cumorah Visitors Center** (603 State Rte. 21, Palmyra; © **315/597-5851;** www.hillcumorah.org); anyone who wants to learn more about the Mormon faith can drop in for some low-pressure information about the church and find out about Mormon-related sights in the area, such as Smith's log cabin. However, the big event in these parts is the annual **Hill Cumorah Pageant ★**, an incredible spectacle and the largest outdoor theatrical production in the U.S., with a costumed cast of 700, a nine-level stage, and music by the Mormon Tabernacle Choir. Every July its seven free productions draw thousands of believers and the curious. For more information, call © **315/597-5851** or visit **www.hillcumorah.com**.

Not far from the Mormons, but on an altogether different spiritual plane, is the **Finger Lakes Race Track** (© **585/935-5252;** www.fingerlakesracetrack.com), in Farmington, also north of Canandaigua (1 mile south of I-90, exit 44 on Rte. 332). Thoroughbred horses race here from April to November.

Visitors interested in the region's Native American roots should head to the **Ganondagan State Historic Site ★**, 1488 State Rte. 444, Victor (© **585/924-5848;** www.ganondagan.org), a real find located northwest of Canandaigua. A former center of the democratically inclined Seneca people, one of the six nations composing the Iroquois Confederacy, the site today features a replica 17th-century Seneca bark longhouse, as well as marked ethnobotanical, Native American–themed trails that aim to teach visitors about Seneca customs and beliefs. Trails are open year-round from 8am to sunset; the visitor center is open May through September Tuesday to Sunday from 9am to 5pm, October Tuesday to Saturday from 9am to 5pm. Interpreted trail walks are offered year-round Saturday at 10am and 2pm, Sunday at noon and 2pm. Visits are $3 for adults, $2 for children, though self-guided walks along the trails are free.

Sports & Outdoor Activities

Public-access beaches on Canandaigua Lake include **Butler Beach,** West Lake Road (© **585/396-2752;** free admission), on the west side of the lake; **Deep Run Park,** East Lake Road (© **585/396-4000**), on the east side of the lake; and **Kershaw Park,** Lakeshore Drive (© **585/396-5060;** fee charged), which has a sand beach and an 8-acre park.

If you'd rather see the lake from a boat, the *Canandaigua Lady* (© **585/396-7350;** www.steamboatlandingonline.com) is a replica 19th-century paddle-wheel steamboat, available for lake excursions and lunch and dinner cruises. From May to mid-September, it departs from Steamboat Landing, 205 Lakeshore Dr. (at the north end of Canandaigua Lake). Fall foliage cruises (mid-Sept to Oct) board at Woodville dock, Route 21 South (south end of Canandaigua Lake), and there are wine-tasting excursion cruises each Wednesday in season, with a different New York State winery

pe Festival ★ (last weekend of Sept) is a fun-filled weekend
n's tradition of making grape pies. The festival has been held in
n 40 years and draws bumper-to-bumper traffic along routes 64
. 50,000 grape pies are sold in that single weekend. For more
585/374-2240, or visit www.naplesgrapefest.org. Grape pies, of
sly labor-intensive to make (you have to peel the grapes first),
they haven't exactly taken off outside of Naples. They are avail-
round at the Arbor Hill Grapery & Winery.

AY & EAT

rea is **Monier Manor ★★**, 54 N. Main St., Naples, NY 14512
com; ✆ 585/374-6719; $150–$190 double; 2-night weekend
une to Nov 1), an elegant B&B. The rooms in this nicely con-
ntury, red Federal-style mansion are very spacious and well deco-
ne fabrics and luxurious period furnishings. The room names,
pretty much describe the ambience and decor: Opulence, Seren-
dulgence. Amenities range from fireplaces and Persian rugs to a
he lovely grounds are a great place to relax. Check out specials
as the wine tour package) online, which make Monier Manor an
nother B&B, and a good value for the money, is **Bristol Views**
932 County Rd. 12, Naples, NY 14512 (www.bristolviews.com;
$125–$180 double), a renovated old farmhouse with four attrac-
y appointed rooms. There's Wi-Fi, a large deck with a hot tub,
lake views.

local spot is **Brown Hound Bistro ★★**, 6459 State Rte. 64,
✆ 585/374-9771; www.brownhoundbistro.com; main courses
aurant with a big regional draw, in an intimate century-old house
wn Naples. The menu is committed to creative application of the
. Try the Browndog yellowfin tuna or the "Big Pork Chop" with
arians will be pleased with dishes like aubergine pouches, egg-
d basil, fresh mozzarella, and roasted tomatoes. The Brown
hrough October, daily 4:30 to 9pm and Saturday to Sunday 8am
sual dining, check out the **Naples Diner,** a longtime fixture at
85/374-5420), or the **Naples Hotel,** 111 S. Main St. (✆ 585/
Federal-style hotel with a great old lounge bar.

STER ★

lls; 45 miles W of Geneva; 105 miles NW of Corning; 330 miles NW of New

thern edge of Lake Ontario, is where the Finger Lakes meet the
cities are perhaps not what most visitors associate with the
Rochester, one of the northern gateways to the lakes, is a sur-
d historic city that's well worth a visit for its trio of excellent
rants, and enjoyable festivals. The third-largest city in New York
an early boomtown and industrial giant in the early 19th cen-
as the flour-milling epicenter of the U.S. and the Erie Canal
ale shipping of grain and flour to New York City. The city today
n for the modern corporate success stories that got their start

canandaigua WINE TRAIL

The seven small wineries clustered around Canandaigua Lake have joined forces to form the Canandaigua Wine Trail (✆ 800/554-7553; www.canandaigua winetrail.com), making it easy for visitors to group them together for tours and tastings. They include **Casa Larga Vineyards ★**, an impressive facility producing a collection of very nice wines, including ice wines, just outside Rochester, 2287 Turk Hill Rd., Fairport (✆ 585/223-4210; www.casalarga.com; year-round Mon–Sat 10am–6pm, Sun noon–6pm); **Arbor Hill Grapery,** 6461 Rte. 64, Bristol Springs,

Naples (✆ 800/554-2406; www. thegrapery.com; May–Dec Mon–Sat 10am–5pm, Sun 11am–5pm; Jan–Apr Sat–Sun 11am–5pm), which features a shop selling a large selection of wine, food, and gift items (including grape pies), and a great little bakery/cafe—excellent for breakfast or lunch. Also of interest is the **Finger Lakes Wine Center** at Sonnenberg Gardens, 151 Charlotte St., Canandaigua (✆ 585/394-9016; daily mid-May to mid-Oct noon–5pm), which offers samples and the sales of more than 30 Finger Lakes wineries.

providing free tastings aboard. Cruise prices range from $15 to $49. Scuba diving, windsurfing, kayaking, and sailboarding rentals and instruction are available from **Canandaigua Sailboarding,** 11 Lakeshore Dr. (✆ 585/394-8150).

Golfers will not want to miss the **Bristol Harbour Resort Golf Course** (✆ 800/288-8248; www.bristolharbour.com), a beautiful 18-hole Robert Trent Jones–designed course right on Lake Canandaigua. Greens fees are $29 to $69.

Good hiking and cycling are available on **Ontario Pathways,** 200 Ontario St., Canandaigua (✆ 585/394-7968; www.ontariopathways.org), 23 miles of rails-to-trails. In winter months, you can ski at **Bristol Mountain Winter Resort,** 5662 Rte. 64, Canandaigua (✆ 585/374-6000; www.bristolmountain.com).

Shopping

Along Canandaigua's Main Street, an "artwalk" takes you to **Gallery on Main Street** (131 S. Main St.; ✆ 585/394-2780), **The Christopher Wheat Gallery** (92 S. Main St.; ✆ 585/399-1180), and **Nadal Glass** (20 Phoenix St.; ✆ 585/374-7850), which features glass hand blown in an old firehouse. The top shopping destination in the area, however, is the **Bloomfield Antique Country Mile,** a cluster of seven antiques dealers along Routes 5 and 20 in Bloomfield (just west of Canandaigua). Several are multidealer shops, such as **Alan's Antique Alley,** 6925 Routes 5 and 20 (✆ 585/657-6776). **Wizard of Clay,** 7851 Rte. 20A, Bristol (✆ 585/229-2980), is a cool stoneware pottery shop. A couple of very large antiques malls are located in Farmington (Rochester Rd., or Rte. 332): **Ontario Mall Antiques** (1740 Rochester Rd.; ✆ 585/398-3030), with more than 600 dealers, and **Antique Emporium of Farmington** (1780 Rochester Rd.; ✆ 585/398-3997), with some 60 dealers.

Where to Stay

Low-key Canandaigua, with three of the loveliest inns in the state and some lower-priced hotels along the lake, makes an excellent base for exploring the western section of the Finger Lakes.

The Chalet of Canandaigua ★★★ 🎁 Ordinarily, I wouldn't find myself seduced by a log cabin, but this extraordinary luxury B&B—one of the finest small properties in the region—is leagues removed from expectations of a rustic, Adirondack-style cabin. Secluded at the end of a long approach past a pond of ducks and tall trees, technically it is constructed of logs. But it's as if the Four Seasons hotel chain decided to do a three-room inn as an alpine cottage. The rustic elements of this unique 1960s abode combine with inviting furnishings, high-tech features, and stunning attention to detail. Rooms are almost impossibly large and enveloping—then there's the expansive deck; the savvy, open-minded owners; and those ridiculous three-course gourmet breakfasts. Look online for last-minute specials.

3770 State Rte. 21, Canandaigua, NY 14424. www.chaletbandb.com. (📞 **585-394-9080.** Fax 585/394-9088. 3 units. $235–$295 suite. Check online for specials and packages. Rates include full breakfast. AE, DC, MC, V. Free parking. *In room:* A/C, flatscreen cable TV/DVD player, minibar, Wi-Fi.

The Inn at Bristol Harbour ☺ This small resort hotel, right on the west bank of Canandaigua Lake, features some excellent outdoors amenities, such as a great golf course (ask about special golf packages), a private beach, and an outdoor swimming pool. The cozy Adirondack-style rooms aren't merely an afterthought; they all have fireplaces and balconies, many with superb panoramic views of the lake. The Lodge restaurant, recommended below, is quite good, and the Tavern is a great place to unwind after a round of golf or touring the area.

5410 Seneca Point Rd., Canandaigua, NY 14424. www.bristolharbour.com. (📞 **800/288-8248** or 585/396-2200. Fax 585/394-9254. 31 units. $129–$295 double. AE, DISC, MC, V. Free parking. **Amenities:** Restaurant; bar; outdoor 18-hole golf course; Jacuzzi; outdoor pool; private beach. *In room:* A/C, TV/VCR, CD player.

Morgan Samuels B&B Inn ★★ 🎁 On 46 sylvan acres, this private and rather prim and proper inn occupying an 1810 English-style mansion is a nice retreat if you're looking for tranquillity. Guest rooms are pretty and romantic, and each is uniquely decorated, with such touches as Oriental rugs and antiques, French doors, and fireplaces (there are an incredible 11 in the house). The enclosed garden porch is a lovely spot to sip afternoon tea, and the library is a private nook in which to plunge into a good book. The emphasis on elegance and old-world refinement will not suit everyone, though many visitors will be in heaven.

2920 Smith Rd., Canandaigua, NY 14424. www.morgansamuelsinn.com. (📞 **585/394-9232.** Fax 585/394-8044. 5 units. $149–$325 double. Rates include full breakfast. AE, MC, V. Free parking. **Amenities:** Hot-springs Jacuzzi; tennis court. *In room:* A/C.

1795 Acorn Inn ★★★ A charming, serene, and meticulously kept B&B—enough to earn a four-diamond rating from AAA—this 1795 Federal Stagecoach Inn west of Canandaigua Lake is one of the most distinguished small country inns in New York State. The entire place, surrounded by gardens and woods, is carefully designed and maintained. The common room is cozy, lined with several thousand books and warmed by a roaring fire in cold months. In addition to the large and very handsomely appointed, colorful rooms on the second floor, all with romantic canopied beds and a couple with fireplaces, guests can luxuriate under the stars in a splendid outdoor hot tub set among the gardens near the carriage house. The candlelit gourmet breakfast is a lovely affair, served on antique English china with heirloom silver.

4508 Rte. 64 S., Bristol Center, Canandaigua, NY 14424. www.acorninnbb.com. (📞 **888/665-3747** or 585/229-2834. 4 units. $160–$245 double; $210–$275 suite. Rates include full breakfast. 2-night minimum weekends June–Oct, also for holidays and special events. AE, MC, V. Free parking. **Amenities:** Outdoor Jacuzzi. *In room:* A/C, TV/VCR, CD player.

Where to Eat

The **New York Wine & Culinar** bar ★★, with a continually chang a tasting room serving New York S dinner, or predinner wine tasting. gua Inn on the Lake has a good re an outdoor terrace. Restaurants ir tro (p. 344), are also worth the dr

Bristol Harbour's Lodge Rest ern Lake Canandaigua, this wood upscale golf resort is a fine place t kind of masculine-looking place th New York strip steak with a bran nivorous entrees, however, includ in phyllo. Even if you're not stayi breakfast or lunch before hitting restaurant or the tavern; in nice w An inexpensive grill menu is also

5410 Seneca Point Rd., Bristol Harbor. (📞 ommended. Main courses $14–$32. AE, Thurs 5–9pm; Fri-Sat 5–10pm.

Canandaigua After

The **Finger Lakes Performing** Canandaigua (on the campus of open-air theater, hosts the Roch events throughout the summer (📞 **716/325-7760**; tickets are **500**). The Rochester Broadway **ger Lakes Elegant Picnic** in such big-name acts as Diana Kra

Naples ★

At the southern end of Canand quintessential small Finger Lak tury buildings. It's a peaceful summer to autumn and for the l **Grape Festival** takes over.

EXPLORING NAPLES

Area wineries worth a visit incl **ery & Winery;** see "Canandaig

Trout **fishing** is good on Cana known for walleye and largemo Cohocton St., Naples (📞 585/3

Duffers should check out the Cohocton St. (📞 **585/374-68**

The **Bristol Valley Theater** org), schedules professional su

The **Naples G** built around the to Naples for more th and 21; as many a information, call (📞 course, are notorio perhaps the reason able, however, year

WHERE TO S

The top inn in the (www.moniermano stay required, mid served, mid-19th-c rated, with handso while a bit preciou ity, Elegance, and Greek soaking tub and packages (such even better value. A **Bed & Breakfast,** (📞 **585/374-8875** tive, clean, and nic and beautiful distar

For dining, the t in Bristol Springs $21–$26), a tiny res not far from downto best local ingredien apricot brandy. Veg plant wrapped arou Hound is open May to 2pm. For more c 139 S. Main St. (📞 **374-5630**), an 189

ROCHES

85 miles W of Niagara York City

Rochester, at the so Great Lakes. Thoug Finger Lakes region prisingly agreeable museums, fine resta State, Rochester wa tury, when it ranke permitted the large-s is perhaps best kno

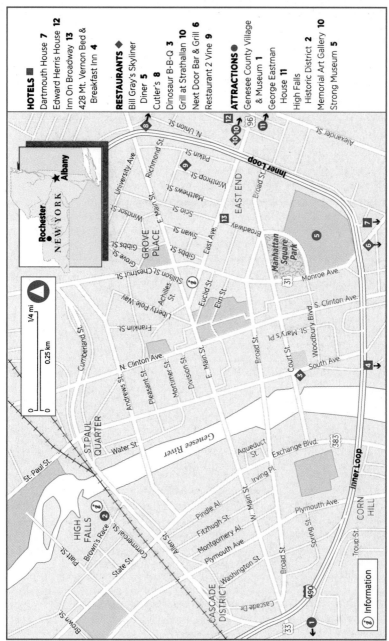

HOTELS ■
Dartmouth House **7**
Edward Herris House **12**
Inn On Broadway **13**
428 Mt. Vernon Bed &
  Breakfast Inn **4**

RESTAURANTS ◆
Bill Gray's Skyliner
  Diner **5**
Cutler's **8**
Dinosaur B-B-Q **3**
Grill at Strathallan **10**
Next Door Bar & Grill **6**
Restaurant 2 Vine **9**

ATTRACTIONS ●
Genesee County Village
  & Museum **1**
George Eastman
  House **11**
High Falls
Historic District **2**
Memorial Art Gallery **10**
Strong Museum **5**

here, including Eastman Kodak, Xerox, and Bausch & Lomb. An extremely livable, family-friendly, and attractive small city, which many locals and visitors contend feels more Midwestern than East Coast, Rochester has an enviable surfeit of gardens and parks, but is predominantly characterized by its residents' modesty and industry.

Essentials

GETTING THERE

BY PLANE   **Greater Rochester International Airport** (ROC), 1200 Brooks Ave. (© 716/464-6000; www.rochesterintlairport.com), is 4 miles southwest of Rochester. The airport is serviced by American, AirTran, Continental, Delta, JetBlue, Northwest, United, and US Airways.

BY CAR   Rochester is about 10 miles north of I-90 (New York State Thruway), reached by either Route 390 or 490.

BY BUS   **Greyhound** and **Trailways** travel to the terminal at 187 Midtown Plaza (© 585/232-5121).

VISITOR INFORMATION   Rochester's **Downtown Visitor Information Center** is located at 45 East Ave., Ste. 400 (© 800/677-7282 or 585/279-8300; www.visitrochester.com). The Events line (© 585/546-6810) is a 24-hour recorded message highlighting current events and activities in the Rochester area. You will also find tourism information centers on the first floor of the Greater Rochester International Airport and at the rest stop of the New York State Thruway (westbound lane) near exit 45.

GETTING AROUND   **Regional Transit System (RTS)** buses traverse the major routes downtown. An All-Day Freedom Pass ($3) is good for unlimited rides and can be purchased on buses. Call © 888/288-3777, or visit www.rgrta.org for information.

Exploring Rochester

Start your visit in the **High Falls Historic District,** the one-time mill area at the edge of the Genesee River and a 96-foot urban waterfall. The **High Falls Heritage Area Visitors Center,** 60 Browns Race (© 585/325-3020; www.centerathighfalls. org), has a small museum on the history of Rochester and some great views of the falls.

Genesee Country Village & Museum ★★ ☺   About 20 miles southwest of Rochester, this assembly of 58 historic buildings gathered from around upstate New York re-creates a working 19th-century village, a living museum on more than 600 acres of rural land. Interpreters in period costume bring the 1800s to life with demonstrations of pottery making, blacksmithing, basket and cheese making, quilting, spinning, and cooking over an open hearth. Buildings include a tavern, a general store, an Italianate villa mansion, an octagon-shaped home, and the boyhood home of George Eastman (of Kodak fame). The buildings are further enlivened by period gardens, roaming animals, and even a baseball diamond, where New York State's vintage teams in period dress play games according to 19th-century rules. Year-round, there is a full calendar of activities, such as a Civil War candlelight tour or country yuletide celebrations; check the website for the schedule. Finally, there's an extensive gallery of wildlife and sporting art (as well as itinerant exhibitions), plus a 175-acre nature center with walking trails (both the gallery and the nature trails can be visited separately from the historic village and museum). Allow at least a full morning or afternoon here.

1410 Flint Hill Rd., Mumford (near intersection of routes 383 and 36). © **585/538-6822.** www.gcv.org. Admission (all-day attractions pass) $15 adults, $12 seniors and students, $9 children 4-16, free for children 3 and under. Mid-May to mid-Oct Tues-Fri 10am-4pm, Sat-Sun and holidays 10am-5pm (gallery weekends only, mid-May to mid-Oct).

George Eastman House ★★ ☺   George Eastman, the founder of the legendary company Kodak and known as the father of popular photography, was born in upstate New York and reared in Rochester. An innovator, philanthropist, and consummate businessman, Eastman endowed the Eastman School of Music at the University of Rochester—just one of many civic-minded projects—and he left his magnificent mansion, now a National Historic Landmark and the oldest photography museum in the world, to the university (in fact, for a time, university presidents lived there). Visitors can tour several rooms and the wonderful formal gardens of his magnificent 1905 Colonial Revival mansion. Every bit as interesting, if not more so, are the extraordinary itinerant exhibitions featuring well-known artists such as Ansel Adams as well as more avant-garde shows and permanent photography collections that include more than 400,000 prints and negatives. Most children love the "Discovery Room" (Tues–Sun 1–4pm) that allows them to inspect antique cameras and make filmstrips and sun prints. The extraordinary gardens may be visited without admission to the house and museum. On-site are a terrific gift shop and a cafe.

900 East Ave. © **585/271-3361.** www.eastmanhouse.org. Admission $12 adults, $10 seniors, $5 students, free for children 12 and under; special exhibitions extra. Tues-Sat 10am-5pm (Thurs until 8pm); Sun 1-5pm.

Memorial Art Gallery ★   One of the country's best regional museums, the Memorial Art Gallery (MAG), part of the University of Rochester, covers the gamut from medieval to contemporary art, and occasionally hosts excellent traveling shows. Very good galleries of 17th- to 19th-century European art have paintings by Rubens, Rembrandt, Monet, Cézanne, and Matisse. The beautiful central gallery with a skylight over the museum's collection of 20th-century sculpture is a pleasant place to relax among works by Henry Moore and others. The gallery's restaurant, **Max at the Gallery,** is an especially nice place for lunch (Tues–Sun), brunch (Sat–Sun), or a light tapas dinner (Thurs 5–8pm in the pavilion).

500 University Ave. © **585/473-7720.** www.mag.rochester.edu. Admission $10 adults, $6 seniors and college students, $5 children 6-18, free for children 5 and under; Thurs evening (5-9pm) half-price admission. Director's audio tour free with admission. Tues-Sun 10am-5pm (Thurs until 9pm); Sun 11am-5pm. Docent-led tours (free with admission) Thurs 6:30pm; Fri 2pm; Sun 1pm.

Strong Museum ★★★ ☺   This imaginative place—a "national museum of play"—is a splendid interactive museum for children and almost certain to entertain adults, too. It is simply one of the finest children's museums in the country. There's a re-creation of Sesame Street, a miniature grocery store where kids can shop and even scan their own groceries, and a fantastic dance lab and radio station where kids make their own sound effects—a real wonderland. Plenty of local families buy annual passes to make it their own personal playground and theme park. The museum even operates its own minibranch of the local library system, and there are books at every turn. The museum began as an outgrowth of a local woman's 20,000-strong collection of dolls, dollhouses, and toys (one of the largest collections in the world, it is impressive but comparatively static given all the activity going on elsewhere in the building). Adults will surely feel a tinge of nostalgia viewing the National Toy Hall of Fame. Plan on a visit of several hours if you're in the presence of curious children. Also on-site

The Erie Canal

Lauded as the most important engineering feat of its day, the **Erie Canal,** completed in 1825, created an international highway from the Great Lakes to the Atlantic Ocean. Shipping costs of flour and other raw materials and manufactured goods were reduced by as much as 90%. The canal stretched 360 miles from the Niagara River and Lake Erie in the west to the Hudson River in the east. It turned Rochester into a boomtown and was instrumental in transforming New York City into a major port, in the process opening up parts of the West for commercial expansion.

The canal diminished in importance as railroads quickly began to crisscross the country, but it is being rediscovered as a tourism waterway. In addition to boating and cruises on the canal, the New York State Erie Canal Heritage trail follows the original towpath along the canal and is ideal for walking, biking, and skiing in winter. Anyone interested in following the canal, by either boat or car, and seeing sights along it should request a copy of *Canal Connections* from any of the country tourism offices. See also www.canals.ny.gov.

are a great gift shop and an actual 1950s Skyliner Diner (Bill Gray's), a great place to take a break and refuel for more playing.

1 Manhattan Sq. ✆ **585/263-2700.** www.strongmuseum.org. Admission $12 adults, $11 seniors, $10 students and children 2–15, free for children 1 and under. Mon–Thurs and Sat 10am–5pm; Fri 10am–8pm; Sun noon–5pm.

Sports & Outdoor Pursuits

Beaches on the Lake Ontario shoreline, north of the city, are very popular with locals. **Ontario Beach Park,** often called "the Port of Rochester," at the mouth of the Genesee River, has piers, a boardwalk, and an antique carousel in addition to a pleasant lake beach.

The farm team of baseball's Minnesota Twins, the **Rochester Red Wings** (✆ **800/447-2623** or 585/454-1001; www.redwingsbaseball.com), play at Frontier Field, downtown, across from High Falls. Tickets are $5.50 to $12. The PGA Championship and the Ryder Cup have been held at **Oak Hill Country Club** (www.oakhillcc.com), and the women play the LPGA Wegmans Rochester International at **Locust Hill Country Club** (www.locusthill.org).

Since 1892, the annual **Lilac Festival ★★**, held in early May at 150-acre Highland Park, has been a magnet for nature lovers: Some 1,200 lilac bushes burst with spring color. The festival also draws musical entertainment and a commercial, carnival-like atmosphere (✆ **585/256-4960;** www.lilacfestival.com). Highland Park, designed in 1888 by Frederick Law Olmsted (who also created NYC's Central Park) and full of beautiful gardens and plantings, is a lovely place for a stroll.

Erie Canal and Genesee River cruises (75–90 min.) are offered aboard the *Mary Jemison Patch,* a 1931 wooden vessel that departs daily from Corn Hill Landing in downtown Rochester, May to October. Call ✆ **585/262-5661,** or visit www.samandmary.org for schedules and additional information.

Especially for Kids

The outstanding **Strong Museum** and the 19th-century **Genesee Country Village & Museum** (see above) are musts for kids visiting Rochester. Also of interest is the

Seneca Park Zoo, 222 St. Paul Blvd. (© 585/336-7200; www.senecaparkzoo.org), which has polar bears, African elephants, and Eurasian Arctic wolves. High Falls is also a good place for families. Kids will enjoy the urban waterfall and laser-light show, shown there on weekend nights in the summer; the High Falls Visitors Center also has an educational exhibit aimed at youngsters. Lake Ontario's beaches and the nearby Seabreeze Amusement Park, 4600 Culver Rd. (© 800/395-2500; www.seabreeze.com), open mid-June to Labor Day, are great spots in the heat of summer.

Shopping

The biggest mall in the area is Eastview Mall, 7979 Pittsford-Victor Rd., Victor (© 585/223-3693), about 20 minutes south of Rochester. Craft Antique Co-op, 3200 W. Ridge Rd. (© 888/711-3463 or 585/368-0670), is one of the state's largest craft-and-antiques co-ops, with 210 shops. Antiques hounds will want to visit the Bloomfield Antique Country Mile corridor along Routes 5 and 20 in Bloomfield, on the way to Canandaigua, where a few dozen antiques shops are located. Craft Company No. 6, 785 University Ave. (© 585/473-3413), which deals in all manner of contemporary American crafts, including jewelry, art glass, and home decor, occupies a Victorian firehouse 1 block from the George Eastman House. One of the best strolling and shopping areas downtown is along Park Avenue and Alexander Street, with lots of food and drink pit stops along the way. Don't forget the excellent gift shops at the Strong Museum and George Eastman House.

Where to Stay

Rochester has two very nice B&Bs in residential neighborhoods, as well as a handful of large chain hotels downtown, including the Hyatt Regency Rochester, 125 E. Main St. (www.rochester.hyatt.com; © 585/546-1234; fax 585/546-6777; $150–$230 double), probably the best of the lot; and the Crowne Plaza, 70 State St. (www.crowneplaza.com; © 585/546-3450; $119–$199 double).

Dartmouth House ★   This ideally located 1905 English Tudor inn, nestled in a residential area near the East Avenue entertainment district and Park Avenue, is a fine place to stay. It claims to be the only B&B in Rochester with central air-conditioning. Rooms are elegantly decorated, with nicely edited period antiques and bold wallpaper. The public rooms feature a grand piano, a fireplace, and window seats, as well as handsome Arts and Crafts details; breakfast, served by candlelight, is a highlight. The Canterbury Suite, with a full kitchen, can accommodate four and is a very good deal.

215 Dartmouth St., Rochester, NY 14607. www.dartmouthhouse.com. © 800/724-6298 or 585/271-7872. 5 units. $109–$165 double; $189–$209 suite. Rates include full breakfast. AE, MC, V. Free parking. In room: A/C, TV/VCR, Wi-Fi.

Edward Harris House ★★   In a handsomely restored, 1896 Victorian, this formally decorated, professionally run inn offers real romance. The home, on the National Register of Historic Places, is in a lovely residential neighborhood near the Park Avenue urban village, full of shops and cafes. Rooms are large and very well equipped, with excellent bedding and linens, decorated with a flair for color and feminine and French Country touches. Breakfast is a bounteous, professional affair. For real peace and quiet (a nice option for families or couples), check out the Cottage, a cute 1940s-era "Fireman's Cottage" that the owners also operate on the banks of the Genesee River, in the small village of Scottsville, New York (15 min. away).

35 Argyle St., Rochester, NY 14607. www.edwardharrishouse.com. © 800/419-1213 or 585/473-9752. 5 units. $169–$189 double. Rates include full breakfast. AE, MC, V. Free parking. In room: A/C, TV, Wi-Fi.

428 Mt. Vernon Bed & Breakfast Inn ★ ⬧   A stately 1917 home on a nice wooded lot just off Highland Park, south of downtown, this relaxed and comfortable place, popular with visiting professors and business travelers, is one of the best places to stay in town. The house has Victorian-style furnishings, but is understated and not fussy. Its biggest advantage is a countrylike atmosphere along with a location that provides travelers a peaceful sanctuary in the midst of the city. Breakfasts are hearty. No children 11 and under are permitted.

428 Mt. Vernon, Rochester, NY 14620. www.428mtvernon.com.© **800/836-3159** or 585/271-0792. 7 units. $140 double. Rates include full breakfast. AE, MC, V. Free parking. *In room:* A/C, TV, Wi-Fi.

Inn on Broadway ★★★   A rarity in Rochester, a luxury boutique inn, this small hotel is a welcome refuge of elegance and relaxed charm in the heart of the East End Theater District, a great downtown location. The stately building began life as the University Club of Rochester, a social club, in the late 1920s. Great architectural details remain, including a series of wonderfully restored murals. Rooms aren't huge, but they have a lovely old-world character, with handsome wallpaper and rich color, and excellent amenities (such as premium Egyptian cotton sheets and fluffy towels). The Luxury Rooms are perhaps worth the splurge, with hardwood floors, stone bathrooms, and gas fireplaces or kitchenettes. The Double Suites, with kitchenettes and pullout sofa beds, are great for small families or extended stays. The on-site restaurant, Tournedos, is an upscale steakhouse and favorite of local wine and beef lovers.

26 Broadway, Rochester, NY 14607. www.innonbroadway.com.© **877/612-3595** or 585/232-3595. Fax 585/546-2164. 23 units. $189–$269 double; $259–$350 suite. Rates include full breakfast. AE, MC, V. Free parking. **Amenities:** Restaurant, 24-hr. concierge. *In room:* A/C, TV, Wi-Fi.

Where to Eat

Rochester has a surprisingly lively dining scene. Much of it is clustered around two areas, East Avenue, or the so-called "East End entertainment district," and Park Avenue and Alexander Street. Two restaurants worth visiting, especially when you're out sightseeing, are actually located in museums: **Max at the Gallery** ★ (© **585/473-6380**) is an upscale option just off the modern sculpture gallery at the Memorial Art Gallery (p. 347), serving lunch Tuesday through Sunday, 11:30am to 2pm; and **Bill Gray's at the Skyliner Diner** (© **585/232-5284**) is the Strong Museum's authentic 1950s diner, with food that kids will love (p. 347).

The Grill at Strathallan ★ AMERICAN   The only Mobil four-diamond restaurant in the state west of New York City, this is the place in Rochester for haute cuisine and fine wine. Entrees are classic, like dry-aged strip steak, veal chop, and slow-roasted salmon, with just a few twists (such as the peach-lacquered duck breast with squash gnocchi and foie gras). Gourmands and oenophiles should check into the periodic six-course wine dinners, with pairings for each course. The restaurant features live jazz until late on Thursday through Saturday nights.

550 East Ave. (in Strathallan Hotel).© **585/454-1880.** www.strathallan.com/grill-at-strathallan.php. Reservations required. Main courses $24–$38. AE, DISC, MC, V. Mon–Thurs 11:30am–2pm and 5:30–9pm; Fri–Sat 5–10pm.

Next Door Bar & Grill ★ AMERICAN   This restaurant, owned by Wegmans, the upstate grocery store empire, replaced Tastings Restaurant, a longtime local favorite. It's less ambitious, with a trendy interior and an emphasis on casual dining and cocktails (the popular, mod lounge bar is open until 1am Sun–Thurs and 2am Fri–Sat). The grill has an open kitchen and focuses on grilled meats and fish, with Robata,

Japanese-style grilled items using white-oak charcoal (the Robata grill mix, with beef, pork, eggplant, and vegetables, is the Japanese answer to an Argentine *paradilla*). Sushi and thin-crust pizzas are also popular. The restaurant can get quite boisterous, with occasionally ear-splitting acoustics, so if you're going for dinner, expect a fun, barlike environment.

3220 Monroe Ave. (Pittsford). © **585/249-4575.** www.nextdoorbarandgrill.com. Reservations recommended. Main courses $16–$35. AE, DISC, MC, V. Daily 5–10pm.

Restaurant 2 Vine ★★ BISTRO/SEAFOOD   In a renovated 1890s ambulance garage, this cheery and casual, often-crowded restaurant and lively bar—a consistent local award winner—is a great place for dinner before or after a show at Little Theatre, next to the restaurant. The space is large, handsome, and warm, with subdued lighting and a beautiful long bar. Choose from elegant entrees like roasted halibut with mushroom-watercress risotto or classic bistro dishes such as mussels steamed in white wine with *pommes frites*. Big appetites and wallets can be steered toward towering iced platters of seafood. In keeping with its name, 2 Vine has an excellent wine list, even though local Finger Lakes wines hardly make an appearance.

24 Winthrop St. © **585/454-6020.** www.2vine.com. Reservations recommended. Main courses $15–$32. AE, DISC, MC, V. Mon–Thurs 11:30am–11pm; Fri 11:30am–midnight; Sat 5pm–midnight.

Rochester After Dark

The **Eastman School of Music** ★ presents more than 700 concerts a year, including jazz, classical, chamber, and opera, among others, at the Eastman Theatre and other venues in Rochester. For concert information, call © 585/274-1100 or visit www.rochester.edu/Eastman. The **Rochester Philharmonic Orchestra** also plays at the Eastman Theatre. Call the box office at © 585/454-2100, or see the schedule at www.rpo.org. The **Xerox Rochester International Jazz Festival** ★ (2nd week of June), one of the city's biggest festival and music draws, features more than 50 concerts by major players (both jazz and jazz-inflected pop and rock) at 15 venues. Contact the hot line at © 585/234-2002, or visit www.rochesterjazz.com.

The **Geva Theatre Center,** 75 Woodbury Blvd. (© 585/232-4382; www.geva theatre.org), is the major venue in town for theater productions, and the most attended regional theater in New York State.

Free laser light shows are projected in the gorge at High Falls on Friday and Saturday nights beginning at 9:30pm from Memorial Day to Labor Day; families and couples on dates hang out on the Rennes bridge that spans the river. The High Falls district is on the way up, with a number of new pubs and restaurants moving in. Expect more on the way. The **East End "entertainment district"** ★, along East Avenue, is one of the best spots to hang out on weekends. The cool Art Deco **Little Theatre,** 240 East Ave. (© 585/232-3906), shows independent and foreign art house films and often has live music in its cafe. The **St. Paul Quarter,** along St. Paul and Main streets, is also replete with lively bars and restaurants. Among its hot nightspots is **Club Industry,** 155 St. Paul St. (© 585/262-4570). **Dinosaur Bar-B-Que,** 99 Court St. (© 585/325-7090; www.dinosaurbarbque.com), a biker bar and lively ribs joint in the old Lehigh Valley Train Station downtown, has live blues bands on weekends and can get pretty raucous. **Next Door Bar & Grill** (p. 350) has a cool lounge bar that has great cocktails and is popular after work and well into the night.

GENEVA & NORTHERN SENECA LAKE ★★

10 miles W of Seneca Falls; 54 miles W of Syracuse; 19 miles E of Canandaigua; 45 miles SE of Rochester

Geneva, tucked midway between the region's two largest cities, Rochester and Syracuse, is a gracious and historic small city hugging the north end of Seneca Lake. With about 15,000 residents, it's one of the larger towns in the region, an eminently livable small city and classic college town (it's home to Hobart and William Smith colleges). During the 19th century, Geneva was the major commercial hub of central New York; today, its revitalized downtown boasts an architecture fan's cornucopia of restored and stately century-old row houses and Victorian mansions with stunning backyards fronting the lake. The deepest of the Finger Lakes at 632 feet and more than 200 feet below sea level, Seneca Lake is a huge draw for outdoor activities.

Essentials

GETTING THERE

BY CAR   Geneva is south of I-90 along Route 14 and right on Routes 5 and 20, coming either west from Seneca Falls or east from Canandaigua.

BY BUS   **Greyhound** and **Trailways** deposit and pick up passengers at the Chalet Coffee Pot, 48 Lake St., Geneva (© **315/789-2582**).

VISITOR INFORMATION   The **Finger Lakes Visitors Connection** can be contacted at © **585/394-3915** or www.visitfingerlakes.com. The nearest walk-in information center is in Seneca Falls at the **Seneca Falls Heritage Area Visitor Center,** 89 Fall St. (© **315/568-1510;** www.senecafalls.com/history-heritage.php); it's open Monday to Saturday from 10am to 4pm and Sunday from noon to 4pm.

Exploring Geneva

Geneva, which grew up at the end of the 18th century on the banks of Seneca Lake, has an unexpected, eclectic collection of well-preserved **mansions ★★** of historic and architectural significance, including examples of Greek Revival, Federal, Victorian Gothic, and Jeffersonian styles, most from the first 3 decades of the 19th century. **South Main Street** is lined with row houses, resembling those of Georgetown in Washington, D.C., and grand mansions overlooking Seneca Lake. Besides the "South Main Street" walking tour brochure, pick up another one called "Architectural Landmarks" (available at the Prouty-Chew House & Museum; see below). Have a look at **Pulteney Park,** the original village green, and Washington, Genesee, Castle, and Jay streets to survey Geneva's architectural feast.

The **Rose Hill Mansion ★**, Route 96A, 1 mile south of Routes 5 and 20 (© **315/789-3848;** www.genevahistoricalsociety.com/Rose_Hill.htm), just east of Geneva and Seneca Lake, is an architectural landmark and excellent example of the Greek Revival style. Built in 1839, it reflects the grandeur of Geneva's early development. Once part of a sprawling lakefront farm, today it is a handsomely restored mansion with Empire furnishings; note the historically accurate and bold wallpaper. On the premises are a good information center, a short film about the house, and two antiques dealers in old carriage houses. The museum is open May through October Monday to Saturday from 10am to 4pm, and Sunday from 1 to 5pm. Admission is $7 adults, $6 seniors, $4 students ages 10 to 18, and $15 for families.

The **Finger Lakes Railway**, with trains operated by the central New York chapter of the National Railway Historical Society, offers occasional scenic trips through Cayuga and Seneca counties, including nine different Memorial Day Weekend excursions (for example, btw. Cayuga and Waterloo, and btw. Skaneateles and Solvay) and themed passenger trains (such as "Cartoon Capers," or "Ride the Rails with 19th-Century Women's Rights Enactors"). Round-trips generally range between $15 and $30. For more information call ℂ 315/209-1029, or for online ticketing, visit www.fingerlakesscenicrailway.com.

The **Prouty-Chew House & Museum,** 543 S. Main St. (ℂ **315/789-5151;** www.genevahistoricalsociety.com/PC_House.htm), is run by, and the headquarters of, the Geneva Historical Society. The building is an 1829 Federal-style home with significant late-19th-century modifications. Visitors are welcome to have a look around the house's two floors. You can also pick up **a self-guided architectural walking tour** map with details on about 50 buildings in Geneva. The Prouty-Chew House is open Tuesday to Friday from 9:30am to 4:30pm and Saturday (and Sun in July–Aug) from 1:30 to 4:30pm. Admission is $5.

A $2-million renovation has returned **The Smith Opera House ★★★**, 82 Seneca St. (ℂ **866/355-LIVE** [5483] or 315/781-5483; www.thesmith.org), to its original glory as a grand movie palace. Built in 1894 but given a whimsical Deco-baroque makeover in the 1930s, with fantastic murals and Moorish touches, the 1,400-seat theater was first an opera house and later a vaudeville theater. Today, it has carved out a niche showing independent and foreign art films and hosting rock and other concerts. Try to take in a movie or show; otherwise, if the box office is open and nothing is going on, ask for a peek inside.

Many of the two dozen wineries on the **Seneca Lake Wine Trail** are within easy reach of Geneva; see the sidebar on p. 322.

Sports & Outdoor Activities

Seneca Lake is one of the 2 largest of the 11 Finger Lakes. Pontoon and fishing-boat rentals are available from **Roy's Marina,** West Lake Road (Rte. 14; ℂ **315/789-3094). Seneca Lake State Park,** Routes 5 and 20, is on the north end of the lake; it's a good spot for strolls, and small kids will love the new playground and water sprays for cooling off in the summer heat. Seneca Lake is known for its **lake trout fishing,** and catches at the annual National Lake Trout Derby sometimes almost top the 100-pound mark.

Shopping

Waterloo Premium Outlets, 655 Rte. 318, Waterloo (ℂ **315/539-1100;** www. premiumoutlets.com/outlets/outlet.asp?id=9), near I-90 and between Geneva and Seneca Falls, has dozens of outlet stores, including Polo Ralph Lauren, Coach, and Mikasa. Two antiques shops operate on the premises of the **Rose Hill Mansion** (see above), selling furniture and antique collectibles on consignment. There are several antiques dealers downtown, including **Geneva Antique Co-op,** 473 Exchange St. (ℂ **315/789-5100). Red Jacket Orchards,** 957 Routes 5 and 20 (ℂ **315/781-2749),** has a nice array of fresh-picked apples and food items, including salsas,

Amish cheeses, and cider from Mennonite farmers. There are several pick-your-own orchards along Routes 5 and 20. The **Amish Country Store at Weaver-View Farms,** 1190 Earls Hill Rd. (🕾 **315/781-2571**), about 7 miles south of Geneva along Seneca Lake, stocks a good selection of quilts, homemade food items, and oak and pine Amish-made furnishings.

Where to Stay

Geneva has some of the grandest places to stay in the Finger Lakes, making it a good place to splurge. Although I'm not a fan of its bulky, suburban yellow-and-blue presence right on the north end of Seneca Lake, marring the beauty of the lakefront, the **Ramada Geneva Lakefront,** 41 Lakeshore Blvd., Geneva, NY 14456 (www.ramada.com; 🕾 **800/990-0907;** 148 units; $109–$199 double), does have good views, an indoor pool, and more affordable prices than some of the chic, historic inns in town.

Chambers in the Belhurst Castle/Vinifera Inn ★★ 🍷 A late-19th-century castle facing Seneca Lake, this is a unique and extraordinary place to stay in the Finger Lakes region. It truly is a castle, with incredible old-world style and massive proportions. All of the rooms are very different, so it's worthwhile taking a look at the website before deciding. Several years ago, Belhurst added a modern wing called **Vinifera Inn** and a wine-themed gift shop. The addition's 20 rooms are large and comfortable, but the design is a tad uninspired, and some of the decorating choices (a Jacuzzi tub in the middle of the room) are questionable. Within the old castle is a sumptuous restaurant—the site of many a wedding—and complimentary wine is always available from a second-floor spigot. A recent addition is the Isabella Spa & Salon. Off-season accommodations rates, especially in smaller rooms, are a true bargain.

Rte. 14 S., Geneva, NY 14456. www.belhurst.com. 🕾 **315/781-0201.** 36 units (14 castle and 20 Vinifera Inn). Belhurst Castle $90–$260 double, $185–$365 suite; Vinifera Inn $145–$295 double, $175–$355 suite. Rates include buffet breakfast. AE, DISC, MC, V. Free parking. **Amenities:** Restaurant; bar; spa; private beach; winery gift shop. *In room:* A/C, TV.

Geneva on the Lake ★ This grandiose—exclusive, elegant, and historic—lakeside hotel is one of the most distinguished in the Finger Lakes. It's a pretty incredible property, but it's also awfully pricey, and at least to me feels slightly out of sync with the mostly low-key Finger Lakes region. Still, that may be a selling point for some, and plenty of well-heeled folks don't seem to mind shelling out. Accommodations are handsomely appointed with Stickley or Chippendale furnishings, if a tad fussy, and all have kitchenettes. Oddly, some of the rooms have Murphy beds. The 70-foot pool perched at the end of the gardens and with lake views is positively Gatsby-like. To me, it seems more like a place to attend an over-the-top wedding than a place to stay for vacation, and judging from the roster of fancy nuptials held here, plenty of people agree.

1001 Lochland Rd., Rte. 14, Geneva, NY 14456. www.genevaonthelake.com. 🕾 **800/3-GENEVA** (343-6382) or 315/789-7190. Fax 315/789-0322. 29 units. $235–$715 double. Rates include full breakfast. AE, DISC, MC, V. Free parking. **Amenities:** Restaurant; bar; canoes; fishing dock; formal gardens; paddle boats; large outdoor pool; sailboats; windsurfer. *In room:* A/C, TV, Wi-Fi (in suites).

White Springs Manor ★★ 🍷 This grand Greek Revival farm mansion, a mile or so up the road away from the lake, has incredibly large rooms. It may not be at the edge of the lake, but it has plenty of character and splendid distant views of the Geneva area. Rooms are equipped with antiques and many have Jacuzzis. For privacy, rent the Playhouse, a free-standing little house with a stone fireplace and Jacuzzi in the front sitting room for those romantic evenings (you might want to close the

curtains on the front door); it's a very good value. Breakfast is served down at Belhurst Castle (where you'll also check in).

White Springs Lane, Geneva, NY 14456. www.belhurstcastle.com. (✆) **315/781-0201.** 16 units. $75–$195 double; $115–$255 suite. Rates include continental breakfast. AE, DISC, MC, V. Free parking. *In room:* A/C, TV.

Yale Manor Bed & Breakfast ★ 👔   A peaceful B&B on the east side of Seneca Lake (7 miles southeast of Geneva), this early-1900s manor house on 10 acres with lake views is a very nice place to stay. Visitors can trek down to the lakefront, where there's a little A-frame house with a deck, a nice spot to relax or swim. Rooms are elegant and understated; particularly nice is the Monticello Room. Families can take over the two simplest rooms, which share a bathroom. From May to October, there is a 2-night minimum stay on weekends.

563 Yale Farm Rd., Romulus, NY 14541. www.yalemanor.com. (✆) **315/585-2208.** Fax 315/585-6438. 6 units, 4 with private bathrooms. $130–$165 double; $240 family suite. Rates include full breakfast. AE, MC, V. Free parking. **Amenities:** Lakefront swimming area. *In room:* A/C, Wi-Fi.

Where to Eat

In addition to the restaurants below, **Belhurst Castle** (see "Where to Stay," above) has a sumptuous formal restaurant, Edgar's, and a more casual grill, Stonecutter's, overlooking the lake. The latter's outdoor terrace can't be beat for lake views.

The Cobblestone Restaurant NORTHERN ITALIAN   An elegant restaurant in an attractive Greek Revival house (inhabiting a former stagecoach stop and the original tavern of a 1790 gentleman's farm), this is the top dining spot in town. There's an atmospheric small dining room downstairs and several others upstairs, where there's a deck with nice long views over Geneva. The menu focuses on classic dishes, such as wood-grilled steaks and chops, chicken parmigiana, fresh lobster, and veal scaloppine. The small and affordably priced wine list includes a number of the Finger Lakes' best.

3610 Pre-Emption Rd. (at Hamilton St./Routes 5 and 20, west of downtown). (✆) **315/789-8498.** www. cobblestonegeneva.com. Reservations recommended. Main courses $18–$28. AE, DISC, MC, V. Tues–Fri 11:30am–3pm; daily 5–10pm.

Parker's Grille & Tap House GRILL/PUB FARE   Down the street from the Smith Opera House, this is a good, casual place for a meal before or after the show, and it's also a fine spot for a drink. The pub fare of burgers, finger foods, hot sandwiches, and Tex-Mex isn't surprising, but it's inexpensive and solidly prepared. The baby back ribs are a local favorite. A nice selection of beers and a number of local wines are good accompaniment for anything on the menu.

100 Seneca St. (✆) **315/789-4656.** Reservations recommended. Main courses $11–$23. AE, DISC, MC, V. Tues–Sun 11:30am–midnight.

Red Dove Tavern ★ 🍴 CREATIVE PUB FARE/TAPAS   With a nice beer selection, tasty seasonal cocktails, and fun atmosphere, this casual pub and restaurant— where the small menu on a chalkboard changes weekly—has become a local favorite. Calling itself "the Finger Lakes' answer to a gastropub," it looks to be a down-and-dirty bar, but the interior is cool, clean, and contemporary, with local artists' work on the walls. In addition to expected pork and veggie sandwiches, you'll find unexpected items such as grilled octopus, tuna tartare, and creative tapas. Saturday brunch is well worth checking out.

30 Castle St. (✆) **315/781-2020.** www.reddovetavern.com. Reservations accepted for parties of 6 or more. Main courses $12–$19. AE, DISC, MC, V. Tues–Fri 11am–1am; Sat 11am–2am.

Geneva After Dark

The Smith Opera House ★★★, 82 Seneca St. (© **866/355-LIVE** [5483] or 315/781-5483; www.thesmith.org), is the coolest after-dark spot in town and one of the best venues in upstate New York. Whether you catch a concert, such as Blues Traveler or the Dave Matthews Band, or see a movie on its huge screen, this 1930s gem has superb acoustics and is just a fantastic place to hang out. There's a neat little bar downstairs, though it doesn't serve alcohol during film sessions. The **Geneva Summer Arts Festival** (July–Aug) features dance, theater, music, and art exhibits. Among the performances, held at several venues including the Smith Opera House, are Lakefront Gazebo concerts, featuring everything from jazz to choral music. For a schedule of events, ask at the Visitor Information Center, or visit www.geneva.ny.us/ Rec/rec-Concerts.html. The restaurant **Hamilton 258,** 258 Hamilton St. (© **315/781-5323**), has a cool martini bar.

SENECA FALLS & NORTHERN CAYUGA LAKE ★★

10 miles E of Geneva; 48 miles E of Syracuse; 42 miles N of Ithaca

Perched on the falls of the Seneca River and a section of the legendary Erie Canal, and cradled between the two largest of the Finger Lakes, Seneca Falls was such a quintessential American small town that Frank Capra apparently used it as the model for Bedford Falls in his classic movie *It's a Wonderful Life.* Yet the town is more significantly known for its rabble-rousing past. In the mid–19th century, Seneca Falls was home to political activists who fought for women's suffrage and civil rights for African Americans. The town is considered the birthplace of women's rights, and some women enamored of that history have moved to Seneca Falls to make it their home.

Cayuga Lake is the longest of the Finger Lakes, 42 miles from end to end.

Essentials

GETTING THERE

BY CAR   Seneca Falls is south of I-90 along Route 414 and equidistant on Routes 5 and 20 between Geneva and Auburn.

VISITOR INFORMATION   Seneca Falls Heritage Area Visitor Center, 89 Fall St. (© **315/568-2703;** www.senecafalls.com), is open Monday to Saturday from 10am to 4pm and Sunday from noon to 4pm. **Cayuga County Office of Tourism,** 131 Genesee St., Auburn (© **800/499-9615** or 315/255-1658; www.tour cayuga.com), is open Monday to Friday from 9am to 5pm, Saturday 9am to 2pm.

Exploring Seneca Falls

The first Women's Rights Convention, the foundation for the modern struggle for civil rights, was held at the Wesleyan Methodist Chapel in Seneca Falls in 1848. The **Women's Rights National Historical Park** ★★, 136 Fall St. (© **315/568-2991;** www.nps.gov/wori), which is run by the National Park Service, commemorates the struggle initiated by Elizabeth Cady Stanton, Lucretia Mott, Susan B. Anthony, Frederick Douglass, and others (the abolitionist and women's rights movements were linked from early on); such happenings at Seneca Falls expanded the definition of liberty in the United States. The extant remains of the original chapel, where 300 people gathered on July 19, 1848, and the landmark "Declaration of Sentiments" was drafted, is next to a museum that's jampacked with information about women's and civil rights history. The museum does an excellent job raising issues to think about for visitors of both genders and all ages, which is why it's also a great place for kids, who can also be made "Junior Rangers." The museum is open daily from 9am to 5pm; admission is free.

Seneca Falls has, quite understandably, become a place of pilgrimage for people with a specific interest in women's and civil rights. A host of related sights, including the **Elizabeth Cady Stanton House,** 32 Washington St. (© **315/568-2991;** www.nps.gov/wori/historyculture/elizabeth-cady-stanton.htm; guided tours $1; sign up at Park Visitor Center), are located in and around Seneca Falls; pick up the booklet *Women's Rights Trail,* at the museum gift shop. Down the street from the Historical Park is the **National Women's Hall of Fame,** 76 Fall St. (© **315/568-8060;** www.greatwomen.org), which is a good place to see, in name and achievement, how far women have come since the days of that legendary convention. It honors the achievements of American women in diverse fields. It's open May through September Monday to Saturday 10am to 5pm and Sunday noon to 5pm; October through April Wednesday to Saturday 11am to 5pm; admission is adults $3, students and seniors $1.50, families $7. Also worth a brief look, especially for those with an interest in the upstate canal system across the street, is the **Seneca Museum of Waterways and Industry,** 89 Fall St. (© **315/568-1510**), which tells the story of transportation and industrialization in the region.

Today, Seneca Falls is relatively quiet and unassuming as compared to its tumultuous past. **Van Cleef Lake,** forged as an expansion of the New York State Barge Canal, is one of the prettiest (and most photographed) spots in the Finger Lakes. The banks of the Cayuga-Seneca Canal are being prettified with benches and paths. The downtown area, essentially a main street with two bridges over the canal (one of which distinctly recalls that pivotal scene in *It's a Wonderful Life*), is charming, and Fall Street is lined with nice shops, including the very appropriate **WomanMade Products** (91 Fall St.; © **315/568-9364;** www.womanmadeproducts.com), a very enjoyable place to while away an afternoon.

At the north end of Cayuga Lake and 5 miles east of Seneca Falls, **Montezuma National Wildlife Refuge ★★**, 395 Routes 5 and 20 east, Seneca Falls (© **315/568-5987;** www.fws.gov/r5mnwr; daily 8am–5pm; visitor center Apr–Oct Mon–Fri 10am–3pm, Sat–Sun 10am–4pm; Nov weekends only 10am–3pm; closed Dec–Mar), established in 1938, is a magnificent spot for birding and a fantastic spot for families to get up close and personal with wildlife. The marshes in this part of the Finger Lakes are a preferred rest stop along the Atlantic Migratory Flyway, and the 7,000 acres of wetlands attract thousands of waterfowl and other water birds—including Canada geese, blue herons, egrets, and wood ducks—on their long journeys from nesting areas in Canada (at the height of migration, as many as two million birds occupy the area). During the fall migration, the peak for geese and ducks is mid- to late November; for shorebirds and wading birds, mid-August to mid-September. During the spring migration that is less flashy than fall, waterfowl peak in late February through April, while the peak of warbler migration is mid-May. In addition to walking trails, there's a self-guided Wildlife Drive (in winter, there are cross-country skiing and snowshoeing). Ask in the visitor center for the location of the bald eagle's nest.

For more information on visiting the area's wineries, particularly those around Cayuga Lake, see the sidebar on the **Cayuga Wine Trail,** on p. 312.

Sports & Outdoor Activities

The Cayuga branch of the Erie Canal system leads directly to Cayuga Lake and flows directly through Seneca Falls. Outdoors enthusiasts could hardly have a better or more historic place to hike or bike than the **Erie Canal Trail ★★**, which runs along the historic canal towpath from the village of Jordan to Montezuma and the Seneca River. For more information, call ✆ **315/252-2791. Liberty Boat Tours** (✆ **877/472-6688**) in Seneca Falls does canal and lake tours, and the **River Otter Boat Tour,** Riverforest Park, 9439 Riverforest Rd., off Route 34 in Weedsport, operates 2-hour tours (Mon and Sat at 10am and 2pm) of the Seneca River and Erie Canal (for reservations, call ✆ **315/252-4171**). **Cayuga Lake State Park** (✆ **315/568-5163**), 2678 Lower Lake Rd., on the west side of the lake, has campgrounds (✆ **315/568-0919**), nature trails, playgrounds, a launch site, and docking. Cayuga Lake is known for its bass fishing, while Seneca Lake has superb trout fishing. On the shores of the two lakes are four state parks and numerous sites for swimming, boating, and picnicking. For fishing charters on Cayuga Lake, try **Eagle Rock Charters** (✆ **315/889-5925;** www.ctbw.com/eaglerock). *Note:* If you want to sail your own boat along the Erie Canal, get a brochure with more information about docking and attractions from Rochester to Syracuse by calling ✆ **800/499-9615.**

For bird-watching, don't miss the spectacular **Montezuma National Wildlife Refuge** (see above). And if you want to fly like a bird, check out **Sunset Adventures Balloon Rides,** Beech Tree Road, Auburn (✆ **315/252-9474;** www.fingerlakes-ballooning.com).

Where to Stay

There are a couple of good B&Bs in Seneca Falls, a chic new boutique hotel, and a large and clean, inexpensive chain motel (**Microtel Inn & Suites;** 1966 Routes 5 and 20; www.microtelinn.com; ✆ **315/539-8438**) on the outskirts of town.

Barrister's B&B ★   This cozy and attractive small inn on one of Seneca Falls' loveliest streets (within walking distance of downtown and the canal), now under new ownership, is an 1888 Colonial Revival that has been very nicely restored and converted into a B&B. The house, run by a local couple, retains handsome details like carved fireplaces and original stained-glass windows, and the comfortable rooms, many of which get great light, have been attractively decorated. Grandmother's Room has a very large bathroom, the Grace Yawger room is nice and quiet, and Erin's Retreat is a large suite with an adjoining sitting room.

56 Cayuga St., Seneca Falls, NY 13148. www.sleepbarristers.com. ✆ **800/914-0145** or 315/568-0145. 5 units. $130–$185 double. Rates include full breakfast. 2-night minimum weekends Apr–Dec. AE, MC, V. Free parking. *In room:* A/C, Wi-Fi.

Hotel Clarence ★★   Surprisingly contemporary, chic, and urban in this historic small town, the Hotel Clarence—named for the angel in *It's a Wonderful Life* (supposedly based on Seneca Falls), this 2-year-old midsize hotel with a boutique feel is a welcome addition to the northern reaches of Cayuga Lake—and a great alternative to chain motels and homey B&Bs. From the attractive redbrick exterior to the interior's clean lines, chandeliers, boldly colored modern furnishings, and large black-and-white photo stills from the movie, the hotel is committed to its aesthetic. The accommodations aren't large, but they have high ceilings and hardwood floors and are very nicely outfitted, with plush linens and robes and flatscreen TVs. Service might not always match the aims of the hotel, though the on-site Vineyard 108 Restaurant is the town's best.

108 Fall St., Seneca Falls, NY 13148. www.hotelclarence.com. ℂ **877/788-4010.** 48 units. $119–$159 double, weekends $179–$219 double AE, DISC, MC, V. Free parking. *In room:* A/C, MP3 docking station, Wi-Fi (free).

Hubbell House A charming 1855 Gothic Revival meticulously decorated and chock-full of Victorian goodies, including dolls, pictures, and books, this professionally run inn is a very nice place to stay, partly due to its location on Van Cleef Lake. The house (all nonsmoking) has a walkway down to gardens and a sweet little pier on the lake; some rooms, as well as the dining room and screened porch, have picturesque lake views. Breakfast is served on china with fresh-squeezed orange juice and items like "Victorian French toast." The Laura Hoskins Hubbell room is over-the-top Victoriana, while other rooms are more sedate and very cozy.

42 Cayuga St., Seneca Falls, NY 13148. www.hubbellhousebb.com. ℂ **315/568-9690.** 4 units. $145–$165 double. Rates include full breakfast. AE, DISC, MC, V. Free parking. *In room:* A/C, Wi-Fi.

John Morrison Manor Bed & Breakfast ★ 🍴 About 3 miles from downtown Seneca Falls, and set on nearly 6 acres of pretty hilltop grounds, this 1838 Greek Revival manor is a fine place to decamp. The five rooms are quite different in size and decor, ranging from country elegant to understated cool (the "pool room" is the most sedate, while others feature more decorative flourishes). The house has several parlors, a fireside den, and an in-ground pool. The country breakfast may be served on the porch or poolside patio in season. A rarity among small B&Bs—no doubt because the two gentleman innkeepers are enamored of their own dogs—the inn has two rooms that are designated pet-friendly.

2138 Rte. 89, Seneca Falls, NY 13148. www.johnmorrismanor.com. ℂ **866/484-4218** or 315/568-9057. 5 units. $115–$175 double. Rate includes full breakfast. AE, DISC, MC, V. Free parking. Pets accepted in 2 units. **Amenities:** Outdoor pool. *In room:* A/C.

Where to Eat

Downtown Deli, 53 Fall St. (ℂ **315/568-9943**), sporting a deck facing the canal, is a good stop for New York–style sandwiches, salads, and soups. **Bailey's,** 95 Fall St. (ℂ **315/568-0929**), is an ice-cream parlor and sandwich shop named, of course, for the character of the same name in *It's a Wonderful Life.* The popular neighborhood joint, **Henry B's,** picked up and moved west to Rochester.

DiVine Restaurant & Bar (Hotel Clarence) ★★ ☺ AMERICAN/BBQ An open and airy, high-ceilinged, contemporary restaurant off the lobby of the Hotel Clarence, this dinner-only eatery is as much a departure from the small-town feel of Seneca Falls as is the hotel that is its home. Its glistening wood floors, painted brick walls and wood tables give it a casual, but urban feel. Start by sharing "vineyard tapas" (including goat cheese and house-smoked chorizo sausage) or house-made Gorgonzola kettle chips. With its own BBQ smoker and wood-fired grill, the specialties are items like beef brisket, pulled pork sliders, Black Angus burgers, and wood-fired grilled rib-eye, but non–meat eaters can opt for pastas or pan-seared scallops and risotto. There's a nice little menu of children's plates and a gourmet version of mac and cheese that should keeps the kids happy.

108 Fall St.ℂ **877/712-4000.** www.hotelclarence.com/dining.html. Reservations recommended. Main courses $15–$28. AE, DISC, MC, V. Daily 5–10pm (tavern opens at 3pm).

Seneca Falls After Dark

Seneca Falls has a surprisingly bustling little cluster of bars on Fall Street. Part of a dying breed, the **Finger Lakes Drive-In,** Routes 5 and 20, Auburn (ℂ **315/252-3969**),

THE underground RAILROAD

After passages of the Fugitive Slave Law in 1850, even the free states of the North were considered unsafe for run-away slaves. The Underground Railroad, the secretive lines of communication and safe houses that carried many slaves along a very dangerous path from the South to freedom in Canada, was active throughout central New York State. Many stops were in the Finger Lakes region. Auburn was home of Harriet Tubman, a former slave who conducted more than 300 people to freedom. The Seward House in Auburn was also an important stop on the Underground Railroad. Frederick Douglass, abolitionist and publisher of the newspaper *The North Star,* lived in Rochester and is buried in Mt. Hope Cemetery there. For more information on the Underground Railroad in New York and principal abolitionist activists, see **www.nyhistory.com/ugrr/links.htm**.

shows first-run movies from April to October, and is a popular spot in summer months.

Auburn

East of Montezuma and midway to Skaneateles is the town of **Auburn,** which, though larger than Seneca Falls, doesn't have quite the charms of its neighbor; it does, however, possess a handful of historic sights. Chief among them is the **Willard Memorial Chapel,** 17 Nelson St. (© **315/252-0339;** www.willardchapel.org), the surviving piece of the once-grand Auburn Theological Seminary, built in 1818. But this Romanesque chapel holds a treasure: an interior designed by Louis Comfort Tiffany, apparently the only existing example of a complete and unaltered Tiffany interior. The series of stained-glass windows, including a nine-paneled Rose Window, and leaded-glass chandeliers are stunning. The chapel is open Tuesday to Friday from 10am to 4pm; suggested donation is $3.

The **Seward House ★**, 33 South St. (© **315/252-1283;** www.sewardhouse. org), is a National Historic Landmark and former home of the 19th-century statesman who served as U.S. secretary of state, U.S. senator, and New York governor. The handsome 19th-century home is very nearly a national library, so extensive is its collection of family artifacts, historical documents, and items collected from the life and travels of William H. Seward. Seward was known principally for negotiating the purchase of Alaska, derided in the press at the time as "Seward's Folly," and as Abraham Lincoln's Secretary of State, attacked and seriously stabbed by a would-be murderer as part of the conspiracy that felled Lincoln. The museum is open mid-October to December 31 and February through June Tuesday to Saturday from 11am to 4pm; from July to mid-October, it's also open Sunday from 1 to 4pm. Admission is $8 adults, $7 seniors, $5 students, free for children 5 and under.

SKANEATELES LAKE ★★★

23 miles W of Syracuse; 32 miles E of Geneva

Hard to pronounce and about as complicated to spell, Skaneateles ("Skinny-atlas") is perhaps the most beautiful and photogenic town in the Finger Lakes region, the only one whose main street backs right up to the curved shore of a sinewy Finger Lake. A small village surprisingly well endowed with creature comforts for visitors, it is deservedly one of the most popular stops in the region. With a moneyed past and long favored by those in the know, it gained a considerable amount of attention several years ago when President Clinton and his wife vacationed here at the home of a wealthy friend. Skaneateles comes as close to emitting a chic Hamptons vibe as you'll find in upstate New York, though it's much more relaxed and personable. At Christmastime, the village defines quaint, becoming a Dickensian postcard with costumed carolers parading around the streets.

Essentials

GETTING THERE

BY CAR   Skaneateles is on Route 20 west of Syracuse; from the south, take Route 41 North, which traces the east side of Skaneateles Lake, off I-81.

VISITOR INFORMATION   The **Skaneateles Chamber of Commerce** is located at 22 Jordan St. (© **315/685-0552;** www.skaneateles.com).

Exploring Skaneateles

Skaneateles's charming and **historic downtown ★★★**, which lovingly cradles the northern shore of Skaneateles Lake, is the prettiest in the Finger Lakes region. A graceful collection of 19th-century Greek Revival and Victorian homes and charming independent shops, it looks and feels more like a classic New England village than one in upstate New York. But Skaneateles is endowed with incredible natural gifts as well: Transparent Skaneateles Lake—one of the cleanest lakes in North America—cuts a gorgeous, 16-mile-long, gently curved swath through low hills and dense green forest. Former New York State Governor and Secretary of State William Seward called it "the most beautiful body of water in the world." On the lakefront are a picturesque gazebo and a long pier that juts out over the water.

East Genesee Street, which in any other town would be called Main Street, is lined with quaint boutiques and antiques shops, as well as restaurants and inns. Inside the impressive gray-stone town library, at 49 E. Genesee St., is the **John D. Barrow Art Gallery** (© **315/685-5135;** www.barrowgallery.org; Memorial Day to Labor Day Mon–Sat 1–4pm, May and Labor Day–Dec Sat 1–4pm; free admission), where you'll find a nice collection of paintings by the library's namesake, a Skaneateles-born artist and painter of Hudson Valley landscapes. **The Creamery,** 28 Hannum St., off West Genesee Street (© **315/685-1360;** May–Sept Thurs–Sat 1–4pm, Oct–May Fri 10am–4pm [Call for more specific hours]; free admission), is a restored creamery dating from 1899 and home to the Skaneateles Historical Society and Museum and its small collection of town historical artifacts. **Walking tours** of Skaneateles are conducted by Historical Society members during summer months; call © **315/685-1360** or 315/485-6841 for information.

Skaneateles's emphasis on culture and the arts is disproportionate to its small size. The town hosts festivals throughout the summer, including free band concerts at the gazebo in Clift Park on Skaneateles Lake during Friday and Saturday evenings in summer; the **Finger Lakes Antique and Classic Boat Show** the last week of July; and the widely attended **Skaneateles Festival ★**, 97 Genesee St. (© **315/685-7418;** www.skanfest.org), which features chamber music as many as 5 nights a week at several venues throughout August and early September. However, the biggest event in Skaneateles doesn't take place in summer. The **Dickens Christmas ★★** celebration revels in old-world Victoriana, with costumed Dickens characters parading about the streets, interacting with visitors and singing Christmas carols. There are free carriage rides around Skaneateles and free roasted chestnuts and hot chocolate. The celebration, a great family event, begins the day after Thanksgiving and is held every Saturday and Sunday from noon to 4pm through December 22.

Sports & Outdoor Activities

Clift Park on Skaneateles Lake has open public swimming. **Thayer Park,** east of the downtown shops, is a quiet, beautiful park for relaxing and enjoying the view. **Austin Park,** 1 Austin St. (btw. Jordan and State sts.), has a playground, basketball and tennis courts, and a track for walking, biking, or skating. The **Charlie Major Nature Trail,** along the Old Short line, between Old Seneca Turnpike and Crow Hill Road, is good for hiking. **Biking** the 32-mile perimeter around the Skaneateles Lake is big with cycling clubs (and, of course, with motorcyclists).

However, the best outdoor activity in Skaneateles is getting out on the lake, and a great way to do so is by cruise boat. **Mid-Lakes Navigation Co. ★,** 11 Jordan St. (② 800/545-4318 or 315/685-8500; www.midlakesnav.com), a longtime local, family-run business, organizes cruises on Skaneateles Lake, including 1-hour sightseeing, Sunday brunch, champagne dinner, and luncheon cruises. If that's too typical, try boarding a U.S. mail boat as it delivers mail to old-fashioned camps on the lake. Call for more information. They also do cruises along the Erie Canal. Most cruises are in July and August. For kayaking instruction and rentals, try **NorthWind Expedition Kayaks,** 2825 W. Lake Rd. (② 315/685-4808; www.northwindkayaks.com); for pontoon, sailboat, canoe, and kayak rentals, see **The Sailboat Shop,** 1322 E. Genesee St. (② 315/685-7558).

The Sherwood Inn owns an antique Chris Craft, *The Stephanie,* on which it offers sunset cruises and sightseeing tours; call ② 800/3-SHERWOOD (374-3796) for more information. For fishing charters and sunset cruises on the lake, contact **Lakeview Charters,** 2478 E. Lake Rd. (② 315/685-8176).

Shopping

Skaneateles is, with the exception of the two largest cities, Rochester and Syracuse, the top shopping destination in the Finger Lakes. The compact downtown area of the village, with just a couple of streets intersecting Genesee Street, is full of unique and quaint shops. **Skaneateles Antique Center,** 12 E. Genesee St. (② 315/685-0752), has several dealers and lots of china, mission furniture, and pottery. Another nice antiques shop 12 miles south of town, on the west side of the lake, is **New Hope Antiques,** 5963 New Hope Rd., in—you guessed it—New Hope (② 315/497-2688). It's housed in a 1920s farmhouse and has a good selection of furnishings and collectibles; it's open from the end of May to October, but closed Tuesday and Wednesday. **Cate & Sally,** 58 E. Genesee St. (② 315/685-1105), is a very chic clothing store for women's fashions; I had to usher my wife out of there in a hurry on a recent trip. **Pomodoro,** 61 E. Genesee St. (② 315/685-8658), is a very feminine, sweet little shop in an adorable house that's packed to the rafters with home furnishings, candles, and all manner of gift items. **Rhubarb Kitchen & Garden Shop,** 59 E. Genesee St. (② 315/685-5803), carries an excellent selection of cookbooks, kitchen and garden items, and even gourmet foods. Quilters will be in heaven at **Patchwork Plus Quilt Shop,** 36 Jordan St. (② 315/685-6979), which stocks more than 5,000 bolts of fabric and has quilting classes.

Where to Stay

Skaneateles has a superb supply of B&Bs, inns, and small hotels clustered around the lake and downtown, including a couple of the best inns in the entire region. Among the very nice (predominantly Victorian in style) B&Bs—apart from the real standouts, reviewed below—in Skaneateles are **The Benjamin Porter House ★**, 10 State St. (www.benjaminporterhouse.com; ✆ **315/685-8611;** $225 double), a handsome, elegantly decorated and sophisticated 1805 Federal building in the heart of the village, walking distance to the lake; and **Frog Pond Bed & Breakfast ★**, 680 Sheldon Rd. (www.frogpondbandb.com; ✆ **315/685-0146;** $150 double), a 180-year-old stone house on the National Historic Register, with just two large rooms a couple miles north of Skaneateles on 130 acres.

Less expensive lodging is available in motels on the outskirts of town on the way to either Syracuse or Auburn, such as **Whispering Winds Motel,** Route 20 (www.whisperingwindsmotel.net; ✆ **800/396-7719;** $79–$109 double), with a large, heated outdoor pool; open May through mid-October.

EXPENSIVE

Hobbit Hollow Farm B&B ★★★ 🛏   This serene and princely estate with luxuriously appointed rooms is a place to pamper yourself. The house, a 100-year-old Colonial Revival, sits on 400 acres about 3 miles from town, next to a large horse barn, with panoramic lake views. The house is first-class in every detail, from the antique furnishings to the crisp linens and beautiful bathrooms. Breakfast is served with silver and Waterford crystal. All the accommodations are different in decor and size; my favorite is the Lake View room, with a four-poster bed and a massive bathroom and Jacuzzi. The Master Suite has a private veranda and fireplace, while the Chanticleer room is sunny and charming, with a funky "pencil" bed. Less expensive rooms are smaller, but cozy and also quite charming; if you're looking for a bargain stay in a rarified place, check out the Twin Room, which ranks as a steal.

3061 W. Lake Rd., Skaneateles, NY 13152. www.hobbithollow.com. ✆ **800/3-SHERWOOD** (374-3796) or 315/685-2791. Fax 315/685-3426. 5 units. $150–$250 double; $250–$300 suite. Rates include full breakfast. AE, DISC, MC, V. Free parking. *In room:* A/C, TV, Wi-Fi.

Mirbeau Inn & Spa ★★   Located about 2 blocks west of downtown, this property strikes out in a bold direction all its own. Rooms are decorated in a modern French country style with rich fabrics, fireplaces, and huge bathrooms, and are set around a Monet-like garden and pond and 12 acres of woodlands. The spa facilities, with a sumptuous palazzo of a relaxation room, are extraordinary; the massage rooms are some of the most inviting I've seen. The inn's restaurant stands very much on its own merits; though not inexpensive, it provides one of the finest dining experiences in the region. For a splurge for both body and soul, Mirbeau is among the best. A number of packages, with spa treatments and dinner included, are available; check the website for current offers. The 12,000-square-foot spa is also open to the public as a day spa, though advance booking is essential.

851 W. Genesee St., Skaneateles, NY 13152. www.mirbeau.com. ✆ **877/647-2328** or 315/685-1927. Fax 315/685-5150. 34 units. $229–$415 double. Rates include continental breakfast. AE, DISC, MC, V. Free parking. **Amenities:** Restaurant; bar; sauna; spa w/exercise room; steam room. *In room:* A/C, TV/DVD, CD player, Wi-Fi.

MODERATE

Sherwood Inn ★★   Right in the heart of Skaneateles, this cozy and sensitively restored inn on the main drag, once a stagecoach stop in the early 1800s, has wide-open lake views from its porch. You'll find hardwood floors in the hallways, four-poster and canopy beds in the rooms, and a genteel, lived-in, old-money feel. My favorite is the swank and romantic Red Room (no. 31), with a fireplace, a Jacuzzi, and a funky light fixture. The elegant restaurant has a beautiful porch with unequaled lake views, and a clubby tavern, a Euro-style pub with wooden booths and green leather chairs. If it's full, you may want to inquire about the nearby Packwood House (www.packwoodhouse.com; $180–$225 double), managed by Sherwood but with a decidedly more corporate look and feel.

26 W. Genesee St., Skaneateles, NY 13152. www.thesherwoodinn.com. (℗ **800/374-3796** or 315/685-3405. Fax 315/685-8983. 25 units. $150–$245 double. AE, DISC, MC, V. Free parking. **Amenities:** Restaurant; bar. *In room:* A/C, TV, Wi-Fi.

The Village Inn of Skaneateles   Just a block off Genesee Street, this tiny, no-smoking inn, like a cross between a European boutique hotel and a B&B, is a smart place to stay. Wholly renovated, it is very well equipped and has a modern feel, though the building dates from 1830. All rooms have gas fireplaces, whirlpool bath-tubs, and Stickley furniture. The Cottage Room has exposed-brick walls, while the Terrace Room has a private balcony overlooking Skaneateles Lake. If you choose, you can take breakfast on the porch at the Sherwood Inn.

25 Jordan St., Skaneateles, NY 13152. www.villageinn-skaneateles.com. (℗ **800/374-3796** or 315/685-3405. 4 units. May–Dec $190–$220 double (inquire about off-season rates). Rates include continental breakfast. AE, DISC, MC, V. Free parking. *In room:* A/C, TV, high-speed Internet access.

Where to Eat

In addition to the restaurants listed below, **Sherwood Inn** (see above), which has a large formal dining room and an inexpensive tavern, offers a large and varied menu and is a popular dining spot—so popular, in fact, that in high season you'll definitely have to wait. For fantastic artisanal breads and pastries, don't miss the exceptional French bakery **Pâtisserie ★**, 4 Hannum St. (℗ **315/685-2433**), located just behind the Sherwood Inn.

EXPENSIVE

The Dining Room at Mirbeau ★ FRENCH COUNTRY   At this innovative small spa hotel, the dining room is elegant French Provincial, with a serene terrace overlooking the pond for outdoor dining. Though the space is refined and sophisti-cated, patrons are as likely to wear jeans as jackets (or spa robes during the day). The evening menu is like that of a country steakhouse, with classic French sauces, a raw bar, and entrees like Hudson Valley duck, steak fritte, rack of lamb, and fresh seafood flown in daily. However, dining here isn't quite the experience it was a few years ago, and service can be spotty, and some diners find it overly expensive. Lunch features lighter items—"spa cuisine"—and a good-value, three-course tasting menu for $25 (the same price as the indulgent Sun brunch). Desserts are worth saving room for, and the wine list is extensive and superbly chosen.

851 W. Genesee St. (℗ **877/MIRBEAU** (647-2328) or 315/685-5006. www.mirbeau.com/dining. Reser-vations required. Main courses $17–$40. AE, DISC, MC, V. Daily 11:30am–2pm and 5–10pm.

Rosalie's Cucina ★ TUSCAN   A friendly, family-run, and vibrant Tuscan restau-rant, a few blocks west of the center of town, Rosalie's is a local favorite with very loyal customers—though others grouse about the prices. The casually attractive Tuscan-style dining room and kitchen are inviting, service is outstanding, and the food is hearty and deliciously authentic. The antipasto is a perfect way to start, and though there are a few choices of homemade pastas, the main courses concentrate on very substantial, country-style meat dishes, such as *vitello Marsala* (veal in Marsala wine), braciola (prime sirloin scaloppine stuffed with prosciutto), and *arrosto di maiale* (slow-roasted pork). Out back is an excellent bakery, with hand-rolled pastries and specialty breads, and the desserts are terrific.

841 W. Genesee St. (©) **315/685-2200.** www.rosaliescucina.com. Reservations recommended. Main courses $22–$40. AE, MC, V. Sun–Thurs 5–9pm; Fri–Sat 5–10pm.

MODERATE

KaBuki SUSHI/PAN-ASIAN   This cute, hip, colorful—and tiny—sushi and Asian restaurant isn't perhaps what you might expect in this traditional town, but locals have embraced it. Start with Thai lettuce wraps and move on to a Szechuan tangerine stir-fry or sake-steamed salmon. Or sit at the bar and enjoy sushi and cut rolls to your heart's content.

12 W. Genesee St. (©) **315/685-7234.** www.kabukiofskaneateles.com. Reservations recommended. Main courses $10–$19. No credit cards. Tues–Thurs 5–9pm; Fri–Sat 5–10pm.

Skaneateles After Dark

Morris's Grill, 6 W. Genesee St. (© **315/685-7761**), a laid-back bar next to KaBuki, is the local hangout. The tavern at the **Sherwood Inn** (see above), which has a cozy bar and a fireplace, as well as fantastic lake views, is also a popular spot for a drink. In summer, evening activities tend to center on the music festivals in town; on Friday and Saturday nights, there's live music at the gazebo in **Clift Park** on the north shore of Skaneateles Lake.

SYRACUSE

145 miles W of Albany; 245 miles NW of New York City; 58 miles NE of Ithaca

It may not have a romantic ring to it, as do many villages in the Finger Lakes, and as a modern, rather industrial upstate city, Syracuse isn't vitally connected to the natural beauty of the region; however, the second-largest city in the area is the principal eastern gateway to the Finger Lakes. Syracuse is perhaps best known as the home of basketball's former NCAA National Champion Orangemen, but this city grew up on the Erie Canal and was once known as "Salt City," when its role was to supply the U.S. with salt. Today, Syracuse is staking its future on the largest mall in the U.S., Destiny USA, the current Carousel Center that developers are slowly remaking into a massive (and largely green) resortlike shopping experience. Beyond those outsized shopping experiences, Syracuse is a city that appeals mostly to passersby and business travelers. However, it is also a good, brief gateway stop for families.

Essentials

GETTING THERE

BY PLANE   **Syracuse Hancock International Airport** (SYR), 2001 Airport Blvd., Syracuse (© **315/454-4330;** www.syrairport.org), 10 minutes from downtown, is serviced by Air Canada, American, Continental, Delta, JetBlue, Northwest, United, and US Airways. **Century Transportation** (© **315/455-5151**) provides taxi and van service at Syracuse Hancock International Airport. There are five major car-rental agencies at the airport.

BY CAR   Syracuse is located at the intersection of two major highways: Interstate 81, running north-south, and the New York State Thruway, I-90, running east-west.

BY BUS Greyhound and **Trailways** stop in Syracuse at the Regional Transportation Center, 130 P and C Pkwy., Syracuse (© **315/472-4421** or 472-5338).

BY TRAIN Amtrak (© **800/USA-RAIL** [872-7245]; www.amtrak.com) travels to Syracuse from New York City, Buffalo, Boston, and other cities. The Regional Transportation Center is located at 130 P and C Pkwy.

GETTING AROUND

OnTrack City Express trains (© **315/424-1212**) run from Syracuse University to the main station at Armory Square, 269 W. Jefferson St., and Carousel Center mall. Trains operate Wednesday to Sunday 11:25am to 6:20pm (in summer Fri–Sun); tickets are $1.50 one-way (pay as you board).

CENTRO buses (© **315/685-7075;** www.centro.org; $1.25) travel to Skaneateles and Auburn.

VISITOR INFORMATION The principal font of tourism information is the **Syracuse Convention and Visitors Bureau,** 572 S. Salina St. (© **800/234-4797** or 315/470-1910; www.visitsyracuse.org). The **Syracuse Urban Cultural Park Visitor Center,** 318 Erie Blvd. E (within Erie Canal Museum; © **315/471-0593**), offers guided tours of downtown for $2.

Exploring Syracuse

Principal among Syracuse's attractions is the **Museum of Science & Technology (MOST)** ★★, 500 S. Franklin St. (© **315/425-0747;** www.most.org), which is located in an old armory and filled on three levels with terrific interactive science exhibits, science demonstrations, simulator rides that will entertain both youngsters and their parents, a cool domed IMAX theater, and a planetarium. It's open Wednesday to Sunday from 10am to 5pm. Museum-only admission is $7 adults, $6 seniors and children 11 and under, planetarium admission $2 extra; combination IMAX/museum ticket is $12 adults, $9.50 seniors and children 11 and under. For IMAX showtimes and tickets, call © **315/473-IMAX** (4629).

The **Everson Museum of Art** ★, 401 Harrison St. (© **315/474-6064;** www.everson.org; Tues–Fri and Sun noon–5pm, Sat 10am–5pm; suggested donation $5), was the first building designed by noted architect I. M. Pei. It contains a superb collection of American ceramics. Architecture buffs may want to go from Everson to one of the finest Art Deco buildings in Syracuse, the **Niagara-Mohawk building,** 101–105 N. Franklin St., a miniature Chrysler Building that's illuminated at night. The **Erie Canal Museum,** 318 Erie Blvd. E. (Rte. 5) at Montgomery Street (© **315/471-0593;** www.eriecanalmuseum.org; Mon–Sat 10am–5pm, Sun 10am–3pm; free admission), is in the original 1850 weigh-lock building designed to determine tolls for boats on the canal. It may not be the most exciting museum you've ever visited, but it makes for an interesting historical stop, depicting as it does six vignettes of 19th-century life along the canal.

Finally, while visiting a bakery might not seem like much of an attraction, the **Columbus Baking Company,** 502 Pearl St. (© **315/422-2913**), is an old-style, family-owned and -operated Italian bakery that continues to make only four types of artisanal, traditional Italian bread (with no preservatives), as it has for over a century. The deep, old-school ovens are right out of the movie *Moonstruck.*

Where to Stay

Bed & Breakfast Wellington ★ This large and very lovely house, a 1914 brick-and-stucco Tudor named for its architect, is a National Historic Landmark. It is embellished with fine Arts and Crafts details, such as rich woods and fireplaces with Mercer tiles. The guest rooms are spacious and pleasant, if not overly fancy (that may be a good thing), though they are decorated with nice antiques and Stickley furniture and carpets, and there's a collection of Wallace Nutting paintings throughout the house. For a small B&B, it's equipped with lots of amenities, such as high-speed Internet access, central air-conditioning, and a couple of relaxing porches. Downstairs is a huge apartment with a dining room and an efficiency kitchen. The sunny Stickley and Lakeview rooms are my favorites.

707 Danforth St., Syracuse, NY 13208. www.bbwellington.com.✆ **800/724-5006** or 315/474-3641. Fax 315/472-4976. 5 units. $99–$150 double. Rates include continental breakfast on weekdays, full gourmet breakfast on weekends. AE, DC, DISC, MC, V. Free parking. *In room:* A/C, TV/VCR/DVD, high-speed Internet access.

The Craftsman Inn & Conference Center 🛋 This Arts and Crafts hotel, just a few miles east of downtown Syracuse, has the amenities of a large hotel, but some of the intimacy of a smaller inn. Rooms are spacious and nicely decorated, with understated color schemes and full sets of handsome Stickley furniture (in mission, Colonial, or Shaker style)—a pretty extraordinary look. The Frank Baum room, named for the author of the *Wizard of Oz,* who was born nearby, has nice Oz artwork on the walls. About a quarter of the rooms are in the new, adjoining Craftsman Lodge. Studio and Executive suites are particularly good for businesspeople in Syracuse for longer stays. The Limestone Grille restaurant, next door, is also decorated with Stickley furniture. The hotel offers pet-friendly rooms.

7300 E. Genesee St., Fayetteville, NY 13066. www.craftsmaninn.com.✆ **800/797-4464** or 315/637-8000. Fax 315/637-2440. 90 units. $139 double; $159–$199 suite. Rates include continental breakfast. AE, DC, DISC, MC, V. Free parking. **Amenities:** Restaurant; bar. *In room:* A/C, TV/VCR, high-speed Internet access, kitchen.

Hotel Skyler ★★★ 🛏 In the University Hill neighborhood, in the heart of Syracuse University, this new, engaging boutique hotel is a very welcome, contemporary surprise in this upstate city—and perhaps a model for future developments. Not only is it chicly designed, in a historic 1920s building that had former lives as a Jewish temple and then a theater, but it's also eco-conscious and Syracuse's first LEED Platinum Designed hotel, with a number of cool sustainable technologies and environmentally friendly materials. Rooms are very stylish and warm, with bursts of bold patterns, color, and textured fabrics, and comfy beds, as well as interesting architectural details, such as columns, reclaimed wood, angled ceilings, and unique windows. Tree House suites, two-story loftlike space with a gallery and solarium at the nearby Golisano Children's Hospital, is the perfect place for families, especially those who might be visiting a child in the hospital (a percentage of revenues for the room is even donated to the hospital).

601 S. Crouse Ave., Syracuse, NY 13210. www.hotelskyler.com.✆ **800/365-4663.** 58 units. $169–$199 double; $218–$299 suite. AE, DISC, MC, V. Free parking. **Amenities:** Bar, fitness center. *In room:* A/C, TV/DVD, fridge, Wi-Fi.

Jefferson Clinton Hotel ★ Across from the MOST (Museum of Science & Technology), in the historic center of Syracuse, this perfectly located modern (and all nonsmoking) hotel in a nicely renovated historic building has large and attractive suites (some are one-bedrooms and others studios, all with fully equipped kitchens) that are perfect for business travelers and other visitors who want to be in the midst of the restaurant and bar action of Armory Square.

416 S. Clinton St. (Armory Sq.), Syracuse, NY 13202. www.jeffersonclintonhotel.com.✆ **315/425-0500.** Fax 315/472-4976. 60 units. $169–$239 studio; $229–$269 1-bedroom suite. Rates include breakfast

buffet. AE, DISC, MC, V. Free parking. **Amenities:** Bar; 24-hr. fitness center. *In room:* A/C, TV/DVD, kitchen, Wi-Fi.

Where to Eat

The Craftsman Inn (see above) operates a nice restaurant called **Limestone Grille** (© 315/637-9999), which serves items like New York strip steak, prime rib, and brook trout.

Coleman's IRISH/PUB FARE   A sprawling, handsome Irish pub and restaurant in the heart of the very Irish neighborhood Tipperary Hill, Coleman's has been around since 1933. The menu is a comfortable mix of simple bar food and Irish specialties, such as Guinness beef stew, Irish roast chicken, and homemade chili, as well as pastas and fresh seafood. For dessert, if you want to stick with the Irish theme, try Bailey's cheesecake or the Irish cream bash. There's live music, from pop to traditional Irish tunes and Celtic rock, from Thursday to Saturday, and nightly beer specials.

110 S. Lowell Ave. © **315/476-1933.** www.colemansirishpub.com. Reservations recommended on weekends. Main courses $8–$22. AE, MC, V. Mon–Sat 11:30am–3pm; Mon–Thurs 5–10pm; Fri–Sat 5–11pm; Sun noon–9pm.

Dinosaur Bar-B-Que ★★ ☺ BARBECUE   A ribs-and-juke joint/biker bar and honky-tonk, this is the original Dinosaur Bar-B-Que, a local legend that looks ripped straight out of Memphis (there are now versions in New York City and Rochester). Don't let the tough-girl waitresses and Harley fanatics intimidate you; at mealtimes the place is a pretty even mix of suits, families, and leather-clad bikers. On weekends when there's live blues until late, the environment is rowdy and fun. The best menu items are classic barbecue: the "Big Ass" pulled-pork plate, pit platters of ribs, and "ass-kickin'" chili, as well as the ⅓-pound barbecued burgers and spicy mojito chicken. Live music rocks every night but Sunday. Older kids will get a kick out of the place.

246 W. Willow St. © **888/476-1662** or 315/476-4937. www.dinosaurbarbque.com. Reservations not accepted. Main courses $8–$25. AE, DC, DISC, MC, V. Mon–Thurs 11am–midnight; Fri–Sat 11am–1am; Sun 2–9pm.

Syracuse After Dark

The **Landmark Theatre** ★★, 362 S. Salina St. (© **315/475-7980;** www.landmark theatre.org), the last-remaining Depression-era movie palace in central New York and listed on the National Register of Historic Places, recently underwent a $16-million renovation in efforts to transform it into a state-of-the-art performing arts center. It should again be a spectacular place to take in a concert or other performances when the work is completed (2012). The streets in **Armory Square** are lined with hopping bars, and nearby the **IMAX Theater** at the MOST has Friday- and Saturday-evening showings until 9pm. **Coleman's,** 110 S. Lowell Ave. (© **315/476-1933**), is a classic Irish pub and a good place to hoist a pint of Guinness.

Syracuse is host to the **New York State Fair** ★ at the 375-acre Empire Expo Center, 581 State Fair Blvd. (© **800/475-FAIR** [3247]; www.nysfair.org; adjacent to Rte. 690 just west of downtown), the last 2 weeks of August. The fair, which hosts all kinds of big-name musical acts and other exhibitions and entertainment, draws more than a million visitors annually. If you're in town during basketball season, try to catch a game of the **Syracuse Orangemen** (national champions in 2003 and a perennial Big East/NCAA contender) at the cavernous Carrier Dome; call © **315/443-2121** or see www.suathletics.com for schedules and information.

THE NORTH COUNTRY

by Marc Lallanilla

Colorado has its Rockies, Europe has its Alps, but what does New York have? The spectacular Adirondack Mountains. The largest park in the continental United States, Adirondack Park is the wildest, most rugged, and possibly the most beautiful part of New York. The park sprawls across 6 million acres of the state, forming a vast wilderness of primeval forests, craggy mountains, pristine lakes, and gin-clear, bubbling streams.

ACTIVE PURSUIT   Kayaking or canoeing across the **Fulton Chain of Lakes**—a total of eight lakes spanning 16 miles—is a great way to spend a summer weekend in the Adirondacks. But this wonderland of outdoor recreation doesn't shut down when winter comes—in fact, some parts of the Adirondacks don't even wake up until the snow starts falling and downhill skiers flock to Olympic-class destinations like the **Whiteface** ski resort near Lake Placid.

RELAXATION   If resting your weary bones in an Adirondack chair while gazing at a sapphire-blue lake doesn't help you unwind, try your hand at **fly-fishing** on the Ausable, St. Regis, or Raquette rivers. Another great way to experience the natural beauty of the Adirondacks is from the comfort of a classic rail car: The **Adirondack Scenic Railroad** takes passengers through the lush forests between Lake Placid and Saranac Lake year-round.

FACILITIES   Most of the "Great Camps" that defined luxury in the Adirondacks are long gone, but you can still get a flavor of classic hunting-lodge accommodations at places like the historic **Big Moose Inn** in Eagle Bay, the lakeside **Woods Inn** in Inlet, and the luxurious **Lake Placid Lodge.** Local New York produce and seasonal specialties can be found at **The View** in Lake Placid and Lake George's **Farmhouse at Top of the World.**

SOUTHERN ADIRONDACKS ★★★

Beautiful spring-fed Lake George is the heart of the southeastern Adirondacks. The area around the 32-mile-long lake—particularly the kitschy village of Lake George—teems with fun-seeking tourists in the summer and fall foliage season, but it shuts down the rest of the year. Nearby, less commercial Bolton Landing is also busy, but the smaller lakes to the west—Schroon, Brandt, and Luzerne—are considerably quieter. To the northeast, the Champlain Valley, too, is less developed, and more bucolic. Route 28, the only east-west road in the region, takes you past tiny villages, the magnificent Fulton Chain of Lakes, and over into Old Forge, which also bustles with activity. It's about 90 miles from Lake George to Old Forge, but it's a beautiful drive (as are all the drives in the park). The areas around Raquette, Blue Mountain, and Indian lakes are particularly charming, with laid-back towns and serene lakes. The southwestern section of the park stays partially open in the winter to accommodate the thousands of snowmobilers who power through here each year. Enter the park via Route 30 and you'll pass the huge Great Sacandaga Lake, along with even more tiny villages and lakes.

Essentials

GETTING THERE

BY PLANE   **Continental Airlines** (© 800/523-3273; www.continental.com) and **Cape Air** (© 800/352-0714; www.flycapeair.com) fly into the **Adirondack Regional Airport** in Saranac Lake (© 518/891-4600) in the northern part of the park. **Spirit Airlines** (© 800/772-7117; www.spirit.com) and **US Airways Express** (© 800/428-4322; www.usairways.com) serve the **Plattsburgh International Airport.** Other nearby airports include Burlington, Vermont (1 hr. from the eastern section of the region), Albany (1 hr. from the southern border), and Montreal (1 hr. from Plattsburgh).

BY BUS   **Adirondack Trailways** (© 800/776-7548; www.trailwaysny.com) serves Lake George, Warrensburg, Chestertown, Pottersville, Saranac Lake, Lake Placid, Keene Valley, Schroon Lake, Malone, Massena, Potsdam, Canton, and Plattsburgh. The daily service from Albany to Lake Placid takes about 4 hours.

BY CAR   You'll likely drive here; north of Albany, I-87 becomes the Adirondack Northway and speeds you along the eastern edge of the park. **Enterprise** (© 800/325-8007; www.enterprise.com) and **Hertz** (© 800/654-3131; www. hertz.com) operate out of Glens Falls (Queensbury), Plattsburgh, and Utica. (Many of these locations will pick you up and deliver you to their rental office without charge—call to confirm.) Both also have rental desks at the Adirondack Regional Airport (above) with limited hours.

BY TRAIN   **Amtrak** (© 800/872-7245; www.amtrak.com) stops in Glens Falls, Whitehall, Ticonderoga, Port Henry, Westport, Port Kent, Plattsburgh, and Rouses Point.

BY FERRY   **Lake Champlain ferries** (© 802/864-9804; www.ferries.com) go from Grand Isle, Vermont, to Plattsburgh, New York; Chimney Point, Vermont to Crown Point, New York; Burlington, Vermont, to Port Kent, New York; and Charlotte, Vermont, to Essex, New York. Schedule depends on season.

VISITOR INFORMATION   The **Adirondack Regional Tourism Council** (© 800/ 487-6867 or 518/846-8016; www.visitadirondacks.com) hosts a comprehensive

The Adirondack Mountains

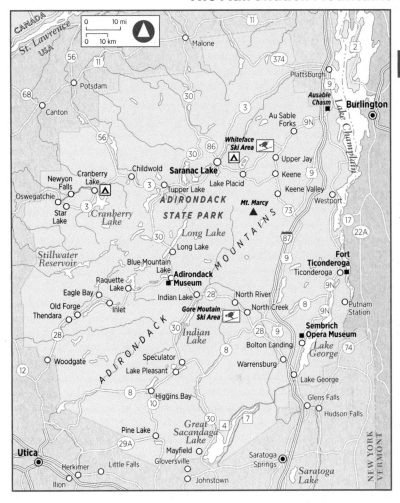

website with suggested itineraries, news updates, videos, weather information, and more. For information on Lake George, you can also contact **Warren County Tourism,** Municipal Center, 1340 State Rte. 9, Lake George (📞 **800/95-VISIT** [958-4748]; www.visitlakegeorge.com). Farther west in the region, contact **Inlet Information** (📞 **866/GO-INLET** [464-6538]; www.inletny.com) or **Old Forge Tourism** (📞 **315/369-6983;** www.oldforgeny.com).

Sports & Outdoor Pursuits

BOAT TOURS   Explore Lake George by hopping aboard a **sightseeing cruise,** generally available from May to October. With the **Lake George Steamboat Company,** 57 Beach Rd., Lake George (📞 **800/553-BOAT** [2628] or 518/668-5777;

www.lakegeorgesteamboat.com), you can choose from 1- to 4-hour narrated cruises—with or without a meal—on the steamship paddle-wheeler or one of the other old-time ships. Just be aware that these tours are often filled to capacity. Another option is *The Morgan,* **The Sagamore** hotel's 72-foot replica of a 19th-century wooden vessel, active from Memorial Day to Columbus Day in October (© **518/644-9400;** www.thesagamore.com); their Thursday evening fireworks cruises are especially popular. For the Fulton Chain of Lakes, take a sightseeing cruise with **Old Forge Lake Cruises** (© **315/369-6473;** www.oldforgelake cruises.com). You can ply Raquette Lake's waters with the **Raquette Lake Naviga-tion Co.** (© **315/354-5532;** www.raquettelakenavigation.com) year-round—their winter ice boat features chili, hot beverages, tacos, and thousands of twinkling white lights.

CANOEING & KAYAKING   The best way to explore this beautiful part of the park just might be with a paddle in hand. With lakes at every turn, canoeing and kayaking bring you up close to the waters that are such an essential part of the Adiron-dack experience. This is a great way to spot wildlife: Keep an eye toward the shoreline for white-tailed deer, red fox, black bear, coyote, moose, beaver, and numerous bird species. The Fulton Chain of Lakes is a popular and heavily trafficked route, with eight lakes spanning 16 miles. From First through Fifth lakes, you'll find a continuous waterway lined with summer cottages. But you'll have to carry your boat to reach the remaining lakes, which are less developed. Lake George is also a gorgeous place to paddle, with crystal-clear, spring-fed waters and a wealth of islands and small bays. It's 32 miles long, so you'll be better off in a sea kayak if you want to do some serious exploring. Rent your canoe or kayak from **Mountainman Outdoor Supply Com-pany,** Route 28 in Old Forge (© **877/226-6369** or 315/369-6672; www.mountain manoutdoors.com). In the Lake George area, try **Lake George Kayak Co.,** Main Street, Bolton Landing (© **518/644-9366;** www.lakegeorgekayak.com); they also offer stand-up paddleboard rentals and demos. Rates at both places range from $16 to $56 for a half-day rental, $24 to $75 for a full day, depending on the type of boat you choose.

DOWNHILL SKIING   Lake Placid's Whiteface (p. 383) it ain't, but **Gore Moun-tain** (© **518/251-2411;** www.goremountain.com) isn't exactly your neighbor's backyard, either. It boasts some serious expert trails and a gondola of its own, making

The Adirondack Cure

In 1876, when Dr. Edward Livingston Trudeau—great-grandfather of cartoon-ist Garry Trudeau (author of the *Doonesbury* comic)—was ailing from tuberculosis, he came to Saranac Lake. Rather than succumbing to the disease, he made a surprise recovery. Attribut-ing his improved health mostly to rest and the region's distinct cold mountain air, Dr. Livingston established the first sanatorium devoted exclusively to the treatment of TB in America. Soon thou-sands of people (including Robert Louis Stevenson) were flocking to the world-renowned Trudeau Sanatorium (now closed), and the little village was trans-formed into a health resort. "Cure cot-tages"—Victorian houses with wide, glassed-in porches where patients could rest—sprang up all around Sara-nac Lake, and you can still see some of them today.

bowling WITH THE VANDERBILTS

"Roughing it" means different things to different people. To the Vanderbilts and their contemporaries, it meant heading off into the woods . . . and setting up camp in absolutely luxurious estates. These sprawling "Great Camps"—many built in the late 19th and early 20th centuries—spanned countless acres of prime forest, with small fiefdoms of beautifully crafted buildings providing shelter and other necessities, such as hot water and indoor plumbing. Several are still standing today, while remnants of others can also be found.

One Great Camp you can visit is the rustic, deserted **Camp Santanoni** in Newcomb, just north of Route 28N (📞 **518/834-9328**). Its 45 buildings are spread out over 12,900 acres. There are no furnishings anymore, and the buildings are closed to the public, but come here to enjoy the beautiful architecture from the outside in this serene, mysterious setting. The camp is open year-round, but there's a catch: You have to hike or ski 5 miles to get here. Guided tours are seldom offered, but interpreters are on-site from late June to August.

Great Camp Sagamore ★★, 4 miles south of Raquette Lake (📞 **315/354-5311;** www.sagamore.org), lets you see how the Vanderbilts themselves went camping. Their 27-building summer retreat for over 50 years even included its own bowling alley. Tours are offered daily from late June to Labor Day at 10am and 1:30pm, daily from Labor Day to mid-October at 1:30pm, and weekends from Memorial Day to late June at 1:30pm.

The two camps are about 40 miles apart; on these winding roads, that could take some time to drive, so don't expect to see both in the same day, especially with the hiking involved at Santanoni. Great Camp Sagamore is about 17 miles west of the Adirondack Museum in Blue Mountain Lake, and Santanoni about 25 miles east.

for a fun day on a 3,600-foot summit and 90 trails. Their recently reopened North Creek Ski Bowl—one of the most historic ski areas in the East, it once hosted ski trains from New York City—increases the amenities at this overlooked jewel of a ski resort. **Bonus:** Because the folks up in Whiteface run this place, too, special passes are available for both mountains if you must get your Olympic fix.

GOLF **The Sagamore** (📞 866/385-6221; www.thesagamore.com) has the area's most renowned links; the work of famous course designer Donald Ross, it dates to 1929. The first tee starts off with a spectacular view of Lake George, but the lake disappears after that. Greens fees for the visiting public are $150 for 18 holes, or $125 after 2pm. Over on the western side, **Thendara Golf Course** (📞 315/369-3136; www.thendaragolfclub.com) is another well-known Donald Ross creation, from 1921 (the back 9 were added in 1959). Greens fees are $37, or $25 if you tee off after 3pm. Just beware—at dusk in summer, the mosquitoes come out with a vengeance.

HIKING **Bald Mountain,** east of Old Forge, is a steep but short (2-mile round-trip) climb that offers several open vistas and a fantastic open summit with views of the Fulton Chain of Lakes. **Cascade Lake,** just north of Eagle Bay, is a 5.5-mile easy loop that takes you to a scenic lake with a beautiful narrow waterfall at its eastern end. Around Lake George, the climb up **Black Mountain** runs 8.5 miles round-trip with a 1,100-foot vertical rise. The payoff? A rocky summit with amazing views. The **Buck Mountain** trail (6.6 miles round-trip) is another good option for a moderate hike. For more hikes, pick up a copy of Barbara McMartin's *50 Hikes in the Adirondacks: Short Walks, Day Trips, and Backpacks Throughout the Park,* 4th Edition (Countryman Press), or contact the **Adirondack Mountain Club,** 814 Goggins Rd., Lake George (© **800/395-8080** or 518/668-4447; www.adk.org). The club also does group outings several times a year. For maps and supplies, try **Mountainman Outdoor Supply Company,** Route 28 in Old Forge (© **877/226-6369** or 315/369-6672; www.mountainmanoutdoors.com).

RAFTING The **Lower Moose River,** near Old Forge, is serious white water—April and early May bring Class IV and V rapids (on a scale of I to V). The **Middle Moose River** is mellower, perfect for families and inexperienced rafters, from May to October. You can do either with **Whitewater Challengers** in Old Forge (© **800/443-RAFT** [7238]; www.whitewaterchallengers.com) or **A.R.O. Adventures** (© **800/525-7238**; www.aroadventures.com).

SNOWMOBILING With some 15 feet of snow each year, the **Old Forge** area often makes national news. When the snow hits, adventurers race up here to plow through the backwoods of Old Forge, race across frozen Lake Champlain, or roar across the Tug Hill plateau. The most popular snowmobile route connects Old Forge and Inlet to the Sargent Ponds area, the Moose River Recreation Area, and the Jessup River Wild Forest. For a trail map and other information, check out www.hamilton county.com or http://visitadirondacks.com. For trail conditions and a downloadable permit application, go to www.inletny.com or call the **Town of Inlet Information Office** (© **866/GO-INLET** [464-6538]).

Especially for Kids

The Lake George area is a veritable wonderland for children, providing plenty of indoor and outdoor amusements. For kids—and adults with a weakness for nostalgia—it doesn't get any better than Old Forge's **Enchanted Forest/Water Safari,** 3183 Rte. 28 (© **315/369-6145;** www.watersafari.com), with giant, colorful statues of Santa Claus, Smokey the Bear, and Uncle Sam; amusement park rides; and a huge water theme park featuring their new "Curse of the Silverback" double-tube water ride (daily May to Labor Day). Speaking of huge, **Six Flags' Great Escape,** 1172 State Rte. 9, Queensbury (© **518/792-3500;** www.sixflags.com), includes Storytown, Ghost Town, and the Splashwater water park featuring the Mega-Wedgie (May to early Sept). In Lake George, there are thrills of a creepier kind: **Dr. Morbid's Haunted House,** 115 Canada St. (© **518/668-3077;** www.drmorbid.com), and **House of Frankenstein Wax Museum,** 213 Canada St. (© **518/668-3377;** www.frankensteinwaxmuseum.com). Lovers of kitschy minigolf shouldn't miss **Around the World Golf,** Beach Road (© **518/668-2531;** www.aroundtheworld golf.com), ranked as one of the top miniature golf courses in the world—where else can you get a geography lesson by putting around the United States (complete with the Empire State Building) or the world (with the Egyptian pyramids)?

Attractions

Adirondack Museum ★★ ☺   History buffs will devour this extensive collection that traces the transportation, tourism, and personal past of this massive park, and displays a rundown of its flora and fauna. The interactive "Great Outdoors" exhibit is fun for the kids as well. They'll love trying out different backpacks, snowshoes, and fishing rods, while everyone will get into the virtual reality rides: flying in a helicopter over the high peaks, rafting Hudson River white water, and bobsledding down the Olympic track. Allow 3 hours to see the exhibits and grounds, and bring a picnic lunch to enjoy the view—the museum's setting, overlooking the lovely **Blue Mountain Lake,** is spectacular. Admission is good for any 2 days within 1 week.

Rte. 30 on Blue Mountain Lake. ℂ **518/352-7311.** www.adkmuseum.org. Admission $18 adults, $16 seniors, $12 students and teens, $6 children 6–12, free for active military and children 5 and under; late May to mid-Oct only, daily 10am–5pm. From I-87, take exit 23, turn left, and then right onto Rte. 9N. Drive through Warrensburg to Rte. 28 and drive west for 1 hr. until Blue Mountain Lake. At the T-intersection, follow Rte. 30 N for 1 mile.

Sembrich Opera Museum ★★   World-renowned soprano Marcella Sembrich, a star of the New York Metropolitan Opera, used this estate as her summer retreat and studio. The museum now houses exhibits celebrating the "golden age of opera" with music, photographs, costumes, paintings, and the diva's personal effects. Her glorious estate overlooking Lake George also hosts concerts and symposiums by music historians.

4800 Lake Shore Dr., Bolton Landing ℂ **518/644-2431.** http://thesembrich.org. Admission free, donations appreciated. June 15–Sept 15 daily 10am–12:30pm and 2–5:30pm. From Route 9N, ½ mile south of the traffic light in Bolton Landing, turn left into the entrance.

Fort Ticonderoga ★★   Military-history fans will be in heaven at this star-shaped fort, which lords over Lake Champlain. Built by the French in the 1750s, the high-perched bastion protected the narrow strip of waterway connecting Lake George to Lake Champlain. Since 1909, it's been open to the public, detailing the important military history of the region. The museum is anything but dry: In addition to historical reenactments with hundreds of uniformed actors, and live performances by the fife-and-drum corps, the fort holds nearly 1,000 muskets, bayonets, pistols, and swords from the 18th century, as well as an extensive collection of period art. Spend some time strolling through the gorgeous gardens surrounding the fort, and drink in the amazing views, stretching from Vermont's Green Mountains to the Adirondacks.

On Lake Champlain, Ticonderoga. ℂ **518/585-2821.** www.fort-ticonderoga.org. Admission $15 adults, $14 seniors, $7 children 7–12, free for local residents and children 6 and under. Mid-May to mid-Oct only, daily 9:30am–5pm. King's Garden early June to mid-Oct only, daily 9:30am–4pm. From I-87, take exit 28, then Rte. 74 east 18 miles to Ticonderoga. Continue straight on Rte. 74 for 1½ miles. Turn left, continuing on Rte. 74E. Proceed straight ⅝ mile to fort entrance.

Where to Stay

Honky-tonk Lake George Village constantly bustles in the summer season, which means busy motels and crowded restaurants. Nearby Bolton Landing is quieter, with a few more upscale options. Farther west, Old Forge is the center of activity, but you'll find serenity in the area around Inlet and Raquette Lake.

While many of the handsome grand inns and lodges that used to pepper these parts are long gone, there are a few still standing—along with full-blown resorts, quiet and simple retreats, and plenty of rustic (and often run-down) roadside motels in between.

EXPENSIVE

The Sagamore ★★★ ☺   Drive onto this 72-acre island and up to the spectacular Colonial-style main building and you'll immediately see what has drawn well-heeled vacationers here since 1883: peace, quiet, and luxury. Jutting out into Lake George, this private getaway offers impressive amenities on its beautifully landscaped grounds, including water activities, a great golf course, and an excellent spa.

A recent multimillion-dollar renovation—along with new management—means some major changes for the property, including a new recreation center, a 10,000-square-foot pool, and an overhauled dining room, bar, lobby, and lakeside restaurant, The Pavilion. The contemporary "lodge" rooms are not actually in the hotel proper, but with balconies and fireplaces, these offer the best bang for your buck. Accommodations in the main building—including 35 spanking-new rooms—are spacious and well appointed, with flatscreen TVs and marble bathrooms; many have a view of the lake. The eye-popping, privately owned Wapanak Castle, with its five fireplaces and a formal living room, is also for rent. The Sagamore also offers a broad array of family-friendly activities and amenities, including babysitting services, ice-cream socials, complimentary boat rides on *The Morgan* (see above), and the Teepee Club for kids.

110 Sagamore Rd., Bolton Landing, NY 12814. www.thesagamore.com. ✆ **866/385-6221** or 518/644-9400. Fax 518/743-6036. 388 units. Late June to Labor Day $199–$560 double, from $569 suite; rest of the year $199–$385 double, from $559 suite. Packages available. AE, DC, DISC, MC, V. Free valet parking. From I-87, get off at exit 22 and take Rte. 9N north for 10 miles to the town of Bolton Landing. At the 2nd traffic light, turn right onto Sagamore Rd. **Amenities:** 6 restaurants; babysitting; children's programs; off-premises golf course; large exercise room; small Jacuzzi; 2 large pools (1 indoor and 1 outdoor); room service; 5 lighted outdoor tennis courts; watersports rentals. *In room:* A/C, TV/VCR w/ pay movies, hair dryer, kitchenette.

MODERATE

The Big Moose Inn ★ 📷
This historic inn, a 1903 former hunting lodge, comes pretty close to my idea of the quintessential Adirondack experience. Located on tranquil, remote Moose Lake—with simple yet cozy rooms, a front porch filled with rocking chairs, a fireplace in the common area, and an appealing tavern—the old inn is also linked to an intriguing slice of American history: the Chester Gillette scandal, the real-world inspiration for Theodore Dreiser's *American Tragedy* (see below). Gillette was convicted of murdering Grace Brown on this very lake, and guests can read all about the trial in framed clippings throughout the place. While rooms are on the small side—it is an old inn, after all—all of them have private bathrooms, and most of them overlook the water. Another plus: The dining room, headed up by a new executive chef, turns out some hearty, satisfying meals like rack of lamb and baked salmon, as well as seasonal specials using locally sourced ingredients.

1510 Big Moose Rd., Eagle Bay, NY 13331. www.bigmooseinn.com. ✆ **888/924-4666** or 315/357-2042. 16 units. Late June to Oct $89–$235 double; rest of the year $69–$215 double. Holiday rates are higher. Rates include continental breakfast. Some weekends have 2-night minimums. AE, DISC, MC, V. Take Rte. 28N to Eagle Bay, then turn left onto Big Moose Rd. Continue for 5 miles until you see Inn on the right. **Amenities:** Restaurant; lounge; complimentary use of canoes and kayaks. *In room:* A/C, TV/DVD, hair dryer, no phone, Wi-Fi.

The Georgian Resort ★
Busy, colorful, and right smack in the heart of the Lake George madness, the Georgian is the kind of place where you'd expect to find dinner theater—and you'd be right. Set beside the lake with 400 feet of private beach with boat rentals and an inflatable slide for the kids, the resort has some rooms with gorgeous views. However, the standard rooms are without a trace of charm. You'll find two rows of motel-style rooms, many of which face the oh-so-lovely parking lot. Of course, you'll want to stay in the *other* building, closer to the lake, and preferably in room nos. 191 to 198, where nothing but shimmering water will be in front of you. Suites have slightly nicer furniture and generally lots more space; some of the biggest sport—yes—heart-shaped Jacuzzis. Really.

scandal IN THE ADIRONDACKS

Even if the names Chester Gillette and Grace Brown don't ring a bell, chances are their story will sound familiar. The two were at the center of a tragedy that gripped the nation in the summer of 1906—and it occurred right on Big Moose Lake. The turn of events went on to inspire Theodore Dreiser's classic novel, *An American Tragedy,* which later informed the 1951 film *A Place in the Sun,* starring Elizabeth Taylor, Shelley Winters, and Montgomery Clift.

Socially ambitious playboy Chester Gillette was working for a wealthy uncle in upstate New York when he became romantically involved with Grace Brown, a farmer's daughter employed at his uncle's factory. After Brown learned that she was pregnant with Gillette's child, the two traveled to the Adirondacks. On July 11, witnesses saw them rowing out on Big Moose Lake; the next day, Brown's body was found at the bottom of the lake. A couple of days later Gillette was arrested for murder, and jailed in Herkimer County.

The press jumped on the sordid story, with reporters and photographers crowding the inns and bars of the usually sleepy region. During the trial, the prosecution charged that Gillette planned the murder, striking Brown with a tennis racket and pushing her into the lake. Gillette was found guilty, and electrocuted on March 30, 1908.

384 Canada St., Lake George, NY 12845. www.georgianresort.com. © **800/525-3436** or 518/668-5401. 162 units. Late May to early Oct $99–$289 double, $179–$389 suite; early Oct to late May $69–$199 double, $129–$299 suite. Some weekends have 2- or 3-night minimums. AE, DC, DISC, MC, V. **Amenities:** Restaurant; lounge; outdoor heated pool; limited room service. *In room:* A/C, TV, fridge (suites only), hair dryer, Wi-Fi.

North Woods Inn & Resort ★   North of Old Forge and along the shore of gorgeous Fourth Lake, this smallish hotel has a lovely setting and some nice amenities, including a restaurant and a pub. Some rooms are in the main lodge, and others are laid out motel-style. All of them are a good size and comfortable, though finished in somewhat drab colors. Your best bet is to stay in a lakefront room on the lodge's second floor—all have access to a shared covered porch. Jacuzzi suites have the same decor, but offer more space and (right again!) a Jacuzzi tucked into the corner; one even has a wood-burning fireplace.

4920 Rte. 28 and Fourth Lake, Old Forge, NY 13420. www.northwoodsinnresort.com. © **315/369-6777.** Fax 315/369-2575. 28 units. Mid-week $120–$150 double; weekends $130–$200 double. Stay 3 nights, next night is free. 2-night minimum on holiday weekends. AE, DISC, MC, V. **Amenities:** 2 restaurants; lounge; outdoor heated pool; limited room service; boat rentals and complimentary use of canoes. *In room:* A/C, TV (suites have VCR or DVD), CD player (in suites), fridge (in some units), Internet, Jacuzzi (in some suites).

The Woods Inn ★★   I love the look of this welcoming, historic inn on Fourth Lake, the only original Adirondack hotel remaining in Inlet. Outside, the building is painted a cheerful yellow, while inside the place is just as appealing, with a friendly staff, and airy and comfortable rooms done up loosely in the Great Camp style. Some rooms lean toward the woodsy with twig tables, chairs, and lamps, while others are more Victorian in spirit, with dark wood and antique furnishings. All are spacious and bright; especially room no. 103, which comes with a private balcony overlooking the lake. Feeling outdoorsy? Stay in one of the three "Adirondack Guide" tents, built on wooden platforms and tricked out with wood-burning stoves, electric lights, and granite sinks. Another bonus: The public beach is just a short walk away.

Rte. 28 (P.O. Box 678), Inlet, NY 13360. www.thewoodsinn.com. ✆ **315/357-5300.** Fax 315/357-5311. 20 units and 3 guide tents. $110–$175 double. Call for off-season rates, which can be considerably cheaper. Rates include light breakfast. 2-night minimum on holiday weekends. DISC, MC, V. **Amenities:** Restaurant; lounge. *In room:* No phone, Wi-Fi.

INEXPENSIVE

Green Harbor Motel and Cottages　This small motel with cottages boasts a terrific setting, off in the woods and right on Long Lake. You'll find a beach, hiking trails, and plenty of serenity. Rooms and cottages are nothing amazing, but for the price and location, they're not bad. Some cottages are decked out with more of an Adirondack-y feel, while others are more sterile. And for those who get a hankering for a midnight dip, a couple of cottages are right on the water.

Rte. 30, Long Lake, NY 12847. www.greenharbormotel.com. ✆ **518/624-4133.** 15 units. May–Oct $75–$130 double for motel rooms; June–Sept cottages rent by the week only, $750 and up; May and Oct cottages $100 less per week. Motel rooms 3-night weekend minimum in high season; off season cottages 3-night minimum. MC, V. Cottages are cash or check only. Closed Nov–Apr. **Amenities:** Public tennis courts nearby, Wi-Fi in some public areas. *In room:* A/C (in some units), TV, fridge (in some units), full kitchens (in cottages), no phone.

The Lake Champlain Inn ★★ 🛏　If your tastes run more toward quaint than woodsy, and you're in the market for a quiet, secluded retreat, this gorgeous 1870 Victorian home is a good bet. Set right by Lake Champlain, the inn has views of the lake, the Adirondacks, and even Vermont's Green Mountains. While rooms aren't the biggest, they boast nice touches like wrought-iron beds, claw-foot tubs, original woodwork—and lots of frilly knickknacks, cutesy pillows, and teddy bears. For more space, the Lakeview Suite offers two connected rooms, while the Schoolhouse—a large, Victorian-style house with two very modern rooms inside—sits nearby on 130 acres. The adjacent state land is perfect for hiking or cross-country skiing, though perhaps the best part of this B&B is sitting on the porch watching the hummingbirds feed.

428 County Rte. 3, Putnam Station, NY 12861. www.tlcinn.com. ✆ **518/547-9942.** 6 units. $105–$135 double. Rates include full breakfast. 2-night weekend minimum in high season. AE, MC, V. Take I-87 to exit 20, turn left onto Rte. 9. At light, turn right onto Rte. 149 for 12 miles, left on Rte. 4 for 10 miles. Go straight through intersection on Rte. 22 for 15 miles. Turn right onto Lake Rd., go 2 miles, bear right, go ½ mile. *In room:* A/C, hair dryer, no phone, Wi-Fi.

CAMPGROUNDS

Glen Hudson Campsite in Warrensburg (http://glenhudson.com; ✆ **518/623-9871**) is a nice riverside campground close to Lake George that offers wooded river and open sites for RVs and tents from mid-May to mid-October. To get away—far away—from the crowds and the RVs, head to **Lake George Islands** (www.lake george.com; ✆ **518/623-1200**). Accessible by boat only, the 398 isolated shoreline campsites are on 44 state-owned islands. It's an amazing back-to-nature experience; some sites have grills and fireplaces and are perfect for parties. The camping fee is $35 ($30 for New York residents) and sites are available mid-May through Columbus Day. They fill up fast, so reserve as early as possible. **Golden Beach Campground** (✆ **315/354-4230**) has a prime perch on the southeast shore of Raquette Lake, and its 207 tent and trailer sites accommodate everyone from backpackers to 40-foot RVs. The fee is $20 per night, $140 per week, and it's open mid-May to Labor Day.

Where to Eat

While there's not much in the way of fine dining up here, some of the hotels and inns offer decent meals, such as the Sagamore's new **La Bella Vita** (✆ **518/743-6101;** www.labellavitaristorante.com) and **The Pavilion** (✆ **518/743-6101**). **Friends Lake Inn,** 963 Friends Lake Rd., Chesterton (✆ **518/494-4751;** www.friendslake. com), turns out high-quality New American cooking using local ingredients. You'll also find a few roadside options for hearty and delicious Adirondack breakfasts, such as the **Muffin Patch,** Route 28, Old Forge (✆ **315/369-6376**).

EXPENSIVE

Farmhouse at Top of the World ★★ 🎒 NEW AMERICAN   Far away—in location and in spirit—from the uninspired, touristy eateries you'll find chockablock throughout Lake George, this green-minded restaurant on a golf course uses produce grown on-site and ingredients from sustainable family farms in the area. The dishes are simple yet creative, and the wine list is one of the best in the region. Choose from their small-plates menu, which includes such items as duck croquettes, or splurge with a five-course tasting menu developed by chef Kevin London; Thursday evenings feature a hearty seasonal Harvest Dinner with seven courses served family style.

441 Lockhart Mountain Rd., Lake George. ✆ **518/668-3000.** www.topoftheworldgolfresort.com. Reservations recommended. Main courses $9–$29; lunch $5–$13. AE, DISC, MC, V. From I-87, take exit 21 to Rte. 9N North. Turn right on Rte. 9L, then turn right onto Lockhart Mountain Rd. May–Oct Wed–Sun 11am–3pm and 5:30–10pm. Seasonal hours vary; call to confirm.

Seventh Lake House ★★★ NEW AMERICAN   You could easily drive right by this unassuming house sitting between Inlet and Raquette Lake, but don't: Inside is probably the best food in the southern Adirondacks. The quiet dining room, facing a lake, is decorated in warm tones and has a stone fireplace; you could also choose to sit out on the screened-in deck. The ever-changing seasonal menu combines "comfortable old favorites" with more cutting-edge "contemporary creations." Start with something inventive, like won-ton shrimp served with orange-mango sweet-and-sour sauce, and follow up with something irresistible, like the triple meatloaf—veal, beef, and pork baked with herbs and spices, wrapped in pastry, and served with an onion sherry sauce.

Rte. 28, Inlet (btw. Inlet and Raquette Lake). ✆ **315/357-6028.** www.seventhlakehouse.com. Reservations recommended. Main courses $15–$27. MC, V. June–Sept daily 5–10pm; Oct–May Wed–Sun 5–9pm. Call ahead to confirm hours in the off season.

MODERATE

East Cove ★ AMERICAN   This local favorite is—thankfully—off Lake George's beaten path. Like many area restaurants, it's a small Adirondack-style log cabin; the interior is fairly charming, with exposed posts and beams and historic photos lining the walls. The food, though it's all basic American favorites, is what keeps diners coming back. The menu spans the meat/fish/pasta realms, and includes pork chops with a Jack Daniels–flavored sauce and caramelized onions, and the delicious sea scallops casino, baked with green and red peppers in garlic butter with crumb topping. On the lighter side, burgers, fish and chips, and chicken sandwiches are also available, and they serve a popular Champagne buffet brunch on Sundays.

3873 Rte. 9L (east of Rte. 9N), Lake George. ✆ **518/668-5265.** www.eastcove.com. Main courses $12–$40. AE, DC, DISC, MC, V. May–Oct daily 5–10pm, Sun 11am–2:30pm; rest of the year Tues–Sun only.

Lanzi's on the Lake ★★ AMERICAN   This great restaurant—run by the five Lanzi brothers—takes full advantage of its lakefront setting (a rarity on Sacandaga) with floor-to-ceiling windows in the restaurant, and a massive outdoor deck. Not only is there a great view outside, but usually a big party as well: Crowds of up to 4,000 have been known to gather for themed parties, such as reggae festivals or chili cook-offs. The kitchen serves up homemade everything, from the salad dressing to the pasta. The portions are huge and very rich. Consider the Lake Chicken, grilled breast topped with sautéed lobster meat, baked under provolone cheese and topped with hollandaise sauce—you may need to join the dance party to work it all off.

Rte. 30, Mayfield. ✆ **518/661-7711.** www.lanzisonthelake.net. Reservations suggested. Main courses $16–$40. AE, MC, V. May–Oct daily 11:30am–10pm (or later, depending on the crowd); Nov–Apr Thurs–Fri 4–10pm, Sat–Sun 11:30am–10pm.

INEXPENSIVE

Keyes Pancake House & Restaurant AMERICAN   The all-day breakfast menu—including nine different flavors of pancakes and four different kinds of syrup—keeps locals and tourists alike coming back to this Old Forge mainstay. It doesn't hurt that the servers are so friendly, either. Though breakfasts of pancakes and omelets are what this place does best, you can still order a sandwich or a meal of chicken Parmesan, steak, roast beef, or meatloaf at lunchtime.

Main St., Old Forge. ✆ **315/369-6752.** www.keyespancakehouse.com. Breakfast $2–$11; lunch entrees $7–$11. MC, V. Late June to Labor Day daily 7am–2pm; Labor Day to early June Fri–Wed 7am–2pm.

Southern Adirondacks After Dark

Nobody comes here for the nightlife, but that doesn't mean there's nothing to do. The **Adirondack Lakes Center for the Arts** in Blue Mountain Lake (✆ **877/752-7715** or 518/352-7715; www.adirondackarts.org) hosts theatrical performances, parties, art classes and exhibits, concerts, movie screenings, and more. They even take their shows "on the road," sponsoring performances in towns throughout the region.

NORTHERN ADIRONDACKS ★★★

Keene Valley and Plattsburgh to Cranberry Lake

The High Peaks, New York's mightiest mountain range, lord over the northern part of the Adirondacks, which seems to operate at full speed 365 days a year. Summer brings hikers, bikers, and paddlers, while winter beckons snowboarders, skiers, and snow-tubers to the state's best mountains. The village of **Lake Placid,** home to two winter Olympics and the birthplace of winter sports in America, is ground zero for all the action. (Call it one of the ironies of geography that this town sits on **Mirror Lake**—the actual Lake Placid is a few miles outside of town.) Here you'll find lots of year-round recreation, along with myriad options for lodging and dining, and a hopping nightlife scene. West of Lake Placid, Route 73 becomes Route 86, which will take you right into the idyllic village of **Saranac Lake.** Even though the town may not have the quality of restaurants that Lake Placid does, you'll see why Saranac Lake is considered the number one small town in New York State by many experts. It has a beautiful setting, and not nearly as many tourists as its larger neighbor to the east. Cut north up Route 30 and you'll be in one of the most remote and prettiest canoeing areas in America: the **St. Regis Canoe Wilderness Area.** Back on 86, the road takes you past two more huge lakes with countless opportunities for fishing, hiking, camping, and canoeing. Head east from Lake Placid and you'll run right into Lake Champlain; though not heavily developed for recreation or tourism, it's a gorgeous sight.

Essentials

GETTING THERE   I-87 cuts north right through the forest, making it easily accessible. Swing east on Route 73 and you'll be headed toward Lake Placid. **Amtrak** (**800/USA-RAIL** [872-7245]; www.amtrak.com) stops in Westport and Plattsburgh, both 50 miles from Saranac Lake. Westport is the closest stop to Lake Placid; book your transfer with Amtrak when you buy your ticket and the limousine service **Ground Force 1,** 2 Main St., Lake Placid (✆ **866/226-1152** or 518/523-0294; also in Plattsburgh, 4 Smithfield Blvd., ✆ **518/563-4444,** www.groundforce1.net), will shuttle you back and forth for about $25 each way. For bus and plane information, see section 1, "Southern Adirondacks," earlier in this chapter.

GETTING AROUND   You'll need a car. **Rent-A-Wreck** (✆ **800/698-1777** or 518/523-4804; www.rentawreck.com) in Lake Placid and in Plattsburgh (✆ **518/562-8462**) offers free pickup/drop-off service to customers in the local vicinity. **Enterprise,** also offering free pickup service, has an office in Saranac Lake (✆ **800/325-8007** or 518/891-9216; www.enterprise.com), as does Hertz (✆ **800/654-3131;** www.hertz.com). From late December to March, the free **Mountain Valley Shuttle** links Lake Placid with Whiteface, Wilmington, Jay, and Ausable Forks. The white-and-blue shuttle runs hourly and picks up at a few hotels in town—Mirror Lake Inn, Golden Arrow, High Peaks Resort, and Art Devlin's—but if you flag them down on Main Street, they'll stop. From town, the shuttle runs direct to Whiteface.

VISITOR INFORMATION   The **Adirondack Regional Tourism Council** (✆ **518/846-8016;** www.adirondacks.org) no longer hosts an information center on I-87, but their website offers comprehensive listings and travel suggestions. Additional information is available from the **St. Lawrence Chamber of Commerce** (✆ **877/228-7810;** northcountryguide.com). The **Lake Placid/Essex County Visitors Bureau,** Olympic Center, 49 Parkside Dr., Lake Placid (✆ **800/447-5224** or 518/523-2445; www.lakeplacid.com), is open year-round Monday to Friday from 8am to 5pm and Saturday and Sunday from 9am to 4pm. The office is closed on Sunday from September to May.

Seeing the Olympic Sights

As recently as 30 years ago, few Americans—save for hikers, skiers, and other outdoors-minded folks—had even heard of Lake Placid, even though the region hosted the 1932 Winter Olympics, where an unknown 16-year-old Norwegian figure skater named Sonja Henie charmed the world. When Lake Placid was once again chosen to host the sports spectacle, this peaceful mountain village was thrust into the international spotlight one more time. Now you can see some of the sites where two generations of legends were made, including the Miracle on Ice hockey victory of the Americans over the Russians (see above). **The Olympic Regional Development Authority** (✆ **518/523-1655;** www.orda.org) handles it all.

Skip the Olympic Training Center (196 Old Military Rd.); there's not much open to the public. Whatever the season, make sure to take a ride on Whiteface's **Cloudsplitter Gondola** ★★ (✆ **518/946-2223**), which offers amazing views of the High

miracle ON ICE

For those of us old enough to remember it, the "Miracle on Ice" was not only a highlight of the 1980 Lake Placid games, but one of the most unforgettable upsets in sports history—a deeply moving story of a scrappy team of underdogs who pulled together to topple the reigning Goliaths of the game. Even more than that, it stands out as one of those rare athletic achievements that transcend sports entirely. In the midst of the Cold War, this little hockey team did nothing less than unite a nation. It gave Americans a much-needed sense of pride after years of disillusionment from the Vietnam War, the Soviet invasion of Afghanistan, an energy crisis, and economic uncertainty.

The mostly college-level U.S. team, seeded 7th out of 12 teams at the start of the Winter Games, began to garner attention when they tied Sweden in the first round, 2-2. They then pulled off a surprising 7-3 victory over the talented Czech team, followed by wins against Norway, Romania, West Germany, and Germany. On a roll, they were now facing the Soviets—not only their Cold War rivals but the team heavily favored to win the Olympic gold.

The Americans were down 3-2 in the final period of the momentous match when a shot by Mark Johnson tied them up. Shortly after, U.S. captain Mike Eruzione scored again, causing the stadium—and just about the entire country—to erupt in chants of "USA! USA!" This unforgettable fourth goal propelled the American team to victory against their formidable Cold War opponents, and secured their place in sports and American history. The U.S. went on to defeat Finland in the final round and take home the gold medal.

Peaks and the Ausable River. (For downhill skiing on Whiteface, see "Sports & Outdoor Pursuits," below.) At the **Verizon Sports Complex ★★**, Route 73 (© **518/523-2811**), 20 minutes west of Lake Placid, don't miss the **bobsled/luge/skeleton track,** where, in winter, you'll watch athletes bomb down on crazy machinery. For a rare treat, strap yourself into a bobsled and race down the .5-mile track with a guide and brakeman—you'll never watch the Olympics the same way again ($79 adults, $74 teens, $69 children 12 and younger; Wed–Sun). The sleds are on wheels in summer, but they go much faster on the winter ice. Drive 10 minutes back toward town to the imposing ski jump towers at the **MacKenzie-Intervale Ski Jumping Complex ★**, Route 73 (© **518/523-2202**). From December to March and May through October, watch athletes soar off these ramps. Ride the lift alongside it and take the 26-story elevator to the top of the 394-foot tower to get the skiers' terrifying perspective ($10). From May to October, you can see the freestylers jump, too—into a 750,000-gallon pool at the adjacent **Aerial Training Center.** Drive back into town and spend a half-hour in the **Winter Olympic Museum ★** (© **518/523-1655**) at the **Olympic Center,** 2634 Main St.; it's just $6 ($4 for seniors and children) to check out a good history of the Games in Lake Placid, with tons of memorabilia, such as Olympic torches from the 1932 games and goalie Jim Craig's hockey stick from 1980. While at the Center, go skating on the rinks where legends like Sonja Henie and Eric Heiden made history (see below), and pay respects at the Herb Brooks Arena, site of the Miracle on Ice.

Sports & Outdoor Pursuits

CANOEING It's rare to find a stretch of water reserved solely for nonmotorized boats, but the St. Regis Canoe Wilderness beckons with the promise of quiet. In fact, the only sounds you'll hear in this remote part of the park are birdcalls and the sound of your paddle as it slices through the water. Just be prepared to carry your canoe: There are lots of portages here. But whether you're interested in 1 day on the water or a weeklong trip, you can get outfitted, with or without a guide. **St. Regis Canoe Outfitters,** 73 Dorsey St., Saranac Lake (© **888/SR-KAYAK** [775-2925] or 518/891-1838; www.canoeoutfitters.com), can set you up with canoe and kayak rentals, guided trips, and camping-gear rentals. **Adirondack Lakes and Trails Outfitters,** 541 Lake Flower Ave., Saranac Lake (© **800/491-0414;** www.adirondackoutfitters. com), is another great place for canoeing advice and/or rentals; they offer a wealth of self-guided and guided trips.

CROSS-COUNTRY SKIING Just outside Lake Placid, **Mount Van Hoevenberg X-C Center** at the Olympic Sports Complex, Route 73 (© **518/523-2811**), is where Olympic athletes train; trail fees are $20 per day for adults (reduced rates for seniors, teens, children, and dogs) and equipment rental is available. **Dewey Mountain Ski Center,** Route 3, just outside Saranac Lake (© **518/891-2697;** www.deweyskicenter.com), is another fun place to explore. Hard-core skiers up for a challenge can head into the backcountry and take on the **Jack Rabbit Trail.** Pick up this or several other trails (and any equipment you need) at the **Cascade Cross Country Center,** on Route 73, 5 miles from Lake Placid (© **518/523-9605;** www. cascadeski.com). Don't miss their full moon parties and other events, from January to March, when the trails are set with bonfires, and hot chocolate, beer, burgers, and hot dogs are served.

DOWNHILL SKIING **Whiteface,** Route 86, Wilmington (© **877/SKI-FACE** [754-3223] or 518/946-2223; www.whiteface.com), is the East's only Olympic mountain (elevation 4,400 ft.) and has the best skiing in the state. With the greatest vertical drop in the East (3,430 ft.), it has a variety of terrain that will appeal to all levels. In fact, 20% of the trails are rated for novices. There are 86 trails and 11 lifts in all. A 1-day lift ticket costs $34 to $57. **Titus Mountain,** 215 Mountain Rd., Malone (© **518/483-3740;** www.titusmountain.com), has 10 lifts that service 27 trails; they also offer night skiing, snowboarding, and tubing on their lower slopes. **Mount Pisgah,** Mt. Pisgah Road, Saranac Lake (© **518/891-0970**), is decidedly less Olympic, and good skiers will get bored here; with only five trails, it's a nice hill for beginners and families. It also boasts a fun tubing hill and the only fully lit night skiing in the Saranac Lake area. Lift tickets cost just $15 to $20.

FLY-FISHING The Ausable River offers tumbles and flows, twists and turns, and a pristine environment in which to cast your line. The village of Wilmington, about a 20-minute drive northeast from Lake Placid, is your headquarters. World-renowned fisherman Fran Betters has passed away, but the guides at his **Adirondack Sport Shop,** Route 86, Wilmington (© **518/946-2605;** www.adirondackflyfishing.com), are continuing his legacy. A full day out with the guides will run you $195 per day, including lunch and a box of flies. Guide Richard Garfield also offers trips all over the region through his **Fly Fish the Adirondacks** service, Lake Placid (© **518/637-2124;** www.flyfishtheadirondacks.com). A full day costs $250, with an additional charge for trips to the Salmon, St. Regis, or Raquette rivers.

FLYING Soar high over the treetops and peer down at the mountain peaks on a scenic airplane flight with **Adirondack Flying Service,** Lake Placid Airport, Route 73, Lake Placid (✆ **866/439-2399;** www.flyanywhere.com). A 20-minute flight, any time of year, is $40 per person (two-person minimum); family discounts and charter air taxi services are available.

GOLF There are lots of places to tee up in this part of the park. The **Whiteface Club & Resort,** Whiteface Inn Lane, Lake Placid (✆ **518/523-2551;** www.whitefaceclubresort.com), was rated four stars by *Golf Digest*; greens fees are $100 ($60 off-season) and club rental is available. Or hit the links at a municipal par-72 course, the **Craig Wood Golf Course,** Route 73, Lake Placid (✆ **877/999-9473;** www.craigwoodgolfclub.com). Greens fees May to June, $28; July to November, $34; add $32 for a cart.

HIKING Everyone wants to climb the Adirondacks' highest peak, Mount Marcy, and its 5,344 feet of rock. On summer weekends, the paths can seem more like midtown Manhattan than wilderness. The most popular (and crowded) approach is from the north, but the more scenic and less busy route (and also the most demanding) is the **Range Trail.** The trail is about 12 miles, and very steep in some places. The hike starts from a parking lot off Route 73 in the center of Keene Valley; there's a small parking fee. **High Falls Gorge,** 8 miles east of Lake Placid on Route 86 (✆ **518/946-2278;** www.highfallsgorge.com), affords a beautiful stroll along the Ausable River, past 700 feet of waterfalls in summer or winter. You'll cross bridges and follow trails as the water spills over ancient granite cliffs. Admission in winter is $14 for adults, $9.50 for kids 4 to 12; summer is $11 for adults, $7.95 for kids. To take a guided hiking tour, talk to the folks at **High Peaks Mountain Adventures Guide Service,** 2733 Main St., Lake Placid (✆ **518/523-3764**); they also offer rock climbing, mountain biking, and kayaking trips.

Llama Trekking

Sure, the Grand Canyon has its burros, but if you're on the lookout for a unique way to see the Adirondack peaks, consider **Adirondack Llama Treks** on Route 2 in Westport (✆ **518/962-8373**). Experienced guides offer half-day or full-day sojourns with meals included (call for seasonal rates).

ICE SKATING Skate on the same rink where Eric Heiden won his record five gold medals in 1980. Lake Placid's Olympic Center on Main Street (✆ **518/523-1655**) gets you onto the outdoor rink in winter nightly from 7 to 9pm; the rink is reserved for speed skaters from 4 to 6pm. On summer weeknights, you can skate indoors at the 1932 arena where Sonja Henie won Olympic Gold. Admission to both rinks costs $8 for adults, $5 for seniors and children 12 and under; skate rentals are $3.

RAFTING Nothing quite beats the rush of white-water rafting, especially when the water is high from snow runoff in the spring. **Adirondack Rafting Company** (✆ **800/510-RAFT** [7238] or 518/523-1635; www.lakeplacidrafting.com) provides everything you need for a guided run of the Hudson River Gorge. Their rafting season runs from April to mid-October; rates range from $65 to $85 per person. Fall foliage runs take place on weekends in September. For a low-key raft ride, plus a walk along nature trails through old-growth Adirondack forest, check out **Ausable Chasm** on Route 9, 12 miles south of Plattsburgh (✆ **518/834-7454;** www.ausablechasm.com). The attraction is now open year-round; walking the entire rim and peering down into the chasm is pretty spectacular. The entrance fee is $16 for adults, $9 for kids 5 to 12, and free for children 4 and under; the raft ride (weather permitting) is $10 for everyone.

TOURING LAKE CHAMPLAIN Unfortunately, the tour boat that left from Plattsburgh is no more, but fortunately, you can still paddle the lake yourself in search of eagles, osprey, and other wildlife. Rent powerboats from **Westport Marina,** 20 Washington St., Westport (✆ **518/962-4356;** www.westportmarina.com), or rent a kayak or canoe to tour the lake from the **Kayak Shack,** 3999 Rte. 9, Plattsburgh (✆ **518/566-0505;** www.kayak-shack.com).

TRAIN Climb aboard for a 45-minute rail journey through the forest (btw. Lake Placid and Saranac Lake) on the **Adirondack Scenic Railroad** ★ (✆ **800/819-2291;** www.adirondackrr.com). Trains depart Wednesday through Sunday from the end of May to mid-October from Saranac Lake (19 Depot St.) or Lake Placid (Station St.); themed rides, like the Polar Express and the Elvis-inspired Doo-Wop '50s train, take place year-round. Round-trip tickets are $19 adults, $17 seniors, and $11 for kids 2 to 12.

Especially for Kids

In winter, nothing in town is as much fun as screaming down onto the ice of Mirror Lake, gripping your toboggan for dear life. On the **Lake Placid Toboggan Chute,** you'll slide down a converted ski jump (✆ **518/523-2591**); get a four-person toboggan and a 40-mph rush ($5 per toboggan, $5 per adult, $3 per child). The slide is near the Olympic Center and the Best Western. You can also go mushing on and around Mirror Lake with **Thunder Mountain Dog Sled Tours** (✆ **518/891-6239**), located across from the High Peaks Resort ($10 per person). For a true Christmas experience (for part of the year, anyway), take the kids to **Santa's Workshop,** 324 Whiteface Memorial Hwy. (Rte. 431), 1½ miles northwest of Route 86 in Wilmington (✆ **518/946-2211;** www.northpoleny.com), where they can hop on rides, feed reindeer, and see Santa's house. The place is geared toward the wee ones; older kids will get bored quickly. Open Tuesday through Saturday 9:30am to 4pm from the end of June to Labor Day; weekends only (10am–3:30pm) Labor Day to Columbus Day and 5 weekends prior to Christmas (10am–3pm). Admission is $20 adults, $18 for seniors and for kids 2 to 16.

The wonderful **Wild Center/Natural History Museum of the Adirondacks** ★★★, 45 Museum Dr., Tupper Lake (✆ **518/359-7800;** www.wildcenter. org), makes for an excellent 2- to 3-hour (or more) excursion. With such exhibits as a giant glacial wall, an indoor "Living River," and the "Find Out Forest," this state-of-the-art, highly interactive museum does an admirable job of explaining the constantly evolving natural characteristics of the Adirondack park. Besides that, it's great fun. There are plenty of live animals inside: turtles, a huge tank of trout, and, best of all—otters! Kids in particular (well, us "adults" too) get a kick out of watching them swim and splash around. There are also such hands-on exhibits as a smelling station, where you can learn the different aromas of an otter, a beaver, and a mink. I found myself strangely mesmerized by a clever keyboard of mating calls: Press one key to hear a bullfrog, another to hear a loon, or play a virtual symphony of mating-season cacophony as the mosquitoes and red-eyed vireos join in. With more outdoor exhibits; a "Naturalist Cabinet" filled with butterfly, egg, and other collections; and a panoramic movie theater with an ever-growing film schedule, trust me: You won't be bored.

THE ADIRONDACK chair

If you've ever sat in one, you know how satisfying the classic Adirondack chair can be. With its straight, steeply angled back and armrests as wide as canoe oars, this icon of American furniture design always brings to mind a relaxing summer afternoon with a tall glass of iced tea.

The earliest version of the Adirondack chair was designed in 1903 by Thomas Lee. While vacationing with his family near the shores of Lake Champlain in Westport, he needed some comfortable seating for his sloped yard. Using just 11 pieces of wood cut from a single board, he fashioned a simple chair that, when placed on a downhill angle, was still comfortable enough for spending hours gazing at the mountain scenery.

According to legend, Lee gave his design to Harry Bunnell, a friend who was short on cash but long on creative carpentry skills. Bunnell immediately saw the potential in Lee's outdoor chair, and in 1904 he filed a patent for a slightly modified version. One year later, Bunnell received U.S. Patent 794,777 for the chair he dubbed the "Westport Chair."

Bunnell spent the next several years as a successful businessman, making Westport chairs crafted from the area's plentiful hemlock wood. The originals were painted green or dark brown and were signed with the company's insignia. If you find one at a yard sale, buy it—these rare chairs are considered valuable collector's items.

Shopping

If you're after outdoor gear, there is an **EMS** at 2453 Main St., Lake Placid (© **518/523-2505;** www.ems.com). For unique Adirondack crafts, visit the **Adirondack Craft Center,** 2114 Saranac Ave., Lake Placid (© **518/523-2062**), where you'll find works from more than 300 artisans. Another good bet is **Adirondack Reflections,** Main Street, Keene (© **518/576-9549;** www.adirondackreflections. com). Keene is also home to **Dartbrook Rustic Goods,** Route 73 (© **518/576-4360;** dartbrookrustic.com), purveyors of beautiful rustic furniture.

Where to Stay

Saranac Lake is a lovely, quiet place to spend the night, but Lake Placid is where the action is in the northern part of the park. If you want proximity to nightlife, spas, and restaurant options—fine dining and otherwise—stay here. Remember that even in the off season, when events like major hockey tournaments take place, you may find rates rivaling those of the summer season.

VERY EXPENSIVE

Lake Placid Lodge ★★★ This much-loved Relais & Châteaux retreat is filled with an enchanting mix of textures, colors, and styles: Reclaimed French oak floors mingle with Hudson River school paintings, handcrafted birch and twig stools, and antique red leather barrel seats. While there's a lot to look at here, the lodge is by no means museum-stiff; it's remarkably welcoming and comfortable. There are 11 rooms in total, including the six spacious suites in the lakeside building next door, with private lakeview porches, as well as 19 private cabins. The accommodations are decorated in the Lodge's signature upscale-rustic style. The cabins afford the ultimate in luxury and privacy—most are set right on the lake's shore, with huge stone fireplaces, giant feather beds, and picture windows.

144 Lodge Way, Lake Placid, NY 12946. www.lakeplacidlodge.com. © **877/523-2700** or 518/523-2700. 30 units. $675–$1,650 suite; $400–$1,650 cabin. Packages available. Rates include breakfast. AE, MC, V. From Main St. Lake Placid, turn left on Rte. 86, turn right at the Lake Placid Lodge sign (Whiteface Inn Rd.). Dogs allowed in cabins. No children 13 or under. **Amenities:** Restaurant; lounge; complimentary bikes; access to health club; room service; watersports rentals. *In room:* A/C, fridge, hair dryer, Wi-Fi.

EXPENSIVE

Mirror Lake Inn ★★★ Just beyond Lake Placid's busy Main Street, on a hill overlooking Mirror Lake, sits this gorgeous inn. Dating from 1883, it maintains a very traditional upscale feel—rustic it's not. Mahogany walls, walnut floors, and chandeliers fill the lobby and its cozy nooks. With the exception of the smallish "Cobble Hill" accommodations, standard rooms are extremely spacious and comfortable, with an understated luxury—there's nothing overly grand or unique about them. Many, however, boast beautiful views of the lake and mountains—some even have balconies. Suites are huge, with graceful furnishings like four-poster beds in some; they're the most elegant rooms in the town. Best of all, a renovation and expansion have given this excellent inn even more suites in buildings across the street, right on the lake. Two major pluses: **The View** restaurant (reviewed below) is outstanding, as is the state-of-the-art spa.

77 Mirror Lake Dr., Lake Placid, NY 12946. www.mirrorlakeinn.com. © **518/523-2544.** Fax 518/523-2871. 131 units. Mid-June to mid-Oct, some holiday weeks, and some off-season weekends $300–$400 double, $450 and up suite; Jan–June, excluding some holiday weeks, and mid-Oct to mid-Dec $195–$290 double, $370 and up for suites. Packages available. AE, DC, DISC, MC, V. **Amenities:** 3 restaurants; lounge; concierge; exercise room; Jacuzzi; 2 pools (1 indoor, 1 heated outdoor); room service; sauna; spa; tennis court; complimentary use of canoes, kayaks, paddle boats, and rowboats. *In room:* A/C, TV/DVD, CD player, fridge, hair dryer, Wi-Fi (added cost).

MODERATE

Dartbrook Lodge ★★ Visitors who are fond of the Great Camp style—but don't want to fork over bundles of dough to get it—need look no farther than this surprising Keene gem. It's particularly good for hikers, as several trail heads are located right in Keene Valley. The property consists of seven individual cabins and suites, all with cathedral ceilings and private porches. While cabins are not far from the road, they feel secluded and quiet once you step inside. Bright, airy, and comfortable, each one boasts colorful rugs, gas fireplace, flatscreen TV, slate rainfall shower, and, of course, Adirondack-style furnishings hand-hewn by talented local artisans (even the in-room soaps are locally crafted). The Cedar Run restaurant at the lodge serves fresh-baked goods, along with a delicious breakfast and lunch.

2835 Rte. 73, Keene, NY 12942. www.dartbrooklodge.com. © **518/576-9080.** 7 units. $175–$195 double; $325 2-bedroom cottage. 2-night weekend minimum sometimes applies. AE, DISC, MC, V. **Amenities:** Restaurant next door. *In room:* A/C, TV/DVD, fridge, kitchen (in some), Wi-Fi.

Golden Arrow Lakeside Resort ★★ ☺ This resort sits right in the heart of Lake Placid and directly on Mirror Lake. Most of the rooms have balconies, and the views (on the lakeside) are great. You can also grab a complimentary kayak and go paddling on the water, right outside your door. Another plus: The property is a sustainability standard setter, earning a four-green-leaf rating from Audubon International. The hotel is justifiably proud of its "green roof"—there's also an allergen-free floor, a guest room recycling program, and a white-sand limestone beach (which minimizes the effects of acid rain). While rooms are a bit bland, they are very comfortable, and with all the other amenities, like the heated indoor pool, health club, and sauna—plus a very affable staff—does it really matter? Suites aren't worth the extra money, though they have nice touches like fireplaces or whirlpool tubs.

2559 Main St., Lake Placid, NY 12946. www.golden-arrow.com. (C) **800/582-5540** or 518/523-3353. 166 units. Mid-June to Columbus Day $129–$279 double, $249–$499 suite; Columbus Day to mid-June weekdays $99–$229 double, $129–$459 suite, weekends high-season rates apply. Packages available. AE, DC, DISC, MC, V. Pets allowed with $50 fee. **Amenities:** Restaurant; lounge; elaborate health club; 2 Jacuzzis; indoor heated pool; limited room service; sauna; complimentary watersports equipment; massage. *In room:* A/C, TV w/pay movies, fridge, hair dryer, kitchenette (in some units), Wi-Fi.

High Peaks Resort ★★

Smack in the middle of town, this remodeled resort sprawls across two streets in two different buildings, one of which is right on the water. While the rooms still feel slightly Hilton-esque, all are spacious and spanking new, and come kitted out with balconies or patios, overstuffed chairs, supercomfy beds, flatscreen TVs, and—my favorite part—beautiful showers with natural stone tiling and rainfall shower heads. For huge, comfortable rooms that look straight down on the water, reserve in the Waterfront Building. (Just be aware that they can book up far in advance.) The resort also has loads of amenities, from three pools to a terrific fitness center, complimentary boats for use on the lake, and an Aveda spa and salon. Because about half the guests are here with a group, the place constantly buzzes. Plus, their lively and popular Dancing Bears restaurant has a nice beer selection, and serves up a good burger.

2384 Saranac Ave., Lake Placid, NY 12946. www.highpeaksresort.com. (C) **800/755-5598** or 518/523-4411. Fax 518/523-1120. 133 units. Mid-June to Aug $169–$369 double; Sept–Dec $149–$289 double; Jan to mid-June $129–$269 double, unless there's an event or holiday, when high-season rates apply. Packages available. AE, DC, DISC, MC, V. Pets allowed. **Amenities:** 3 restaurants; 3 lounges; concierge; state-of-the-art fitness center; Jacuzzi; 3 pools (1 indoor, 2 heated outdoor); room service; spa; complimentary boat rentals. *In room:* A/C, TV w/pay movies, fridge, hair dryer, MP3 docking station, Wi-Fi.

INEXPENSIVE

Adirondack Motel ★ 🍴

Head to this small, friendly lakeside motel to stay right on Saranac Lake at a great value. Rooms are nothing unique, but they are spacious and comfortable—and very clean—and even the most inexpensive have views of the water. If you're staying for a while, consider a boathouse room or cottage, both of which have kitchen facilities and are right at the lake; cottages even have fireplaces. The property definitely takes advantage of its setting; you can take a dip in the lake or grab one of the canoes and paddle away a few steps from your door.

248 Lake Flower Ave., Saranac Lake, NY 12983. www.adirondackmotel.com. (C) **800/416-0117** or 518/891-2116. 13 units. $69–$139 double; $89–$235 boathouse room and suites. Rates vary seasonally, and special holiday rates apply. Rates include muffins and coffee. AE, DISC, MC, V. From Lake Placid, take Rte. 86 north; Lake Flower and the inn will be on your left. Dogs allowed with $10 charge. **Amenities:** Complimentary use of paddle boats and canoes. *In room:* A/C, TV, fridge, hair dryer, kitchenettes in boathouse or full kitchens in cottages, Wi-Fi.

Art Devlin's Olympic Motor Inn ★ 🍴

If you enjoy the kitsch value of Lake Placid, you'll adore this small hotel just 3 blocks from the Olympic Center—in the lobby, you'll find some 450 trophies and medals from ski jumper Art Devlin. Now run by Art's son (also Art), this hotel is a little less than extraordinary, but remains a good-value option. Rooms are simple but spacious, and painted in nice bright colors. Some give you a glimpse of high peaks, even from a balcony, while others look out onto the less-romantic parking lot. Rooms in the back building are bigger, but you should splurge on one of the "upscale" rooms. The best ones have plasma TVs, 180-degree-view balconies, Jacuzzi tubs, and lots of space—one of the best values in town.

2764 Main St., Lake Placid, NY 12946. www.artdevlins.com. ✆ **518/523-3700.** Fax 518/523-3893. 50 units. Mid-June to mid-Sept midweek $72–$184 double, weekend $98–$264 double; rest of year midweek $72–$184 double, weekend $82–$258 double. Rates include continental breakfast. 2-night minimum some weekends. AE, DC, DISC, MC, V. Dogs allowed. **Amenities:** Heated outdoor pool (summer only). *In room:* A/C, TV, fridge, hair dryer, microwave (some rooms), Wi-Fi.

CAMPGROUNDS

For a truly unique experience, canoe out to one of the 87 solitary sites on **Saranac Lake Islands,** Saranac Lake (www.dec.ny.gov/outdoor/24496.html; ✆ **518/891-3170**), and pitch your tent away from the crush of car campers. Sites cost $22 and are available mid-May to Columbus Day. **Whispering Pines Campground,** Route 73, Lake Placid (✆ **518/523-9322**), is a sprawling campground right on the outskirts of Lake Placid. You can set up deep in the woods, but be prepared for loud partiers in RVs. If you're one of them, you'll love it here; tent campers in search of a back-to-nature experience will want to look elsewhere. Tent sites are $19; water and electric hookups are $25 to $29. **Ausable Point Campground** (www.dec.ny.gov/outdoor/24452.html; ✆ **518/561-7080**) sits on a stunning patch of land overlooking Lake Champlain with 123 sites. There's a shoreline of natural sand, and the campground borders a wildlife management area with a hiking trail; sites are $22. Open mid-May to mid-October, **Cranberry Lake Campground,** off Route 30 in Lake Cranberry (www.dec.ny.gov/outdoor/24460.html; ✆ **315/848-2315**), sits on a crystalline lake in one of the most undeveloped parts of the park, yet the campground is easily accessible. Their 173 campsites rent for $20 a night.

Where to Eat

Dining options range from romantic lakeside hideaways to busy food feasts in Lake Placid. For exquisite farm-to-table meals with an excellent wine selection and great views, make a reservation at **Artisans** at the Lake Placid Lodge (✆ **518/523-2700**). For a hearty homemade breakfast, try **Chair 6,** 46 Sentinel Rd. (✆ **518/523-3630**), or Keene's **Cedar Run Bakery & Café,** 2835 Rte. 73 (✆ **518/576-9929;** http://cedarrunbakery.com).

EXPENSIVE

The View ★★★ AMERICAN   Like the Mirror Lake Inn to which it's attached, this restaurant is upscale, traditional, classic, and unfailingly excellent. The change from black-tie servers to a more casually attired staff better reflects the lake view out the picture windows. However, the less formal atmosphere doesn't mean a more casual kitchen—the award-winning restaurant turns out seasonally inspired, consistently creative dishes accompanied by an equally impressive wine list. Start off with some Maine lobster bisque or fried oysters on the half shell with Himalayan pink salt and citrus crème fraîche. Then dig into such fork-tender entrees as osso buco with braised porcini mushroom demi-glace or a grilled Chinook salmon with fruitwood smoked bacon. The View is also open for breakfast.

77 Mirror Lake Dr. (inside the Mirror Lake Inn), Lake Placid. ✆ **518/302-3000.** Reservations recommended. Casual dress. Main courses $25–$44. AE, DC, DISC, MC, V. Daily 7:30–11am and 5:30–9pm.

MODERATE

Brown Dog Cafe & Wine Bar ★★ CONTINENTAL   Beloved by local foodies and discerning tourists, the Brown Dog serves up delicious sandwiches with imported cheeses and house-roasted meats on artisanal breads during the day. But in the evening, the little eatery on Main Street is transformed into a sophisticated and charming fine-dining destination, with shimmering Mirror Lake as a backdrop. Thoughtfully prepared dishes include mouthwatering smoked duck quesadillas with sun-dried cranberries; escargot en croûte with scallions, garlic, and Pernod cream; and Virginia crab cakes with a chardonnay sauce. Of course, there's an excellent wine list, with dozens of wines available by the glass.

2409 Main St., Lake Placid. ⓒ **518/523-3036.** Reservations recommended for dinner. Lunch $6–$7; main courses $8–$10. AE, MC, V. June–Aug daily 11:30am–9pm; off season Thurs–Mon 11:30am–9pm.

Caribbean Cowboy ★★ 🍴 FUSION   Hidden at the back of a building on Saranac Avenue, this Caribbean/Asian/Cajun restaurant offers a refreshing change of pace from the usual Adirondack fare. The atmosphere is vibrant and fun and the dishes burst with color and flavor. But don't be fooled by the casual ambience; the prices here ain't cheap. Still, the portions are generous and the cuisine is consistently inspired and tasty. Think sweet and spicy jerk kitchen, fritters, Cajun salmon burgers, bright Thai red curry with mussels and shrimp, and crispy sweet potato fries. Oh, and Key lime pie. Mmmm.

2126 Saranac Ave., Ste. 2, Lake Placid. ⓒ **518/523-3836.** www.placidcowboy.com. Reservations not accepted. Main courses $14–$28. MC, V. June to Labor Day Tues–Sun 5–10pm. Call for off-season hours.

Great Adirondack Steak & Seafood Company ★★ ☺ STEAKHOUSE   A steakhouse and microbrewery in one—a winning combination. Right on Main Street in Lake Placid, this highly popular restaurant comes complete with Adirondack antiques, a fireplace, large bay windows overlooking Mirror Lake, and satisfying meals that keep 'em coming. There's nothing shocking or inventive on the menu, just good pastas, meat, and fish. Try the rack of ribs basted with the house red-ale barbecue sauce, or the shrimp and scallops simmered in a garlic cream sauce with mushrooms and shallots, topped with puff pastry. An extensive kids' menu means the little ones will be happy as well here. The house brews, too, are great, especially the Ausable Wulff Red Ale.

2442 Main St., Lake Placid. ⓒ **518/523-1629.** www.greatadirondacksteakandseafood.com. Reservations not accepted. Main courses $19–$39. AE, DC, DISC, MC, V. July 4 to late Aug 8am–10pm; Sept–July 3 Mon–Fri 11am–10pm, weekends 8am–10pm.

INEXPENSIVE

Blue Moon Cafe ★★ 🍴 COFFEE SHOP   This small cafe has a loyal following that borders on a cult. The Blue Moon gained its reputation as a gathering spot and a great breakfast place, patronized by locals as well as out-of-towners, who return here every time they visit the Adirondacks. The reason? Big, fluffy omelets, huge stacks of moist pancakes, and amazing coffee. And now that they're open for dinner, and they have good Wi-Fi, there are even more reasons to get hooked on this place.

55 Main St., Saranac Lake. ⓒ **518/891-1310.** Omelets and sandwiches $4–$9. AE, DISC, MC, V. Tues–Sat 7am–9pm; Sun 8am–2pm; Mon 7am–3pm.

Noonmark Diner ★ 📷 DINER   Located in tiny Keene Valley, this homey spot is a mainstay among hikers and locals. It's the sort of place you'll think about when you're far away, dreaming about the simpler pleasures of the Adirondacks. While they do tasty big breakfasts—the blueberry pancakes are sublime—and satisfying burgers 'n' such, it's the homemade pies that made them famous in these parts. Choose from black raspberry crumb, mince, maple walnut, apricot crumb . . . the list goes on. Bring a couple home for some friends.

Rte. 73, Keene Valley. ⓒ **518/576-4499.** www.noonmarkdiner.com. Burgers and sandwiches $2–$8; dinner entrees $8–$15. Summer daily 6am–10pm; rest of year 6am–9pm.

BACKCOUNTRY blunders: DO'S & DON'TS

- Don't camp within 150 feet of roads, trails, or bodies of water.
- Lean-tos are for everyone; yes, you must share!
- No outhouse? No problem: Dig a hole 6 to 8 inches deep and at least 150 feet from water or campsites. Cover with leaves and soil.
- I like you smelling fresh, but no regular soap within 150 feet of water.

- Giardia is one bug you can avoid: Boil, filter, or treat water.
- Use only dead and down wood for fires.
- Carry out what you carry in.
- Leave wildlife and plants undisturbed—doing otherwise is not nice *and* it's illegal.

Players Sports Bar & Grill ★ ☺ AMERICAN   This is the cheapest lakeside eats-with-a-view place in Lake Placid. Set downstairs from Main Street right at water level, Players is a simply decorated place that serves up the basics as you gaze out at the water. Come here to chow on burgers, ribs, sandwiches, and salads. You'll find everything from barbecued chicken to pulled pork to hot wings and nachos.

2405 Main St., Lake Placid. ℂ **518/523-9902.** Sandwiches and platters $7–$20. AE, MC, V. June–Aug daily 11am–midnight; closes earlier in the off season.

Lake Placid After Dark

The **Lake Placid Pub & Brewery,** 813 Mirror Lake Dr. (ℂ **518/523-3813;** www. ubuale.com), just might be the best place in town to have a drink. They brew some truly fine ales (try Bill Clinton's fave, Ubu Ale), cook up great burgers and nachos, and have two floors for drinking (downstairs is cozy P.J. O'Neill's Irish pub)—along with an outdoor deck overlooking Mirror Lake. **Dancing Bears Lounge** in High Peaks Resort (ℂ **518/523-4411**) has a good selection of icy-cold beers, plus live music on Friday and Saturday nights. **Zig Zags,** 130 Main St. (ℂ **518/523-8221**), attracts a lively under-30 crowd, while **Roomers,** 137 Main St. (ℂ **518/523-3611**), is the town's nightclub, where dancing lasts till the wee hours. But if your idea of a good time consists of cozying up to a fire with a nice glass of wine or fine liqueur, your place is **The Cottage,** 5 Mirror Lake Dr. (ℂ **518/523-2544**)—part of the Mirror Lake Inn, and set on the water across the street from the hotel. Inside it's quaint, and there's also an outdoor patio that's perfect in summer.

THOUSAND ISLANDS

30 miles NW from Watertown; 90 miles N from Syracuse

Ask a downstate New Yorker about the Thousand Islands and chances are you'd be met with a thousand-yard stare. Formerly one of the nation's prime vacation destinations, these days it's a household name only if you like the salad dressing. While that creamy concoction did originate here (see "The Skinny on Salad Dressing"), this isn't exactly a reason to visit. The real appeal for the faithful is the stunning natural beauty, and an abundance of fish and wildlife.

Spanning a 50-mile stretch on the southern end of the Saint Lawrence River, the islands were carved out of granite formations left some 10,000 years ago by a retreating glacier. Their beauty has long captivated lucky visitors: Iroquois legend describes them as "spilling like flowers from creation's basket." Equally taken by the archipelago, French explorers coined the name we use today. The exact number of islands depends on who's counting, but everyone seems to agree that it's well over 1,000; 1,800 or so is more likely. They range from small, rocky outcroppings to sprawling tracts fit for a king—or at least a castle, and there are two here dating back to the region's heyday.

A century ago, this "Venice of the New World" attracted a who's who of the rich and famous. Millionaires of America's Gilded Age would come north by private rail car and be swept off in private water taxis to glamorous hotels, or to the islands they owned. But the grand hotels have long since burned down; in their place you'll find more modest accommodations. And while many of the islands' mansions are still standing, most are private property.

Today's Thousand Islands experience is one of taking it all in—sitting on the dock or in a boat, watching the day go by on the river. **Alexandria Bay** is at the heart of it all, attracting families and fisherman alike, while the **Antique Boat Museum** of Clayton exhibits one of the world's best collections of recreational freshwater boats. Farther down the coast, don't forget little **Sackets Harbor**—though technically just out of the region, it's only a short drive, and has a history and charm of its own.

Essentials

GETTING THERE   I-81 heads north from the New York State Thruway, passing through Watertown straight up to the Thousand Islands Bridge, which crosses to Canada. Watertown itself, 30 miles to the south, is the closest city to the region, but it's served only by **Adirondack Trailways** (© **800/776-7548;** www.trailwaysny. com). The bus terminal is at 540 State St. Syracuse is the nearest big city, so the major airport in the area is **Syracuse Hancock International** (© 315/454-4330).

VISITOR INFORMATION   The **1000 Islands Welcome Center,** 43373 Collins Landing, Alexandria Bay (© **800/8-ISLAND** [847-5263] or 315/482-2520; www.visit1000islands.com), is your information hub, conveniently located next to the Thousand Islands Bridge. It's open daily from May to October 8am to 6pm, and from November to April Monday to Friday 8am to 4pm.

GETTING AROUND   I-81 passes right through the heart of the region, crossing into Canada over the Thousand Islands Bridge. For the scenic route, take Route 12 as far north as Morristown, or merge onto Route 12E as it hugs the coast south from Clayton. Or take a trip down the 518-mile **Great Lakes Seaway Trail,** which hugs the shorelines of the St. Lawrence River, Lake Ontario, and the Niagara River, and continues down to Lake Erie. The roadway—a designated National Scenic Byway— is dotted with countless historical sites and scenic vistas (see also "Seaway Trail Discovery Center," below; www.seawaytrail.com).

Museums & Other Attractions

For those interested in regional history, the **Thousand Islands Museum,** 312 James St., Clayton (© **315/686-5794;** www.timuseum.org), is worth a brief stop for their collection of historic photos, maps, and hunting decoys. War buffs will want to check out the **Sackets Harbor Battlefield State Historic Site,** 504 W. Main St. (© **315/646-3634;** www.sacketsharborbattlefield.org). During the War of 1812, Sackets Harbor was rife with American naval and military activity. Now, there is an interpretive outdoor "History Trail" (also consider a cellphone tour) at the site, along

Thousand Islands

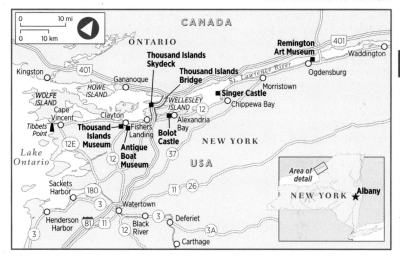

with guided tours of a restored 1860s Commandant's House and summer reenactments of camp life in the 1800s. The battlefield is also just a lovely place to walk around, perched on a bluff overlooking Lake Ontario. Look for upcoming events to commemorate the 200th anniversary of the war.

Antique Boat Museum ★★★   Boating enthusiasts simply cannot skip this museum, which contains the largest collection of inland freshwater boats in the U.S. Even people with a passing interest in boats, or those who appreciate gorgeous woodwork, will like this place. More than 250 boats grace the property, including a Chippewa dugout canoe dating from 1860 and the world's largest runabout, along with old rowboats and sailboats. One of the highlights is a tour of George Boldt's 1903 houseboat, *La Duchesse,* as well as 1920s racing boats and a 100-year-old, 110-foot houseboat owned by Andrew McNally (of Rand McNally fame). Try your hand at rowing a St. Lawrence skiff or (for an extra charge) take a speedboat ride. Show up in August and you can catch the antique boat show, the region's biggest event and the oldest wooden-boat show in the U.S. The museum also hosts regattas, children's activities, and boat-building classes.

750 Mary St., Clayton. (C) **315/686-4104.** www.abm.org. Admission $12 adults, $11 seniors, $6 children 7-17, free for military and children 6 and under. Mid-May to mid-Oct daily 9am–5pm.

Boldt Castle ★★   One of the last remaining symbols of true American grandeur in the Thousand Islands, this sprawling stone mansion built by Waldorf=Astoria Hotel owner George C. Boldt casts a regal presence over Heart Island and the shoreline of Alexandria Bay. With turrets and tunnels, a drawbridge, a Gaudí-like kids' playhouse, its own power house, and formal gardens, the castle and all its pieces are dazzling—and look entirely out of place today. The home comes with a sad tale: Boldt had the castle built over the course of 4 years to give to his wife on her birthday in 1904—Valentine's Day—but she died a month before, and the castle, 80% complete, was never occupied. After falling into disrepair, it's been slowly restored: There's an

| | **The Skinny on Salad Dressing** |

Yes, Thousand Island dressing did indeed originate in these here parts—to be specific, in the town of Clayton. A fishing guide named George LaLonde offered this new and unusual dressing as part of his shore dinners served after a long day of fishing. The dressing went public at the hotel that's now called the 1000 Islands Inn, and the recipe ended up in the hands of George Boldt, Thousand Islands resident and owner of New York City's Waldorf=Astoria Hotel, who put it on his hotel's menu. You can still get "original recipe" dressing right at the 1000 Islands Inn if you're lucky: Only 5,000 bottles are produced each year and are sold between mid-May and mid-September for $6.95 each.

oval stained-glass window in the foyer ceiling, a formal dining room, an impressive billiards room, and the bedroom areas. But most of the house is still gutted, so you won't spend as much time as expected during your self-guided tour. Still, bring a picnic lunch and enjoy the 5-acre island's grounds. Then take the shuttle to the Yacht House and check out Boldt's amazing collection of antique wooden boats, including the exquisite steam-powered vessel *Kestrel*.

Heart Island. ℂ **800/847-5263.** www.boldtcastle.com. Admission $7 adults, $4.50 children 6–12. May to end of June and early Sept to early Oct daily 10am–6:30pm; July to early Sept daily 10am–7:30pm; early to mid-Oct 10am–5:30pm. Yacht House admission $3 adults, $2 children; mid-May to end of Sept daily 10:30am–6:30pm. Uncle Sam Boat Tours, on the water in Alexandria Bay (ℂ **315/482-2611**; http://usboattours.com), runs a shuttle for the 10-min. trip to the castle, with frequent departures early May to mid-Oct, $7 adults, $4.50 children.

Frederic Remington Art Museum ★ ☺   Fans of Remington's Western-themed paintings and bronzes will have much to savor here. And for those unfamiliar with his work—cowboys, Indians, and the horses they rode on, depicted in lifelike grandeur, cast in action poses for eternity—this impressive collection in sleepy Ogdensburg is a nice introduction. Cast no. 14 of his iconic *Rattlesnake*—a horse rears away in terror from a snake, as the rider clutches his hat—is particularly riveting, the drama rendered in vivid, realistic detail. (The sculpture was rumored to have been Ronald Reagan's favorite artwork.) But what makes this museum interesting is its treasure-trove of Remington's later-in-life Impressionist landscape paintings of his beloved New York State North Country. **Bonus:** My docent was wonderfully engaging, full of anecdotes about Remington's life and work.

303 Washington St., Ogdensburg. ℂ **315/393-2425.** www.fredericremington.org. Admission $9 adults, $8 seniors and students 16 and older, $5 active military, free for children 15 and under. May–Oct Mon–Sat 10am–5pm, Sun 1–5pm; Nov–Apr Wed–Sat 11am–5pm, Sun 1–5pm.

Seaway Trail Discovery Center ★ ☺   This historic limestone building, an old hotel built after the War of 1812, houses a series of interactive kid-oriented exhibits exploring different aspects of the Seaway Trail. Natural history, war history, lighthouses, maritime history, recreation, and agriculture are just a few areas covered; it's worth at least an hour's stop for families with kids. There's a nature room where you can listen to bird songs, a section highlighting some important figures from the area— Susan B. Anthony, Frederic Remington, George Eastman—and . . . wait for it . . . a talking cow. Really, who among you can resist a talking cow?

410 W. Main St., Sackets Harbor. ℂ **800/SEAWAY-T** (732-9298). www.seawaytrail.com. Admission $4 adults, $3 seniors and military, $2 children. May–Oct daily 10am–5pm; Nov–Apr Tues–Sat 10am–5pm.

Singer Castle ★★ Opened to the public only since 2003, this dramatic medieval castle is worth going out of your way to see. It's a stunning creation, made of the same granite used for Boldt Castle and erected at the same time in the first years of the 20th century. Unlike its sister castle, however, Singer was actually occupied, and it's still furnished with period pieces. Its builder and owner, Commodore Frederick Gilbert Bourne, was a self-made millionaire who became the director and president of the Singer Sewing Company at age 36. He bought the island and built this 28-room gem with a four-story tower as a retreat for himself and his family. It's sprawling and beautiful, with plenty of parking space for his boats and oddities like underground passageways and dungeons. In order to see the property, you have to take a 45-minute tour, but it's an interesting one: Guides point out Bourne's secret passageways and peepholes used to spy on guests. If you really fall in love with the place, consider an overnight stay in the Royal Suite—a luxurious wing of the castle available for rent—and the entire island is yours for the evening.

Dark Island. ℂ **315/324-3275.** www.singercastle.com. Admission $14 adults, $11 seniors, $6 children 4-12. No strollers allowed. Mid-May to mid-June and early Sept to mid-Oct Sat–Sun 10am–5pm; mid-June to early Sept daily 10am–5pm. Last tour begins at 4pm. Private boaters can land anytime; Uncle Sam Boat Tours, on the water in Alexandria Bay (ℂ **315/482-2611**; http://usboattours.com), runs a 3½-hr. 2-castle tour with a 1-hr. stop at Singer ($46 adults, $23 kids), which includes admission to Singer (admission to Boldt Castle is optional). Call or check website for schedule.

1000 Islands SkyDeck ★ ☺ Every place with a view must have an observation tower, right? Even the relatively undeveloped Thousand Islands have a candy-cane-looking deck hovering high in the sky. Take the elevator up 400 feet and on a good day you'll get a 25-mile view over the St. Lawrence River. Three decks (one of them is enclosed) let you take in the scattered islands sitting in the river. Of course, it's on the Canadian side, so bring your passport, eh?

Hill Island, Lansdowne, Ontario. ℂ **613/659-2335.** www.1000islandsskydeck.com. Admission C$9.75 adults, C$5.75 children 6–12, free for children 5 and under. Spring and fall daily 9am–6pm; summer daily 9am–8pm.

Sports & Outdoor Pursuits

BOAT TOURS Lots of tour boats run the island circuit all summer, offering close-up views of the islands and occasionally interesting narration peppered with the standard bad jokes. You can stop at Singer Castle, as well as Boldt Castle (with an unlimited stop to jump off and check out the grounds), Millionaire's Row (with amazing mansions, called "cottages"), and interesting points, like **Tom Thumb Island**—the region's smallest at 3 square feet. You'll cross over into Canadian waters, pass under the international bridges, and see that some islands are just big enough for a shack, while others are a whopping 45 square miles in area. Go with **Uncle Sam Boat Tours** ★★, 47 James St., Alexandria Bay (ℂ **800/253-9229;** http://usboat tours.com), and those 12 and under will get to drive the boat for a few seconds and get a captain's license. The two-nation, 2-hour tour is $17; a 1-hour tour is $19 for adults, $9.25 for children 4 to 12 years old. Uncle Sam also offers lunch and dinner cruises, fireworks cruises, and other special-event boat tours ($7.50–$46).

FISHING To say that the St. Lawrence is a haven for fishermen would be an understatement. The creatures that ply these waters are the main reason many people venture up this way during the season (which generally runs Apr–Nov)—it's truly a world-class area for fishing. Why? Because of areas like Henderson Trench, a glacier-cut area west of Henderson Harbor between Stony Island and Stony Point, which averages 120 feet in depth. In late summer, the waters attract mature king salmon; as they wait for their ancient call to head up the Black River to spawn and die, they gorge themselves and grow to some 30 pounds or more. In eastern Lake Ontario, you'll hook lake trout, steelhead, and walleye. On the St. Lawrence, there's also walleye, pike, perch, bass, and muskellunge (get your muscles ready—these monsters can grow up to 35 lb.). In the inland waters, anglers find trout, walleye, muskellunge, and pike. Some of the less expensive fishing charters are out of Clayton, and cost from $100 to $200 per person for a full day. Consider: **Ferguson Fishing Charters** (© **315/686-3100;** www.fergusonfishingcharters.com), **St. Lawrence Charters** (© **315/686-1216;** www.thousandislands.com/fishingcharters), and **1000 Islands Fishing Charters** (© **877/544-4241**).

GOLF   The flat, lush riverside terrain makes for some nice golf courses. Play in the middle of the river out on Wellesley Island at the **Thousand Islands Country Club,** 21496 Clubhouse Dr. (© **800/928-TICC** [8422]; www.ticountryclub.com), which boasts two 18-hole courses, including one designed in 1894 by George Boldt (he of Boldt Castle). Greens fees are $22 to $35 weekdays, $25 to $45 weekends. Or try the par-71 **C-Way Golf Club,** Route 12, Clayton (© **315/686-4562;** www.cwayresort.com), where greens fee are $20 to $32.

KAYAKING   Get an up-close-and-personal tour of the islands as you skim along the surface in a kayak. With all the water traffic out here, especially the enormous tankers, it's good to go with a guide. Besides, it's easy to get lost among all the islands! Kayak past **Grass Point Marsh** and keep an eye out for wildlife as you work your way toward historic **Rock Island,** with some of the area's most beautiful cottages. Paddle through the **French Creek Wildlife Preserve** and look for birds. Or take on something seriously adventuresome and spend the day circumnavigating the region's third-largest land plot, **Grindstone Island.** Go with **T.I. Adventures,** 1011 State St., Clayton (© **315/686-2500;** www.tiadventures.com). Rentals start at about $30 for a half-day; weekly rentals also available.

BALLOONING   Because this region doesn't have many mountains, it's hard to get a bird's-eye perspective on the natural splendor of the Thousand Islands. **Champagne Balloon Adventures,** 27 James St., Alexandria Bay (© **315/686-2500;** www.balloonadventures.com), solves that problem by offering sunrise and sunset hot-air balloon trips, weather permitting, for $175 per person. Actual time in the air lasts up to an hour, followed by a reception of champagne, hors d'oeuvres, and other refreshments. Don't forget your camera!

RAFTING   The Thousand Islands are home to some of the nation's most renowned white water, namely the **Black River Canyon.** From May to October, the Black

---

 The Eagles Have Landed

In the early 1900s, bald eagles thrived in the Thousand Islands. Unfortunately, years of pollution, pesticide use, and habitat loss contributed to the bird's gradual disappearance in the region. But now, bald eagles are slowly making a comeback. Groups on both the American and Canadian sides are involved in efforts to protect the eagles' nesting and overwintering habitats. Recently, there were three nests with a total of six eaglets on the St. Lawrence River—a promising sign.

Among the Wreckage

The clear waters of the St. Lawrence River offer some excellent opportunities for world-class wreck diving. Not only is there evidence of 3 centuries of canoe, boat, and shipwrecks, but many of these sunken vessels are very well preserved. Some of the best dive sites include the *Keystorm,* a steamer that sank in 1912; the *Vickery,* a schooner that struck a rock and dropped to its grave in 1889; and the *Wolfe Islander,* a car ferry that was intentionally sunk in 1985. Go with **1000 Islands Diving Adventures,** 335 Riverside Dr., Clayton (✆ **315/686-3030;** www.1000-islands.com/diving). On the Canadian side, **Arctic Kingdom Expeditions** (✆ **888/737-6818;** www.arctickingdom.com) is now offering January and February ice dives for thick-blooded adventurers. Heated airboats transport divers, who are given an unparalleled opportunity to explore the wrecks and "Lost Villages" of submerged power stations and lake locks underneath winter's ice, when visibility is near crystal-clear.

gushes with pounding white water—with May and June having the most powerful white water—and scores of paddlers fly down it on rafts. It's Class III and IV, which means there's some serious rollicking going on (and you must be at least 14 years old to go). As you cruise through Rocket Ride and Cruncher, you'll see fabulous waterfalls cascade from the canyon walls. Go with **Whitewater Challengers** (✆ **800/443-RAFT** [7238] or 315/639-6100; www.whitewaterchallengers.com); it's $51 to $74 for a day trip. **ARO Adventures** (✆ **800/525-RAFT** [7238]) is another good choice; a day trip will set you back $50 to $69.

Especially for Kids

You can get your speed on at **Alex Bay 500 Go-Karts** on Route 12, ¼ mile north of the Thousand Islands Bridge (✆ **315/482-2021;** www.1000islands.com/alexbay500); there's also a miniature golf course and an immense game arcade on-site. Or get lost in the 7-foot-high hedges of **Mazeland,** also on Route 12, ¾ mile north of the bridge (✆ **315/482-2186**). The whole family will get a kick out of seeing movie stars under the stars at the **Bay Drive-In Theatre,** Route 6 and Bailey Settlement Road, Alexandria Bay (✆ **315/482-3874;** www.baydrivein.com).

Where to Stay

You'll find the most lodging options in Alexandria Bay, which is also where you'll find the most people. If you stay in charming little Sackets Harbor (my favorite), there are some good restaurants and bars all within walking distance. And don't forget the Canadian side: The **Frontenac Club Inn,** 225 King St. E., Kingston, Ontario (www.frontenacclub.com; ✆ **613/547-6167**), is an excellent choice. (Bring your passport!)

Unfortunately, all the old grand hotels patronized by the Vanderbilts and their ilk at the turn of the 20th century were claimed by fire, so you won't find any classics like the Adirondacks' Sagamore. The historic properties were replaced by motels and two-story resorts, which have the benefit of being on the water, but generally promise little else. Fortunately, there are a couple of exceptions (reviewed below). Few spots are open year-round, and many hotels require a 2-night minimum stay on summer weekends.

EXPENSIVE

Riveredge Resort ★★   Sitting on the water in the heart of Alexandria Bay, this is the area's most expansive accommodations, boasting two pools, a great restaurant with amazing views, and some of the best amenities around. (There's even a poolside tiki bar.) The comfortable standard rooms are rather spacious, with comfortable beds and decent-size bathrooms; loft suites have two stories (beds are upstairs in the "loft"), and some come with a Jacuzzi. The fourth-floor concierge level comes complete with turndown service. Most rooms have balconies that come with water views; try to score one that looks out on spectacular Boldt Castle.

17 Holland St., Alexandria Bay, NY 13607. www.riveredge.com. © **800/365-6987.** Fax 315/482-5010. 128 units. Room rates vary based on availability. Summer $162–$303 double; fall and spring $132–$223 double; winter $59–$133 double. Packages available. 2-night minimum on weekends. AE, DC, DISC, MC, V. At Rte. 12 and Church St. turn left, turn right onto Walton St. and left onto Holland St. Pets allowed with $25 fee. **Amenities:** Restaurant; lounge; concierge; concierge-level floor; exercise room; 2 Jacuzzis; small indoor and outdoor heated pools; limited room service; sauna. *In room:* A/C, TV w/pay movies, hair dryer, Wi-Fi.

MODERATE

Candlelight Bed & Breakfast ★★ 📖   This historic redbrick 1832 inn is perhaps the most pleasant, peaceful place to stay in charming Sackets Harbor. Location-wise, you can't do much better, as it's just a 2-minute stroll to the town's great brewpub, restaurants, and marina. But it's also in a very quiet part of Sackets, a couple minutes' walk from Lake Ontario. All three tastefully appointed rooms are pretty, well maintained, and comfortable, with ceiling fans, wing chairs, four-poster beds, and nice-sized bathrooms; two of three have views of the lake. The owners are friendly and helpful, and you'll be treated to a delicious big breakfast, including delights like blueberry strata or baked apple pancakes.

501 W. Washington St., Sackets Harbor, NY 13685. www.imcnet.net/candlelight. © **800/306-5595** or 315/646-1518. 3 units. $89–$135 double year-round. Rates include full breakfast. MC, V. *In room:* A/C, TV, hair dryer, Wi-Fi.

Edgewood Resort ★★   This 40-acre waterfront property is set far back from the road, so the grounds are nice and quiet. All rooms have balconies or porches, and many look directly over the water—some people even fish from their balconies! Some rooms have mahogany decks and cedar posts, giving an upscale, woodsy touch to the spacious but otherwise basic sleeping areas. Done in earthy greens and browns, the guest rooms are simply furnished with industrial carpeting, scratchy sofas, and wildlife stencils on the walls. But with your own deck, you'll hardly want to sit indoors. In addition to a log cabin for rent, the Edgewood also has a great lounge and snack bar—open only on weekends—with a huge deck overlooking the water.

Edgewood Park Rd., Alexandria Bay, NY 13607. www.theedgewoodresort.com. © **888/EDGEWOOD** (334-3966) or 315/482-9923. 107 units. July–Aug Sun–Thurs $129–$509 double, Fri–Sat $169–$589 double; May–June and Sept–Oct Sun–Thurs $99–$409 double, Fri–Sat $129–$489 double. June–Sept 2-night weekend minimum. AE, DISC, MC, V. **Amenities:** 2 restaurants; 2 lounges; large outdoor pool; Wi-Fi in the lobby. *In room:* A/C, TV, hair dryer, Jacuzzis and kitchenettes (in suites).

Ontario Place   With an excellent location in Sackets Harbor—it's spitting distance to great dining and fun—this privately owned hotel offers a range of rooms from standards to suites to Jacuzzi suites. It's worth paying the extra money for the suites, as they are higher up in the hotel and therefore sunnier—and quieter—with some nice views of the water. While the first-floor "Travelers' Staterooms" are enormous—with king beds and bathrooms with two showers—some are rather dark.

103 General Smith Dr., Sackets Harbor, NY 13685. www.ontarioplacehotel.com. ✆ **800/564-1812** or 315/646-8000. 46 units. Memorial Day to Labor Day $109–$119 double, $175–$245 suite; rest of year $89–$99 double, $155–$225 suite. AE, DISC, MC, V. Pets allowed with $25 fee. *In room:* A/C, TV, fridge, microwave, Wi-Fi.

INEXPENSIVE

Capt. Thomson's Resort ★

Occupying the prime waterview grounds of the historic Frontenac Hotel, this two-story motel is decidedly less glamorous but has an equally grand view. Rooms are nothing more than standard motel-type accommodations—industrial carpeting, IKEA-ish furniture, cramped bathrooms—though with historic photos on the walls. The payoff is in the views: Those rooms not facing the parking lot offer picture-perfect scenes of the river and islands. Their new restaurant, Riley's by the River, is open 7 days a week from 7am to 9pm in summer; call for off-season hours.

47 James St., Alexandria Bay, NY 13607. www.captthomsons.com. ✆ **800/ALEXBAY** (253-9229). Fax 315/482-5013. 68 units. $59–$176 double and queen; $99–$219 efficiency apartments; $119–$199 Jacuzzi room. Packages available. 2-night minimum weekends; 3-night minimum July 4 and Labor Day weekends. AE, DC, DISC, MC, V. Closed mid-Oct to May. **Amenities:** Restaurant; outdoor heated pool. *In room:* A/C, TV, hair dryer, free Wi-Fi.

Channelsyde Motel

This small motel takes advantage of its riverside location without breaking the bank. It's set on a large lawn with a small beach; you can swim in the river here or just relax on one of the lawn chairs. Rooms are done in light colors and floral patterns. They're hardly huge and are set up motel-style, but are not uncomfortable. Still, the big benefit to the Channelsyde is its location, 3 miles from downtown Alex Bay and just steps from the water.

21061 Pt. Vivian Rd., Alexandria Bay, NY 13607. www.channelsyde.com. ✆ **315/482-2281.** 14 units. Summer season $115 double; off-season $80 double; $10 dockage fee. 2-night minimum some summer weekends. DISC, MC, V. **Amenities:** Restaurant (snacks only). *In room:* A/C, TV, fridge, Wi-Fi.

Tibbetts Point Lighthouse Hostel

If you're a lover of lighthouses—or a fan of romantic overnight experiences of the no-frills variety—do yourself a favor and stay here. One of the oldest (and still functioning) lighthouses in the Great Lakes, the Tibbetts is set on a beautiful spot—where Lake Ontario meets the St. Lawrence—at the end of a lovely drive along the river. Guests stay in the Victorian-era light keeper's quarters, with their choice of one of the private rooms (which contain from two to six beds), or a bunk in the dorm room. As this is truly a hostel, it's bare-bones indeed (and cheap!), with simple beds and shared bathrooms (even for the private rooms). But it's very well kept, with a full kitchen, hot showers, and lockers. Though this place is pretty off the radar, there are some groups that pass through.

Tibbetts Point Rd., Cape Vincent, NY 13618. www.capevincent.org/lighthouse. ✆ **315/654-3450.** 26 beds. Reservations recommended, especially for the private rooms. Mid-May to mid-Oct $20 dorm beds, $23 beds in private rooms. From Cape Vincent, go west on Broadway. After about ½ mile, where Broadway intersects Pleasant Valley Rd., continue west on Tibbetts Point Rd., about 2 miles to the end. **Amenities:** Kitchen w/fridge, microwave, oven.

CAMPGROUNDS

Fortunately, some very choice properties in this region are state parklands, making for fantastic campsites with great views. One of the best options is **Long Point State Park,** 7495 State Park Rd., Three Mile Bay (✆ **800/456-2267** or 315/649-5258), on a long, narrow peninsula facing one of Lake Ontario's bays. With 80 campsites, only 16 of them are electric, ensuring a relatively peaceful experience. **Cedar Point**

State Park, 36661 Cedar Point State Park Dr., Clayton (© **315/654-2522**), also offers some tent sites right on the water. Off by itself is **Association Island RV Resort and Marina,** 15530 Snowshoe Rd., Henderson (www.associationisland resort.com; © **800/393-4189** or 315/955-6522), which juts out into Lake Ontario. The entire 65-acre island is devoted to camping, but with 305 RV sites, along with five cottages and a marina, you'll hardly be alone.

Where to Eat

The key to dining around here is to manage expectations: With few exceptions, restaurants follow the hotel trend—decent and reliable without being anything fancy. However, some are located right on the water, and most brim with personality. The food is mostly okay, but remember, it's about the whole experience. Eating a seafood dinner on the river as the sun sets is about as Thousand Island–y as it gets—don't miss it.

That said, if you're looking for something interesting—culinarily speaking—Sackets Harbor has a few gems. Also consider a jaunt across the bridge into Kingston, Ontario, where your options will multiply: fish and chips, Southeast Asian, gourmet pizza, French, and other eclectic fare can all be found "over there."

EXPENSIVE

Clipper Inn ★★AMERICAN   Ask most locals where they go for a "night out" and they'll direct you to this building on Route 12. One of the nicest places not on the water, the Clipper caters to a hometown crowd, with references to locals and inside jokes typed on the menu's specials page. Get a table in back, where fans and a huge skiff hang from the ceiling. It's the type of place that calls its own appetizers unnecessary because food comes with salad, a loaf of warm bread, and the de rigueur relishes (which are better than average). The menu is standard American but has some dashes of brilliance, like the Chicken Alaska, with crabmeat, broccoli, and béarnaise sauce. There's also scrod prepared several different ways. Homemade desserts are good; the white-chocolate raspberry bread pudding with white-chocolate sauce is not to be missed. One drawback: The service, while friendly, is frustratingly slow.

126 State St., Clayton. © **315/686-3842.** www.clipperinn.com. Reservations suggested. Main courses $18–$38. AE, DC, DISC, MC, V. Apr–mid-June Wed–Sun 5–10pm; mid-June to Oct Tues–Sun 5–10pm.

Tin Pan Galley ★★★ NEW AMERICAN   Open for breakfast, lunch, and dinner, with a flower-filled stone courtyard, an inspired wine list, and knowledgeable and friendly servers, this is one of the finest restaurants in the North Country. The cuisine is the most creative—and consistently flavorful—in this part of the state. For starters, there's a five-spiced calamari with a Thai sweet chili sauce, and homemade garlic potato chips with a fantastic Maytag blue cheese dip. Entrees include a mouthwatering panko coriander crusted grilled ahi tuna and a "French Quarter" chicken stuffed with andouille, white corn, and jack cheese. But it's the breakfasts here that are legendary, with such imaginative options as blueberry fritters, sausage poblano gravy and biscuits, beef tenderloin Benedict with portabella mushrooms, and breakfast chimichangas. The stuffed French toast—loaded with strawberries and dollops of ricotta and cream cheese—is a revelation. Have we mentioned how much we like this place?

110 W. Main St., Sackets Harbor. © **315/646-3812.** www.tinpangalley.com. Reservations suggested for lunch and dinner. Breakfasts $5–$14; main dinner courses $19–$29. AE, DC, DISC, MC, V. Mon–Fri 8am–9pm; weekends 7am–9pm.

A FISHIN' tradition

In this hugely popular fishing destination, it only makes sense to find traditions surrounding the consumption of fish. One that began in the early 1900s is the shore dinner: River guides would set out in their skiffs, fish all morning, and set up on one of the islands to prepare and eat the feast. Thankfully, this practice continues today.

Here's how it works: After a full morning of fishing, you'll stop on a deserted or nearly deserted island and relax around picnic tables as the guide sets up, starting with a fire. Traditional shore dinners begin with the guide putting sliced fatback in the skillet—100% fat from the back of a pig. Why all fat? The grease that's rendered from the fatback is used to fry the fish and dessert. As the fat fries, slices of bread are loaded up with sliced onion and pieces of fat and folded into a sandwich. There's your appetizer. You may also be served a salad (with Thousand Island dressing, of course). Meanwhile, the guide is frying up the just-caught fish, as well as cooking potatoes and corn on the cob.

As you chow on the fish, dessert preparations begin. Eggs, sugar, and cream go into a dish, along with bread that has been drying in the sun. When the mixture is thrown into the hot fatback grease, the batter puffs up, making the French toast–like concoction resemble a puff pastry. Top it with butter, maple syrup, cream, and brandy.

Note: Most of the fishing companies mentioned in "Fishing," above, offer a traditional shore dinner for an extra charge.

MODERATE

Cavallario's Steak & Seafood ★ AMERICAN   While steaks are the specialty in this large restaurant with a faux castle facade, the menu actually features only a few red-meat options; the rest focuses on seafood, chicken, and veal. You can even get an entire "shore dinner" brought to your table. While the standard menu offers no surprises, the well-prepared food gets high marks. You'll find sautéed honey-dipped chicken breast with a macadamia-nut crust, along with classics like baked manicotti and sautéed shrimp with vodka cream sauce.

26 Church St., Alexandria Bay. ✆ **315/482-9867.** www.cavssteak.com. Main courses $14–$27; most seafood at market prices. AE, DC, DISC, MC, V. May–Oct daily 5–9pm; Nov–Apr daily 5–10pm.

Foxy's ★★ 🎒 ☺ AMERICAN   Another local family favorite that's tucked between Clayton and Alexandria, Foxy's is the best midrange restaurant on the water, and those lucky enough to find it return year after year. Unfortunately, there's very little outdoor seating, but come to watch the sunset from one of the many windows. The atmosphere is congenial and casual—it's a terrific spot to spend the evening. The food is better than the plastic tablecloths and paper napkins would suggest. The menu leans Italian American, so expect pizzas and lasagna, but there's also the predictable mix of steak and seafood. Desserts are generously sized and good, like fried ice cream or turtle cheesecake.

Fishers Landing. ✆ **315/686-3781.** Main courses $10–$24. AE, MC, V. Mother's Day to mid-June Wed–Sun 4–9pm; mid-June to late Sept daily 4–10pm. From Rte. 12, turn west on Rte. 195, at the blinking light btw. Clayton and Alexandria Bay.

Sackets Harbor Brew Pub ★★ BREW PUB   Located in a refurbished railway station of the now-extinct New York Central Railroad and right on the shore of Lake

Ontario, this friendly spot serves up great views and inspired pub food (and beyond) complemented by award-winning beers that are growing in popularity. Dine outside on the patio, or in the dining room that's decked out in deep reds with lots of wood, brass, and ceiling fans. Sample the signature 1812 amber ale or a Black River Lager, and tuck into duck nachos, pecan-crusted Brie with raspberry coulis, lemon caramelized sea bass, or tuna Wellington with wasabi cream cheese.

212 W. Main St., Sackets Harbor. © **315/646-2739.** www.sacketsharborbrewpub.com. Main courses $18–$26. AE, DISC, MC, V. Mon–Fri 5–9:30pm; Sat–Sun noon–10pm.

INEXPENSIVE

Aubrey's Inn ★★ ☺AMERICAN   This homey place with the lumpy booth seat cushions is a local fave that's hopping anytime it's open. Why? Very simple: mammoth portions of good food at reasonable prices and friendly service to boot. The only water views are of the murals on the walls, but you don't come for the ambience. You're here for the heaping plate of spaghetti or the fresh fish from the St. Lawrence or pancakes the size of manhole covers. Kids' menu $4 to $5.

550 Broadway, Cape Vincent. © **315/654-3754.** Main courses $10–$16. AE, DISC, MC, V. Winter daily 7am–8pm; summer daily 7am–9pm.

Bella's Bistro ★ LIGHT FARE   Specializing in homemade breads and baked goods, this bistro also turns out some terrific coffee and breakfasts, like banana walnut French toast, along with a wide variety of freshly made sandwiches and salads for lunch. The Round Island Raspberry Chicken comes with sweet Vidalia onions, raspberry sauce, and melted provolone cheese, while the Murray Island has roasted beef, zesty horseradish mayo, and Swiss. It's a great place to pick up a picnic.

602 Riverside Dr., Clayton © **315/686-2341.** www.bellasonlinenow.com. Breakfast $5–$9; lunch $6–$10. Summer and fall Mon–Fri daily 7am–6pm, Sun 8am–5pm; call for off-season hours.

Thousand Islands After Dark

The newly renovated **Clayton Opera House,** 405 Riverside Dr., Clayton (© 315/686-2200; www.claytonoperahouse.com), is open year-round, hosting music, theater, and comedy performances, while the **Lyric Coffee House,** 246 James St., Clayton (© 315/686-4700; lyriccoffeehouse.com), features regional musical acts on weekends (and delicious gelato every day). Across the river, the **Thousand Islands Playhouse** in Gananoque, Ontario, boasts two theaters: the Springer Theatre, at 690 Charles St. S., and the Firehall Theatre, 185 South St. (© 866/382-7020 or 613/382-7020; www.1000islandsplayhouse.com). They present dramas, musicals, and comedies from May to October. Or try your luck at the **O.L.G. Casino** (formerly the Thousand Islands Charity Casino), 380 Hwy. 2, Gananoque, Ontario (© 888/942-6224).

Some of the bars in Alexandria Bay hop till the wee hours. Check out the **Dockside Pub,** 17 Market St. (© 315/482-9849), for their popular pub food and outside patio in season; **Rum Runner Wharf Bar & Grill,** 219 Holland St., at the Bonnie Castle Resort (© 315/482-4511); or **Skiffs,** 12 Jane St. (© 315/482-7543). And you can't visit Sackets Harbor without having a pint (or two) at the friendly **Sackets Harbor Brewing Company** (212 W. Main St., Sackets Harbor; © 315/646-2739; www.sacketsharborbrewpub.com).

WESTERN NEW YORK

by Marc Lallanilla

Even the most jaded traveler leaves western New York with a sense of surprise, if not amazement, especially after seeing Niagara Falls. Yes, it has become a tourist attraction, but there's simply no way to crowd out one ele-mental fact: Niagara Falls is utterly breathtaking. "It is with roses and locomotives . . . and Niagara Falls that my poems are competing," e e cummings wrote, and millions of visitors each year view the falls with the same kind of stunned silence. Of course, if you still want to have a soak in a heart-shaped Jacuzzi, be wowed by an IMAX theater, tiptoe through a haunted house, or just get your passport stamped, you can do all of that here, too.

Only a short ride to the south, the city of Buffalo has all sorts of delights waiting to be discovered beneath its rugged exterior: an astounding assort-ment of architecture, including a handful of Frank Lloyd Wright designs that have been preserved or reconstructed; a vital regional and interna-tional arts scene; walkable neighborhoods lined with galleries, boutiques, and hip little bars; and seriously good food, ranging from top-tier restau-rants to old-world taverns serving up some of the best hot dogs and roast beef sandwiches you'll ever have.

As you move away from the big city, the population thins quickly and rolling hills give way to farmland. Out here you'll come across some of the quirkier destinations the state has to offer, with museums dedicated to kazoos, Lucille Ball, and even JELL-O, while nearby Lily Dale is a mecca for mediums and those with a spiritualist bent. In little East Aurora, the legacy of the Roycrofters, a fine crafts collective from the late 19th cen-tury, lives on. Heading east, deeper into rural New York, you'll find Letch-worth State Park, home to a breathtaking natural gorge and one of the state's best-kept secrets. Finally, not far from the Pennsylvania border lies the Chautauqua Institution, a learning vacation retreat that attracts faith-ful devotees as well as major talents every summer for their lectures and performances.

BUFFALO

70 miles W of Rochester; 398 miles NW of New York City

New York's second-largest city is one of the state's oft-overlooked gems, and is brimming with attractions that are as surprising as they are delightful. Buffalo is home to some world-class cultural institutions, abundant venues for outdoor recreation, and inventive restaurants that leave chicken wings back on the farm. Add in the city's vibrant nightlife and passion for professional sports, and you have the making of a great weekend getaway.

Things to Do Visitors to the Queen City are often surprised by the many art treasures to be found in the **Albright-Knox Gallery,** home to some of the best works by Picasso, Gauguin, and Warhol. If your tastes are more outdoorsy, however, spend some time in one of the city's many outstanding parks; the **Buffalo and Erie County Botanical Gardens** and Frederick Law Olmsted's **Delaware Park** are among the finest in the country.

Shopping Take a stroll through **Elmwood Village,** home to a dazzling variety of bistros, boutiques, art galleries, and specialty shops. After scouring the delights at **Everything Elmwood,** grab a well-deserved snack at **Delish.** Buffalo's North Park neighborhood is home to dozens of antiques shops along **Hertel Avenue,** including **Buffalo Wholesale Antiques** and the **Antique Lamp Company.**

Restaurants and Dining Why fight it? You have to try the local culinary favorites, so tuck into some of Buffalo's best wings at **Duff's,** and don't miss the less well-known but equally delicious Beef on Weck at **Charlie the Butcher's.** For a more upscale dining experience, try the innovative cuisine at **Left Bank,** or the fantastic wine cellar at Bacchus.

Nightlife and Entertainment While **Shea's Performing Arts Center** and **Tralf Music Hall** host big-name acts, you can find more cutting-edge entertainment at Ani DiFranco's **Babeville.** But to see how Buffalo natives *really* let their hair down, grab tickets for a local sporting tradition—a home game of the **Buffalo Bills** or the NHL's **Sabres.**

Getting There

BY PLANE The **Buffalo Niagara International Airport** (© 716/630-6000; www.buffaloairport.com), 10 miles east of downtown, is served by a number of airlines, including **JetBlue** (© 800/538-2583; http://jetblue.com), which has lots of cheap one-way flights from other parts of New York; **AirTran Airways** (© 800/AIRTRAN [247-8726]; www.airtran.com); **American** (© 800/433-7300; www.aa.com); **Continental** (© 800/525-0280; www.continental.com); **Southwest** (© 800/435-9792; www.southwest.com); **United** (© 800/241-6522; www.united.com); and **US Airways** (© 800/428-4322; www.usairways.com).

The **ITA Shuttle** (© **800/551-9369** or 716/633-8294) can take you from the airport to the downtown hotels. It's $18 per person one-way and shuttles leave every hour on the hour from 6am to 10pm.

BY CAR If you'd prefer to rent a car—and you'll need one if you want to get beyond the downtown Buffalo attractions—**Alamo** (© 800/327-9633; www.alamo.com), **Avis** (© 800/331-1212; www.avis.com), **Budget** (© 800/527-0700; www.budgetbuffalo.com), **Enterprise** (© 800/325-8007; www.enterprise.com), **Hertz** (© 800/654-3131; www.hertz.com), and **National** (© 800/227-7368; www.nationalcar.com)

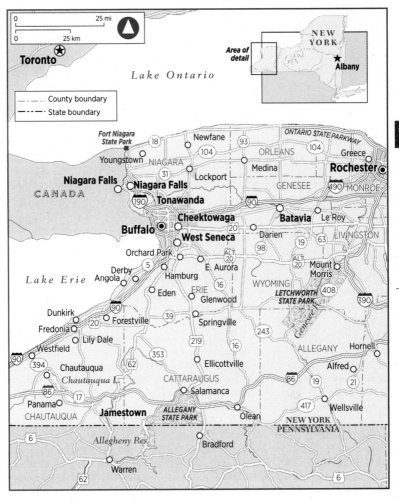

all have rental counters at the airport. Buffalo is reachable from most areas of the United States via the New York State Thruway (I-90).

BY RAIL   Amtrak (📞 **800/USA-RAIL** [872-7245]; www.amtrak.com) rolls into Buffalo's tiny train station at 75 Exchange St. (at Washington St.).

BY BUS   Greyhound (📞 **800/231-2222**; www.greyhound.com) and **New York Trailways** (📞 **800/295-5555**; www.trailwaysny.com) make their way to the station at 181 Ellicott St. (at N. Division). **Megabus** (**877/462-6342**; http://us.megabus. com) serves Buffalo (from the Ellicott St. station) and the Buffalo Niagara International Airport.

VISITOR INFORMATION The **Buffalo Niagara Convention & Visitors Bureau,** 617 Main St. (*©* **800/BUFFALO** [283-3256]; www.visitbuffaloniagara. com), is located in the Market Arcade downtown. It's open Monday to Friday 9am to 5pm and Saturday 10am to 2pm. Drop by for helpful information and pick up brochures and coupons.

GETTING AROUND While Buffalo has rail and bus systems, driving is still recommended. The **Metro Rail** (http://metro.nfta.com) runs along Main Street from HSBC Arena to the South Campus of the University at Buffalo (a SUNY school), with several stops in between (it also goes to Niagara Falls and other regional destinations). Along Main Street, aboveground, it's free; once it goes underground at the Theater stop, it's $1.75 per ride (exact change not necessary). If you want a taxi, it's best to call, since they're hard to find on the street. Try **Broadway Taxi** (*©* **716/896-4600**).

Exploring the Area

WALK DOWNTOWN Buffalo's magnificent downtown architecture deserves more than just a drive-by; do yourself a favor and check it out on foot. Start at the E. B. Green and William S. Wicks–designed **Market Arcade** at 617 Main St., just north of Chippewa Street. London's Burlington Arcade served as an inspiration for this Beaux Arts–style precursor to the modern, indoor shopping mall. Sunlight streams through the frosted glass skylights of the building, which now houses shops, cafes, and the Buffalo Niagara Visitors Center. Staying on Main Street, just south of Chippewa is Green's neoclassical **Buffalo Savings Bank Building** (1901)—known as "Gold Dome," but officially the M&T Center. Continue down Main to the Soldiers and Sailors monument in **Lafayette Square.** On your right is the 352-foot **Liberty Building,** adorned with two reduced-scale replicas of the Statue of Liberty, and across the square is the French Renaissance–style **Lafayette Hotel,** designed by Louise Blanchard Bethune—the country's first female professional architect. At Church Street, face right to see the gorgeous **St. Paul's Episcopal Cathedral.** On your left is the **Ellicott Square Building;** with 500,000 square feet, it was the world's largest office building for 16 years after it opened in 1896. Step inside to see the majestic interior courtyard with its glass roof and Italian marble mosaic floor. It's also a good place to stop and have a Beef on Weck—Buffalo's signature roast beef sandwich—from **Charlie the Butcher Express** (716/855-8646; www.charliethe butcher.com), right in the lobby. Cut over Swan Street to Pearl Street, and on your left is E. B. Green's **Dun Building,** named for Robert Dun, founder of the nation's largest credit-reporting agency, Dun & Bradstreet. Walk north on Pearl Street, and on your left just before Church Street is Louis Sullivan's stunning **Guaranty Building** from 1895, dressed up in ornate terra-cotta tiles. Turning left on Church and right on Franklin, you'll find the late-Victorian Romanesque **Old County Hall.** Head farther north on Franklin and you can't miss the massive **Buffalo City Hall,** an Art Deco gem with a brightly colored crown to your left. Go up to the 28th-floor observation deck (free) for a great panoramic view of the city (*©* **716/851-4200;** Mon–Fri 8am–5pm). Turning left out of City Hall, walk north on Delaware Avenue, and take a break for a coffee at **Spot,** 227 Delaware Ave. (*©* **716/332-2299**), at the corner of Chippewa, where people flock at all times of the day and night. If you prefer a guided walking tour, contact **Preservation Buffalo Niagara** (*©* **716/852-3300;** www. preservationbuffaloniagara.org), which offers tours every Friday year-round, weekdays July and August, and weekends May through October. Winter tours take visitors on

Downtown Buffalo

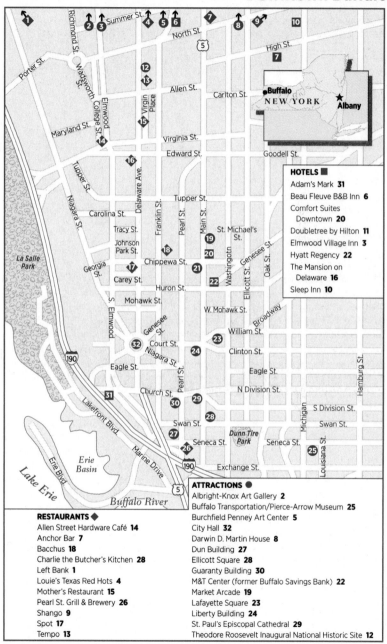

HOTELS ■
Adam's Mark **31**
Beau Fleuve B&B Inn **6**
Comfort Suites
  Downtown **20**
Doubletree by Hilton **11**
Elmwood Village Inn **3**
Hyatt Regency **22**
The Mansion on
  Delaware **16**
Sleep Inn **10**

RESTAURANTS ◆
Allen Street Hardware Café **14**
Anchor Bar **7**
Bacchus **18**
Charlie the Butcher's Kitchen **28**
Left Bank **1**
Louie's Texas Red Hots **4**
Mother's Restaurant **15**
Pearl St. Grill & Brewery **26**
Shango **9**
Spot **17**
Tempo **13**

ATTRACTIONS ●
Albright-Knox Art Gallery **2**
Buffalo Transportation/Pierce-Arrow Museum **25**
Burchfield Penney Art Center **5**
City Hall **32**
Darwin D. Martin House **8**
Dun Building **27**
Ellicott Square **28**
Guaranty Building **30**
M&T Center (former Buffalo Savings Bank) **22**
Market Arcade **19**
Lafayette Square **23**
Liberty Building **24**
St. Paul's Episcopal Cathedral **29**
Theodore Roosevelt Inaugural National Historic Site **12**

an "Inside Downtown" tour that visits more interior sites (for reasons that quickly become obvious during a Buffalo snowstorm).

MUSEUMS

Albright-Knox Art Gallery ★★★ The gorgeous Albright-Knox is one of Buffalo's can't-miss attractions, a world-class treasure-trove of 5,000 works that should draw more attention than it does. This Greek Revival building, with 18 dramatic marble columns on its facade, dates to 1905 and nabs some exhibits that don't even make it to New York City. The Albright has recently intensified its efforts to sell older works and buy more contemporary art, which fit in well at the museum's newer wing that opened in 1962. Gauguin, Picasso, Pollock, de Kooning, and Warhol are all represented in the permanent collection, while some artists of the moment and cutting-edge photographers and video artists are shown here as well. The collection is well organized and not overwhelming; plan on at least a half-day here—and lunch at Muse, the excellent cafe.

1285 Elmwood Ave., Buffalo, NY 14222. *(C)* **716/882-8700.** www.albrightknox.org. Admission $12 adults, $8 seniors and students, $5 children 6–12, free for children 5 and under. Tues–Thurs and Sat–Sun 10am–5pm; first Fri of the month 10am–10pm.

Buffalo Transportation/Pierce-Arrow Museum ★ In the early 20th century, the Pierce-Arrow Company of Buffalo was among the top manufacturers of luxury cars in America. Customers included the White House, the royal families of Japan and Saudi Arabia, Hollywood stars, and wealthy local industrialists. This museum pays tribute with a collection of early autos, as well as bikes and motorcycles the company also made before the Depression sent it spiraling downward. The museum has also secured enough money to build a gas station that was designed by Frank Lloyd Wright—a project that was never realized in his lifetime. *Tip:* Construction of the Wright gas station has affected hours of operation; call ahead for visiting hours.

263 Michigan Ave. (at Seneca St.), Buffalo, NY 14203. *(C)* **716/853-0084.** www.pierce-arrow.com. Admission $7 adults, $6 seniors, $3 children 6–17, free for children 5 and under. Usually open Sat noon–4pm; tours at other times may be possible; always call first.

Burchfield Penney Art Center ★★ ☺ Across the street from the Albright-Knox, this museum—full of works from distinguished Western New York artists—moved into a striking new building in 2008. True to its name, BPAC houses the world's largest collection of watercolors by Charles Burchfield, including his beautifully gritty studies of grain elevators. Sketches, studies, and notes exhibited alongside

The Botanical Gardens

Even in the depths of an icy, dark Buffalo winter, there's always one lively spot of green that delights visitors and locals alike: the **Buffalo and Erie County Botanical Gardens** (*(C)* **716/827-1584;** www.buffalogardens.com). The jewel in this 156-acre park is the enormous greenhouse, designed in the 1890s by Lord & Burnham (the premier greenhouse designers of the era) along the lines of London's famed Crystal Palace. One of only two tri-domed plant conservatories remaining in the United States, the immense Victorian edifice is home to a world-class collection of tropical palms, a reproduction of a Panamanian cloud forest, a colorful orchid house—even an exhibit of the Florida Everglades (minus the alligators and mosquitoes).

the finished paintings provide for a rich experience of Burchfield's process. Other highlights in the permanent collection include work by local notables Elbert Hubbard and Robert Longo. Bringing kids? An interactive "USEUM" space by regional artist Alfonso Volo encourages children to play and learn about art. Another plus: BPAC's dedication to sustainability has made it the first art museum in New York to get LEED certification.

1300 Elmwood Ave., Buffalo, NY 14222. ℂ **716/878-6011.** www.burchfieldpenney.org. Admission $9 adults, $7 seniors and students, free for children 10 and under. Tues–Wed and Fri–Sat 10am–5pm; Thurs 10am–9pm; Sun 1–5pm.

Darwin D. Martin House ★★★ A must for any lover of Frank Lloyd Wright architecture. One of his greatest works—the man himself called it his "opus"—this Prairie-style home was designed and constructed between 1903 and 1906. The 10,000-square-foot residence was built for Mr. Martin, one of Buffalo's wealthy industrialists and perhaps Wright's biggest booster. With its low-slung profile and emphasis on the horizontal, the home was—and remains—an amazing piece of architecture. A tour of the inside reveals the architect's genius for expanding spaces and hiding bookcases. A major, painstaking, and masterful restoration has re-created large parts of the complex from scratch. The spectacular new visitor center—a sleek, glass pavilion designed by Toshiko Mori—opened on the grounds in 2009. *Tip:* Ongoing restoration has affected the visitation hours; call ahead for an updated schedule.

125 Jewett Pkwy., Buffalo, NY 14214. ℂ **716/856-3858.** www.darwinmartinhouse.org. Admission $15 adults, $13 seniors, $10 students. Reservations strongly recommended. Mar–Nov Wed–Mon 4–6 tours a day; Jan–Mar closed Tues and Thurs, 1–3 tours a day. In-depth tours at 11am most days (rates higher). From downtown, take Rte. 33 east to NY 198 west to Parkside Ave. exit, bear right off Rte. 198 onto Parkside Ave., go 2 lights to Jewett Pkwy., and turn right. Martin House is 2 blocks up at Jewett and Summit.

Theodore Roosevelt Inaugural National Historic Site ★ The home of Roosevelt's friend Ansley Wilcox, this mansion became famous on September 14, 1901, when Teddy was sworn in as the 26th president of the United States in the library. (Hours earlier, President William McKinley had succumbed to an infection brought on by an assassin's bullet.) The library has been re-created to reflect what it looked like on the inaugural day, and the rest of the home is an interesting glimpse into how Buffalo's wealthiest families lived at the turn of the 20th century. In 2009, a major renovation introduced new exhibits and re-created the original carriage house, which is now home to the visitor center.

641 Delaware Ave. (btw. North and Allen), Buffalo, NY 14202. ℂ **716/884-0095.** www.nps.gov/thri. Admission $10 adults, $7 seniors and students, $5 children 6–18, free for children 5 and under. Mon–Fri 9am–5pm; Sat–Sun noon–5pm.

Outdoor Pursuits

BOATING Find out what Lake Erie is all about on a trip aboard the *Miss Buffalo II* (ℂ **800/244-8684** or 716/856-6696; www.buffaloharborcruises.com). Narrated tours and lunch cruises, providing views of Buffalo's unique architecture, depart from the Erie Basin Marina downtown from July to Labor Day (Tues–Sun). They also offer special DJ parties and TGIF happy hours. Tours $15 adults, $10 children 6 to 12; additional charges for on-board lunches and special events.

GUIDED TOURS With so much history and so many architectural landmarks, it only makes sense to take advantage of Buffalo's terrific guided tours, which will give you a deeper understanding of the city's rich heritage. **Buffalo Tours,** 617 Main St.

Righteous Babe

Singer-songwriter and Nickel City native Ani DiFranco had long admired the former Asbury Delaware Methodist Church, a striking but rapidly deteriorating Gothic Revival building in downtown Buffalo. Before the city could follow through on its plans to demolish it, DiFranco's recording company—Righteous Babe Records—bought the building in 2003. Now, $10 million in renovations later, the former church has been transformed into **Babeville**, 341 Delaware Ave. (✆ 716/852-3835; www. babevillebuffalo.com), a multi-use facility housing a state-of-the-art performance hall, a live-music basement club, the offices of Righteous Babe, and the Hallwalls Contemporary Arts Center. Visit the website for information about shows and events.

(✆ 716/852-3300; www.buffalotours.org), runs tours focusing on Millionaire's Row, the waterfront revival, grain elevators, the Olmsted-designed Parkside neighborhood, and many others. Run by a local comedian and an amateur historian, **Forgotten Buffalo** (✆ 716/833-5211; www.forgottenbuffalo.com) loads people on a bus and shows them the best of old-school Buffalo. We're talking historic taverns, steel mills, gin mills, gritty neighborhoods, more watering holes, and other nostalgia-laden landmarks. Did we forget to mention the drinking joints?

PLAYING IN THE PARKS   When Buffalo business was booming, the city hired New York City Central Park designer Frederick Law Olmsted to create a parks system that was unrivaled in its era. (An impressed Olmsted proclaimed that Buffalo was "the best designed city in the country, if not the world.") If you have time for only one park, **Delaware Park** is a 350-acre gem with wide-open spaces and quiet walkways. On some summer evenings, you can enjoy concerts and other events alfresco. The other parks are Martin Luther King, Jr.; Front; South; Cazenovia; and Riverside (✆ 716/838–1249; www.bfloparks.org).

WALKING THE WATERFRONT   Buffalo's ambitious waterfront revitalization project (www.eriecanalharbor.com) is transforming 12½ acres of the harbor into a tourism destination. Take a walk around the harbor and the rebuilt Commercial Slip (the passage that joined the canal to the Great Lakes), and check out their schedule of concerts, children's programs, and historical reenactments. Read all about the Erie Canal's heritage on the interpretive exhibits, and then pay a visit to the **Buffalo and Erie County Naval & Military Park,** One Naval Park Cove (✆ 716/847-1773; www.buffalonavalpark.org), where you can explore a submarine, a missile cruiser, and USS *The Sullivans,* a destroyer named after the five brothers who died when their ship was sunk by a Japanese torpedo. The park is open daily April through October; admission $9 for adults, $6 children and seniors.

Shopping

Buffalo's Elmwood Village was recently voted one of the best neighborhoods in the country, and it's no wonder: The tree-lined streets are packed with funky boutiques, art and photography galleries, bistros, and specialty shops, all housed in a mix of Georgian, Italianate, Queen Anne, Colonial Revival, and other architectural styles. Grab a massive cupcake at **Delish,** 802 Elmwood Ave., then scour the eclectic selection of gifts at **Everything Elmwood,** 740 Elmwood Ave. (✆ 716/883-0607;

www.everythingelmwood.org), and edgy women's wear at **Sweet & Dirty,** 585 Potomac Ave. (🕾 716/887-8311; http://sweetndirty.blogspot.com).

For antiques and other home furnishings, head to Hertel Avenue in North Park, where you'll find an ethnically diverse neighborhood and such shops as **Buffalo Wholesale Antiques,** 1539 Hertel Ave. (🕾 716/832-4231), and the **Antique Lamp Co.,** 1213 Hertel Ave. (🕾 716/871-0508; www.antiquelampco.com). Just 12 miles east of Buffalo, Clarence Hollow bills itself as the "Antiques Capital of Western New York." Check out the **Antique World Flea Market and Co-ops,** 1095 Main St., Clarence (🕾 716/759-8483; www.antiqueworldmarket.com), with 10 buildings of collectibles.

An essential Buffalo stop for book lovers is the wonderful **Talking Leaves Books,** with two locations: 51 Elmwood Ave. (🕾 716/884-9524) and 3158 Main St. (🕾 716/837-8554; www.tleavesbooks.com).

Spectator Sports

Buffalo residents are incredibly passionate about their hockey and football teams—the NFL's **Buffalo Bills** regularly sell out their home games, despite not making it to the playoffs since 1994. They hit the gridiron just outside the city in Ralph Wilson Stadium at 1 Bills Dr., Orchard Park (🕾 716/649-0015; www.buffalobills.com). The NHL's **Sabres** play downtown at the HSBC Center, 1 Seymour H. Knox III Plaza (🕾 888/GO-SABRES [467-2273]; www.sabres.com).

Especially for Kids

Buffalo and its surrounding areas have more than a few destinations to help families pass the time on rainy—and sunny—days. The latest addition to the popular **Buffalo Zoo ★★**, 300 Parkside Ave. (🕾 716/837-3900; www.buffalozoo.org), is the **M&T Bank Rainforest Falls.** Opened in 2008, this enclosed, climate-controlled facility simulates a tropical forest. The cascading waterfall, giant anteaters, vampire bats, ocelots, armadillos, and monkeys augment a host of zoo events and programs that are scheduled throughout the summer and autumn months. At **Explore and More Children's Museum,** 300 Gleed Ave., East Aurora (🕾 716/655-5131; www.exploreandmore.org), kids up to 10 are encouraged to learn through interactive play. Infants can climb and explore, while the older tots can construct their own Frank Lloyd Wright–inspired houses, learn about how food is grown and harvested, and get to know other cultures. **Martin's Fantasy Island ★**, 2400 Grand Island Blvd., Grand Island (🕾 716/773-7591; www.martinsfantasyisland.com), has 80 acres with more than 100 rides. Kids love the Silver Comet roller coaster, petting zoo, and water slides.

Where to Stay

Finding accommodations right in downtown Buffalo is mostly a matter of deciding among several large chain hotels. However, smaller and more interesting options can be found in some great walking neighborhoods a bit to the north, such as Elmwood Village, Bryant, and Allentown.

EXPENSIVE

Hyatt Regency ★★★ With a prime spot right on Main Street and next to the convention center, the towering 395-room Hyatt attracts a business-focused clientele, but the location makes this a good option for the leisure traveler, too. A former office building, the rooms were created from variously shaped offices and are now are uniformly styled in a sharp chocolate, blue, and cream decor. I especially like the rooms above the eighth floor facing Lake Erie that have a waterside view.

2 Fountain Plaza, Buffalo, NY 14202. www.buffalo.hyatt.com.✆ **716/856-1234.** Fax 716/852-6157. 395 units. $119–$249 double; $229–$559 suite. Packages available. AE, DC, DISC, MC, V. Self-parking $7. **Amenities:** 2 restaurants; concierge; exercise room; room service; Wi-Fi in public areas. *In room:* A/C, TV w/pay movies, hair dryer, Internet (small fee).

The Mansion on Delaware ★★★ 🛍 This 1860s Second Empire–style building was brought back from the brink of complete collapse to become the city's swankiest place to stay. The interiors are magnificent, with gorgeous black walnut fireplace mantels, detailed plaster moldings, and ornate pocket doors. The superb service and sleekly designed rooms—with very modern furniture, workstations, and amenities— have attracted everyone from Hillary Clinton to Kiefer Sutherland. The "grand" rooms are larger and worth the extra money, and though suites are a little too small for two separate rooms, they come decked out with fireplaces and plasma TVs. I recommend no. 200, a "premium grand" room with high ceilings and huge floor-to-ceiling bay windows; and no. 212, cozy and quietly situated in the back, with a fireplace.

414 Delaware Ave., Buffalo, NY 14202. www.mansionondelaware.com.✆ **716/886-3300.** Fax 716/883- 3923. 28 units. $195–$375 double. Rates include European buffet breakfast, complimentary happy hour cocktails. AE, DC, DISC, MC, V. Free valet parking. **Amenities:** Complimentary downtown transport; concierge; exercise room; room service. *In room:* A/C, TV/DVD, hair dryer, Internet.

MODERATE

Adam's Mark ★★ Walk into the mammoth lobby and it's immediately clear that this 486-room hotel is all business—there are even video monitors listing current airline arrivals and departures in real time. Beyond the dozen-plus meeting facilities catering to everyone from bridge players to motivational speakers, you'll find a bevy of amenities aimed at satisfying the convention crowds, including a nice pool and exercise area. Accommodations range from single rooms to bi-level suites, all sporting suitable business-class furniture, and all guaranteeing the rare treat of windows that actually open.

120 Church St., Buffalo, NY 14202. www.adamsmark.com.✆ **800/444-ADAM** (2326) or 716/845-5100. Fax 716/845-0310. 486 units. $99–$209 double; $325–$650 suite. AE, DISC, MC, V. **Amenities:** Restaurant; lounge; executive-level rooms; exercise room; indoor pool; room service; sauna. *In room:* A/C, TV w/pay movies, hair dryer, Wi-Fi.

Beau Fleuve Bed & Breakfast Inn ★★ With more than 19 years of experience under the owners' belt, Beau Fleuve has earned its reputation as the preeminent B&B of Buffalo. Built in the 1880s, this grand Victorian house occupies a spot on tree-lined Linwood Avenue in Buffalo's Linwood Historic Preservation District, and the owners have maintained its period charm through tasteful renovations. Each room is exquisitely decorated in tribute to one of five ethnicities that have shaped Buffalo's culture: French, Italian, German, Irish (the largest room), and Polish. You'll find pedestal sinks in the bathrooms, stained glass windows, comfortable sitting areas, and antique and artisanal furnishing throughout the house. To top it off, the lavish, candlelit breakfast has a reputation of its own.

242 Linwood Ave., Buffalo, NY 14209. www.beaufleuve.com. ✆ **800/278-0245** or 716/882-6116. 5 units. $135–$175 double occupancy. Rates include full breakfast. 2-night minimums may apply. AE, DISC, MC, V. Parking available. **Amenities:** Fridge in common area. *In room:* A/C, hair dryer, Wi-Fi.

INEXPENSIVE

Comfort Suites Downtown ★★ Formerly the Radisson, this all-suite hotel gives you plenty of living space in a superb location, all for less than the previous owners were charging. While you won't find the same amenities as at, say, the Hyatt, the Comfort Suites gives you some of the best bang for your buck in downtown Buffalo. These rates don't afford you exquisite furniture or enormous bathrooms, but you'll still find plenty of breathing space, with French doors dividing bedroom and living room areas, plus flatscreen TVs and DVD players.

601 Main St., Buffalo, NY 14203. www.comfortsuites.com. © **716/854-5500.** Fax 716/854-4836. 146 units. $119–$229 suite. Rates include continental breakfast. AE, DC, DISC, MC, V. Free self-parking. **Amenities:** Restaurant; exercise room. *In room:* A/C, TV, fridge, hair dryer, microwave, Wi-Fi.

The Elmwood Village Inn: Honu House ★★ Centrally located in Buffalo's colorful Elmwood Village neighborhood, this 1890s house is steps away from oodles of great food and funky boutiques, and a short walk from some of the best art in the city. Not quite a B&B (just coffee and scones for breakfast; no doilies or teddy bears anywhere), Honu House nevertheless has a welcoming, homey atmosphere—especially if your home's decor flows from Burchfield-school originals to Pakistani furniture. The individual rooms boast a distinctive selection of original pieces, antiques, and modern furnishings, though none feels cluttered. Two of the spacious bathrooms feature Caribbean-inspired showers with marble walls, while the master suite has a Jacuzzi. If you're staying longer, consider shacking up in the Skylight Suite, the sleek private apartment perched on the top floor.

893 Elmwood Ave., Buffalo, NY 14222. www.elmwoodvillageinn.com. © **716/886-2397.** 4 units. $95–$130. AE, DC, DISC, MC, V. **Amenities:** Kitchen; 2nd-floor kitchenette. *In room:* A/C, TV (in suites only), hair dryer, kitchen (in Skylight Suite), Wi-Fi.

Sleep Inn You might think you've died and gone to strip mall purgatory in this chain-shopping enclave just off I-290, but the location—15 minutes from downtown—also makes for a convenient home base on the way to or from Niagara. With crisp, new rooms, Sleep Inn has the basics well covered: comfortable beds, relative peace and quiet, and a quick hop on or off the major artery for the area.

75 Inn Keepers Lane, Amherst, NY 14228. www.sleepinn.com. © **866/753-3769** or 716/691-6510. Fax 716/691-3454. 92 units. $95–$149 double. Packages available. Rates include continental breakfast. AE, DC, DISC, MC, V. **Amenities:** Jacuzzi; indoor heated pool. *In room:* A/C, TV, hair dryer, Internet.

Where to Eat

When talking Buffalo and food, it's easy to fixate on the well-known culinary oddities that originated here. (Full disclosure: I am a huge fan of that local masterstroke, Beef on Weck.) And sure, it's kinda cool that you can still get Buffalo wings at the (overrated) **Anchor Bar,** 1047 Main St. (© 716/886-8920), where they were supposedly invented. But because of its ethnically diverse population, Buffalo is in fact a foodie magnet, with an almost astonishingly wide range of cuisine types to choose from.

VERY EXPENSIVE

Tempo ★★★ ITALIAN With an inventive Italian menu and upscale contemporary setting, Tempo has been a favorite on the Buffalo dining scene since it opened. Exposed brick, modern art, and dark wood floors lend classic touches, while candlelight and jazz strains offer a dash of romance. Start with the seared ahi loin, eggplant antipasto, or two towers of beef carpaccio with arugula and shaved Parmesan. Continue on to the prosciutto-wrapped filet topped with warm Gorgonzola, served with homemade melt-in-your-mouth gnocchi. The lengthy wine list (mostly from Italy and California) complements the menu nicely, and desserts are equally well done.

581 Delaware Ave., Allentown. © **716/885-1594.** www.tempobuffalo.com. Reservations recommended. Main courses $22–$49. AE, DC, MC, V. Mon–Thurs 5–10pm; Fri–Sat 5–10:30pm.

EXPENSIVE

Bacchus ★★★ INTERNATIONAL/TAPAS   A hip restaurant in downtown's busiest area, Bacchus is indeed a wine mecca, offering more than 200 bottles, all available by the glass. Often crowded, and sometimes downright noisy, the large space combines a bar with a chic candlelit dining room. You can order delicious larger plates of lamb chops and filet or ahi tuna, but the culinary ingenuity is best found in the small plates. They're larger than traditional tapas (two per person will do) and trade the typical Spanish flair for innovations like a butternut squash risotto with duck confit or roasted quail with Asian pear relish. Crowds form early, but a wait at the bar is hardly a bore.

56 W. Chippewa St.© **716/854-WINE** (9463). www.ultimaterestaurants.com/bacchus. Reservations recommended. Small plates $9–$15; large plates $20–$32. AE, DISC, MC, V. Tues–Thurs 5–11pm; Fri–Sat 5pm–midnight.

Mothers Restaurant ★★★ 🎁 AMERICAN   Step inside from the alleyway and you'll find a quiet, brick-wall-lined, candlelit hideaway that every local will recommend as historic Buffalo's finest. The handwritten menu boasts a plethora of flavors and a wealth of ingredients. Choose from rich entrees like center-cut pork chop with blue cheese walnut stuffing and port glaze or grilled swordfish with orange ginger butter. The equally complex appetizers shine, too, with offerings like potato gnocchi topped with lump crab and white truffle cream. Full dinners served until 3am every night make it ideal for late-night gourmet diners. **Bonus:** There's an outdoor patio.

33 Virginia Place (btw. Virginia and Allen sts.).© **716/882-2989.** Reservations suggested. Main courses $15–$29. AE, MC, V. Mon–Sat 4pm–4am; Sun 1pm–4am.

MODERATE

Left Bank ★★ 🎁 NEW AMERICAN   On the west side of town, with red-brick interiors, vaulted ceilings, an outdoor patio, and a convivial atmosphere, this restaurant is a Buffalonian favorite; I recommend making reservations well ahead of time, as it fills up fast. The cuisine skews slightly Italian, not French as the name might imply. Appetizers are innovative and uniformly excellent: The spicy stuffed banana peppers come baked in a tomato sauce with basil and asiago cheese; grilled tiger shrimp is served on artichoke bottoms with baked goat cheese. For entrees, the carrot pappardelle is sublime, with lobster, shrimp, and crabmeat in a shellfish brandy cream. Another special treat is their Sunday string quartet brunch. I'll say it again—reserve, reserve, reserve.

511 Rhode Island St.© **716/882-3509.** www.leftbankrestaurant.com. Reservations recommended. Main courses $12–$30. AE, DISC, MC, V. Sun 11am–2:30pm and 4–10pm; Mon–Thurs 5–11pm; Fri–Sat 5pm–midnight.

Pearl Street Grill & Brewery ★ AMERICAN BREWPUB   With an enormous tap heralding the entrance from three stories up, you can see Pearl Street from blocks away. Inside is a scene to match: leaded windows, exposed brick, wood beams, and a matrix of ceiling fans impossibly interconnected by a three-tiered belt system. Sure, the warehouse-cum-microbrewery is a stereotype by now, but these four floors of beer, food, and pool do it well, attracting college kids and families alike. The menu has the usual suspects—burgers, pizza, pasta—along with a handful of selections made with their own brews, such as beer-braised pot roast and "beef streetganoff." Their signature beer is the excellent Trainwreck amber, but with a selection ranging from wheat to stout, you'll have plenty of choices. Brewery tours are also available.

76 Pearl St. (at Seneca).© **716/856-BEER** (2337). www.pearlstreetgrill.com. Reservations accepted. Burgers and main courses $8–$22. AE, DC, DISC, MC, V. Kitchen Mon–Sat 11am to at least 9pm; Sun open at noon.

Shango ★ CAJUN/CREOLE   This inviting North Buffalo bistro specializes in wines—with about 20 available by the glass—but they also have an impressive list of microbrews and Belgian beers, along with terrific service. While they do a fine chicken-and-sausage gumbo, and their po' boys are good, let's focus here on the brunch, which is one of the best in the city. French toast stuffed with brie cheese with banana caramel rum sauce; poached eggs, crab, artichoke with a roasted jalapeño cream sauce in a puff pastry shell—yes, they're as mouthwatering as they sound. Other notable entrees, available at brunch and otherwise, are blackened Texas redfish with jambalaya and a Creole bouillabaisse filled with shellfish in a fennel tomato broth. *Note:* Parking might be a bit of a challenge.

3260 Main St. ✆ **716/837-2326.** www.shangobistro.com. Reservations recommended. Main courses $16-$24. AE, MC, V. Mon-Thurs 5-10pm; Fri-Sat 5-11pm; Sun 11am-3pm.

INEXPENSIVE

Allen Street Hardware Café ★ BAR   With a mighty fine selection of scotch and bourbon, 60-odd wines, and a signature IPA, you'd be forgiven for thinking this friendly pub is more about drinking than eating. But the food, while nothing too fancy, is quite good. Choose from dozens of toppings for your 12-ounce burger and hand-cut fries, or grab a portobello panini with goat cheese and roasted red and hot banana peppers. The buttermilk fried chicken or the 10-ounce strip steak on a hoagie roll won't disappoint either. Located in the old Allentown Hardware storefront, the red walls are decorated with the works of local artists, and when the kitchen closes (9:30pm or so) there's live music every Wednesday through Saturday.

245 Allen St. ✆ **716/882-8843.** www.allenstreethardware.com. Burgers, sandwiches, and salads $6-$12. AE, DISC, MC, V. Daily from 5pm.

Charlie the Butcher's Kitchen ★ DELI   Beef on Weck is one of those "only in Buffalo" creations, and Charlie has made it into a science. The basic sandwich consists of sliced, rare roast beef on a salty German Kaiser roll (the weck; *Kummelweck,* that is), and of course Charlie insists on dipping the top of the roll in au jus and adding horseradish. He's set up in the food court of the gorgeous Ellicott building downtown; grab a sandwich and enjoy the Italian mosaic floors and the skylight.

295 Main St. (in the Ellicott Sq. building). ✆ **716/855-8646.** www.charliethebutcher.com. Beef on Weck $6; other sandwiches $5-$8. AE, MC, V. Mon-Fri 10am-5pm.

Louie's Texas Red Hots HOT DOGS   No, the hot dog wasn't invented here, but Buffalonians have embraced it with an unequaled passion. So forget the Texas reference—this is a Buffalo institution. The dogs do taste better here (all that practice cooking 'em); at Louie's, they come nicely seared with mustard, onions, and Louie's special Greek sauce. Best of all, you can "getcha hot dogs" 24 hours a day.

2350 Delaware Ave. ✆ **716/877-6618.** louistexasredhots.com. Hot dogs $2. No credit cards. 24 hr.

Buffalo After Dark

PERFORMING ARTS

Shea's Performing Arts Center, 646 Main St. (✆ **716/847-1410;** www.sheas.org), is a gorgeous former movie palace dating from 1926 and built in the style of a European opera house. It now hosts touring shows, concerts, opera, and dance performances. The **Buffalo Philharmonic Orchestra** performs at the architecturally and acoustically impressive **Kleinhans Music Hall,** 1 Symphony Circle (✆ **800/318-9404;** www. bpo.org), most every week from mid-September to the end of July. The **Studio Arena,**

710 Main St. (✆ **800/77-STAGE** [777-8243]), is one of the finest regional theaters in the country, with several productions each season (Sept–May). The **Paul Robeson Theatre,** 350 Masten Ave. (✆ **716/362-0230;** www.africancultural.org), showcases works of African-American playwrights, directors, and actors, while the **Irish Classical Theater Company** at the Andrews Theater, 625 Main St. (✆ **716/853-ICTC** [4282]; www.irishclassicaltheatre.com), performs classic and modern works in the round. Both seasons run September through June.

NIGHTCLUBS & LIVE MUSIC

Downtown on and around Chippewa Street, you'll find loud bars pouring local brew Genesee as well as countless other beverages. You can party at the **Skybar,** on the roof of **D'Arcy McGees,** 257 Franklin St. (✆ **716/853-3600;** www.buffaloskybar. com). For the well-dressed, over-25 crowd, try **Crocodile Bar,** 88 W. Chippewa St. (✆ **716/853-CROC** [2762]), which offers an extensive martini menu. Allen Street is a bit quieter, but you can also find some good bars like **Colter Bay,** at Delaware and Allen (✆ **716/882-1330**). This is also where you'll find Buffalo's gay scene, in bars like **Cathode Ray,** 26 Allen St. (✆ **716/884-3615**). Another good bet for gays: **Club Marcella,** 622 Main St. (✆ **716/847-6850**), which features drag shows and underwear contests, along with DJs spinning tunes 'til the wee hours.

For live music, check out the **Tralf Music Hall,** 622 Main St. (✆ **716/852-2860;** www.tralfmusichall.com), which hosts a wide assortment of local and (inter-) national acts, tending toward classic and indie rock, with some jazz and experimental music thrown in. On a smaller scale, **Nietzsche's,** 248 Allen St. (✆ **716/886-8539;** www.nietzsches.com), offers Celtic sessions, songwriter showcases, local bands, and comedy. The **Colored Musicians Club** (yes, you read that right) at 145 Broadway (✆ **716/855-9383;** www.coloredmusiciansclub.org) has hosted countless jazz greats—such as Dizzy Gillespie and Billie Holiday—in its 80-odd years, and still offers jazz regularly.

DAY TRIPS FROM BUFFALO

If you'd rather not change accommodations nightly, Buffalo can be your base for exploring much of the surrounding area—it's only about 75 miles to the Pennsylvania border. Niagara Falls, of course, should be one of your destinations and is discussed in section 5. Another thing you'll likely want to do is to take a drive either south along Lake Erie or northeast along Lake Ontario—the views over both of these Great Lakes are spectacular. Follow the **Seaway Trail** (www.seawaytrail.com), which blazes a path from top to bottom, and check out the historic and informative stops along the way. If you head inland, the landscape quickly transforms into mile upon mile of rural farmland. You'll find quirky museums celebrating everything from the kazoo to Lucille Ball, along with one of the nation's premier educational vacation spots and one of the state's best parks.

Essentials

GETTING AROUND   A car is absolutely essential in this rural part of the state. See "Getting There," in section 1, for car-rental options.

VISITOR INFORMATION   **Cattaraugus County Tourism,** 303 Court St., Little Valley (✆ **800/331-0543;** www.enchantedmountains.com), is open Monday to Friday from 8am to 5pm.

Museums & Attractions

Graycliff ★★★ A destination for Frank Lloyd Wright worshipers and design fans alike, this 1927 house set on a 70-foot cliff overlooking Lake Erie was built for Isabelle Martin—wife of Wright's most generous patron, Darwin Martin. The two-story, 6,500-square-foot house on 8 acres served as the Martins' summer home through the mid-1940s, and is a wonderful example of Wright's take on "organic architecture," an attempt to bring the natural world indoors. Ribbons of glass flood the house with light; cantilevered balconies move fresh air throughout the rooms; manmade lines and shapes echo the natural forms outdoors. It's a transitional point from Wright's earlier Prairie style—found in Buffalo's **Martin House** (p. 409)—to his late concrete designs like Fallingwater in Pennsylvania. The basic 1-hour tour is fascinating, but you can also sign up for 2-hour or the even more intensive 4-hour tours with a master architect; true aficionados of Wright can take a tandem tour that includes the Martin House.

6472 Old Lake Shore Rd., Derby. *C* **716/947-9217.** http://graycliffestate.org. Admission $15 for adults, $10 for students ages 10–22 with ID. 1-hr. tours mid-Apr to early Dec Thurs-Tues. Call for information on other tours. Reservations required. I-90 to exit 57, Rte. 75 north to Rte. 20W, go 7 miles, turn right on S. Creek Rd. to end, turn left on Old Lake Shore Rd.

Herschell Carrousel Factory Museum ★ Lovers of old carousels, bygone ages, or just exquisite woodworking shouldn't miss this stop. It's the world's only museum housed in an original carousel factory building, which opened in 1915 to carve wood into fanciful carousel horses. You'll see some 20-odd hand-carved carousel animals and music-roll production equipment from the Wurlitzer Company. There are also two historic carousels to ride, one dating from 1916.

180 Thompson St., North Tonawanda. *C* **716/693-1885.** www.carrouselmuseum.org. Admission $5 adults, $4 seniors, $2.50 children 2-12. Apr to mid-June and early Sept to Dec Wed-Sun noon-4pm; mid-June to early Sept Mon-Sat 10am-4pm, Sun noon-4pm. I-290 to exit 2. Rte. 425 north for 2 miles, left on Christiana, right on Payne, left on Thompson.

Lily Dale Assembly ★★ One hour south of Buffalo, this tiny Victorian enclave has been the spiritual home to, well, spiritualism, since Lily Dale was established in 1879. About 40 registered mediums currently reside here, and from the end of June to early September, travelers descend on the place for daily events that include meditation and healing services, clairvoyant demonstrations, and workshops. Workshops and speakers cost up to $350 (most are in the $40–$50 range), but you can watch the basic activities just by paying the gate fee of $10, good for 24 hours. Two very basic hotels and private homes can put you up for the night, and there's camping as well. There are also hiking trails, a beach, a museum, a sweat lodge, a few shops, and some cafes.

5 Melrose Park, Lily Dale. *C* **716/595-8721.** www.lilydaleassembly.com. Summer day gate fee $10, evening fee $5; fees are discounted for active military, seniors, children, and season passes. From I-90, take exit 59 to Rte. 60 south. Drive 8 miles and turn right on Dale Dr. in Cassadaga, then continue for 1 mile.

Seneca-Iroquois National Museum ★ Located on the Allegany Indian Reservation, this small tribal museum is dedicated to the Six Nations of the Iroquois Confederacy—the Seneca, Oneida, Mohawk, Onondaga, and Cayuga, and eventually the Tuscarora. While one wishes there were a better historical overview here, there's an interesting reproduction of a longhouse, and a nice collection of cornhusk dolls, moccasins, and bead- and basketwork. But the best reason to come here is "This Is Where We Walked," a heart-rending exhibit about the Seneca people who were

OFFBEAT museums IN AND AROUND BUFFALO

JELL-O was discovered in 1897, and the world-famous dessert can trace its roots to this area—in particular, the town of LeRoy. For the entire history of the gelatinous stuff—likely more than you ever wanted to know—visit the **JELL-O Gallery,** 23 E. Main St., LeRoy (© **585/768-7433;** www.jellogallery.org).

At the **Lucy-Desi Museum,** 212 Pine St., Jamestown (© **LUCY-FAN** [582-9326]; www.lucy-desi.com), you'll learn how Jamestown's hometown heroine Lucille Ball and Desi Arnaz met and collaborated on what this museum calls "the most famous comedy series of all time." Yes, that's debatable, but if you're a fan, you'll enjoy the collection of clothes and merch. If you're not, give this place a pass.

Head to the **Kazoo Museum ★**, 8703 S. Main St., Eden (© **716/992-3960;** www.edenkazoo.com), to find kazoos of all shapes and sizes: wooden kazoos, liquor-bottle-shaped kazoos that celebrated the end of Prohibition, silver and gold kazoos, and many more.

Okay, so the **Pedaling History Bicycling Museum ★★**, 3943 N. Buffalo Rd. (Rte. 277), Orchard Park (© **716/662-3853;** www.pedalinghistory.com), may not exactly qualify as offbeat, but it is highly specialized. And, frankly, this place—the world's largest bicycle museum—*is* amazing, with army bikes mounted with machine guns, tandem bikes with side-by-side seating, folding paratrooper bikes from World War II, the only surviving floating marine bike from the 1880s, and a bicycle built for five.

dislocated by the construction of the Kinzua Dam in 1965, and the devastation it wrought on their way of life.

814 Broad St., Salamanca. © 716/945-1760. www.senecamuseum.org. Admission $5 adults, $3.50 seniors and students, $3 children 7-17. May–Nov Thurs–Mon 9am–5pm; call for off-season hours. Take I-90 W. to exit 55 (Rte. 219 S.). Stay on 219 S. for about 50 miles, then turn right at Rte. 417 (which turns into Broad St.).

Shopping

Elbert Hubbard founded the **Roycroft Arts and Crafts Community** more than 100 years ago in the tiny town of East Aurora. Now, craftspeople carry on the fine workmanship of the Roycrofters—makers of furniture, pottery, lamps, metalwork, and handcrafted books, all notable for their sturdiness and clean lines—and have made it a big business here. Browse their galleries and shops; with any luck you'll see them at work. Go to the **Schoolhouse Gallery & Cabinet Shops,** 1054 Olean Rd. (© **716/655-4080;** www.ralaweb.com), for some of the most beautiful works. Other artisans sell their work at **West End Gallery,** 48 Douglas Lane (© **716/652-5860;** www.west-end-gallery.com).

For a step back in time of a different kind, visit **Vidler's 5 & 10,** 676–694 Main St., East Aurora (© **877/VIDLERS** [843-5377]; www.vidlers5and10.com). Since 1930, this quaint store has been selling candies, confections, dry goods, and knick-knacks. There's even a section of the store with the original wood floors—and take note of the brass cash register.

The **Amish** maintain a small enclave on the eastern border of Chautauqua County and the western border of Cattaraugus County, bisected by Route 62 in the Conewango

Valley area. Drive along Route 62 and you'll run across numerous shops selling cheese, crafts, maple syrup, furniture, quilts, and baked goods. Shops aren't open on Sunday, and the Amish request that you not take photographs.

Outdoor Pursuits

ERIE CANAL EXPERIENCES Take a ride on the man-made water route that transformed all of New York state. Get on a boat with **Lockport Locks and Erie Canal Cruises,** 210 Market St., Lockport (© **800/378-0352** or 716/433-6155; www.lockportlocks.com), for the 2-hour experience of being raised through the 49-foot elevation of the Niagara Escarpment in the only double set of locks on the canal (mid-May to mid-Oct; $16 adults, $8.50 kids 4–10). Pass under bridges, see water cascade over locks, and travel through the solid walls of the "rock cut." No, it's no speedboat ride, but if you haven't experienced going through a lock, it's pretty cool. Or take the **Lockport Cave and Underground Boat Ride,** 2 Pine St. (© **716/438-0174;** www.lockportcave.com). You'll walk through a 1,600-foot tunnel, blasted out of solid rock in the 1800s, then ride a boat to see the start of geologic cave formations and miner artifacts (early May weekends only, end of May to mid-Oct daily; $10 adults, $6.50 kids 4–12).

PARKS You can explore cliffs, crevices, cavernous dens, and caves of quartz in two parks with tons of the hardened rock: **Rock City Park,** 505 Rte. 16 S., Olean (© **866/404-ROCK** [7625]; www.rockcitypark.com), open early May 1 to the end of October, and **Panama Rocks,** Route 10, Panama (© **716/782-2845;** www.panama rocks.com), open mid-May to mid-October. Take an hour for either. Or get out among the trees in **Allegany State Park** (© **716/354-9121**): Its 65,000 acres, most of it primitive woodland, make it the largest state park in the system, with sandy beaches, picnic areas, museums, and historic cottages for rent, as well as hiking and nature trails.

SCULPTURE GARDEN If the kids—or their parents—need a place to run around and holler while also soaking up some culture, the **Griffis Sculpture Park,** 6902 Mill Valley Rd., East Otto (© **716/667-2808;** www.griffispark.org), is the perfect destination. Part of the Essex Arts Center, this 400-acre garden, located 8 miles outside Ellicottville, is home to hundreds of immense sculptures and miles of hiking trails. Admission is $5 for adults, $3 for students and seniors, and free for kids 11 and under. Open May through October, the park maintains a "please touch" approach to its artworks, inviting folks to feel and even clamber on the outdoor sculpture.

SKIING It's not exactly Colorado, or Vermont, or even, well, the Adirondacks. But here's where to go when you absolutely must get your swoosh on. At **Kissing Bridge,** in Glenwood (© **716/592-4963;** www.kbski.com), you'll find 38 snow-covered slopes, encompassing 700 acres of terrain and served by 10 lifts. And **Holiday Valley,** in Ellicottville (© **716/699-2345;** www.holidayvalley.com), has 13 lifts, 58 slopes spread over 1,400 acres, and a 750-foot vertical drop—so you'll get good variety no matter what kind of skiing or riding you like.

WINERIES It's not just in the Finger Lakes region that you'll find nice upstate New York State wines. The southern shore of Lake Erie, though it has just a thin strip of soil suitable for grape production, has a generations-old grape-and-wine heritage, and the wineries make for a fun stop-off. Check out **Johnson Estate Winery,** 8419 W. Main Rd., Westfield (© **800/374-6569;** http://johnsonwinery.com); **Woodbury Vineyards,** 3215 S. Roberts Rd., Fredonia (© **716/679-9463;** www.woodbury vineyards.com); and **Merritt Estate Winery,** 2264 King Rd., Forestville (© **888/ 965-4800;** www.merrittestatewinery.com).

Where to Stay

EXPENSIVE

The Roycroft Inn ★★★ 📖   In its current form, this small country inn was opened in 1995, but the property dates from 1895, when the Roycroft Arts and Crafts Community was founded by Elbert Hubbard. Hubbard's self-contained community supported hundreds of craftspeople, and this inn housed some of the many thousands of talented artists and artisans who traveled here from around the world. Common areas are intimately rustic, and though guest rooms aren't huge, they're hardly cramped; in fact, they feel rather airy, with their spare, clean lines and simple wicker furniture. A touch of history is in all of them—they're outfitted with at least one original Roycroft piece, plus some reproductions that lend a distinguished air to your stay. But there's nothing stuffy about the place—it's comfy and thoroughly modern, as are the sizable bathrooms. Their fantastic restaurant is listed separately, below.

40 S. Grove St., East Aurora, NY 14052. www.roycroftinn.com.✆ **716/652-5552.** Fax 716/655-5345. 28 units. $140–$295 double. Packages available. AE, DC, DISC, MC, V. I-90 to Rte. 400 to Maple St. exit, right on Maple, left on Main, and make the 1st right onto S. Grove St. **Amenities:** Restaurant; access to nearby health club; limited room service. *In room:* A/C, TV/VCR, hair dryer, Wi-Fi.

MODERATE

Old Library ★   Right next door to The Old Library Restaurant, and a former Carnegie home, this pink house looks decidedly un-Carnegie, as it's more frilly than stately. Dating from 1895, the historic home is beautifully appointed, with a rich woodwork of oak, blistered maple, and mahogany; parquet floors; gorgeous stained-glass windows; and tons of antiques. Few of the units, however, can boast the charm of the public spaces—some are carpeted and done in pastel colors, and some are cramped—but I am partial to the Major Hoops room. Upgrade to one of the huge suites if you can.

120 S. Union St., Olean, NY 14760. www.oldlibraryrestaurant.com.✆ **877/241-4348** or 716/373-9804. Fax 716/372-7775. 9 units. $85–$97 double; $135–$145 suite. Packages available. Rates include full breakfast. AE, DC, DISC, MC, V. I-86 to exit 26, which leads you right onto S. Union St. **Amenities:** Restaurant; lounge; room service. *In room:* A/C, TV, hair dryer, Wi-Fi.

CAMPGROUNDS

Lake Erie State Park ★★   Set on high bluffs overlooking Lake Erie, this campground has gorgeous views, along with great hiking and cross-country skiing trails. Bring your binoculars, as there are some terrific opportunities for bird-watching (it's a natural stopping place for migratory birds before they fly across the lake). Try to reserve one of the "prime" lakeside sites, which tend to fill up quickly. Cabins are primitive, with bunk beds and no hot water, and you must bring your own bedding.

5905 Lake Rd., Brockton, NY 14716. ✆ **716/792-9214.** 97 campsites, 10 cabins. $15 for nonelectric hookups, $21–$27 for electric; $73 cabins. 1-week minimum cabin rental ($290 late June to late Aug). AE, DISC, MC, V. New York State Thruway W. (I-90) to exit 59 to Rte. 60 north. Left on Rte. 5. Park is located 5 miles west of Dunkirk.

Where to Eat

EXPENSIVE

Roycroft Inn ★★ AMERICAN   Like the distinctive furniture that fills the inn, the dishes at the Roycroft Inn are simple but always well crafted. Get a table in the Larkin Room, which overlooks the serene courtyard garden. The fish here is excellent; you can't go wrong with the seared ahi tuna with a vegetable spring roll. But landlubbers are hardly out of luck: Try the Berkshire pork tenderloin with Swiss chard and currant sauce. Desserts are rich and delicious; because you can order sliver portions, sample a few, like the chocolate truffle cake and the cherry lattice pie.

40 S. Grove St., East Aurora. ℭ**716/652-5552.** www.roycroftinn.com. Reservations recommended. Main courses $9–$30; breakfast $2–$10; lunch $4–$15. AE, DC, DISC, MC, V. Mon–Sat 7–10am and 11:30am–3pm; Mon–Thurs 5–9pm; Fri–Sat 5–10pm; Sun 9am–3pm and 4:30–9pm. Take I-90 to Rte. 400 to Maple St. exit, turn right, turn left on Main and make your 1st right onto S. Grove St.

MODERATE

Ellicottville Brewing Company ★BREWPUB   Whether you're skiing at Holiday Valley or taking a leisurely summer drive around charming Ellicottville, the EBC makes a fun stop. A former mill and carpenters' shop, the popular brewpub has a welcoming atmosphere, a beer garden with a fountain and a fire pit, and some darn good beers, especially their award-winning Two Brothers Pale Ale. Plus, their menu ventures into territory beyond pub fare. Sure, they cook up some good burgers and fries, but they also have some surprises, like a delicious spicy African peanut soup, Thai chili mussels, and a chicken tarragon salad. Get here early on winter weekends—it gets packed.

28A Monroe St., Ellicottville. ℭ**716/699-ALES** (2537). www.ellicottvillebrewing.com. Main courses $9–$22; lunch $5–$14. AE, MC, V. Memorial Day to Labor Day and Dec–Mar Sun–Thurs 11:30am–10pm, Fri–Sat 11:30am–11pm. Closed Mon in off season; closed Apr.

The Old Library ★★AMERICAN   A Carnegie library from 1910 to 1974, this gorgeous brick building now houses an excellent restaurant. Fortunately, it has held onto its book-loving roots without getting old and musty. The interior is decorated with friezes and ornate woodwork—check out the long, beautiful bar from Chicago's notorious Cattleman's restaurant—and laden with antiques and, of course, books. The menu, presented as (what else?) a chapter in a book, offers about 200 wines and a wealth of food options, including appetizers like Oysters Rockefeller and escargot, and entrees ranging from pasta to jumbo lobster tail and rack of lamb with a Dijon-mustard-and-garlic glaze. *Bonus:* They have a nice selection of single malts.

116 S. Union St., Olean. ℭ**877/241-4348** or 716/372-2226. www.oldlibraryrestaurant.com. Main courses $13–$35. AE, DC, DISC, MC, V. Mon–Sat 4–10pm; Sun 10am–2:30pm.

Root Five ★AMERICAN   Set right on Lake Erie—on a magical plot of land that's perfect for sunsets—this joint jumps, especially in summer, when live bands rock the place. The large covered patio area provides tons of room to enjoy the water view. The menu has some typical bar fare, but some interesting upscale choices as well, such as peach-barbecued baby back ribs. But seafood is the specialty here, including a crab-crusted Norwegian salmon with Thai purple rice. And we love the beer selection—25 bottled beers, and 17 drafts, including Lake Placid Brewery's Ubu Ale.

4914 Lakeshore Rd., Hamburg. ℭ**716/627-5551.** www.rootfive.com. Reservations accepted. Main courses $14–$27; lunch $9–$15. AE, DISC, MC, V. Sun–Thurs 4:30–9pm; Fri–Sat 4:30–10pm. Take Rte. 5 south from downtown Buffalo, past Rte. 75.

INEXPENSIVE

Schwabl's ★★★ 🍴DELI   To the uninitiated, the Buffalo specialty known as Beef on Weck sounds simple enough: sliced roast beef on *kummelweck*—a German kaiser roll sprinkled with caraway seeds and pretzel salt—with a touch of au jus and a helping of horseradish. But for the more-than-curious, and the downright fanatical, Schwabl's—around since 1837—is, hands down, *the* place to get one. Clad in white from head to shin, servers have the reassuring air of German nurses, while behind the counter a silent man in shirtsleeves, tie, and apron concentrates on carving your center-cut roast to order. Don't forget to order a side of the German potato salad, which is also outstanding.

789 Center Rd., West Seneca, NY.© **716/674-9821.** www.schwabls.com. Beef on Weck $11; other items $5–$18. AE, MC, V. Mon–Sat 11am–11pm; Sun 1–8:30pm.

Ted's Jumbo Red Hots ☺ HOT DOGS   For more than 75 years, Ted has been perfecting the hot dog—his delectable dogs come regular-size and foot-long, and are served plain, with cheese and/or chili. Buffalo knows hot dogs, and residents flock here to get 'em hot off the charcoal grill, often with an old-fashioned milkshake. Not into hot dogs? You can also order a burger or chicken sandwich. And with seven locations around the Buffalo area, you'll never be too far from one.

2351 Niagara Falls Blvd., Amherst;© **716/691-7883.** 4878 Transit Rd., Depew;© **716/668-7533.** 6230 Shimer Rd., Lockport;© **716/439-4386.** 333 Meadow Dr., North Tonawanda;© **716/693-1960.** 3193 Orchard Park Rd., Orchard Park;© **716/675-4662.** 2312 Sheridan Dr., Tonawanda;© **716/834-6287.** 7018 Transit Rd., Williamsville;© **716/633-1700.** www.tedsonline.com. Hot dogs $2–$3.50. No credit cards. All locations daily for lunch and dinner.

LETCHWORTH STATE PARK

60 miles E from Buffalo; 35 miles S of Rochester

While claims like "The Grand Canyon of the East" tend to invite more than a little skepticism, Letchworth comes closer to living up to this than any of its competition. One of the most magnificent scenic areas in the eastern U.S., this narrow strip of lush woodlands straddling the Genesee River is a destination unto itself. The roaring water cuts a winding gorge through the park's 14,350 acres, breaking into more than 30 waterfalls along the way, including New York's highest plunging cascade, Inspiration Falls. A drive through the park will bring you near the action, but with 66 miles of hiking trails, there are plenty of ways to get even closer. The most dramatic scenery— wonderfully dense forest and cliffs as high as 600 feet—can be found in the southern part of the park; up north, the land flattens out as you approach farm country. Of course, wildlife is abundant throughout the park—look for beavers, deer, eagles, hawks, river otters, and birds galore.

Essentials

GETTING THERE   From Buffalo, take the New York State Thruway (I-90) west to Route 400 south and take the East Aurora exit. Turn left onto Route 20A east and follow 20A to Warsaw. Make a right onto Route 19 south to Route 19A, to Denton Corners Road. Turn left on Denton Corners Road and into the **Castile entrance** (open year-round). From Rochester, take I-390 to exit 7 to the **Mount Morris entrance** (open year-round). *Tip:* Some park entrances, for example the Parade Grounds and Portageville entrances, are closed in winter.

VISITOR INFORMATION   The grounds at Letchworth State Park, Castile (© **585/493-3600;** www.letchworthpark.com), are open daily from 6am to 11pm year-round. There is an $8 entrance fee for cars. The **Visitors Center** (© **585/493-3600**) is located in the southern end of the park.

Outdoor Pursuits

BALLOONING   One of the most unique ways to see this spectacular river canyon is from overhead in a hot-air balloon with **Balloons Over Letchworth** (© **585/493-3340;** www.balloonsoverletchworth.com). Float over the gorge in a seven-story hot-air balloon and look down on the many waterfalls and towering cliffs—and end the ride with a champagne celebration. Flights take place from May to October, weather permitting, at a price of $225 per person; if you can, go in October when the foliage is on full display (though bad weather is common in Oct and flights are more frequently canceled). Plan on 3 hours total; you'll be in the air 45 minutes to an hour. Flights depart from the Middle/Upper Falls picnic area.

HIKING   The most scenic hike here is the **Gorge Trail,** which follows the river as it meanders through the park. It's a 7-mile trail one-way and moderately difficult, so don't do the whole thing unless you're feeling adventuresome. For an easy .75-mile hike—and one you can do with the kids—the **Pond Trail** takes you out to a small pond stocked with fish (no fishing unless you have a license). Another easy stroll is the quarter-mile trail to **Inspiration Point,** from which you can see Inspiration Falls. The trail head is located near the Parade Grounds entrance off Trail 7 (the Genesee Greenway).

RAFTING   See the park from the bottom up, screaming as you course through the rushing white water: Take a 5½-mile trip along the Genesee River through Class II white water with **Adventure Calls Outfitters** (© **888/270-2410** or 585/343-4710; www.adventure-calls.com). The 2½-hour trip is perfect for novices and families. You can even get out of the rafts and go bodysurfing at the New Wave Rapids or get soaking wet at the Leap of Faith. Open April to mid-November Saturday, Sunday, and holidays ($45); from the end of June to the end of August also open Tuesday to Friday ($30).

Where to Stay
EXPENSIVE
Glen Iris Inn ★★★ 🎁   This historic former home of William Pryor Letchworth is the only inn in the park. Rustic yet formal, it's been a hotel since 1914; today the yellow-and-green wooden house has been restored to its roots. Set right on top of a cliff overlooking Middle Falls, it's a magnificent spot: Walk just a few steps from the front porch for a spectacular view of the falls and the Genesee River below. Some of the rooms here are on the small side, but all are tastefully decorated in formal Victorian style—think dark woods, antiques, floral prints, and lacy table coverings. Try to reserve the spacious Cherry Suite, which has exquisite hardwood floors and a private balcony with great views of the falls. There's also a lodge, but rooms there are more modern and have less character; stay at the inn. Three separate homes—Caroline's Cottage, the Stone House, and the Chalet—offer space for the whole family, and your own swath of land in the park. Rooms book up quickly and up to a year in advance, so plan ahead. The restaurant is reviewed below.

7 Letchworth State Park, Castile, NY 14427. www.glenirisinn.com. © **585/493-2622.** Fax 585/493-5803. 25 units. $100–$225 double; $260–$385 cottage. AE, DISC, MC, V. Closed mid-Nov to Good Friday (usually mid-Apr). **Amenities:** Restaurant; lounge; limited room service. *In room:* A/C, TV/VCR in lodge rooms and cottages, fridge and microwave in lodge rooms and cottages.

CAMPING
Letchworth has camping and cabins set deep in the woods. Unfortunately, the 270 tent and trailer sites are located at the northern end of the park—far from the falls—and are open only May to October. A better bet is one of the 82 cabins, which are spread throughout the park. Don't expect anything fancy here—they're simple and rustic cabins, with bunk beds, fridges, stoves, and (in some) cold-water-only sinks. Rates run $41 to $115 a night, with a 2-night minimum with reservation; call © **800/456-2267** to reserve.

Where to Eat

EXPENSIVE

Caroline's at the Glen Iris Inn ★★ 🍴AMERICAN   Set in a formal Victorian dining room, Caroline's is the area's best dining experience. The menu is ambitious, and the kitchen turns out delicious versions of classic dishes. Start with the apple-wood smoked trout with horseradish dill cream sauce, or warm Danish brie topped with seasonal berries. Leave room for the grilled filet mignon with cracked black pepper demi-glace, or the chipotle shrimp and sausage served over cavatappi pasta with shaved asiago cheese. The desserts, prepared on-site, are also worth saving room for: Go for the luscious bananas foster. Breakfast and lunch are also served, and you can dine on the porch, too.

7 Letchworth State Park, Castile. ☎**585/493-2622.** Reservations recommended. Lunch entrees $10–$16; dinner entrees $21–$35. AE, MC, V. Daily 8–10:30am and 11:30am–4pm; dinner daily 5–8:30pm; shorter hours off-season.

THE CHAUTAUQUA INSTITUTION ★★

77 miles S of Buffalo; 142 miles SW of Rochester; 406 miles NW of New York City

Located on a beautiful, 18-mile-long lake in the southwestern corner of the state, the Chautauqua Institution attracts thousands every summer for a vacation like no other. For starters, there's the stunning setting: 750 acres of beautiful wooded grounds, dotted with Victorian mansions and pulled together with a redbrick walkway. In season (end of June to end of Aug), some 7,500 people are in residence daily—attending classes, playing sports, enjoying a symphony, and taking in lectures on anything from Cuban politics to photographing for *National Geographic*.

Founded by Methodists in 1874, the institution was established as an experiment in vacation learning, offering courses of the Sunday school variety, but it quickly broadened its focus to encompass the realms of education, arts, recreation, and religion (the Institution's four pillars). Over the years, it has evolved into an internationally respected forum for the free exchange of ideas—including politics, literature, the arts, and science. Presidents from Ulysses S. Grant to Bill Clinton have stayed here; the latter in the grand Athenaeum Hotel, and the former in a tent, despite the Miller cottage having been built specifically for his visit. And Chautauqua continues to expand: Most recently, the Institution added the Fletcher Music Hall and the Turney Sailing Center, thanks to philanthropic support.

With more than 2,000 events every season, your stay here can be as enriching as you'd like. Daily lectures, tied in with the theme of the week, are held in both the amphitheater and the hall of philanthropy, and are covered by your gate fee. Chamber music is performed every Monday—you'll need to purchase tickets, so get in line early, as they sell out immediately. While the demographics at Chautauqua skew older, there is plenty here for kids as well, from day camp to music lessons. Opportunities for recreation—including swimming, sailing, tennis, and golf—are also plentiful.

Though the institution is nondenominational, there are houses of worship for several Christian congregations, and a Jewish life center. Shops and a refectory are open in season, as is the elegant restaurant at the Athenaeum. Once the summer has passed, there's little activity here outside the library and archive center.

Essentials

GETTING THERE   You'll need to drive here. Chautauqua is 70 miles from Buffalo. From the New York State Thruway (I-90), take exit 60, then Route 394 west. From the Southern Tier Expressway (I-86/Rte. 17) if eastbound, take exit 7, then Route 33 north, and Route 394 east. If westbound, take exit 8, then Route 394 west.

VISITOR INFORMATION   The **Chautauqua County Visitors Bureau** is located at the gates of Chautauqua Institution, Route 394 (© **800/242-4569**). For information on the institution, call © **800/836-ARTS** (2787) or visit www.ciweb.org.

ADMISSION TO THE INSTITUTION   Entering the gates of the institution will cost you $26 for a daytime (7am–8pm) pass, $12 for an afternoon (noon–8pm) pass, plus another $8 if you're spending the night—on top of hotel charges. Weekly passes start at $389 for adults, $150 for children, and season passes range from $1,750 to $3,560 per adult, $322 for children, depending on when you plan to attend. Make it easy and order ahead online. Your gate fee gets you into all the lectures and entertainment (with the exception of opera and theater) that you can fit in. You can also take a dip in the lake. Sporting options (there are many) all cost extra.

Outdoor Pursuits

The institution offers a wealth of activities, all of which cost extra beyond the gate fee. Activities include a state-of-the-art fitness center ($10 a visit), a pool ($2 per swim session), weeklong sailing instruction (call for rates), bike rental (starting at $65 for adults, $45 for kids, per week), tennis ($20 per hour), and golf (greens fees $25 weekdays, $31–$39 weekends), or you can always go swimming in the lake for free.

Where to Stay

Thousands of Chautauqua guests choose to stay right on the institution's grounds in privately owned accommodations that range from quaint rooming houses and inns to luxury homes and condominiums. Some recommended properties include **Ashland Guest House,** 10 Vincent Ave. (www.chautauquaguesthouse.com; © **888/598-5969** or 716/357-2257 [in season] or 716/837-3711 [off season]); **Vera Guesthouse,** 25 S. Terrace (same contact info as the Ashland); **The Cambridge Inn,** 9 Roberts Ave. (www.thecambridgeinn.com; © **716/357-3292** [in season] or 727/866-7965 [off season]); **The Gleason,** 12 N. Lake Dr. (gleasonhotel@netzero.com; © **716/357-2595**); and the **Tally Ho Hotel,** 16–20 Morris Ave. (© **716/357-3325** [in season] or 954/920-2088 [off season]). Rooms may be available by the day, week, and/or season, and amenities run the gamut from a single bed with shared bathroom to gorgeous, fully loaded lakefront condos that go for a few thousand dollars a week. For a complete list of lodgings, look through the accommodations section on the Chautauqua website (www.ciweb.org).

Athenaeum Hotel ★★★   This magnificent Victorian grande dame sits on a tree-shaded hill overlooking Chautauqua Lake on the grounds of the institution. It's open only during the Chautauqua Institution's season (end of June to end of Aug), and at scattered times after that until October, which is a bit of a shame. Around since 1881 (it was the first hotel in the world to have electric lights), it feels very presidential; indeed, no fewer than nine U.S. presidents have stayed here, including Clinton during his reelection campaign. Though rooms have been renovated, the basic structure hasn't been changed since it was built; be prepared for cramped bathrooms. You'll want to spend your time outdoors anyway, enjoying the grounds and the lake, or just lounging on the deck under the soaring arches. *Note:* All guests are on the American plan, so three meals a day are included in the rates.

On S. Lake Dr. (P.O. Box 66), Chautauqua, NY 14722. http://athenaeum-hotel.com. **℃800/821-1881** or 716/357-4444. Fax 716/357-4175. 157 units. $323–$536 double; reduced rates for singles and long-term guests. Rates include 3 meals daily. AE, DISC, MC, V. Parking $6 per day; valet $5 in, $5 out. **Amenities:** Restaurant; room service. *In room:* A/C, TV, hair dryer.

CAMPING

Right on Chautauqua Lake, you'll find 250 campsites with 2,000 feet of lakefront at the sprawling **Camp Chautauqua,** Route 394 (www.campchautauqua.com; ℃ **800/578-4849** or 716/789-3435). Count on lots of RV traffic, though you'll be able to find a spot for yourself to pop a tent. You'll also get tons of amenities like a teen center, coin-op laundry, heated pools, and tennis. Campsite rates range from $25 per night up to $65 for an "Executive Site." There are also another 180 campsites at **Chautauqua Heights,** 5652 Thumb Rd., Dewittville (www.chautauquahgts.com; ℃ **716/386-3804**).

Where to Eat

In addition to meals at the stately Athenaeum (see below), casual dining for breakfast, lunch, or dinner is available on the institution's grounds at the **Refectory.** In Mayville, 4 miles away, there's **The Watermark,** 188 S. Erie St. (℃ **716/753-2900;** www.watermarkrestaurant.net); **Webb's Captain's Table,** 115 W. Lake Rd., Route 394 (℃ **716/753-3960;** www.webbsworld.com), overlooking Chautauqua Lake at Webb's hotel; and **Olive's at the Country Grill,** 43 S. Erie St. (℃ **716/753-2331**).

Athenaeum Hotel ★★ AMERICAN   Though most people who dine here are guests of the hotel, you can still enjoy a meal in this grand hotel with a reservation and proper attire. The dining room is traditional and elegant, and the view of the lake is a nice accompaniment to your five-course dinner. You might start off with a smoked salmon or tortellini Bolognese, move through soup and salad, and have your choice of four or five entrees, such as roast half duck or crab cakes a la Newport. For the past several years, the Athenaeum has also had a successful Farm to Table program using seasonal ingredients harvested from the surrounding rich farmland.

On S. Lake Dr. (P.O. Box 66), Chautauqua. ℃ **800/821-1881** or 716/357-4444. Business casual attire required for dinner. Reservations required. Breakfast $15; buffet lunch $27; 5-course dinner $69; Sun brunch $45. AE, DISC, MC, V. Summer Mon–Sat 8am–9:30am, noon–1:30pm, and 5–7:30pm, and Sun 11:30am–1:30pm.

NIAGARA FALLS ★★★

21 miles NW of Buffalo; 165 miles NW of Ithaca

"I have seen the falls and I am all rapture and amazement," declared Henry James. Years later, thousands of visitors every day experience the same sense of wonder when they first see Niagara Falls. Despite its development into a tourist destination, the American Falls and Horseshoe Falls continue to spellbind honeymooners, retirees, and teenagers alike. While hundreds of thousands of gallons pour over the rocks and ledges, a wide range of amenities make it easy for visitors for experience the power and drama of this natural wonder of the world up close.

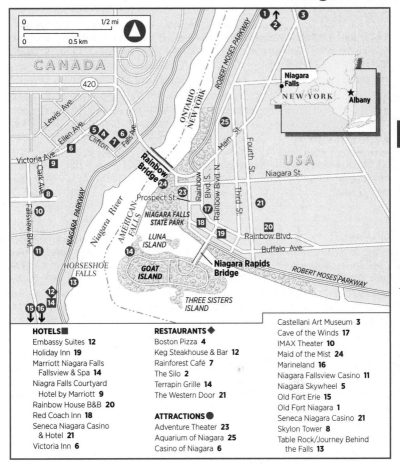

Niagara Falls

HOTELS ■
Embassy Suites **12**
Holiday Inn **19**
Marriott Niagara Falls
Fallsview & Spa **14**
Niagra Falls Courtyard
Hotel by Marriott **9**
Rainbow House B&B **20**
Red Coach Inn **18**
Seneca Niagara Casino
& Hotel **21**
Victoria Inn **6**

RESTAURANTS ◆
Boston Pizza **4**
Keg Steakhouse & Bar **12**
Rainforest Café **7**
The Silo **2**
Terrapin Grille **14**
The Western Door **21**

ATTRACTIONS ●
Adventure Theater **23**
Aquarium of Niagara **25**
Casino of Niagara **6**

Castellani Art Museum **3**
Cave of the Winds **17**
IMAX Theater **10**
Maid of the Mist **24**
Marineland **16**
Niagara Fallsview Casino **11**
Niagara Skywheel **5**
Old Fort Erie **15**
Old Fort Niagara **1**
Seneca Niagara Casino **21**
Skylon Tower **8**
Table Rock/Journey Behind
the Falls **13**

ACTIVE PURSUITS   To get a different perspective on the region, take a bike ride on the path that runs along the Niagara River from the falls all the way up to the charming, historic village of **Niagara-on-the-Lake.** If you're looking for a little more adrenaline, however, nothing beats the rush—or the view—you'll get from a **helicopter trip** over Niagara Falls.

TOURS   You really can't miss the **Cave of the Winds** tour that takes visitors along a wooden walkway built directly on the rocks next to Bridal Veil Falls. And since you're wet anyway, you might as well enjoy the world-renowned **Maid of the Mist** boat ride that brings passengers on a once-in-a-lifetime journey to the very base of the thundering falls.

FACILITIES   There's no shortage of restaurants and accommodations in Niagara Falls, though some may seem dated or a bit too kitschy for some folks. The **Seneca Niagara Casino & Hotel** is the big player in the area, while the **Red Coach Inn**

13

WESTERN NEW YORK | Niagara Falls

is homier and more comfortable. And visitors looking for something beyond standard tourist cuisine will enjoy the **Terrapin Grille's** distinctive fusion menu.

Essentials

GETTING THERE   Niagara Falls International Airport (www.niagarafallsairport. com) serves mostly charter and cargo planes—the only passenger options are **Direct Air** (© **877/432-DIRECT** [3473]; www.visitdirectair.com) and **Spirit Airlines** (**800/772-7117;** www.spirit.com). Otherwise, plan to fly into **Buffalo Niagara International Airport** (4200 Genesee St.; © 716/630-6000; www.buffaloairport. com). See section 1 of this chapter for all airline listings. **ITA Shuttle** runs from Buffalo Niagara International Airport to both the American and the Canadian sides of the falls (© **800/551-9369** or 716/633-8294). The cost is $45 per person one-way to the American side, $60 to the Canadian side.

Driving from I-90, take Route 290 to Route 190 to the Robert Moses Parkway, which goes right to the heart of downtown Niagara Falls, New York; you'll see signs for the Rainbow Bridge to Canada. The **Greyhound station** (© **800/231-2222;** www.greyhound.com) is at 303 Rainbow Blvd.; **Amtrak** (© **800/USA-RAIL** [872-7245]; www.amtrak.com) stops at the Niagara Falls station at 27th Street and Lock-port Road.

VISITOR INFORMATION   On the American side, the **Niagara Tourism and Convention Corporation** is at 10 Rainbow Blvd., Niagara Falls (© **877/FALLS-US** [325-5787] or 716/282-8992; www.niagara-usa.com). Office hours are Monday to Friday from 8:30am to 5pm. In Canada, **Niagara Falls Tourism,** 5400 Robinson St., Niagara Falls, Ontario (© **800/563-2557;** www.niagarafallstourism.com), is open June to August Monday to Friday from 8am to 5pm, Saturday and Sunday from 10am to 4pm; rest of the year 9am to 5pm daily.

WHEN TO GO   A visit during the dead of winter may have its particular charms (the massive, otherworldly ice formations are fascinating), but many of the top falls attractions, like *Maid of the Mist* and Cave of the Winds, operate only when the ice has melted—anywhere from early April to sometime in May. The season usually runs through October, but most hotels and restaurants are open year-round.

GETTING AROUND   A car is not essential for getting around on either side of the falls. In fact, if you're just planning to see the in-town attractions, you might be better off without one—traffic and parking in the summer are nightmarish, and parking lots are expensive year-round. Most attractions are fairly close to one another, but you don't even have to walk: Shuttles on both sides of the falls will take you to both the major hotels and the major attractions.

CROSSING THE BORDER   You're welcome to drive over to Canada, though I recommend the walk over the bridge. It's only a couple of city blocks long and you'll get great views along the way. As a bonus, you'll avoid the lineup of cars—the wait can be an hour or more in summer. Either way, be sure to carry proper proof of U.S. citizenship. Americans are now required to present either a passport or another approved documentation (visit www.getyouhome.gov for details) when arriving by land or by sea. Customs folks on both sides will inquire why you're going and how long you'll be; upon your return, they'll ask if you've brought anything back with you. If you're in a car, be prepared to pop the trunk.

Seeing the Falls

Head straight for the **Niagara Falls State Park** (© 716/278-1796; www.niagara fallsstatepark.com), the oldest state park in the United States. Designed by Frederick Law Olmsted, its natural beauty is still the best thing about the American side of the falls. In winter it's quiet and serene; summer is a different story. Parking here costs $8 to $10, and you can either walk through the park or ride the trolley ($2 adults, $1 kids 6–12; year-round) along its 3-mile route. Don't miss the stunning view from the **Observation Tower,** which stretches out over the Niagara River ($1 Apr–Oct; free Nov–Mar).

For a closer encounter with the falls, visit **Cave of the Winds ★★** (© 716/278-1730; Apr–Oct; $11 adults, $8 kids 6 to 12); the entrance is right in the park. An elevator takes you down 175 feet, where you'll walk out along wooden scaffolding constructed right on the rocks, bringing you up alongside the Bridal Veil Falls. You'll be given a raincoat and sandals beforehand—and you'll want to use them.

Accessible both from the New York Observation Tower and from the Canadian side is the famous ***Maid of the Mist*** boat ride **★★★** (© 716/284-8897; www. maidofthemist.com; Apr or May–Oct; $14 adults, $7.85 kids 6–12). This is the most popular attraction here, and for good reason. Aboard this famous boat you'll cruise right up to the base of both the American and the Horseshoe Falls, surrounded by a deafening roar while mist sprays up on your face. Don't worry, they provide slickers to keep you dry. The downside: The trip lasts only 30 minutes, and the boat will be jampacked.

Over on the Canadian side, the view is pure panorama and absolutely stunning. A walkway winds along the edge of the Niagara River, offering a picture-perfect view with every step. When you get out to the newly renovated Table Rock, take the **Journey Behind the Falls** (© 905/354-1551; www.niagaraparks.com). An elevator brings you down to tunnels, where you'll get to view the blur of water right behind Horseshoe Falls through little portholes cut in the rock. There's also a midfalls platform that provides a dramatic view of Horseshoe, just off to its side. Admission is C$11 for adults, C$6.95 for kids 6 to 12, and free for children 5 and under. Also at Table Rock is **Niagara's Fury** (© 877/642-7275), a "4D" multimedia—and multisensory—experience that simulates the creation of the falls. It costs C$15 for adults, C$9.75 for children 6 to 12, and free for children 4 and under.

The falls are illuminated by cascades of colored lights every night of the year—the best view is from the Canadian side, though along the bridge it's not bad either. There's also a concert on the Canadian side every Friday and Sunday from 8 to 10pm, May to September, followed by a fireworks show.

Biking the Niagara River

There's an excellent paved path that runs the length of the Niagara River from Niagara Falls all the way up to picturesque Niagara-on-the-Lake, a historic 19th-century village known for its charm and its wines. Part of the Niagara River Recreation Trail, it's a beautiful ride through scenic countryside. (You can also continue south on the trail, all the way down to Fort Erie; the entire trail is 35 miles long.) Rent a bike, helmet, and lock from **Zoom Leisure,** 6289 Fallsview Blvd., Niagara Falls, Ontario (© 866/811-6993; http://zoomleisure.com).

Niagara Falls Attractions Passes

If you plan on doing several of the falls attractions, consider buying a pass. On the American side, the Park Service's **Discovery Pass** (© 716/278-1796) gets you into all of the state park attractions, including *Maid of the Mist* and Cave of the Winds, plus unlimited free rides on the Niagara Scenic Trolley ($33 adults, $26 for ages 6–12). You can get these online at www.niagarafallsstatepark.com,

or at the visitor center inside the park. On the Canadian side, the **Niagara Falls Adventure Pass,** available online at **www. niagaraparks.com,** gets you into the Journey Behind the Falls, *Maid of the Mist,* Niagara's Fury, and the White Water Walk C$50 adults, C$37 for children 6 to 12. On both sides of the falls, admission to the attractions is free for kids 5 and under.

Bird's-Eye Views

Niagara Falls' skyline is punctuated by the distinctive **Skylon Tower,** 5200 Robinson St., Niagara Falls, Ontario (© 905/356-2651; www.skylon.com), which rises 775 feet above the *Maid of the Mist* pool. It's been taking people high above the falls since 1965, and on a good day you can see Toronto and Buffalo. Ride one of the yellow elevators up the outside of the tower for the view (C$14 adults, C$8.10 children 12 and under), but skip the overrated restaurant at the top. Helicopter tours are more expensive but do make for the most rarefied experience of the falls. The rides last less than 12 minutes; **Niagara Helicopters,** 3731 Victoria Blvd., Niagara Falls, Ontario (© 905/357-5672; www.niagarahelicopters.com), costs C$132 (C$82 for kids 11 and under), and **Rainbow Air,** 454 Main St., Niagara Falls, NY (© 716/284-2800; www.rainbowairinc.com), charges $85 ($50 for "small" kids). If you want to stay closer to the Earth, there's the **Niagara SkyWheel,** 4946 Clifton Hill, Niagara Falls, Ontario (© 905/358-4793; www.cliftonhill.com). The gondolas circle up to 175 feet in the air, year-round, and it's open late. Tickets are C$10 for adults, C$7 for kids 3 to 12.

Other Attractions

On the Canadian side, take a ride on the **Whirlpool Aero Car,** 3 miles north of the falls, at 3850 Niagara Pkwy. (© 905/354-5711), a cable car that takes you high above the churning white water of the **Niagara Whirlpool,** created by an abrupt change in the river's direction. Admission is C$12 for adults, C$7.95 for children 6 to 12, and free for children 5 and under (May–Nov). It closes down in the heart of winter. The **Botanical Gardens,** 9 miles north of the falls, 2565 Niagara Pkwy. (© 905/358-0025; www.niagaraparks.com), boasts 100 acres of formal and informal gardens open dawn to dusk. Admission is free. On the grounds, kids and nature lovers will love the **Butterfly Conservatory,** where more than 2,000 tropical butterflies flutter around in a rainforest-like setting. Admission is C$12 adults, C$7.95 children 6 to 12, and free for children 5 and under. Both of these are open year-round.

On the American side, the small, year-round **Aquarium of Niagara,** 701 Whirlpool St. (© 800/500-4609 or 716/285-3575; www.aquariumofniagara.org), lets you get up close and personal with penguins, sea lions, and sharks, as well as rare species of fish. The best time to come is at the penguins' mealtime—either 10am or 3pm.

Time it right and you can also catch the sea lion training session (11am and 1, 3:30, and 6pm), shark feedings (11:30am every other day), or the seal show (10:30am and 4:30pm). Admission is $10 for adults, $8 for seniors, $6 for kids 3 to 12. On the Canadian side, **Marineland,** 7657 Portage Rd. (© **905/356-9565;** www. marineland.ca), is a lot more like SeaWorld (with prices to match)—a huge, summer-time-only park with killer and beluga whales jumping out of the water, a petting zoo, and amusement park rides. Hours vary throughout the summer, so be sure to call ahead. Admission is C$42 for adults, C$35 for kids 5 to 9.

On a rainy day, head to Canada's IMAX theater, 6170 Fallsview Blvd. (© **866/405-IMAX** [4629]; imaxniagara.com), to catch "**Legends and Daredevils**" or "**The Falls.**" Either one costs C$15 for adults and C$10 for kids 4 to 12. Or, on the American side, check out "**Niagara: Legends of Adventure,**" a dramatic 40-minute action movie shown hourly on the 45×25-foot screen at the **Adventure Theater,** 1 Prospect Park (© **866/750-4629;** www.niagaramovie.com). Admission is $11 for adults, $7 for kids 6 to 12.

Old Fort Niagara, in Youngstown, NY (© **716/745-7611;** http://oldfortniagara. org), is a 17th-century fort on one of the most scenic (and strategic) pieces of land in upstate New York—right on Lake Ontario at the mouth of the Niagara River. Believed to be the longest continuously operating fort in North America, it has been used by the French, British, and Americans over its more than 300-year history. Cannons, living quarters decked out for the time period, and underground gunpowder-holding rooms are on display, along with a preserved 24×28-foot 1812 flag that once flew here. The fort is open at 9am daily year-round; admission is $10 adults, $6 children 6 to 12 (closing hours vary throughout the season, so call ahead). Over in Canada, **Old Fort Erie,** 50 Lakeshore Rd., Fort Erie, Ontario (© **905/871-0540;** www. oldforterie.com), is a series of flint-stone buildings 17 miles south of the falls, which saw action only during the War of 1812. Interiors are also reconstructed, with gun-powder storage, officers' quarters, and soldiers' living areas giving insight into the conditions at the time. Open mid-May to mid-October from 10am to 5pm; admission is C$12 adults and C$7.95 kids 6 to 12. Be on the lookout for events commemorating the 200th anniversary of the War of 1812.

Back on the American side, the **Castellani Art Museum,** at Niagara University, Senior Drive, Niagara Falls, NY (© **716/286-8200;** www.castellaniartmuseum.org), has a small but impressive collection of modern works, including lesser-known pieces by Dalí, Haring, de Kooning, Picasso, and Warhol. There's also a fascinating exhibit exploring the Buffalo Niagara region's Underground Railroad activity. Admission is free (donations welcomed); the museum is open Tuesday to Saturday 11am to 5pm and Sunday 1 to 5pm. (See the sidebar "The Underground Railroad & Buffalo Niagara.")

Looking for something a bit more active? If you've never been in a jet boat (okay, even if you have), get ready for an exhilarating ride with **Whirlpool Jet Boat Tours** (© **905/468-4800;** www.whirlpooljet.com). Tours leave from 115 S. Water St., Lewiston, and 61 Melville St., Niagara-on-the-Lake, Ontario. The cost is C$52 for adults and C$42 for kids 6 to 13—and everyone must be at least 44 inches tall. The "Wet Jet" boat skims along the Niagara River at speeds up to 65 mph, barreling through the Niagara Gorge and into the Whirlpool on this 1-hour, 18-mile ride. Yes, you will get wet—drenched is more like it. Either bring a change of clothes or take the less extreme "Jet Dome" boat (available on the Canadian side).

Finally, oenophiles will want to head to the utterly charming historic village of Niagara-on-the-Lake, Ontario, to hit the wine trail. Some must-visits: **Hillebrand Winery,** 1249 Niagara Stone Rd. (© **800/582-8412;** www.hillebrand.com); **Peller Estates,** 290 John St. E. (© **905/468-4678;** www.peller.com); **Stratus Vineyards,** 2059 Niagara Stone Rd. (© **905/468-1806;** www.stratuswines.com); and **Jackson-Triggs Winery,** 2145 Niagara Stone Rd. (© **905/468-4637;** www.jacksontriggs winery.com).

Shopping

It should be no surprise that there are tons of souvenir shops on either side of the falls, selling everything from commemorative Niagara spoons to waterfall snow globes. There are also a couple of things you can get only on the Canadian side, such as Cuban cigars (of course, you're not supposed to bring them back over the border). Lots of places sell them (you'll see the signs). One of the better shops is **Gordon's Cigars and Pipes,** 5856 Ferry St., Niagara Falls, Ontario (© **905/358-7425**). His best cigars are in the back room. For a souvenir emblazoned with the red coats of the Canadian Mounties, head to the **Mounted Police Trading Post,** 5685 Falls Ave. (© **800/372-0472**).

Where to Stay

Accommodations range from huge chains to quaint B&Bs to disgusting motels; the Canadian side has more and better choices. Rates from June to August are decidedly higher than those for the rest of the year and may fluctuate wildly depending on the particular week, whether any events are in town, and, of course, availability. So if you call to book and the quotes are astronomical, try the following week.

If you're like me—and prefer calm over crass commercialism—I recommend staying in nearby Lewiston, New York, at the pleasant **Barton Hill Hotel & Spa,** 100 Center St. (www.bartonhillhotel.com; © **800/718-1812** or 716/754-9070), located just steps away from the Niagara River, or in Canada's Niagara-on-the-Lake, where there are some decidedly more charming lodging options.

The Underground Railroad & Buffalo Niagara

For many fugitive slaves traveling through the Underground Railroad in the early to mid–19th century, the Buffalo Niagara region represented the final stretch in their long journey to freedom. Two major escape routes passed through Buffalo and Niagara Falls, helping thousands of African Americans make the crossing into Canada. The courageous men and women escaping slavery, the "passengers," were aided by the "conductors," heroic people who fed and cared for the fugitives as they fled. Dozens of farmhouses, houses, and churches served as "stations," places where the refugees could find temporary shelter. For a good overview, check out **"Freedom Crossing, The Underground Railroad in Greater Railroad,"** an exhibit at the Castellani Art Museum, 5795 Lewiston Rd., Niagara Falls (© **716/286-8200;** www.castellaniartmuseum.org). Better still, take an Underground Railroad Heritage Tour with **Motherland Connextions,** 176 Bridge St. Station, Niagara Falls (© **716/282-1028;** www.mother landconnextions.com), which includes visits to some of the churches, farms, and other "stations" in the area.

kid STUFF IN CANADA'S CLIFTON HILL

A veritable Disneyland of the north, the Clifton Hill area on the Canadian side (www.cliftonhill.com) abounds with haunted houses, theme rides, and tons of video games. At the **Ripley's 4D Moving Theater,** 4983 Clifton Hill (✆ **905/356-2261**), ride the virtual roller coaster (buckle up—your seat heaves and pitches in sync with the roller coaster movie). You might want to skip the **Ripley's Believe It or Not! Museum;** the **Guinness World Records**

Museum, 4943 Clifton Hill (✆ **905/356-2299**), is more interesting—you'll learn useless trivia like the largest collection of navel fluff (.54 oz.). Itching for a terror fix? **The Nightmares Fear Factory,** 5631 Victoria Ave. (✆ **905/357-FEAR** [3327]), actually claims to be for adults—but they let kids in, too. Creep through at your own pace, if you dare—but wimp out in the middle and you'll be added to their "chicken list."

EXPENSIVE

Marriott Niagara Falls Fallsview & Spa ★★★   Put simply, if you want to stay as close to the falls as possible, book here. Built in a curving design that allows virtually every room an unobstructed view, this luxury hotel sits just 300 feet from Horseshoe Falls—closer than any competitor. The service is good and amenities are plentiful, including an extensive spa. Standard rooms are big with large bathrooms; upgraded rooms let you take a whirlpool bath with the falls just a glance away. With comfy beds, a great restaurant (reviewed below), a spa and pool, and the best falls view in town, you may never want to leave this place.

6740 Fallsview Blvd., Niagara Falls, Ontario, Canada L2G 3W6. www.niagarafallsmarriott.com. ✆ **888/501-8916** or 905/357-7300. Fax 905/357-0490. 432 units. C$119–C$629 double. Packages available. AE, DC, DISC, MC, V. Valet parking C$20. **Amenities:** Restaurant; lounge; children's programs; concierge; executive-level rooms; small exercise room; 2 Jacuzzis; massage; large indoor pool; room service; sauna; spa. In room: A/C, TV w/pay movies, hair dryer, minibar, Wi-Fi.

Red Coach Inn ★★ 🛍   Just across the street from the rapids, this 1920s-era Tudor-style hotel with a distinctive gabled roof is one of the few luxury properties on the American side, and the most comfortably intimate hotel on either side. Skip the tiny standard rooms and go with a suite; these are more like apartments, with full kitchens, dining tables, comfy chairs and sofas, and tons of amenities. All the rooms are tastefully done up with antique furnishings—and some come with canopy beds—but the inn feels distinctly homey rather than stuffy. In fact, there's not even a formal front desk—you just check in at the restaurant. All suites have a view of the rapids, a separate bedroom, and spacious bathrooms.

2 Buffalo Ave., Niagara Falls, NY 14303. www.redcoach.com. ✆ **866/719-2070** or 716/282-1459. 19 units. Guest rooms $99–$199; 1-bedroom suites $139–$259; 2-bedroom suites $179–$399. Packages available. AE, DISC, MC, V. **Amenities:** Restaurant; lounge. In room: A/C, TV/VCR, CD player, fridge, hair dryer, kitchens (in some units), microwave, Wi-Fi.

Seneca Niagara Casino & Hotel ★★★   Rising 26 stories above the low-slung landscape, this property has become the luxury standard-bearer for the area. No, you won't get a view of the falls—they're a few blocks away—but for a combination of modern amenities and comfort, it's hard to do better on either side of the river. Rooms are spacious, with earthy hues and plump furniture, along with Native American design touches, in honor of the Seneca Indian owners. Upgrade to an enormous corner suite and you'll get two full walls of floor-to-ceiling windows and a Jacuzzi tub (some have a dramatic view of the river and the Canadian skyline). Flatscreen TVs and great sound systems make it hard to leave the rooms, but you'll want to explore the several fine restaurants (their steakhouse is reviewed below), spa, shows, and, of course, lots of gambling space.

310 Fourth St., Niagara Falls, NY 14303. www.senecaniagaracasino.com. © **877/873-6322.** 594 units. May–Oct $139–$229 double, $349 suite; Nov–Apr $99–$189 double, $199–$299 suite. Packages available. AE, DC, DISC, MC, V. **Amenities:** 6 restaurants; deli; 3 lounges; concierge; exercise room; Jacuzzi; massage; large indoor pool; room service; spa; high-roller rooms. *In room:* A/C, TV/DVD w/pay movies, fridge, hair dryer, Internet, minibar.

MODERATE

Embassy Suites ★★ With spacious suites that rise 42 stories directly above the falls, the Embassy Suites doesn't disappoint with its square footage or its views. Up top, the best rooms have fireplaces, Jacuzzis, and curving windows with dramatic views of both falls. There's also the bonus of the extensive breakfast buffet each morning and a happy hour (includes two complimentary alcoholic beverages) each evening, plus a large indoor pool. Still, this is no Ritz-Carlton, so while the furniture is comfy and serviceable, it's not exactly high-end. Also, be prepared: Some of the living rooms areas are windowless and dark.

6700 Fallsview Blvd., Niagara Falls, Ontario, Canada L2G 3W6. www.embassysuitesniagara.com. © **800/420-6980** or 905/356-3600. Fax 905/356-0472. 512 units. End of May to Labor Day C$129–C$299 double midweek, C$199–C$399 double weekend; Labor Day to end of May C$199–C$399 double. Packages available. Rates include full breakfast buffet and 2 complimentary drinks during evening happy hour. AE, DC, DISC, MC, V. Valet parking C$30 **Amenities:** 2 restaurants; coffee shop; lounge; concierge; small exercise room; Jacuzzi; indoor pool; room service; Wi-Fi in public spaces. *In room:* A/C, TV w/pay movies, hair dryer, kitchenette, minibar, Wi-Fi (C$13).

Holiday Inn ★ 🍴 This Holiday Inn benefits from recent renovations—with a good mix of amenities and comfy furniture, the wood floors and Sealy Pillowtop mattresses are nice additions to these mostly bright and airy rooms—though it appears they may have forgotten about the hallways, which could use a pick-me-up. Another downside: Many of the bathrooms are quite small. Still, this hotel offers decent value for the area. Try for one of the higher-floor rooms—from some you can see the rapids as they approach the falls, which is about as good as a view gets on the U.S. side.

114 Buffalo Ave., Niagara Falls, NY 14303. www.holidayinn.com. © **877/863-4780** or 716/285-2521. Fax 716/285-0963. 189 units. Summer season $130–$170 double, $220–$280 suite; off season $99–$119 double, $130 suite. Packages available. AE, DC, DISC, MC, V. **Amenities:** Restaurant; lounge; concierge; exercise room; Jacuzzi; indoor pool; room service. *In room:* A/C, TV w/pay movies, hair dryer, kitchenette (in suites), Wi-Fi.

Niagara Falls Courtyard Hotel by Marriott ★★ Right across the street from HoJo's, the Courtyard offers rooms that are a little larger in a hotel that's decidedly newer and less kitschy. You'll find an upscale restaurant and a large pool area, and all in the same great location—close to everything without being in the middle of the Clifton Hill mayhem. Rooms are spacious and simply furnished. It's a great option for families, but with fireplace and Jacuzzi rooms available, it's also an affordable option for couples.

5950 Victoria Ave., Niagara Falls, Ontario, Canada L2G 3L7. www.nfcourtyard.com. © **800/321-2211** or 905/358-3083. Fax 905/358-8720. 258 units. July–Aug C$149–C$359 double; Sept–June C$99–C$299 double. Packages available. AE, DC, DISC, MC, V. Self-parking C$10. **Amenities:** 2 restaurants; small exercise room; Jacuzzi; indoor-outdoor pool; sauna. *In room:* A/C, TV w/pay movies, hair dryer, Internet, minibar.

INEXPENSIVE

Rainbow House B&B ★★ Staying at this small inn is like visiting your favorite grandmother's house. Owner Laura Lee's home is charmingly cluttered and extremely cheery and welcoming, and her cinnamon rolls are legendary. The front porch is filled with colorful flowers, while the rooms are decked out in wicker and wood furnishings and are stuffed with knickknacks. Though they aren't huge, they all have private bathrooms, and the honeymoon suite has its own balcony with a bench swing. While you don't have to be newlyweds to book here, Laura Lee will be happy to tie the knot for you in the downstairs chapel if you so desire.

423 Rainbow Blvd., Niagara Falls, NY 14303. www.rainbowhousebb.com. © **800/724-3536** or 716/282-1135. 4 units. Mid-Mar to mid-Nov $80–$150 double; mid-Nov to mid-Mar weekdays $65–$110 double, weekends $75–$125 double. Rates include breakfast. MC, V. Take Robert Moses Pkwy. to Fourth St., turn right onto Rainbow Blvd. *In room:* A/C, no phone.

Victoria Motor Inn Even the budget chains in the heart of Clifton Hill push their rates through the roof in summer, but this family-run inn is holding fast to its menu of decent accommodations at good prices. No, the digs are nothing fancy, but they are clean, and some even have balconies overlooking the street. And cheap prices aren't the only thing holding fast; this is one of the few places left to still offer heart-shaped Jacuzzi tubs in some rooms.

5869 Victoria Ave., Niagara Falls, Ontario, Canada L2G 3L3. www.victoriamotorinn.com. © **905/374-6522.** Fax 905/374-3038. 33 units. Memorial Day to Labor Day midweek C$80–C$120 double, weekend C$140–C$170 double, C$20 more for suite; early Sept to late May midweek C$50–C$75 double, weekend C$80–C$110 double. DISC, MC, V. **Amenities:** Restaurant (breakfast only); outdoor pool; Wi-Fi in lobby. *In room:* A/C, TV, no phone.

CAMPGROUNDS

Set right on the shore of Lake Ontario, **Four Mile Creek State Park,** 1055 Lake Rd., Youngstown (© **716/745-3802**), is a huge expanse of park with 275 campsites and great views—on a clear day you can see Toronto. Pay a few bucks extra for a prime site and you'll be right on the water. There's lots of exploring to do around here: Hiking trails unfold along densely wooded bluffs, while the marsh at the mouth of Four Mile Creek is home to many varieties of wildlife, including great blue herons and white-tailed deer.

Where to Eat

Twenty minutes away in Niagara-on-the-Lake you'll find some of the best food (and wines, of course) in the Canadian Niagara region. Here you'll find excellent upscale dining at the elegant Georgian-style **Charles Inn,** 209 Queen St. (© **905/468-4588;** www.charlesinn.ca), as well as local favorite **Stone Road Grille,** 238 Mary St. (© **905/468-3474;** www.stoneroadgrille.com), a casual bistro known for their artisanal cheeses and house-made charcuterie.

EXPENSIVE

Terrapin Grille ★★★ AMERICAN Combining one of the best restaurants in town with the best unobstructed falls view, the Marriott Hotel's restaurant offers an exceptional—if pricey—fine-dining experience. Yes, every table has a view of the falls, but with just one wall of floor-to-ceiling windows, some tables are better than others—try to get one as close as possible to the windows. The food is some of the city's best, incorporating local produce and fusing traditional Italian, French, and Asian cuisines. There are pastas on the menu, but you'll want to come for steak and/or seafood, the restaurant's specialties. Consider delicious entrees, such as rack of lamb with a red-wine reduction, or the signature dish: sea bass with a cilantro-chili rub and a raspberry reduction. There's also an extensive wine list featuring local and international wines.

At the Marriott Fallsview, 6740 Fallsview Blvd., Niagara Falls, Ontario. ℂ **905/357-7300,** ext. 4220. Reservations suggested. Lunch C$12–C$45; dinner main courses C$22–C$72. AE, DC, DISC, MC, V. Daily 6:30am–9pm (10pm on Sat).

The Western Door ★★★ STEAKHOUSE Setting the standard for luxury on the American side, the Seneca Niagara Hotel has no fewer than seven dining options under its roof, with the Western Door at the top of the heap. Back away from the siren song of the slots and head upstairs to this hideout styled in dark woods and swirling carpets. Inspect your meat at the counter in back: perfectly marbled rib-eyes and filets that will be cooked exactly how you like them. The usual steakhouse sides are decent, but save room for one of the wonderful desserts, like sweet-potato-glazed cheesecake or lemon crème brûlée. And if you really want to dine like a high roller, be sure to reserve one of the tables that overlook the casino floor.

At the Seneca Niagara Casino & Hotel, 310 Fourth St., Niagara Falls, NY 14303. ℂ **877/873-6322.** www. senecaniagaracasino.com. Reservations suggested. Main courses $27–$75. AE, DC, DISC, MC, V. Sun–Thurs 5–9:30pm; Fri–Sat 5–10pm.

MODERATE

Keg Steakhouse & Bar ★ STEAKHOUSE This Canadian steakhouse chain feels more expensive than it is, with its classic wood decor, relaxed setting, and stone fireplace. The food is also a cut above chain-restaurant cuisine; steaks are the specialty, but don't overlook the chicken and ribs. There's no need to order appetizers—everything here is keg-size (read: "supersized"). Sides, on the other hand, are a good idea; the steamed asparagus, garlic cheese toast, and others are big enough to share. This particular Keg is located on the ninth floor in the Embassy Suites, so ask for a table by the window for a great view of the falls. There is also a second location in town at the Courtyard by Marriott.

6700 Fallsview Blvd., Niagara Falls, Ontario. ℂ **905/374-5170.** www.kegsteakhouse.com. Dinner main courses C$20–C$49. AE, DC, DISC, MC, V. Daily noon–11:30pm (till midnight on Fri–Sat).

Rainforest Café ★ ☺ AMERICAN Straight out of your most vivid childhood dreams—and predictably set in the kid-centric Clifton Hill neighborhood—this outlet of the Rainforest Café chain boasts faux rain and trees, along with comical touches like bar stools painted to resemble animal "behinds" (complete with tails). There are endless distractions: With an 80-foot erupting volcano and a shark exhibit, it's every kid's dream come true. The food is fine, and who wouldn't enjoy ordering Planet Earth Pasta or a Rumble in the Jungle turkey wrap? Choices run the gamut from chicken-fried steak to coconut shrimp, burgers, and pizza.

5785 Falls Ave., Niagara Falls, Ontario. ℂ **905/374-2233.** www.rainforestcafe.com. Reservations recommended. Main courses C$13–C$26. AE, DC, DISC, MC, V. July to Labor Day Sun–Thurs 11am–10pm, Fri–Sat 11am–midnight; early Sept–June Sun–Thurs 11am–10pm, Fri–Sat 11am–11pm.

INEXPENSIVE

Boston Pizza ★ ☺ PIZZA If the Rainforest Café sounds a bit too mellow for you, head to Boston Pizza, where practically every video game ever made is what's for dinner. You can also get food here. Set in the heart of the Clifton Hill action, this eatery runs at its own pace, which is usually fast-forward. Kids pour into the video game area nonstop, occasionally returning to their tables for a bite of burger, while adults crowd around the noisy bar to watch sports on the many TVs. As the name implies, pizza is the specialty here; you'll find more than 20 variations on the menu.

4950 Clifton Hill, Niagara Falls, Ontario. ✆ **905/358-2750.** Main courses C$12–C$25. AE, DC, DISC, MC, V. Daily 11am–2am.

The Silo ☺ AMERICAN For a change of pace, take a quick drive up to Lewiston, to this cylindrical coal silo that has been transformed into a restaurant. Choose from burgers, salads, chicken sandwiches, hot dogs, and more, but the real treat here is the signature "haystack" sandwich: steak on a sub roll, topped with melted mozzarella and overflowing with shredded hash browns. The Silo is set right on the Niagara, so take your order out to the picnic tables that ring the restaurant and chow down overlooking the shimmering water.

115 N. Water St., Lewiston. ✆ **716/754-9680.** www.lewistonsilo.com. Sandwiches $2.50–$6. DISC, MC, V. May–Sept daily 10am–10pm. From the Robert Moses State Pkwy., take Lewiston exit, follow Center St. all the way to the water.

Niagara Falls After Dark

GAMBLING In 2002, **Seneca Niagara Casino,** 310 Fourth St., Niagara Falls (✆ **877/8-SENECA** (873-6322) or 716/299-1100; www.senecaniagaracasino.com), opened on the American side, and this Seneca Indian–operated casino just keeps growing. Over the river, the **Niagara Fallsview Casino Resort,** 6380 Fallsview Blvd., Niagara Falls, Ontario (✆ **888/FALLSVU** [325-5788]; www.fallsviewcasino resort.com), is a sprawling complex of 180,000 square feet with more than 3,000 slot machines and 150 gaming tables. **Casino Niagara,** 5705 Falls Ave., Niagara Falls, Ontario (✆ **888/946-3255;** www.casinoniagara.com), is another good spot. Both the Americans and the Canadians have lots of slots, as well as blackjack, craps, roulette, music, bars, restaurants, and nonstop action.

NIGHTCLUBS The drinking age in Ontario is 19, and most clubs on the Canadian side of the falls appeal to the younger set. Both **Club Mardi Gras,** 4967 Clifton Hill (✆ **905/356-9165;** www.clubmardigrasniagara.com), and **Rumours Night Club,** 4960 Clifton Hill (✆ **905/358-6152;** www.rumoursnightclub.com), are smack in the middle of the tourist district—look for lines out the door. **Club Rialto,** 5875 Victoria Ave. (✆ **905/356-5646**), is one place that caters to an over-30 crowd, with music that's a little less hip-hop and a little more Billy Joel. If Vegas-like shows are your thing, check out the **Seneca Niagara Events Center** (at the **Seneca Niagara Casino**) on the U.S. side, 310 Fourth St. (✆ **716/852-5000**), where you'll find big names like Bill Cosby and Aretha Franklin—or hit the other bars in this huge complex. Performers like Crosby, Stills & Nash, and Jay Leno take the stage at the **Avalon Theatre** (at the **Niagara Fallsview Casino Resort**), 6380 Fallsview Blvd., Niagara Falls, Ontario (✆ **888/836-8118**). You can also chill out in **R5** or catch big-screen sports at the **Splash Bar,** both located in the same resort. Call their main number (✆ **888/FALLSVU** [325-5788]) for information. Lewiston's outdoor venue **Artpark,** 450 S. 4th St. (✆ **716/754-4375;** www.artpark.net), right on the Niagara River, is the summer home of the Buffalo Philharmonic, and has hosted such acts as Ani DiFranco, The Black Keys, and Cheap Trick.

PLANNING YOUR TRIP TO NEW YORK STATE

by Neil Edward Schlecht

14

New York is the third-biggest state in the U.S. by population and is the largest state in the northeast, and while it may not be as large as some states out west, its size and geography mean that zipping from New York City upstate to the Adirondacks or Finger Lakes is not the simple matter some believe it to be. Crossing the state takes considerable time and effort, making regional vacations the way to go for most travelers. Most people want to include New York City on their itinerary, and it can easily be combined with a trip to another region, whether that means Long Island, the Hudson River Valley, the Catskill Mountain Region, or even something farther removed in upstate New York.

Of course, New York City requires its own unique preparation. Travelers should be prepared for the expense of staying and eating in the city, which, in most cases, is considerably higher than in other parts of the state, as well as the sheer size and bustle that many people from smaller hometowns may not be familiar with (though for a city of its size, New York is considered very safe). Getting around the city requires a mastery of public transportation, walking, or the added expense of taxis, while traveling beyond the city requires renting a car or taking a combination of trains and buses. International visitors will find themselves at home in New York City, an extremely international city with many languages spoken; the rest of the state is much less so.

GETTING THERE
By Plane

With flights from across the country and around the world converging in New York City, many visitors to New York State, regardless of where they're headed, may find it convenient to arrive in New York City first and move on from there.

The Port Authority of New York and New Jersey operates three major airports in the New York City area: **John F. Kennedy International Airport (JFK), LaGuardia Airport (LGA),** and **Newark-Liberty International Airport (EWR).** Together they're served by most major domestic airlines.

However, arriving in New York City isn't the only option. For those traveling elsewhere in the state, several of the airlines listed above offer direct or connecting flights to Albany (ALB), Buffalo (BUF), Islip (ISP), Rochester (ROC), Syracuse (SYR), Ithaca (ITH), and 10 other cities. US Airways covers more New York destinations than any other carrier. AirTran Airways, American Airlines, Continental, Delta, JetBlue Airways, Northwest, and United also offer service to many of these cities, as do **Air Canada** and **Southwest.**

To find out which airlines travel to New York, see "Airline Websites," p. 453.

By Car

Drivers approaching from the west or east can take **I-90,** a toll road that crosses the country from Seattle to Boston and runs straight through New York, connecting Buffalo, Rochester, Syracuse, Utica, Schenectady, and Albany. **Route 17 (I-86** in western New York) roughly follows the state's southern border through Jamestown, Olean, Corning, Elmira, and Binghamton, then heads southwest into the Catskills and Orange County.

I-95 connects major cities along the East Coast from Florida to Maine, including New York City. **I-87** runs north to south, from New York City to Newburgh, Kingston, Albany, Saratoga Springs, and Plattsburgh; it then crosses into Canada where the road extends to Montreal.

Travelers from the south can also use **I-81,** which enters the state near Binghamton and continues north to Cortland, Syracuse, and Watertown. **I-88** links Binghamton and Schenectady. **I-390** provides a route between I-90 and NY Route 17 in the Finger Lakes region.

There is a toll on the **New York State Thruway,** which is I-90 from western New York to Albany and I-87 from Albany to New York City. The New York State Thruway Authority hot line dispenses recorded updates on road conditions; dial ✆ **800/ THRUWAY** (847-8929), or check the website for construction schedules at www. thruway.state.ny.us.

The **American Automobile Association** (✆ **800/836-2582;** www.aaa.com) will help members find the best routes to their destinations and provide free customized maps. AAA also offers emergency roadside assistance; members can call ✆ **800/ AAA-HELP** (4357).

Another great way to plan your route is on **MapQuest** (www.mapquest.com) or **Google maps** (www.google.com). Simply type in your start and end points and receive full step-by-step directions to your destination. A free state map is also available from the **New York State Division of Tourism.** See "Visitor Information," in "Fast Facts," in this chapter.

For information on car rentals and gasoline (petrol) in New York, see "By Car," under "Getting Around," later in this section.

By Train

Rail travel can be less cramped than airline flights and affords some amazing views of the American landscape. **Amtrak** (✆ **800/USA-RAIL** (872-7245); www.amtrak. com) connects New York with many American cities from coast to coast, and a handful of Canadian cities, too. However, a cross-country trip can last for days (Los Angeles to NYC is about 70 hr.) and requires one or more connections. Unfortunately, despite the extended travel time, there isn't much savings here; train reservations cost almost as much as air travel, and sometimes more.

Three main Amtrak routes cross New York State, connecting major metropolitan areas and the towns along the way. Several trains, including **Metroliner** shuttle service and high-speed **Acela Express** trains, travel the Northeast Corridor from Washington, D.C., to Philadelphia, New York City, and Boston. **Empire Service** runs north from New York City to Albany, then west to Syracuse, Rochester, Buffalo, and Niagara Falls; the *Maple Leaf* runs daily, extending the same route through Toronto, Canada. The *Adirondack* travels the Hudson River Valley north to Albany (making stops in Yonkers, Croton-on-Hudson, Poughkeepsie, Rhinecliff, and Hudson), then follows along Lake Champlain to Plattsburgh and finally Montreal, Canada.

Check the website for Internet-only deals or ask your phone representative about regional and seasonal promotions before you reserve tickets. Seniors automatically receive 15% off regular fares, and membership discount programs are available to veterans and students. Families should note that for each adult ticket purchased, two kids 14 and under may ride for half-price, and one child 1 and under comes along for free.

Amtrak Vacations (✆ **877/YES-RAIL** [937-7245]; www.amtrak.com) can put together a complete travel package including train, hotel, car rental, and sightseeing. Through a partnership with United Airlines, Amtrak has created the **Air Rail** program, which allows travelers to explore destinations at leisure by rail, then make a speedy return home by plane.

GETTING AROUND

New York State is considerably larger than many people realize; the drive from New York City to Niagara Falls can take 7 or 8 hours, while the nearest point in the Finger Lakes is nearly 5 hours from the city. Before you commit to hours of drive time, you may want to weigh the alternatives.

By Plane

CommutAir (www.commutair.com), a partner of **Continental Airlines** (✆ **800/ 525-0280;** www.continental.com), offers flights to Albany, Buffalo, Rochester, Syracuse, and Ithaca. Reservations must be made through Continental.

JetBlue Airways (✆ **800/538-2583;** www.jetblue.com) is hard to beat, with consistently low ticket prices and daily runs from New York City (JFK Airport) to Buffalo, Rochester, and Syracuse.

US Airways (✆ **800/428-4322;** www.usairways.com) and its partner **Colgan Air** (www.colganair.com), also partnered with Continental and United, provide direct flights from New York City to Albany, Buffalo, Ithaca, Rochester, and Syracuse, as well as service from Albany to Buffalo and Islip. **Northwest Airlines** (✆ **800/225-2525;** www.nwa.com) flies to Ithaca.

Attention visitors to the U.S. from abroad: Some major airlines offer transatlantic or transpacific passengers special discount tickets under the name **Visit USA,** which allows mostly one-way travel from one U.S. destination to another at very low prices. Unavailable in the U.S., these discount tickets must be purchased abroad in conjunction with your international fare. This system is the easiest, fastest, cheapest way to see the country. Inquire with your air carrier.

By Car

Unless you plan to spend the bulk of your vacation in a city where walking is the best way to get around (read: NYC), the most cost-effective way to travel in New York State is by car. (See "Car Rental Agencies," at the end of this chapter.)

Check out **Breezenet.com,** which offers domestic car-rental discounts with some of the most competitive rates around.

For an explanation of major New York State roadways and the cities they connect, see "By Car," under "Getting There," earlier in this chapter.

Gas prices in New York State tend to be at least 10¢ higher than the national average. Of the major cities, Albany and Binghamton have the cheapest gas. Not surprisingly, New York City's is the most expensive (as much as 50¢ higher per gallon). Taxes are already included in the printed price. One U.S. gallon equals 3.8 liters or .85 imperial gallons. Fill-up locations are known as gas or service stations.

All the major rental-car companies operate in New York State, including **Alamo, Avis, Budget, Dollar, Enterprise, Hertz, National,** and **Thrifty.** It's worth noting that the only companies located at Kennedy, LaGuardia, and Newark airports are Avis, Budget, Dollar, Hertz, and National. Enterprise is also available at LaGuardia and Newark, but not at Kennedy. When you're renting a car, there is always some kind of deal to be found—check company websites or ask reservations agents about specials before you rent. If you're a member of AAA, AARP, or another organization, find out if you qualify for a discount.

If you plan to travel between December and March, be advised that winter weather can present significant obstacles, such as wet or icy pavement, poor visibility, or routes that are just plain shut down. Make sure that your vehicle is adequately prepared with snow tires and working windshield wipers, battery, and defrosters.

Highway speed limits are 55 or 65 mph. The speed limit in New York City is 30 mph unless otherwise posted. "Right on red" (making a right turn at a red light after coming to a complete stop) is permitted in most parts of New York State, but not in New York City. Motorcyclists must wear helmets, and goggles if helmets are not equipped with face shields. State law requires drivers, front-seat passengers, and children 9 and under to wear seat belts. Children 3 and under must ride in safety seats. Fines can run up to $100. Talking on a hand-held cellphone while driving (without an earpiece) is punishable by a fine of up to $100 (exceptions are made for emergency situations, such as calls to the police). Drivers can be charged with driving while intoxicated (DWI) for having a blood alcohol content of .08% or higher and sentenced to a fine or jail time upon conviction.

By Train

The train won't get you where you're going any faster, but it will cut down on the amount of time you have to spend behind the wheel. When you get where you're going, though, you'll probably need to rent a car anyway because public transportation is not very extensive beyond New York City.

Amtrak (© **800/USA-RAIL** [872-7245]; www.amtrak.com) basically follows the same paths as the New York State Thruway and the Adirondack Northway (routes 90 and 87), leaving much of the state inaccessible by rail. For more information on cities served by Amtrak, see "Getting There," earlier in this chapter.

Visitors to Long Island can take the **Long Island Rail Road** (**LIRR;** © **718/217-5477;** www.mta.nyc.ny.us/lirr). With service from New York City's Penn Station, the LIRR is the main mode of transportation for commuters as well as Manhattanites weekending in the Hamptons. Because seating is normally unreserved, trains are often standing-room-only during the summer vacation season. **Hamptons Reserve Service** (© **718/558-8070**) guarantees passengers a seat on the Friday express train for an extra fee in addition to the regular fare.

Metro-North Railroad (© **800/METRO-INFO** [638-7646] or 212/532-4900; www.mta.nyc.ny.us/mnr/index.html) makes the Hudson Valley region easily reachable from New York City's Grand Central Station with commuter lines extending as far north as Poughkeepsie and Wassaic, and west to Port Jervis.

By Bus

Greyhound (© **800/231-2222,** or 001/214/849-8100 outside the U.S. with toll-free access; www.greyhound.com) is the sole nationwide bus line. International visitors can obtain information about the **Greyhound North American Discovery Pass.** The pass, which offers unlimited travel and stopovers in the U.S. and Canada, can be obtained from foreign travel agents or through www.discoverypass.com. Travelers to Long Island (particularly the Hamptons and North Fork) often find the local bus service from Manhattan aboard the **Hampton Jitney** (© **212/362-8400;** www.hamptonjitney.com) preferable to the slower train. **Megabus** (© **877-GO2-MEGA** [462-6342]; http://us.megabus.com) travels to New York City, Albany, Rochester, Syracuse, Binghamton, and Buffalo; **BoltBus** (© **877/265-8287;** www.boltbus.com) offers daily express service to New York City from Washington, D.C., as well as Boston and Philadelphia; and **Vamoose** (© **212/695-6766;** www.vamoosebus.com) serves New York City from Arlington, Virginia, and Bethesda, Maryland.

TIPS ON ACCOMMODATIONS

New York offers a wide range of accommodations—from the superchic (and super-expensive) luxury hotels of Manhattan and the Victorian B&Bs of Saratoga Springs to the rustic mountain retreats of the Catskills and Adirondacks and the salty seaside motels of Long Island.

The **New York State Hospitality and Tourism Association** (© **518/465-2300;** www.nyshta.org) covers the gamut of hotel and motel options and provides a free map listing the names and basic rates of its members statewide.

The perfect bed-and-breakfast can be hard to track down because few are well known outside their local areas. The **Empire State Bed & Breakfast Association** (© **800/841-2340;** www.esbba.com) makes the task easier with its free, color guide to 150 inns and B&Bs across the state. Another good bet is **Bed & Breakfast Inns Online** (www.bbonline.com), where you can view interior and exterior photos of almost every property profiled, including several listed on the National Register of Historic Places. The site offers last-minute, midweek, and seasonal specials besides a variety of other packages.

House swaps aren't for everyone—clean freaks and people with control issues should probably skip this option. However, you may consider staying in a private home while the owners stay in yours to be a comfortable and cost-effective alternative to booking a hotel. **HomeLink International** (☏ **800/638-3841** or 813/975-9825; www.homelink.org) is an established house-swapping service. Apartment swaps in Manhattan, Brooklyn, and other New York City boroughs can be found through **Craigslist.org.** People over 50 may register their homes with **Seniors Home Exchange** (www.seniorshomeexchange.com). **HomeAway** (www.homeaway.com), one of the nation's largest vacation rentals sites (with homeowners across the country offering both short- and long-term rentals), has all kinds of listings for homes and apartments in New York City, Long Island, and more.

For tips on surfing for the best hotel deals online, visit Frommers.com.

FAST FACTS

Area Codes Major area codes include these: New York City (212, 646, 917, 718, 437); Long Island (518, 631); Eastern New York (518); Central New York (315, 617); Western New York (585, 716). For a full list of New York State area codes, go to www.verizon.com.

Business Hours Business hours in New York State don't differ much from those of the rest of the country, and are generally 9am to 5pm, with one notable exception: It may be a tired cliché, but they don't call New York City "the city that never sleeps" for nothing. Although some stores close at 7pm, many are open until 9pm, and a few as late as 11pm. Most restaurants serve until 11pm, and later on weekends. Some diners serve breakfast all night to bar-crawlers and club kids, and there are 24-hour convenience stores on every block.

Car Rental See "By Car," under "Getting Around," earlier in this chapter.

Cellphones See "Mobile Phones," below.

Crime See "Safety," later in this section.

Customs For details regarding U.S. Customs and Border Protection, consult your nearest U.S. embassy or consulate, or **U.S. Customs** (www.cbp.gov).

For information on what you're allowed to bring home, contact one of the following agencies:

Canadian Citizens: Canada Border Services Agency (☏ **800/461-9999** in Canada, or 204/983-3500; www.cbsa-asfc.gc.ca).

U.K. Citizens: HM Customs & Excise at ☏ **0845/010-9000** (from outside the U.K., 020/8929-0152), or consult their website at **www.hmce.gov.uk**.

Australian Citizens: Australian Customs Service at ☏ **1300/363-263,** or log on to **www.customs.gov.au**.

New Zealand Citizens: New Zealand Customs, The Customhouse, 17–21 Whitmore St., Box 2218, Wellington (☏ **04/473-6099** or 0800/428-786; **www.customs.govt.nz**).

Doctors Except in the most rural areas, such as the Adirondack Mountains, you should have no trouble finding a doctor or getting prescriptions filled. Without proof of insurance, you pay as a walk-in in a hospital emergency room. Also see "Health," below.

Drinking Laws The legal age for purchase and consumption of alcoholic beverages is 21; proof of age is required and often requested at bars, nightclubs, and restaurants, so it's always a good idea to bring ID when you go out. In general, grocery and convenience stores sell beer and other products that are less than 6% alcohol by volume (like wine coolers). Wine and spirits are sold at liquor stores, also called package stores.

Restaurants and bars can't serve drinks before 8am Monday through Saturday, or before noon on Sunday. Closing time for bars, taverns, and nightclubs varies by county. Albany, Buffalo, and New York City bars close at 4am; in Rochester and Syracuse they close at 2am. In quieter areas, closing time comes as early as 1am. Do not carry open containers of alcohol in your car or any public area that isn't zoned for alcohol consumption. The police can fine you on the spot. And nothing will ruin your trip faster than getting a citation for DWI ("driving while intoxicated"), so don't even contemplate drinking and driving.

Driving Rules See "Getting Around," earlier in this chapter.

Electricity Like Canada, the United States uses 110 to 120 volts AC (60 cycles), compared to 220 to 240 volts AC (50 cycles) in most of Europe, Australia, and New Zealand. Downward converters that change 220 to 240 volts to 110 to 120 volts are difficult to find in the United States, so bring one with you.

Embassies & Consulates All embassies are in the nation's capital, Washington, D.C. Some consulates are in major U.S. cities, and most nations have a mission to the United Nations in New York City. If your country isn't listed below, call for directory information in Washington, D.C. (© **202/555-1212**), or check **www.embassy.org/embassies**.

The embassy of **Australia** is at 1601 Massachusetts Ave. NW, Washington, DC 20036 (© **202/797-3000;** www.usa.embassy.gov.au). Consulates are in Honolulu, Houston, Los Angeles, New York, and San Francisco.

The embassy of **Canada** is at 501 Pennsylvania Ave. NW, Washington, DC 20001 (© **202/682-1740;** www.canadainternational.gc.ca/washington). Other Canadian consulates are in Buffalo (New York), Detroit, Los Angeles, New York, and Seattle.

The embassy of **Ireland** is at 2234 Massachusetts Ave. NW, Washington, DC 20008 (© **202/462-3939;** www.embassyofireland.org). Irish consulates are in Boston, Chicago, New York, San Francisco, and other cities. See website for complete listing.

The embassy of **New Zealand** is at 37 Observatory Circle NW, Washington, DC 20008 (© **202/328-4800;** www.nzembassy.com). New Zealand consulates are in Los Angeles, Salt Lake City, San Francisco, and Seattle.

The embassy of the **United Kingdom** is at 3100 Massachusetts Ave. NW, Washington, DC 20008 (© **202/588-6500;** http://ukinusa.fco.gov.uk). Other British consulates are in Atlanta, Boston, Chicago, Cleveland, Houston, Los Angeles, New York, San Francisco, and Seattle.

Emergencies Call © **911** to report a fire, call the police, or get an ambulance anywhere in the United States. This is a toll-free call. (No coins are required at public telephones.) In New York City, some issues may also be resolved by calling © **311,** the main hotline for all things metropolitan. If you encounter serious problems, contact the **Traveler's Aid Society International** (© **202/546-1127;** www.travelersaid.org). This nationwide, nonprofit, social-service organization geared to helping travelers in difficult straits offers services that might include reuniting families separated while traveling, providing food and/or shelter to people stranded without cash, or even emotional counseling. If you're in trouble, seek them out.

Family Travel A good source for family vacation suggestions is the **I Love NY** website (www.iloveny.com/kids). It features travel ideas for families (children's museums and amusement parks; click on Travel Fun) as well as a history brief on the state, puzzles and games, and an interactive coloring book. New York City's official tourism website (www.nyc.gov) details restaurants, museums, and tours designed to fascinate kids, plus gives a list of activities and neighborhoods that even the most blasé teen might enjoy.

To locate accommodations, restaurants, and attractions that are particularly kid-friendly, look for the "Kids" icon throughout this guide.

Gasoline Please see "By Car," under "Getting There," earlier in this chapter.

Health In general, vacationers in New York State generally need take no more health precautions than they would at home. There's no shortage of doctors, hospitals, and pharmacies across the state. But it's true that cities have more facilities than rural areas. The New York State Department of Health provides a list of hospitals by county at www.health.state.ny.us/nysdoh/hospital/main.htm.

Pharmacy chains, such as **Rite Aid** (www.riteaid.com), **CVS** (www.cvs.com), and **Walgreens** (www.walgreens.com), are easy to find should you need to fill or refill a prescription. Bring your doctor's telephone number with you so that the pharmacist can confirm the prescription with your doctor's office. It's also helpful to have the number of your home pharmacy on hand in case your doctor can't be reached.

The United States **Centers for Disease Control and Prevention** (© **800/311-3435;** www.cdc.gov) provides up-to-date information on health hazards by region or country and offers tips on food safety. For the latest information about health issues affecting travelers, visit the **Centers for Disease Control and Prevention**'s travel page at www.cdc.gov/travel, or call the **Travelers' Health Hotline** at © **877/FYI-TRIP** (394-8747). The **New York State Department of Health** website (www.health.state.ny.us) is geared toward residents rather than visitors, but provides more specifics about issues concerning New York.

BUGS/BITES

Mosquitoes are a familiar annoyance, particularly in late summer and early fall when New York's mosquito population peaks. They were upgraded from pest to public health issue, however, when the first U.S. case of the mosquito-borne **West Nile virus** was reported in New York City back in 1999. The virus can lead to a flulike bout of West Nile fever, or more serious diseases such as West Nile encephalitis or meningitis. Even if you get a few bites, though, the risk of illness is low. Not all mosquitoes carry the virus, and most people who are infected never become sick, although people over 50 are more susceptible. Symptoms include fever, headache, stiff neck, body ache, muscle weakness or tremors, and disorientation. If you think you've been infected, see a doctor right away or go to the emergency room.

Ticks are common in the Northeast. They stay close to the ground and prefer damp, shady grass and stone walls. **Lyme disease** is carried by deer ticks, which are 2mm or less in size (smaller than dog ticks or cattle ticks). Removing the offender within the first 36 hours usually prevents transmission of the harmful bacteria. Seek medical aid if symptoms develop, such as the trademark "bull's-eye" bruise or red rash that grows outward from the area of the bite, or other signs like joint pain, fever, fatigue, or facial paralysis.

OTHER WILDLIFE CONCERNS

Raccoons, foxes, skunks, and bats are the most likely to spread **rabies.** The virus can be transmitted through the bite or scratch of an infected animal, or by contact with the animal's saliva or nervous tissue through an unhealed cut. This means it's unsafe to poke around dead carcasses as well. If contact occurs, wash the wound thoroughly with soap and water and report to a doctor or hospital for treatment. Let a park ranger or another official know so the animal can be captured and tested for the disease.

Black bears are indigenous to the Adirondack, Catskill, and Allegheny mountains. Although they're naturally inclined to avoid humans, they'll often raid campsites in search of food. Tuck food away and clean up campsites after meals to keep them from sniffing around. A useful source for black bear safety tips is the Citizens for Responsible Wildlife Management website at **www.responsiblewildlifemanagement.org/bear_safety.htm**.

See also "Medical Requirements" and "Doctors," in this section.

Insurance For information on traveler's insurance, trip-cancellation insurance, and medical insurance while traveling, please visit www.frommers.com/planning.

Internet & Wi-Fi   Cybercafes and FedEx Offices (formerly Kinko's) are good places to go for Internet access in cities. To find a cybercafe, try www.cybercafe.com. New York's most rural areas, such as parts of the Catskill and Adirondack mountains and the North Country, are not well connected.

Most major airports have **Internet kiosks** that provide basic Web access for a per-minute fee that's usually higher than cybercafe prices. More and more hotels, resorts, airports, cafes, and retailers are going Wi-Fi (wireless fidelity), becoming "hotspots" that offer free high-speed Wi-Fi access or charge a small fee for usage. Wi-Fi is often found in campgrounds, RV parks, and even entire towns. Most laptops sold today have built-in wireless capability. To find public Wi-Fi hotspots at your destination, visit **www.jiwire. com**; its Hotspot Finder holds the world's largest directory of public wireless hotspots.

For information on electrical currency conversions, see "Electricity," earlier in this section.

Legal Aid   While driving, if you are pulled over for a minor infraction (such as speeding), never attempt to pay the fine directly to a police officer; this could be construed as attempted bribery, a much more serious crime. Pay fines by mail, or directly into the hands of the clerk of the court. If accused of a more serious offense, say and do nothing before consulting a lawyer. In the U.S., the burden is on the state to prove a person's guilt beyond a reasonable doubt, and everyone has the right to remain silent, whether he or she is suspected of a crime or actually arrested. Once arrested, a person can make one telephone call to a party of his or her choice. The international visitor should call his or her embassy or consulate. If you find yourself in need of legal representation, contact the **New York State Bar Association's Lawyer Referral and Information Service** (© **800/ 342-3661** or 518/487-5709; www.nysba.org).

LGBT Travelers   New York is now the sixth state in the nation to make same-sex marriages legal. And New York City—where the gay liberation movement got its beginning with the Stonewall riot in Greenwich Village in 1969—today is home to a gay, lesbian, bisexual, and transgender community of more than a million strong by some estimates. The highlight of the events calendar is the annual **Pride Week** (p. 29), but visitors year-round have plenty to explore in the many gay-owned restaurants, bars, boutiques, bookstores, and art galleries found largely in Manhattan's Greenwich Village and Chelsea neighborhoods. The central bulletin board for meetings, cultural events, and resources in New York City is **The Lesbian, Gay, Bisexual, and Transgender Community Center** (© **212/620-7310;** www.gaycenter.org).

There's more to gay and lesbian life in the Empire State than cruising Chelsea and the Village. Travelers will find thriving networks in upstate, central, and western New York. **Outcome Buffalo** (www.outcomebuffalo.com) and **Pride Center of the Capital Region** (© **518/462-6138;** www.capitalpridecenter.org) are great sources of information about nightlife, social groups, news, and links to other gay and lesbian organizations in and around Albany. **Sullivan County** in the Catskill Mountain region is proudly gay-friendly in tourist matters, and it operates a website with plenty of information for gay and lesbian travelers (© **845/747-4449;** www.outinthecatskills.com).

The International Gay and Lesbian Travel Association (**IGLTA;** © **800/448-8550** or 954/776-2626; www.iglta.org) is the trade association for the gay and lesbian travel industry, and offers an online directory of gay- and lesbian-friendly travel businesses and tour operators.

Mail   At press time, domestic postage rates were 28¢ for a postcard and 44¢ for a letter. For international mail, a first-class letter of up to 1 ounce costs 98¢ (75¢ to Canada and 79¢ to Mexico); a first-class postcard costs the same as a letter. For more information go to **www.usps.com**.

Medical Requirements Unless you're arriving from an area known to be suffering from an epidemic (particularly cholera or yellow fever), inoculations or vaccinations are not required for entry into the United States. Also see "Health," earlier in this section.

Mobile Phones Just because your cellphone works at home doesn't mean it'll work everywhere in the U.S. (thanks to our nation's fragmented cellphone system); New York City can be complicated, depending on your carrier, as can many rural areas. Take a look at your wireless company's coverage map on its website before heading out; T-Mobile, Sprint, and Nextel are particularly weak in rural areas. If you need to stay in touch at a destination where you know your phone won't work, **rent** a phone that does from **InTouch USA** (✆ 800/872-7626; www.intouchglobal.com) or a rental-car location, but beware: You'll pay $1 a minute or more for airtime. In New York City, you can rent cellphones at **Roberts Rent-a-Phone,** 226 E. 54th St., New York, NY 10022 (✆ **800/964-2468** or 212/832-7143; www.roberts-rent-a-phone.com), or **Cellhire USA,** 45 Broadway, 20th Floor, New York, NY 10006 (✆ **866/235-5447;** www.cellhire.com).

If you're venturing deep into national parks, you may want to consider renting a **satellite phone** ("satphone"). It's different from a cellphone in that it connects to satellites rather than ground-based towers. Unfortunately, you'll pay at least $2 per minute to use the phone, and it works only where you can see the horizon (that is, usually not indoors). In North America, you can rent Iridium satellite phones from **RoadPost** (www.roadpost. com; ✆ **888/290-1606** or 905/272-5665). InTouch USA (see above) offers a wider range of satphones but at higher rates.

If you're not from the U.S., you'll be appalled at the poor reach of the **GSM (Global System for Mobile Communications) wireless network,** which is used by much of the rest of the world. Your phone will probably work in most major U.S. cities; it definitely won't work in many rural areas. To see where GSM phones work in the U.S., check out www.t-mobile. com/coverage. And you may or may not be able to send SMS (text messaging) home.

Money & Costs

THE VALUE OF THE U.S. DOLLAR ($) VS. OTHER POPULAR CURRENCIES

US$	A$	C$	€	NZ$	£
1.00	1.00	1.00	0.73	1.31	0.63

Frommer's lists exact prices in the local currency. The currency conversions quoted above were correct at press time. However, rates fluctuate, so before departing consult a currency exchange website such as www.oanda.com/currency/converter to check up-to-the-minute rates.

New York City is consistently ranked among the top 15 most expensive cities in the world, and the most expensive in the U.S. Hotel costs in the city far outstrip those of pretty much anywhere else in the country. Thankfully, costs elsewhere in the state are closer to the national average, and even in New York City there are deals to be found.

Credit cards and traveler's checks are accepted at almost all hotels, restaurants, shops, and attractions, plus many grocery stores; and ATMs are practically everywhere.

For help with currency conversions, tip calculations, and more, download Frommer's convenient Travel Tools app for your mobile device. Go to www.frommers.com/go/mobile and click on the Travel Tools icon.

Newspapers & Magazines The *New York Times, New York Daily News,* the *Wall Street Journal,* and *USA Today* are sold at newsstands everywhere in New York City and are generally available in hotels and corner newspaper boxes throughout the state. Major cities have their own daily papers. The largest of these are the *Buffalo News, Rochester Democrat and Chronicle, Syracuse Post-Standard,* and *Albany Times Union.*

WHAT THINGS COST IN NEW YORK STATE

ITEM	MANHATTAN	UPSTATE NEW YORK
Cup of coffee	$2.00	$1.50
Taxi from airport	$30.00 (LGA)	$15.00 (ALB)
Bus fare	$2.25	$1.50 (Albany)
Gallon unleaded gas (press time)	$4.25	$3.99
Moderate 3-course dinner (for one w/o alcohol)	$70.00	$40.00
Night in a moderately priced hotel room	$275.00	$150.00
Concert/theater ticket	$90.00	$40.00

Passports Virtually every air traveler entering the U.S. is required to show a passport. All persons, including U.S. citizens, traveling by air between the United States and Canada, Mexico, Central and South America, the Caribbean, and Bermuda are required to present a valid passport. **Note:** U.S. and Canadian citizens entering the U.S. at land and sea ports of entry from within the western hemisphere must now also present a passport or other documents compliant with the Western Hemisphere Travel Initiative (WHTI; see www.getyouhome.gov for details). Children 15 and under may continue entering with only a U.S. birth certificate, or other proof of U.S. citizenship.

PASSPORT OFFICES

- **Australia** Australian Passport Information Service (℡ **131-232,** or visit www. passports.gov.au).
- **Canada Passport Office,** Department of Foreign Affairs and International Trade, Ottawa, ON K1A 0G3 (℡ **800/567-6868;** www.ppt.gc.ca).
- **Ireland Passport Office,** Setanta Centre, Molesworth Street, Dublin 2 (℡ **01/671-1633;** www.foreignaffairs.gov.ie).
- **New Zealand Passports Office,** Department of Internal Affairs, 47 Boulcott St., Wellington, 6011 (℡ **0800/225-050** in New Zealand, or 04/474-8100; www. passports.govt.nz).
- **United Kingdom** Visit your nearest passport office, major post office, or travel agency, or contact the **Identity and Passport Service (IPS),** 89 Eccleston Sq., London, SW1V 1PN (℡ **0300/222-0000;** www.ips.gov.uk).
- **United States** To find your regional passport office, check the U.S. State Department website (http://travel.state.gov/passport) or call the **National Passport Information Center** (℡ **877/487-2778**) for automated information.

Petrol Please see "By Car," under "Getting Around," earlier in this chapter.

Police In nonemergency situations, call the nearest police station. Local police precinct telephone numbers can be found in the blue "government" pages of the phone book. In an emergency, call ℡ **911,** a toll-free call (no coins are required at public telephones). For issues of safety, call the **Statewide Public Security Tips Hotline** at ℡ **866/SAFE-NYS** (723-3697), or ℡ **888/NYC-SAFE** (692-7233) in New York City.

Safety The crime rate in New York State has been steadily dropping for the past decade or more. New York City, once famous for muggings, is now—improbably, some might say—considered one of the safest large cities in the country. That said, it's never a good idea to take your safety for granted.

First and foremost, know where you're going. If you look lost or distracted, you may seem like an easy mark. Ask for directions at the front desk before leaving your hotel, and try not to be obvious about checking maps on the street. Be wary of strangers who offer to act as guides. They may expect you to tip them, or they may try to lead you to a secluded place where they can rob you. Try not to use the subway to get around late at night; opt for the bus or a taxi instead.

Since the September 11, 2001, terrorist attacks, counteracting terrorism in New York has been a major concern. The police urge everyone to report unattended bags or suspicious-looking packages through the **Statewide Public Security Tips Hotline** at ℂ **866/SAFE-NYS** (723-3697), or ℂ **888/NYC-SAFE** (692-7233) in New York City.

Senior Travel Members of **AARP,** 601 E St. NW, Washington, DC 20049 (ℂ **888/687-2277;** www.aarp.org), get discounts on hotels, airfares, and car rentals. AARP offers members a wide range of benefits, including *AARP The Magazine* and a monthly newsletter. Anyone 50 and over can join.

The U.S. National Park Service offers an **America the Beautiful—National Park and Federal Recreational Lands Pass—Senior Pass** (formerly the **Golden Age Passport**), which gives seniors 62 years or older lifetime entrance to all properties administered by the National Park Service—national parks, monuments, historic sites, recreation areas, and national wildlife refuges—for a one-time processing fee of $10. The pass must be purchased in person at any NPS facility that charges an entrance fee. For more information, go to www.nps.gov or call ℂ **888/467-2757.**

Smoking The legal age to purchase cigarettes and other tobacco products in New York State is 18. But you won't find many places left to smoke them. A state law passed in 2003 prohibits smoking in almost all public venues and in the workplace. This includes bars and restaurants, although smokers can still light up in cigar bars, designated outdoor areas of restaurants, and some private clubs. The law does not affect Native American-run casinos, and smoking is still permitted there. An outdoor ban on smoking in New York City parks, in plazas (including the pedestrian plazas in Times Square and Herald Square, as well as the Coney Island Boardwalk), and at nearby beaches went into effect in May 2011.

Student Travel Check out the **International Student Travel Confederation (ISTC)** website (www.istc.org) for comprehensive travel services information and details on how to get an **International Student Identity Card (ISIC),** which qualifies students for substantial savings on rail passes, plane tickets, entrance fees, and more. It also provides students with basic health and life insurance and a 24-hour help line. The card is valid for a maximum of 18 months. You can apply for the card online or in person at **STA Travel** (ℂ **800/781-4040** in North America; ℂ **132-782** in Australia; ℂ **0871/2-300-040** in the U.K.; www.statravel.com), the biggest student travel agency in the world; check out the website to locate STA Travel offices worldwide. If you're no longer a student but are still 25 or under, you can get an **International Youth Travel Card (IYTC)** from the same people, which entitles you to some discounts. **Travel CUTS** (ℂ **800/592-2887;** www.travelcuts.com) offers similar services for both Canadians and U.S. residents. Irish students may prefer to turn to **USIT** (ℂ **01/602-1904;** www.usit.ie), an Ireland-based specialist in student, youth, and independent travel.

Taxes Sales tax in New York State varies between 7.25% and 8.75% (the state tax is 4.25%, and counties generally tack on another 3% or 4%). On top of the sales tax, hotel occupancy taxes can add as much as 5% to hotel and motel bills; an additional 5% typically applies to car rentals as well. The United States has no value-added tax (VAT) or other indirect tax at the national level. Every state, county, and city may levy its own local tax on all purchases, including hotel and restaurant checks and airline tickets. These taxes will not appear on price tags.

Telephones Many convenience groceries and packaging services sell **prepaid calling cards** in denominations up to $50. Many public pay phones at airports now accept American Express, MasterCard, and Visa. **Local calls** made from most pay phones cost either 25¢ or 35¢. Most long-distance and international calls can be dialed directly from any phone. **To make calls within the United States and to Canada,** dial 1 followed by the area code and the seven-digit number. **For other international calls,** dial 011 followed by the country code, the city code, and the number you are calling.

Calls to area codes **800, 888, 877,** and **866** are toll-free. However, calls to area codes **700** and **900** (chat lines, bulletin boards, "dating" services, and so on) can be expensive—charges of 95¢ to $3 or more per minute. Some numbers have minimum charges that can run $15 or more.

For **directory assistance** ("Information"), dial 411 for local numbers and national numbers in the U.S. and Canada. For dedicated long-distance information, dial 1, then the appropriate area code plus 555-1212.

Time The continental United States is divided into **four time zones:** Eastern Standard Time (EST), Central Standard Time (CST), Mountain Standard Time (MST), and Pacific Standard Time (PST). Alaska and Hawaii have their own zones. For example, when it's 9am in Los Angeles (PST), it's 7am in Honolulu (HST),10am in Denver (MST), 11am in Chicago (CST), noon in New York City (EST), 5pm in London (GMT), and 2am the next day in Sydney.

Daylight saving time (summertime) is in effect from 1am on the second Sunday in March to 1am on the first Sunday in November, except in Arizona, Hawaii, the U.S. Virgin Islands, and Puerto Rico. Daylight saving time moves the clock 1 hour ahead of standard time.

For help with time translations, and more, download our convenient Travel Tools app for your mobile device. Go to www.frommers.com/go/mobile and click on the Travel Tools icon.

Tipping Tips are a very important part of certain workers' income, and gratuities are the standard way of showing appreciation for services provided. (Tipping is certainly not compulsory if the service is poor!) Particularly in New York City, tipping is a way of life that residents and visitors have to accept; waiters have grown accustomed to some Europeans' and other nationalities' lack of familiarity with accepted tipping norms in the U.S., and even have been known to chase customers out the door when they receive anything less than 20% (and some restaurants frequented by tourists have also tried to institute mandatory gratuities into their billing).

Toilets You won't find public toilets or "restrooms" on the streets in most areas of New York, but they can be found in hotel lobbies, bars, restaurants, museums, department stores, railway and bus stations, and service stations. Large hotels and fast-food restaurants are often the best bet for clean facilities. Restaurants and bars in resorts or heavily visited areas may reserve their restrooms for patrons. There are now smart-phone apps for locating public toilets in New York City (and other cities around the world); the best is called SitOrSquat. Another similar app for New York City is Best Bathroom.

Travelers with Disabilities Most disabilities shouldn't preclude anyone from traveling. There are more options and resources out there than ever before.

AbilityTrip.com (http://abilitytrip.com/category/north_america/usa/new-york) has a destination review of New York City, detailing everything from airport, hotel, and restaurant facilities to wheelchair-accessible activities, tours, and arts. Several travel agencies offer services for travelers with disabilities who are eager to explore the natural and cultural wonders of New York State. **People and Places** (📞 **716/937-1813** or 716/496-8826;

www.people-and-places.org) offers escorted tours for vacationers with developmental disabilities to the Adirondacks, Catskills, Thousand Islands, Finger Lakes, and other destinations in New York State. **Next Stop New York** (✆ **800/434-7554** or 718/264-2300; www.nextstopnewyork.com) designs theater, food-tasting, and sightseeing tours of Manhattan for groups or individuals, and can design custom programs for groups of travelers with physical or mental challenges. **Alternative Leisure Company & Trips Unlimited** (✆ **781/275-0023**; www.alctrips.com) offers group excursions in New York and New England, as well as a "Traveling Companion" program, which provides staff members to accompany individuals on customized trips.

The **America the Beautiful—National Park and Federal Recreational Lands Pass—Access Pass** (formerly the **Golden Access Passport**) gives travelers who are visually impaired or have permanent disabilities (regardless of age) free lifetime entrance to federal recreation sites administered by the National Park Service, including the Fish and Wildlife Service, the Forest Service, the Bureau of Land Management, and the Bureau of Reclamation. This may include national parks, monuments, historic sites, recreation areas, and national wildlife refuges. For more information, go to www.nps.gov or call ✆ **888/467-2757.**

Organizations that offer a vast range of resources and assistance to travelers with disabilities include **MossRehab** (✆ **215/663-6000**; www.mossresourcenet.org); the **American Foundation for the Blind (AFB)** (✆ **800/232-5463**; www.afb.org); and **SATH (Society for Accessible Travel & Hospitality**; ✆ **212/447-7284**; www.sath.org). **Air Ambulance Card** (www.airambulancecard.com) is now partnered with SATH and allows you to preselect top-notch hospitals in case of an emergency.

Many travel agencies offer customized tours and itineraries for travelers with disabilities. Among them are **Flying Wheels Travel** (✆ **507/451-5005**; www.flyingwheelstravel. com) and **Accessible Journeys** (✆ **800/846-4537** or 610/521-0339; www.disabilitytravel. com).

Flying with Disability (www.flying-with-disability.org) is a comprehensive information source on airplane travel. **Avis Rent A Car** (✆ **888/879-4273**) has an "Avis Access" program that offers services for customers with special travel needs. These include specially outfitted vehicles with swivel seats, spinner knobs, and hand controls; mobility scooter rentals; and accessible bus service. Be sure to reserve well in advance.

Also check out the quarterly magazine ***Emerging Horizons*** (www.emerginghorizons. com), available by subscription ($16.95 per year U.S.; $21.95 outside the U.S.).

VAT   See "Taxes," earlier in this section.

Visas   The U.S. State Department has a **Visa Waiver Program (VWP)** allowing citizens of the following countries to enter the United States without a visa for stays of up to 90 days: Andorra, Australia, Austria, Belgium, Brunei, Czech Republic, Denmark, Estonia, Finland, France, Germany, Greece, Hungary, Iceland, Ireland, Italy, Japan, Latvia, Liechtenstein, Lithuania, Luxembourg, Malta, Monaco, the Netherlands, New Zealand, Norway, Portugal, San Marino, Singapore, Slovakia, Slovenia, South Korea, Spain, Sweden, Switzerland, and the United Kingdom. (***Note:*** This list was accurate at press time; for the most up-to-date list of countries in the VWP, consult http://travel.state.gov/visa.) Even though a visa isn't necessary, in an effort to help U.S. officials check travelers against terror watch lists before they arrive at U.S. borders, visitors from VWP countries must register online through the Electronic System for Travel Authorization (ESTA) before boarding a plane or a boat to the U.S. Travelers must complete an electronic application providing basic personal and travel eligibility information. The Department of Homeland Security recommends filling out the form at least 3 days before traveling. Authorizations will be valid for up to 2 years or until the traveler's passport expires, whichever comes first. Currently, there is a $14 fee for the online application. Existing ESTA registrations remain valid through their expiration dates. ***Note:*** Any passport issued on or after October 26, 2006, by a VWP country must be an **e-Passport** for VWP travelers to be eligible to enter the U.S. without a visa. Citizens of these nations also need to present a round-trip air or cruise ticket upon arrival. E-Passports contain computer chips capable of storing biometric information, such as the required digital photograph of the holder. If your passport doesn't have this feature, you can still travel without a visa if the valid passport was issued before October 26, 2005, and includes a machine-readable zone; or if the valid passport was issued between October 26, 2005, and October 25, 2006, and includes a digital photograph. For more information, go to **http://travel.state.gov/visa**. Canadian citizens may enter the United States without visas, but will need to show passports and proof of residence.

Citizens of all other countries must have (1) a valid passport that expires at least 6 months later than the scheduled end of their visit to the U.S.; and (2) a tourist visa.

For information about U.S. visas go to **http://travel.state.gov** and click on "Visas." Or go to one of the following websites:

Australian citizens can obtain up-to-date visa information from the **U.S. Embassy Canberra,** Moonah Place, Yarralumla, ACT 2600 (✆ **02/6214-5600**), or by checking the U.S. Diplomatic Mission's website at **http://canberra.usembassy.gov/visas.html**.

British subjects can obtain up-to-date visa information by calling the **U.S. Embassy Visa Information Line** (✆ **09042-450-100** from within the U.K. at £1.20 per minute; or ✆ **866/382-3589** from within the U.S. at a flat rate of $16, payable by credit card only) or by visiting the "Visas to the U.S." section of the American Embassy London's website at **http://london.usembassy.gov/visas.html**.

Irish citizens can obtain up-to-date visa information through the **U.S. Embassy Dublin,** 42 Elgin Rd., Ballsbridge, Dublin 4 (✆ 1580-47-VISA [8472] from within the Republic of Ireland at €2.40 per minute; **http://dublin.usembassy.gov**).

Citizens of **New Zealand** can obtain up-to-date visa information by contacting the **U.S. Embassy New Zealand,** 29 Fitzherbert Terrace, Thorndon, Wellington (✆ **644/462-6000; http://newzealand.usembassy.gov**).

Visitor Information   Call or write the **New York State Division of Tourism,** P.O. Box 2603, Albany, NY 12220-0603 (✆ **800/CALL-NYS** [225-5697] or 518/474-4116; www.iloveny.com), for a stack of free brochures, including the informative *I Love New York Travel Guide,* the *Official NYC Guide,* and pamphlets about seasonal events. They even throw in a free state map that's just as useful as any for which you'd pay $5 at the gas station. You can also download state and regional maps from its website. While on the road, you can pick up brochures at one of the state's **information centers.** Call the toll-free number above or check the *I Love New York Travel Guide* for the locations along your route. For regional tourist offices and websites, see the listings in destination chapters later in this book.

If you're planning a tour of the great outdoors, contact the **New York State Office of Parks, Recreation and Historic Preservation,** Albany, NY 12238 (✆ **518/474-0456,** or 518/486-1899 for callers with hearing or speech impairments; www.nysparks.state.ny.us), to request a free brochure, order admission passes, or find out about camping, hiking, and a host of other activities within the state's parks and historic sites. To reserve a campsite or other accommodations, book online or call ✆ **800/456-2267.** You can find a list of Frommer's travel apps at www.frommers.com/go/mobile.

Wi-Fi   See "Internet & Wi-Fi," earlier in this section.

AIRLINE WEBSITES

MAJOR AIRLINES

Aeroméxico
www.aeromexico.com

Air France
www.airfrance.com

Air India
www.airindia.com

Air Jamaica
www.airjamaica.com

Air New Zealand
www.airnewzealand.com

Alitalia
www.alitalia.com

Alaska Airlines/ Horizon Air
www.alaskaair.com

American Airlines
www.aa.com

Bahamasair
www.bahamasair.com

British Airways
www.british-airways.com

Cape Air
www.flycapeair.com

Caribbean Airlines (formerly BWIA)
www.caribbean-airlines.com

China Airlines
www.china-airlines.com

Continental Airlines
www.continental.com

Cubana
www.cubana.cu

Delta Air Lines
www.delta.com

EgyptAir
www.egyptair.com

El Al Airlines
www.elal.co.il

Emirates Airlines
www.emirates.com

Finnair
www.finnair.com

Frontier Airlines
www.frontierairlines.com

Hawaiian Airlines
www.hawaiianair.com

Iberia Airlines
www.iberia.com

Icelandair
www.icelandair.com

Israir Airlines
www.israirairlines.com

Japan Airlines
www.jal.co.jp

JetBlue Airways
www.jetblue.com

Korean Air
www.koreanair.com

Lan Airlines
www.lan.com

Lufthansa
www.lufthansa.com

Midwest Airlines
www.midwestairlines.com

North American Airlines
www.flynaa.com

Olympic Airlines
www.olympicairlines.com

Qantas Airways
www.qantas.com

Pan Am Clipper Connection
www.flypanam.com

Philippine Airlines
www.philippineairlines.com

South African Airways
www.flysaa.com

Swiss Air
www.swiss.com

TACA
www.taca.com

Thai Airways International
www.thaiair.com

Turkish Airlines
www.thy.com

United Airlines
www.united.com

US Airways
www.usairways.com

Virgin America
www.virginamerica.com

Virgin Atlantic Airways
www.virgin-atlantic.com

BUDGET AIRLINES

AirTran Airways
www.airtran.com

Frontier Airlines
www.frontierairlines.com

JetBlue Airways
www.jetblue.com

Southwest Airlines
www.southwest.com

Spirit Airlines
www.spiritair.com

WestJet
www.westjet.com

Airline Websites

PLANNING YOUR TRIP TO NEW YORK STATE

Index

See also Accommodations index, below.

General Index

A

ABC Carpet & Home (New York City), 133
Academic trips, 34–35
Accommodations, 442–443
    best, 1, 4–6
Active vacations, 48–57
Adair Vineyards (New Paltz), 230
Adirondack Balloon Festival (Glens Falls), 31–32
Adirondack Canoe Route, 52–53
Adirondack chairs, 386
Adirondack Craft Center (Lake Placid), 386
Adirondack Lakes Center for the Arts (Blue Mountain Lake), 380
Adirondack Mountain Club (ADK), 55
Adirondack Mountains, 369–402
    northern, 380–391
    southern, 370–380
    suggested itinerary, 42–44
Adirondack Museum (Blue Mountain Lake), 374–375
Adirondacks, hiking, 54
Adirondack Scenic Railroad, 385
Adirondack Sport Shop (Wilmington), 383
Adventure and wellness trips, 35–36
Adventure Cycles & Sports, 152
African-American Family Day (Albany), 283
Air-Ride, 59
Air travel, 438–441
Albany, 39, 260, 276–288
    accommodations, 284–285
    exploring, 278–283
    festivals, 283
    getting around, 278
    layout of, 278
    nightlife, 287–288
    outdoor pursuits, 283–284
    restaurants, 286–287
    traveling to, 261
    visitor information, 276
Albany Alive at Five, 283
Albany Area Visitors Center, 282
Albany Institute of History & Art, 278–279, 282
Albany LatinFest, 283
Albany Pump Station, 288
Albany-Rensselaer Rail Station, 261
Albany Riverfront Jazz Festival, 283
Albany Tulip Festival, 283

Albright-Knox Art Gallery (Buffalo), 408
Alexandria Bay, 392
Alex Bay 500 Go-Karts, 397
Alice in Wonderland (sculpture, New York City), 124
Allegany State Park, 419
All New York Tours, 36
Americana Manhasset, 143–144
American Ballet Theatre (New York City), 136
American Family Immigration History Center (New York City), 111
American Immigrant Wall of Honor (New York City), 111
American Museum of Natural History (New York City), 110, 129
The Amish, 418–419
Amish Country Store at Weaver-View Farms (near Geneva), 354
An American Tragedy (Dreiser), 377
Ananda Ashram (Monroe), 36
Anthony Road Wine Company (Penn Yan), 323
Antique Boat Museum (Clayton), 393
Antique Boat Show & Auction (Clayton), 31
Antiques
    best places to find, 7–8
    Buffalo, 411
    Canandaigua Lake area, 341
    Catskill Mountain region, 233–234, 241–242
    Geneva, 353
    Hammondsport, 335–336
    Hudson, 218
    Long Island, 143, 154, 170
    Lower Hudson Valley, 193
    Mid-Hudson Valley, 207–208
    Rochester, 349
    Saratoga Springs, 270
    Skaneateles, 361, 362
    Sullivan County, 255
    Upper Hudson Valley, 219
A1 Trails, 51, 55
Apollo Theater (New York City), 135
Appalachian National Scenic Trail, 49
Apple Pond Farm and Renewable Energy Education Center (Callicoon), 34, 254
Aquarium of Niagara (Niagara Falls), 430–431
Arbor Hill Grapery (Naples), 341
Arctic Kingdom Expeditions (Canada), 397
Area codes, 443
Arkell Museum (Canajoharie), 299
Around the World Golf (Lake George), 374
Art Forms (Woodstock), 231
Asher House Antiques (Rhinebeck), 207

Ashokan Reservoir, 232
Association Island RV Resort and Marina (Henderson), 400
Atlantic Kayak Tours (Saugerties), 233
Atlantis Marine World (Riverhead), 155
Atwater Estate Vineyards (Hector), 322
Auburn, 360
Aurora, 320
Ausable Chasm, 384–385
Ausable Point Campground, 52, 389
Austin Park (Skaneateles), 362
Autumn, 27

B

Babeville (Buffalo), 410
The Baggage Room (Ithaca), 321
Bald eagles, 256, 396
Bald Mountain, 373
Ballooning. *See* Hot-air ballooning
Balloons Over Corning, 330
Ballston Spa, 270
Bardavon Opera House (Poughkeepsie), 215
The Barn (Windham), 241
Baseball, 130, 284, 348
Baseball Hall of Fame (Cooperstown), 30–31, 289–292
Basketball, New York City, 130
Battery Park (New York City), 62
Bay & Main (Greenport), 159
Bay Drive-In Theatre (Alexandria Bay), 397
B.B. King Blues Club & Grill (New York City), 137
Beaches
    Long Island, 143, 151, 160–162, 168–169
    Shelter Island, 178
    Utica area, 301
Beacon, 202, 215
Beacon Hill Antiques, 207
Beacon Theatre (New York City), 135
Bear Mountain Loop, 209
Bear Mountain State Park, 192, 193
Bearsville Theater, 231
Beaverkill, 254
Bed & breakfasts, best, 5–6
Bedell Cellars (Cutchogue), 152
Beekman Arms Antique Market (Rhinebeck), 207
Belleayre Mountain, 233
Belleayre Music Festival (Highmount), 30
Belmont Stakes (Elmont), 29
Belvedere Castle (New York City), 123, 126
Benmarl Wine Company (Marlboro-on-Hudson), 214
Bergdorf Goodman (New York City), 134

Accommodations

ACCOMMODATIONS INDEX